# Engineering Graphics with AutoCAD® 2023

James D. Bethune

David Byrnes

**Engineering Graphics with AutoCAD® 2023**

For government sales inquiries, please contact governmentsales@pearsoned.com.

For questions about sales outside the U.S., please contact intlcs@pearson.com.

**Editor-in-Chief:** Mark Taub
**Acquisitions Editor:** Anshul Sharma
**Development Editor:** Patrice Rutledge
**Managing Editor:** Sandra Schroeder
**Senior Project Editor:** Tonya Simpson
**Copy Editor:** Kitty Wilson
**Cover Designer:** Chuti Prasertsith
**Composition:** codeMantra
**Proofreader:** Jen Hinchliffe
**Indexer:** Erika Millen

Library of Congress Control Number: 2022940668

ISBN 10: 0-13-792999-4
ISBN 13: 978-0-13-792999-3

1  2022

# Pearson's Commitment to Diversity, Equity, and Inclusion

Pearson is dedicated to creating bias-free content that reflects the diversity of all learners. We embrace the many dimensions of diversity, including but not limited to race, ethnicity, gender, socioeconomic status, ability, age, sexual orientation, and religious or political beliefs.

Education is a powerful force for equity and change in our world. It has the potential to deliver opportunities that improve lives and enable economic mobility. As we work with authors to create content for every product and service, we acknowledge our responsibility to demonstrate inclusivity and incorporate diverse scholarship so that everyone can achieve their potential through learning. As the world's leading learning company, we have a duty to help drive change and live up to our purpose to help more people create a better life for themselves and to create a better world.

Our ambition is to purposefully contribute to a world where

- Everyone has an equitable and lifelong opportunity to succeed through learning

- Our educational products and services are inclusive and represent the rich diversity of learners

- Our educational content accurately reflects the histories and experiences of the learners we serve

- Our educational content prompts deeper discussions with learners and motivates them to expand their own learning (and worldview)

While we work hard to present unbiased content, we want to hear from you about any concerns or needs with this Pearson product so that we can investigate and address them.

Please contact us with concerns about any potential bias at https://www.pearson.com/report-bias.html.

This text teaches technical drawing and uses AutoCAD 2023 as its drawing instrument. Although it follows the general format of many technical drawing texts and presents much of the same material about drawing conventions and practices, the emphasis is on creating accurate, clear drawings. For example, the text shows how to locate dimensions on a drawing so that they completely define the object in accordance with ASME Y14.5-2009 national standards, but the presentation centers on the AutoCAD's **Dimensions** panel and its associated tools and options. The standards and conventions are presented and their applications are shown with the use of AutoCAD 2023. This integrated teaching concept is followed throughout the text.

Most chapters include drawing problems. The drawing problems are varied in scope and are open-ended, which means that there are several correct solutions. This is intended to encourage student creativity and increase their problem-solving abilities.

**Chapters 1 through 3** cover tools on the **Draw** and **Modify** panels of the **Home** tab of AutoCAD's ribbon, and other commands needed to set up and start drawings. The text starts with simple **Line** commands and proceeds through geometric constructions. The final sections of Chapter 3 describe how to bisect a line and how to draw a hyperbola, a parabola, a helix, and an ogee curve. Redrawing many of the classic geometric shapes will help students learn how to use the **Draw** and **Modify** panels and other associated commands with accuracy and creativity.

**Chapter 4** presents freehand sketching. Simply stated, there is still an important place for sketching in technical drawing. Many design ideas start as freehand sketches and are then developed on a computer. This chapter now includes extensive exercise problems associated with visual orientation.

**Chapter 5** presents orthographic views. Students are shown how to draw three views of an object using AutoCAD 2023. The discussion includes projection theory, hidden lines, compound lines, oblique surfaces, rounded surfaces, holes, irregular surfaces, castings, and thin-walled objects. The chapter ends with several intersection problems. These problems serve as a good way to pull together orthographic views and projection theory. Several new, more difficult, exercise problems have been added to this edition. The chapter also includes an explanation of the differences between first- and third-angle projections as defined by ANSI and ISO conventions. Appropriate exercise problems help reinforce the understanding of the differences between the two standards.

**Chapter 6** presents sectional views and introduces the **Hatch** and **Gradient** commands. The chapter includes multiple, broken-out, and partial sectional views and shows how to draw an S-break for a hollow cylinder.

**Chapter 7** covers auxiliary views and shows how to use the **Snap**, **Rotate** command to create axes aligned with slanted surfaces. Secondary auxiliary views are also discussed. Solid modeling greatly simplifies the determination of the true shape of a line or plane, but a few examples of secondary auxiliary views help students refine their understanding of orthographic views and, eventually, the application of user coordinate systems (UCSs).

**Chapter 8** shows how to dimension both two-dimensional shapes and orthographic views. The **Dimension** tools and their associated commands are demonstrated, and examples of how to use the **Dimension Styles** tool are included. The commands are presented as needed to create required dimensions. The conventions demonstrated are in compliance with ANSI Y14.5-2009.

**Chapter 9** introduces tolerances. The chapter shows how to draw dimensions and tolerances using the **Dimension** and **Tolerance** commands, among others. The chapter ends with an explanation of fit types, and shows how to use the tables included in the Appendix to determine the maximum and minimum tolerances for matching holes and shafts.

**Chapter 10** discusses the use of geometric tolerances and explains how AutoCAD 2023 can be used to create geometric tolerance symbols directly from dialog boxes. Both profile and positional tolerances are explained. The overall intent of the chapter is to teach students how to make parts fit together. Fixed and floating fastener applications are discussed, and design examples are given for both conditions.

**Chapter 11** covers how to draw and design with the use of standard fasteners, including bolts, nuts, machine screws, washers, hexagon heads, square heads, set screws, rivets, and springs. Students are shown how to use the **Wblock** command to create drawings of the individual thread representations and how to use them for different size requirements.

**Chapter 12** discusses assembly drawings, detail drawings, and parts lists. Instructions for drawing title blocks, tolerance blocks, release blocks, and revision blocks, and for inserting drawing notes are also included to give students better preparation for industrial practices.

**Chapter 13** presents gears, cams, and bearings. The chapter teaches how to design by using gears selected from manufacturers' catalogs and websites. The chapter shows how to select bearings to support gear shafts and how to tolerance holes in support plates to maintain the desired center distances of meshing gears. It also explains how to create a displacement diagram and then draw the appropriate cam profile.

**Chapter 14** introduces AutoCAD 3D capabilities. Both parallel (isometric) and perspective grids, as well as the world coordinate system (WCS) and user-defined coordinate systems (UCSs) are demonstrated so students learn the fundamentals of 3D drawings before drawing objects.

**Chapter 15** shows how to create three-dimensional solid models. It includes examples of both parallel and perspective grids and using different **Visual Style** options. The chapter shows how to union, subtract, and intersect primitive shapes to create more complex models and orthographic views from those models.

**Chapter 16**, which is available online, presents two project problems: a milling vise and a tenon jig. These problems can be used for group or individual projects. These projects are intended to help students learn to work in groups and work on large, complex projects. This chapter can be found on the web as a supplement to the Instructor's Manual by registering your book at https://www.pearson.com/us/higher-education/subject-catalog/download-instructor-resources.html. Instructors may distribute this URL to students.

## Online Instructor Supplementary Materials

Instructor materials are available from Pearson's Instructor Resource Center. Go to https://www.pearson.com/us/higher-education/subject-catalog/download-instructor-resources.html to register or to sign in if you already have an account.

## Acknowledgments

Many thanks to my family, and Dave Byrnes for an excellent revision.

James D. Bethune

My thanks to Anshul Sharma, Patrice Rutledge, Kitty Wilson, and Tonya Simpson at Pearson; also thanks to Jim Bethune for creating such a fine edition to update.

David Byrnes

# Brief Contents

You can find Chapter 16 and the Appendix at informit.com/title/9780137929993.
Click the *Downloads* tab to access the PDF file.

# Contents

**You can find Chapter 16 and the Appendix at informit.com/title/9780137929993. Click the** *Downloads* **tab to access the PDF file.**

# chapter **one**

# Getting Started

Figure 1-1

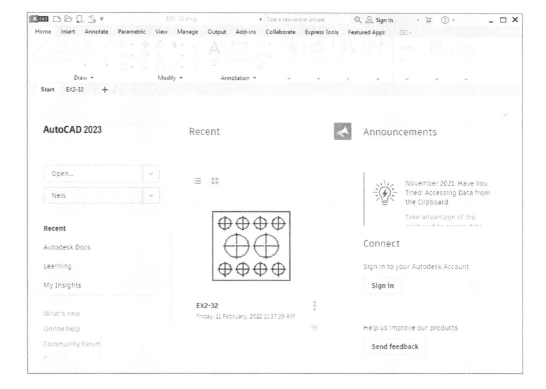

## 1-1 Introduction

This chapter introduces you to AutoCAD 2023. It covers basics such as using the **Application** menu, starting new drawings, making settings and entering data in dialog boxes, and saving your work.

Figure 1-1 shows the initial AutoCAD drawing screen, which appears when the program is first started.

### Starting a New Drawing

**1** Click the down arrow beside the **New** button on AutoCAD's opening screen.

A list of recently used templates appears in the drop-down menu (Figure 1-2). You will use various templates throughout the text, but for a start, you will use the **acad.dwt** template. The **acad.dwt** template defines inches as its primary units. If the **acad.dwt** template does not appear in the drop-down, click **Browse templates...** and select it from there.

Figure 1-2

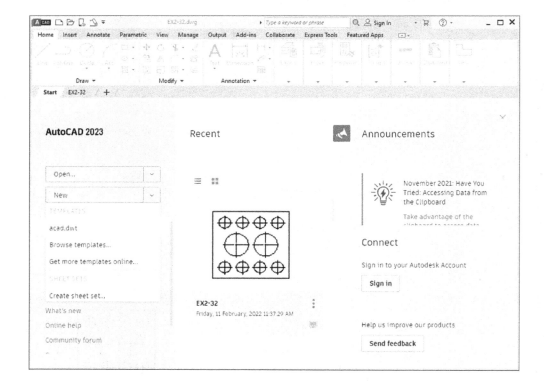

**2** Click **acad.dwt** on the **Templates** list.

The drawing screen appears (Figure 1-3).

**NOTE**

The tool panels in the figure have a light-colored background—for printing clarity. Your background may be dark.

Figure 1-3

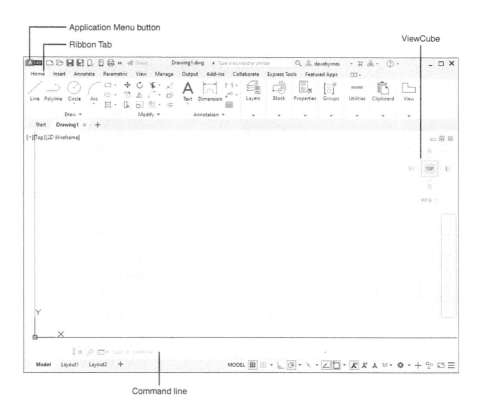

## An Alternative Method to Starting a New Drawing

**1** Click the **Application Menu** button in the upper-left corner of the drawing screen to display the **Application** menu.

A list of drawing commands and utilities appears (Figure 1-4).

**2** Click **New**.

The **Select Template** dialog box appears (Figure 1-5).

Figure 1-4

**3** Select the **acad** template and click **Open**.

Figure 1-5

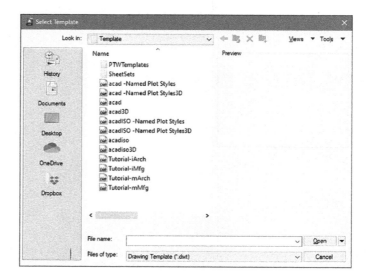

The AutoCAD drawing screen appears (Figure 1-6). The Ribbon appears at the top of the screen, showing a group of tabs and panels. Select different tabs to access other groups of panels. Panels contain commands.

Figure 1-6

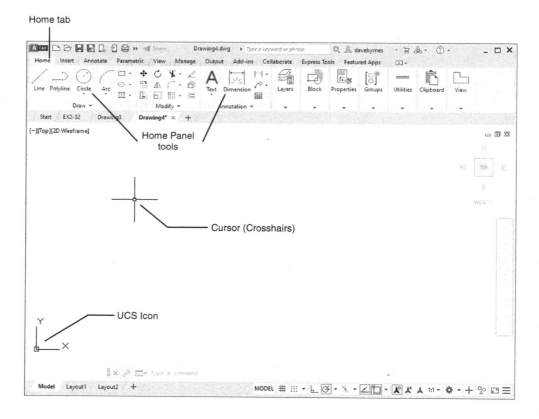

The command line is located at the bottom of the screen, as are other tools (icons) for commands such as **Grid** and **Snap**. Use the command line to enter inputs for the commands, among other uses.

The drawing's name appears at the top of the screen. In Figure 1-4, for example, the drawing name is Drawing1.dwg. This is a default name created by AutoCAD. If a drawing name had been entered, it would appear where the Drawing1.dwg title currently appears.

The large open area in the center of the screen is the *drawing area* or *drawing editor*. You create drawings in this area.

The symbol at the bottom-left corner of the drawing area is called the **User Coordinate System (UCS)** icon. It shows the direction of positive X and Y coordinates.

## 1-2 Tabs and Panels

The headings across the ribbon at the top of the screen (**Home**, **Insert**, etc.) are called *tabs*, and the groups of commands on the tabs are called *panels*. Figure 1-7 shows the **Home** panels and the **Annotate** panels.

**Figure 1-7**

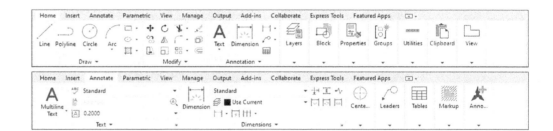

## Accessing Additional Commands Within a Panel

Each panel shows a group of the most commonly used commands. Additional commands are available by clicking the arrow to the right of the panel's name. Figure 1-8 shows the additional **Draw** commands available.

**Figure 1-8**

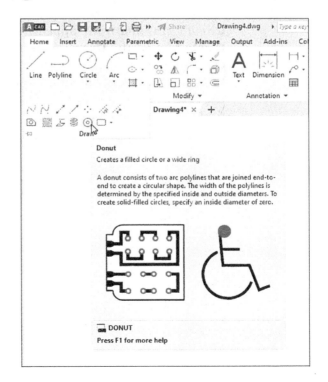

## Tooltips for Commands

A *tooltip* is a pop-up help window that appears when the cursor is hovered over a command's icon (Figure 1-8). Initially, when you place the cursor over a command icon but don't click, a tooltip appears, identifying the command. After a few seconds the tooltip expands to further define the command.

## Accessing Other Help Information

If you cannot find a command or if you need further instructions for operating a particular command, type a keyword into the text box in the program's title bar, and press **Enter** or click the **Access to Help** button located in the top-right section of the screen (Figure 1-9). The icon for the **Access to Help** tool is a question mark within a circle. The **Help** dialog box appears. Type in the name of what you are seeking and click the magnifying glass icon just to the right of the search box.

**Figure 1-9**

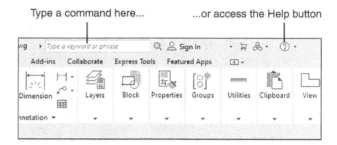

## 1-3 The Command Line Window

The command line window is located at the bottom of the drawing screen. Use it to access commands that do not have their own icons or to select options associated with the command. Figure 1-10 shows a circle. The word CIRCLE automatically appears in the command line when you click the **Circle** tool on the **Draw** panel. As presented, the circle will be defined by entering a radius value. Enter the radius value into the box with the blue background before clicking the left mouse button to complete the circle. If the radius value does not appear, press the F12 function key and ensure that the Dynamic Input is **ON**.

**Figure 1-10**

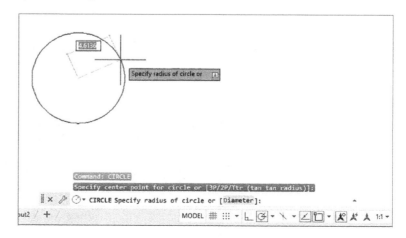

The command line shows the word Diameter in brackets: [Diameter]. Follow the next steps to use the **Circle** command's **Diameter** option.

## Entering a Diameter Value

**1** Click the **Circle** tool on the Home panel and draw a circle.

**2** Click the command line box.

**3** Type **d** and press **Enter**.

The system is now set for a diameter value for the circle.

**4** Enter a value for the diameter of the circle and press **Enter**.

The options shown at the command line always include one uppercase letter. It may not always be the first letter. Type that letter and press **Enter** to access the option.

Diameter values may also be entered by first clicking the arrowhead next to the **Circle** tool and selecting the **Center, Diameter** option.

## 1-4 Command Tools

A *tool button* displays a picture (icon) that represents an AutoCAD command. Most commands have equivalent tool buttons.

### Determining the Command That a Tool Button Represents

Figure 1-11 shows the steps to find the name and description of the command that the tool button executes.

**Figure 1-11**

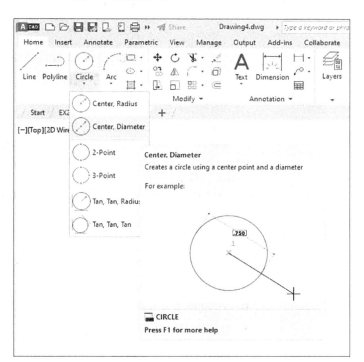

**1** Hover the cursor arrow over the selected tool button.

In the example shown, the **Circle** command tool button with the **Diameter** option is selected.

**2** Hold the arrow still without pressing any mouse buttons.

The command name appears in a tooltip. If you continue to keep the cursor arrow on the tool button, an expanded tooltip that further describes the command appears.

## 1-5 Starting a New Drawing

When you start a new drawing, AutoCAD assigns a drawing name. The drawing units are specified, the drawing limits are modified, if needed, and **Grid** and **Snap** values are defined. The following four sections show you how to start a new drawing.

## 1-6 Naming a Drawing

You can use any combination of letters and numbers as a file name. Either uppercase or lowercase letters can be used, since AutoCAD file names are not case sensitive. The symbols $, -, and _ (underscore) can also be used. Other symbols, such as % and *, cannot be used (Figure 1-12).

Figure 1-12

**Correct drawing names:**
    FIRST      EK-131-1      PA1-1a

**Incorrect drawing names:**
    100%      *.*

**To locate a file on a the C: drive:**
    C:FIRST

All AutoCAD drawing files will automatically have the extension .dwg added to the given file name by default. If you name a drawing **FIRST**, it will appear in the files as **FIRST.dwg**. (A default setting is one that AutoCAD will use unless specifically told to use some other value.)

If you want to locate a file on another drive, specify the drive letter followed by a colon in front of the drawing name. For example, in Figure 1-12 **C:FIRST** will locate the drawing file **FIRST** on the C: drive.

### Creating a New Drawing

There are three ways to access the **Create New Drawing** dialog box that is used to name a new drawing:

- Select **New** from the **Application** menu (Figure 1-13).

- Type the word **new** at a command prompt.

- Hold down the **Ctrl** key and press **N**.

**Figure 1-13**

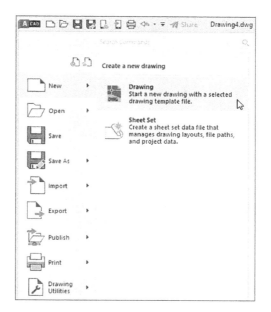

Any of these methods will open the **Select Template** dialog box (Figure 1-14). The **acad** template will set up a drawing with inch values and ANSI style dimensions. The **acadiso** template will set up a drawing with millimeter values and ISO-style dimensions.

**Figure 1-14**

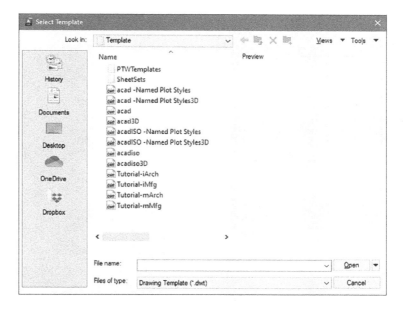

## Saving a New Drawing File

The first time you use one of the **Save** tools to save your drawing, you must give your drawing a name (Figure 1-15). When you click **Save** for the first time in a new drawing, the **Save Drawing As** dialog box appears (Figure 1-16). Select a folder in which to save your work and enter a file name in the text box.

**Figure 1-15**

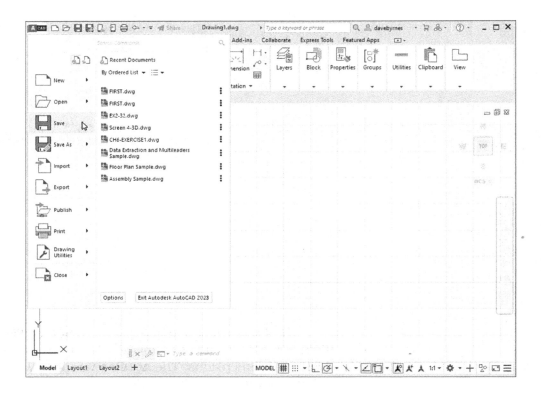

**Figure 1-16**

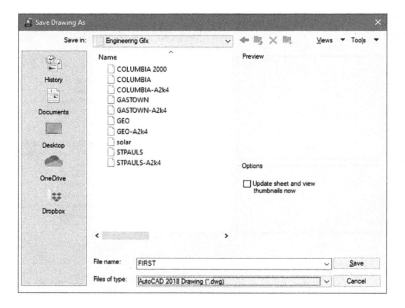

It's a good idea to save your work frequently. AutoCAD can be configured to save your drawings automatically, but it's a much better process to actively save your work. After you've created your drawing file in the **Save Drawing As** dialog box, using the **Save** command creates a backup version (*filename*.bak) and updates your saved file.

To save your work after you've given it a name, click the **Save** button in the **Quick Access Toolbar** at the top of the screen, or you can use the standard Windows shortcut: **Ctrl+S**.

**1** Click the large **Application Menu** button in the upper-left corner of the screen.

**2** Click **Save**.

Since you have not yet named and saved this drawing file, the **Save Drawing As** dialog box appears (Figure 1-16).

The **Save Drawing As** dialog box lists all existing drawings. Click on the thumbnail option to change the list to thumbnail drawings.

**3** Enter the drawing name.

In this example, the drawing name **FIRST** was used.

**4** Click **Save**.

The name of the drawing appears at the top of the screen.

## 1-7 Drawing Units

AutoCAD 2023's **Drawing Units** dialog box allows for either English or metric units to be used as default values; however, AutoCAD can work in any of five different unit systems: scientific, decimal, engineering, architectural, or fractional. The default system is the decimal system, and it is used with either English values (inches) or metric values (millimeters). See Figure 1-17.

**Figure 1-17**

Access the Drawing Units dialog box by first opening the **Application** menu and then selecting **Drawing Utilities**.

### Specifying or Changing the Drawing Units

**1** Select **Drawing Utilities** in the **Application** menu.

**2** Select **Units** (Figure 1-18).

The **Drawing Units** dialog box appears (Figure 1-19).

**Figure 1-18**

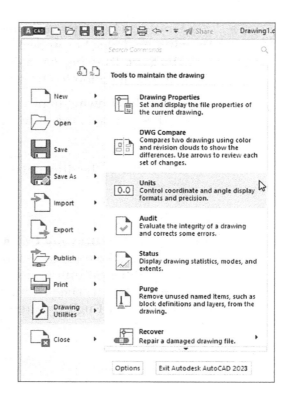

**Figure 1-19**

**3** In the **Length** area, select architectural units by clicking the arrow to the right of the **Type** text box.

A list of the five unit options cascades down.

**4** Select **Architectural**.

Note that the **Sample Output** section, located slightly below the center of the **Drawing Units** dialog box, shows fractional inches.

**5** Repeat the procedure and set the drawing units back to **Decimal**.

## Specifying or Changing the Precision of the Units System

Unit values can be expressed with decimal places from zero to eight or in inches from 0 to 1/256 inch.

**1** Access the **Drawing Units** dialog box as explained previously.

**2** In the **Length** area, click the arrow to the right of the current precision value display box below the word **Precision**.

A drop-down list of the possible decimal precision values cascades from the box (Figure 1-20).

**Figure 1-20**

**3** Select **0.00**.

The value 0.00 appears in the **Precision** box.

**4** Click **OK**.

The original drawing screen appears.

## Specifying or Changing the Angle Units Value

You can specify angles in one of five different units: **Decimal Degrees**, **Degrees/Minutes/Seconds**, **Gradians**, **Radians**, or **Surveyor** units. **Decimal Degrees** is the default value.

Change the angle units in the **Angle** area by selecting the desired units in the drop-down menu under **Type**. The precision of the angle units is changed in the same way as for linear units.

## 1-8 Drawing Limits

You can use **drawing limits** to set the boundaries of a drawing. The drawing boundaries are usually set to match the size of a sheet of drawing paper. This means that when the drawing is plotted and a hard copy is made, it will fit on the drawing paper.

Figure 1-21 shows a list of standard flat-size drawing sheets for engineering applications, Figure 1-22 shows standard metric sizes, and Figure 1-23 shows standard architectural sizes.

Figure 1-21

```
Standard Drawing Sheet Sizes—Inches

        A = 8.5 × 11
        B = 11 × 17
        C = 17 × 22
        D = 22 × 34
        E = 34 × 44
```

Figure 1-22

```
Standard Drawing Sheet Sizes—Millimeters

        A4 = 210 × 297
        A3 = 297 × 420
        A2 = 420 × 594
        A1 = 594 × 841
        A0 = 841 × 1189
```

Figure 1-23

```
Standard Drawing Sheet Sizes—Architectural
                                      USA
        A = 9 × 12
        B = 12 × 18
        C = 18 × 24
        D = 24 × 36
        E = 36 × 48
```

A standard 8.5" × 11" letter-size sheet of paper as used by most printers is referred to as an *A-size* sheet of drawing paper.

> **NOTE**
>
> A sheet of paper can be sized to match standard sheet sizes by the capabilities of the printer or plotter. Many printers and plotters have built-in scaling features, and some list standard sheet sizes that can be applied to a drawing.

## Aligning the Drawing Limits with a Standard A3 (Metric) Paper Size

**1** Click the **Application Menu** button in the upper-left corner of the screen.

**2** Click **Print**, then click **Page Setup** (Figure 1-24).

The **Page Setup Manager** dialog box appears.

**Figure 1-24**

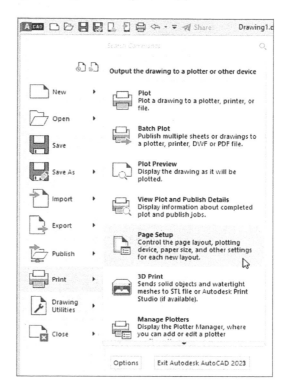

**3** Click **Modify…** (Figure 1-25).

The **Page Setup - Model** dialog box appears.

**Figure 1-25**

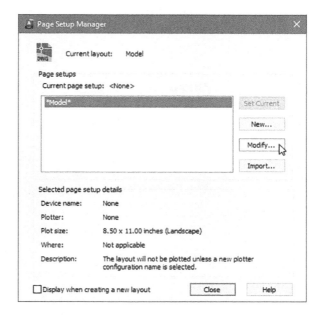

**4.** Click the arrow to the right of the **Paper size** box.

A drop-down list of available paper sizes appears (Figure 1-26).

**5.** Select the **ISO A3 (420.00 x 297.00)** size.

The dimensions in the preview box in the **Printer/plotter** area of the **Page Setup-Model** dialog box change to the selected values.

**Figure 1-26**

**6.** Click **OK**.

The drawing screen is now sized to the 420.00 × 297.00 ISO A3 dimensions.

---

**NOTE**

The sheet size may also be set with the **Limits** command. Type **Limits** at a command prompt and define the drawing limits by specifying the lower-left corner of the drawing as **0.00,0.00** (which is the default setting) and the upper-right corner as needed. If the new limits exceed the current screen limits, type zoom at a command prompt, then type a for **Zoom All**. The new drawing limits are matched to the screen size. The default sheet size for the acad template is 8.5 × 11 (ANSI A), and for the **acadiso** template the default is 210 × 297 (ISO A4).

## 1-9 Grid and Snap

The **Grid** command is used to place a grid background on the drawing screen. This background grid is helpful for establishing visual reference points for sizing and for locating points and lines. The grid may appear as lines or dots. You can specify the type of grid in the **Drafting Settings** dialog box.

> **NOTE**
> A graph paper-style grid background is used in most figures in this book.

The **Snap** command limits the movement of the cursor to predefined points on the screen. For example, if the **Snap** command values are set to match the **Grid** values, the cursor will snap from intersection to intersection (or dot to dot) on the grid.

The default **Grid** and **Snap** setting for the **acad** template is **.50** inch, and the default setting for **Grid** and **Snap** for the **acadiso** template is **10** millimeters.

> **NOTE**
> The **Grid** function can be toggled off and on with the **F7** key, and the **Snap** function can be toggled with the **F9** key.

### Setting the Grid and Snap Values

**1** Start a new drawing and select the **acadiso** template (where values are in millimeters).

**2** Right-click the **Snap** tool located at the bottom of the screen and click **Snap Settings** (Figure 1-27).

**Figure 1-27**

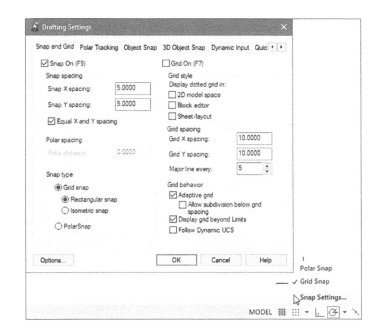

The **Drafting Settings** dialog box appears (Figure 1-27). If it is not already selected, click the **Snap and Grid** tab.

**3** Click the **Grid On** and **Snap On** checkboxes. A check mark appears in each of the boxes.

**4** Place the cursor in the **Snap X spacing** text box to the right of the given value under the **Snap On** heading.
A vertical flashing cursor appears.

**5** Backspace out the existing value and type in **5**.

**6** Click the **Snap Y spacing** box.

The Y spacing automatically equals the X spacing value. You can create rectangular grid spacing by specifying different X and Y spacing values.

**7** Select the **Grid X spacing** text box under the **Grid spacing** heading.

**8** Backspace out the existing value and type in **10** if needed.

**9** Click the **Grid Y spacing** box to make the X and Y values equal.

**10** Click **OK**.

Figure 1-28 shows the result. Since the **Snap** values have been set to exactly half of the **Grid** values, the cursor can be located either directly on grid intersections or halfway between them.

**Figure 1-28**

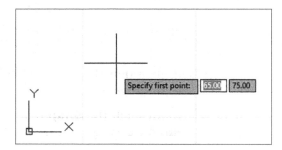

You can turn the grid on and off either by double-clicking the **Grid** icon at the bottom of the screen or by pressing the **F7** key on the keyboard. Turn Snap on and off by double-clicking the **Snap** icon at the bottom of the screen or by pressing the **F9** key on the keyboard. You can also turn **Grid** and **Snap** off and on by clicking their respective buttons on the status bar located at the bottom of the screen.

## 1-10 Drawing Problem

Set up a drawing that uses millimeter dimensions and the following parameters:

Sheet size = **297,420 (A3)**

Grid = **10** spacing

Snap = **5** spacing

Whole-number precision

## Specifying the Drawing Units

**1** Click the **Application Menu** button in the upper-left corner of the drawing screen and then select **New**, then **Drawing**.

The **Select Template** dialog box appears (Figure 1-29).

Figure 1-29

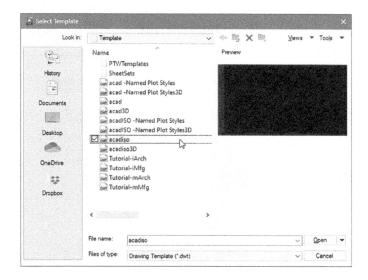

**2** Select the **acadiso** template and click **Open**.

## Defining the Units Precision

**1** Click the **Application Menu** button in the upper-left corner of the drawing screen and then select **Drawing Utilities**, then **Units**.

The **Drawing Units** dialog box appears (Figure 1-30). In this example, only whole numbers will be used, so the **0** option is selected.

**2** Select the **0** precision and click **OK**.

Figure 1-30

## Setting the Sheet Size

The default values for an **acadiso** template are $210 \times 297$, but this drawing problem calls for $297 \times 420$, an A3 sheet size.

**1** Open the **Application** menu and select **Print**, then **Page Setup**.

The **Page Setup Manager** dialog box appears.

**2** Click **Modify**.

The **Page Setup - Model** dialog box appears (Figure 1-31).

Figure 1-31

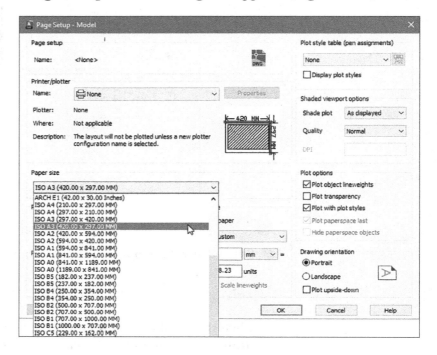

**3** Scroll down the available **Paper size** options and select the **ISO A3 (420.00 x 297.00)** option.

**4** Click **OK**.

## Setting Grid and Snap Values

**1** Right-click the **Grid** button at the bottom of the screen.

**2** Click **Grid Settings**.

The **Drafting Settings** dialog box appears (Figure 1-32).

**3** Select **Grid On** and **Snap On** and set the snap spacing to **5** and the grid spacing to **10**.

**4** Enter **Zoom** at the command prompt, type **A**, and press **Enter**.

The screen is now ready for starting a drawing using millimeter values.

**Figure 1-32**

## 1-11 Save and Save As

Use the **Save** command to save your work. If you start a new drawing, the first time you click **Save**, the **Save As** command displays the **Save Drawing As** dialog box. You can select **Save As** at any time if you want to save your drawing using a different name or in a different location, but most of the time you will use the **Save** command to simply save your work.

## Using the Save and Save As Commands

**1** Click the **Save** button on the **Quick Access Toolbar** at the top of the screen, above the Home panel (Figure 1-33).

**Figure 1-33**

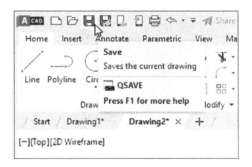

**NOTE**

The small group of tool buttons to the right of the **Application Menu** button and above the ribbon is called the **Quick Access Toolbar**. You will find frequently used commands here, including New, Open, Save, and Print. You can customize the Quick Access Toolbar to add your own frequently used commands.

Because this drawing has not yet been saved, the **Save Drawing As** dialog box appears (Figure 1-34). In this example, the file name **Drawing1. dwg** appears. This is the default name that was created automatically when the new drawing was opened.

Figure 1-34

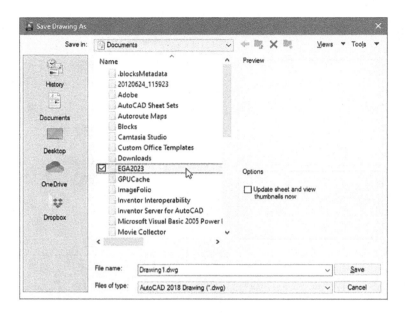

2 Create a new folder where you can save your work.

Figure 1-34 shows a folder named **EGA2023** created under **Documents**.

3 Save the drawing in the folder **EGA2023** located in the **Documents** folder and enter the name **Box** (Figure 1-35).

Figure 1-35

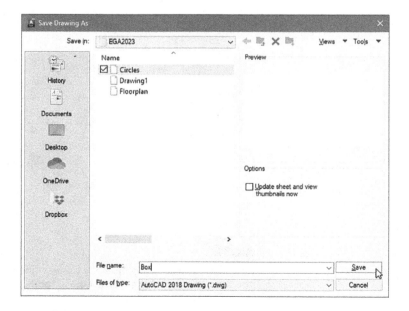

**4** Click **Save**.

## 1-12 Open

Use the **Open** command to call up an existing drawing so that you can continue working on it.

### Using Open

Access existing drawings using **Open** and the **Select File** dialog box.

**1** On the **Application** menu, click **Open** (Figure 1-36), then click **Drawing**.

**Figure 1-36**

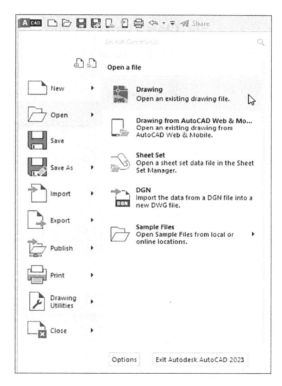

The **Select File** dialog box appears (Figure 1-37).

**2** Click the **Views** option at the top of the **Select File** dialog box and click the **Thumbnails** and **Preview** options.

Thumbnails of the drawing files appear.

**3** Click the desired file.

A preview appears.

**4** Click **Open**.

Figure 1-37

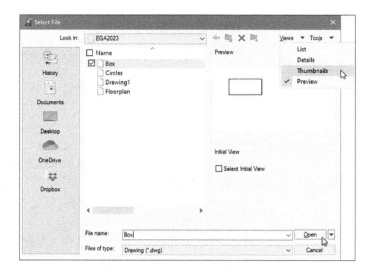

## 1-13 Close

The **Close** command allows you to close the current drawing.

**1** On the **Application** menu, click **Close** and then click **Current Drawing** (Figure 1-38).

The system exits the AutoCAD program.

Figure 1-38

# 1-14 EXERCISE PROBLEMS

### EX1-1

Create a drawing screen as shown in Figure EX1-1. Select the **acadiso** template, turn on the **Grid** and **Snap** functions, and set the grid spacing to **10** and snap spacing to **5**. Set the sheet size to **ISO A3 (297.00 x 420.00)**. Name the drawing **Screen 1**.

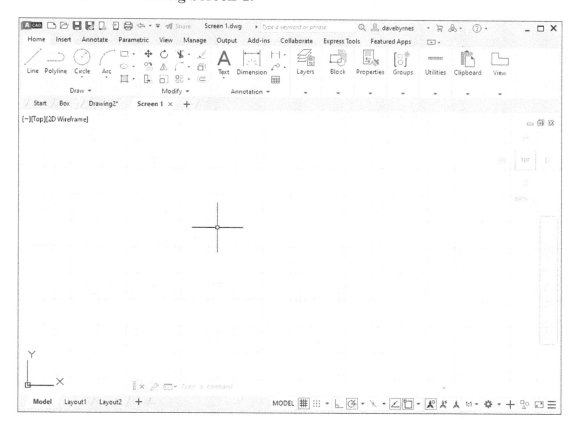

### EX1-2

Create a drawing screen as shown in Figure EX1-2. Select the **acad** template, turn on the **Grid** and **Snap** functions, and set the grid spacing to **0.50** and snap spacing to **0.25**. Locate the origin in the lower-left corner of the drawing screen. Name the drawing **Screen 2**.

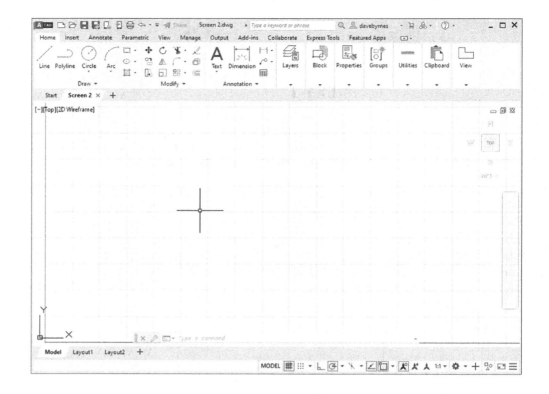

## EX1-3

Create a drawing screen as shown in Figure EX1-3. Select the **acadiso** template, turn on the **Grid** and **Snap** functions, and set the grid spacing to **50** and snap spacing to **10**. Set the grid background to **dotted**. Name the drawing **Screen 3**.

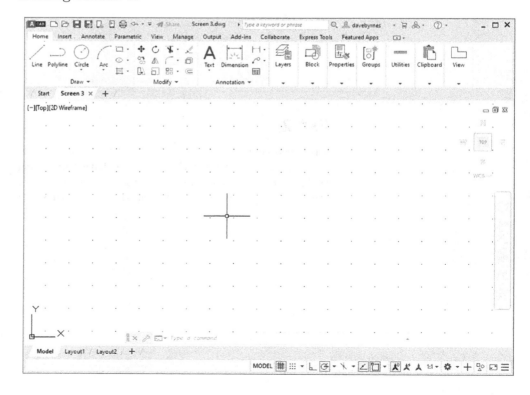

## EX1-4

Create a drawing screen as shown in Figure EX1-4. Select the **acadiso3D** template, turn on the **Grid** and **Snap** functions, and set the grid spacing to **20** and snap spacing to **5**. Name the drawing **Screen 4-3D**.

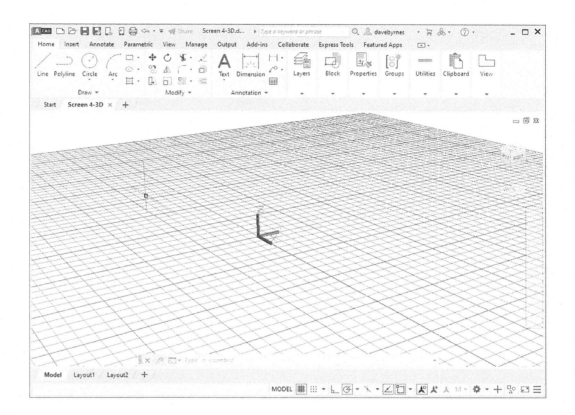

# chapter **two**

# Fundamentals of 2D Construction

## 2-1 Introduction

This chapter demonstrates how to work with AutoCAD commands. You can execute AutoCAD commands by using command tools and a series of prompts. The prompts appear in the command line window and ask the user for a selection or numeric input so that a command sequence can be completed. This chapter uses the **Line** command to show the various input and prompt sequences that are typical with AutoCAD commands.

Most of the commands contained in the **Draw** and **Modify** panels are demonstrated in this chapter. Enough commands are presented for you to be able to create simple 2D shapes. Chapter 3 presents more advanced applications for these commands and introduces some new commands as well.

## 2-2 Line—Random Points

Use the **Line** command to draw a straight line between two defined points.
There are four ways to define the length and location of a line:

- Randomly select points

- Set a specific value for the **Snap** function and select points with the **Snap** spacing values

- Enter the coordinate values for the starting point and endpoint

- Use relative inputs and specify the starting point, the length, and the direction of the line

### Randomly Selecting Points

**1** Start a drawing using the **acadiso** template and select the **Line** tool on the **Draw** panel on the **Home** tab (Figure 2-1).

You can also access the **Line** command by typing the word **line** or the letter **L** in response to a command prompt.

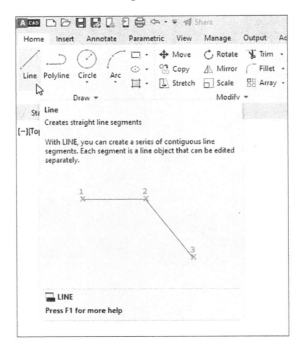

The following command sequence appears in the command line window:

```
Command: _line Specify first point:
```

**2** Place the cursor anywhere on the drawing screen and press the left mouse button.

AutoCAD responds:

```
Specify next point or [Undo]:
```

As you move the cursor from point to point, dynamic input appears on the screen (Figure 2-2). Dynamic input includes an absolute angle box and a length change box. Dynamic input is discussed in Section 2-5.

**NOTE**

If you do not see dynamic input on the screen, press the **F12** function key to turn it on.

**3** Pick another random point on the screen.

AutoCAD responds:

```
Specify next point or [Undo]:
```

AutoCAD keeps asking for another point until you press either the **Enter** key or the right mouse button. When you press the right mouse button (that is, right-click), the right-click menu appears.

**4** Press the right mouse button and click **Enter** to end the **Line** command sequence.

**Figure 2-2**

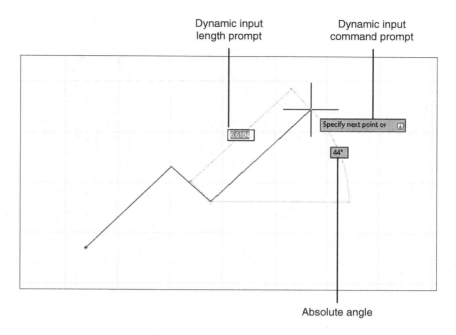

Dynamic input length prompt

Dynamic input command prompt

Absolute angle

You can restart the **Line** command by pressing the right mouse button immediately after selecting **Enter**. A right-click menu appears (Figure 2-3). Select **Repeat LINE** to restart the **Line** command.

**Figure 2-3**

## Exiting a Command Sequence

If, as you work, you need to exit a command sequence, press the **Esc** key, and you return to a command prompt. The **Esc** key allows you to exit almost any AutoCAD command.

## Creating a Closed Area

**1** Select the **Line** tool from the **Draw** panel.

AutoCAD responds:

```
Command: _line Specify first point:
```

**2** Click a random point (such as P1 in Figure 2-4).

```
Specify next point or [Undo]:
```

Figure 2-4

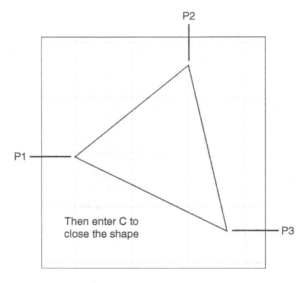

Then enter C to
close the shape

**3** Click a second random point.

```
Specify next point or [Undo]:
```

**4** Click a third random point.

```
Specify next point or [Close Undo]:
```

**5** Type **c** and then press **Enter** to activate the **Close** option.

AutoCAD draws a line from the third point to the starting point, creating a closed area. You can also create an enclosed area by using the **Object Snap Endpoint** option. As you move the cursor toward a line, a box appears at the line's endpoint. Clicking within the endpoint box attaches the line to that endpoint. Right-click the **Object Snap** icon at the bottom of the screen for a list of other **Object Snap** options.

## 2-3 Erase

You can erase any line by using the **Erase** command. There are two ways to erase lines: Select individual lines or use a selection box to choose a group of lines. The **Erase** tool is located on the **Modify** panel on the **Home** tab (Figure 2-5).

Figure 2-5

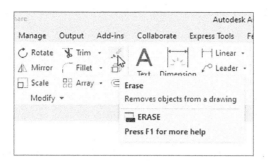

## Erasing Individual Lines

**1** Click the **Erase** tool on the **Modify** panel.

The following prompt appears in the command line window:

Command: _erase

Select objects:

The normal crosshairs are replaced by a rectangular selection box called the *pickbox*. Any time you see the pickbox, AutoCAD expects you to select an entity—in this example, a line.

If you change your mind and do not want to erase anything, select the next command that you want to use, and the **Erase** command is terminated.

**2** Select the two open lines by placing the rectangular cursor on each line, one at a time, and pressing the left mouse button. The left side of Figure 2-6 shows a single object selected.

Figure 2-6

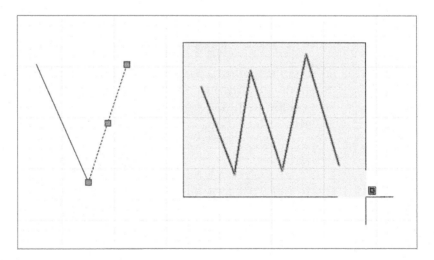

The lines are highlighted and display grips at their midpoints and endpoints. The highlight indicates that the line has been selected. The selection is confirmed by a change in the prompt:

Select objects: 1 found

Select objects:

**3** Right-click or press the **Enter** key to complete the **Erase** sequence.

The two lines disappear from the screen.

## Erasing a Group of Lines

**1** Click the **Erase** tool.

```
Command: _erase
Select objects:
```

**2** Place the rectangular select cursor above and to the left of the lines to be erased and click the left mouse button (Figure 2-6). Do not hold the mouse button down.

**3** Move the mouse, and a shaded window drags from the selected first point.

The right side of Figure 2-6 shows a window selection.

**4** When all the lines to be erased are completely within the window, press the left mouse button.

All the lines completely within the window are selected and change to a faint hue. The number of lines selected is indicated in the command line box.

**5** Right-click or press the **Enter** key to complete the command sequence.

The lines disappear from the screen. You can use the **Undo** tool to return all the lines, if needed.

If you create the **Erase** window from right to left, any line even partially within the **Erase** window is erased. If the left mouse button is held down and dragged across the object, an irregularly shaped window is formed.

## 2-4 Line—Snap Points

You can draw lines by using calibrated snap spacing. This technique is similar to drawing points randomly, but because the cursor is limited to specific points, the lengths of lines can be determined accurately (Figure 2-7).

Figure 2-7

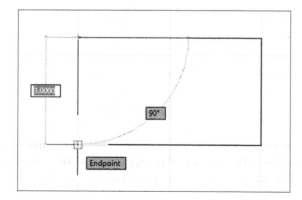

## Drawing Problem

**1** Turn on both the **Grid** and **Snap** functions and set both grid spacing and snap spacing to **.5**. Zoom the grid in or out to fit the screen.

> **NOTE**
> See Section 1-9 for instructions on how to use the **Grid** and **Snap** functions.

**2** Select **Line** from the **Draw** panel.

```
Command: _line Specify first point:
```

**3** Click a grid point.

```
Specify next point or [Undo]:
```

**4** Move the cursor horizontally to the right **10** grid spaces and press the left mouse button.

Because the snap spacing has been set to .5, 10 spaces equal 5 units. Watch the dynamic input readings as you move the cursor. The X value should increase by 5, and the Y value should stay the same.

```
Specify next point or [Undo]:
```

**5** Move the cursor vertically **6** spaces and press the left mouse button.

```
Specify next point or [Close Undo]:
```

**6** Move the cursor horizontally to the left **10** spaces and press the left mouse button.

```
Specify next point or [Close Undo]:
```

**7** Type **c** and press **Enter** or place the endpoint of the left vertical line on the starting point of the first line. Right-click and select **Enter**.

You can save or erase the drawing as desired.

## 2-5 Line—Dynamic Input

Using the **Dynamic Input** mode allows you to add both angular and distance values to a drawing through the use of screen prompts.

By default, AutoCAD 2023 does not display the **Dynamic Input** button on the status bar. Use the following steps to turn it on:

**1** Click the **Customization** button at the right end of the status bar (Figure 2-8).

**Figure 2-8**

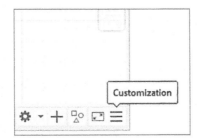

**2** Select **Dynamic Input** from the pop-up menu to place a check mark next to it and turn it on (Figure 2-9).

The **Dynamic Input** button now appears on the status bar (Figure 2-10).

Figure 2-9

Figure 2-10

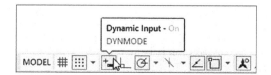

**3** Click anywhere in the drawing area to close the Customization menu.

**Dynamic Input** mode is enabled when the status bar button is highlighted (Figure 2-10).

## Creating Lines Using Dynamic Input

This example was created using inch values.

**1** Click the **Line** command tool on the **Draw** panel and select a starting point.

Figure 2-11 shows the dynamic input for the next point.

**Figure 2-11**

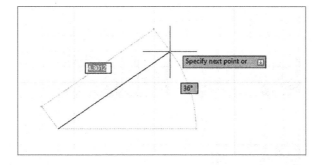

**2** Move the cursor to the approximate location of the second line point.

The distance and angular values for this new point are displayed in dynamic input labels. Do not click the mouse.

Angular values assume that 0° is a horizontal line to the right of the first line point.

**3a** Move the cursor to the command line window and type in the desired distance and angle value.

Use the format @*Distance<angle*. In this example, the input **@3.5<45** was entered (Figure 2-12).

**Figure 2-12**

**3b** You can also enter the distance and angle for the line by typing the values starting with @. The values appear in the dynamic input boxes on the screen. When the **<** symbol is entered, a lock icon appears next to the distance value (Figure 2-13). Press **Enter** when the values are entered.

**Figure 2-13**

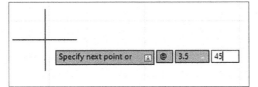

**4** Press **Enter**.

The angular value is applied to the line, and the dynamic input label prepares for the next line point input.

**5** Complete the desired shape and press **Enter**.

## Accessing Dynamic Input Settings

Use the **Drafting Settings** dialog box to access dynamic input settings (Figure 2-14).

Figure 2-14

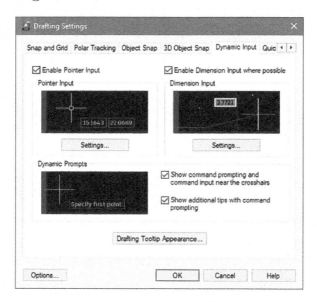

**1** Right-click the **Dynamic Input** tool at the bottom of the screen and select **Dynamic Input Settings**.

The **Drafting Settings** dialog box appears.

The **Dynamic Input** tab of this dialog box controls the pointer input, dimension input, and dynamic prompts aspects of dynamic input. The default values are used throughout the text.

## 2-6 Construction Line

The **Construction Line (Xline)** command is used to draw lines of infinite length. Construction lines are very helpful during the initial layout of a drawing. They can be trimmed as needed during the creation of a drawing.

> **NOTE**
>
> If you trim a construction line so it now has an endpoint, the remaining part of the construction line becomes a *ray*. You can create rays directly using the **Ray** command, which is on the expanded **Draw** panel.

**1** Select the **Construction Line** tool from the expanded **Draw** panel (Figure 2-15).

AutoCAD prompts:

```
Command:_ xline Specify a point or [Hor Ver Ang Bisect Offset]:
```

**Specify a point** is the default option.

**NOTE**

The **Construction Line** tool is located on a flyout from the **Draw** panel. Click the arrow next to the word **Draw** to access the flyout.

**Figure 2-15**

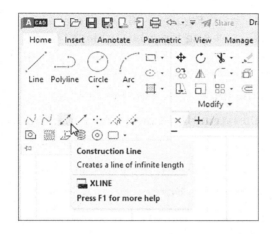

☐2 Select or define a starting point.

You can position the direction of the line by moving the cursor or by using dynamic input, as defined in Section 2-5, to define the line's direction.

☐3 Select or use dynamic input to define a through point.

```
Specify through point:
```

A line pivots about the designated throughpoint and extends an infinite length in both directions through the cursor. You can position the angle of the line by moving the cursor (Figure 2-16).

**Figure 2-16**

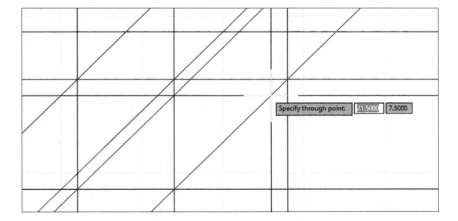

**4** Select or define a through point.

An infinitely long line is drawn through the two designated points.

`Specify through point:`

**5** Press **Enter** to end the **Construction Line** command sequence.

You can reactivate the sequence and draw another construction line by pressing the **Enter** key a second time.

## Using Other Construction Line Commands: Hor, Ver, and Ang

The lines shown in Figure 2-16 were created by using the **Hor** (horizontal), **Ver** (vertical), and **Ang** (angular) options. A grid was created, and **Snap** was turned on so that the lines could be drawn through known points. Figure 2-16 was created as follows:

**1** Set up the drawing screen with grid and snap spacings of **.5**.

**2** Select **Construction Line** in the expanded **Draw** panel.

AutoCAD prompts:

`Command:_ xline Specify a point or [Hor Ver Ang Bisect Offset]:`

**3** Type **H** and press **Enter**.

A horizontal line appears through the cursor.

`Specify through point:`

**4** Pick or define a point on the drawing screen.

A horizontal line appears through the point. As you move the mouse, another horizontal line appears through the cursor.

`Specify through point:`

**5** Pick or define a second point.

`Specify through point:`

**6** Pick or define a third point.

`Specify through point:`

**7** Right-click, right-click again, and select **Repeat XLINE**.

`Command:_ xline Specify a point or [Hor Ver Ang Bisect Offset]:`

**8** Type **V** and press **Enter**.

`Specify through point:`

**9** Draw vertical lines, right-click twice, and select the **Repeat XLINE** option.

`Command:_ xline Specify a point or [Hor Ver Ang Bisect Offset]:`

**10** Type **A** and press **Enter**.

`Enter angle of xline (0) or [Reference]:`

**11** Type **45** and press **Enter**.

`Specify through point:`

An infinite line at 45° appears through the crosshairs.

▣ Draw **45°** lines.

`Specify through point:`

▣ Press **Enter**.

Your drawing should look approximately like Figure 2-16.

## Using Another Construction Line Option: Offset

The **Offset** option allows you to draw a construction line parallel to an existing construction line, regardless of the line's orientation, at a predefined distance (Figure 2-17).

**Figure 2-17**

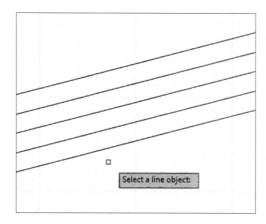

Select a line object:

▣ Select **Construction Line** in the expanded **Draw** panel.

`Command:_ xline Specify a point or [Hor Ver Ang Bisect Offset]:`

▣ Draw a line approximately **15°** to the horizontal.

AutoCAD prompts:

`Specify through point:`

▣ Double-click the **Enter** key to restart the **Construction Line** command sequence.

`Command:_ xline Specify a point or [Hor Ver Ang Bisect Offset]:`

▣ Type **O** and press **Enter**.

The **O** appears in the dynamic input box.

`Offset distance or through <Through>:`

▣ Type **.5** and press **Enter**.

`Select a line object:`

▣ Select the line.

`Pick side to offset:`

▣ Select a point above the line.

`Select a line object:`

▣ Select the line just created by the **Offset** option.

`Pick side to offset:`

**9** Again select a point above the selected line.

```
Select a line object:
```

**10** Draw several more lines below the original line.

```
Select a line object:
```

**11** Right-click and select **Enter** to end the **Construction Line Offset** sequence and return to the command prompt.

## 2-7 Circle

The **Circle** tool button is on the **Draw** panel. A circle can be defined by a center point and either a radius or a diameter, by two or three points on the diameter, or by the tangents to either two existing lines or arcs and a radius value or to three objects. Each of these command options has a separate tool button on the **Draw** panel in the **Circle** tool button's drop-down (Figure 2-18).

**Figure 2-18**

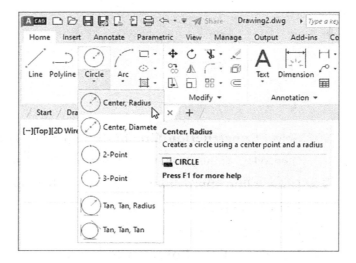

## Drawing a Circle—Radius

**1** Click **Circle** on the **Draw** panel.

```
Command: _circle Specify a center point for circle or
[3P 2P Ttr (tan tan radius)]
```

**2** Pick a point or use dynamic input to define a center point.

```
Specify radius of circle or [Diameter]:
```

**3** Type **3.50** and press **Enter**.

The radius value appears in the dynamic input box.

## Drawing a Circle—Diameter

**1** Click the down arrow on the **Circle** tool button and then click **Center, Diameter** in the drop-down menu.

```
Command: _circle Specify a center point for circle or
[3P 2P Ttr (tan tan radius)]:
```

**2** Pick a point or define a center point.

```
Specify radius of circle or [Diameter]:
```

**3** Type **8.00** and press **Enter**.

## Drawing a Circle—Two Points

**1** Click the down arrow on the **Circle** tool button and then click **2-Point** in the drop-down menu.

```
Command: _circle Specify a center point for circle or [3P 2P Ttr
(tan tan radius)]: _2p Specify first end point of circle's diameter:
```

**2** Select or define a first point.

```
Select second end point of circle's diameter:
```

**3** Select or define a second point.

The circle is automatically drawn through the first and second points, as shown on the left side of Figure 2-19.

**Figure 2-19**

## Drawing a Circle—Three Points

**1** Click the down arrow on the **Circle** tool button and then click **3-Point** on the drop-down menu.

```
Command: _circle Specify a center point for circle or
[3P 2P Ttr (tan tan radius)]: _3p Specify first point on circle:
```

**2** Pick or define a first point.

```
Specify second point on circle:
```

**3** Pick or define a second point.

```
Specify third point on circle:
```

**4** Pick or define a third point.

The circle is automatically drawn through the three points, as shown on the right side of Figure 2-19.

## Drawing a Circle—Tangent Tangent Radius

The **tangent tangent radius** option allows you to draw a circle tangent to two entities and then specify a radius. Figure 2-20 shows a circle drawn tangent to two lines.

**1** Click the down arrow on the **Circle** tool button and then click **Tan, Tan, Radius** on the drop-down menu.

```
Command: _circle Specify a center point for circle or [3P 2P Ttr
(tan tan radius)]: _ttr Specify point on object for first tangent of
circle:
```

**Figure 2-20**

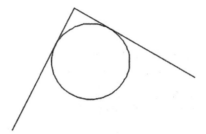

**2** Select an entity.

```
Specify point on object for second tangent of circle:
```

**3** Select the other entity.

```
Specify radius of circle <value>:
```

**4** Type a radius value and press **Enter**.

Drawing a circle using the **Tan, Tan, Tan** option is similar to the steps for **Tan, Tan, Radius**. Simply select three objects—lines, arcs, or circles— rather than two objects and a radius.

## Quadrant-Sensitive Applications

The **Circle** command's **TTR** option is quadrant sensitive—that is, the final location of the tangent circle depends on the location of the tangent spec points. In Figure 2-21, the **TTR** option was used to draw a large circle tangent to two smaller circles, and in both examples, the larger tangent circle was created by using the same radius. Note the difference in results depending on where on the smaller circles the tangent points were chosen.

**Figure 2-21**

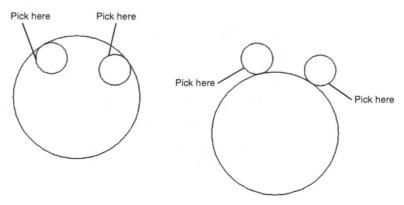

## 2-8 Circle Centerline

Standard drawing convention includes centerlines with all circles. Circles usually represent holes. The circle's center point locates the hole and, during manufacture, serves as the location point for a drill.

### Creating Center Marks

**1** Click the **Annotate** tab on the ribbon.

A new set of ribbon panels appears (Figure 2-22).

**Figure 2-22**

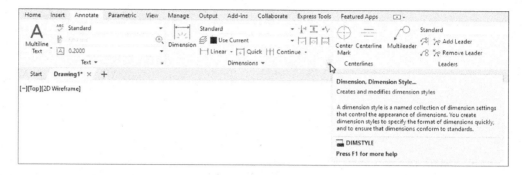

**2** Click the arrow in the lower-right corner of the **Dimensions** panel.

The **Dimension Style Manager** dialog box appears (Figure 2-23).

**Figure 2-23**

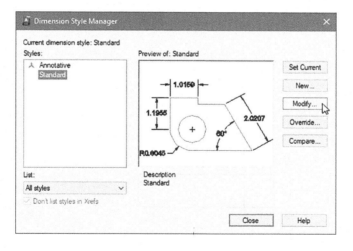

**3** In the **Dimension Style Manager** dialog box, click **Modify**.

The **Modify Dimension Style: Standard** dialog box appears.

**4** Select the **Symbols and Arrows** tab, then in the **Center marks** area, click the **Line** option (Figure 2-24).

Figure 2-24

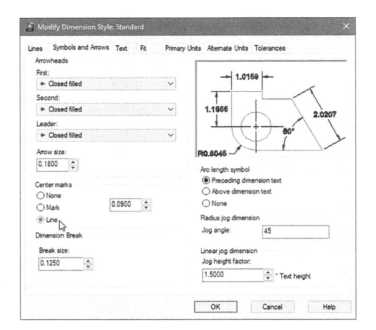

The preview screen displays centerlines.

5️⃣ Click **OK** and then **Close** to return to the drawing screen.

6️⃣ Click the **Center Mark** tool on the **Centerlines** panel, and then click the given circle, as shown in Figure 2-25.

Figure 2-25

Centerlines appear on the circle.

## 2-9 Polyline

A *polyline* is a linear object made from a series of individual, connected line or arc segments that act as a single entity. Polylines can be used to generate curves and splines and can also be used in three-dimensional applications to produce solid objects.

## Drawing a Polyline

**1** Select **Polyline** from the **Draw** panel.

AutoCAD prompts:

Command: _pline

Specify start point:

**2** Pick or define a starting point.

Specify next point or [Arc Close Halfwidth Length Undo Width]:

**3** Pick or define a second point.

Specify next point or [Arc Close Halfwidth Length Undo Width]:

**4** Pick or define several more points (Figure 2-26).

Specify next point or [Arc Close Halfwidth Length Undo Width]:

**Figure 2-26**

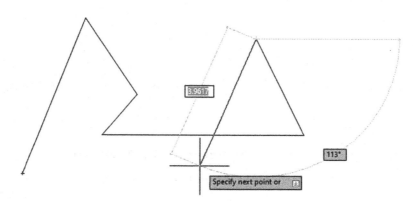

**5** Right-click and then select **Enter**.

## Verifying That a Polyline Is a Single Entity

Figure 2-26 shows a polyline.

**1** Select **Erase** from the **Modify** panel or enter the word **erase**.

AutoCAD prompts:

Select objects:

**2** Pick any one of the line segments in the polyline.

Select objects:

The entire polyline, not just the individual line segment, is selected because in AutoCAD, the polyline is a single entity.

**3** Press **Enter**.

The entire polyline disappears.

**4** Click **Undo** on the **Quick Access Toolbar**.

The object reappears.

## Drawing a Polyline Arc

Figure 2-27 shows a polyline drawn using the **Arc** option.

**Figure 2-27**

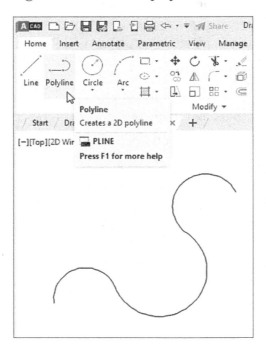

**1** Select **Polyline** from the **Draw** panel.

AutoCAD prompts:

```
Specify start point:
```

**2** Pick or define a starting point.

```
Specify next point or [Arc Close Halfwidth Length Undo Width]:
```

**3** Type **A** and press **Enter**.

```
Specify endpoint of arc or [Angle CEnter Direction Halfwidth Line
Radius Second pt Undo Width]:
```

**4** Pick or define another point.

```
Specify endpoint of arc or [Angle CEnter Direction Halfwidth Line
Radius Second pt Undo Width]:
```

**5** Pick or define another point.

**6** Right-click, and then select **Enter**.

## Other Options with a Polyline Arc

Figure 2-28 shows examples of polyline arc options.

**1** Select **Polyline** from the **Draw** panel.

```
Command: _pline
```

```
Specify start point:
```

Figure 2-28

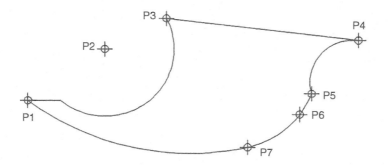

2 Pick or define a starting point (such as P1 in Figure 2-28).

Specify next point or [Arc Halfwidth Length Undo Width]:

3 Draw a short horizontal line segment.

Specify next point or [Arc Close Halfwidth Length Undo Width]:

4 Type **A** and press **Enter**.

Specify endpoint of arc or [Angle CEnter CLose Direction Halfwidth Line Radius Second pt Undo Width]:

5 Type **CE** and press **Enter**.

**CE** activates the **Center** option. You can now define an arc that will be part of the polyline by defining the arc's center point and its angle, chord length, or endpoint.

Specify center point of arc:

6 Pick or define a center point (such as P2 in Figure 2-28).

Specify endpoint of arc or [Angle Width]:

7 Pick or define an endpoint (such as P3 in Figure 2-28).

Specify endpoint of arc or [Angle CEnter Direction Halfwidth Line Radius Second pt Undo Width]:

8 Type **L** and press **Enter**.

The **Line** option is used to draw straight-line segments.

Specify next point or [Arc Close Halfwidth Length Undo Width]:

9 Pick or define an endpoint (such as P4 in Figure 2-28).

Specify next point or [Arc Close Halfwidth Length Undo Width]:

10 Type **A** and press **Enter**.

Specify endpoint of arc or [Angle CEnter Direction Halfwidth Line Radius Second pt Undo Width]:

11 Type **R** and press **Enter.**

Specify radius of arc:

12 Type **1.5** or another value and press **Enter**.

Specify endpoint of arc or [Angle]:

13 Pick or define an endpoint (such as P5 in Figure 2-28).

Specify endpoint of arc or [Angle CEnter CLose Direction Halfwidth Line Radius Second pt Undo Width]:

**14** Type **S** and press **Enter**.

```
Specify second point on arc:
```

**15** Pick or define a point (such as P6 in Figure 2-28).

```
Specify endpoint of arc:
```

**16** Select or define an endpoint (such as P7 in Figure 2-28).

```
Specify endpoint of arc or [Angle CEnter CLose Direction Halfwidth
Line Radius Second pt Undo Width]:
```

**17** Type **CL** and press **Enter**.

The **CL** (close) option joins the last point drawn to the first point of the polyline by use of an arc.

## Drawing Different Line Thicknesses

**1** Select **Polyline** from the **Draw** panel.

```
Specify start point:
```

**2** Select or define a starting point.

```
Specify next point or [Arc Close Halfwidth Length Undo Width]:
```

**3** Type **W** and press **Enter**.

The **Width** option defines the width of a line. The **Halfwidth** option is used to define half of the width of a line.

```
Specify starting width <0.0000>:
```

**4** Type **1.00** and press **Enter**.

```
Specify ending width <1.0000>:
```

**5** Press **Enter**.

```
Specify next point or [Arc Close Halfwidth Length Undo Width]:
```

**6** Draw several line segments (Figure 2-29).

**Figure 2-29**

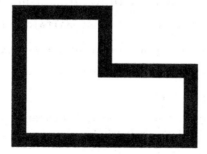

## 2-10 Spline

A *spline* is a non-radial curved line created through (*fit spline*) or near (*control vertex spline*) a series of points. If the curve forms an enclosed area, it is called a *closed spline*. Curved lines that do not enclose an area are called *open splines*. See Figure 2-30.

**NOTE**

There are two ways of drawing splines: using either the **Fit** or **Control Vertex** tool buttons on the expanded **Draw** panel. Fit splines pass through the points you pick onscreen. Control vertex splines are created using inflection points that you pick.

**Figure 2-30**

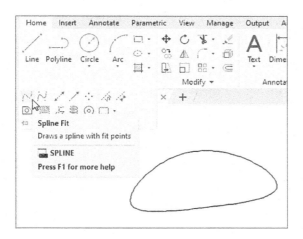

1. Select **Spline Fit** from the **Draw** panel. AutoCAD prompts:

   Command: _spline

   Specify first point or [Method Knots Object]:

2. Pick or define a starting point.

   Specify next point:

3. Pick or define a second point.

   Specify next point or [Close Fit tolerance] <start tangent>:

4. Select or define two more points.

   Specify next point or [Arc Close Halfwidth Length Undo Width]:

5. Type **C** and press **Enter** (Figure 2-30).

## 2-11 Ellipse

The **Ellipse** command has two options. These options allow you to define an ellipse by using the lengths of its major and minor axes or by picking a center point and specifying axis lengths. You can also draw elliptical arcs using the third option on the **Ellipse** tool button.

### Drawing an Ellipse—Axis Endpoint

1. On the **Draw** panel, click the down arrow next to the **Ellipse** tool and then click **Axis, End**.

   AutoCAD prompts:

   Specify axis endpoint of ellipse or [Arc Center]:

**2** Pick or define a starting point for one of the axes.

`Specify other endpoint of axis:`

**3** Pick or define an endpoint that defines the length of the axis.

`Specify distance to other axis or [Rotation]:`

**4** Pick or define a point that defines half of the length of the other axis.

The distance specified in step 4 is the radius of the axis. In the example shown in the extended tooltip (Figure 2-31), points 1 and 2 define the major axes, and point 3 defines the minor axis. The sample ellipse drawn in Figure 2-31 shows an object in which points 1 and 2 were used to define the minor axes, and point 3 was used to define the major axis.

**Figure 2-31**

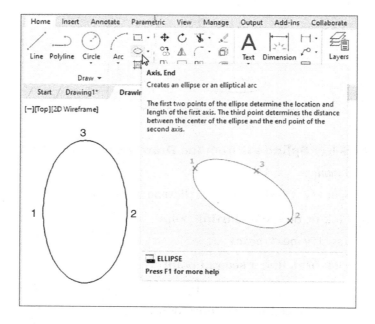

## Drawing an Ellipse—Center

**1** On the **Draw** panel, click the down arrow next to the **Ellipse** tool and then click **Center**.

AutoCAD prompts:

`Specify axis endpoint of ellipse or [Arc Center]:`

`Specify center of ellipse:`

**2** Pick or define the center point of the ellipse (such as P1 in Figure 2-32).

`Specify axis endpoint:`

**3** Pick or define one of the endpoints of one of the axes (such as P2 in Figure 2-32).

The distance between the center point and the endpoint is equal to the radius of the axis.

`Specify distance to other axis or [Rotation]:`

**Figure 2-32**

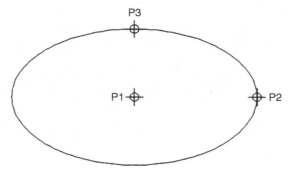

4 Pick or define a point that defines half of the length of the other axis (such as P3 in Figure 2-32).

## Drawing an Elliptical Arc

1 On the **Draw** panel, click the down arrow next to the **Ellipse** tool button and then click **Elliptical Arc**.

```
Specify axis endpoint of elliptical arc or [Center]:
```

2 Select or define a point (such as P1 on Figure 2-33).

```
Specify other endpoint of axis:
```

**Figure 2-33**

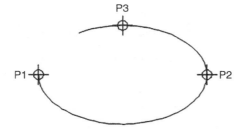

3 Select or define a point (such as P2 in Figure 2-33).

The distance between points 1 and 2 defines the length of the major axis.

```
Specify distance to other axis or [Rotation]:
```

4 Select or define a point that defines the minor axis (such as P3 in Figure 2-33).

```
Specify start angle or [Parameter]:
```

5 Type **0** and press **Enter**.

```
Specify end angle or [Parameter Included angle]:
```

6 Type **315** and press **Enter**.

## 2-12 Rectangle

Use the **Rectang** command to draw rectangular polylines. If you select one of the lines that constitute the rectangle, the entire rectangle is highlighted because it's a single object. The **Explode** command, whose tool button is located on the **Modify** panel, can reduce any block to its individual elements. If a rectangle is exploded, it is changed from a single polyline object to four individual straight lines.

### Drawing a Rectangle

**1** Select the **Rectangle** tool from the **Draw** panel.

AutoCAD prompts:

```
Specify first corner point or [Chamfer Elevation Fillet Thickness
Width]:
```

**2** Pick or define a starting point.

```
Specify other corner point:
```

**3** Pick or define a point.

The two points define the length and width of the rectangle. (Figure 2-34).

Figure 2-34

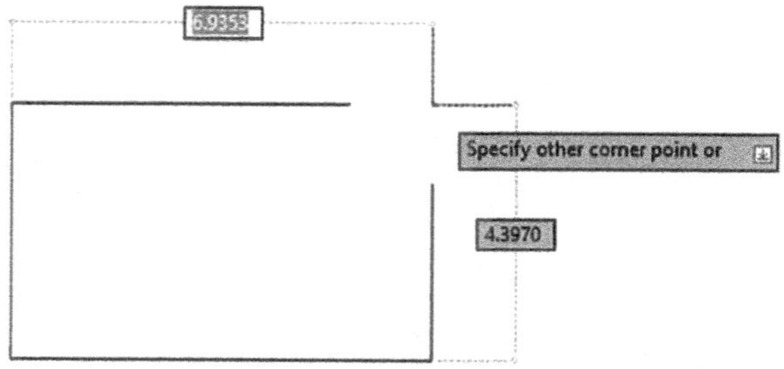

Once you have picked the first corner, you can also choose an option to enter the dimensions, the area, or a non-orthogonal rotation.

### Exploding a Rectangle

**1** Select **Explode** from the **Modify** panel (Figure 2-35).

```
Select object:
```

**2** Select the rectangle.

```
Select object:
```

**3** Press **Enter**.

There is no visible change in the rectangle, but it is now composed of four individual straight lines. As a test, use the **Erase** command to remove one of the lines.

Figure 2-35

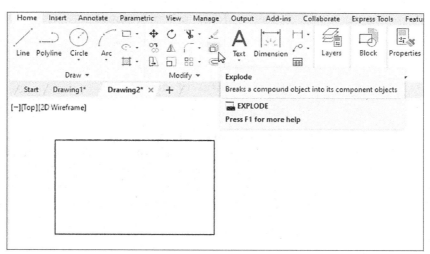

Figure 2-35

## 2-13 Polygon

A *polygon* is a closed polyline object bounded by straight lines. The **Polygon** command draws only regular polygons, in which all sides and angles are equal. A regular polygon with four equal sides is a square. This example shows how to draw a six-sided polygon, or hexagon.

### Drawing a Polygon—Center Point

The **Polygon** and **Rectangle** commands share a tool button in the **Draw** panel. If the tool button shows a rectangle, click the down arrow beside the button and select **Polygon**.

**1** Select **Polygon** from the **Draw** panel (Figure 2-36).

AutoCAD prompts:

```
Command: _polygon
Enter number of sides <4>:
```

Figure 2-36

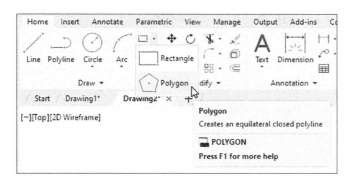

**2** Type **6** and press **Enter**.

```
Specify center of polygon or [Edge]:
```

**3** Select or define a center point.

`Enter an option [Inscribed in circle Circumscribed about circle]:`

**4** Type **C** and press **Enter**.

`Specify radius of circle:`

**5** Type a value and press **Enter**.

The **Circumscribe** option was selected here because the diameter of the designated circle will equal the distance across the flats of the hexagon. The distance across the flats is often used to specify hexagon head bolt sizes and the wrench sizes used to fit them. The **Inscribe** option creates a polygon where the radius specifies the distance between the corners (see Figure 2-37).

**Figure 2-37**

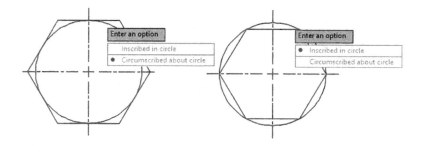

## Drawing a Polygon—Edge Distance

**1** Select the **Polygon** tool from the **Draw** panel.

AutoCAD prompts:

`Command: _polygon`

`Enter number of sides <4>:`

**2** Type **6** and press **Enter**.

`Specify center of polygon or [Edge]:`

**3** Type **E** and press **Enter**.

`Specify first endpoint of edge:`

**4** Pick or define a point.

`Specify second endpoint of edge:`

**5** Pick or define a point.

## 2-14 Point

The **Point** command creates point objects on a drawing. You can set the appearance and size of point objects in the **Point Style** dialog box. By default, a point object is dimensionless and always appears as a single pixel, regardless of zoom magnification. If you select the **Point** tool from the **Draw** menu, you can place multiple point objects until you press **Esc** to exit the command.

## Changing the Shape of a Point

Start with the cursor at the command prompt. Do not click the **Point** tool.

**1** Type **Ptype** on the command line and press **Enter**.

The **Point Style** dialog box appears, displaying 20 different visual appearances for point objects (Figure 2-38).

Figure 2-38

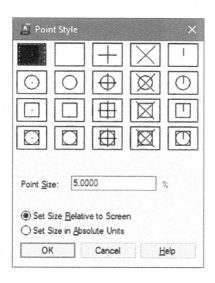

**2** Click the icon in the middle of the top row and click **OK**.

**3** On the expanded **Draw** panel, click **Multiple Points** and add several points to the screen.

**4** Press the **Esc** key to exit the **Point** tool.

## Changing the Size of a Point

**1** Type **Ptype** at a command prompt and press **Enter**.

**2** In the **Point Size** edit box, type **2.0** and press **Enter**.

If you change the point type or point size value, all existing and new point objects take on the new values.

## 2-15 Text

You can add drawing text with the **Multiline Text** tool found on the **Annotate** panel of the **Home** tab.

### Creating Multiline Text

Use the **Multiline Text** command to enter drawing text. First, define the area in which the text is to be entered. Enter text in the **Multiline Text Editor**, just as you would with a word processing program. You can move text objects to different locations on the drawing screen by using the **Move** command.

**1** Select the **Multiline Text** tool button from the **Annotate** panel.

AutoCAD prompts:

```
Specify first corner:
```

**2** Pick or define a point.

The area that you are about to define is for the entire text entry, but it can be modified. Text can be created with different fonts (Figure 2-39).

```
Specify opposite corner or [Height Justify Line spacing Rotation
Style Width]:
```

**Figure 2-39**

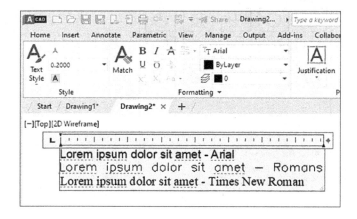

**3** Define the other corner of the area.

The **Multiline Text Editor** window appears in the drawing area, and the **Text Editor** tab opens at the right end of the ribbon (Figure 2-40).

**Figure 2-40**

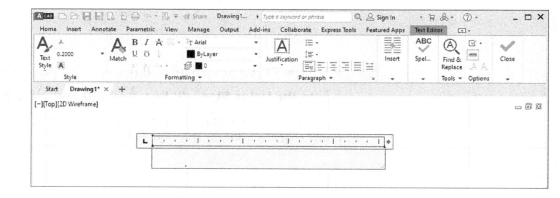

**4** Type in your text and then click the screen outside the text box.

The text will be located on the drawing screen within the specified area.

## The Multiline Text Editor

You can use the **Multiline Text Editor** to change the text height, color, font style, and justification.

## Accessing the Multiline Text Editor

The **Multiline Text** tool is available in the **Text** panel of the **Annotate** tab.

**1** Click the **Annotate** tab.

**2** Click the **Multiline Text** tool.

**3** Define an area for text.

The **Text Editor** tab now appears at the end of the ribbon (Figure 2-40).

The **Text Editor** tab and its panels are not normally visible. It appears only in concert with the **Multiline Text** command.

## Changing Text Height

**1** Click the **Multiline Text** tool and type the desired text.

**2** Highlight the text in the text editor.

**3** In the **Style** panel of the **Text Editor** tab, click and highlight the text height box and type in a new text height (Figure 2-41).

**Figure 2-41**

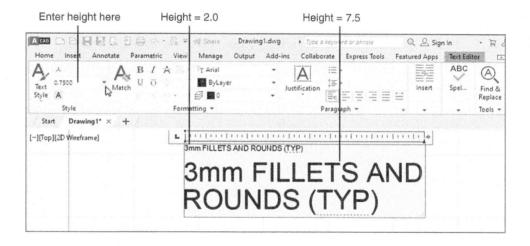

**4** Press **Enter**.

## Changing the Text Font

**1** Click the **Multiline Text** tool and type the desired text.

**2** Highlight the text.

**3** Access the drop-down list of fonts in the **Formatting** panel of the **Text Editor** tab by clicking the arrow on the right side of the drop-down and then scroll down the list and select the **Times New Roman** font.

The font of the selected text changes to Times New Roman (Figure 2-42).

Figure 2-42

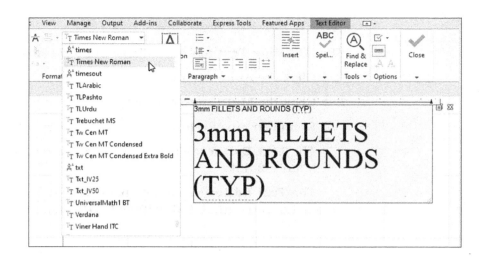

Figure 2-42 shows multiple lines of text, one typed in Arial font and the other in Times New Roman font.

## Justifying Text

AutoCAD justifies text to the left unless otherwise specified. Figure 2-42 shows text created with the default left justification.

## Justifying Text to the Right

In the next steps, the **Properties** palette is used to change the text justification.

**1** Use a window to select the lines of text shown in Figure 2-42 (that is, select them so that they appear in a selection window).

**2** With the text selected, right-click and select the **Properties** (not **Quick Properties**) option.

The **Properties** palette appears (Figure 2-43).

Figure 2-43

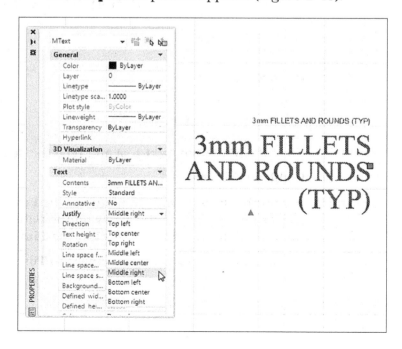

**3** In the **Text** section of the **Properties** palette, click the **Justify** line and then click the arrow on the right side of the box.

**4** Scroll down the drop-down list and click **Middle right** (Figure 2-43).

The text justifies to the right. Note that the justification is dynamic—that is, as you scroll, the lines of text change.

Figure 2-43 shows a list of other possible justifications available. Figure 2-44 shows examples of the nine possible justifications shown in the drop-down list.

**Figure 2-44**

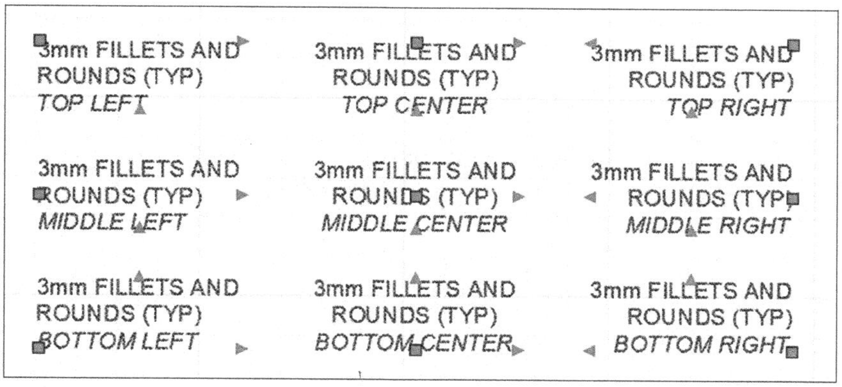

## Using the Symbol Options

In AutoCAD, you can type some basic characters to display three common symbols used in drawing text:

**%%C** = Ø (diameter symbol)
**%%P** = ± (plus/minus symbol)
**%%D** = ° (degree symbol)

As you type a symbol with one of these options, it begins by appearing just as you type it (in the **%%** form) in the **Multiline Text Editor**, but when you type the third character, it changes to the actual symbol.

You can also create these symbols by using the **Windows Character** chart, as follows:

**Alt+0216** = Ø
**Alt+0177** = ±
**Alt+0176** = °

## Changing Text Color

You can change the color of a text object by using the **Color** option located on the **Text Editor** tab (Figure 2-45). Click the arrow to the right of the **Color** box, and a chart of available colors appears.

Figure 2-45

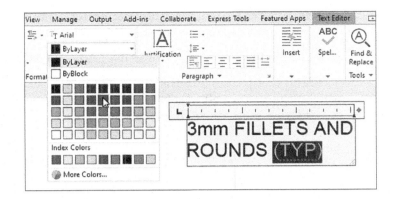

## 2-16 Move

The **Move** command relocates selected objects to a new location or locations on a drawing (Figure 2-46).

Figure 2-46

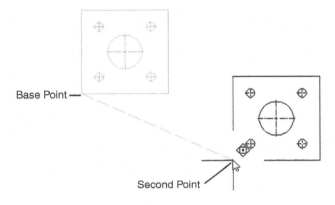

Base Point

Second Point

## Moving an Object

**1** Select the **Move** tool button from the **Modify** panel on the **Home** tab.

Select objects:

**2** Window the entire object.

Select objects:

**3** Press **Enter** or right-click.

Specify base point or [Displacement]:

**4** Pick or define a base point.

You can select any point. Snap points are usually used as base points because they can define precise displacement distances and accurate new locations.

Specify second point or <use first point as displacement>:

**5** Pick or define a second point, which is the displacement point (that is, the new location of the objects relative to the base point).

The object moves relative to the first point to its new location, relative to the second point.

## 2-17 Copy

The **Copy** command makes an exact duplicate of an existing object. You can use **Copy** to create more than one copy without reactivating the command. **Copy** is similar to **Move** in that you pick a base point and a second point, but **Copy** leaves the original object.

### Copying an Object

**1** Select **Copy** from the **Modify** panel.

```
Select objects:
```

**2** Window the entire object.

```
Select objects:
```

**3** Press **Enter** or right-click.

```
Specify base point:
```

**4** Pick or define a base point.

In the example shown in Figure 2-46, the lower-left corner of the object was selected as the base point.

```
Specify second point of displacement or <use first point as
displacement>:
```

**5** Pick or define a second point, which is the displacement point.

The original object remains in its original location, and a new object appears relative to the displacement point (Figure 2-47).

Figure 2-47

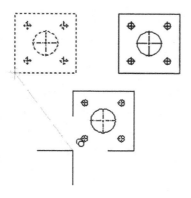

**6** Right-click and select **Enter** to create the copy and end the command.

## Making Multiple Copies

AutoCAD continues to make copies of a selected object until all of the copied objects are made.

**1** Make as many copies as you like.

After you make each copy, you see this prompt:

`Select a second displacement point:`

**2** Move the cursor to a new displacement point or right-click and select **Enter** to confirm that the objects have been copied (Figure 2-48).

**Figure 2-48**

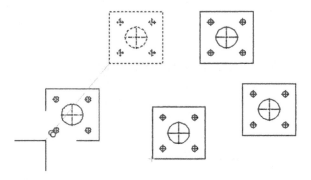

## 2-18 Offset

**1** Select **Offset** from the **Modify** panel.

`Specify offset distance or [Through Erase Layer] <Through>:`

**2** Specify the offset distance by typing a value and then press **Enter**.

In this example (Figure 2-49), a distance of **.25** was selected.

`Select object to offset or <exit>:`

**Figure 2-49**

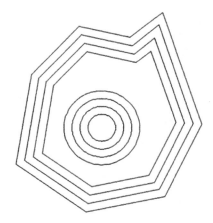

**3** Select an object.

`Specify point on side to offset:`

**4** Select a point on the side of the object you want to offset.

`Select object to offset or <exit>:`

You can repeat the process by double-clicking the right mouse button and selecting the **Repeat Offset** option.

## 2-19 Mirror

The **Mirror** command is very useful when drawing symmetrical objects because only half of the object needs be drawn. The second half can be created by using the **Mirror** command.

**1** Select **Mirror** from the **Modify** panel.

`Select objects:`

**2** Window the object.

`Select objects:`

**3** Press **Enter** or right-click.

`Specify first point of mirror line:`

**4** Select a point on the mirror line.

`Specify second point of mirror line:`

**5** Select a second point on the mirror line.

`Delete source object? [Yes No]<N>:`

**6** Press **Enter** or right-click.

Any line can be used as a mirror line, including lines within an object. Figure 2-50 shows an object mirrored about one of its edge lines.

**Figure 2-50**

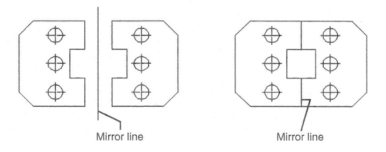

Mirror line          Mirror line

## 2-20 Array

An array is a group of objects arranged in a regular pattern. You can put objects in arrays using the **Rectangular Array**, **Path Array**, and **Polar Array** commands. Figure 2-51 shows a rectangular array.

Figure 2-51

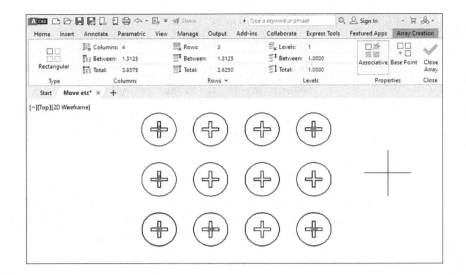

## Using the Rectangular Array Option

**1** Select **Rectangular Array** from the **Modify** panel.

**2** Select the object to be arrayed and right-click.

The screen changes. The array creation panels appear on the **Array Creation** tab (Figure 2-51). The default setting is for a 4-by-3 array. Edit the default array by entering values in the panels on the **Array Creation** tab. In the example in Figure 2-52, a 5-by-2 array was created.

Figure 2-52

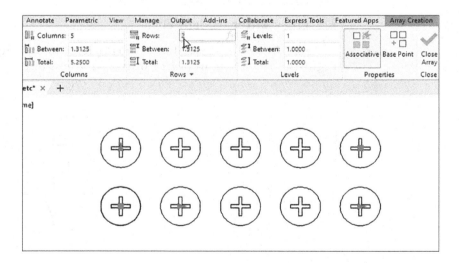

**3** Enter the array values.

**4** Right-click and select the **Enter** option.

## Using the Polar Array Option

With the **Polar Array** option, objects are arrayed in a circular pattern around a center point (Figure 2-53).

**1** Select the **Polar Array** tool from the **Modify** panel.

Figure 2-53

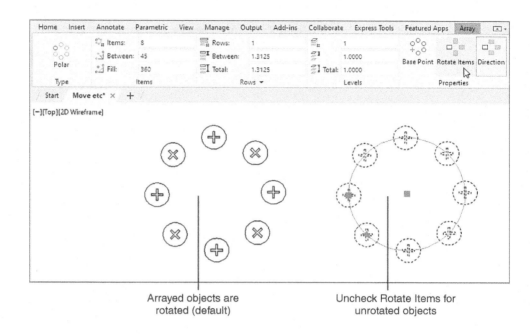

Arrayed objects are
rotated (default)

Uncheck Rotate Items for
unrotated objects

**2** Select the object to be arrayed and right-click.

`Specify center point of Array or [Base point Axis of rotation]:`

**3** Select a center point for the array.

The screen changes. The array creation panels appear on the **Array Creation** tab (Figure 2-51). The default setting is for six items in the array. The default array can be edited by using the panels on the **Array Creation** tab. In this example, eight items were selected, and the **Direction** tool was activated. Arrayed items can be rotated (the default) or unrotated.

**4** Enter the array values.

**5** Right-click and select the **Enter** option.

## Using the Path Array Option

Use **Path Array** when you want to create multiple objects along a defined path. The path can be a line, circle, polyline, spline, or any linear or curved object. You can also create 3D path arrays by selecting a helix (see Chapter 3) or a 3D polyline as a path. 3D polylines are not covered in this book.

**1** Select the **Path Array** tool from the **Modify** panel.

**2** Select the object to be arrayed and right-click.

`Specify center point of Array or [Base point Axis of rotation]:`

**3** Select the path object.

`Select path curve:`

The **Array Creation** tab appears at the end of the ribbon.

**4** Enter values for the array numbers and distances, and indicate whether the object should be aligned to the path as it is arrayed.

**5** Right-click and select **Enter** (Figure 2-54).

**Figure 2-54**

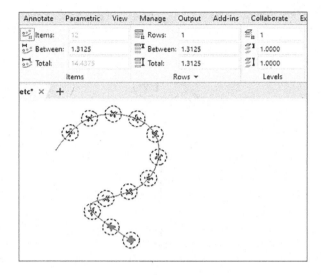

## 2-21 Rotate

The **Rotate** command rotates an object about a specified base point (Figure 2-55).

By default in AutoCAD, **0°** is to the east, or three o'clock on a clock face. Angles in the counterclockwise direction are positive angles.

**Figure 2-55**

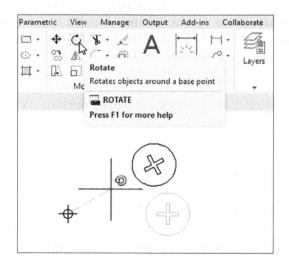

## Rotating an Object

**1** Select **Rotate** from the **Modify** panel.

```
Select objects:
```

**2** Select the object or objects to be rotated.

```
Select objects:
```

**3** Press **Enter** or right-click.

```
Specify base point:
```

**4** Pick or define a base point.

The base point may be anywhere on the screen.

```
Specify rotation angle or [Reference]:
```

**5** Type a value and press **Enter**.

The object rotates about the base point by the specified angle in the counterclockwise direction. To rotate the object in a clockwise direction, enter a negative value.

## 2-22 Trim

Use the **Trim** command to remove parts of objects that are crossed by other objects. By default, starting the command selects all objects that can be trimmed. You can hover the cursor over parts of lines or other objects and click to remove them. **Trim** is a very important AutoCAD command and is used frequently.

## Using Trim

**1** Select **Trim** from the **Modify** panel.

```
Select cutting edges:
Select objects:
```

**2** Move the cursor over a part of any object you want to remove and click when you see the red X over the object.

**3** Press **Enter** or right-click.

```
Select object to trim or [Project Edge Undo]:
```

As shown in Figure 2-56, the left portion of the circle, and the portion of the line within the circle, are deleted.

Figure 2-56

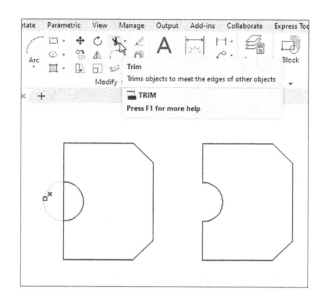

**4** Press **Enter**.

Selected portions of the objects disappear. Figure 2-57 shows an example similar to the one presented in Figure 2-56, but in this example, different portions of the line and circle are trimmed.

Figure 2-57

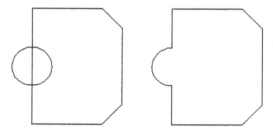

## 2-23 Extend

The **Extend** command extends selected lines, arcs, or polylines to new borders (Figure 2-58). **Extend** and **Trim** work similarly to each other and share a tool button on the **Modify** panel.

**1** Select **Extend** from the **Modify** panel.

```
Select boundary edges:

Select objects:
```

**2** Move the cursor over a part of any object you want to extend to a new boundary and click when you see the object highlighted and extended (Figure 2-58).

**3** Right-click, and then select **Enter**.

Figure 2-58

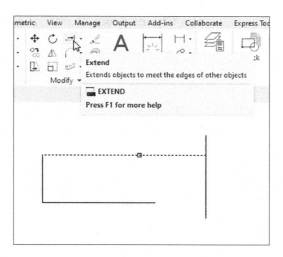

## 2-24 Break

Use the **Break** command to remove portions of an object. It is similar to the **Trim** command but does not require edges to be cut. Break distances are defined between points (Figure 2-59).

Figure 2-59

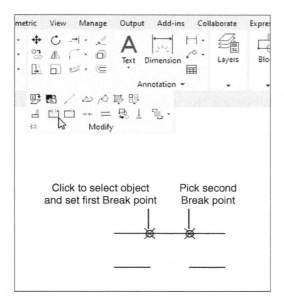

Click to select object and set first Break point     Pick second Break point

## Using the Break Command

**1** Select **Break** from the expanded **Modify** panel.

```
Select object:
```

**2** Select a point on the line.

Selecting the object also sets the first point of the break at the same place. If object snap is enabled and selected points are getting in the way, toggle off the **Object Snap** button or press **F3** to turn off the feature.

```
Specify second break point or [First point]:
```

**3** Pick a second point.

The length of the break will be equal to the distance between the two selected points.

> **NOTE**
>
> Use the **Break at Point** command to break a line into two parts. It does not remove part of the line but simply breaks the line into two parts.

## Using the First Point Option

The **F**, or **First point**, option allows you to first select a line and then define the starting point of the break. This means that unlike with the default **Break** command sequence, as just described, the first selection captures only the line, not the line and the first break point.

**1** Select **Break** from the **Modify** panel.

```
Select object:
```

**2** Select the line.

```
Specify second break point or [First point]:
```

**3** Type **F** and press **Enter**.

```
Specify first break point:
```

**4** Pick or define the first point of the break. Toggle off **Object Snap** in the status bar, if necessary.

```
Specify second break point:
```

**5** Pick or define the second point of the break.

## 2-25 Chamfer

A *chamfer* is a straight-line corner cut, usually cut at 45°. Other angles may be used (Figure 2-60).

**Figure 2-60**

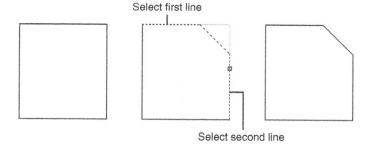

Select first line

Select second line

## Creating a Chamfer

The **Chamfer** and **Fillet** commands share a tool button on the **Modify** panel. Click the down arrow next to the button and select the desired command.

**1** Select **Chamfer** from the **Modify** panel.

AutoCAD prompts:

```
(TRIM mode) Current chamfer Dist1 = 0.0000, Dist2 = 0.0000
Select first line or [Polyline Distance Angle Trim Method] <Select
first line>:
```

**2** Type **D** and press **Enter**.

```
Specify first chamfer distance <0.0000>:
```

**3** Type **.75** and press **Enter**.

```
Specify second chamfer distance <0.7500>:
```

AutoCAD assumes that the chamfer will be at 45° and automatically sets the second distance equal to the first.

**4** Select the first line to be chamfered, then hover the cursor over the second line. The lines and the chamfer are highlighted (Figure 2-60).

**5** Click on the second line to complete the chamfer.

## 2-26 Fillet

A *fillet* is a rounded corner (Figure 2-61).

**Figure 2-61**

## Creating a Fillet

**1** Select **Fillet** from the **Modify** panel. Click the **Fillet/Chamfer** tool button if necessary.

```
Current settings: Mode = Trim, Radius = 0.5000
Select first object or [Polyline Radius Trim]:
```

**2** Type **R** and press **Enter**.

```
Specify fillet radius <0.0000>:
```

**3** Type **.5** and press **Enter**.

```
Command:
Select first object or [Polyline Radius Trim Multiple]:
```

**4** Select a line.

```
Select second object:
```

**5** Hover the cursor over the second line. The lines and the fillet are highlighted.

**6** Click on the second line to complete the fillet.

You can also create fillets between circles (Figure 2-62). The **Fillet** command is location sensitive, meaning that the location of the selection points will affect the shape of the resulting fillet.

**Figure 2-62**

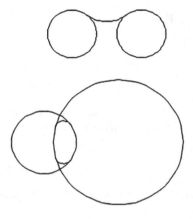

## 2-27 Table

The **Table** command is used to create tables such as the one shown in Figure 2-63. Tables are used on drawings to define multiple hole dimensions, to define coordinate data, and to create parts lists, among other uses.

**Figure 2-63**

| LOCATION | X COORD | Y COORD | Ø |
|----------|---------|---------|-------|
| A1 | 15.00 | 85.00 | 20.00 |
| A2 | 15.00 | 15.00 | 20.00 |
| A3 | 145.00 | 85.00 | 20.00 |
| A4 | 145.00 | 15.00 | 20.00 |
| B1 | 55.00 | 70.00 | 30.00 |
| B2 | 110.00 | 70.00 | 30.00 |
| C1 | 80.00 | 30.00 | 40.00 |

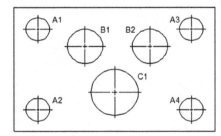

## Creating a Table

Follow the steps below to create a table object:

**1** Click **Table** on the **Annotate** panel.

The **Insert Table** dialog box opens (Figure 2-64).

Figure 2-64

Open Table Style dialog box

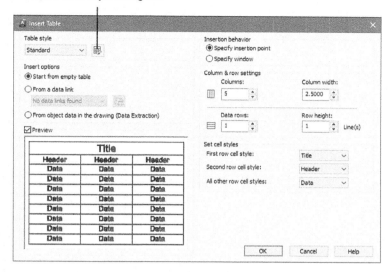

Click the button under **Table style** at the top of the **Insert Table** dialog box.

The **Table Style** dialog box appears (Figure 2-65).

Figure 2-65

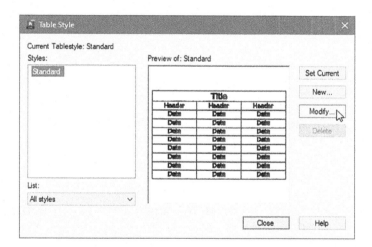

Click **Modify**.

The **Modify Table Style: Standard** dialog box appears.

Click the **Text** tab in the **Cell styles** area (Figure 2-66).

The word **Data** at the top of the **Cell styles** area indicates that the modifications will be made on the text used in the data cells.

Click the ellipsis button to the right of **Text style: Standard** (Figure 2-66).

Figure 2-66

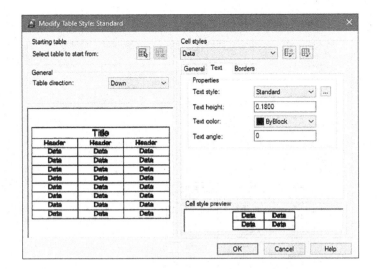

The **Text Style** dialog box appears (Figure 2-67).

Figure 2-67

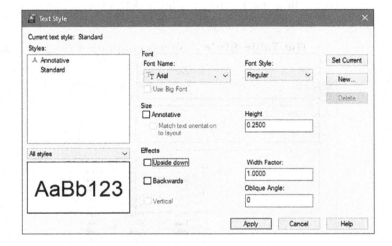

**6** Select the **Arial** font and set the height to **0.25**. Then click **Apply** and **Close**.

The **Modify Table Style: Standard** dialog box reappears (Figure 2-66).

**7** Click the arrow to the right of **Data** under **Cell styles** and select the **Title** option.

**8** Confirm that the text height for the Title cells is set to **0.25**. Click **OK** and close the **Modify Table Style: Standard** and the **Table Style** dialog boxes.

**9** Return to the **Insert Table** dialog box and set the number of data rows and columns and the size of boxes; then click **OK** (Figure 2-68).

Figure 2-68

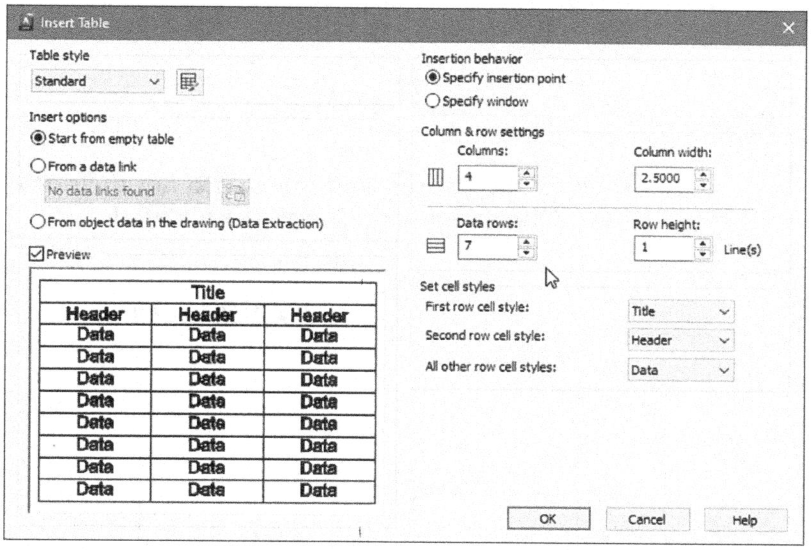

Note that the number of data rows does not include the column headings. A blank table appears on the screen (Figure 2-69).

Figure 2-69

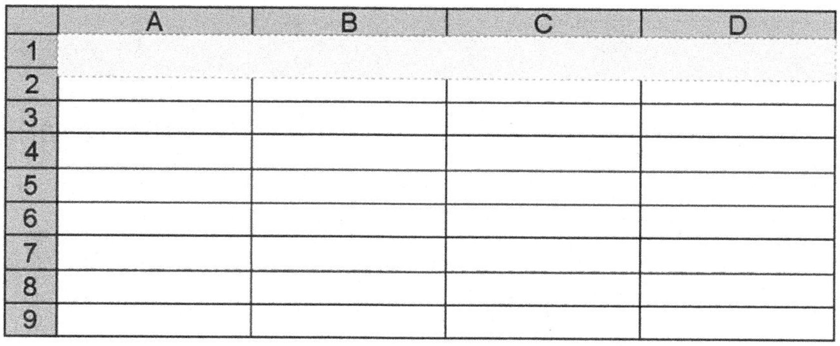

**10** Click on the appropriate box and type in the required data. Use the arrow keys to move from one box to another and continue entering data.

# 2-28 EXERCISE PROBLEMS

Redraw the figures that follow. Do not include dimensions in your drawings. Dimension values are as indicated.

## EX2-1 Inches

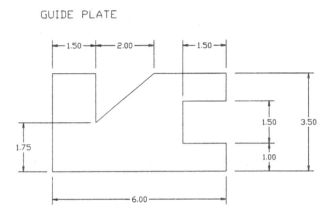

## EX2-2 Inches

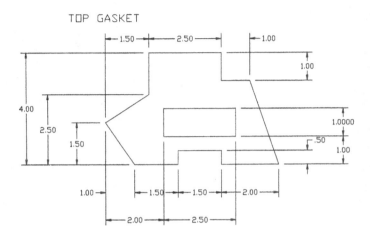

## EX2-3 Millimeters

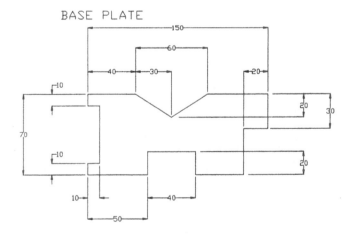

## EX2-4 Millimeters

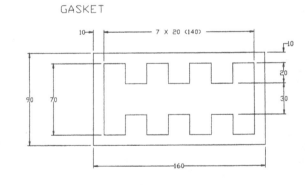

## EX2-5 Inches

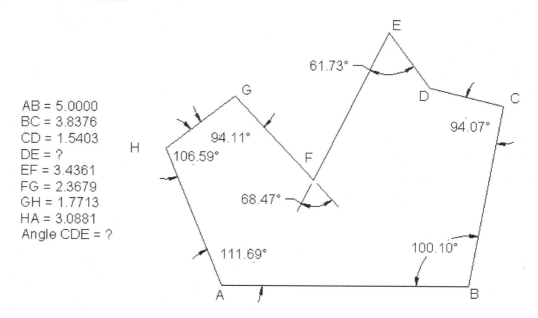

AB = 5.0000
BC = 3.8376
CD = 1.5403
DE = ?
EF = 3.4361
FG = 2.3679
GH = 1.7713
HA = 3.0881
Angle CDE = ?

## EX2-6 Millimeters

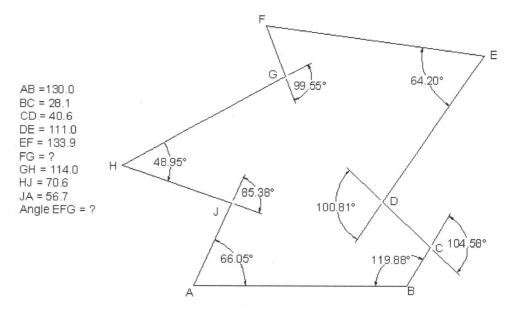

AB =130.0
BC = 28.1
CD = 40.6
DE = 111.0
EF = 133.9
FG = ?
GH = 114.0
HJ = 70.6
JA = 56.7
Angle EFG = ?

## EX2-7 Inches

SIDE BRACKET

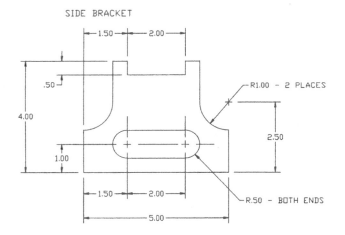

## EX2-8 Inches

FILTER PLATE

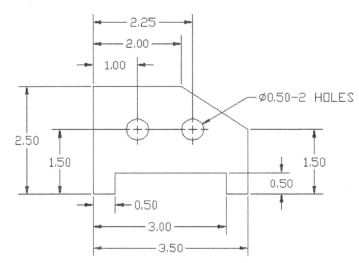

## EX2-9 Millimeters

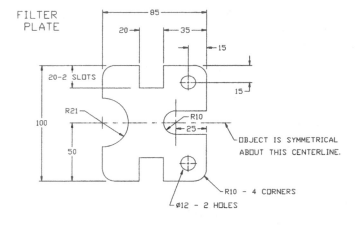

## EX2-10 Inches

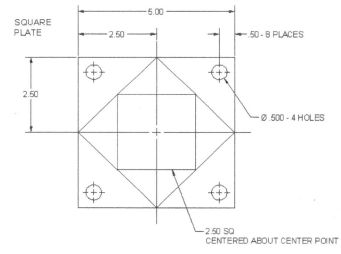

## EX2-11 Inches

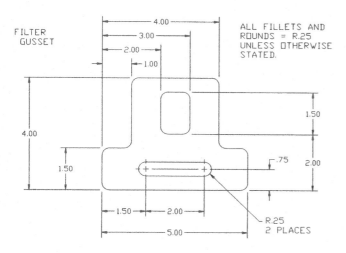

FILTER GUSSET

ALL FILLETS AND ROUNDS = R.25 UNLESS OTHERWISE STATED.

## EX2-12 Millimeters

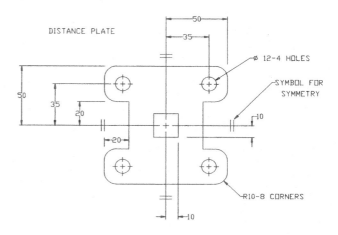

DISTANCE PLATE

Ø 12-4 HOLES

SYMBOL FOR SYMMETRY

R10-8 CORNERS

## EX2-13 Millimeters

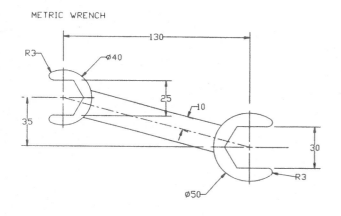

METRIC WRENCH

## EX2-14 Inches

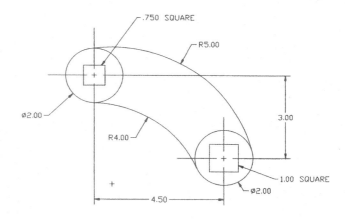

.750 SQUARE

R5.00

1.00 SQUARE

## EX2-15 Millimeters

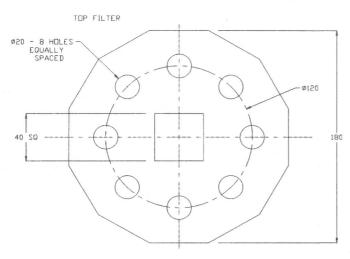

TOP FILTER

Ø20 - 8 HOLES EQUALLY SPACED

Ø120

40 SQ

## EX2-16 Millimeters

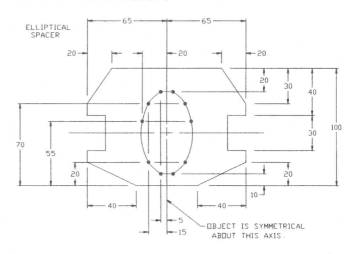

ELLIPTICAL SPACER

OBJECT IS SYMMETRICAL ABOUT THIS AXIS.

## EX2-17 Inches

GUIDE GASKET

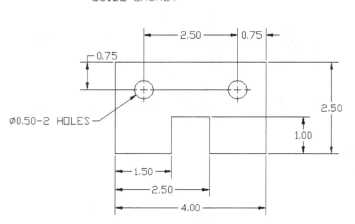

## EX2-18 Millimeters

STAR SPACER

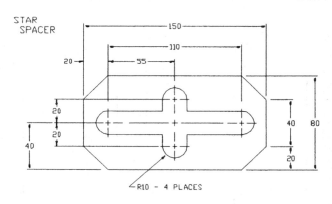

## EX2-19 Inches

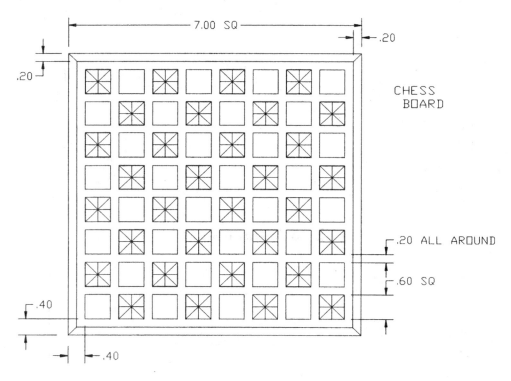

CHESS BOARD

## EX2-20 Millimeters

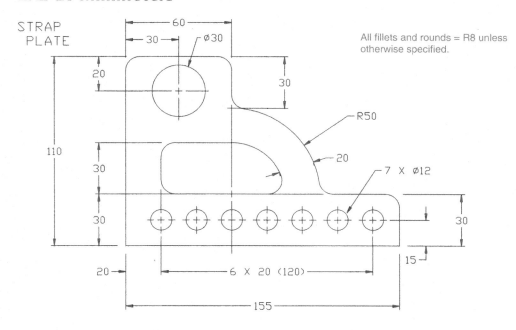

STRAP PLATE

All fillets and rounds = R8 unless otherwise specified.

## EX2-21 Inches

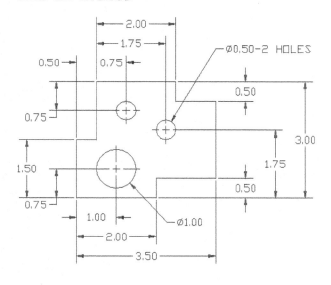

## EX2-22 Millimeters

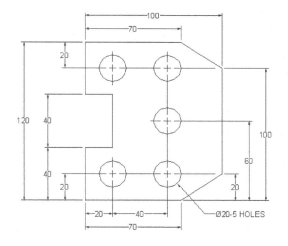

## EX2-23 Millimeters

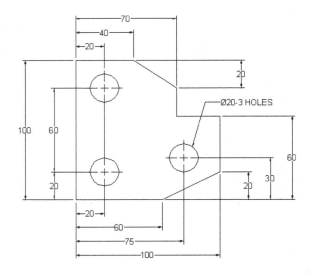

## EX2-24 Inches

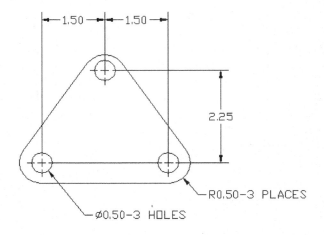

## EX2-25 Millimeters

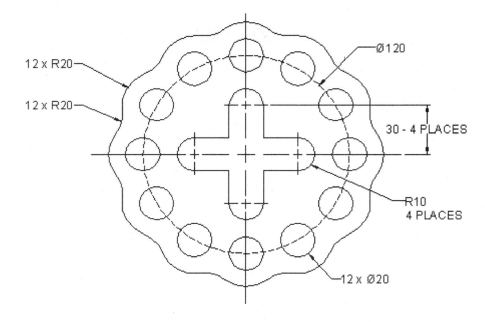

## EX2-26 Millimeters

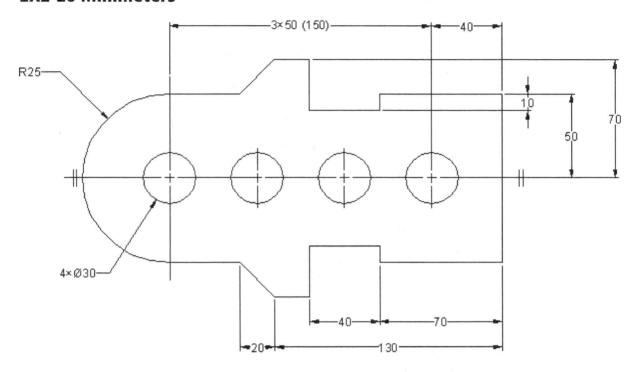

## EX2-27 Millimeters

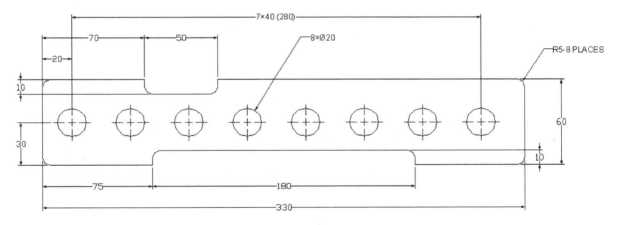

## EX2-28 Inches

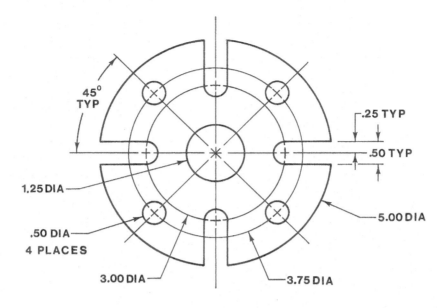

45°
TYP

.25 TYP

.50 TYP

1.25 DIA

.50 DIA
4 PLACES

3.00 DIA

3.75 DIA

5.00 DIA

MATL .25 STEEL

## EX2-29 Millimeters

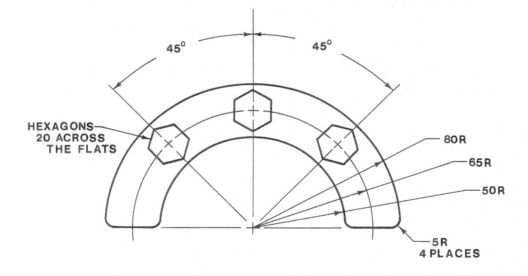

45°        45°

HEXAGONS
20 ACROSS
THE FLATS

80R

65R

50R

5R
4 PLACES

## EX2-30 Millimeters

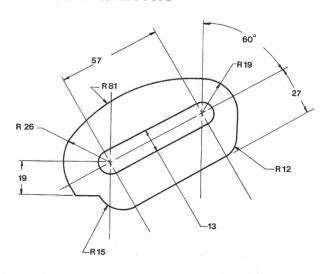

## EX2-31 Millimeters

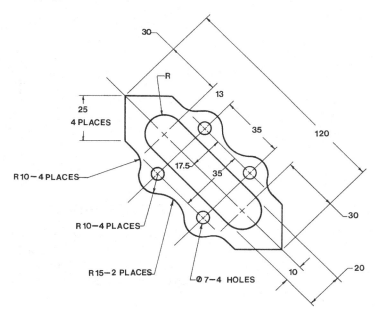

## EX2-32 Inches

Redraw the hole plate shown below. Do not include the dimensions on your drawing. Draw and complete the hole table outlined below. Set the text style to **Arial**. The data text is **.18** high, the heading text is **.25** high, and the title text is **.375** high.

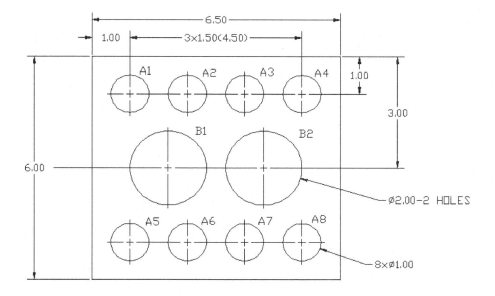

## Hole Table

| Location | X-dim | Y-dim | Ø |
|----------|-------|-------|---|
| A1 | | | |
| | | | |
| | | | |
| | | | |
| | | | |
| | | | |
| | | | |
| | | | |
| | | | |
| | | | |

## EX2-33 Millimeters

Redraw the hole plate shown below. Do not include the dimensions on your drawing. Draw and complete the hole table outlined below. Set the text style to **Arial**. The data text is **5** high, the heading text is **10** high, and the title text is **15** high.

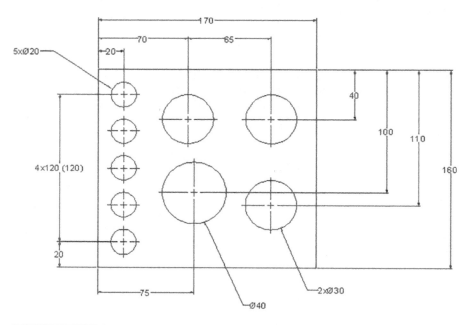

## Hole Table

| Location | X-dim | Y-dim | Ø |
|----------|-------|-------|---|
| A1 | | | |
| | | | |
| | | | |
| | | | |
| | | | |
| | | | |
| | | | |
| | | | |
| | | | |
| | | | |

# 3 chapter **three**

## Advanced Commands

### 3-1 Introduction

This chapter explains how to use some of the more advanced AutoCAD commands. Included are the **Object Snap (Osnap)**, **Grips**, **Layer**, **Block**, and **Attribute** commands and settings.

### 3-2 Object Snap

*Object snap modes* allow you to snap to specific points on entities on the drawing screen rather than just to points, as does the **Snap** command. Object Snap—**Osnap** for short—can snap to the endpoint of a line, to the intersection of two lines, or to the center point of a circle, as well as to other items. The **Object Snap** tab in the **Drafting Settings** dialog box allows you to access the various **Osnap** modes.

> **NOTE**
>
> Do not confuse the **Snap** command with **Object Snap**. **Snap** lets you move the cursor at regular intervals in the drawing area and has no relationship to objects themselves. **Object Snap**, as its name indicates, refers to specific points on existing AutoCAD objects.

### Accessing the Object Snap Modes

**1** Locate the **Object Snap** tool button on the status bar at the bottom of the screen.

**2** Click the down arrow next to the button.

A list of object snap modes appears (Figure 3-1).

Figure 3-1

Object snap modes can also be accessed by holding down the **Ctrl** key and pressing the right mouse button. This feature can be activated during any command sequence. A right-click menu appears on the screen, listing the **Osnap** modes (Figure 3-2).

**Figure 3-2**

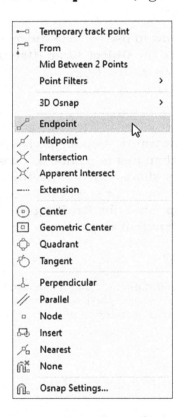

Clicking **Object Snap Settings** at the bottom of the menu in Figure 3-1 opens the **Object Snap** tab on the **Drafting Settings** dialog box (Figure 3-3). The **Object Snap** tab can turn on an **Osnap** option permanently; that is, the option remains on until you turn it off. If **Endpoint** mode is on, the cursor snaps to the nearest endpoint every time a point selection is made. When object snap modes are enabled in this way, the process is referred to as *running object snaps*.

**Figure 3-3**

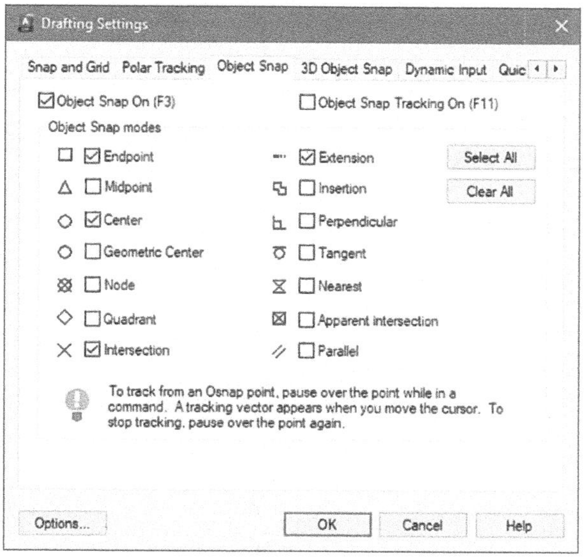

Turning on an **Osnap** mode is very helpful when you know that you are going to select several points of the same type; however, in many cases, it is more practical to activate an **Osnap** option as needed by using the right-click menu. When object snap modes are enabled in this as-needed way, the process is called *object snap overrides*.

## Enabling Object Snap Modes

**1** Access the **Drafting Settings** dialog box's **Object Snap** tab in one of two ways: Right-click the **Object Snap** icon at the bottom of the screen and click the **Object Snap Settings** option, or hold down the **Ctrl** key, right-click, and click the **Osnap Settings** option.

The **Drafting Settings** dialog box appears (Figure 3-3).

**2** Click the box to the left of the object snap mode that you wish to activate. A check mark appears, indicating that the mode is active.

**3** Close the **Drafting Settings** dialog box.

The **Options** button on the **Drafting Settings** dialog box allows you to access the **Options** dialog box, where you can change the size or color of the **AutoSnap Markers** used to identify **Osnap** points.

## Changing the Size of the Osnap Marker

The **Options** dialog box contains an **Aperture Size** option. This option allows you to change the size of the rectangular box on the cursor (Figure 3-4). A larger box makes it easier to grab objects, but a box that is too large may grab more than one object or the wrong object.

Figure 3-4

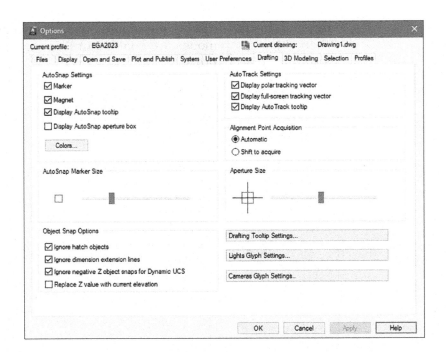

## 3-3 Osnap—Endpoint

**Endpoint** mode is used to snap to the endpoint of an existing entity (Figure 3-5).

Figure 3-5

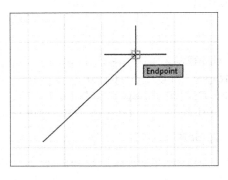

## Snapping to the Endpoint of an Existing Line

**1** Select **Line** from the **Draw** panel.

```
Command: _line Specify first point:
```

**2** Hold down the **Ctrl** key and right-click. Select **Endpoint** from the right-click menu.

```
Specify next point or [Undo]: _endp of
```

**Osnap** modes do not work independently but in conjunction with other commands. In this example, the **Line** command must be activated first, and then the **Osnap** mode is selected. Note that a marker appears at the endpoint of the line, indicating that the **Endpoint** mode has selected the line's endpoint. **Endpoint** mode also works with arcs, polylines, and 3D applications.

## 3-4 Osnap—Midpoint

**Midpoint** mode is used to snap to the midpoint of an existing entity. In the example presented in Figure 3-6, a circle is to be drawn with its center point at the midpoint of the line.

**Figure 3-6**

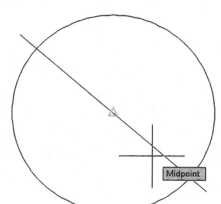

### Drawing a Circle About the Midpoint of a Line

**1** Select **Circle** from the **Draw** panel.

```
Command: _circle Specify center point for circle or [3P 2P Ttr
(tan tan radius)]:
```

**2** Hold down the **Ctrl** key and right-click. Select **Midpoint** from the right-click menu.

```
Command:_circle Specify center point for circle or [3P 2P Ttr
(tan tan radius)]:_mid of
```

**3** Select the line.

```
Specify radius of circle or [Diameter]:
```

**4** Select a radius value.

## 3-5 Osnap—Intersection

The **Intersection** option is used to snap to the intersection of two or more entities. Figure 3-7 shows a set of projection lines that are to be used to define an ellipse.

**Figure 3-7**

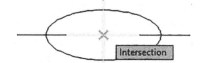

## Using Osnap Intersection Mode to Define an Ellipse

In this example, use **Intersection** mode to create an ellipse tangent to the sides of the rectangle, centered at the intersection of the lines.

**1** Select **Ellipse** from the **Draw** panel.

```
Specify axis endpoint of ellipse or [Arc Center]:
```

**2** Select **Intersection** from the **Object Snap** right-click menu and pick an intersection of the box and a line.

```
Specify axis endpoint of ellipse or [Arc Center]: _int of
```

**3** Select the first point for the ellipse.

```
Specify other endpoint of axis:_int of
```

**4** Select the **Intersection** option and then select the second point.

Select the intersection that defines the length of one of the axes from the ellipse center point. In this example, the distance between the two points selected equals the length of the major axis of the ellipse.

```
Specify distance to other axis or [Rotation]:_int of
```

**5** Select the **Intersection** tool from the **Object Snap** dialog box and select the intersection that defines the other axis length.

## 3-6 Osnap—Apparent Intersection

**Apparent Intersection** mode is used to snap to an intersection that would be created if the two entities were extended to create an actual intersection. Figure 3-8 shows two lines that do not intersect, but that, if continued, would intersect.

Figure 3-8

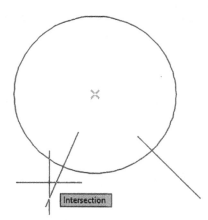

## Drawing a Circle Centered About an Apparent Intersection

While there is an **Apparent Intersect** object snap mode in the **Drafting Settings** dialog box and the object snap right-click menu, this mode is most often used in 3D work. In 2D drafting, **Intersection** mode finds the apparent intersection of objects that do not meet but that would if they were long enough. Choosing **Intersection** and selecting a line displays the intersection marker with an ellipsis (three dots) beside it. This marker means AutoCAD expects you to select another object. When you hover the cursor over the other object, the intersection point then appears.

**1** Select the **Circle** tool from the **Draw** panel.

```
Command: _circle Specify center point for circle or [3P 2P Ttr
(tan tan radius)]:
```

**2** Select **Intersection** from the **Object Snap** right-click menu.

```
Command: _circle Specify center point for circle or [3P 2P Ttr
(tan tan radius)]: _appint of
```

**3** Select one of the lines.

```
Command: _circle Specify center point for circle or [3P 2P Ttr
(tan tan radius)]: _appint of
```

**4** Select the other line.

```
Specify radius of circle or [Diameter]:
```

**5** Define a radius value for the circle.

## 3-7 Osnap—Center

The **Center** option is used to draw from a given point directly to the center point of a circle (Figure 3-9).

**Figure 3-9**

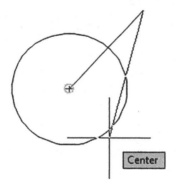

## Drawing a Line to the Center Point of a Circle

**1** Select **Line** from the **Draw** panel.

```
Command: _line Specify first point:
```

**2** Pick the starting point for the line.

```
Specify next point or [Undo]:
```

**3** Select **Center** mode from the right-click menu.

```
Specify next point or [Undo]: _cen of
```

**4** Select any point on the circle.

Do *not* try to select the center point directly. Select any point on the edge of the circle or arc; the center point is calculated automatically.

## 3-8 Osnap—Quadrant

The **Quadrant** option is used to snap directly to one of the quadrant points of an arc, a circle, or an ellipse. Figure 3-10 shows the quadrant points for an arc, a circle, and an ellipse.

**Figure 3-10**

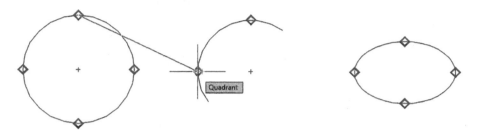

### Drawing a Line to One of a Circle's Quadrant Points

**1** Select **Line** from the **Draw** panel.

    Command: _line Specify first point:

**2** Select a starting point for the line.

    Specify next point or [Undo]:

**3** Select **Quadrant** from the **Osnap** right-click menu.

    Specify next point or [Undo]: _qua of

**4** Select a point on the circle near the desired quadrant point.

## 3-9 Osnap—Perpendicular

The **Perpendicular** option is used to draw a line perpendicular to an existing entity (Figure 3-11).

**Figure 3-11**

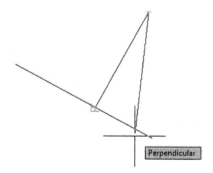

## Drawing a Line Perpendicular to an Existing Line

**1** Select **Line** from the **Draw** panel.

    Command: _line Specify first point:

**2** Pick a starting point for the line.

    Specify next point or [Undo]:

**3** Select **Perpendicular** on the **Osnap** right-click menu.

    Specify next point or [Undo]: _per to

**4** Select the line or entity that will be perpendicular to the drawn line.

## 3-10 Osnap—Tangent

The **Tangent** option is used to draw lines tangent to existing circles and arcs (Figure 3-12).

**Figure 3-12**

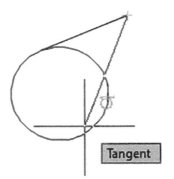

## Drawing a Line Tangent to a Circle

**1** Select **Line** from the **Draw** panel.

    Command: _line Specify first point:

**2** Pick the starting point for the line.

    Specify next point or [Undo]:

**3** Select **Tangent** from the **Osnap** right-click menu.

    Specify next point or [Undo]: _tan to

**4** Select the circle.

## 3-11 Osnap—Nearest

The **Nearest** option is used to snap to the nearest available point on an existing entity (Figure 3-13).

Figure 3-13

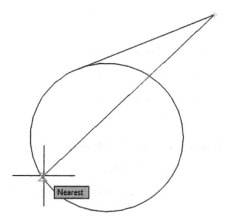

## Drawing a Line from a Point to the Nearest Selected Point on an Existing Line

**1** Select **Line** from the **Draw** panel.

Command: _line Specify first point:

**2** Pick a starting point for the line.

Specify next point or [Undo]:

**3** Select **Nearest** from the **Osnap** right-click menu.

Specify next point or [Undo]: _nea to

**4** Select the existing line.

The existing line need be only within the aperture on the cursor. The line endpoint is snapped to the nearest available point on the line.

## 3-12 Drawing Problem

Redraw the object shown in Figure 3-14. Do *not* include dimensions. Use **Osnap** commands whenever possible.

**1** Create a new drawing called **SP3-1**.

Figure 3-14

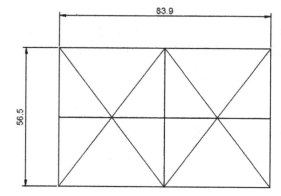

**2** Use the following drawing setup:

Limits: lower left = **<0.0000,0.0000>**

Limits: upper right = **297,210**

Zoom All

Grid = **10**

Snap = **5**

**3** Draw an **83.9** × **56.5** rectangle. Use dynamic input values to draw the rectangle's edge lines and enable **Snap** (Figure 3-15).

**Figure 3-15**

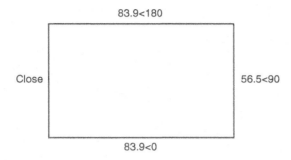

**4** Draw line **A–B–C**. Point **A** is a grid snap point, so it may be selected directly. Point **B** is selected by using **Osnap Midpoint**, and point **C** is selected by using **Osnap Endpoint** (or **Intersection**) (Figure 3-16).

**Figure 3-16**

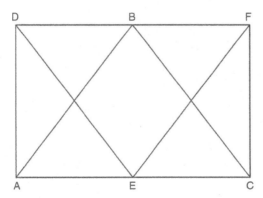

**5** Draw line **D–E–F** by using **Endpoint**, **Midpoint**, and **Endpoint**, respectively.

**6** Draw line **B–E** by using **Intersection** (Figure 3-17).

**Figure 3-17**

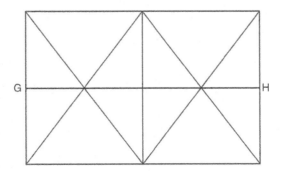

**7** Draw line **G–H** by using **Midpoint**.

**8** Save the drawing if desired.

## 3-13 Drawing Problem

Redraw the object shown in Figure 3-18. Do not include dimensions.

**1** Create a new drawing called **SP3-2**.

**Figure 3-18**

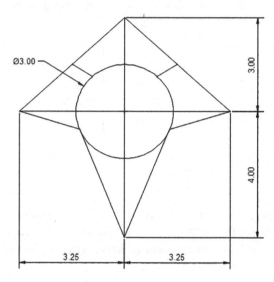

**2** Use the following drawing setup:

Limits: Accept the default values

Grid = **.50**

Snap = **.25**

**3** Draw lines **A–B**, **C–D**, **A–C**, and **C–B**. The endpoint of each of these lines is located on a grid snap point, so the points may be selected directly.

**4** Draw circle **O** (Figure 3-19). Respond to the center point prompt by selecting **Intersection** from the **Osnap** pop-up menu.

**Figure 3-19**

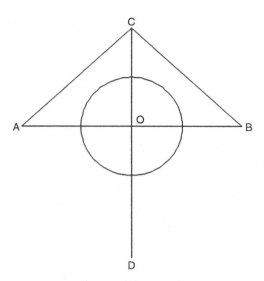

5️⃣ Draw lines **G–I** and **H–J**, using **Midpoint** and **Nearest** (Figure 3-20).

**Figure 3-20**

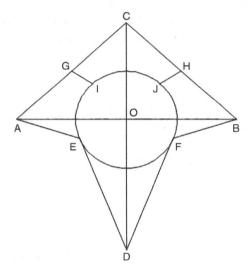

6️⃣ Draw lines **D–E** and **D–F**, using **Tangent**. Draw lines **A–E** and **B–F**, using **Endpoint**. Points **A**, **B**, and **D** are grid snap points and also are endpoints.

7️⃣ Save the drawing if desired.

## 3-14  Grips

*Grips* are small squares that appear on an object when you select the object with no command active. For example, when you select a line, grips appear at the endpoints and at the midpoint. When you select a circle, grips appear at the center and at the four quadrants. Arcs show grips at the endpoints and midpoint, and polylines show grips at their vertices and midpoints.

Grips appear on any AutoCAD object when it's selected and no command is active. Figure 3-21 shows some examples of grips.

**Figure 3-21**

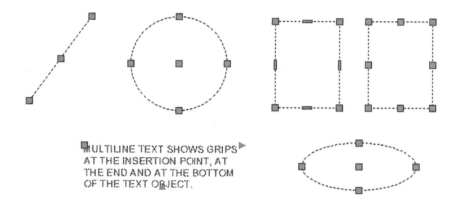

MULTILINE TEXT SHOWS GRIPS
AT THE INSERTION POINT, AT
THE END AND AT THE BOTTOM
OF THE TEXT OBJECT.

Grips provide a helpful alternative to editing objects without actually running any of the **Modify** commands. For example, if a line is to be rotated about its center point, you can use a grip to first identify the line's center point (pickbox) and then lock onto it as the center point (base point) for the rotation. You can use the center point of a circle to move the circle to a new location, or you can drag a quadrant grip to change a circle's radius.

## Turning Grips Off

By default, grips are automatically enabled. You can turn off grips by changing the value of the **Grips** system variable as follows:

**1** Type **Grips** at a command prompt.

```
Enter new value for GRIPS <1>:
```

The three possible **Grips** values are as follows:

- 0 = Grips are off.
- 1 = Grips are on.
- 2 = Grips are on, and polylines display midpoint grips between vertices. This the default setting.

**2** Type **0** and press **Enter**.

Grips are now turned off.

## Accessing the Grips Dialog Box

**1** Grip an existing line—that is, place the cursor on the line and press the left mouse button.

A line is gripped when a command prompt is displayed and no other command sequence is active.

**2** Click on one of the grip points.

In this example, the lower endpoint was selected.

```
<Stretch to point>/Basepoint/Copy/Undo/eXit:
```

**3** Right-click.

The **Grips** menu appears (Figure 3-22).

Figure 3-22

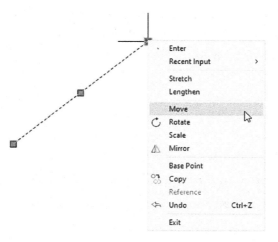

## 3-15  Grips—Extend

### Extending the Length of a Line

Extend a line 1.25 inches.

**1** Draw an angled line as shown in Figure 3-23 and then draw a circle of radius **1.25** centered on one of the line's endpoints.

Figure 3-23

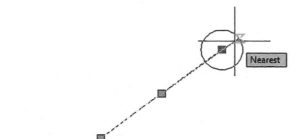

**2** Press the **Esc** key to ensure a command prompt.

**3** Select the line.

Blue grips appear at the two endpoints and at the midpoint.

**4** Select the endpoint that also serves as the circle's center point.

The blue pickbox changes to a solid-red square box.

**5** Right-click and select the **Stretch** option from the **Grips** menu.

```
**STRETCH**
Specify stretch point or [Base point Copy Undo eXit]:
```

Stretch the endpoint of the line to the edge of the 1.25 circle by accessing the **Osnap** menu (press the **Ctrl** key and right-click) and selecting the **Nearest** option.

**6** Select a point on the circle that aligns the line through the three grip points; then press the left mouse button.

**7** Erase the circle.

## 3-16 Grips—Move

### Moving an Object Using Grips

Draw a circle in a new location on the drawing.

**1** Press the **Esc** key to ensure a command prompt.

**2** Select any point on the circle.

Blue grips appear at the circle center point and at each of the quadrant points.

**3** Select the circle's center point.

The center point grip changes to a solid-red square box.

```
**STRETCH**
Specify stretch point or [Base point Copy Undo eXit]:
```

**4** Move the circle to a new location and press the left mouse button (Figure 3-24).

**Figure 3-24**

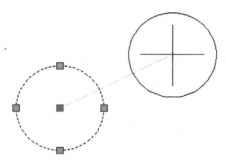

The circle's new location can be located by using dynamic input.

## 3-17 Grips—Rotate

### Rotating an Object Using Grips

Rotate a line 35° about its midpoint.

**1** Press the **Esc** key to ensure a command prompt.

**2** Select the line.

Blue grips appear at the line's two endpoints and at its midpoint.

**3** Select the line's midpoint.

The blue grip at the midpoint changes to solid red.

**4** Right-click and select **Rotate** from the **Grips** menu.

```
**ROTATE**
Specify rotation angle or [Base point Copy Undo eXit]:
```

**5** Type **35** and press **Enter** (Figure 3-25).

**Figure 3-25**

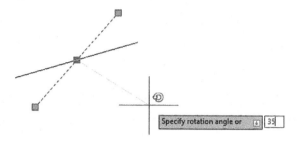

## 3-18 Grips—Scale

### Changing the Scale of an Object

Reduce an object to half of its original size.

**1** Press the **Esc** key to ensure a command prompt.

**2** Select the objects by first windowing them and then pressing the left mouse button.

Blue grips appear all around the object.

**3** Select any one of the grips.

The selected grip changes to a solid-red square box.

**4** Right-click to activate the **Grips** options box.

**5** Select **Scale** from the menu.

```
**SCALE**
Specify scale factor or [Base point Copy Undo Reference eXit]:
```

**6** Type **.5** and press **Enter** (Figure 3-26).

**Figure 3-26**

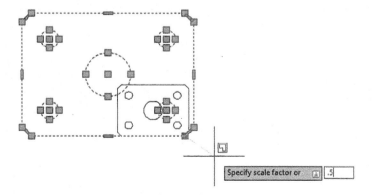

## 3-19 Grips—Mirror

### Mirroring an Object

Draw a mirror image of an object.

**1** Press the **Esc** key to ensure a command prompt.

**2** Window the object and then press the left mouse button.

Blue grips appear at end-, mid-, and center points of all objects.

**3** Select any grip.

The selected grip changes to a solid-red square box.

**4** Right-click to activate the **Grips** menu.

**5** Select **Mirror**.

```
**MIRROR**
Specify second point or [Base point Copy Undo eXit]:
```

**6** Select the grip vertically above the selected upper-right pickbox (Figure 3-27).

Figure 3-27

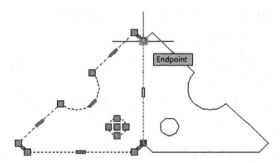

**7** Press the **Esc** key twice to fix the mirrored object.

## 3-20 Blocks

*Blocks* are groups of entities saved as a single object. Blocks save shapes and groups of shapes that are used frequently when creating drawings. Once created, blocks can be inserted into drawings, thereby saving drawing time.

The **Block** tools are located in the **Block** and **Block Definition** panels on the **Insert** tab (Figure 3-28). Blocks are first created by using the **Block** tool. They are then saved and, when needed, inserted into a drawing by use of the **Insert** tool. Blocks can be edited after they are created.

Figure 3-28

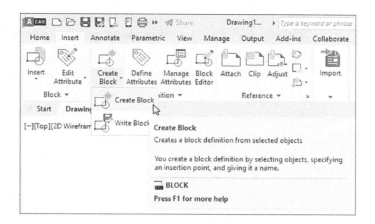

## Creating a Block

Figure 3-29 shows an object. A block can be made from this existing drawing as follows:

**1** Select the **Create** tool from the **Block Definition** panel.

Figure 3-29

The **Block Definition** dialog box appears.

**2** Click the **Select objects** box.

```
Select objects:
```

**3** Window the objects and press **Enter**.

The **Block Definition** dialog box reappears.

**4** Type **GASKET** in the **Name** box.

Block names may contain up to 31 characters.

**5** Click the **Pick point** box.

**6** Define the centerline insertion as the base point for the block.

The **Block Definition** dialog box reappears. **Osnap** may be used to locate an insertion point. The values listed in the **Block Definition** dialog box are XYZ values relative to the current origin (Figure 3-29).

The insertion base point will be a point on the object that will align with the screen cursor during the block insertion process.

In this example, **Intersection object snap** was used to define the intersection of the shape's centerlines as the insertion point.

**7** Click **OK**.

## Inserting a Block

**1** Click the **Insert** tab and select **Insert** from the **Block** panel.

**2** Click the **Recent Blocks** option (Figure 3-30).

Previews of blocks defined in the current drawing appear in the **Blocks** palette (Figure 3-31).

**Figure 3-30**

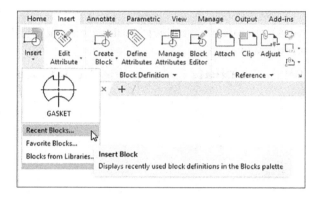

**Figure 3-31**

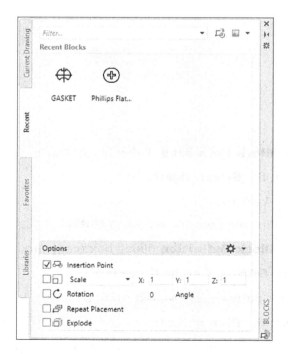

**3** Drag and drop the **GASKET** block onto the screen.

The **GASKET** block appears on the screen with its insertion point aligned with the cursor.

**4** Select the insertion point and click the mouse.

The block appears drawn to the original scale at which it was created. The scale and angle of rotation can be edited.

The default scale factor is 1. This means that if you accept the default value by pressing **Enter**, the shape is redrawn at its original size.

## Changing the Scale of a Block

**1** Select **Insert** from the **Block** panel.

**2** Select the **GASKET** block.

```
Specify insertion point or [Basepoint Scale X Y Z Rotate]:
```

**3** Type **S** and press **Enter**.

```
Specify scale factor for XYZ axes:
```

**4** Type **2** and press **Enter**.

```
Specify insertion point:
```

**5** Pick a point.

The **Rotation** option is used to rotate a block about its insertion point. AutoCAD assumes that a horizontal line to the right of the insertion point is 0° and that counterclockwise is the positive angular direction.

The block is now part of the drawing; however, the block in its present form may not be edited. A block is treated as a single entity and not as individual lines. You can verify this by trying to erase any one of the lines in a block. The entire object is erased. The object can be returned to the screen by clicking the **Undo** tool.

## Exploding a Block

Blocks can be edited in the **Block Editor**, or they can be exploded, individual objects can be edited, and then the objects can be reblocked.

**1** Select **Explode** from the **Modify** panel.

```
Command: _explode
Select objects:
```

**2** Pick anywhere on the object to select it.

```
Select objects:
```

**3** Press **Enter**.

The object is now exploded and can be edited. There is no visible change in the block on the screen, but there is a short blink after the **Explode** command is executed.

## 3-21 Working with Blocks

Figure 3-32 shows a resistor circuit. It was created from an existing block called **RESISTOR**. The drawing used decimal units with **Grid** set to **0.5** and **Snap** set to **0.25**. The default drawing limits were accepted.

**Figure 3-32**

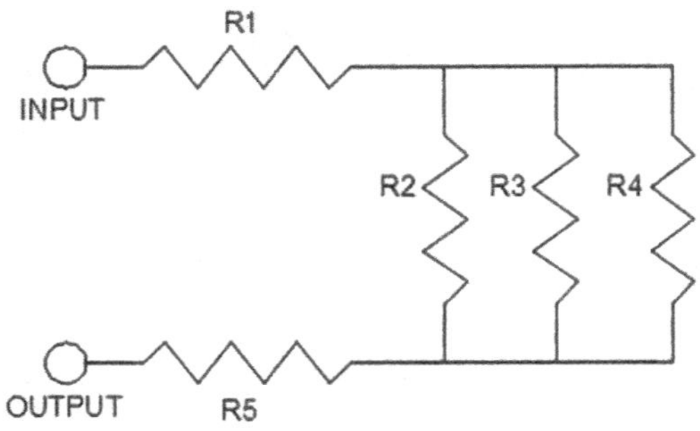

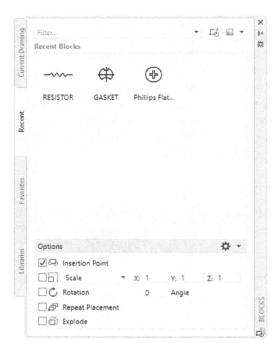

### Inserting Blocks at Different Angles

**1** On the **Block** tab of the **Insert** panel, select **Insert** and then click **Recent Blocks**.

The **Blocks** palette appears (Figure 3-33).

**Figure 3-33**

**2** Select the cascade menu on the right side of the **Name** box.

**3** Click the **RESISTOR** block in the **Recent Blocks** tab.

The **RESISTOR** block appears attached to the crosshairs at the predefined insertion point (Figure 3-34).

**Figure 3-34**

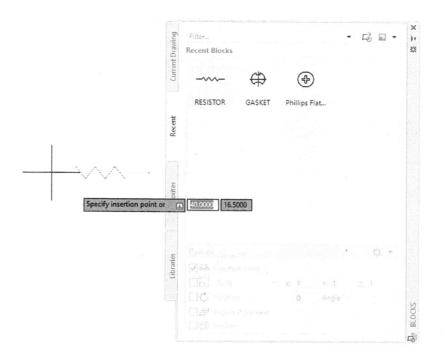

The resistor is too large for the drawing, so a reduced scale is used to generate the appropriate size.

`Specify insertion point or [Basepoint Scale X Y Z Rotate]:`

**4** Type **S** and press **Enter**.

`Specify scale factor for XYZ axes:`

**5** Type **0.50** and press **Enter**.

`Specify insertion point:`

Locate the resistor on the screen.

You can continue inserting blocks without restarting the **Insert** command as long as the **Blocks** palette is open.

**6** Select the **RESISTOR** block again, and in the **Options** area of the **Recent** tab, set the **X**, **Y**, and **Z** scale factors to **0.5** (Figure 3-35).

**Figure 3-35**

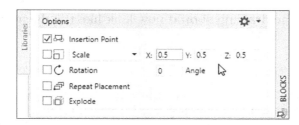

`Specify insertion point or [Scale X Y Z Rotate PScale PX PY PZ PRotate]:`

**7** Type **R** and press **Enter**.

`Specify rotation angle:`

⌗8 Type **90** and press **Enter**.

    Specify insertion point:

⌗9 Pick an insertion point (Figure 3-36).

**Figure 3-36**

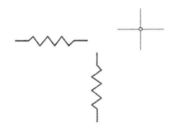

⌗10 Use the **Copy** command (**Modify** panel) to add the additional required resistors (Figure 3-37).

**Figure 3-37**

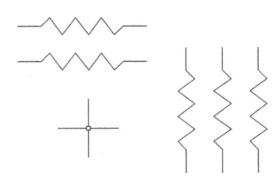

⌗11 Use the **Line** command (**Draw** panel) to draw the required lines.

⌗12 Select **Circle** (**Draw** panel) and draw a circle of diameter **0.250**.

⌗13 Use the **Copy** command (**Modify** panel) to create a second circle.

⌗14 Use the **Move** command to position the circles so that they touch the ends of the two horizontal resistor blocks. Move the other resistors to create the circuit drawing (Figure 3-32).

⌗15 Use the **Dtext** command to add the appropriate text.

The drawing should now look like the diagram presented in Figure 3-32.

## Inserting Blocks with Different Scale Factors

Figure 3-38 shows four different-sized threads, all created from the same block. The block labeled A used the default scale factor of 1, so it is exactly the same size as the original drawing used to create the block. The block labeled B was created with an **X** scale factor equal to **1**, and a **Y** scale factor equal to **2**. The procedure is as follows:

⌗1 Select the **Insert** tool from the **Draw** panel.

Figure 3-38

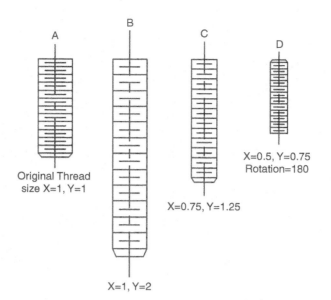

**2** Select the **THREAD** block.

The **THREAD** block is not included in AutoCAD. **THREAD** was created specifically for this example.

```
Specify insertion point or [Scale X Y Z Rotate PScale PX PY PZ
PRotate]:
```

**3** Type **X** and press **Enter**.

```
Specify X scale factor:
```

**4** Type **1** and press **Enter**.

```
Specify insertion point:
```

**5** Type **Y** and press **Enter**.

```
Specify Y scale factor:
```

**6** Type **2** and press **Enter**.

```
Specify insertion point:
```

**7** Specify a point.

The thread labeled C has an **X** scale factor of **0.75** and a **Y** scale factor of **1.25**. The thread labeled D has an **X** scale factor of **0.5**, a **Y** scale factor of **0.75**, and a rotation angle of 180°.

## Using the Blocks Palette to Change the Shape of a Block

The D thread scale factors and rotation angle were defined through the **Blocks** palette. The procedure is as follows:

**1** Select **Insert** and then select **Recent Blocks**.

The **Blocks** palette appears, with the **Recent** tab active (Figure 3-39).

Figure 3-39

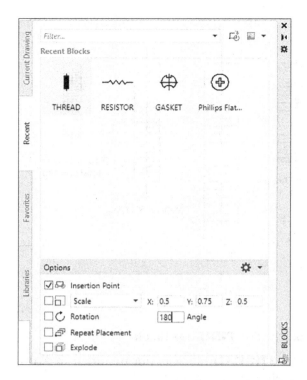

In the **Options** area at the bottom of the **Recent** tab, enter new **Scale** and **Rotation** values.

If you click the **THREAD** block before changing the values, the **Options** settings are grayed out. Press **Esc** to cancel the insertion. The **Blocks** palette remains open, and the **Options** settings are now available.

Place the cursor arrow inside the **X** scale box, backspace to remove the existing value, and type **.50**.

Change the **Y** scale to **.75**.

Change the **Rotation** to **180**.

In this case, the insertion point was defined on screen.

## Combining Blocks

Figure 3-40 shows a hex head screw that was created from two blocks. The threaded portion of the screw was created first; then the head portion was added. Note that when the hex head block was created, the insertion point was deliberately selected so that it could easily be aligned with the center-line and the top surface of the thread block.

Figure 3-40

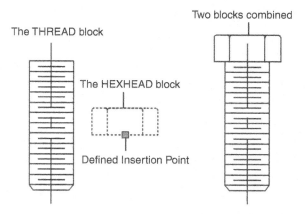

The THREAD block

The HEXHEAD block

Defined Insertion Point

Two blocks combined

## 3-22 Wblock

The **Wblock** command creates a new drawing file from a block that exists in the current drawing. When a block is created, it is unique to the drawing on which it was defined. This means that if you create a block on a drawing and then save and exit the drawing, the block is saved with the drawing but cannot be used on another drawing. If you start a new drawing, the saved block is not available.

Any block can be defined and saved, however, with the **Wblock** command. **Wblock** creates individual drawing files that can be inserted into any drawing.

### Using Wblock to Create a New Drawing File

This section shows how to use **Wblock** to create a drawing file from existing objects to form the gasket in Figure 3-29. You can use **Wblock** to create a new drawing file from objects shown on the screen.

**1** Open the drawing containing the gasket objects.

**2** Click the **Insert** tab and in the **Block Definition** panel, select the down arrow on the **Create Block** tool button. Select **Write Block** (Figure 3-41).

The **Write Block** dialog box appears (Figure 3-42).

Ensure that the **Objects** radio button is on.

Figure 3-41

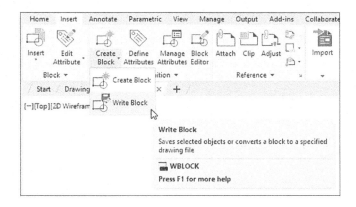

Figure 3-42

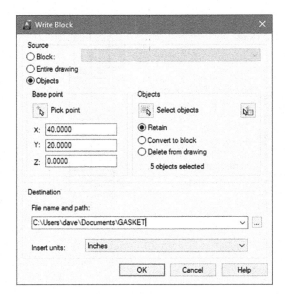

**3** Click **Select objects**.

The **Write Block** dialog box vanishes.

**4** Select the objects and click the right mouse button to confirm.

The **Write Block** dialog box appears.

**5** Click **Pick point**.

**6** Select the base point for the new drawing. In this example, the intersection of the centerlines is selected. This will be the insertion point when the drawing is inserted into another drawing.

**7** Enter a new file name for the drawing.

In this example, the name **GASKET** is entered.

**8** Click **OK**.

## Verifying That Wblock Created a New Drawing

**1** Click the **Insert** tab, click the **Insert** tool, and click **Recent Blocks**.

The **Blocks** palette appears, with the **Recent** tab active (Figure 3-43). The name **GASKET.dwg** confirms that **Wblock** created a new drawing file.

**2** Click the **GASKET.dwg** icon and move it onto the drawing field.

A wblocked file is an independent drawing file that can be inserted into any other drawing. Figure 3-44 shows **GASKET.dwg** listed in the document files.

**Figure 3-43**

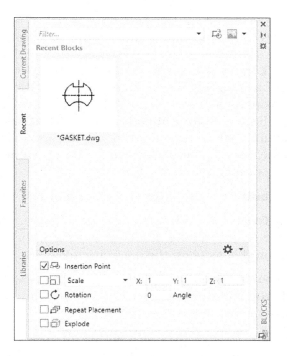

**Figure 3-44**

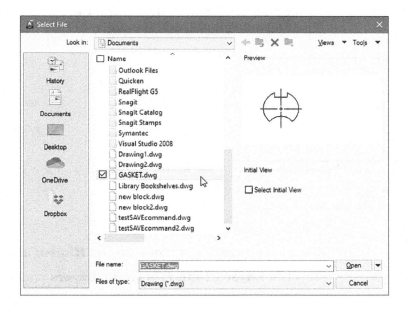

**NOTE**

You can use the **Options** section of the **Blocks** palette to change the size and rotation angle of a wblocked object in the same way as for any other block in the drawing.

## 3-23 Layers

A *layer* is like a clear piece of paper that you can lay directly over the drawing. You can draw on the layer and see through it to the original drawing. Layers can be made invisible, and information can be transferred between layers.

In the example in this section, a series of layers will be created, and then a group of lines will be moved from the initial layer, called **Layer 0**, to the other layers.

The **Layers** panel is located on the **Home** tab (Figure 3-45). There are five indicators in the layer name drop-down that indicate the status of some of the properties of an individual layer. For example, in Figure 3-45 the open padlock icon indicates that layer **Text-Large** is unlocked. A closed padlock indicates a locked layer. The icons on the drop-down are toggles, which means you can click them to change values. The icons represent the following properties:

- **Lightbulb:** Toggles layer visibility off or on.

- **Sun:** Toggles the freeze/thaw state of layers, which is a deeper form of setting layer visibility. If a layer is frozen, the icon changes to a snow-flake, and objects on the layer are invisible.

- **Viewport with sun:** Toggles layer visibility within a specific layout view-port. You can freeze a layer in a viewport and keep it thawed in other parts of the drawing.

- **Padlock:** Toggles layer lock status off and on. If the padlock is unlocked, the layer can be edited or drawn on.

- **Filled square:** Shows the default color of the layer. Objects drawn on that layer will take on this color.

Figure 3-45

## Creating New Layers

This exercise creates two new layers: **Hidden** and **Center**.

**1** Click **Layer Properties** on the **Layers** panel of the **Home** tab (Figure 3-46).

Figure 3-46

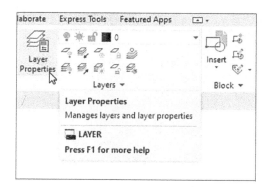

The **Layer Properties Manager** dialog box appears (Figure 3-47). You may have to extend the box to the right to see all its contents.

**Figure 3-47**

Click **New Layer**

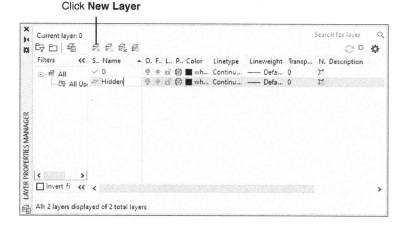

**2** Click **New Layer**.

A new layer named **Layer1** appears.

**3** Type **Hidden** in place of the **Layer1** name (Figure 3-47).

The name **Hidden** appears under the **0** layer heading in the **Name** column.

**4** Click the **New Layer** box again, and add another new layer named **Center**.

The name **Center** appears in the **Name** column. There are now three layers in the drawing (Figure 3-48). The **0** layer is the current layer, as indicated by the green checkmark beside its name.

**Figure 3-48**

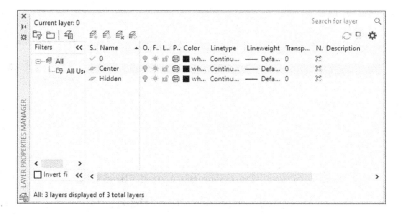

## Changing the Color and Linetype of a Layer

Layer properties and settings appear in columns to the right of the **Name** column in the **Layer Properties Manager**.

**1** Find the **Color** column in the **Layer Properties Manager**.

**2** Hover the cursor over **wh**... in the **Hidden** layer row.

The word **white** appears in a tooltip, indicating that the layer's color is white (Figure 3-49).

Figure 3-49

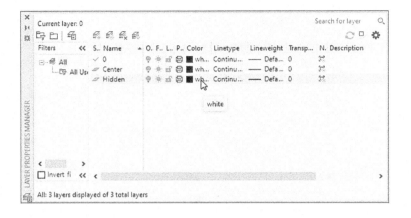

**3** Click on the letters **wh**... or the square color tile.

The **Select Color** dialog box appears (Figure 3-50).

Figure 3-50

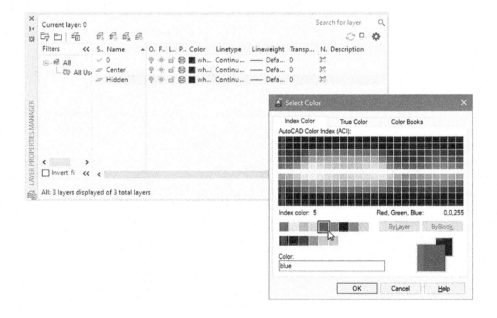

**4** Select the color **blue** and click **OK**.

All lines drawn on the **Hidden** layer are now blue, and the color box for the **Hidden** layer is blue.

**5** Click the word **Continuous** on the **Hidden** layer row under the **Linetype** column.

The **Select Linetype** dialog box opens (Figure 3-51).

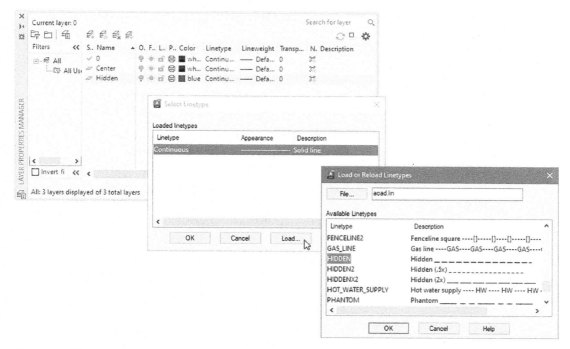

**Figure 3-51**

6. Click **Load**.

   The **Load or Reload Linetypes** dialog box appears.

7. Scroll down the **Available Linetypes** list and select **HIDDEN** by clicking on the linetype name or the pattern preview.

8. Click **OK**.

9. Click the word **Continuous** on the **Center** layer row under the **Linetype** column.

   The line is highlighted.

10. Change the **Center** layer's color to **red** and its linetype to **CENTER**.

    The **Layer Properties Manager** dialog box should look as shown in Figure 3-52.

**Figure 3-52**

Click the X to close the Layer Properties Manager

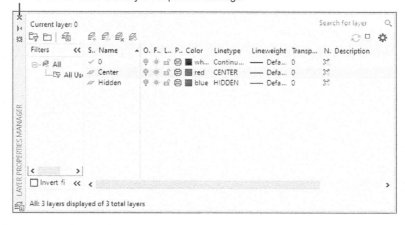

To close the **Layer Properties Manager** dialog box, click the **X** at the top of the dialog box's title bar (Figure 3-52).

## Drawing on Different Layers

Only the layer designated as the current layer may be worked on, even though other layers may be visible. There are three ways to make a layer the current layer:

- Use the **Layer** drop-down list located on the **Layers** panel under the **Home** tab. Click a layer's name. The layer becomes the current layer. The current layer is the name displayed in the **Layer** drop-down after the cascading list disappears. In Figure 3-53, for example, **Text-Large** appears as the current layer, and **Metal** is selected to become the new current layer.

**Figure 3-53**

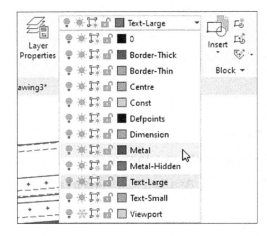

- Use the **Layer Properties Manager** tool to access the **Layer Properties Manager** dialog box. Click on a layer name, click the current box, and then click **OK**. The layer name appears in the **Layer control** box, indicating that it is the current layer (Figure 3-54).

**Figure 3-54**

Set selected layer current

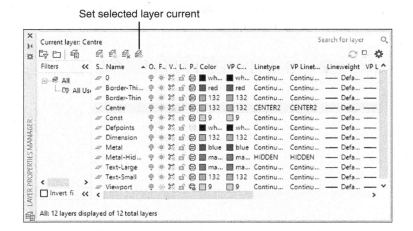

- Use the **Make Current** tool by clicking an entity on the screen. The entity's layer becomes the current layer (Figure 3-55).

Figure 3-55

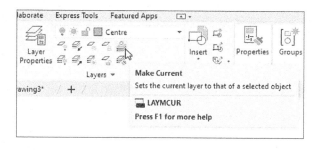

Once a current layer has been established, objects may be drawn and modified on that layer.

## Changing an Object's Layer

An object can be drawn on one layer and moved to another layer. This capability is helpful when designing; for example, an original layout may be created in a single layer, and then lines can be changed to different layers as needed. As a line changes layers, it assumes the color and linetype of the new layer. Figure 3-56 shows a circle and a line drawn on the **0** layer. Change the line to a centerline and the circle to a hidden line by moving the objects to the appropriate layers.

Figure 3-56

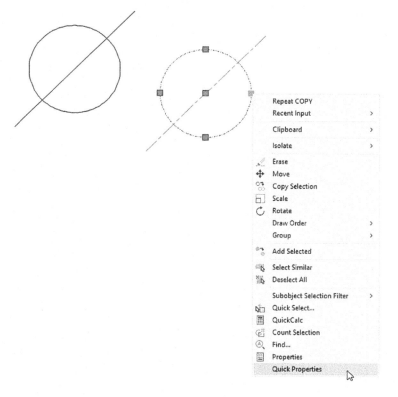

**1** Click the circle and right-click one of the grip pickboxes. Then click the **Quick Properties** option.

The **Circle Properties** dialog box appears.

**2** Click the **Layer** line and scroll down and click the **Hidden** option.

The circle's color turns blue, and the linetype changes to a hidden pattern.

**3** Transfer the line to the **Center** layer by using the same procedure.

Figure 3-57 shows the results of the layer changes.

**Figure 3-57**

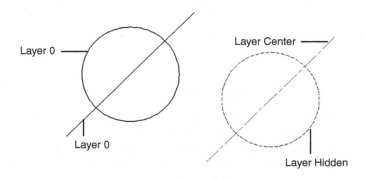

## Changing the Scale of a Linetype

Figure 3-58 shows two parallel lines drawn on the **Hidden** layer.

**Figure 3-58**

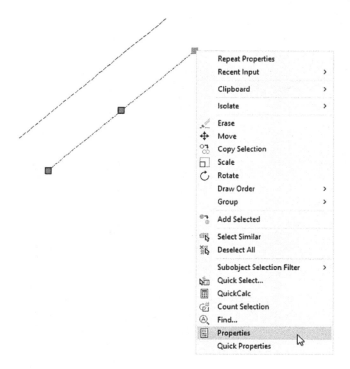

**1** Click the lower line.

Grips appear on the line.

**2** Right-click one of the grips.

A right-click menu appears.

**3** Click **Properties**.

The **Properties** palette appears (Figure 3-59).

**Figure 3-59**

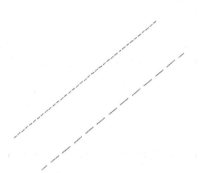

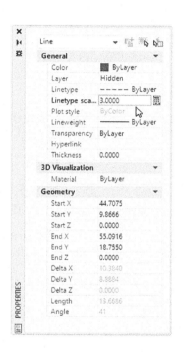

**4** Change **Linetype scale** to **3.0000**.

**5** Close the **Properties** palette by clicking the **X** in the upper-left corner of the box and press the **Esc** key.

Figure 3-59 shows the resulting changes in the lower line. The new line has a different linetype scale and therefore different spacing.

## Using the Match Layer Tool

Figure 3-60 shows two lines. The lower line is on the **Hidden** layer, and the upper line is on layer **0**. The **Match Layer** tool is used to change the layer of the upper line (layer **0**) to the layer of another object (**Hidden** layer).

**1** Click the **Match Layer** tool.

```
Select objects:
```

Figure 3-60

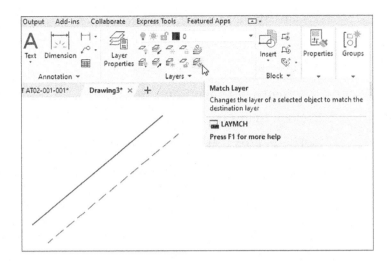

2 Click the line on the layer **0** (the upper line).

Select object:

3 Right-click.

Select object on destination layer or [Name]:

4 Click the line on the **Hidden** layer (the lower line).

The lines are now both on the **Hidden** layer. (The lower line had a different linetype scale.)

## Turning Layers Off

1 Select **Layer Properties**.

A list of current layers appears in the drop-down list.

2 Click the lightbulb icon on the **Center** layer.

The lightbulb icon changes from yellow to blue, indicating that the layer is off.

## 3-24 Attributes

*Attributes* are sections of text added to a block that prompt the drafter to add information to the drawing. For example, a title block may have an attribute that prompts the user to add the date to the title block as it is inserted into a drawing. Attributes are located on the **Attributes** panel on the **Insert** tab.

## Adding an Attribute to a Block

Figure 3-61 shows a block named **GASKET**. It was added to a new drawing by using the **Insert** command on the **Insert** tab's **Block** panel. This example adds attributes that request information about the product's part number, material, quantity, and finish.

**Figure 3-61**

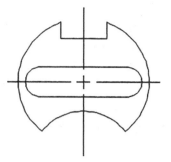

1 Access the **Block Definition** panel under the **Insert** tab and click the **Define Attributes** tool (Figure 3-62).

**Figure 3-62**

The **Attribute Definition** dialog box appears (Figure 3-63).

**Figure 3-63**

2 In the **Attribute** area, type **NUMBER** in the **Tag** edit box.

A *tag* is the name of an attribute and is used for filing and reference purposes. A tag name must be one word with no spaces.

3 Click in the **Prompt** edit box and type **Enter Part Number:** followed by a space.

The prompt line appears at the bottom of the screen when a block containing an attribute is inserted into a drawing. If you do not define a prompt, the tag name is used as a prompt.

**4** Leave the **Default** edit box empty.

The value in the **Default** edit box is the default value if nothing is entered when the prompt appears. Based on the defined prompt and value inputs, the following prompt line appears in the **Edit Attributes** dialog box:

```
Enter Part Number:
```

**5** Select **Specify on-screen** and click **OK**.

The text of the first attribute appears with crosshairs. Select a location for the attribute tag by moving the crosshairs and then press the left mouse button (Figure 3-64).

**Figure 3-64**

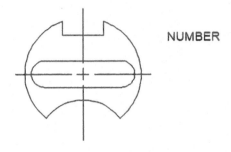

Figure 3-65 shows another **Attribute Definition** dialog box. Note that the **Align below previous attribute definition** checkbox is selected. Figure 3-66 shows the resulting drawing.

**Figure 3-65**

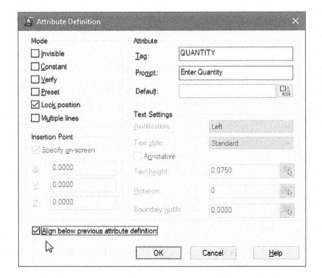

**Figure 3-66**

## Creating a New Block That Includes Attributes

**1** Select **Create Block** from the **Block Definition** panel of the **Insert** tab.

The **Block Definition** dialog box appears.

**2** Name the new block **GASKET-2**.

**3** Select a base point.

In this example, the center point was selected.

**4** Finish block creation by selecting the block and all the attribute tags (Figure 3-67).

**Figure 3-67**

**5** Click **OK**.

The Edit Attributes dialog box appears. Verify that the attributes are correct. If all entries are correct, click **OK** (Figure 3-68).

**Figure 3-68**

## Inserting an Existing Block with Attributes

**1** Select **Insert** on the **Block** tab of the **Insert** panel.

A preview panel appears, displaying blocks defined in the current drawing (Figure 3-69).

**Figure 3-69**

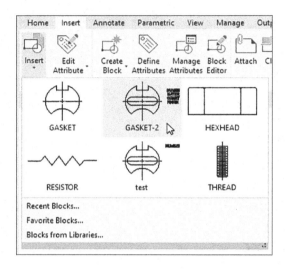

**2** Select **GASKET-2**.

```
Specify the insertion point or [Scale X Y Z Rotate PScale PX PY PZ
PRotate]:
```

**3** Pick an insertion point.

As soon as you pick the insertion point, the **Edit Attributes** dialog box appears. You need to enter values in the edit boxes of the **Edit Attributes** dialog box to complete the insertion (Figure 3-70).

**4** Click inside the **Enter Part Number** edit box, type **BU-AM311**, and press **Tab**.

**5** In the **Enter Material** edit box, type **CARBON STEEL** and press **Tab**.

**6** In the **Enter Quantity** edit box, type **4** and press **Tab**.

**7** In the **Enter Finish** edit box, type **BLACK**.

**8** Click **OK** to close the **Edit Attributes** dialog box and finish inserting the block.

**Figure 3-70**

Figure 3-71 shows the resulting block insertion.

**Figure 3-71**

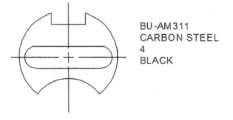

BU-AM311
CARBON STEEL
4
BLACK

## Editing an Existing Attribute

Once a block with attributes has been created and inserted, it can be edited by using the **Advanced Attribute Editor** dialog box. The procedure is as follows. Note that the block to be edited must be on the drawing screen.

**1** Double-click the block containing the attribute values you want to edit.

The **Enhanced Attribute Editor** dialog box appears (Figure 3-72).

**Figure 3-72**

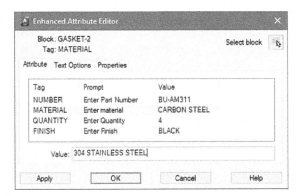

**2** Click the **MATERIAL** line and then click inside the **Value** edit box.

**3** Replace the words **CARBON STEEL** with the text **304 STAINLESS STEEL**.

**4** Click **OK**.

Figure 3-73 shows the resulting changes.

Figure 3-73

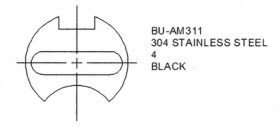

**3-25 Title Blocks with Attributes**

Figure 3-74 shows a title block that has been saved as a block. It would be helpful to add attributes to the block so that when it is inserted into a drawing, the drafter will be prompted to enter the required information.

Figure 3-74

Note that text may be added to an AutoCAD template by use of the **Mtext** command. Create the desired text and use the **Move** command to position it within the title block. The title block shown in Figure 3-74 was custom drawn for a special application.

Figures 3-75, 3-76, 3-77, 3-78, and 3-79 show the five **Attribute Definition** dialog boxes used to define the title block attributes. Note that the **Text height** setting in Figures 3-75 through 3-79 may be varied if desired. Also note that no attribute defaults were assigned. This means that the space on the drawing is left blank if no prompt value is entered. Figure 3-80 shows the resulting title block with the attribute tags in place.

Figure 3-75

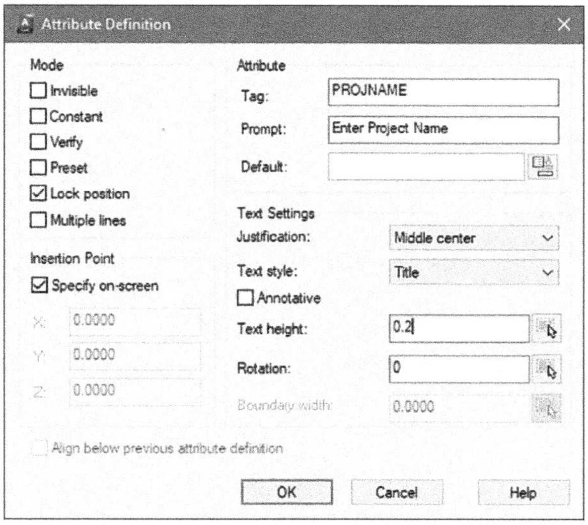

Figure 3-76

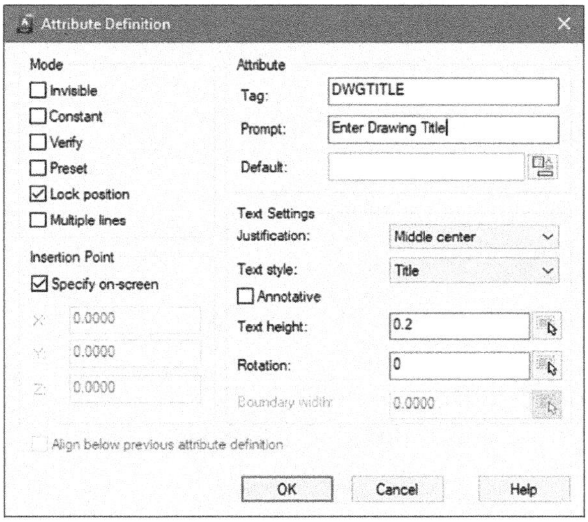

Figure 3-77

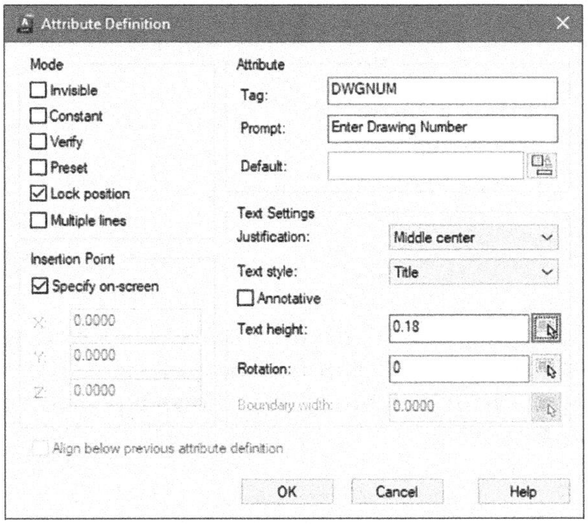

**Figure 3-78**

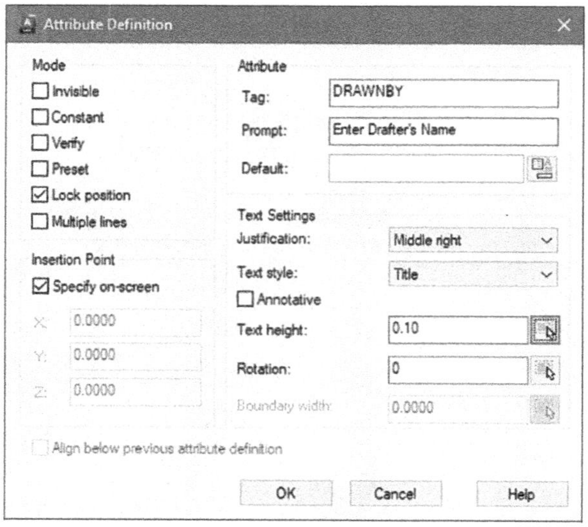

Attribute Definition

Mode
- [ ] Invisible
- [ ] Constant
- [ ] Verify
- [ ] Preset
- [x] Lock position
- [ ] Multiple lines

Attribute
Tag: DRAWNBY
Prompt: Enter Drafter's Name
Default:

Text Settings
Justification: Middle right
Text style: Title
- [ ] Annotative
Text height: 0.10
Rotation: 0
Boundary width: 0.0000

Insertion Point
- [x] Specify on-screen
X: 0.0000
Y: 0.0000
Z: 0.0000

- [ ] Align below previous attribute definition

OK    Cancel    Help

**Figure 3-79**

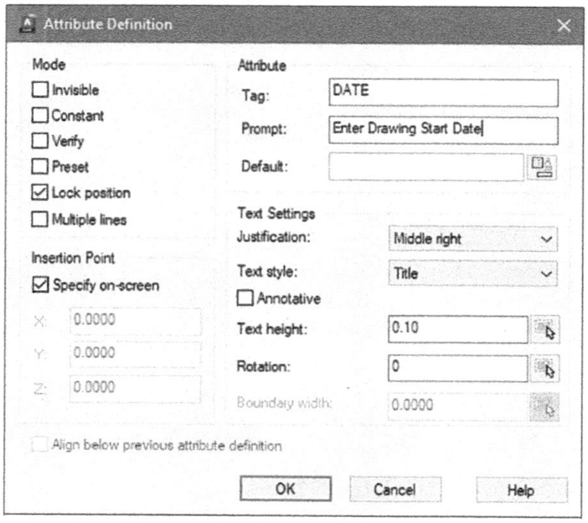

Attribute Definition

Mode
- [ ] Invisible
- [ ] Constant
- [ ] Verify
- [ ] Preset
- [x] Lock position
- [ ] Multiple lines

Attribute
Tag: DATE
Prompt: Enter Drawing Start Date
Default:

Text Settings
Justification: Middle right
Text style: Title
- [ ] Annotative
Text height: 0.10
Rotation: 0
Boundary width: 0.0000

Insertion Point
- [x] Specify on-screen
X: 0.0000
Y: 0.0000
Z: 0.0000

- [ ] Align below previous attribute definition

OK    Cancel    Help

**Figure 3-80**

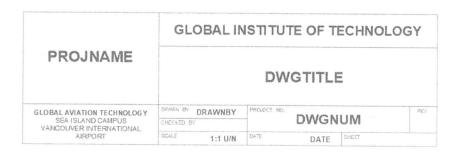

The new block with attributes was saved as **TITLE-A** by using the **Block** command. It can now be wblocked to a new drawing file and used on future drawings. Figure 3-81 shows a possible title block created from the **TITLE-A** block.

**Figure 3-81**

| 737 SKIN REPAIR MODULE | GLOBAL INSTITUTE OF TECHNOLOGY | | | |
|---|---|---|---|---|
| | GENERAL ASSEMBLY END VIEW & PARTS LIST | | | |
| GLOBAL AVIATION TECHNOLOGY SEA ISLAND CAMPUS VANCOUVER INTERNATIONAL AIRPORT | DRAWN BY    DMB | PROJECT NO. | AVST 2100-P11 | REV |
| | CHECKED BY | | | |
| | SCALE    1:1 U/N | DATE    2022.02.28 | SHEET | |

## 3-26  Edit Polyline

The **Edit Polyline** tool, which is on the expanded **Modify** panel of the **Home** tab, is used to change the shape of a polyline. In the next example, the **Edit Polyline** command is used to create a splined polyline from a given polyline.

### Creating a Splined Polyline from a Given Polyline

**1** Draw a polyline, using the **Polyline** tool on the **Draw** panel.

**2** Select the **Edit Polyline** tool from the **Modify** panel.

    Command: _pedit Select polyline:

**3** Select the polyline.

    Select an option [Close Join Width Edit vertex Fit Spline Decurve
    Ltype gen Reverse Undo]:

**4** Select the **Spline** option.

    Figure 3-82 shows the edited polyline.

**Figure 3-82**

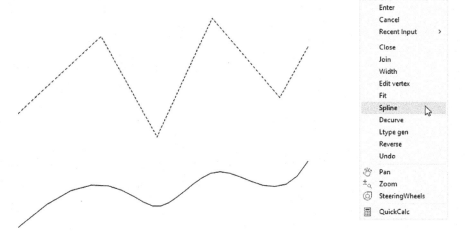

## 3-27 Edit Spline

**Edit Spline**, also found on the expanded **Modify** panel of the **Home** tab, is used to change the shape of a spline.

### Editing a Spline

**1** Select the **Edit Spline** tool from the expanded **Modify** panel.

    Command: _splinedit
    Select spline:

**2** Select a spline.

A series of control points appears on the screen (Figure 3-83). These points are the original data points used to define the spline. In this example, one of the points is moved.

    Enter an option [Close Join Fit data Edit vertex convert to Polyline
    Reverse Undo eXit]<exit>:

**Figure 3-83**

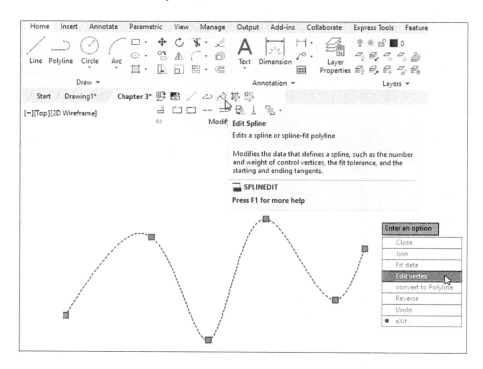

**3** Select the **Edit vertex** option and press **Enter**.

    Enter a vertex editing option [Add Delete Elevate order and Kink
    Move Weight eXit] <exit>:

**4** Select the **Move** option; and press **Enter**.

The first square data point changes color, and a rubber-band-type line extends from the point. A small cross appears within the point.

**5** Select a new location for the point and click the mouse; then right-click and type **X** to exit the **Move** option.

**6** Type **X** again to exit the command.

**NOTE**

If you want to edit one of the inner control points on the spline, use the **Next** and **Previous** options from within the **Move** option.

Figure 3-83 shows the edited spline. The chosen location becomes the new location for the first point. If a point other than the first point needs to be moved, press **Enter** when the **X** appears, and the **Edit** command advances to the next point. Every time the **Enter** key is pressed, the **Edit** command advances to the next point. Only the **X** option allows you to exit the command sequence.

## 3-28 Edit Text

Figure 3-84 shows a line of text that contains a typing error. When the word *worf* was typed, the **f** key was mistakenly struck instead of **d**.

**Figure 3-84**

THIS IS A SAMPLE LINE OF
TEXT. EDIT THIS WORF.

| | |
|---|---|
| | Repeat MTEXT |
| | Recent Input > |
| A▸ | Mtext Edit... |
| | Annotative Object Scale > |
| | Clipboard > |
| | Isolate > |
| | Erase |
| | Move |
| | Copy Selection |
| | Scale |
| | Rotate |
| | Draw Order > |
| | Group > |
| | Add Selected |
| | Select Similar |
| | Deselect All |
| | Subobject Selection Filter > |
| | Quick Select... |
| | QuickCalc |
| | Count Selection |
| | Find... |
| | Properties |
| | Quick Properties |

## Changing Existing Text

**1** Click the existing text.

Grips appear on the text object (Figure 3-84).

**2** Right-click and select **Mtext Edit**.

The text appears inside the **Multiline Text Editor**, and the **Text Editor** contextual tab appears at the end of the ribbon.

**3** Edit the word (Figure 3-85) and click the mouse to close the **Multiline Text Editor**.

Figure 3-85

## 3-29 Constructing the Bisector of an Angle, Method I

Bisect angle **A–O–B** (Figure 3-86).

**1** Select **Draw**, **Circle**.

Figure 3-86

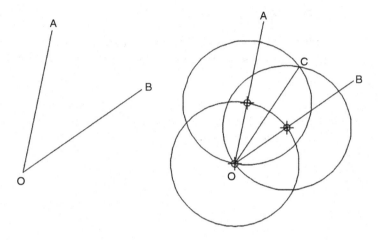

**2** Draw a circle with a center point located at point **O**. The circle may be of any radius. This is an excellent place to take advantage of AutoCAD's **Drag** mode. Move the cursor until the circle appears to be approximately the same size as shown.

**3** Copy the circle twice. Locate the new circles' center points on intersections of the first circle and angle **A–O–B**. Use **Osnap Intersection** to ensure accuracy.

**4** Draw a line from point **O** to intersection **C**, as shown. Use **Osnap Intersection** to ensure accuracy.

## 3-30 Constructing the Bisector of an Angle, Method II

Bisect angle **A–O–B** (Figure 3-87).

**1** Draw a circle with a center point located at point **O**. The circle may be of any radius. This is an excellent place to take advantage of AutoCAD's **Drag** mode. Move the cursor until the circle appears to be approximately the same size as shown.

**Figure 3-87**

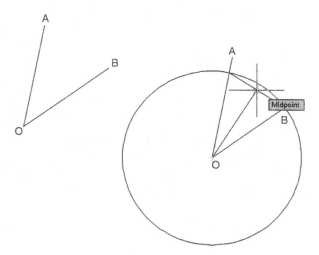

■2■ Draw a line between the intersection point created by the circle and angle **A–O–B**. Use **Osnap Intersection** to ensure accuracy.

■3■ Draw a line between point **O** and the midpoint of the line. Use **Osnap Midpoint** to ensure accuracy.

## 3-31 Constructing an Ogee Curve (S-Curve) with Equal Arcs

Construct an ogee curve between lines **A–B** and **C–D** (Figure 3-88).

■1■ Draw a straight line between points **B** and **C**. Use **Osnap Endpoint** to ensure accuracy.

**Figure 3-88**

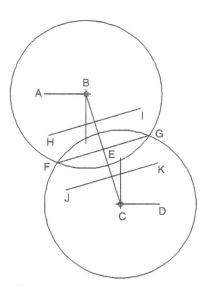

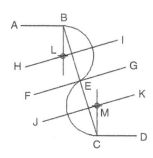

**2** Draw lines perpendicular to lines **A–B** at **B** and **C–D** at **C**, as shown.

Use **Osnap Endpoint** to accurately start the lines on points **B** and **C**. Use relative coordinates to draw the lines. The lines may be of any length greater than half the perpendicular distance between lines **A–B** and **C–D**.

**3** Construct a perpendicular bisector of line **B–C**.

Draw circles centered at points **B** and **C** with a radius slightly more than half the length of line **B–C**. Draw a line to connect the two points where the circles intersect (points **F** and **G** in Figure 3-88). This line forms the perpendicular bisector of line **B–C**. Erase the two circles.

Further bisect the two halves of line **B–C** by offsetting line **B–C** using the **Mid2Pt** object snap mode.

**4** Click **Offset** on the **Modify** panel. Make sure the default command option in the prompt is **<Through>** and then press **Enter**. Press **Shift** and right-click; select **Mid Between 2 Points**. Using the **Endpoint** and **Midpoint** object snaps, pick points **B** and **E**.

**5** Repeat step 4, offsetting line **F–G** to the other side of the line. Using **Mid Between 2 Points**, use object snaps to pick points **E** and **C**.

The center points of the two arcs forming the ogee curve (points **L** and **M**) will be the intersections of the two offset lines, **H–I** and **J–K**, and the two vertical lines you drew in step 2.

**6** Draw a circle centered at point **L** that passes point **B**.

**7** Draw a circle centered at point **M** that passes point **C**. Trim the two circles to create the smooth ogee curve (Figure 3-88).

The two arcs of steps 6 and 7 define an ogee curve by equal arcs. Figure 3-89 shows the construction of an ogee curve with unequal arcs. The construction techniques are similar to those presented previously.

**Figure 3-89**

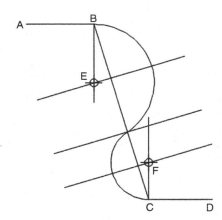

## 3-32 Constructing a Parabola

A *parabola* is the locus of a point such that its distance from a fixed point, the *focus*, is equal to its distance to a fixed line, the *directrix*.

Given a focus point **A** and a directrix **B–C**, construct a parabola (Figure 3-90).

**Figure 3-90**

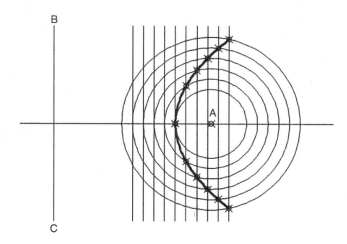

1. Draw a line parallel to **B–C** so that it intersects the midpoint between line **B–C** and point **A**. Use **Offset**.

2. Draw a circle centered about point **A** whose radius is equal to half the distance between line **B–C** and point **A**.

3. Offset lines and a circle **0.2 inch** from the parallel line and the circle created in steps 1 and 2.

4. Identify the intersections of the lines and circles created in step 3. In this example, point objects identify the points.

5. Draw a polyline connecting all the intersection points.

6. Use the **Edit Polyline, Fit** option to change the polyline to a parabolic curve.

## 3-33 Constructing a Hyperbola

A *hyperbola* is the locus of points equidistant between two fixed foci.

Given foci points **F1** and **F2** equidistant from a vertical line and two other vertical lines drawn through points **A** and **B**, draw a hyperbola. See Figures 3-91 and 3-92.

Figure 3-91

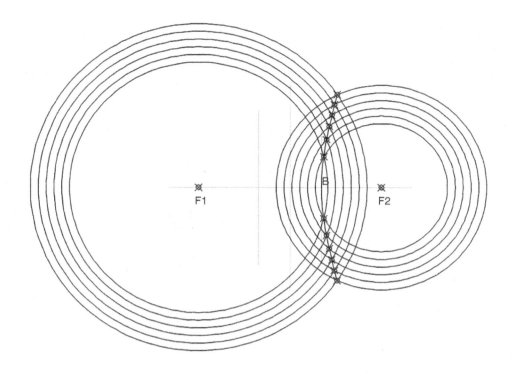

Figure 3-92

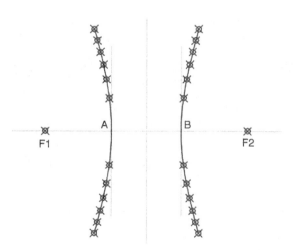

**1** Draw a circle of arbitrary radius, using point **F2** as the center. If possible, set up the drawing so that both points **F1** and **F2** are on snap points. If this is not possible, draw a vertical line through point **F2** so that the **Osnap Intersection** option can be used to locate the center accurately.

**2** Draw a circle centered about **F2** with radius equal to the radius of the circle drawn in step 1, plus the distance between points **A** and **B** (Figure 3-91).

**3** Draw concentric circles around the circles centered about **F1** and **F2**. The distance between all the circles should be equal. Use **Offset**.

**4** Mark the intersections between the smaller and larger circles, as shown in Figure 3-91. Use filled circles to define the points.

**5** Draw a polyline connecting the intersection points.

**6** Use the **Edit Polyline, Fit** option to draw the hyperbola.

**7** Use **Mirror** to create the opposing hyperbola (Figure 3-92).

## 3-34 Constructing a Spiral

Construct a spiral of Archimedes (Figure 3-93).

**Figure 3-93**

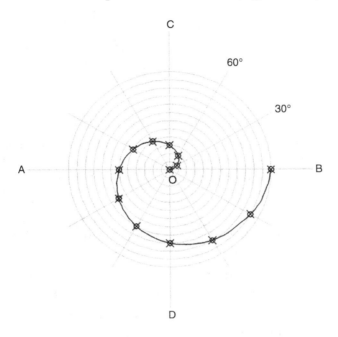

**1** Draw two perpendicular centerlines **A–B** and **C–D**, as shown.

**2** Draw **12** concentric circles about center point **O**. Use **Offset** to draw circles.

**3** Draw 12 equally spaced lines **30°** apart, as shown. Array either the horizontal or vertical line by using the **Polar Array** command. Use point **O** as the center of rotation.

**4** Draw a polyline starting at point **O**. The second point is the intersection of the 30° ray with the first circle. Point 2 is the intersection of the 60° ray and the second circle. Continue through all 12 rays and circles.

**5** Use the **Edit Polyline, Fit** option to change the polyline to a spiral (Figure 3-93).

## 3-35 Constructing a Helix

Construct a helix that advances 1.875 inches every 360°.

**1** Draw a vertical line **1.875** inches long and a horizontal line **4.0** inches long, as shown (Figure 3-94).

Figure 3-94

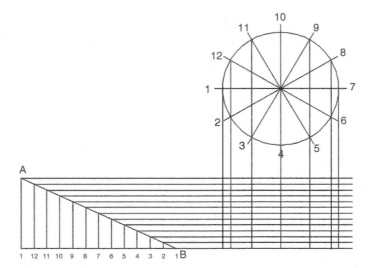

**2** Draw a horizontal line that can easily be divided into **12** equal spaces. The length of the horizontal line is arbitrary. Set up a grid so that the 12 equal spaces can easily be identified.

**3** Draw a circle as shown. Make sure the circle is clearly above and to the right of the original lines. Use **Array** and divide the circle by **12** equally spaced rays. Use the **Polar Array** command with the circle's center point as the center of rotation.

**4** Draw line **A–B** as shown. Draw **12** equally spaced vertical lines between the horizontal line and line **A–B**.

**5** Label the circle and the horizontal line as shown. The number of divisions must be the same for both the circle and the horizontal line.

**6** Draw vertical lines from the intersections of the 12 equally spaced rays and the circle's circumference, as shown in Figure 3-94. Use the **Osnap Intersection** option to ensure accuracy.

**7** Draw horizontal lines from the intersections on line **A–B** so that they intersect the vertical lines from step 6. Use the **Osnap Intersection** option to ensure accuracy.

**8** Mark the intersections of the lines from steps 6 and 7 as shown.

**9** Use a polyline to connect the horizontal and vertical intersections as shown.

**10** Use the **Spline, Fit** option to draw the helix (Figure 3-95).

Figure 3-95

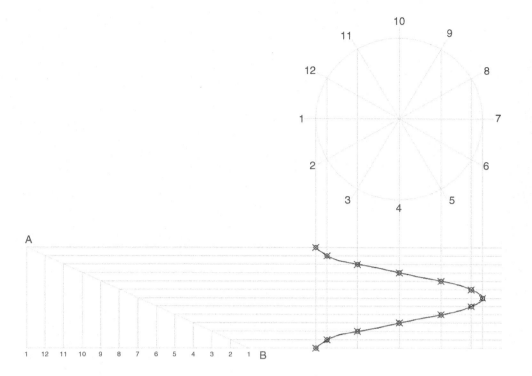

**NOTE**

In AutoCAD, the **Helix** command is used to create 2D or 3D open-ended spiral shapes. A *helix* is three-dimensional, with height as well as radius dimensions. If the helix has a height of zero, it is referred to as a *spiral*.

## 3-36 Designing by Using Shape Parameters

An elementary design problem often faced by beginning designers is to create a shape based on a given set of parameters. This section presents two examples of this type of design problem.

### Drawing Problem

Design a shape that will support the hole pattern shown in Figure 3-96, subject to the given parameters. Design for the minimum amount of material. All dimensions are in millimeters.

- The edge of the material may be no closer to the center of a hole than a distance equivalent to the radius of the hole.

- The minimum distance from any cutout to the edge of the part may not be less than the smallest distance calculated in step 1.

- The minimum inside radius for a cutout is R = **5** millimeters.

Figure 3-96

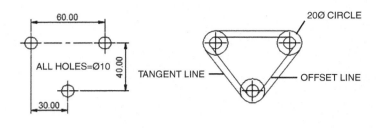

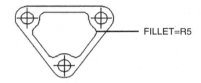

The solution is as follows:

**1** Calculate the minimum edge distances for the holes.

In this problem, the three holes are all the same diameter: 10 millimeters. Given the parameter that an edge may be no closer to the center of the hole than a distance equivalent to the size of the hole's diameter, the distance from the outside edge of the hole to the edge of the part must be no less than 5 millimeters, or a circular shape of diameter 20 millimeters.

**2** Draw **Ø20** circles, using the existing circle's center point, as shown in Figure 3-96.

**3** Draw outside tangent lines between the Ø20 circles.

The second parameter limits the minimum edge distance to the minimum edge distance calculated in step 2, or 5 millimeters.

**4** Use the **Offset** command to draw lines **5** millimeters from the outside tangent lines drawn in step 3 to define the internal cutout.

**5** Use the inside radius parameter of **5** millimeters, and add fillets to the internal cutout.

**6** Erase any excess lines.

Figure 3-96 shows the final shape.

## Drawing Problem

Design a shape that will support the hole pattern shown in Figure 3-97. Support the center hole with four perpendicular webs. All dimensions are in inches.

• The edge of the material may be no closer to the center of a hole than a distance equivalent to the radius of the hole.

• The minimum distance from any cutout to the edge of the part may not be less than the smallest distance calculated in step 1.

• The minimum inside radius for a cutout is R = **.125** inch.

Figure 3-97

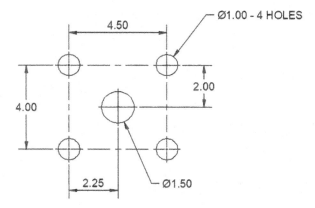

The solution is as follows:

**1** Calculate the minimum edge distances for the holes.

In this example, the hole diameters are 1.00 and 1.50 inches.

**2** Add circles of radius **2.00** and **3.00**, as shown (Figure 3-98).

Figure 3-98

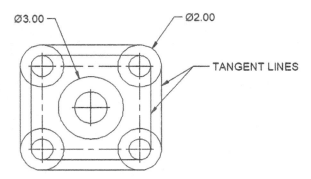

The minimum edge distance based on the Ø1.00 of the smaller hole equals 0.50 inch.

**3** Use the minimum edge distance and define the inside edge of the internal cutouts.

**4** Use the minimum edge distance to define the four supporting webs for the center hole.

**5** Add the inside bend radii.

The inside bend radii were added by using the **Fillet** command. This causes a portion of the internal edge to disappear. Use the **Offset** command again to replace the line defining the edge of the internal cutout (Figure 3-99).

**6** Remove all excess lines.

**Figure 3-99**

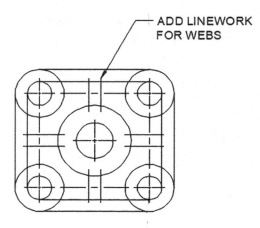

**Figure 3-100**

Figure 3-100 shows the final drawing.

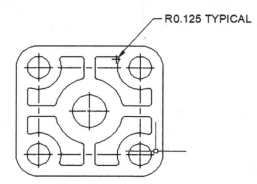

# 3-37 EXERCISE PROBLEMS

Redraw to scale the figures that follow, using the given dimensions. Do not include dimensions on the drawings.

## EX3-1 Inches (Hint: Use Osnap)

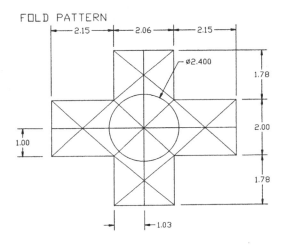

## EX3-2 Millimeters (Hint: Use Osnap)

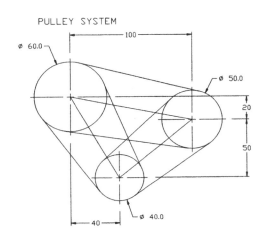

## EX3-3 Millimeters (Hint: Use Osnap)

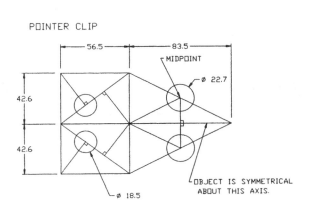

## EX3-4 Millimeters (Hint: Use Osnap)

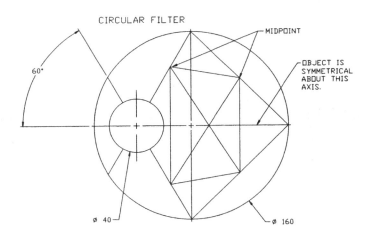

## EX3-5

Draw a 54° angle; construct the bisector.

## EX3-6

Draw an 89.33° angle; construct the bisector.

## EX3-7 Inches

Given points **A** and **B**, as shown next, construct an ogee curve of equal arcs.

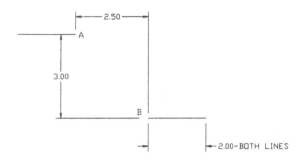

## EX3-8 Millimeters

Given points **A**, **B**, and **C**, as shown next, construct an ogee curve that starts at point **A**, passes through point **C**, and ends at point **B**.

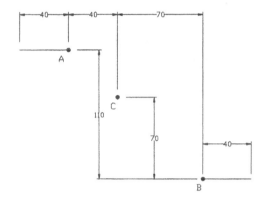

## EX3-9

Construct a hexagon inscribed within a 3.63-inch diameter circle.

## EX3-10

Construct a hexagon inscribed within a 120-millimeter diameter circle.

## EX3-11 Inches

Given point **A** and directrix **B–C**, as shown, construct a parabola.

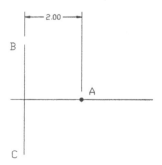

## EX3-12 Millimeters

Given point **A** and directrix **B–C**, as shown next, construct a parabola.

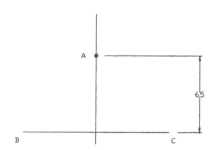

## EX3-13 Inches

Given foci **F1** and **F2**, as shown next, draw a hyperbola.

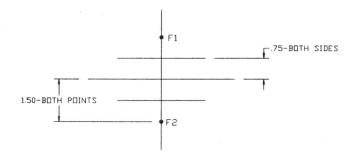

## EX3-14 Millimeters

Given foci **F1** and **F2**, as shown next, draw a hyperbola.

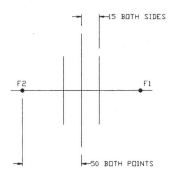

## EX3-15 Inches

Given the concentric circles and rays shown next, construct a spiral.

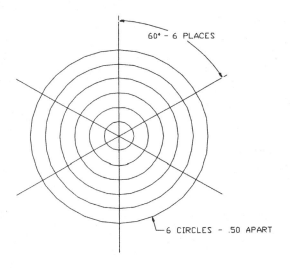

## EX3-16 Millimeters

Given the concentric circles and rays shown next, construct a spiral.

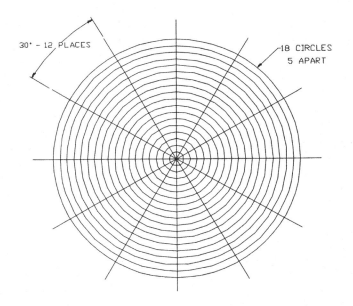

## EX3-17 Inches

Given the setup shown next, construct a helix.

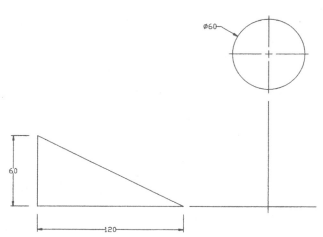

## EX3-18 Millimeters

Given the setup shown next, construct a helix.

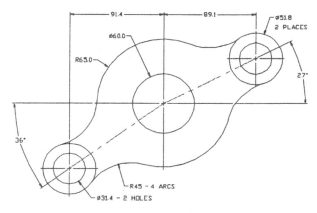

## EX3-19 Millimeters

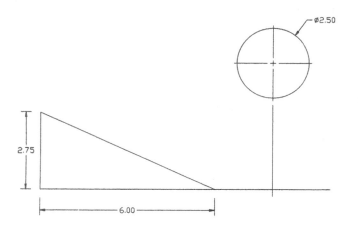

## EX3-20 Millimeters

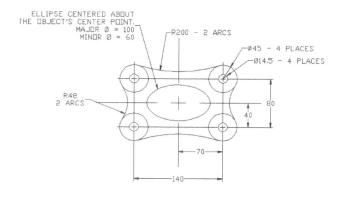

## EX3-21 Inches

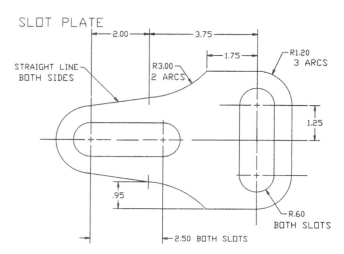

## EX3-22 Inches

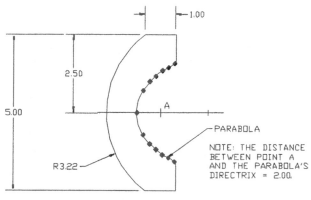

## EX3-23 Millimeters

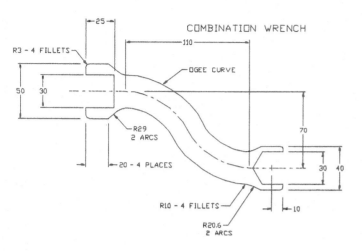

## EX3-24 Millimeters

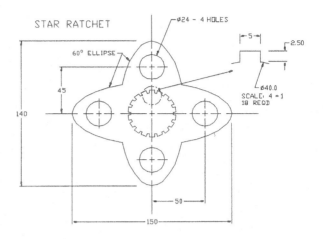

## EX3-25 Millimeters

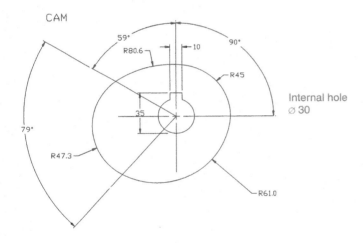

## EX3-26 Millimeters

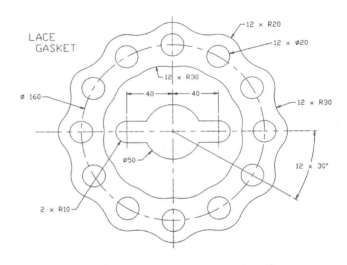

## EX3-27 Millimeters

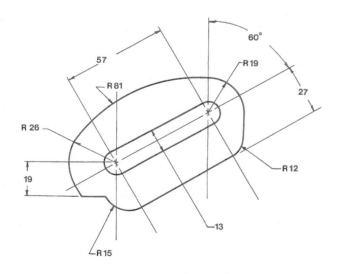

## EX3-28 Millimeters

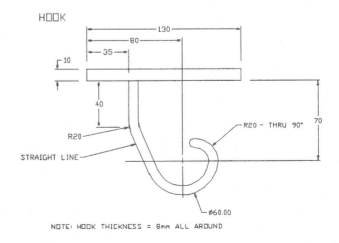

## EX3-29 Inches

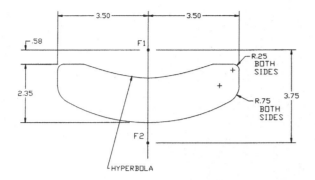

## EX3-30 Inches

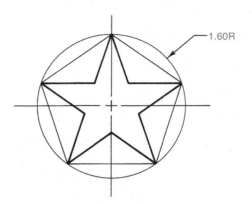

## EX3-31 Millimeters

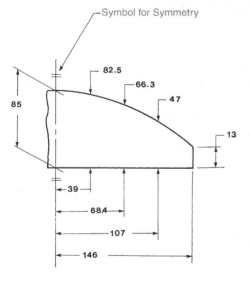

## EX3-32 Millimeters

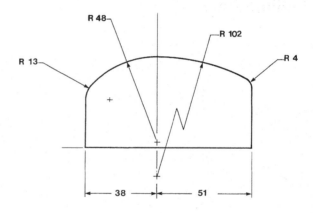

## EX3-33 Millimeters

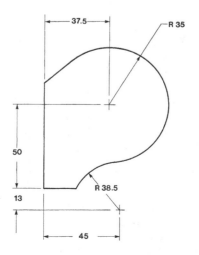

## EX3-34 Millimeters

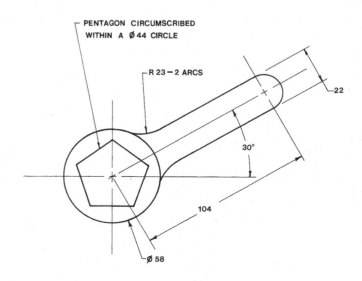

## EX3-35 Inches

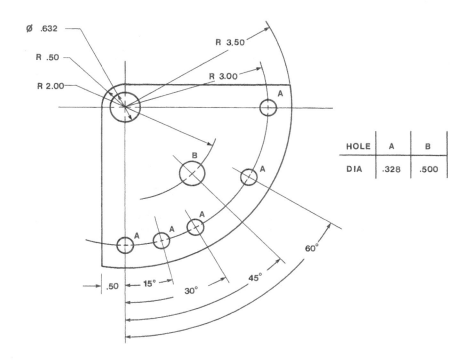

| HOLE | A | B |
|------|------|------|
| DIA | .328 | .500 |

## EX3-36 Inches

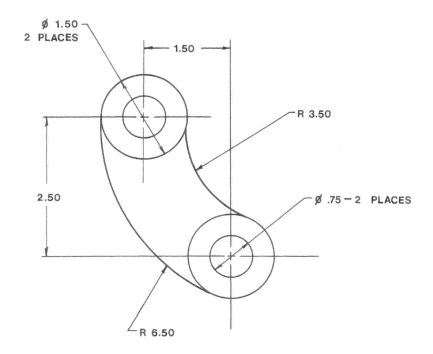

## EX3-37 Inches

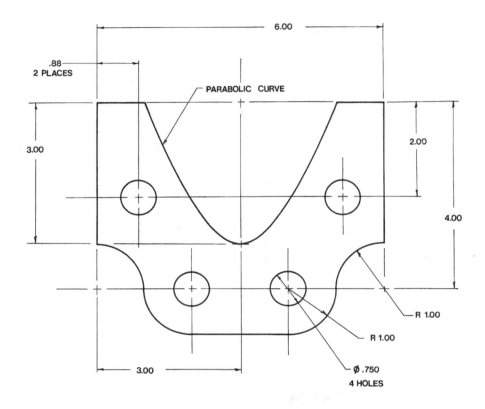

## EX3-38 Millimeters

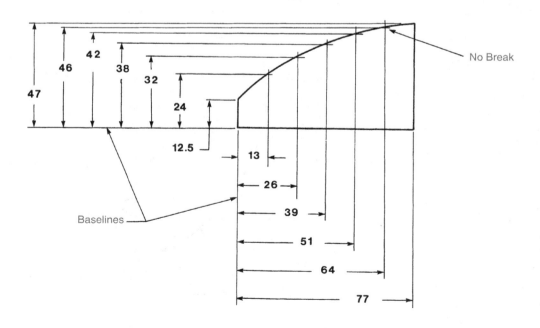

## EX3-39 Centimeters

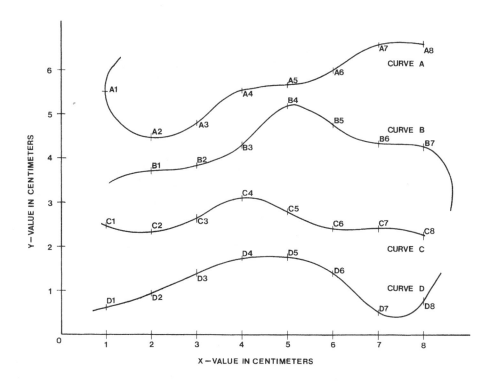

## EX3-40 Inches

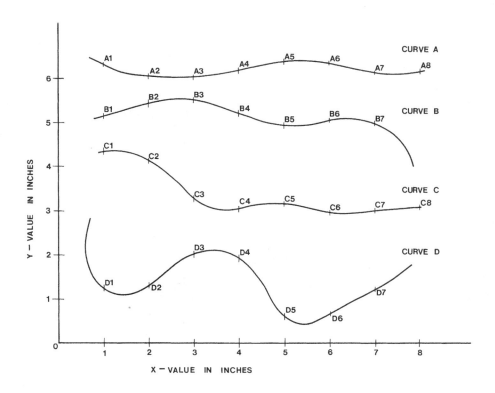

## EX3-41 Millimeters

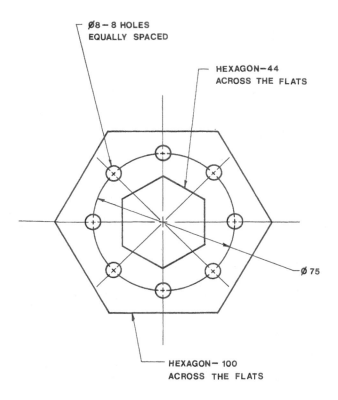

Ø8 – 8 HOLES
EQUALLY SPACED

HEXAGON – 44
ACROSS THE FLATS

Ø 75

HEXAGON – 100
ACROSS THE FLATS

## EX3-42 Millimeters

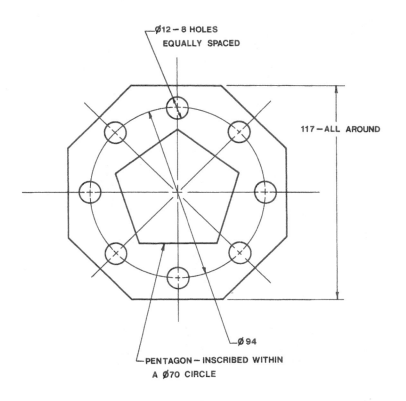

Ø12 – 8 HOLES
EQUALLY SPACED

117 – ALL AROUND

Ø 94

PENTAGON – INSCRIBED WITHIN
A Ø70 CIRCLE

## EX3-43

Draw a circle, mark off 24 equally spaced points, and then connect each point with every other point by using only straight lines.

## EX3-44 Millimeters

**1** Create a block of the drawing layout that follows.

**2** Add the following attributes:

Tag = **DATE**

Prompt = Enter today's date

Value = (leave blank)

Tag = **Drawing**

Prompt = Enter the drawing number

Value = (leave blank)

Tag = **NAME**

Prompt = Enter your name

Value = (leave blank)

Align the attribute tags on the drawing.

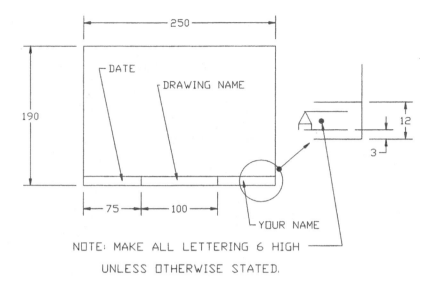

DRAWING LAYOUT — 2(MILLIMETERS)

## EX3-45 Millimeters

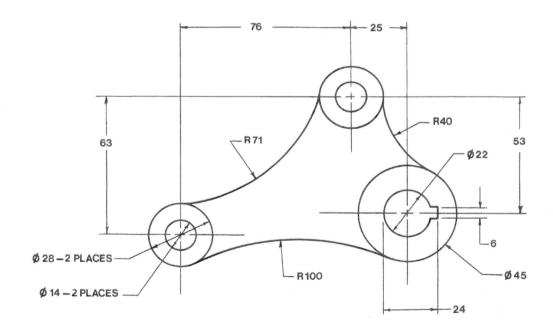

## EX3-46 Millimeters

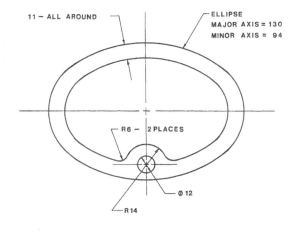

11 – ALL AROUND

ELLIPSE
MAJOR AXIS = 130
MINOR AXIS = 94

R6 – 2 PLACES

Ø 12

R14

## EX3-47 Millimeters

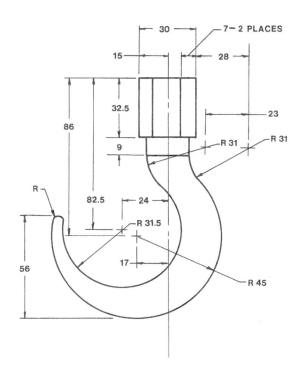

30

7 – 2 PLACES

15

28

32.5

23

86

9

R 31

R 31

R

82.5

24

R 31.5

56

17

R 45

## EX3-48 Inches

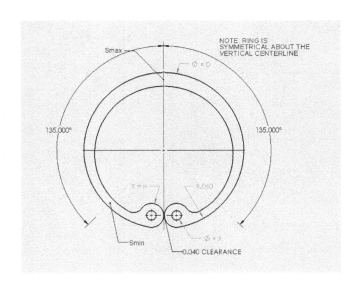

NOTE: RING IS
SYMMETRICAL ABOUT THE
VERTICAL CENTERLINE

Smax

Ø = D

135.000°

135.000°

R = H

R.060

Smin

Ø = J

0.040 CLEARANCE

### Retaining Ring - Internal - Inches

| PART NO | ØD | Smax | Smin | H | A | ØJ | Thk |
|---|---|---|---|---|---|---|---|
| BU-25 | .25 | .025 | .015 | .065 | .030 | .031 | .020 |
| BU-50 | .50 | .053 | .035 | .114 | .042 | .047 | .035 |
| BU-75 | .75 | .070 | .040 | .142 | .055 | .060 | .040 |
| BU100 | 1.00 | .091 | .052 | .155 | .060 | .060 | .042 |
| BU125 | 1.25 | .120 | .062 | .180 | .070 | .075 | .050 |
| BU150 | 1.50 | .127 | .066 | .180 | .070 | .075 | .050 |

### Retaining Ring - Internal - Millimeters

| PART NO | ØD | Smax | Smin | H | A | ØJ | Thk |
|---|---|---|---|---|---|---|---|
| MBU-20 | 20 | 2.3 | 1.9 | 4.1 | 2.0 | 2.0 | 1.0 |
| MBU-30 | 30 | 3.0 | 2.3 | 4.8 | 2.0 | 2.0 | 1.2 |
| MBU-40 | 40 | 3.9 | 3.0 | 5.8 | 2.5 | 2.5 | 1.7 |
| MBU-50 | 50 | 4.6 | 3.8 | 6.5 | 2.5 | 2.5 | 2.0 |
| MBU-60 | 60 | 5.4 | 4.3 | 7.3 | 2.5 | 2.5 | 2.0 |
| MBU-70 | 70 | 6.2 | 5.2 | 7.8 | 3.0 | 3.0 | 2.5 |

## EX3-49 Millimeters

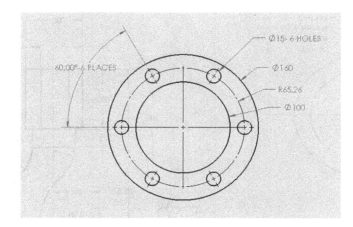

## EX3-50 Inches

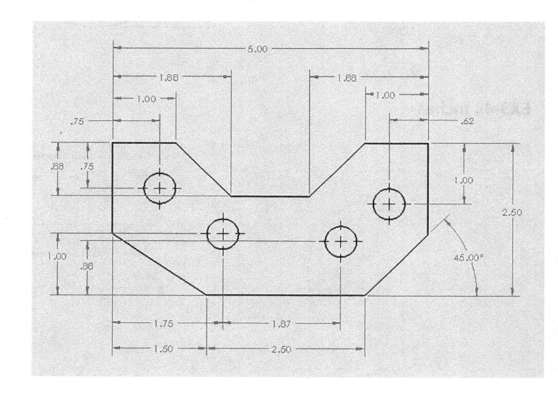

## EX3-51 Millimeters

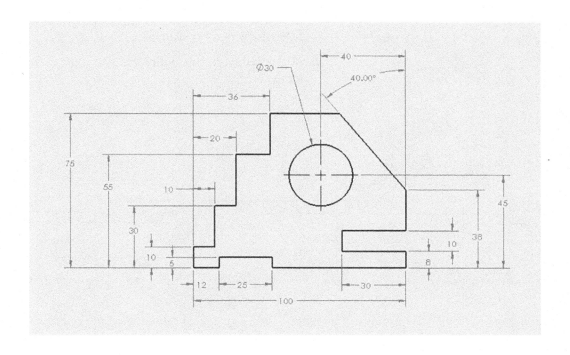

## EX3-52 Inches

Create a block for the standard tolerance blocks shown.

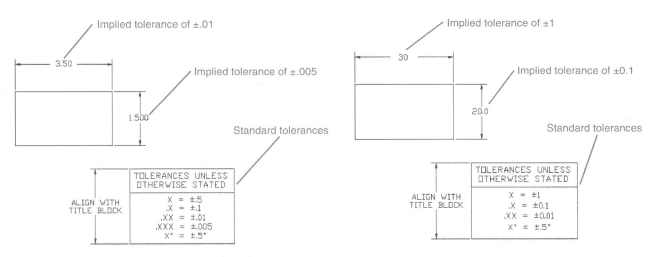

### EX3-53 Inches

**1** Create a block for one of the title blocks shown. A sample completed title block is also shown.

**2** Add attributes that will help the user complete the title block satisfactorily.

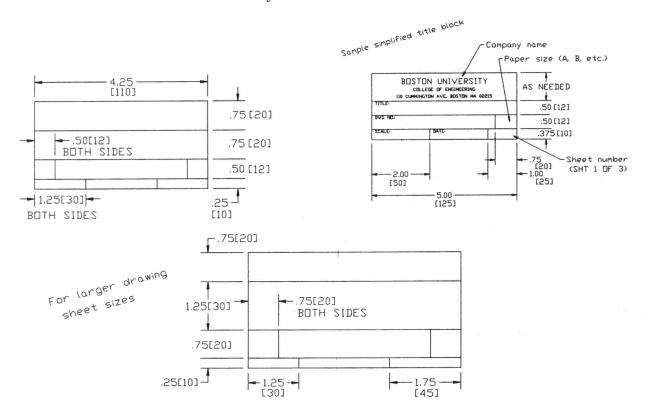

### EX3-54 Inches

Create a block of the following release block.

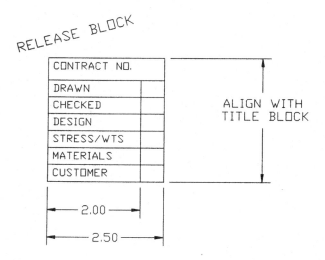

## EX3-55 Inches

Create blocks for the parts list formats that follow. Add the appropriate attributes.

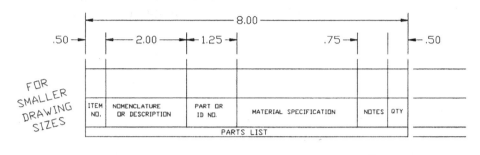

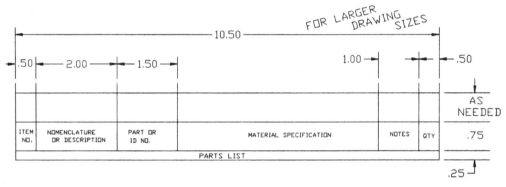

## EX3-56

Create blocks for the given revision block formats. The dimensions within the dimension lines are inches; the dimensions within the brackets are millimeters.

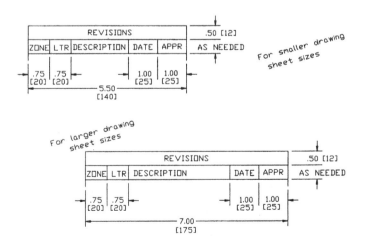

Design a shape that will support the hole patterns shown in Exercises EX3-57 through EX3-61. Design for a minimum amount of material and to satisfy the following parameters:

- The edge distance of the material may be no closer to the center of a hole than a distance equal to the radius of the hole.

- The minimum edge distance from any internal cutout to the edge of the part may be no less than the distance calculated above.

- The minimum inside radius for a cutout is 5 millimeters, or 0.125 inch.

## EX3-57 Inches

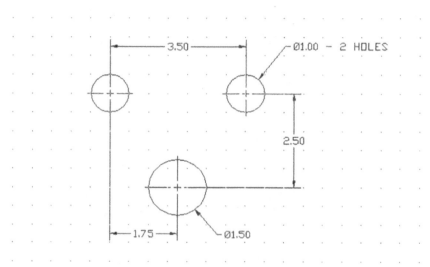

## EX3-58 Millimeters

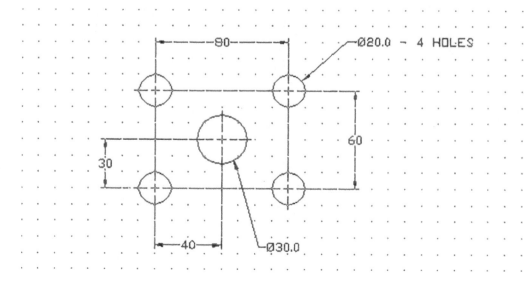

## EX3-59 Millimeters

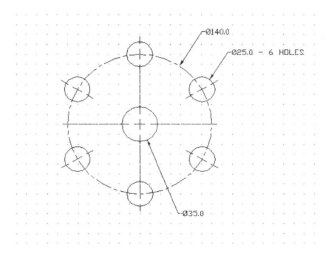

## EX3-60 Millimeters

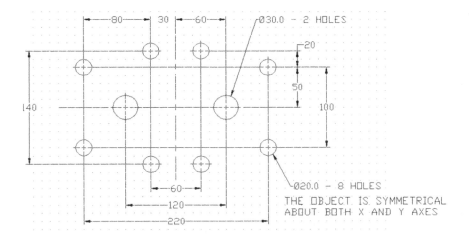

## EX3-61 Millimeters

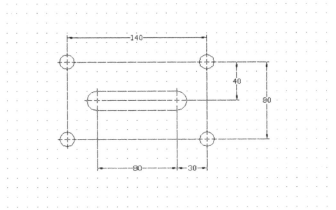

# chapter **four**
## Sketching

### 4-1 Introduction

The ability to create freehand sketches is an important skill for engineers and designers to acquire. The old joke about engineers and designers not being able to talk without a pencil in their hand is not far from the truth. Many design concepts and ideas are very difficult to express verbally, so they must be expressed visually. Sketches can be created quickly and used as powerful aids in communicating technical ideas.

This chapter presents the fundamentals of freehand sketching as applied to technical situations. It includes both two-dimensional and three-dimensional sketching. Like any other skill, freehand sketching is best learned through lots of practice.

### 4-2 Establishing Your Own Style

As you learn how to sketch and practice sketching, you will find that you develop your own way of doing things—your own style. This is very acceptable, as there is no absolutely correct method for sketching but only recommendations.

The most important requirement of freehand sketching is that you be comfortable. As you practice and experiment, you may find that you prefer a certain pencil lead hardness, a certain angle for your paper, and a certain way to make your lines, both straight and curved. You may find that you prefer to use oblique sketches rather than isometric sketches when sketching three-dimensional objects. Eventually, you will develop a style that is comfortable for you and that you can consistently use to create good-quality sketches.

Try all the types of sketches presented in the chapter. Only after you have tried and practiced all of the different types will you be able to settle on the technique and style that work best for you.

## 4-3 Graph Paper

Graph paper is very helpful when preparing freehand sketches. It helps you to sketch straight lines, allows you to set up guide points for curved lines, and can be used to establish proportions. It is recommended that you start by doing all two-dimensional sketches on graph paper. As you become more proficient with sketching, you can sketch on plain paper, but because most technical sketching requires some attention to correct proportions, grid paper will always be helpful.

Graph paper is available in many different scales and in both inch and metric units. Some graph paper is printed with light-blue lines, since many copying machines cannot easily reproduce blue lines. This means that copies of the sketches done on light-blue guidelines will appear to have been drawn on plain paper and will include only the sketch.

## 4-4 Pencils

Pencils are made with many grades of lead hardness (Figure 4-1). Hard leads can produce thin, light lines and are well suited for the accuracy requirements of board-type drawings but that are usually too light for sketching. Soft leads produce broad, dark lines but tend to smudge easily if handled too much.

**Figure 4-1**

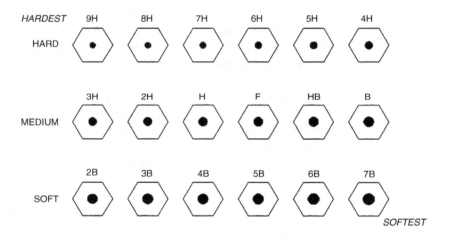

The choice of lead hardness is a personal one. Some designers use 3H leads very successfully; others use HB leads with equally good results. You are probably used to a 2H lead, as this is the most commonly available. Start sketching with a 2H lead, and if the lines are too light, try a softer lead; if the lines are too dark, try a harder lead until you are satisfied with your work. Pencils with different grades of lead hardness are available at most stationery and art supply stores.

Most sketching is done in pencil because it can easily be erased and modified. If you want the very dark lines that ink produces, it is recommended that you first prepare the drawing in pencil and then use a pen to trace over the lines that you want to emphasize.

## 4-5 Lines

Straight lines are sketched using one of two methods: by drawing a series of short lines—called *feathering*—or by drawing a series of line segments. The line segments should be about 1 to 2 inches or 25 to 50 millimeters long. It is very difficult to keep line segments reasonably straight if they are much longer. As you practice, you will develop a comfortable line segment length (Figure 4-2).

**Figure 4-2**

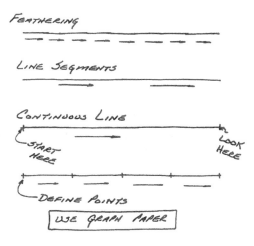

You can also sketch long, continuous lines. First, locate the pencil at the line's starting point; then, look at the endpoint as you sketch. This will help you develop straighter long lines. As you sketch continuous lines on graph paper, the graph lines will serve as an additional guide for keeping the lines straight.

Long lines can be created using a series of shorter lines, and very long lines can be sketched by first defining a series of points and then using short segments to connect the points.

It is usually more comfortable to turn the paper slightly when sketching, as shown in Figure 4-3. Right-handers turn the paper counterclockwise, and left-handers, clockwise.

**Figure 4-3**

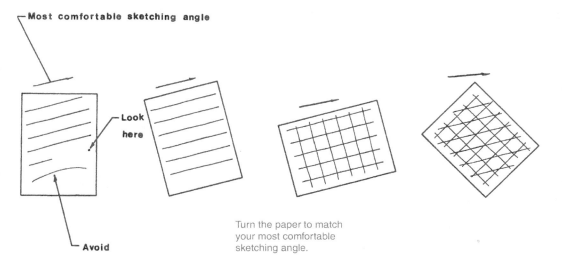

Turn the paper to match your most comfortable sketching angle.

It is also easier to sketch all lines in the same direction—that is, with your hand motion always the same. Rather than change your hand position for lines of different angles, simply change the position of the paper and sketch the lines as before. Horizontal and vertical lines are sketched by using exactly the same motion; the paper is just turned 90°. Straight lines of any angle can be sketched in the same manner.

Sketch lines by using a gentle, easy motion. Don't squeeze the pencil too hard. Sketch lines with more of an arm motion than a wrist motion. If too much wrist motion is used, the lines will tend to curve down at the ends and look more like arcs than straight lines.

## 4-6 Proportions

Sketches should be proportional. A square should look like a square and a rectangle like a rectangle. Graph paper is very helpful for sketching proportionally, but it is still sometimes difficult to be accurate even with graph paper. Start by first sketching very lightly and then checking the proportionality of the work (Figure 4-4). Go back over the lines, making corrections if necessary, and then darken the lines. The technique of first sketching lightly, checking proportions, making corrections, and then going over the lines is useful regardless of the type of paper used.

**Figure 4-4**

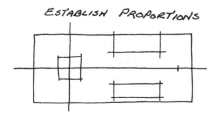

ESTABLISH PROPORTIONS

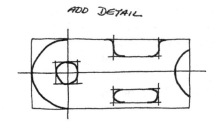

ADD DETAIL

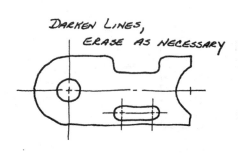

DARKEN LINES,
ERASE AS NECESSARY

It is often helpful to sketch a light grid background based on the unit values of the object being sketched. This is true even if you are working on graph paper because it helps to emphasize the unit values you need (Figure 4-5).

**Figure 4-5**

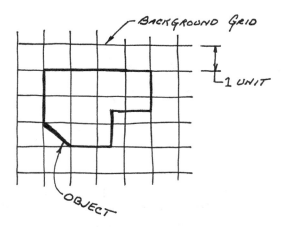

You don't always know the exact proportions of an object. A simple technique to approximately measure an object is to use the sketching pencil (Figure 4-6). Hold the pencil at arm's length and sight the object. Move your thumb up the pencil so that the distance between the end of the pencil and your thumb represents a distance on the object. Transfer the distance to the sketch. Continue taking measurements and transferring them to the sketch until you've created reasonable proportions.

**Figure 4-6**

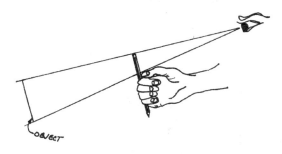

## 4-7 Curves

Curved shapes are best sketched by first defining points along the curve and then lightly sketching the curve between the points (Figure 4-7). Evaluate the accuracy and smoothness of the curve, make any corrections necessary, and then darken the curve.

**Figure 4-7**

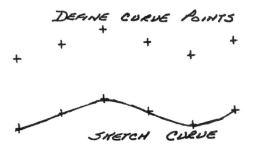

Sketch circles by sketching perpendicular centerlines and marking off four points equally spaced from the center point along the centerlines. The distance between the center point and the points on the centerlines should be approximately equal to the circle's radius (Figure 4-8).

Figure 4-8

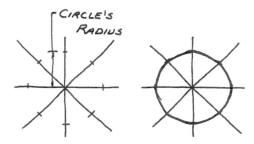

Draw a second set of perpendicular centerlines approximately 45° to the first. Again mark four points approximately equal to the radius of the circle. Sketch a light curve through the eight points and check the curve for accuracy and smoothness. Make any corrections necessary and darken the circle.

You can sketch an ellipse by first sketching a perpendicular axis and then locating four marks on the centerlines that are approximately equal to major and minor axis distances. Sketch a light curve, make any corrections necessary, and darken in the elliptical shape (Figure 4-9).

Figure 4-9

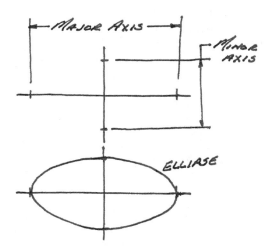

Figure 4-10 shows how to sketch a slot. To sketch the slot, locate and sketch centerlines for the two end semicircles. Add two additional radius points and then lightly sketch the overall shape of the slot. Make corrections and darken the final lines.

**Figure 4-10**

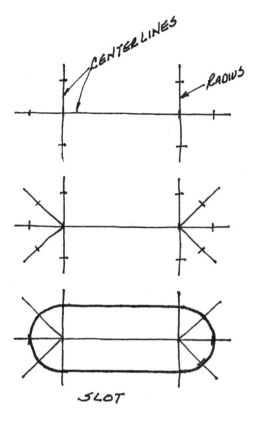

## 4-8 Drawing Problem

Sketch the object shown in Figure 4-11.

**1** Sketch the overall rectangular shape of the object (Figure 4-12).

**2** Add proportional guidelines for the outside shape of the object and lightly sketch the outside shape.

**3** Locate and sketch guidelines and axis lines for the other features.

**4** Lightly sketch the object and make any corrections necessary.

**5** Darken the final lines.

**Figure 4-11**

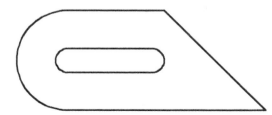

Figure 4-12

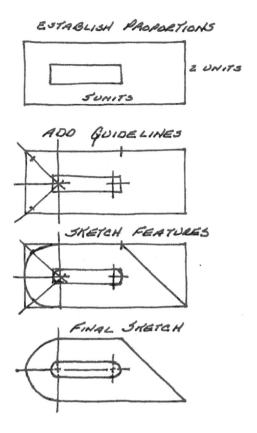

## 4-9 Isometric Sketches

*Isometric sketches* are based on three isometric axes that are three equal 120° apart (Figure 4-13). The isometric axis can also be drawn in a modified form that contains a vertical line and two 30° lines. The modified axis is more convenient for sketching and is the more commonly used form (Figure 4-14).

**Figure 4-13**

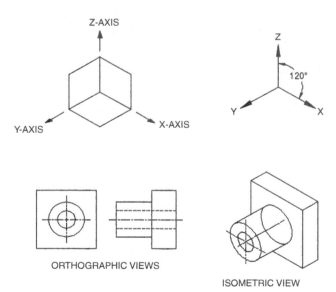

Figure 4-14

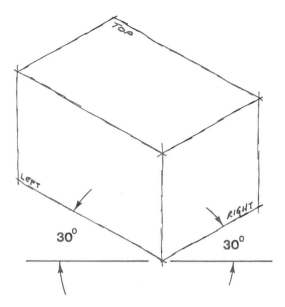

The receding lines of an isometric sketch are parallel. This is not visually correct, as the human eye naturally sees objects farther away as smaller than those that are closer. In reality, railroad tracks appear to converge; however, it is easier to draw objects with parallel receding lines, and if the object is not too big, the slight visual distortion is acceptable. See Section 4-12 for an explanation of perspective drawings whose receding lines are not parallel but convergent.

The three planes of an isometric drawing are defined as the left, right, and top planes, respectively (Figure 4-14). When creating isometric sketches, it is best to start with the three planes drawn as if the object were a rectangular prism or cube. Think of creating the sketch from these planes as working with a piece of wood and trim away the unnecessary areas. Figure 4-15 shows an example of an isometric sketch. In the example, the overall proportions of the object were used to define the boundaries of the object, and then other surfaces were added as necessary.

Figure 4-15

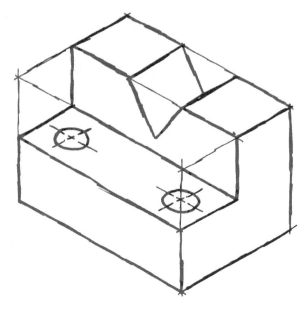

Isometric sketches may be sketched in different orientations. Figure 4-16 shows six possible orientations. Note how orientation 1 makes the object look as if it is above you, and orientation 6 makes it look as if it is below you. Orientation can also serve to show features that would otherwise be hidden from view. The small cutout is clearly visible in only one of the orientations. Always try to orient an isometric sketch so that it shows as many of the object's features as possible.

Figure 4-16

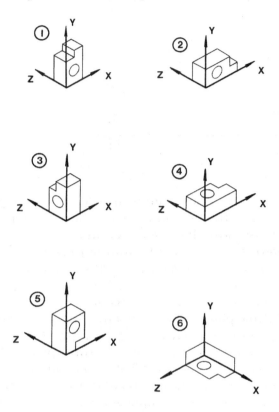

Figure 4-17 shows an isometric drawing of a cube that has a hole in the top plane. Notice that the hole is circular in the top orthographic view but elliptical in the isometric view. The hole must be sketched as an ellipse to appear visually correct in the isometric drawing. The axis lines for the ellipse are parallel to the edge lines of the plane. The proportions of the ellipse are defined by four points equidistant from the ellipse center point along the axis lines. The ellipse is then sketched lightly, checked for accuracy, and darkened.

**Figure 4-17**

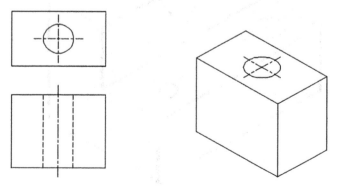

## 4-10 Drawing Problem

Sketch the object shown in Figure 4-18. Do not include dimensions but keep the object proportional.

**1** Use the overall dimensions of the object to sketch a rectangular prism of the correct proportions. This is a critical step. If the first attempt is not proportionally correct, erase it and sketch again until a satisfactory result is achieved (Figure 4-19).

**Figure 4-18**

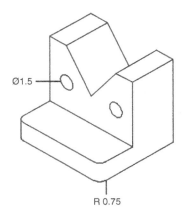

**Figure 4-19**

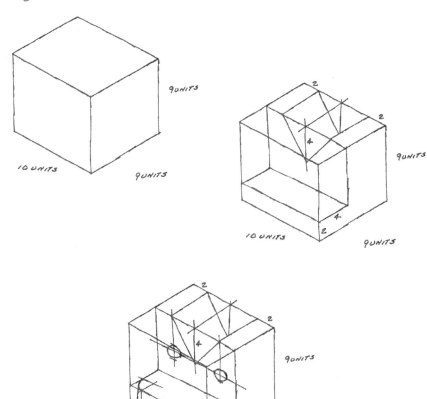

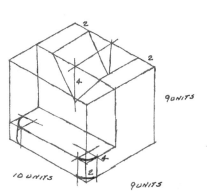

**2** Sketch the cutout.

**3** Sketch the rounded surfaces. Note how axis lines are sketched and the elliptical shape is added. Tangency lines are added, and visually incorrect lines are erased.

**4** Sketch the holes. The holes are located by locating their centerlines and then sketching the required ellipses.

## 4-11 Oblique Sketches

An *oblique sketch* is based on an axis system that contains one perpendicular set of axis lines and one receding line (Figure 4-20). The front plane of an oblique axis is perpendicular, so the front face of a cube will appear as a square and the front face of a cylinder as a circle. The receding lines can be at any angle, but 30° is most common.

Figure 4-20

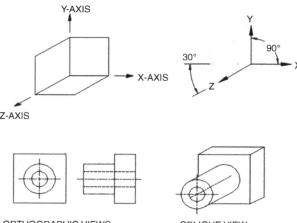

ORTHOGRAPHIC VIEWS          OBLIQUE VIEW

The receding lines of oblique sketches are parallel. As with isometric sketches, this causes some visual distortions, but unless the object is very large, these distortions are acceptable.

Sketch holes in the front plane of an oblique sketch as circles but sketch holes in the other two planes as ellipses (Figure 4-21). The axis lines for the ellipse are parallel to the edge lines of the plane. The proportions of the ellipses are determined by points equidistant from the center point along the axis.

Figure 4-22 shows an example of a circular object sketched as an oblique sketch. Oblique sketches are particularly useful in sketching circular objects because they allow circles in the frontal planes to be sketched as circles rather than as the elliptical shapes required by isometric sketches.

**Figure 4-21**

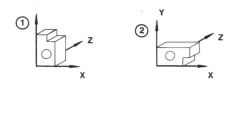

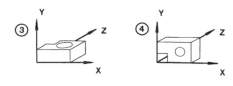

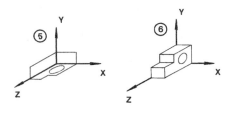

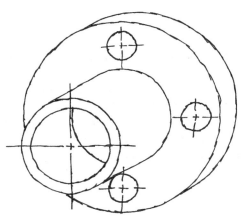

**Figure 4-22**

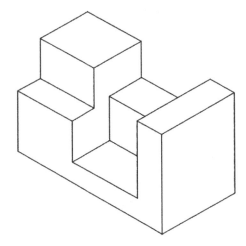

Figure 4-23 shows an object in an isometric view. Figure 4-24 shows how an oblique sketch of the object was developed.

**Figure 4-23**

Figure 4-24

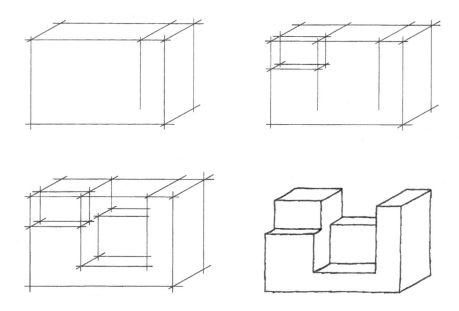

## 4-12 Perspective Sketches

A *perspective sketch* is a sketch whose receding lines converge to a vanishing point. Perspective sketches are visually accurate in that they look like what we see: Objects farther away appear smaller than those that are closer.

Figure 4-25 shows a comparison among the axis systems used for oblique, isometric, and two-point perspective drawings. The receding lines of the perspective drawings converge to vanishing points that are located on a theoretical horizon. The horizon line is always located at eye level. Objects above the horizon line appear to be above you, and objects below the horizon appear to be below you.

Figure 4-25

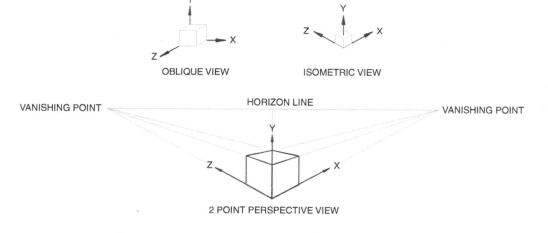

Perspective drawings are often referred to as *pictorial drawings.* Figure 4-26 shows an object drawn twice: once as an isometric drawing and again as a pictorial, or two-point, perspective. Note how much more lifelike the pictorial drawing looks in comparison with the isometric drawing.

**Figure 4-26**

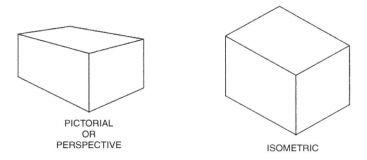

PICTORIAL
OR
PERSPECTIVE

ISOMETRIC

Figure 4-27 shows a perspective sketch based on only one vanishing point. One-point perspective sketches are similar to oblique sketches. The front surface plane is sketched by using a 90° axis, and then receding lines are sketched from the front plane to a vanishing point. As you practice sketching, eventually you will not need to include a vanishing point but will imply its location.

**Figure 4-27**

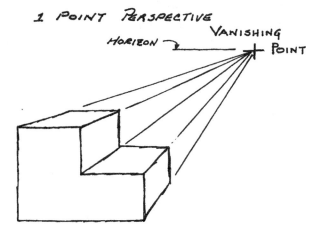

Figure 4-28 shows how to sketch circular shapes in one- and two-point perspective sketches. In each style, the axis lines consist of a vertical line and a line that is aligned with the receding edge lines. Circular shapes in perspective drawings are not elliptical but are irregular splines. Each surface requires a slightly different shape, depending on the angle of the receding lines, to produce a visually accurate circular shape.

Figure 4-28

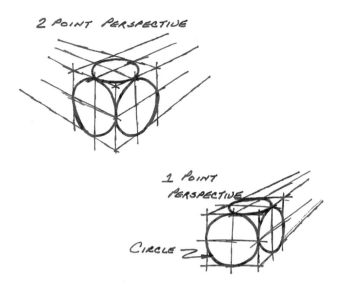

## 4-13 Working in Different Orientations

It is important for a designer to be able to sketch an object in different orientations in order to present a clear representation of all of the design's different facets.

Figure 4-29 shows three different objects sketched in three different orientations. Each sketch used an isometric format. Proportions for each object were determined by using the dot grid background.

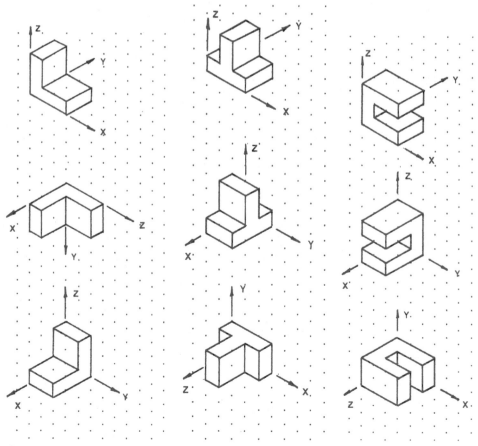

Figure 4-29

## 4-14 EXERCISE PROBLEMS

Sketch the shapes in Exercise Problems EX4-1 through EX4-6. Measure the shapes to determine their dimensions.

**EX4-1**

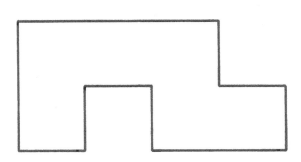

**EX4-2**

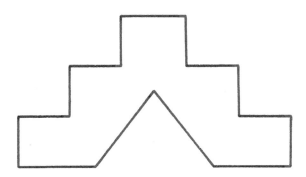

**EX4-3**

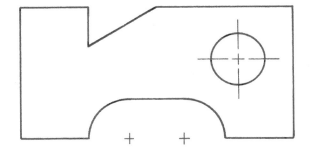

**EX4-4**

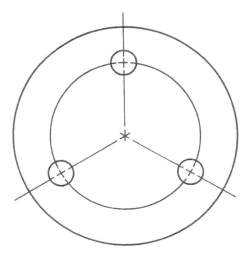

**EX4-5**

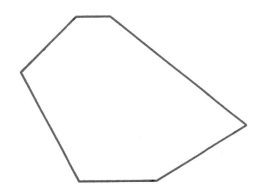

**EX4-6**

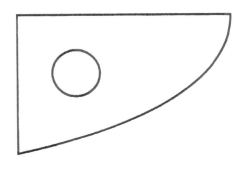

Prepare isometric or perspective sketches of the objects shown in Exercise Problems EX4-7 through EX4-18. Measure the objects to determine their dimensions.

**EX4-7**

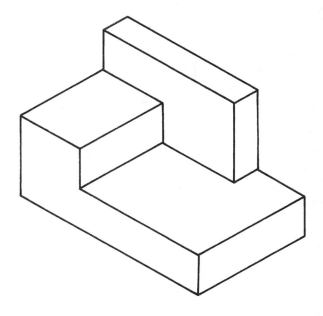

**EX4-8**

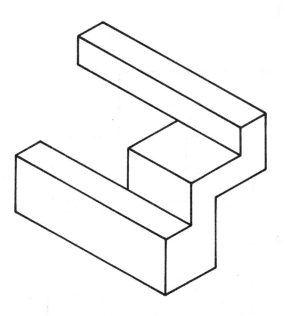

**EX4-9**

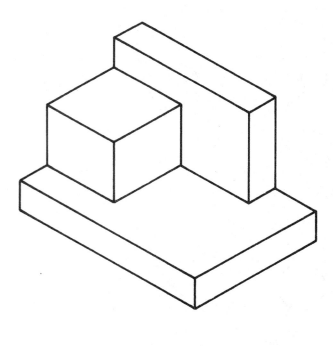

**EX4-10**

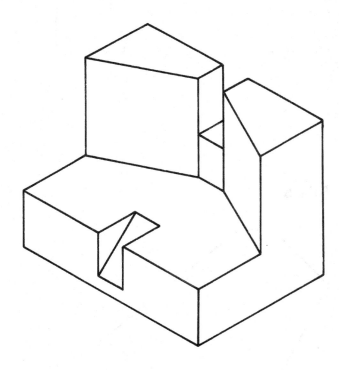

**EX4-11**

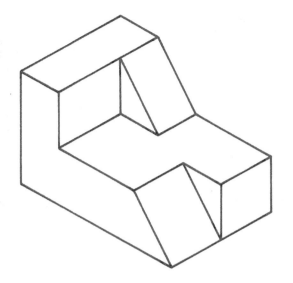

**EX4-12**

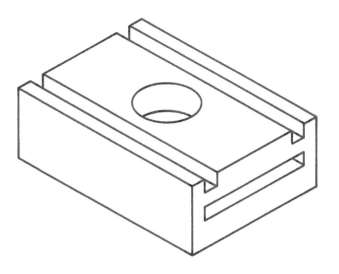

**EX4-13**

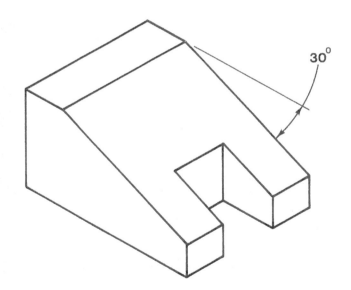

30°

**EX4-14**

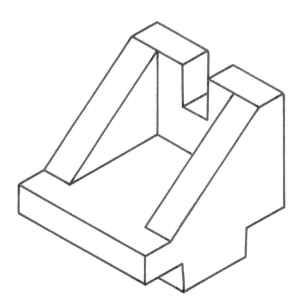

**EX4-15**

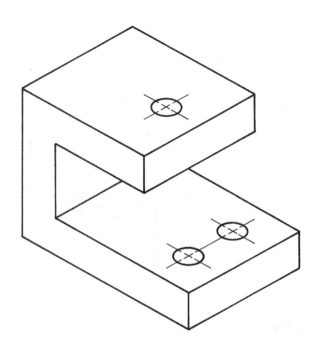

**EX4-16**

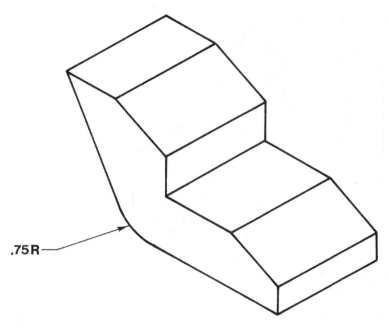

.75R

**EX4-17**

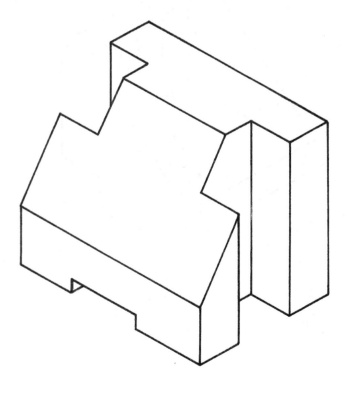

**EX4-18**

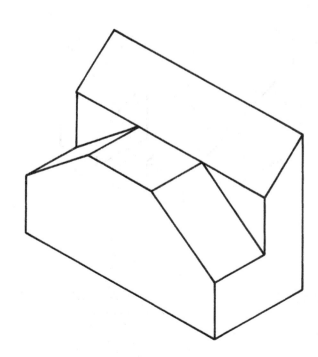

Prepare oblique or perspective sketches of the objects shown in Exercise Problems EX4-19 through EX4-22. Measure the objects to determine their dimensions.

**EX4-19**

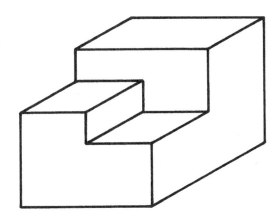

**EX4-20**

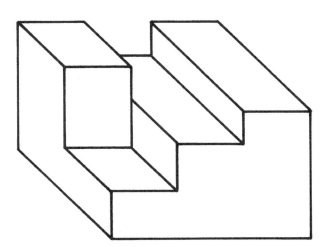

**EX4-21**

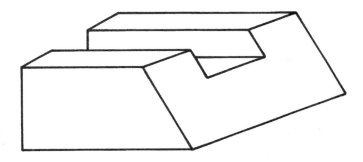

**EX4-22**

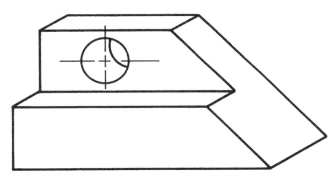

Prepare isometric sketches of the shapes that follow, each in the given orientation, and then sketch the objects in the three different orientations defined by the X, Y, and Z axes. Assume that the spacing between dots in the background grid is approximately 0.25 inch, or 10 millimeters.

## EX4-23

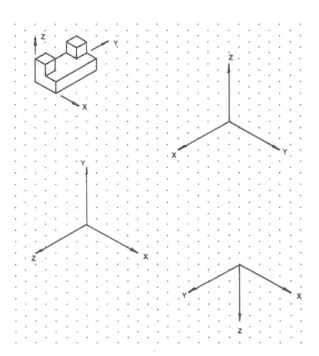

## EX4-24

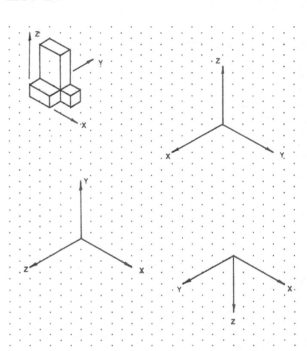

## EX4-25

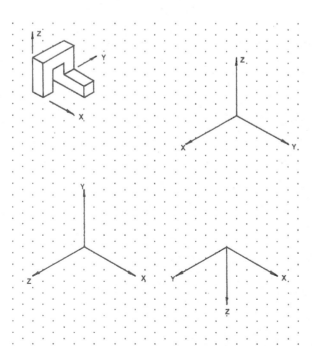

## EX4-26

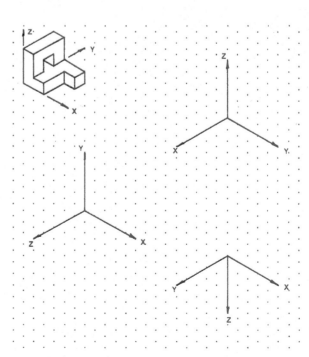

## EX4-27

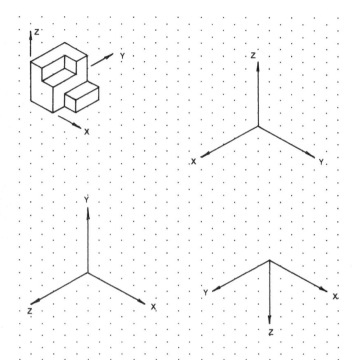

## EX4-28

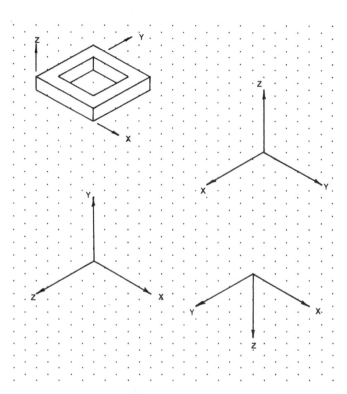

## EX4-29

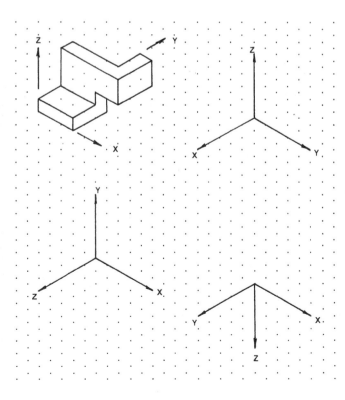

## EX4-30

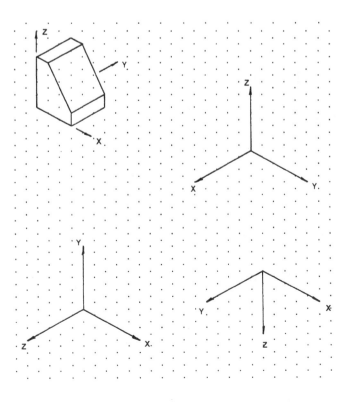

## EX4-31

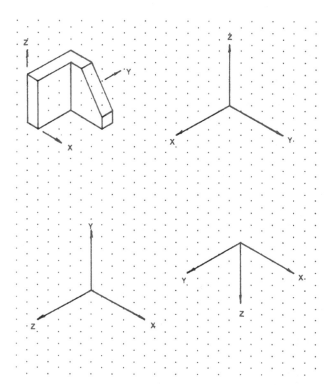

## EX4-32

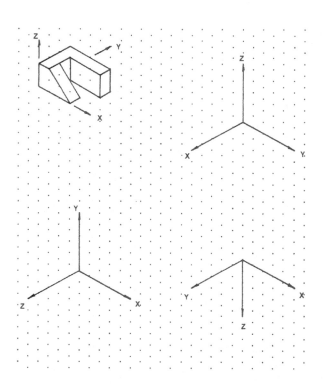

## EX4-33

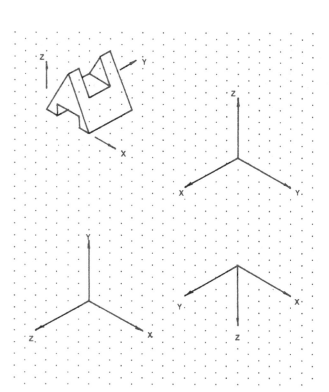

## EX4-34

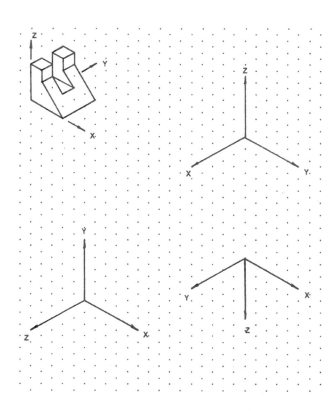

## EX4-35

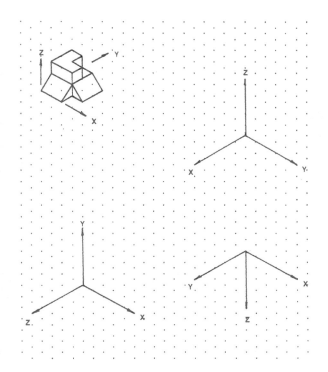

## EX4-36

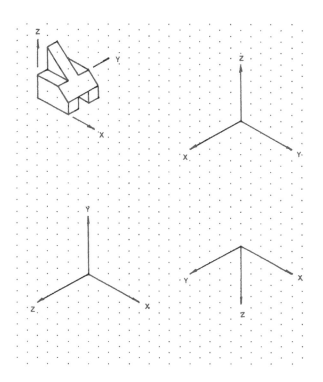

## EX4-37

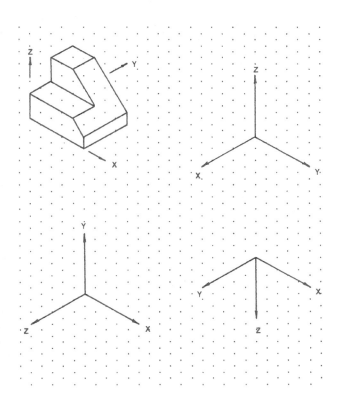

## EX4-38

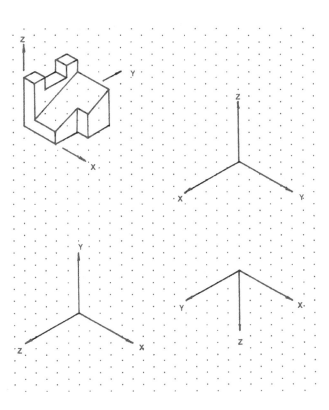

## EX4-39

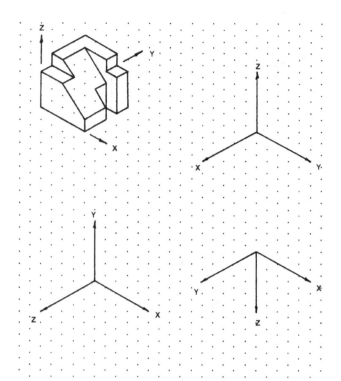

## EX4-40

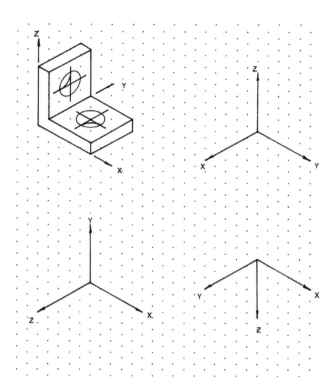

## EX4-41

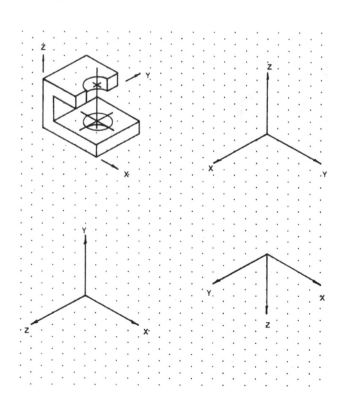

## EX4-42

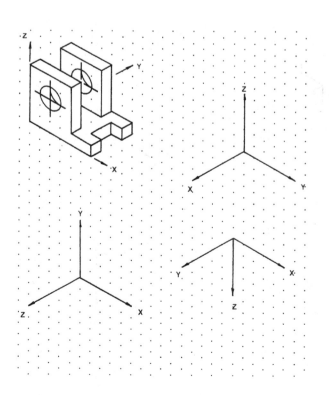

## EX4-43

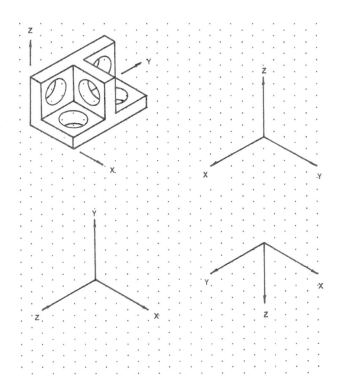

## EX4-44

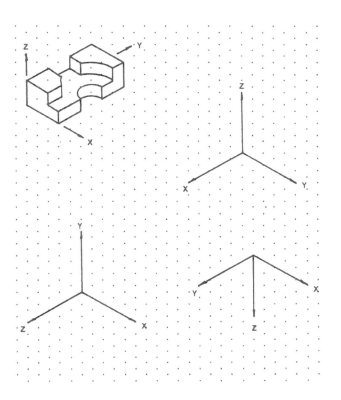

## EX4-45

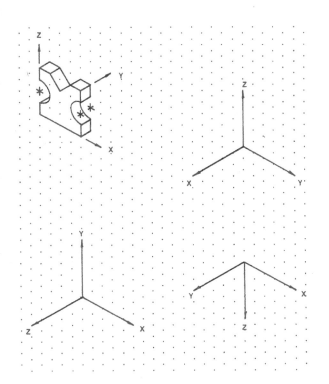

## EX4-46

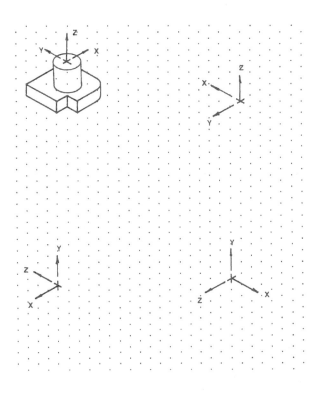

## EX4-47

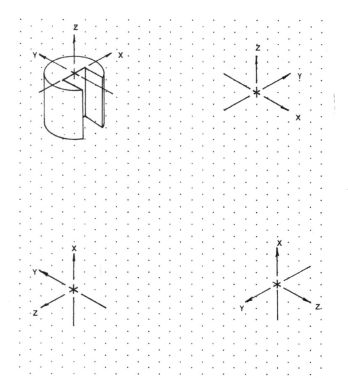

## EX4-48

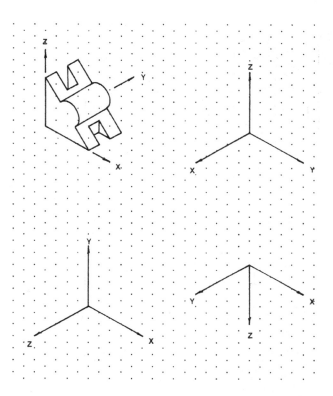

## EX4-49

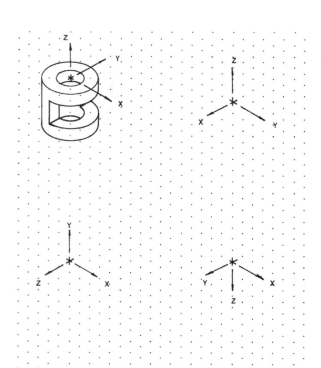

## EX4-50

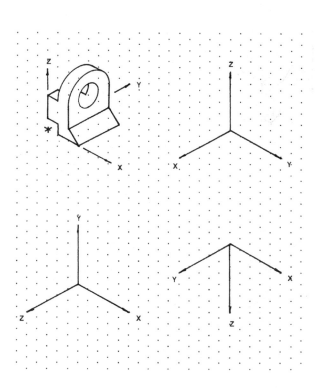

Sketch the following objects.

**EX4-51**

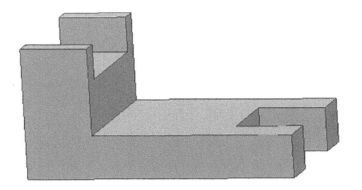

**EX4-52**

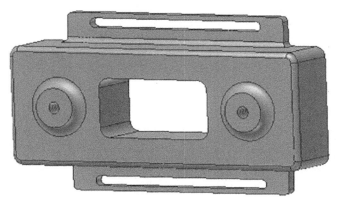

**EX4-53**

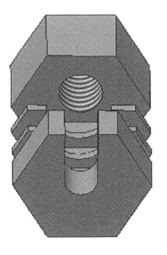

**EX4-54**

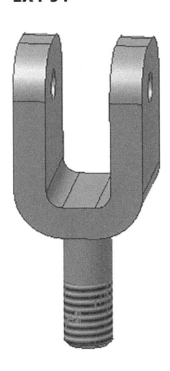

# 5 chapter five

# Orthographic Views

## 5-1 Introduction

This chapter introduces orthographic views. An *orthographic view* is a two-dimensional view of a three-dimensional object. Orthographic views are created by projecting a view of an object onto a plane which is usually positioned so that it is parallel to one of the planes of the object (Figure 5-1).

Figure 5-1

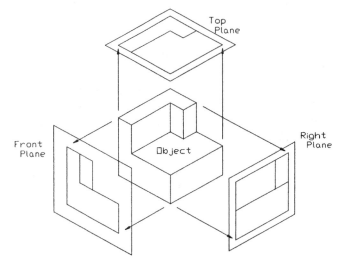

You can position orthographic projection planes at any angle relative to an object, but in general, the six views parallel to the six sides of a rectangular object are used (Figure 5-2). Technical drawings usually include only the front, top, and right-side orthographic views because together they are considered sufficient to completely define an object's shape.

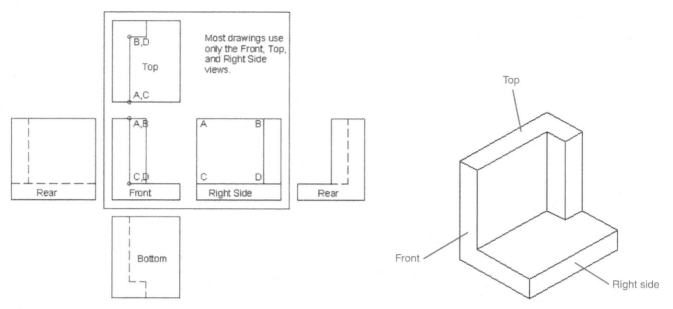

**Figure 5-2**

## 5-2 Three Views of an Object

Orthographic views are positioned on a technical drawing so that the top view is located directly over the front view, and the right side view is directly to the right side of the front view (Figure 5-2). This convention, called *third-angle projection*, is discussed in Section 5-37.

The locations of the front, top, and right side views relative to each other are critical. Correct relative positioning of views allows information to be projected between the views. Vertical lines project information between the front and top views, and horizontal lines project information between the front and right-side views.

Orthographic views are two-dimensional, so they cannot show depth. In Figure 5-2, plane **A–B–C–D** appears as a straight line in both the front and top orthographic views. Edge **A–B** appears as a vertical line in the top view, as a horizontal line in the side view, and as point **AB** in the front view. The end view of a plane is a straight line, and the end view of a line is a point (Figure 5-3).

**Figure 5-3**

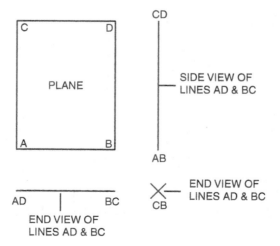

Figure 5-4 shows an object and the front, top, and right-side orthographic views of the object. Plane **A–B–C–D** appears as a rectangle in the front view and as a line in both the top and right-side views.

To help you better understand the relationship between orthographic views and, in particular, the front, top, and side views of an object, place a book on a table as shown in Figure 5-5. Note how the front, top, and side views were projected and then arranged to create a technical drawing of the book.

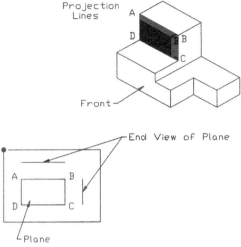

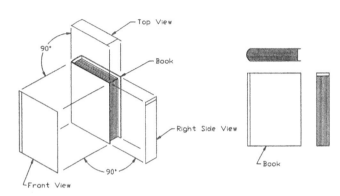

**Figure 5-4**

**Figure 5-5**

## 5-3 Visualization

In engineering drawing, *visualization* is the ability to look at a three-dimensional object and mentally see the appropriate three orthographic views.

It is an important skill for designers and engineers to develop. Visualization also includes the ability to look at two-dimensional orthographic views and mentally picture the three-dimensional object that the views represent.

Figure 5-6 shows a 5 × 3.5 × 2-inch box and three orthographic views of the box. The creation of three-dimensional object drawings is explained in detail in Chapters 14, 15, and 16. This section presents a short exercise to help you better understand how orthographic views are related to three-dimensional objects.

**Figure 5-6**

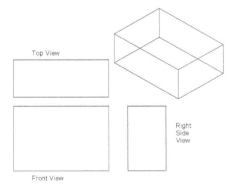

## Drawing a Three-Dimensional Box

**1.** Set the AutoCAD drawing screen for inches. On the **Named Views** panel of the **View** tab, click the drop-down list currently showing **Unsaved View** and then select **SE Isometric** from the menu (Figure 5-7).

**Figure 5-7**

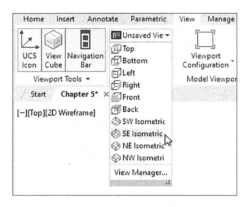

The origin axis reference icon changes to the 3D alignment.

**2.** Enter the command **box** at the command prompt.

```
Specify first corner or [Center]:
```

**3.** Press **Enter**.

```
Specify corner or [Cube/Length]:
```

**4.** Type **L** and press **Enter**.

```
Specify length:
```

**5.** Type **5** and press **Enter**.

```
Specify width:
```

**6.** Type **3.5** and press **Enter**.

```
Specify height:
```

**7.** Type **2** and press **Enter**.

A box in three dimensions appears on the screen.

Before continuing, you may need to turn on the **Navigate** panel on the **View** tab that is off when AutoCAD is installed.

**8.** With the **View** tab selected, right-click in the empty gray area to the right of the last panel on the tab. From the right-click menu, select **Show Panels** and then select **Navigate** (Figure 5-8). The **Navigate** panel appears at the end of the **View** tab (Figure 5-9).

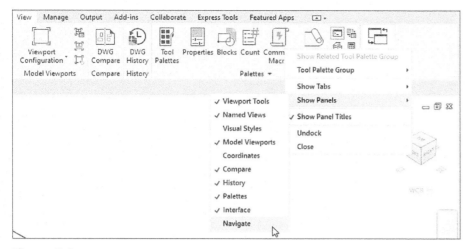

**Figure 5-8**

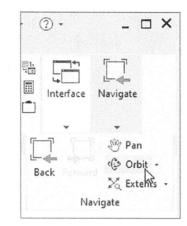

**Figure 5-9**

9. Select **Orbit** from the **Navigate** panel (Figure 5-9). Move the cursor around the drawing screen, holding the left mouse button down. Position the box so as to create each of the three orthographic views shown in Figure 5-6.

Figures 5-10 and 5-11 show two additional objects and their orthographic views.

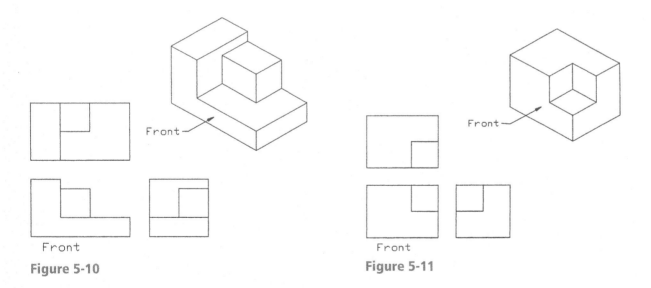

**Figure 5-10**

**Figure 5-11**

## 5-4 Hidden Lines

Hidden lines represent surfaces that are not directly visible in an orthographic view. Figure 5-12 shows an object that contains a surface that is not visible in the right-side view. A hidden line is used to represent the end view of the surface.

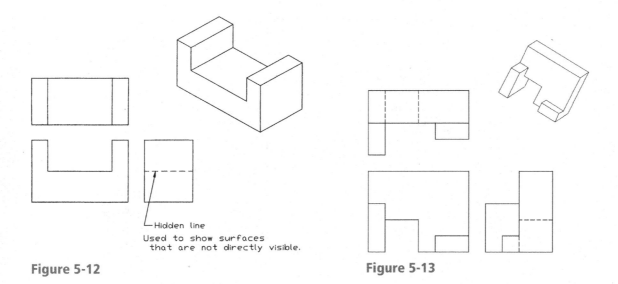

**Figure 5-12**

Hidden line
Used to show surfaces
that are not directly visible.

**Figure 5-13**

Figure 5-13 shows an object and three views of the object. The top and side views of the object contain hidden lines.

Figure 5-14 shows an object that contains an edge line **A–B**. In the top view of the object, line **A–B** is partially hidden and partially visible. When the line is directly visible through the square hole, it is drawn as a continuous line; when it is not directly visible, it is drawn as a hidden line.

**Figure 5-14**

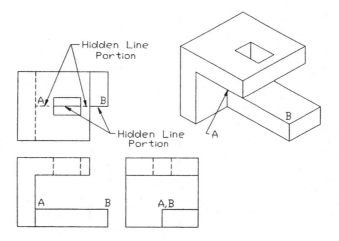

## 5-5 Hidden Line Conventions

Figure 5-15 shows several conventions associated with drawing hidden lines. Whenever possible, show intersections of hidden lines as touching lines, not as open gaps. Corners should also be shown as touching lines.

**Figure 5-15**

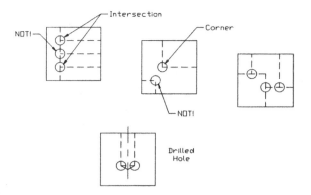

Figure 5-16 shows two hidden lines and a continuous line that are aligned. A small gap should be included between the two types of lines to prevent confusion about where one type of line ends and the other begins. A visual distinction can also be created by selecting a different color for hidden lines. If continuous and hidden lines are drawn with different colors, then gaps are not necessary.

**Figure 5-16**

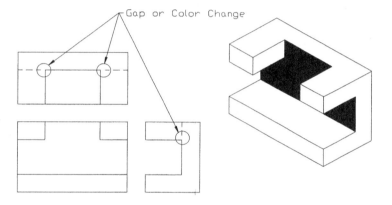

## 5-6 Drawing Hidden Lines

Hidden lines can be created in several different ways, but two of the easiest options are to modify an existing continuous line and to transfer an existing continuous line to a layer created specifically for hidden lines. In the examples presented, both linetype and line color will be changed.

### Adding Hidden Linetypes to a Drawing

**1** Enter the command **Linetype** at the command prompt.

The **Linetype Manager** dialog box appears (Figure 5-17).

**2** Click **Load** in the **Linetype Manager** dialog box.

The **Load or Reload Linetypes** dialog box appears.

**3** Scroll down the linetypes and select **HIDDEN** (Figure 5-18).

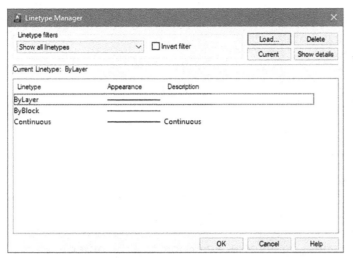

**Figure 5-17**

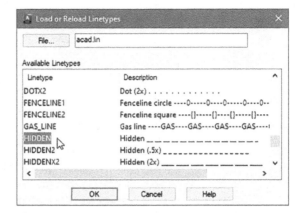

**Figure 5-18**

**4** Click **OK** and then click **OK** again to return to the drawing screen.

**5** Draw a line, as shown in Figure 5-19.

**Figure 5-19**

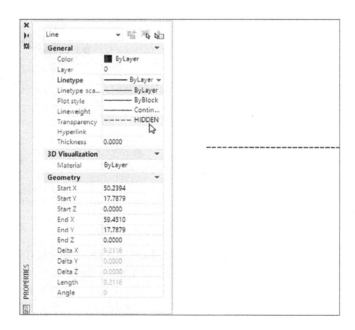

**6** Click the line.

Grips appear on the line.

**7** Right-click and select the **Properties** option.

The **Properties** palette appears.

**8** Click the **Linetype** line, scroll down, and select the **HIDDEN** linetype.

**9** Click the **Color** line and then select the **Blue** color.

As shown in Figure 5-20, the line now has a hidden linetype and is blue.

**Figure 5-20**

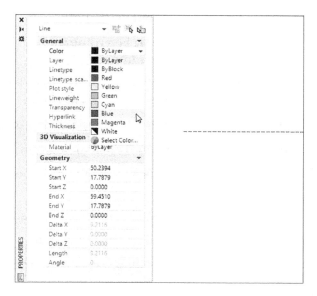

**10** Close the **Properties** palette. Click the large **X** in the upper-left corner of the box.

**11** Press the **Esc** key.

## Creating a Hidden Layer for General Use

Create a hidden layer so that any line can be transferred to that layer, and a hidden blue line will be created.

**1** Click **Layer Properties** on the **Layers** panel under the **Home** tab.

The **Layer Properties Manager** dialog box appears (Figure 5-21).

**NOTE**

Click and drag the right edge of the **Layer Properties Manager** to extend the width of the box.

**Figure 5-21**

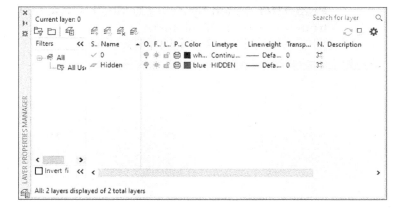

**2** Click **New Layer**.

A new layer listing, **Layer1**, appears below the **0** layer.

**3** Change the name **Layer1** to **Hidden**.

**4** Scroll across the **Hidden** layer line and click the word **Continuous** under the **Linetype** heading.

The **Select Linetype** dialog box appears. The **Hidden** linetype is not available and must be loaded to continue.

**5** Click **Load** in the **Select Linetype** dialog box.

The **Load or Reload Linetypes** dialog box appears.

**6** Scroll down the list of available linetypes, and select **HIDDEN**, and click **OK**.

The **Select Linetype** dialog box reappears.

**7** Click the **Hidden** line and then click **OK**.

The **Select Linetype** dialog box closes, and the **Layer Properties Manager** remains open.

**8** In the Layer Properties Manager, on the **Hidden** row under **Color**, click the square tile and use the **Select Color** dialog box to change the hidden line's color to blue.

**9** Close the **Layer Properties Manager** by clicking the **X** at the top of the palette's title bar.

## Changing Layers

Figure 5-22 shows a continuous line drawn on the **0** layer.

**1** Click the line.

**2** In the **Layers** panel, click the drop-down layer list and scroll down; select the **Hidden** layer (Figure 5-22).

**3** Press the **Esc** key.

The line is now located on the **Hidden** layer, has a hidden linetype, and is blue.

The line's linetype and color could have also be changed by using the **Quick Properties** dialog box shown in Figure 5-23. Access the **Quick Properties** option by right-clicking the line and selecting **Quick Properties** from the bottom of the menu.

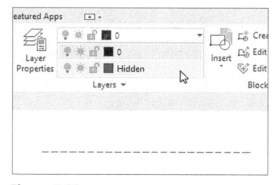

Figure 5-22

Figure 5-23

Figures 5-24 and 5-25 show an object and three views of that object. There are hidden lines in several of the orthographic views.

**Figure 5-24**

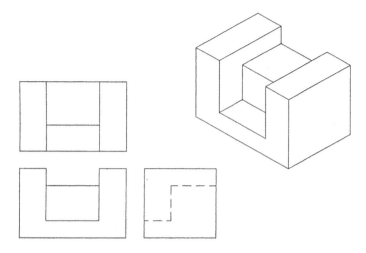

**Figure 5-25**

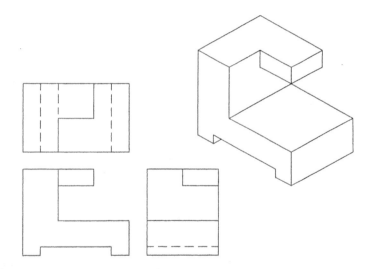

## 5-7 Precedence of Lines

When orthographic views are prepared, it is not unusual for one type of line to be drawn over another type; for example, a continuous line may be drawn over a centerline (Figure 5-26). Drawing convention has established a precedence of lines: A continuous line takes precedence over a hidden line, and a hidden line takes precedence over a centerline.

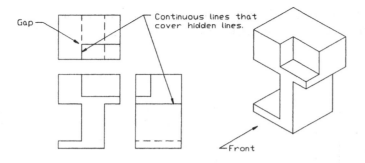

Figure 5-26

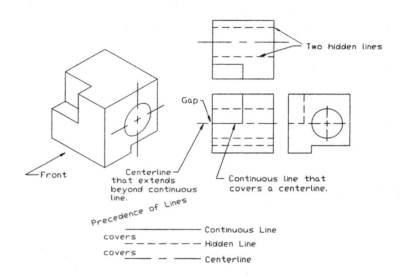

If different linetypes are of different lengths, include a gap where the line changes from continuous to either hidden or center in order to create a visual distinction between the lines. Color or lineweight changes may also be used to create visual distinctions between lines.

## 5-8 Slanted Surfaces

*Slanted surfaces* are surfaces that are not parallel to either the horizontal or vertical axis. Figure 5-27 shows a slanted surface **A–B–C–D**. Slanted surface **A–B–C–D** appears as a straight line in the side view and as a plane in both the front and top views. It is important to note that neither the front view nor top view of surface **A–B–C–D** is a true representation of the surface. Both orthographic views are smaller than the actual surface. Lines **B–C** and **A–D** in the top view are true length, but lines **A–B** and **C–D** are shorter than the actual edge lengths. The same is true for the front view of the surface. The side view shows the true length of lines **A–B** and **D–C**. True lengths of lines and true shapes of planes are discussed again in Chapter 7.

Figure 5-28 shows another object that contains slanted surfaces. Note how projection lines are used between the views. As objects become more complex, the shape of a surface or the location of an edge line is not always obvious, so projecting information between views—and therefore, the exact, correct relative view location—becomes critical. Information can be projected only between views that are correctly positioned and accurately drawn.

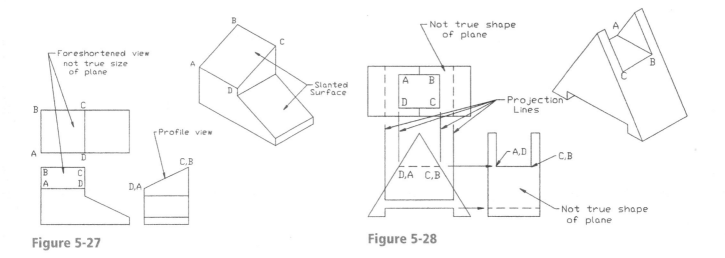

**Figure 5-27**

**Figure 5-28**

## 5-9 Projection Between Views

Information is projected between the front and side views using horizontal lines and between the front and top views using vertical lines. Information can be projected between the top and side views by using a combination of horizontal and vertical lines that intersect a 45° miter line (Figure 5-29).

**Figure 5-29**

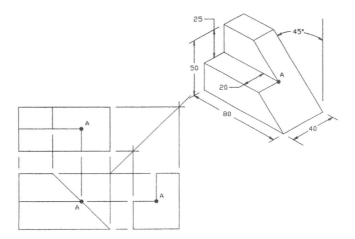

A 45° miter line is constructed between the top and side views. This line allows the project lines to change direction, turn a corner, and change from horizontal to vertical lines. To go from the top view to the side view, horizontal projection lines are constructed from the top view so that they intersect the miter line. Vertical lines are constructed from the intersection points on the miter line into the side view. The reverse process is used to go from the side view to the top view.

The following drawing problem shows how projection lines can be used to create orthographic views through AutoCAD.

# 5-10 Drawing Problem

Draw the front, top, and right-side orthographic views of the object shown in Figure 5-29. Set up the drawing as follows:

**1** Start a new drawing using the **acadiso.dwt** drawing template and make the following settings, creating a separate layer for hidden lines:

Limits = **297** × **210** (metric setup)

Grid  = **10**

Snap  = **5**

Ortho  = **ON** (F8)

Layer  = **HIDDEN** (LType = **HIDDEN**, Color = **Green**)

**2** Use the overall dimensions length = **80**, height = **50**, and depth = **40** to define the overall size requirements of the three orthographic views (Figure 5-30). The **20** spacing between the views is arbitrary. The distance between the front and top views does not have to equal the distance between the front and side views. In this example, the two distances are equal.

**Figure 5-30**

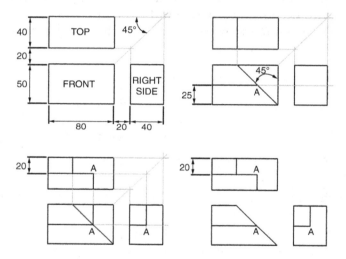

**3** Draw a **45°** miter line starting from the upper-right corner of the front view. This step is possible only if the distances between the views are equal. If the distances are not equal, draw the front and top views, add the miter line, and project the overall size of the side view from the front and top views.

3.a (Optional) Trim away the excess lines to clearly define the areas of the front, top, and side views.

3.b (Optional) The **Layer** tool may be used to create a layer for construction lines and another layer for final drawing lines. The lines for the final drawing may then be transferred to the final drawing layer, and the construction layer can be turned off. This method eliminates the need for extensive erasing or trimming.

**4** Draw the **45°** slanted surface in the front view, as shown in Figure 5-30. Project the intersection of the slanted surface and the top edge of the front view into the top view. Add a horizontal line across the front and right-side views **25** from the bottom edge line. The 25 value comes from the given dimension. Label the intersection of the slanted line and the horizontal line point **A**.

**5** Draw a horizontal line in the top view **20** from the top edge, as shown in Figure 5-30. Continue the line so that it intersects the miter line. Project the line into the side view. Use **Osnap Intersection** with **Ortho** on to ensure an accurate projection. Label point **A** in the side view.

**6** Project point **A** in the front view into the top view (using a vertical line). Label the intersection of the projection line and the horizontal line in the top view as point **A**.

**7** Use **Erase** and **Trim** to remove the excess lines.

**8** Save the drawing, if desired.

## 5-11 Compound Lines

A *compound line* is formed when two slanted surfaces intersect (Figure 5-31). The true length of a compound line is not shown in the front, top, or side views.

Figure 5-32 shows another object that contains compound lines. The three orthographic views of a compound line are sometimes difficult to visualize, making it more important to be able to project information accurately between views. Usually, part of an object can be visualized and part of the orthographic views can be created. The remainder of the drawing can be added by projecting from the known information.

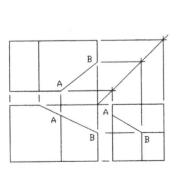
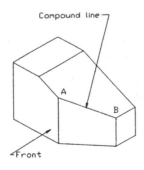

**Figure 5-31**

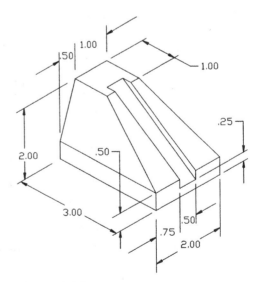

**Figure 5-32**

## 5-12 Drawing Problem

Figure 5-33 shows how the front, top, and side views of the object shown in Figure 5-32 were created by projecting information. The procedure is as follows:

**Figure 5-33**

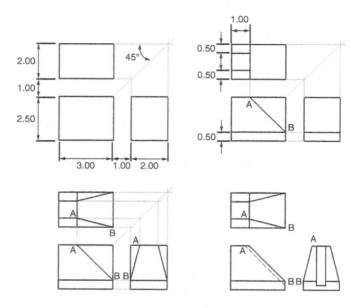

**1** Start a new drawing using the acad.dwt template, where drawing units represent inches. Set up the drawing as follows:

Limits = **Default**

Grid   = **.5**

Snap  = **.25**

**2** Use the overall dimensions to define the space and location requirements for the views. Draw the **45°** miter line.

**3** Use the given dimensions to define the starting point and endpoint on each compound line in the top and front views. One of the lines has been labeled **A–B**.

**4** Draw the compound line in the top view and then project it into the side view, using information from both the top and front views.

**5** Add the dovetailed shape, using the given dimensions. Draw the appropriate hidden lines for the dovetail.

**6** Erase and trim the excess lines.

**7** Save the drawing, if desired.

Figure 5-34 shows the three orthographic views and the pictorial view of another example of an object that includes compound lines. Some of the projection lines have also been included.

**Figure 5-34**

**Chapter 5**

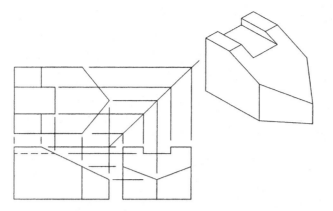

## 5-13 Oblique Surfaces

*Oblique surfaces* are surfaces that do not appear correctly shaped in the front, top, or side views. Figure 5-35 shows an object that contains oblique surface **A–B–C–D**. Figure 5-35 also shows three views of just surface **A–B–C–D**. An oblique surface is projected by first projecting its corner points and then joining the points with straight lines. The orthographic views of oblique surfaces are sometimes visually abstract. This makes the development of their orthographic views more dependent on projection than is the case with other types of surfaces.

Figure 5-36 shows another object that contains an oblique surface. Figure 5-37 shows how the three orthographic views were developed. The oblique surface is defined by using only two angles, but this is sufficient to create the three views because the surface is flat. The edge lines are parallel. Lines **A–B**, **C–D**, and **E–F** are parallel to each other, and lines **C–B**, **D–E**, and **F–A** are also parallel to each other. Figure 5-37 also shows three views of just the oblique surface, along with the appropriate projection lines.

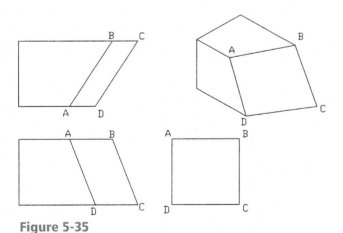

**Figure 5-35**

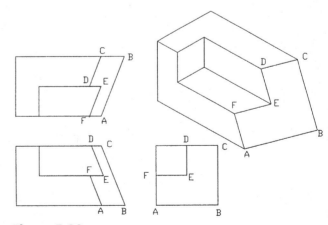

**Figure 5-36**

**Figure 5-37**

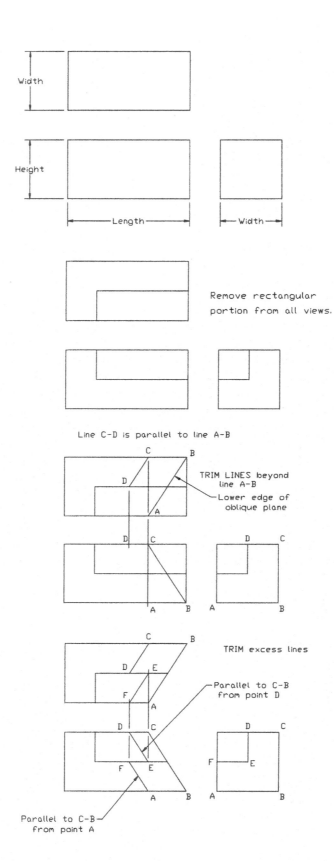

Width

Height

Length

Width

Remove rectangular portion from all views.

Line C-D is parallel to line A-B

C    B

D

TRIM LINES beyond line A-B

A

Lower edge of oblique plane

D    C          D    C

A    B        A    B

C    B

D    E

TRIM excess lines

F

A

Parallel to C-B from point D

D    C          D    C

F    E        F    E

A    B

Parallel to C-B from point A

## 5-14 Drawing Problem

The three views of the object shown in Figure 5-38 may be drawn as follows. (The given dimensions are in millimeters.)

**1** Use the **Line** and **Offset** commands to set up the sizes and locations of the three views. Use **Osnap Intersection** to draw the projection lines (Figure 5-39).

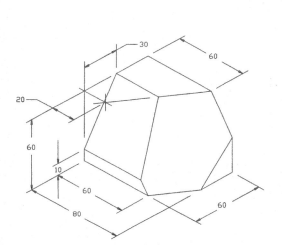

**Figure 5-38**

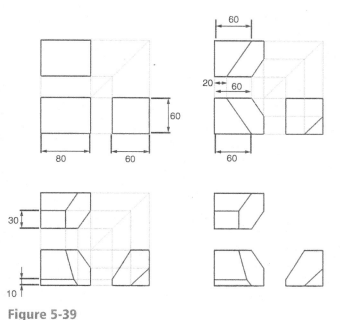

**Figure 5-39**

**2** Draw an oblique surface based on the given dimensions. The edge lines of the oblique surface are parallel.

**3** Draw the slanted surface in the side view and project the surface into the other views. Use the intersection between the slanted surface and flat sections on the top and side of the object to determine the shape of the oblique surface.

**4** Use **Erase** and **Trim** to remove any excess lines. Save the drawing, if desired.

## 5-15 Rounded Surfaces

*Rounded surfaces* are surfaces that have constant radii, such as arcs or circles. Surfaces that do not have constant radii are classified as *irregular surfaces*. See Section 5-24.

Figure 5-40 shows an object with rounded surfaces. Surface **A–B–C–D** is tangent to both the top and side surfaces of the object, so no edge line is drawn. This means that the top and side orthographic views of the object are ambiguous. If only the top and side views are considered, then other interpretations of the views are possible. The object in Figure 5-40 generates the same top and side orthographic views but does not include rounded surface **A–B–C–D**. The front view is needed to define the rounded surfaces and limit the views to only one interpretation.

**Figure 5-40**

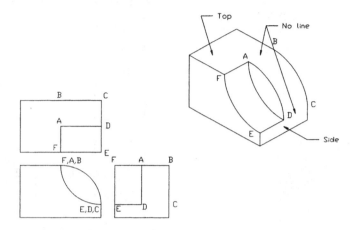

Surfaces perpendicular to an orthographic view always produce lines in that orthographic view. The vertical surface shown in the front view of Figure 5-41A requires an edge line in the top view. The vertical line in the front view is perpendicular to the top views.

**Figure 5-41**

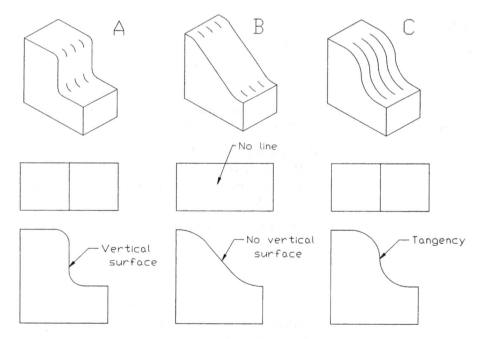

The object shown in Figure 5-41B has no lines perpendicular to the top view, so no lines are drawn in the top view. Figure 5-41C shows two rounded surfaces that intersect at points tangent to their centerlines. The intersection point is considered sufficient to require an edge line in the top view. No line would be visible on the actual object, but drawing convention prescribes that a line be drawn.

Figure 5-42 shows an object that contains two semicircular surfaces. Note how lines representing the widest and deepest point of the surfaces generate lines in the top view. No line would actually appear on the object. Figure 5-43 shows further examples of objects with curved surfaces.

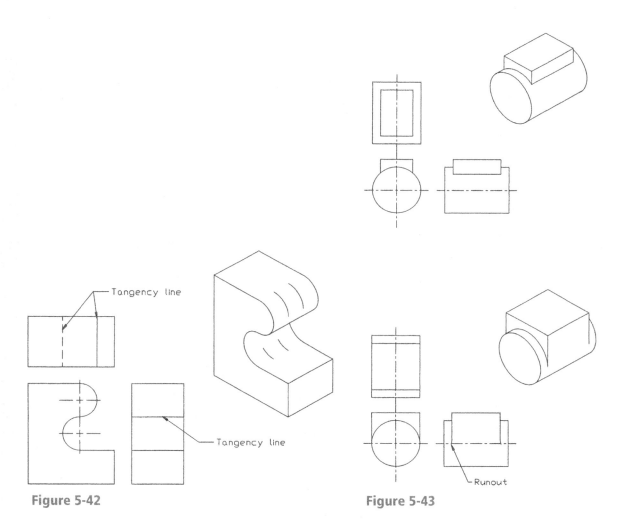

**Figure 5-42**

**Figure 5-43**

## 5-16 Drawing Problem

Figure 5-44 shows an object that includes rounded surfaces, and Figure 5-45 shows how the three views of the object were developed.

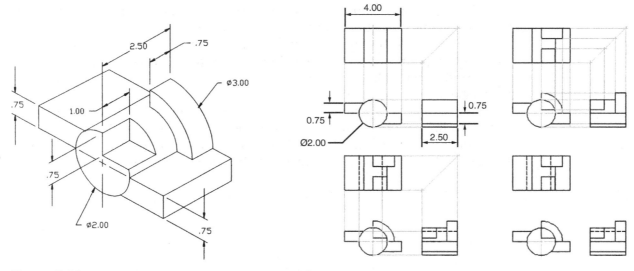

**Figure 5-44**

**Figure 5-45**

The procedure is as follows:

**1** Use the given overall dimensions to lay out the size and location of the three views.

**2** Draw in the external details, the cutout, and the circular extension in all three views.

**3** Add the appropriate hidden lines. Either use the **Modify Properties** option or create a layer for hidden lines.

**4** Erase and trim any excess lines and save the drawing, if desired.

## 5-17 Holes

Holes are represented in orthographic views by circles and parallel hidden lines. All views of a hole always include centerlines (Figure 5-46). In AutoCAD, it is good practice to create a separate layer for centerlines, as was previously done for hidden lines. You can assign the **CENTER** linetype to this layer, and make it a different color so centerline objects stand out from other objects.

Holes that go completely through an object are dimensioned by the use of only a diameter. The notation **THRU** may be added to the diameter specification for clarity.

Holes that do not go completely through an object include a depth specification in their dimension. The depth specification is interpreted as shown in Figure 5-46. Holes that do not go completely through an object must include a conical point. The conical point is not included in the depth specification. Conical points must be included because most holes are produced by using a twist drill with conically shaped cutting edges.

**Figure 5-46**

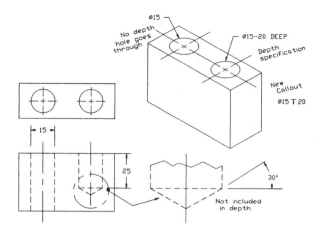

The cutting angles of twist drills vary, but they are always represented by a 30° angle, as shown.

Figure 5-47 shows an object that contains two through holes and one hole with a depth specification. Note how these holes are represented in the orthographic views and how centerlines are used in the different views.

**Figure 5-47**

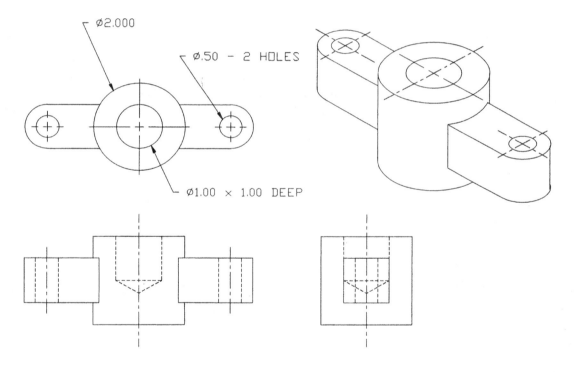

Figure 5-48 is another example of an object that includes a hole. The hole is centered about the edge line between the two normal surfaces. Figure 5-49 shows the same object with the hole's center point offset from the edge line between the two normal surfaces. Compare Figures 5-48 and 5-49 and look for the differences between them.

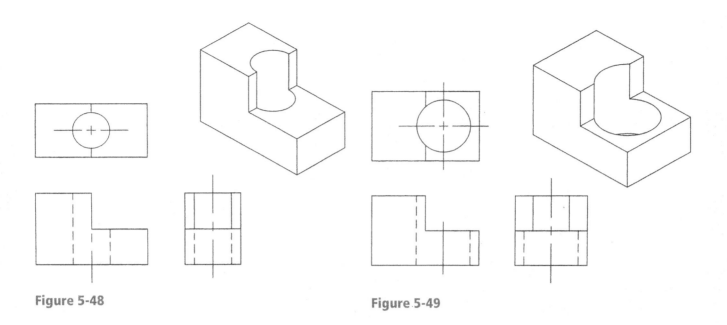

**Figure 5-48**

**Figure 5-49**

## 5-18 Holes in Slanted Surfaces

Figure 5-50 shows a hole that penetrates a slanted surface. The hole is perpendicular to the bottom surface of the object. The top view of the hole appears as a circle because we are looking straight down into it. The side view shows a distorted view of the circle and is represented by an ellipse.

**Figure 5-50**

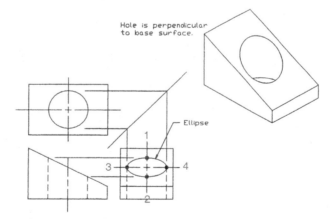

The shape of the ellipse in the side view is defined by projecting information from the front and top views. Points 1 and 2 are known to be on the vertical centerline, so their locations can be projected from the front view to the side view by using horizontal lines. Points 3 and 4 are located on the horizontal centerline, so their locations can be projected from the top view into the side view by the 45° miter line.

The elliptical shape of the hole in the side view is drawn, connecting the projected points, by using the **Ellipse** command.

## Drawing an Ellipse Representing a Projected Hole

Follow these steps to draw the ellipse shown in Figure 5-51:

**Figure 5-51**

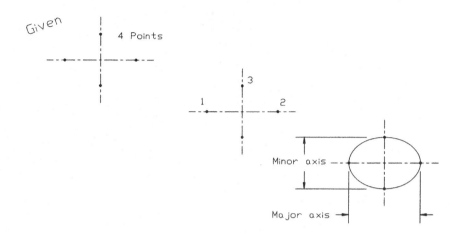

**1** Define the *first point* as one of the points at which the major axis intersects one of the centerlines.

**2** Define the *second point* as the other point on the major axis that intersects the same centerline.

**3** Define the *third point* as one of the points on the minor axis that intersects the centerline perpendicular to the centerline used in steps 1 and 2.

## Drawing Three Views of a Hole in a Slanted Surface

Figure 5-52 shows an object that includes a hole drilled perpendicular to the slanted surface. The hole is 1.00 unit in diameter. The hidden lines in the front view that represent the edges of the hole are drawn parallel to the centerline at a distance of 0.50. The horizontal and vertical centerlines of the hole are located in the top and right views. The intersection of the hole edges with the slanted surface shown in the front view is projected into the top and side views as shown.

The slanted surface shown in Figure 5-52 appears as a straight line in the front view. This means that the hole representations in the top and side views are rotated about only one axis. This, in turn, means that the hole representation is foreshortened in only one direction. The other direction—the other axis length—remains at the original diameter distance on 1.00. The four points needed to define the projected elliptical shape can be defined by the projection lines and the measured 1.00 distance.

The hole also penetrates the bottom surface, forming a different-sized ellipse. The hole's penetration can be shown in the side view by hidden lines parallel to the given centerline. The elliptical shape in the top view is defined by drawing horizontal parallel lines from the intersection of the hole's projected shape with the vertical centerline and by projection lines from the front view that define the hole's length.

Figure 5-52

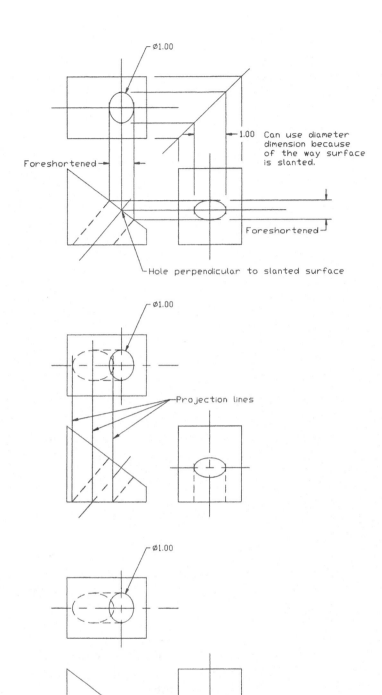

## Drawing Three Views of a Hole Through an Oblique Surface

Figure 5-53 shows a hole drilled horizontally through the exact center of an oblique surface of an object. The oblique surface means that both axes in the top and front views will be foreshortened. The procedure used to create the hole's projection in the front and top views is as follows (Figure 5-54):

**1** Draw the hole in the side view. The hole appears as a circle because it is drilled horizontally.

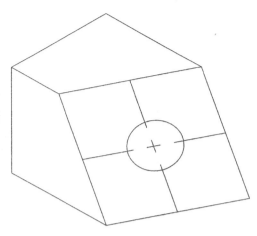

**Figure 5-53**

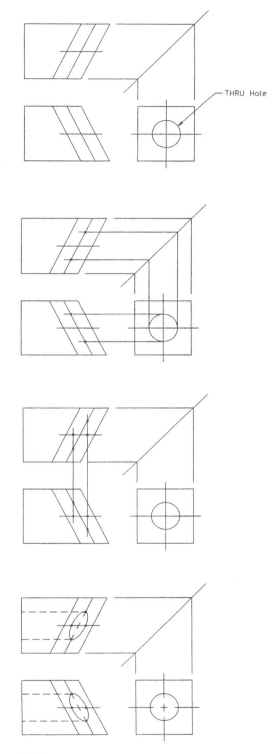

THRU Hole

**Figure 5-54**

**2** Draw the hole's centerlines in the front and top views. The hole is located exactly in the center of the oblique surface, so lines parallel to the surface's edge lines located midway across the surface may be drawn.

**Chapter 5** | Orthographic Views **225**

**3** Project the intersection of the hole and the horizontal centerline into the top view and project the intersection of the hole with the vertical centerline into the front view.

**4** Project the intersections created in step 3 with the horizontal centerline, represented by the slanted centerline, onto the horizontal centerline in the front view. Likewise, project the intersection points created in step 3 on the horizontal centerline in the front view to the slanted centerline in the top view.

**5** Draw the ellipses as required, add the appropriate hidden lines, and erase and trim any excess lines. Save the drawing, if desired.

### 5-19 Cylinders

Figure 5-55 shows three views of a cylinder that is cut along the centerline by surface **A–B–C–D**. Note that each of the three views includes centerlines. The front and top views of a cylinder are called the *rectangular views*, and the side view (end view) is called the *circular view*. The width of the top view is equal to the diameter of the cylinder.

Figure 5-56 shows a cylinder that has a second surface located above the centerline in the front view. The top view of the cylinder shows the flat surface and the rounded portion of the cylinder. Both the flat surface and the two rounded surfaces appear as rectangles.

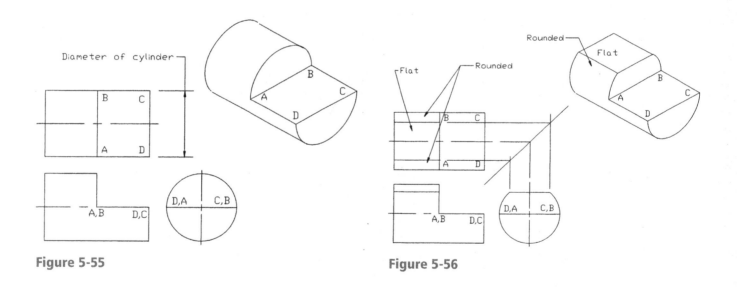

**Figure 5-55**　　　　　　　　　　　　　　**Figure 5-56**

Figure 5-57 shows a cylinder with a surface **J–K–L–M** that is located below the centerline in the front view. The top view of this surface does not include any rounded surfaces because they have been cut away.

Figure 5-57

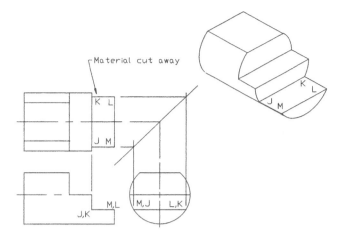

Material cut away

## 5-20 Drawing Problem

Figure 5-58 shows a cylindrically shaped object that has three surface cuts: one above the centerline, one below the centerline, and one directly on the centerline. Figure 5-59 shows how the three views of the object were developed. The procedure is as follows:

**1** Use the given overall length of the cylinder and its diameter to create the two rectangular top and front views and the circular end views.

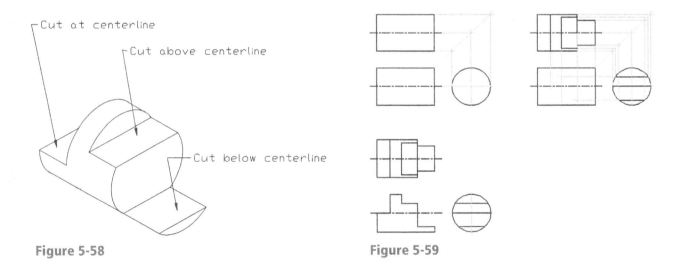

Cut at centerline

Cut above centerline

Cut below centerline

**Figure 5-58**

**Figure 5-59**

**2** Draw horizontal lines in the side view to define the end views of the three surfaces. Project the sizes and locations of the surfaces into the front and top views. Use **Osnap Intersection**, with **Ortho** on, for accurate projection.

**3** Erase and trim the excess lines.

**4** Save the drawing, if desired.

## 5-21 Cylinders with Slanted and Rounded Surfaces

Figure 5-60 shows the front and side views of a cylindrical object that includes a slanted surface. Slanted surfaces are projected by defining points along their edges in known orthographic views and then projecting the edge points.

**Figure 5-60**

TOP VIEW

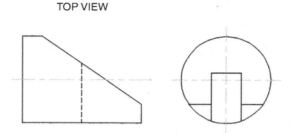

## 5-22 Drawing Problem

At least two known views are needed for accurate projection. This problem shows how to define and project a slanted cylindrical surface into the top view, given the front and side views (Figure 5-61).

**1** Draw the rectangular shape of the top view by projecting the length from the front view and the width from the side view.

**2** Project the centerlines and label points **1**, **2**, **3**, **4**, and **5** in the front and side views. The locations of these points are known from the given information.

**3** Draw three horizontal lines across the front and side views. The locations of the lines are arbitrary. Label the intersections of the horizontal lines with the edge of the slanted surface as shown.

The three horizontal lines serve to define point locations along the surface's edge.

A line contains an infinite number of points, so any six can be used.

**4** Draw vertical projection lines (using **Intersection** object snap) from the six point locations in the front view into the area of the top view.

**5** Project the six point locations from the side view into the area of the top view. Use the 45° miter line to make the turn between the two views. The intersection of the vertical projection lines of step 2 and the projection lines from the side view defines the location of the points in the top view. Label the six points.

**Figure 5-61**

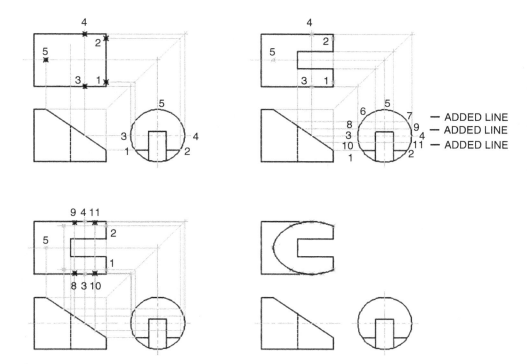

**6** Select **Spline Fit** to create a smooth line between the six projected points.

**7** Remove any excess lines and save the drawing, if desired.

Figure 5-62 shows another cylindrical object that contains a slanted surface along with some of the projection lines.

**Figure 5-62**

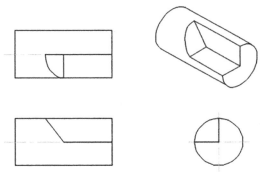

## 5-23 Drawing Conventions and Cylinders

A hole drilled into a cylinder produces an elliptically shaped edge line in a profile view of the hole (Figure 5-63). Drawing convention allows a straight line to be drawn, in place of the elliptical shape, for a small hole. The elliptical shape should be drawn for a large hole in a cylinder—that is, one whose diameter is greater than half the diameter of the cylinder.

Figure 5-63

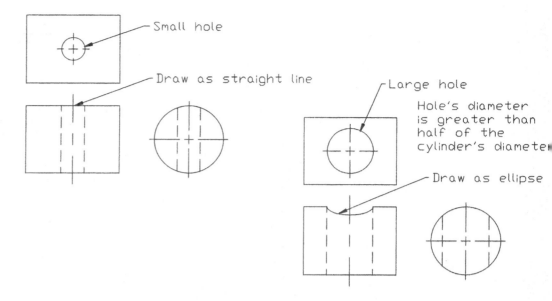

Drawing convention also permits straight lines to show the profile view of a keyway cut into a cylinder (Figure 5-64). As with holes, if a keyway is large relative to a cylinder, the correct offset shape should be drawn. A keyway is considered large if its width is greater than half of the diameter of the cylinder.

Figure 5-64

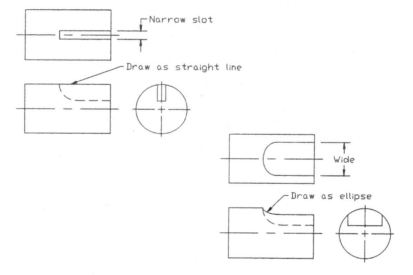

## 5-24 Irregular Surfaces

*Irregular surfaces* are curved surfaces that do not have constant radii (Figures 5-65 and 5-66). Irregular surfaces are defined by the X,Y coordinates of points located on the edge of the surface. The points may be dimensioned directly on the view but are often presented in chart form, as shown in Figure 5-66. Figure 5-66 also shows a wing airfoil section defined relative to a given X,Y coordinate system.

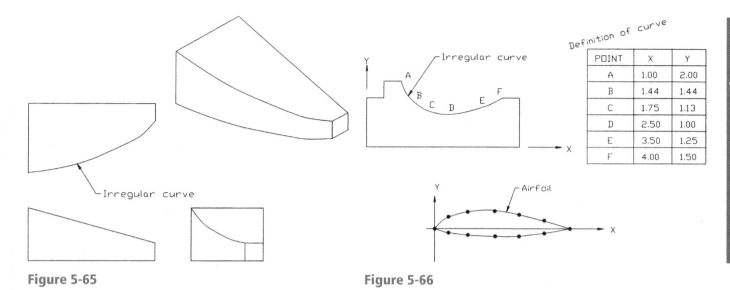

**Figure 5-65**

**Figure 5-66**

| POINT | X | Y |
|-------|------|------|
| A | 1.00 | 2.00 |
| B | 1.44 | 1.44 |
| C | 1.75 | 1.13 |
| D | 2.50 | 1.00 |
| E | 3.50 | 1.25 |
| F | 4.00 | 1.50 |

Irregular surfaces are projected by defining points along their edges and then projecting the points. At least two known views are needed for accurate projection. The more points used to define a curve, the more accurate the final curve shape will be.

## 5-25 Drawing Problem

Figure 5-67 shows an object that includes an irregular surface. The irregular surface is defined by points referenced to an X,Y coordinate system. The point values are listed in a chart. Draw three views of the object shown in Figure 5-67. Your views should look similar to those in Figure 5-68.

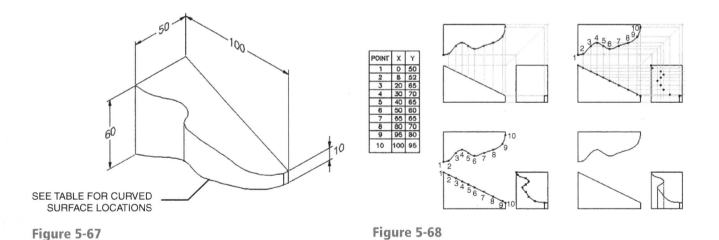

| POINT | X | Y |
|-------|-----|----|
| 1 | 0 | 50 |
| 2 | 8 | 52 |
| 3 | 20 | 65 |
| 4 | 30 | 70 |
| 5 | 40 | 65 |
| 6 | 50 | 60 |
| 7 | 65 | 65 |
| 8 | 80 | 70 |
| 9 | 95 | 80 |
| 10 | 100 | 95 |

**Figure 5-67**

SEE TABLE FOR CURVED SURFACE LOCATIONS

**Figure 5-68**

**1** Draw the front and top views, using the given dimensions and chart values. Draw the outline of the side view, using the given dimensions.

**2** Project the points that define the irregular curve in the top view into the front view. Label the points.

**3** Project the points for the curve from both the top and front views into the side view. Label the intersection points.

**4** Use **Polyline**, **Edit Polyline**, and **Fit** to create a curve that represents the side view of the irregular surface.

**5** Erase and trim any excess lines. Save the drawing, if desired.

Remember that it is possible to create a layer for construction lines and for a final drawing. After the initial drawing is laid out, the final drawing lines may be copied onto another layer and the construction layer turned off. This method eliminates the need for extensive erasing and trimming.

## 5-26 Hole Callouts

Four hole-shape manufacturing processes are used so often that they are defined using standardized drawing callouts: ream, spotface, counterbore, and countersink (Figure 5-69).

A *ream* is a process that smooths out the inside of a drilled hole. A hole created with a twist drill has spiral-shaped machine marks on its surfaces. Reaming is used to remove the spiral machine marks and to increase the roundness of the hole. Ream callouts generally include a much tighter tolerance than do drill diameter callouts.

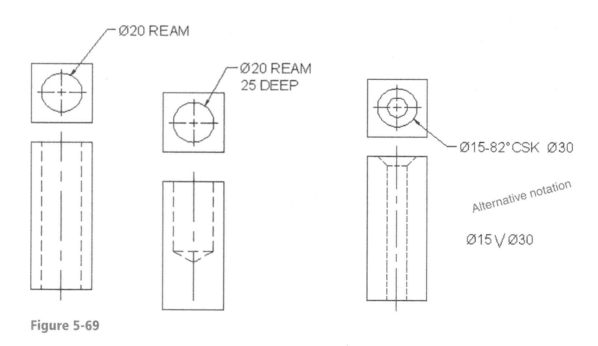

**Figure 5-69**

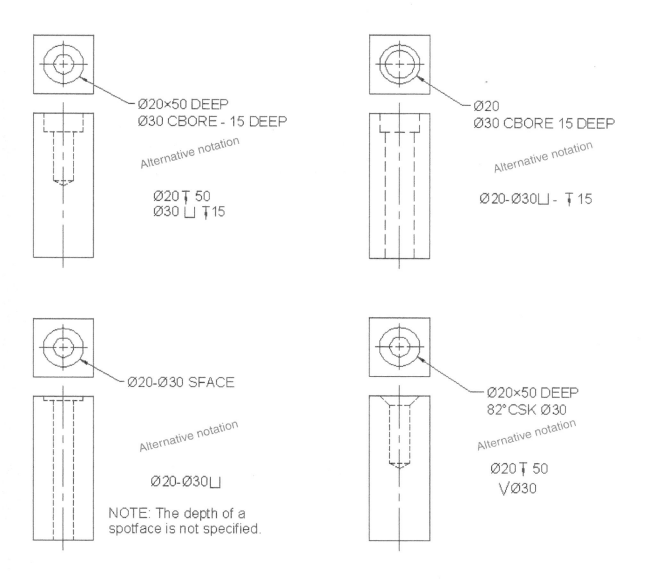

Ø20×50 DEEP
Ø30 CBORE - 15 DEEP

*Alternative notation*

Ø20 ⊤ 50
Ø30 ⊔ ⊤ 15

Ø20
Ø30 CBORE 15 DEEP

*Alternative notation*

Ø20-Ø30⊔ - ⊤ 15

Ø20-Ø30 SFACE

*Alternative notation*

Ø20-Ø30⊔

NOTE: The depth of a
spotface is not specified.

Ø20×50 DEEP
82°CSK Ø30

*Alternative notation*

Ø20 ⊤ 50
∨ Ø30

A *spotface* is a very shallow counterbored hole generally used on cast surfaces. Cast surfaces are more porous than machine surfaces. Rather than machining an entire surface flat, it is cheaper to manufacture a spotface because only a small portion of the surface is machined. Spotfaces are usually used for bearing surfaces of fasteners.

A spotface callout defines the diameter of the hole and the diameter of the spotface. A depth need not be given. When machining was done mostly by hand, the machinist would make the spotface just deep enough to produce a shiny surface (most cast surfaces are more gray in color), so no depth was needed. Automated machines require a spotface depth specification. Usually, the depth is very shallow.

A *counterbore* consists of two holes drilled along the same centerline. Counterbores are used to allow fasteners or other objects to be recessed, thus keeping the top surface uniform in height.

A counterbore drawing callout specifies the diameter of the small hole, the diameter of the large hole, and the depth of the large hole. The information is given in this sequence because it is also the sequence that the manufacturer uses. Note that the hidden lines used in the front view of the counterbored hole clearly show the intersection between the two holes.

Figure 5-70 shows an alternative notation for drawing callouts, as defined by ISO standards (see Section 5-36), that is intended to remove language from drawings. As parts are often designed in one country and manufactured in another, it is important that drawing callouts be universally understood.

**Figure 5-70**

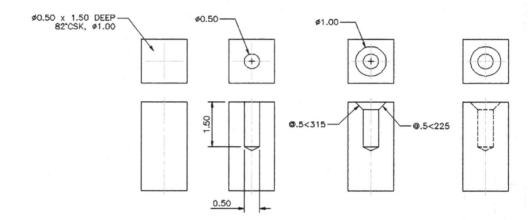

## Drawing a Countersunk Hole

A *countersink* is a conical-shaped hole used primarily for flat-head fasteners. The drawing callout specifies the diameter of the hole, the included angle of the countersink, and the diameter of the countersink as measured on the surface of the object. Almost all countersinks are 82°, but some are drawn at 45°.

**1** Draw a **0.50**-diameter hole in the top view. Project the hole's diameter into the front view.

**2** Draw a **1.00**-diameter hole in the top view and project its diameter into the front view. In the front view, draw **45°** lines from the intersection of the 1.00-diameter hole and the top surface of the front view so that the lines intersect the 0.50-diameter hole's projection lines. Use **Osnap Intersection** to ensure accuracy.

**3** Draw a horizontal line between the lines of the intersection created in step 2. Again use **Osnap Intersection**.

**4** Erase and trim the excess lines.

## 5-27 Castings

Casting is one of the oldest manufacturing processes. Metal is heated to liquid form, poured into molds, and allowed to cool. The resulting shapes usually include many rounded edges and surface tangencies because it is very difficult to cast square edges. Concave edges are called *rounds*, and convex edges are called *fillets* (Figure 5-71). A runout is used to indicate that two rounded surfaces have become tangent to one another. A *runout* is a short arc of arbitrary radius—that is, arbitrary as long as the runout is visually clear.

**Figure 5-71**

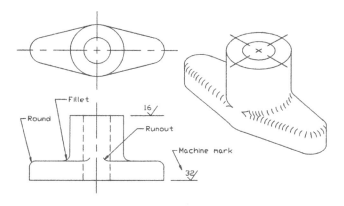

Cast objects are often partially machined to produce flatter surfaces than can be produced using the casting process. Machined surfaces are defined by the use of surface control symbols (machine marks or checkmarks), as shown in Figure 5-71. The numbers within the machine marks specify the flatness requirements in terms of microinches or micrometers. Surface control symbols are explained in greater detail in Section 9-26.

*Bosses* are turret-like shapes that are often included on castings to localize and minimize machining. A boss is defined by its diameter and its height. The sides of a boss are rounded and defined by a radius that is usually equal to the height of the boss (Figure 5-72).

**Figure 5-72**

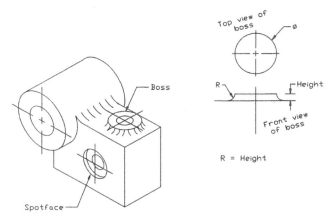

Spotfacing is a machine process often associated with castings. As with bosses, spotfaces help to localize and minimize machining requirements (refer to Section 5-26).

The direction of runouts is determined by the shape of the two surfaces involved. Flat surfaces intersecting rounded surfaces generate runouts that turn out. Rounded surfaces that intersect rounded surfaces generate runouts that turn in (Figure 5-73).

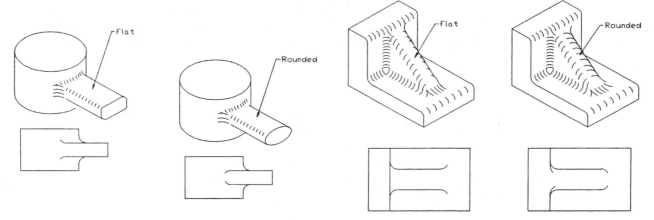

**Figure 5-73**

The same convention is followed for flat and rounded surfaces that intersect flat surfaces.

The location of a runout is determined by the location of the tangent that it represents (Figure 5-74). The location of a tangency point can be determined by first drawing the top view of the tangency line by using **Osnap Tangent**. A line can then be drawn from the center point of the circular top view to the end of the tangency line by using **Osnap Endpoint**. The point of tangency can then be projected from the top view to the front view by using **Osnap Intersection** with **Ortho** on.

**Figure 5-74**

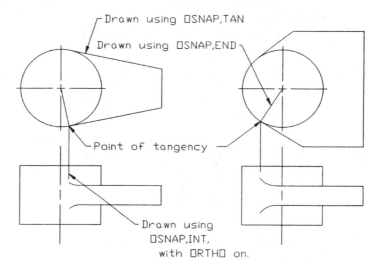

Use **Arc** (type the word **arc** in response to a command prompt) to draw runouts. Any convenient radius may be used, provided that the runout is clearly visible and visually distinct from the straight line. Figure 5-75 shows some further examples of cast surfaces that include runouts.

Figure 5-75

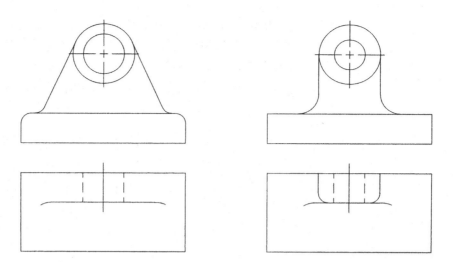

## 5-28 Drawing Problem

Draw three views of the object shown in Figure 5-76. The solution was drawn as follows:

**1** Use the given overall dimensions and draw the outline of the front, top, and side views.

Figure 5-76

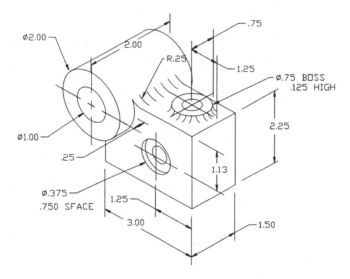

**2** Change the appropriate lines to hidden lines. Draw the fillets and rounds. The **Fillet** command may erase needed lines. You can change the **Fillet** command's **Trim** option to **No Trim** to retain all objects without trimming them away, or you can simply redraw the needed lines after the fillet or round is complete.

**3** Draw the spotface and boss in each of the views. The hole in the boss is 0.500 deep. Clearly show the bottom of the hole, including the conical point. Draw the hole in the front view and use **Copy** to copy the hole into the side view.

**4** Use **Draw, Circle** to draw the 1.00-diameter hole in the front view. Draw the appropriate hidden lines and centerlines in the other views.

**5** Save the drawing, if desired.

Figure 5-77 shows the three standard views creation.

**Figure 5-77**

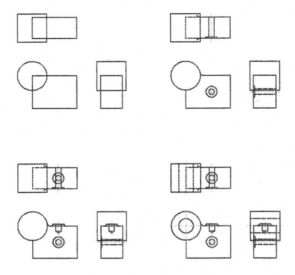

## 5-29 Thin-Walled Objects

Thin-walled objects such as parts made from sheet metal or tubing present some unique drawing problems. For example, the distance between surfaces is usually so small that hidden lines can't be used to define holes, and there isn't enough distance to draw a broken-line pattern (Figure 5-78).

**Figure 5-78**

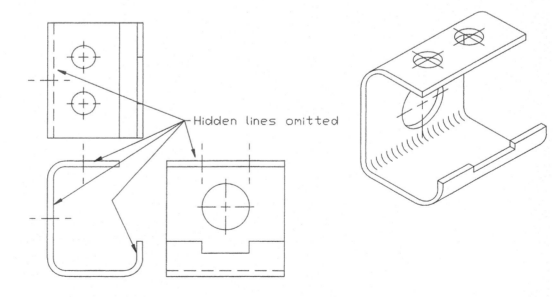

Hidden lines may be applied to thin-walled objects in one of three ways: The lines may be drawn as continuous lines but in a different color from that used for the actual continuous lines; an enlarged detail of the area may be drawn, including the hidden lines; or the hidden lines may be omitted and only a centerline included. Each of these techniques is shown in Figure 5-78. Every hole must include a centerline.

A company is likely to have a drawing manual that states the company policy on drawing hidden lines in thin-walled objects. The most important goal is to be consistent in the representation.

Many sheet-metal parts are manufactured by bending. Bending produces an inside bend radius and an outside bend radius. The inside bend radius plus the material thickness should equal the outside bend radius. See Figure 5-79. The same radius should not be used for both the inside and the outside bends.

**Figure 5-79**

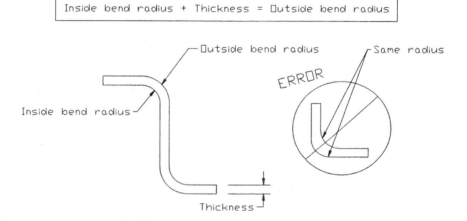

## 5-30 Drawing Problem

Draw three views of the object shown in Figure 5-80. Figure 5-81 shows how the three views were developed.

**Figure 5-80**

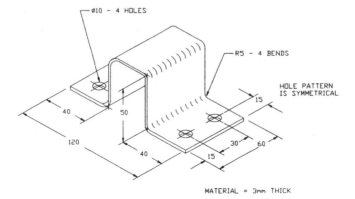

Figure 5-81

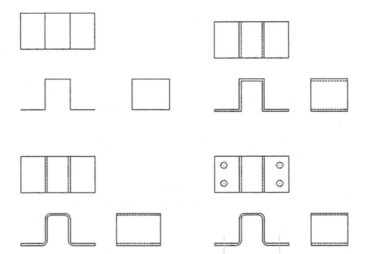

1. Use the given overall dimensions in Figure 5-80 to draw the outline of the three views. Draw the object as if all bends were 90°.

2. Use **Offset**, set to a distance of **3 mm**, to draw the thickness of the object. Use **Extend** and **Trim** to add and remove lines as needed. The thickness can also be drawn by setting the snap spacing equal to the material thickness.

   Change the appropriate lines to hidden lines.

3. Draw fillets, using a radius of **5 mm** for the inside bend radii and **8 mm** for the outside bend radii.

4. Use **Draw, Circle** to draw the holes in the appropriate view and add centerlines as shown.

5. Save the drawing, if desired.

## 5-31 Intersections

An *intersection drawing* is a drawing that shows the intersection of two objects. Figure 5-82 shows the intersection between a triangular prism and a rectangular prism. A discussion of intersections has been included at this point in the book because intersections rely heavily on projection of information between views. They require not only a knowledge of the principles of projection but also an understanding about what the various lines represent. Intersections in 3D solids are discussed in Chapter 15, Advanced Modeling.

Three intersection problems are presented in the following three drawing problems.

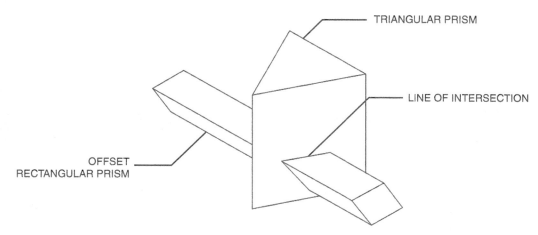

TRIANGULAR PRISM

LINE OF INTERSECTION

OFFSET
RECTANGULAR PRISM

Figure 5-82

## 5-32 Drawing Problem

Given the side and top views of a smaller circle intersecting a larger circle, as shown in Figure 5-83, draw the front view. All dimensions are in inches. Because the object is symmetrical, the intersection for one side will be developed and then mirrored.

Figure 5-83

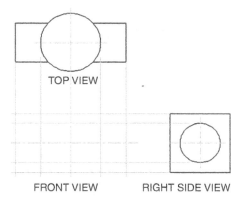

TOP VIEW

FRONT VIEW          RIGHT SIDE VIEW

**1** Draw the outline of the front view by projecting lines from the given top and front views (Figure 5-84).

**2** Define points on the edge of the smaller circle. In this example, 17 points were defined.

**3** Extend the horizontal centerline of the smaller circle in the side view into the area of the front view. Use **Draw, Offset** and add six lines parallel to the horizontal centerline in the side view. Label the intersection of the horizontal lines with the edge of the smaller circle. (In Figure 5-84, for the sake of clarity, not all points are numbered.)

**4** Project points **1**, **2**, **3**, **4**, and **5** into the top view. Use **Draw, Line** along with **Osnap Intersection** to draw vertical lines from the side view so that they intersect the 45° miter line. Then project the intersections on the miter line into the top view by using horizontal lines. Label the points as shown.

Figure 5-84

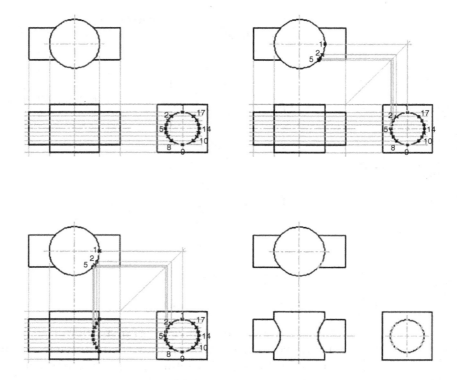

5 Project points **1**, **2**, **3**, **4**, and **5** from the top view into the area of the front view so that they intersect the horizontal lines from the side view. Label the points as shown.

Use the **Mirror** command to mirror the projected points below the horizontal centerline and then to the left of the vertical centerline.

6 Use **Draw**, **Polyline**, **Edit Polyline**, and **Fit** to draw the curves that represent the intersection.

7 Add the lines needed to complete the front view, remove all excess lines, and save the drawing, if desired.

## 5-33 Drawing Problem

Figure 5-85 shows the top and right-side views of a triangular-shaped piece intersecting a hexagonal-shaped piece. What is the shape of the front view?

Figure 5-85

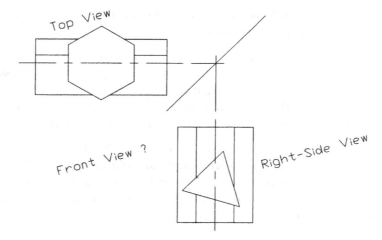

Figure 5-86 shows the solution obtained by projecting lines from the two given views into the front view and shows an enlargement of the intersecting surfaces. Using a straightedge, verify the location of each labeled point by projecting horizontal lines from the front view and vertical lines from the top view into the front view.

**Figure 5-86**

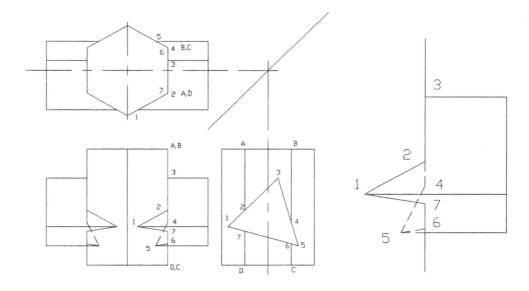

## 5-34 Drawing Problem

Given the side and top views of a circle intersecting a cone, as shown in Figure 5-87, draw the front view.

**Figure 5-87**

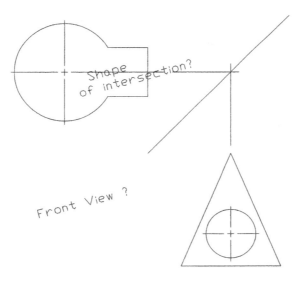

As in the previous drawing problems, the problem is solved by defining intersection points in the given two views and then projecting them into the front view. The cone, however, presents a unique problem because it is both round and tapered. There are few edge lines to work with.

The solution requires that there be a more precise definition of the cone's surface than is presented by the circle and centerlines in the top view and the profile front view.

**1** Figure 5-88, step 1, shows how points **1** and **3**, located on the vertical centerline of the cylinder, are projected from the side view to the front view and then to the top view. The vertical centerline is aligned with the right-side profile line of the cone so that it can be used for projection.

This is not true for points 2 and 4, located on the horizontal centerline in the side view. Currently, the locations of points 2 and 4 are unknown in both the front and top views, so projection lines cannot be drawn. The locations of points 2 and 4 can be determined in the front and top views.

**Figure 5-88**

Step 1

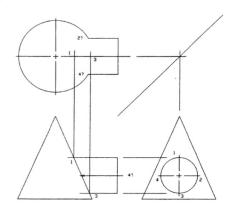

Step 2

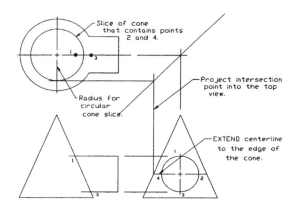

Step 3

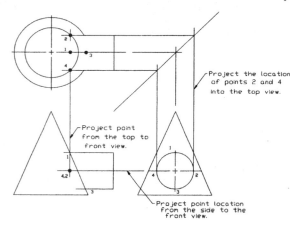

Step 4

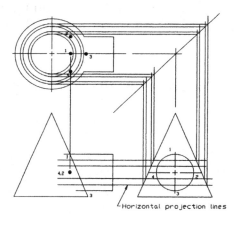

Step 5

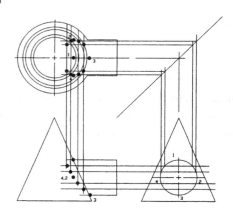

Step 6

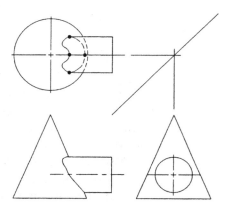

**2** Extend the horizontal centerline in the side view so that it intersects the edge lines of the cone. Use **Osnap Intersection**, with **Ortho** on, and project the intersection of the extended horizontal centerline and the cone's edge line so that it intersects the vertical centerline in the top view. Draw a circle in the top view, using the distance between the center point of the cone and the intersection of the vertical centerline and the projection line as the radius.

The circle in the top view represents a slice of the cone located at exactly the same height as points 2 and 4. Points 2 and 4 must be located somewhere in the slice.

**3** Project points **2** and **4** into the top view from the side view so that the projection line intersects the circular slice drawn in step 2. Label the intersections **2** and **4**.

**4** Project the locations of points **2** and **4** in the top view into the front view, using a vertical line. Project the locations of the points from the side view into the front view, using a horizontal line. The intersection of the vertical and horizontal projection lines defines the locations of points **2** and **4** in the front view.

**5** Expand the procedure explained in steps 2 and 3 by drawing a series of horizontal projection lines between the front and side views, as shown. Use **Draw** for the first line and **Offset** for the other lines. The locations of these additional lines are random.

Use **Osnap Intersection**, with **Ortho** on, to project the intersections of the horizontal lines with the cone's edge lines in the top view.

**6** Draw circles, using the distance between the cone's center point and the projection lines' intersections with the vertical centerline as radii. Use **Osnap Intersection** to locate the circles' center point and radii distances.

**7** Use **Draw**, **Polyline**, **Edit Polyline**, and **Fit** to draw the required curves in the top and front views. Use **Osnap Intersection** to ensure accurate curve point locations. The **Move** option located on the **Edit Polyline** command options line can be used to move vertex points on the curves to make them appear smoother and more continuous.

**8** Trim and erase all excess lines and save the drawing, if desired.

## 5-35 Designing by Modifying an Existing Part

Many beginning design assignments require that an existing part be modified to meet a new set of requirements. Designers must therefore create something different from the original drawing. This ability to look beyond the drawing is an important design skill.

**1** Figure 5-89 shows a dimensioned part, and Figure 5-90 shows the three orthographic views of the part. The part is to be redesigned as follows:

**Figure 5-89**

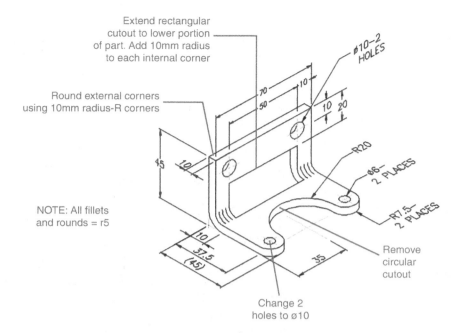

Extend rectangular cutout to lower portion of part. Add 10mm radius to each internal corner

Round external corners using 10mm radius-R corners

NOTE: All fillets and rounds = r5

Ø10—2 HOLES

R20

Ø6—2 PLACES

R7.5—2 PLACES

Remove circular cutout

Change 2 holes to ø10

**Figure 5-90**

Original views

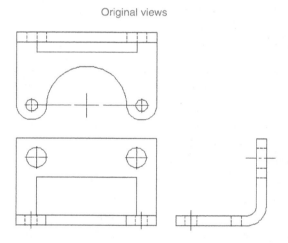

**2** Replace the two **Ø7.5** holes with **Ø10** holes.

**3** Remove the **R20** cutout.

**4** Modify the horizontal portion of the part so that its overall length is **45** millimeters; make the entire part symmetrical about its **90°** axis.

**5** Round the four external and four internal corners, using a **10**-millimeter radius.

Figure 5-91 shows the three resulting orthographic views.

Revised views

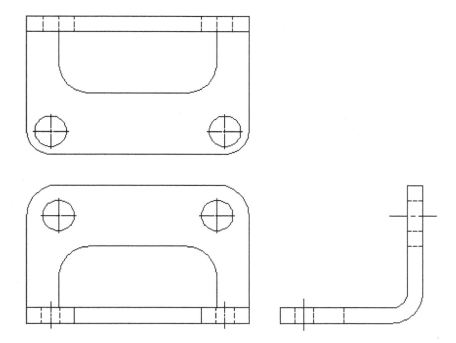

**Figure 5-91**

## 5-36 Drawing Standards

Two standards organizations define the projection and placement of orthographic views: the American National Standards Institute (ANSI) and the International Organization for Standardization (ISO). ANSI calls for orthographic views to be created using third-angle projection; this is the accepted method for use in the United States. See the American Society of Mechanical Engineers publication ASME Y14.3-2018. Some countries other than the United States use first-angle projection. See ISO publication 128-30, available at www.iso.org.

This chapter has presented orthographic views using third-angle projections, as defined by ANSI. However, there is so much international commerce happening today that you should be able to work in both conventions, just as you should be able to work in both inches and millimeters.

Figure 5-92 shows a three-dimensional model and three orthographic views created using third-angle projection and three orthographic views created using first-angle projection. Note the differences and similarities. The front view in both projections is the same. The top views are the same but are in different locations. The third-angle projection presents a right-side view, while the first-angle projection presents a left-side view.

**Figure 5-92**

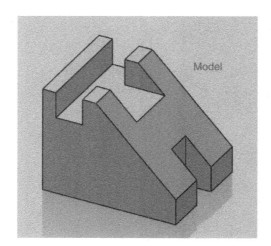

Model

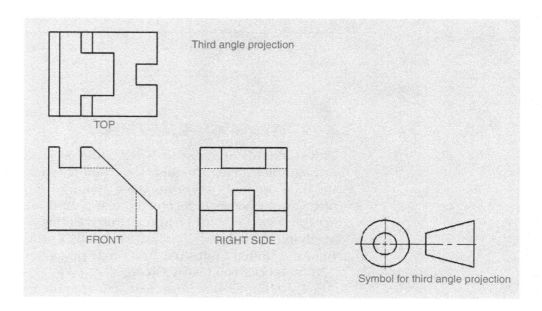

Third angle projection

TOP

FRONT

RIGHT SIDE

Symbol for third angle projection

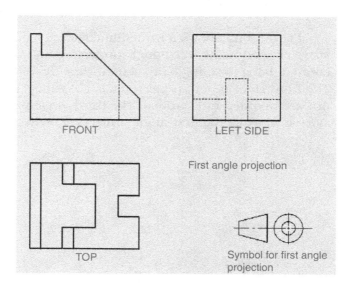

FRONT

LEFT SIDE

First angle projection

TOP

Symbol for first angle projection

Figure 5-92 also shows the drawing symbols for first- and third-angle projections. These symbols can be added to a drawing to help the reader understand which type of projection is being used.

## 5-37 Third- and First-Angle Projections

Figure 5-93 shows an object with a front orthographic view and two side orthographic views: one created using third-angle projection and the other created using first-angle projection. For third-angle projections, the orthographic view is projected on a plane located between the viewer's position and the object. For first-angle projections, the orthographic view is projected on a plane located beyond the object. The front and top views for third- and first-angle projections appear the same, but they are located in different positions relative to the front view.

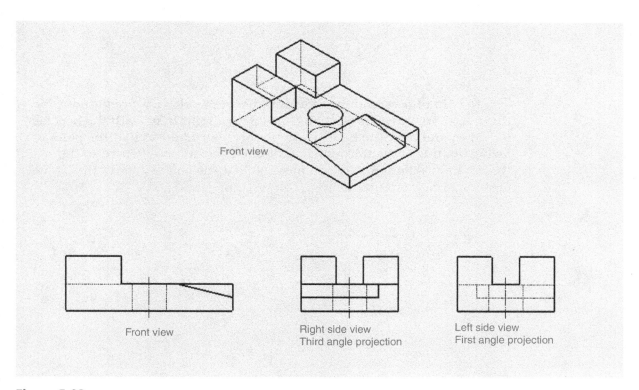

**Figure 5-93**

The side orthographic views are different for third- and first-angle projections. Third-angle projections use a right-side view located to the right of the object. First-angle projections use a left-side view located to the right of the object. Figures 5-94 and 5-95 show the two different side-view projections for the same object. For third-angle projection, the viewer is located on the right side of the object and creates the side orthographic view on a plane located between the view position and the object. The viewer looks directly at the object. For first-angle projection, the viewer is located on the left side of the object and creates the side orthographic view on a plane located beyond the object. The viewer looks through the object.

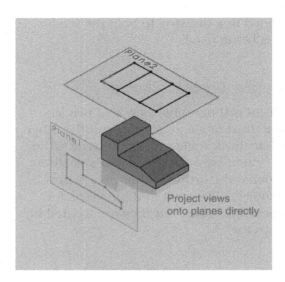

**Figure 5-94**

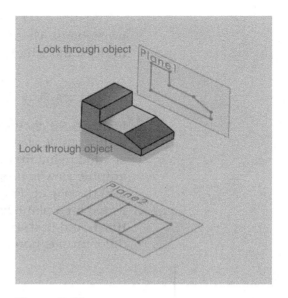

**Figure 5-95**

To help understand the difference between side-view orientations for third- and first-angle projections, locate your right hand with the heel facing down and the thumb facing up. Rotate your hand so that the palm is facing up; this is the third-angle projection orientation. Return to the thumb-up position. Rotate you hand so that the palm is down; this is the first-angle view orientation.

# 5-38 EXERCISE PROBLEMS

Draw a front, top, and right-side orthographic view for each of the objects in Exercise Problems EX5-1 through EX5-94. Do not include dimensions.

## EX5-1 Inches

L-BLOCK

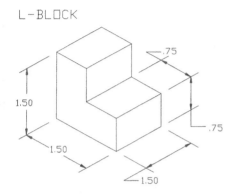

## EX5-2 Millimeters

STEP BLOCK

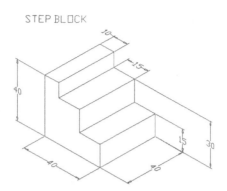

## EX5-3 Millimeters

STEPPER

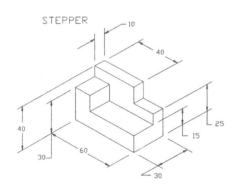

## EX5-4 Inches

PILLAR STOP

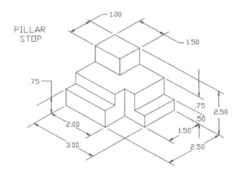

## EX5-5 Millimeters

SPLIT BLOCK

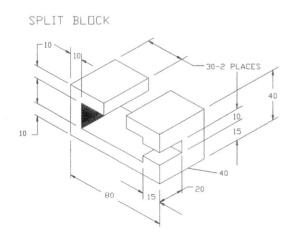

## EX5-6 Millimeters

SQUARE CLIP

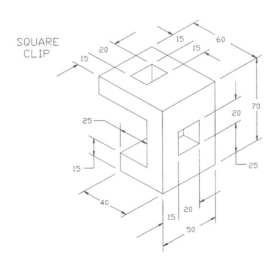

## EX5-7 Millimeters

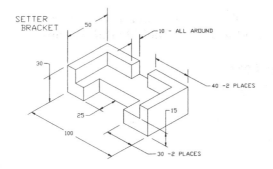

## EX5-8 Millimeters

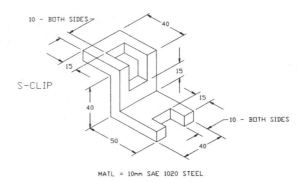

## EX5-9 Inches

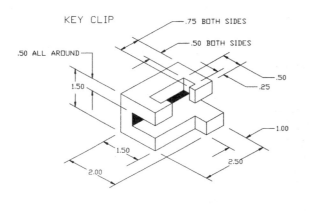

## EX5-10 Millimeters

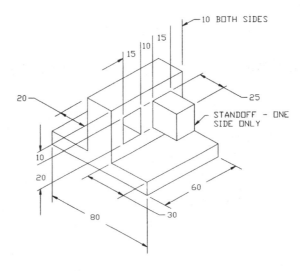

## EX5-11 Millimeters

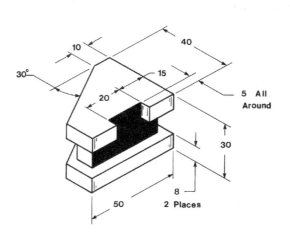

## EX5-12 Inches

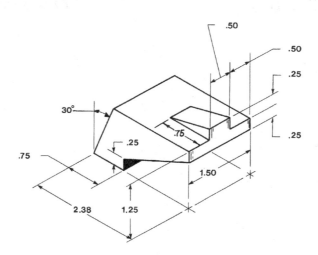

## EX5-13 Millimeters

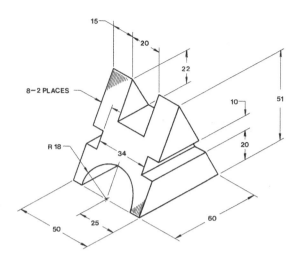

## EX5-14 Millimeters

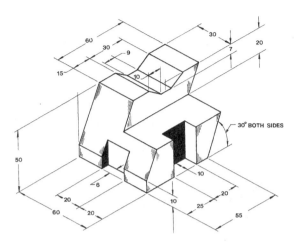

## EX5-15 Millimeters

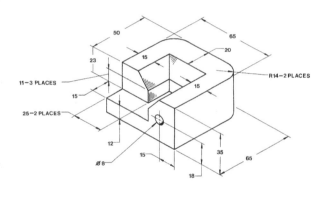

## EX5-16 Millimeters

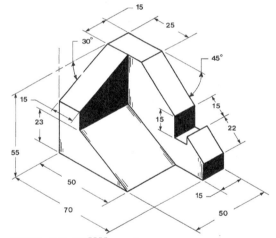

## EX5-17 Millimeters

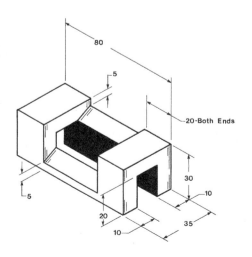

## EX5-18 Millimeters

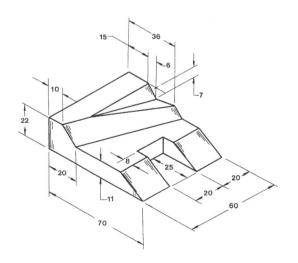

## EX5-19 Millimeters

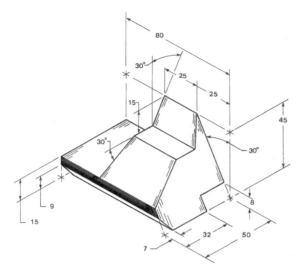

## EX5-20 Millimeters

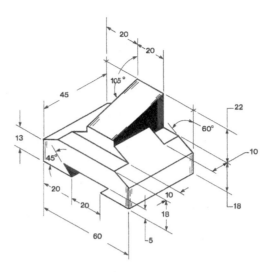

## EX5-21 Inches

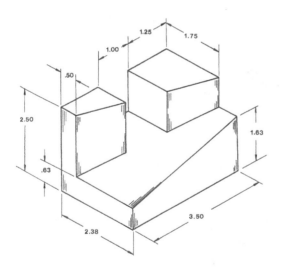

## EX5-22 Millimeters

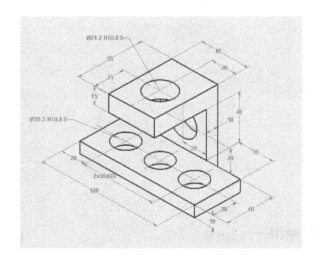

## EX5-23 Millimeters

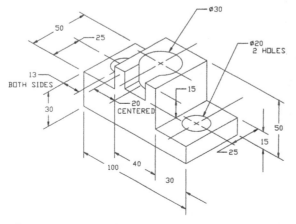

## EX5-24 Inches

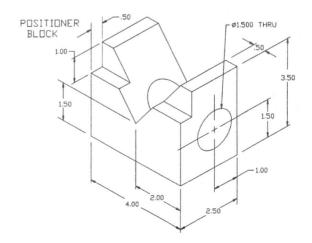

# EX5-25 Millimeters

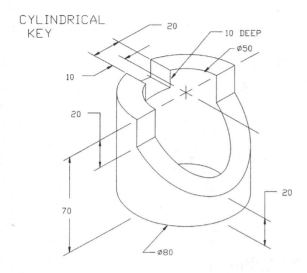

CYLINDRICAL KEY

20
10 DEEP
Ø50
10
20
20
70
Ø80

# EX5-26 Millimeters

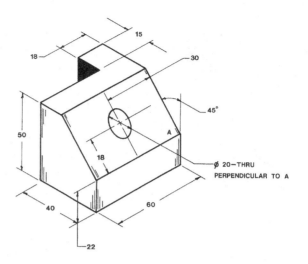

15
18
30
45°
50
18
A
Ø 20—THRU
PERPENDICULAR TO A
40
60
22

# EX5-27 Millimeters

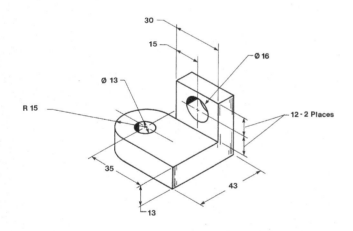

30
15
Ø 16
Ø 13
R 15
12 - 2 Places
35
43
13

# EX5-28 Millimeters

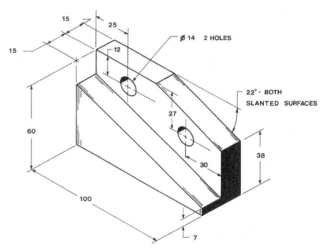

15
25
Ø 14   2 HOLES
15
12
22° - BOTH
SLANTED  SURFACES
60
27
38
100
30
7

# EX5-29 Millimeters

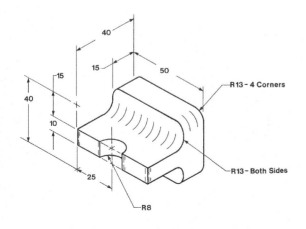

40
15
50
15
R13 - 4 Corners
40
10
R13 - Both Sides
25
R8

# EX5-30 Millimeters

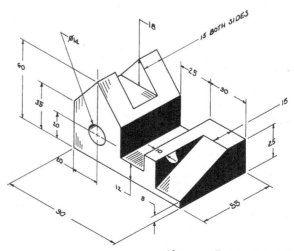

Ø14
18
15 BOTH SIDES
60
25
35
30
20
15
20
10
25
12
8
30
55

## EX5-31 Inches

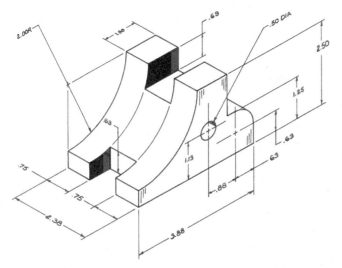

## EX5-32 Millimeters

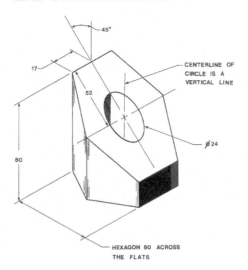

## EX5-33 Inches

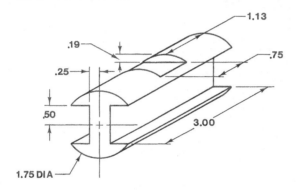

## EX5-34 Millimeters

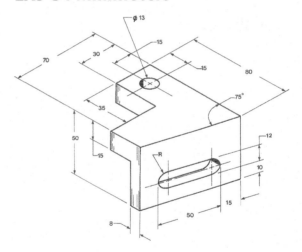

## EX5-35 Millimeters

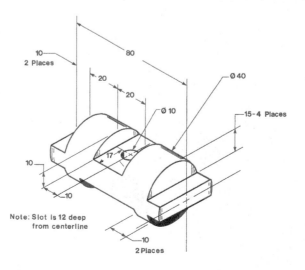

## EX5-36 Inches

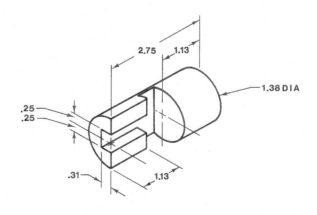

## EX5-37 Millimeters

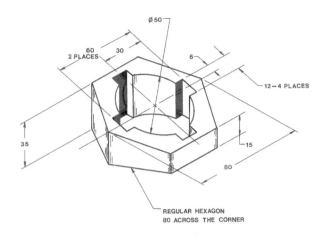

Ø50
60 2 PLACES
30
6
12—4 PLACES
35
15
80
REGULAR HEXAGON
80 ACROSS THE CORNER

## EX5-38 Millimeters

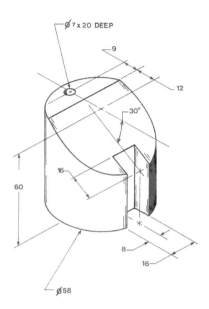

Ø7 x 20 DEEP
9
12
30°
16
60
8
16
Ø58

## EX5-39 Millimeters

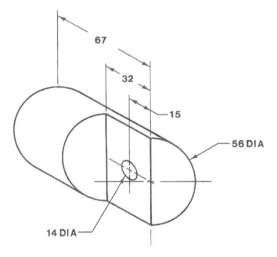

67
32
15
56 DIA
14 DIA

## EX5-40 Millimeters

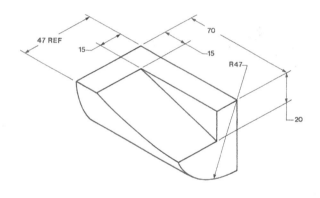

47 REF
15
70
15
R47
20

## EX5-41 Inches

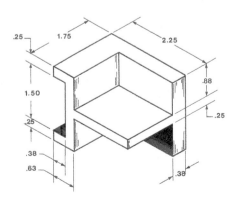

.25
1.75
2.25
.88
1.50
.25
.25
.38
.63
.38

## EX5-42 Inches

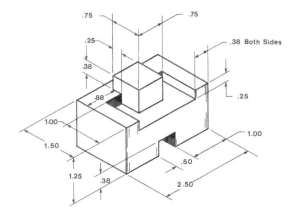

.75
.75
.25
.38 Both Sides
.38
.25
.88
1.00
1.00
1.50
.50
1.25
.38
2.50

## EX5-43 Millimeters

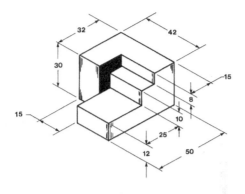

## EX5-44 Millimeters

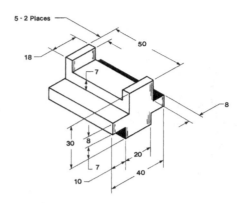

## EX5-45 Millimeters

NOTE: THE SLOT
IS 15 LONG

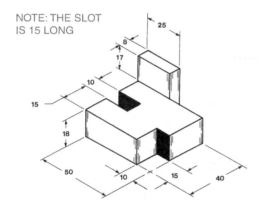

## EX5-46 Millimeters

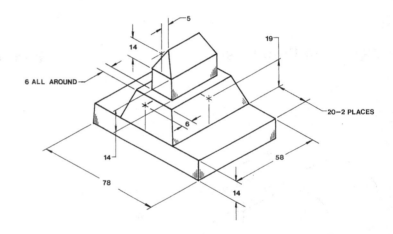

## EX5-47 Inches

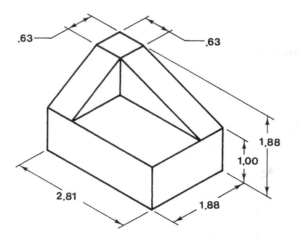

## EX5-48 Inches

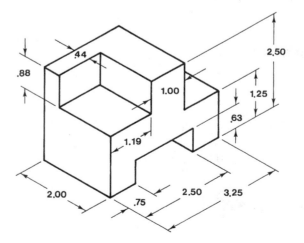

## EX5-49 Millimeters

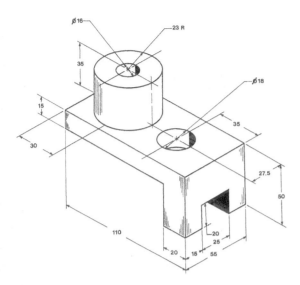

## EX5-50 Inches

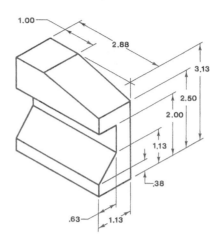

## EX5-51 Inches

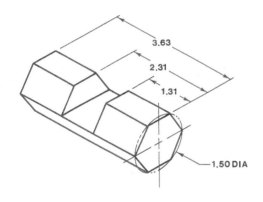

## EX5-52 Millimeters

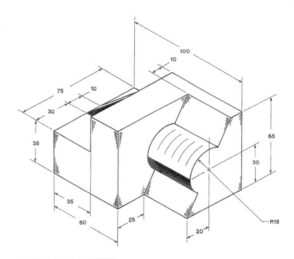

## EX5-53 Inches

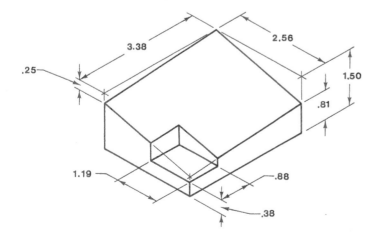

## EX5-54 Millimeters

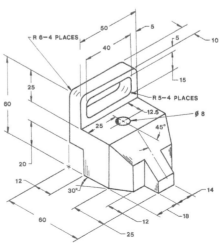

## EX5-55 Millimeters

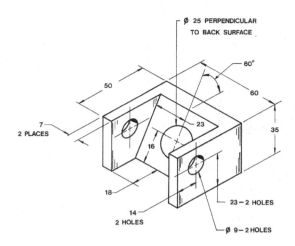

## EX5-56 Millimeters

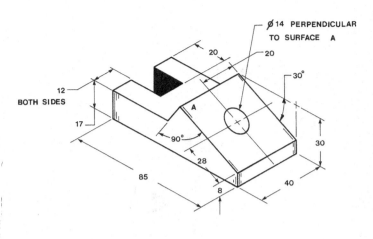

## EX5-57 Millimeters

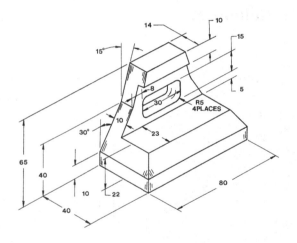

## EX5-58 Millimeters

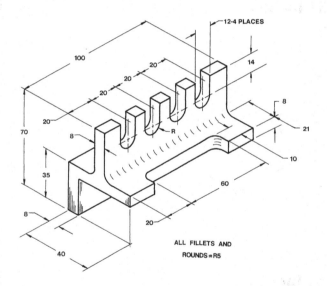

## EX5-59 Millimeters

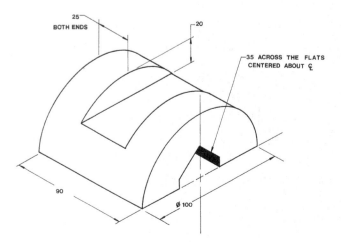

## EX5-60 Inches

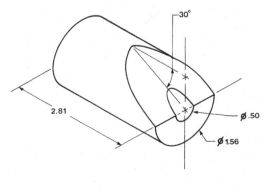

## EX5-61 Millimeters

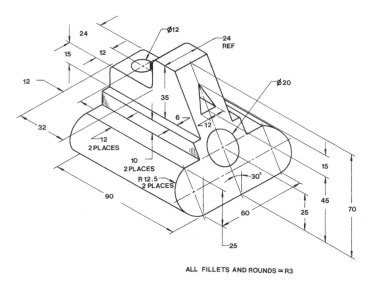

ALL FILLETS AND ROUNDS = R3

## EX5-62 Millimeters

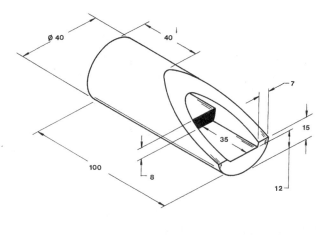

## EX5-63 Millimeters

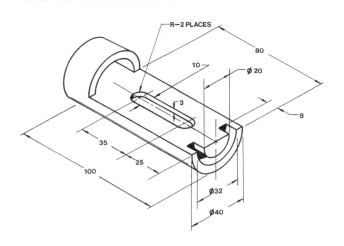

## EX5-64 Millimeters

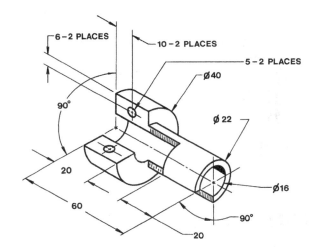

## EX5-65 Millimeters

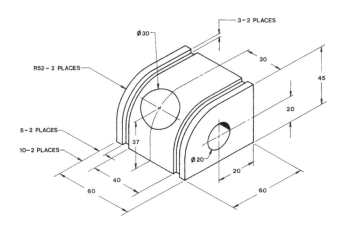

## EX5-66 Millimeters

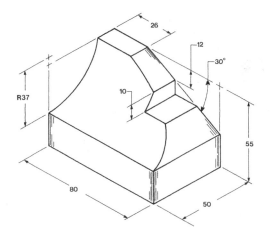

## EX5-67 Millimeters

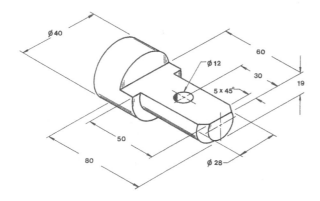

## EX5-68 Millimeters

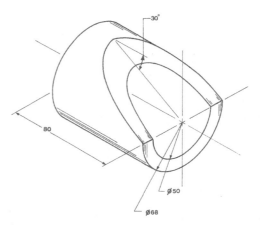

## EX5-69 Millimeters

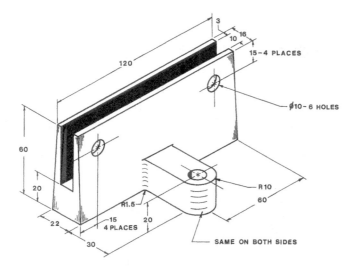

## EX5-70 Millimeters

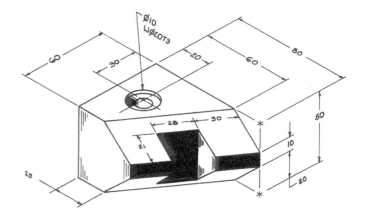

## EX5-71 Millimeters

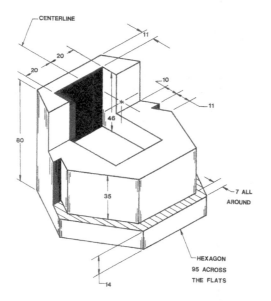

## EX5-72 Millimeters

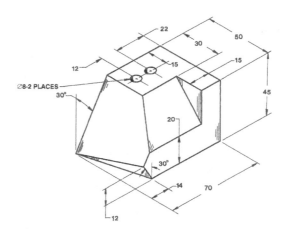

## EX5-73 Millimeters

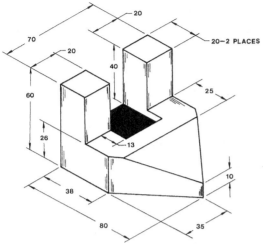

## EX5-74 Inches

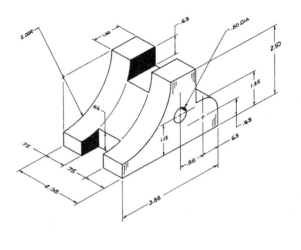

## EX5-75 Inches

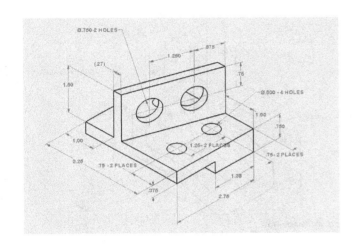

## EX5-76 Millimeters

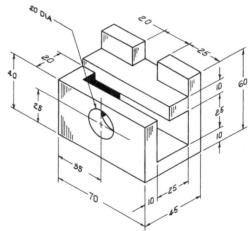

## EX5-77 Millimeters

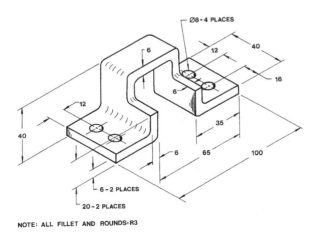

NOTE: ALL FILLET AND ROUNDS=R3

## EX5-78 Millimeters

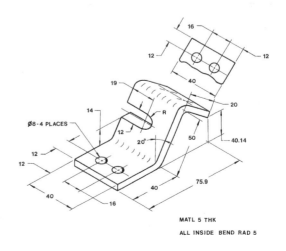

MATL 5 THK

ALL INSIDE BEND RAD 5

## EX5-79 Millimeters

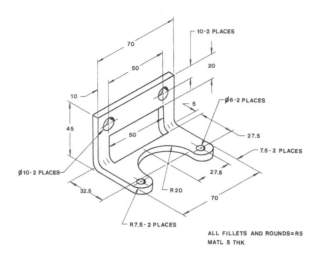

10-2 PLACES
70
50
20
10
45
5
Ø6-2 PLACES
50
27.5
7.5-2 PLACES
Ø10-2 PLACES
27.5
32.5
R 20
70
R7.5-2 PLACES

ALL FILLETS AND ROUNDS = R5
MATL 5 THK

## EX5-80 Millimeters

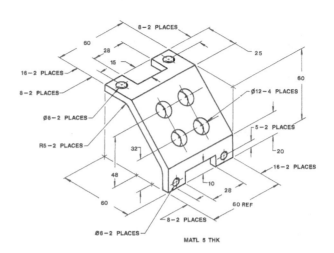

8-2 PLACES
60
28
15
25
16-2 PLACES
60
8-2 PLACES
Ø12-4 PLACES
Ø8-2 PLACES
5-2 PLACES
R5-2 PLACES
32
20
48
16-2 PLACES
60
10
28
60 REF
8-2 PLACES
Ø6-2 PLACES
MATL 5 THK

## EX5-81 Millimeters

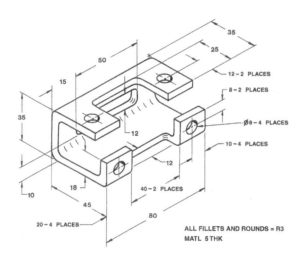

35
25
50
12-2 PLACES
15
8-2 PLACES
35
Ø8-4 PLACES
12
10
10-4 PLACES
12
18
40-2 PLACES
45
80
20-4 PLACES

ALL FILLETS AND ROUNDS = R3
MATL 5 THK

## EX5-82 Millimeters

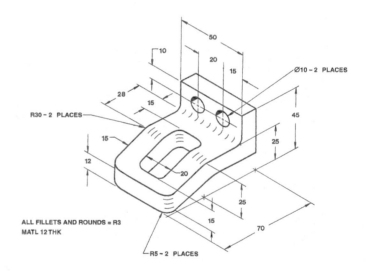

50
10
20
15
Ø10-2 PLACES
28
15
45
R30-2 PLACES
25
15
12
20
25
15
70
R5-2 PLACES

ALL FILLETS AND ROUNDS = R3
MATL 12 THK

## EX5-83 Millimeters

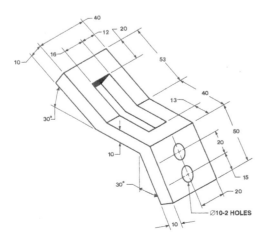

40
12
20
10
16
53
40
13
30°
50
10
20
30°
15
20
Ø10-2 HOLES
10

## EX5-84 Inches

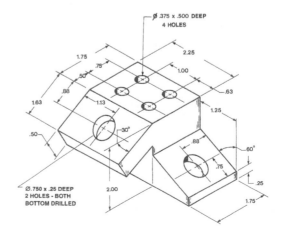

Ø .375 x .500 DEEP
4 HOLES
1.75
2.25
.75
.50
1.00
.88
.63
1.63
1.13
1.25
.50
30°
.88
60°
.75
Ø.750 x .25 DEEP
2 HOLES - BOTH
BOTTOM DRILLED
2.00
.25
1.75

## EX5-85 Millimeters

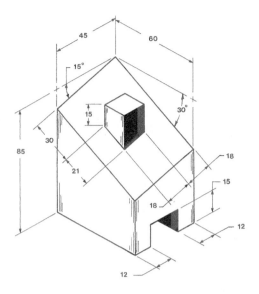

## EX5-86 Millimeters

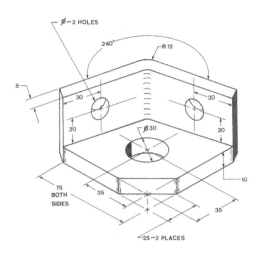

## EX5-87 Inches

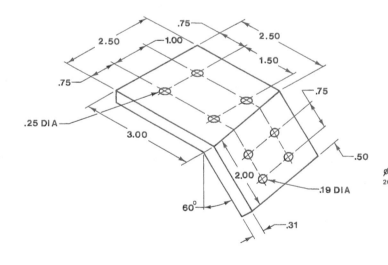

## EX5-88 Millimeters

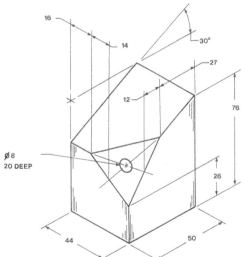

## EX5-89 Millimeters

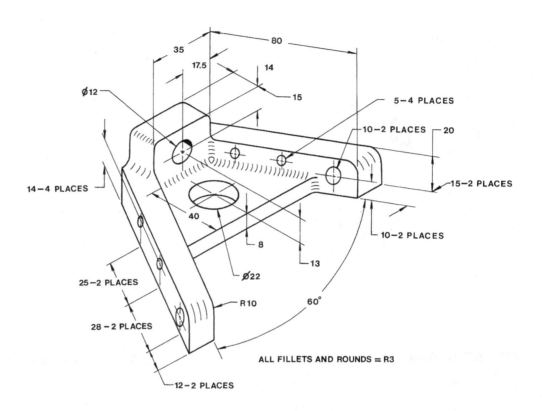

## EX5-90 Millimeters

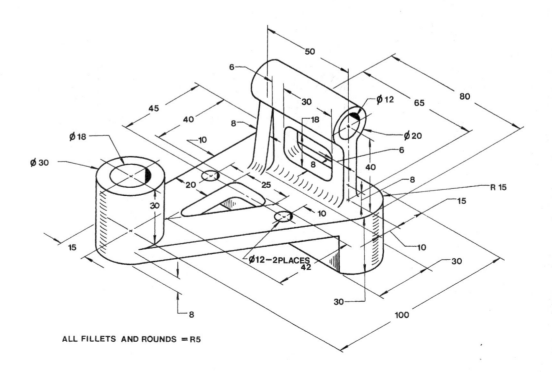

## EX5-91 Millimeters

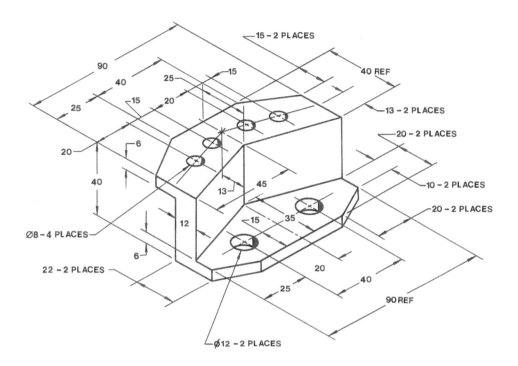

## EX5-92 Millimeters

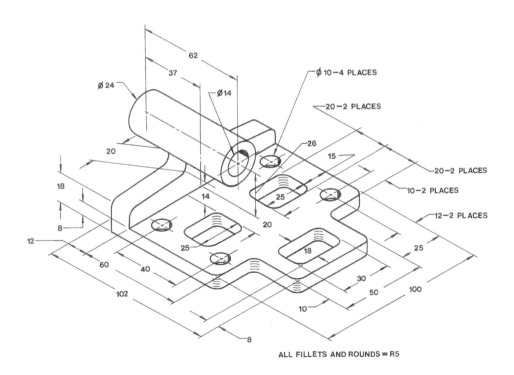

ALL FILLETS AND ROUNDS = R5

## EX5-93 Millimeters

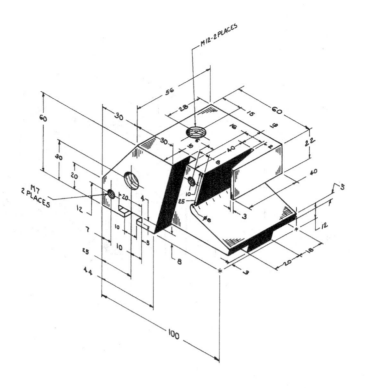

## EX5-94 Millimeters

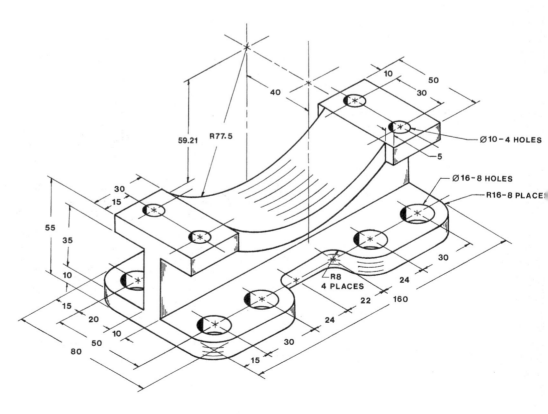

For Exercise Problems EX5-95 through EX5-100:

1. Sketch the given orthographic views and add the top view so that the final sketch includes front, top, and right-side views.

2. Prepare a three-dimensional sketch of the object.

## EX5-95

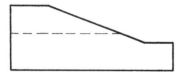

## EX5-96

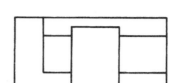
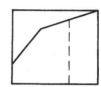

## EX5-97

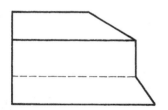
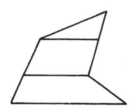

## EX5-98

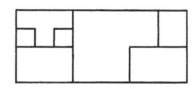

## EX5-99

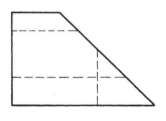
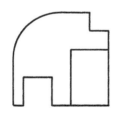

## EX5-100

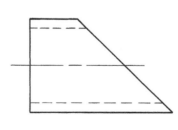
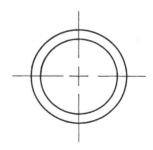

For Exercise Problems EX5-101 through EX5-128:

1. Redraw the given views and draw the third view.

2. Prepare a three-dimensional sketch of the object.

## EX5-101 Inches

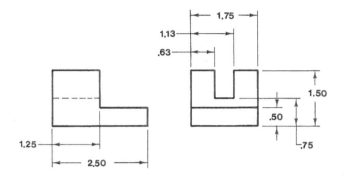

## EX5-102 Inches

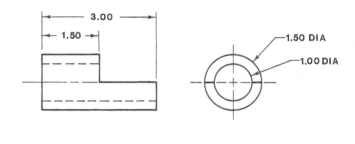

## EX5-103 Inches

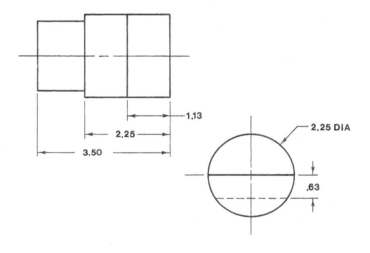

## EX5-104 Inches

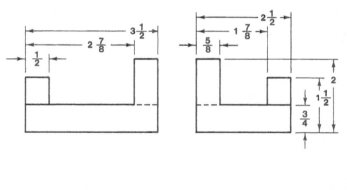

## EX5-105 Inches

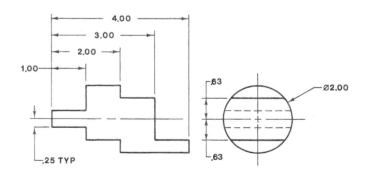

## EX5-106 Inches

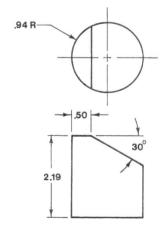

## EX5-107 Inches

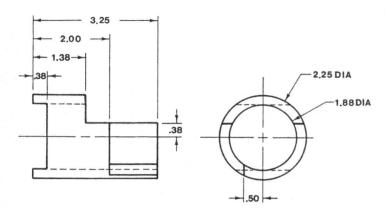

## EX5-108 Inches

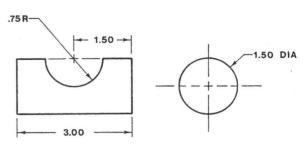

## EX5-109 Inches

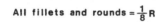

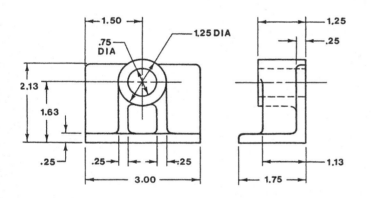

## EX5-110 Inches

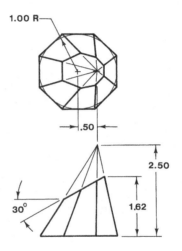

## EX5-111 Inches

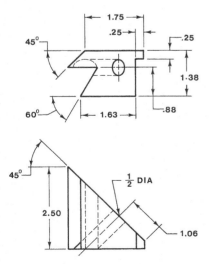

## EX5-112 Inches

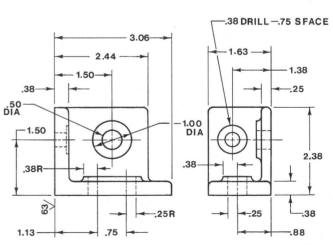

Each exercise on this page is presented on a 10 × 10-mm grid.

## EX5-113

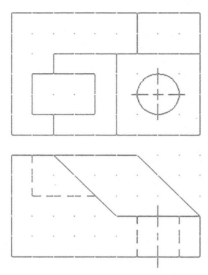

## EX5-114

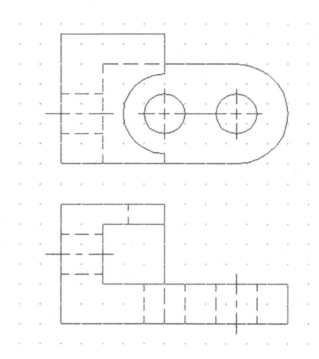

## EX5-115

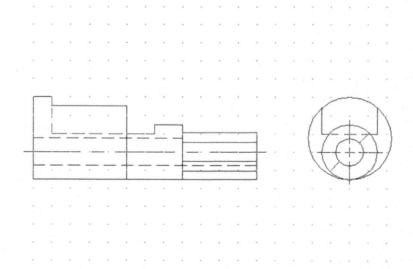

**EX5-116**

Each exercise on this page is presented on a .50" × .50" grid.

**EX5-117**

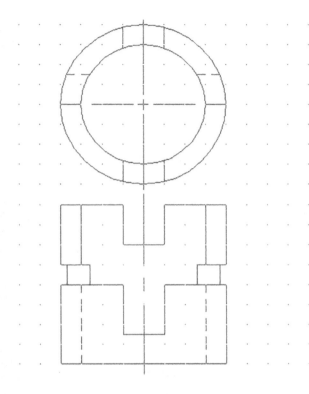

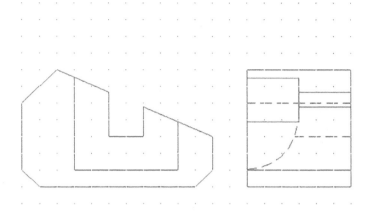

**EX5-118**

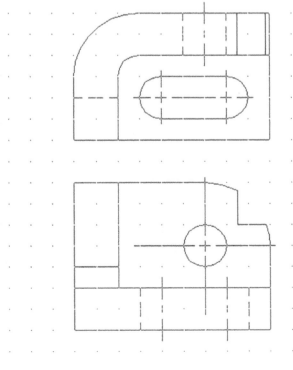

**EX5-119**

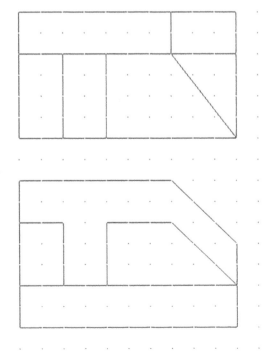

## EX5-120

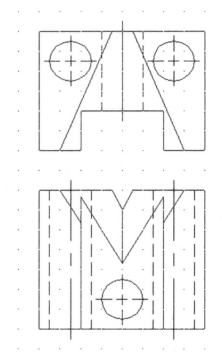

Exercise Problems EX5-121 through EX5-124 are each presented on a .50″ × .50″ grid.

## EX5-121

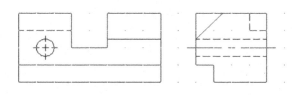

## EX5-122

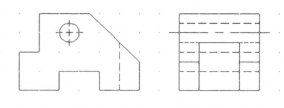

## EX5-123

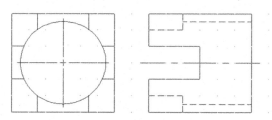

Exercise Problems EX5-125 through EX5-128 are each presented on a 10 × 10-mm grid.

## EX5-124

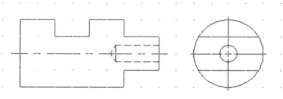

## EX5-125

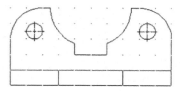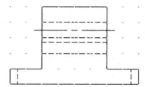

## EX5-126

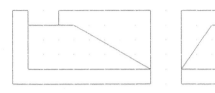

## EX5-127

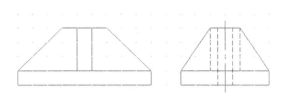

Draw the complete front, top, and side views of the two intersecting objects given in Exercise Problems EX5-129 through EX5-134 on the basis of the given complete and partially complete orthographic views.

## EX5-128

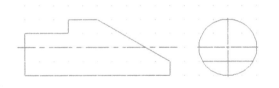

## EX5-129 Millimeters

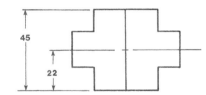

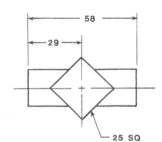

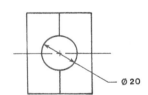

## EX5-130 Millimeters

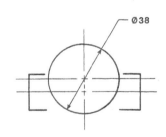

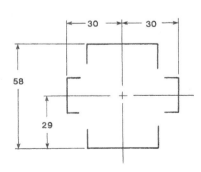

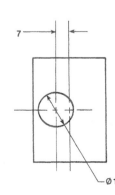

## EX5-131 Inches

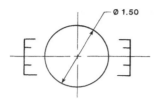

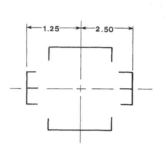

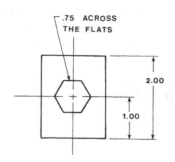

## EX5-132 Inches

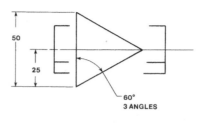

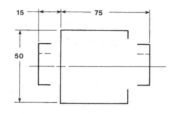

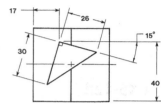

## EX5-133 Millimeters

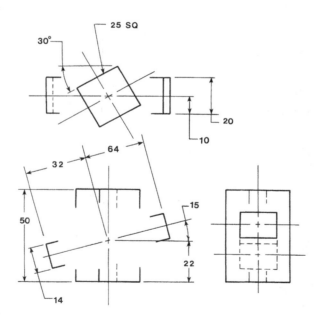

## EX5-134 Millimeters

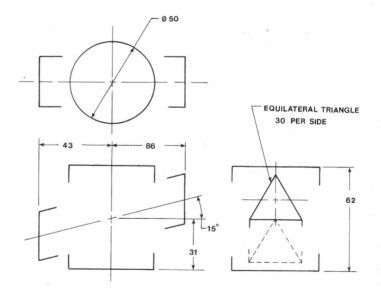

Draw the front, top, and side orthographic views of the objects given in Exercise Problems EX5-135 through EX5-138 on the basis of the partially complete isometric drawings.

## EX5-135 Millimeters

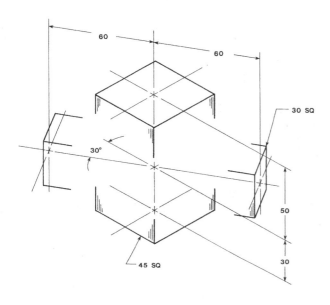

## EX5-136 Millimeters

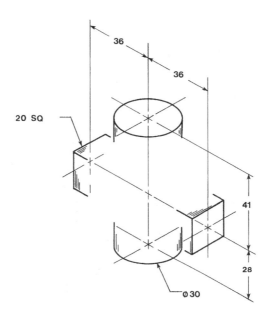

## EX5-137 Inches

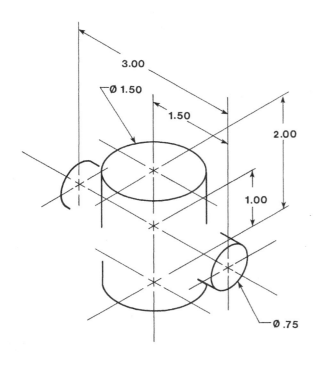

## EX5-138 Inches (Scale: 5=1)

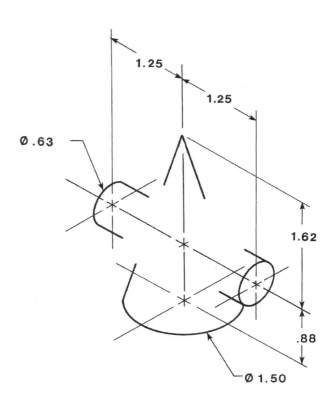

Redesign the existing objects as indicated in Exercise Problems EX5-139 through EX5-142 and then prepare a front, top, and right-side view of each object.

## EX5-139 Millimeters

1. Replace the four existing 12-wide slots with seven slots 16 wide.
2. Increase the distance between the slots from 20 to 24.
3. Modify the overall length as needed.
4. Increase the size of the 60 slot so that it is 20 from both ends.

Change to 16-7 PLACES.

12—4 PLACES

Modify as needed.

100

20

20

20

14

8

21

10

70

20

8

R

35

60

Modify as needed.

8

20

ALL FILLETS AND ROUNDS = R5

40

Maintain at both ends.

## EX5-140 Millimeters

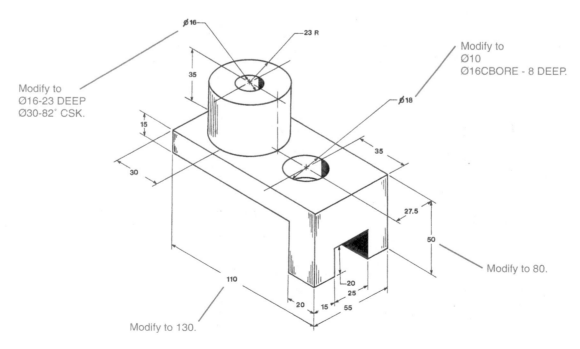

Ø16

23 R

Modify to Ø10 Ø16CBORE - 8 DEEP.

Modify to Ø16-23 DEEP Ø30-82° CSK.

35

Ø18

15

35

30

27.5

50

110

Modify to 80.

20

25

20   15   55

Modify to 130.

## EX5-141 Millimeters

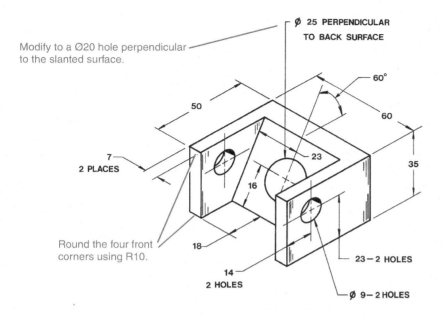

Modify to a Ø20 hole perpendicular to the slanted surface.

Ø 25 PERPENDICULAR TO BACK SURFACE

60°

60

50

35

7
2 PLACES

23

16

Round the four front corners using R10.

18

14
2 HOLES

23 – 2 HOLES

Ø 9 – 2 HOLES

## EX5-142 Millimeters

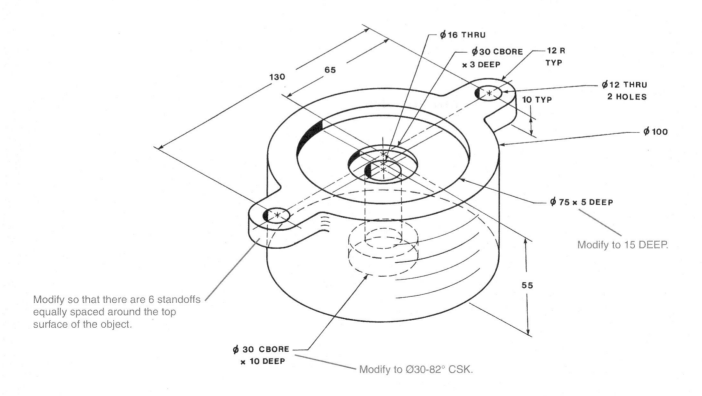

Ø 16 THRU

Ø 30 CBORE
x 3 DEEP

12 R
TYP

Ø 12 THRU
2 HOLES

130

65

10 TYP

Ø 100

Ø 75 x 5 DEEP

Modify to 15 DEEP.

55

Modify so that there are 6 standoffs equally spaced around the top surface of the object.

Ø 30 CBORE
x 10 DEEP

Modify to Ø30-82° CSK.

Given the following orthographic views, create an isometric model of each object.

## EX5-143 Millimeters

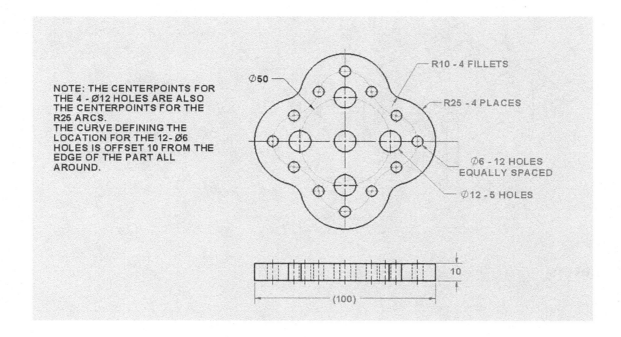

NOTE: THE CENTERPOINTS FOR THE 4 - Ø12 HOLES ARE ALSO THE CENTERPOINTS FOR THE R25 ARCS.
THE CURVE DEFINING THE LOCATION FOR THE 12- Ø6 HOLES IS OFFSET 10 FROM THE EDGE OF THE PART ALL AROUND.

Ø50
R10 - 4 FILLETS
R25 - 4 PLACES
Ø6 - 12 HOLES EQUALLY SPACED
Ø12 - 5 HOLES

10
(100)

## EX5-144 Millimeters

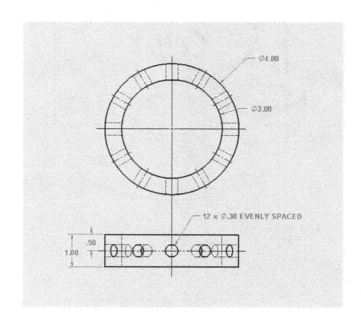

Ø4.00
Ø3.00
12 x Ø.38 EVENLY SPACED
.50
1.00

Each of the following exercise problems is presented using first-angle projection and ISO conventions.

**1** Create an isometric drawing from the given orthographic views.

**2** Draw front, top, and right-side orthographic views of the objects using third-angle projections and ANSI conventions.

## EX5-145

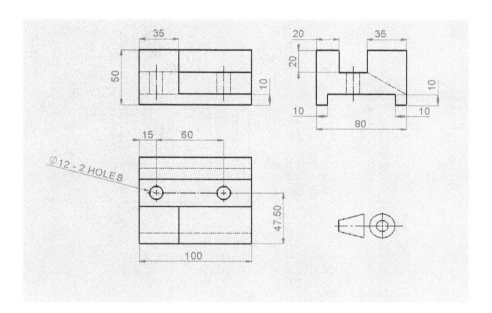

## EX5-146

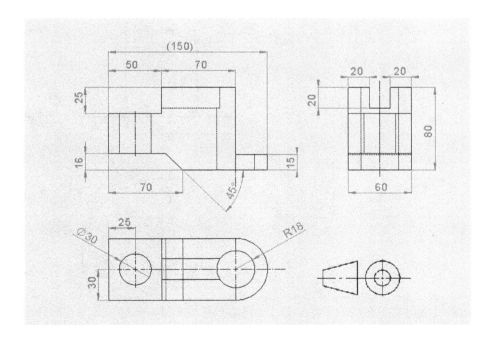

## EX5-147

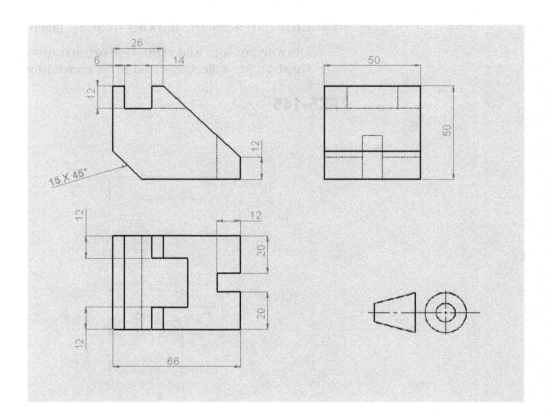

## EX5-148

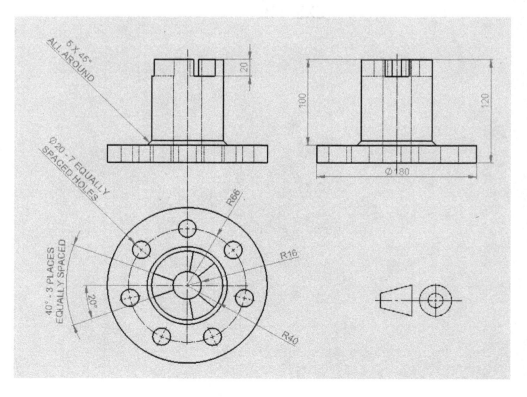

**EX5-149**

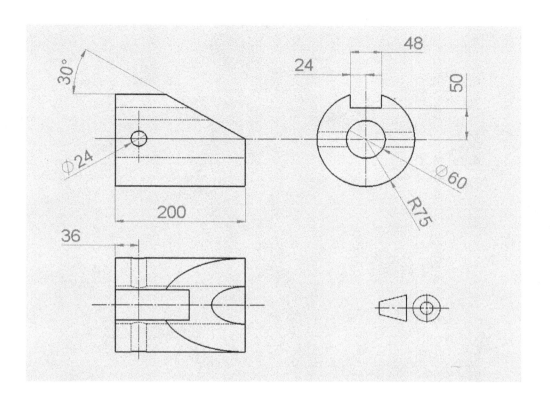

# chapter **six**

## **Sectional Views**

## 6-1 Introduction

*Sectional views* are used in technical drawing to expose internal surfaces. They serve to present additional orthographic views of surfaces that appear as hidden lines in the standard front, top, and side orthographic views.

Figure 6-1 shows an object intersected by a cutting plane. Figure 6-2 shows the same object, with its right side and the cutting plane removed. Hatch lines represent the locations on the surfaces where the cutting plane passed through solid material. The front and right-side orthographic views and a sectional view are also shown. Note the similarity between the sectional view and the cut pictorial view in Figure 6-1.

**Figure 6-1**

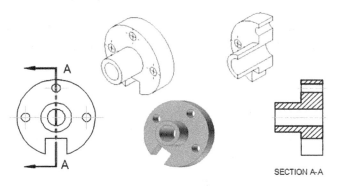

SECTION A-A

**Figure 6-2**

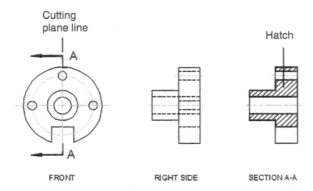

Sectional views do not contain hidden lines, so they are used to clarify orthographic views that are difficult to understand because of excessive hidden lines. Figure 6-3 shows an object with a complex internal shape. The standard right view contains many hidden lines and is difficult to follow. Note how much easier it is to understand the object's internal shape when it is presented as a sectional view.

**Figure 6-3**

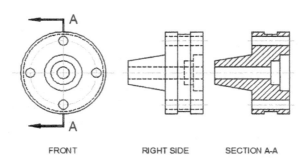

Sectional views *do* include all lines that are directly visible. Figure 6-4 shows an object, a cutting plane line, and a sectional view taken along the cutting plane line. Surfaces that are directly visible are shown in the sectional view. For example, part of the large hole in the back left surface is, from the given sectional view's orientation, blocked by the shorter rectangular surface. The part of the hole that appears above the blocking surface is shown; the part behind the surface is not.

**Figure 6-4**

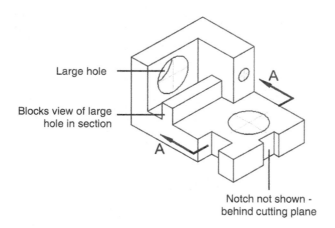

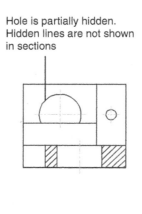

Sectional views are always viewed in the direction defined by the cutting plane arrows. Any surface that is behind the cutting plane is not included in the sectional view. Sectional views are aligned and oriented relative to the cutting plane lines as a side orthographic view is to the front view. The orientation of a sectional view may be better understood by placing your right hand on the cutting plane line so that your thumb is pointing up. Move your hand to the right and place it palm down. Your thumb should now be pointing to the left. Your thumb indicates the top of the view.

Drafters and designers often refer to sectional views as "sectional cuts" or simply "cuts." The terminology is helpful in understanding how sectional views are defined and created.

## 6-2 Cutting Plane Lines

Cutting plane lines are used to define the location for the sectional view's cutting plane. An object is "cut" along a cutting plane line.

Figure 6-5 shows two linetype patterns for cutting plane lines. Either pattern is acceptable, although some companies prefer to use only one linetype for all drawings to ensure a uniform appearance in all of their drawings. The dashed-line pattern is used throughout this book.

**Figure 6-5**

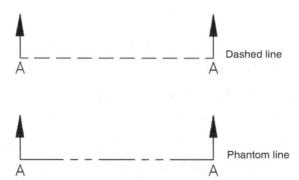

The two patterns shown in Figure 6-5 are included in AutoCAD's linetype library as the **Dashed** and **Phantom** styles. The arrow portion of the cutting plane line is created by the use of the **Multileader** tool, found on the **Leaders** panel of the **Annotate** tab or on the **Annotation** panel of the **Home** tab.

### Drawing a Cutting Plane Line—Method I

Change a given continuous line, **A–A**, to a cutting plane line (Figure 6-6). The **Dashed** linetype must first be added to the list of available linetypes.

**Figure 6-6**

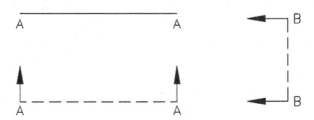

**1** Type the word **linetype** at a command prompt.

The **Linetype Manager** dialog box appears.

**2** Select **Load**.

The **Load or Reload Linetypes** dialog box appears (Figure 6-7).

Figure 6-7

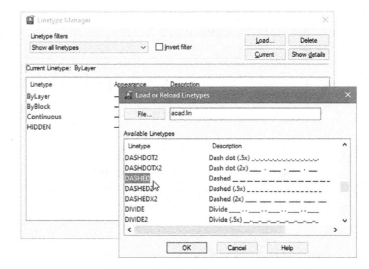

**3** Select **DASHED** and **PHANTOM** and then return to the drawing screen.

**4** Click line **A–A**.

A **Properties** dialog box appears.

**5** Select the **Linetype** line in the **Properties** dialog box.

**6** Scroll down the linetype listing and select the **DASHED** option.

**7** Close the **Properties** dialog box, and press the **Esc** key.

## *Drawing an Arrowhead*

**1** Click the **Multileader** tool and draw a leader line on the drawing screen (Figure 6-8 (a)). Type any letter in the text prompt; you can edit it later.

It is recommended that the leader line be either horizontal or vertical. In this example, a vertical line is drawn.

Figure 6-8

**2** Click **Explode** on the **Modify** panel and explode the leader line.

**3** Use the **Erase** tool from the **Modify** panel to remove the short horizontal section of the line. Move the letter from the leader to a suitable place near the arrow (Figure 6-8 (b)).

**4** Use **Move** and **Copy** to create two leader lines and position them at the ends of the dashed section line (Figure 6-8 (c)).

If necessary, use the **Rotate** command to align the arrowhead and line segment with the sectional line.

## Changing the Size of an Arrowhead

Arrowheads used for cutting plane lines are usually drawn larger than arrowheads used for dimension lines. This serves to make them more distinctive and easier to find. The normal arrowhead size is twice that of a dimension or regular multileader arrow. When creating section arrows with the **Multileader** tool, it's most efficient to create a new multileader style to be used for section marks only.

**1** Select the **Multileader Style Manager** from the **Leaders** panel under the **Annotate** tab.

The **Multileader Style Manager** is accessed by clicking the arrow in the lower-right corner of the **Leaders** panel.

**2** Click **New**.

The **Create New Multileader Style** dialog box appears (Figure 6-9).

**3** Enter the new style name **SectionMark** and click **Continue**.

**Figure 6-9**

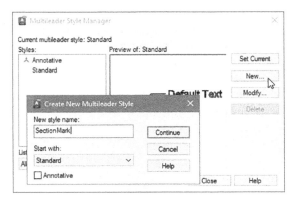

The **Modify Multileader Style: SectionMark** dialog box appears (Figure 6-10).

**4** Select the **Leader Format** tab and use the **Arrowhead Size** box to change the arrowhead's size to **0.3600** (from the default arrow size 0.1800). Click **OK**.

**5** Return to the drawing screen and use the **Multileader** tool to create the needed section marks.

Figure 6-10

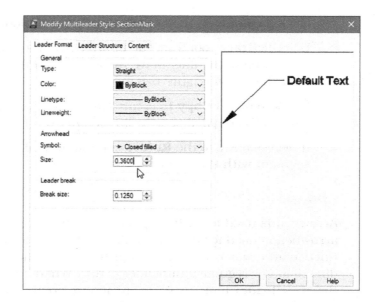

## Drawing a Cutting Plane Line—Method II

A cutting plane can also be created by first defining a separate layer for cutting plane lines. The linetype is **Dashed** or **Phantom**, and a color can be assigned, if desired. (Colors do not display on black-and-white prints, but they can help you when working on the screen.) Section 3-24 describes how to create and work with layers.

### Drawing Cutting Plane Lines

Cutting plane lines should extend beyond the edges of the object (refer to Figures 6-1, 6-2, and 6-3). A cutting plane line should extend far enough beyond the edges of the object so that there is a clear gap between the arrowhead and the edge of the object.

If an object is symmetrical about the centerline and only one sectional view is to be taken, exactly aligned with the centerline, the cutting plane line may be omitted (Figure 6-11).

Figure 6-11

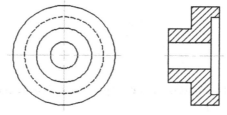

## 6-3 Indicating Solid Cuts

*Hatching* (sometimes called *cross-hatching*) is used to represent areas where solid material has been cut in a sectional view. Hatch lines are evenly spaced at any inclined angle that is not parallel to any existing edge line and should be visually distinct from the continuous lines that define the boundary of the sectional view.

Figure 6-12 shows an area that includes uniform section lines evenly spaced at 45°. The other area shown in Figure 6-12 includes a 45° edge line; therefore, the section lines cannot be drawn at 45°. Lines at 135° (0° is horizontal to the right) were drawn instead.

**Figure 6-12**

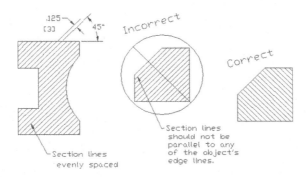

Figure 6-13 shows an object that contains edge lines at both 45° and 135°. The section lines within this area were drawn at 60°.

**Figure 6-13**

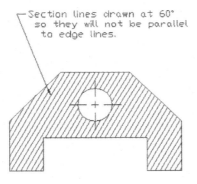

If two or more parts are included within the same sectional view, each part must have visually different section lines. Figure 6-14 shows a sectional view that contains two parts. Part 1's section lines were spaced 3 millimeters apart at 45°; part 2's were spaced 3 millimeters apart at 135° (that is, −45°).

**Figure 6-14**

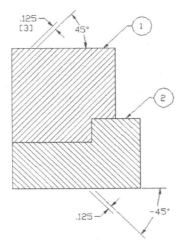

The recommended spacing for hatch lines is 0.125 inch, or 3 millimeters, but smaller areas may use section lines spaced closer together than larger areas (Figure 6-15). Section lines should never be spaced so close together as to look blurry or be so far apart that they are not clearly recognizable as section lines.

Figure 6-15

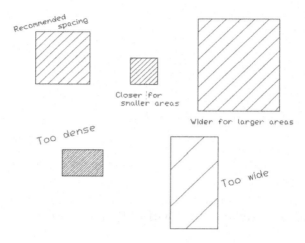

Evenly spaced sectional line patterns drawn at 45° are called *general* or *uniform* patterns; other patterns are available. Different section line patterns are used to help distinguish different materials. The different patterns allow the drawing reader to see what materials are used in a design without having to refer to the drawing's parts list. It should be noted that not all companies use different patterns to define material differences. When you are in doubt, the general pattern is usually acceptable.

How to draw different hatch patterns in AutoCAD is explained in the next section.

## 6-4 Hatch

Solid areas cut by section planes are drawn in AutoCAD with the **Hatch** tool, located in the **Draw** panel on the **Home** tab. **Hatch** offers many different hatch patterns and spacings. The general pattern of evenly spaced lines at 45° is defined as pattern ANSI31 and is the default setting for the **Hatch** command.

### Hatching a Given Area

Given an area, use **Hatch** to indicate cut surfaces of solids.

**1** Select the **Hatch** tool from the **Draw** panel.

The **Hatch Creation** contextual tab, with its own panels, appears at the end of the ribbon (Figure 6-16).

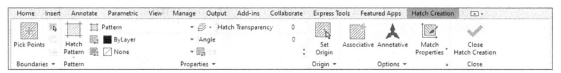

**Figure 6-16**

▣ Select a point within the area to be hatched and click the mouse.

▣ Right-click and select the **Enter** option.

The area is hatched (Figure 6-17).

**Figure 6-17**

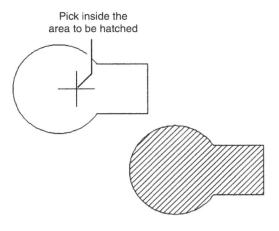

Pick inside the
area to be hatched

## Changing Hatch Patterns

▣ Select **Hatch** from the **Draw** panel.

The **Hatch Creation** contextual tab appears.

▣ Click **Hatch Pattern**. If you see several patterns (which you may, depending on your screen resolution), click the lowest arrow on the right side of the **Pattern** panel.

A selection of hatch patterns appears (Figure 6-18). Additional patterns can be found by scrolling down on the right side of the panel.

▣ Select the desired pattern and apply it as described previously.

**Figure 6-18**

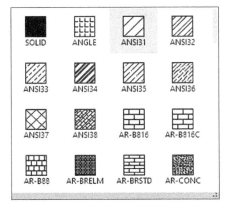

Figure 6-19 shows three intersecting shapes with five different hatch patterns applied.

Figure 6-19

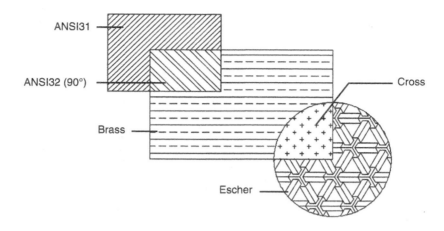

## Changing the Spacing and Angle of a Hatch Pattern

**1** Select the **Hatch** tool from the **Draw** panel.

The **Hatch Creation** contextual tab appears (Figure 6-20).

**Figure 6-20**

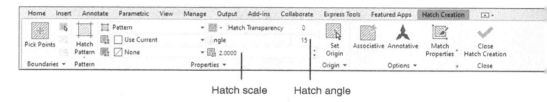

**2** Change the **Angle** option box to **15** and the **Scale** option box to **2**.

Figure 6-21 shows a comparison between an ANSI31 pattern created with the default values 1 and 0° and the adjusted pattern with the values 2 and 20°.

**Figure 6-21**

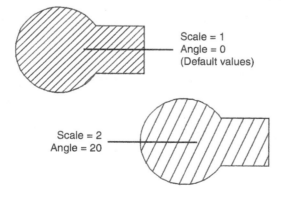

# 6-5 Drawing Problem

Figure 6-22 shows an object with a section mark indicating a cutting plane line. Figure 6-23 shows how a front view and a sectional view of the object are created.

**1** Draw the front orthographic view of the object and lay out the height and width of the object on the basis of the given dimensions.

Sectional views must be directly aligned with the angle of the cutting plane line. Sectional views are, in fact, orthographic views that are based on the angle of the cutting plane line. Information is projected to sectional views as it was projected to top and side views. In this example, the cutting plane line is a vertical line, so horizontal projection lines are used to draw the sectional view.

**Figure 6-22**

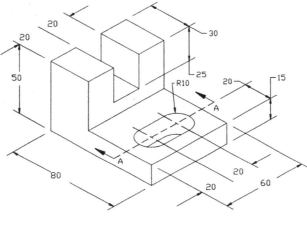

**Figure 6-23**

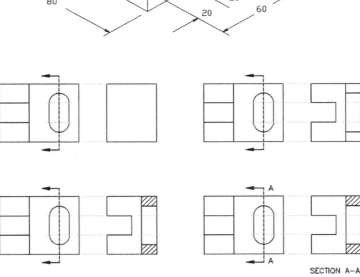

SECTION A–A

**2** Draw the object features. No hidden lines are drawn.

**3** Use **Hatch** to draw section lines within the appropriate areas.

**4** Erase or trim any excess lines.

**5** Modify the color of the section lines, if desired.

**6** Save the drawing, if desired.

## 6-6 Styles of Section Lines

AutoCAD has more than 50 different hatch patterns. You can preview the different patterns in swatches in the **Hatch Creation** tab's **Hatch Pattern** panel. Most of the available patterns (in particular the ones starting with **AR-**) are for architectural use. The patterns can be used to create elevation drawings and to add texture patterns to drawings of houses, buildings, and other structures. Mechanical drawings usually refer to objects made from steel, aluminum, or a composite material. There are hundreds of variations of each of these materials.

In general, if you decide to assign a particular pattern to a material, clearly state which pattern has been assigned to which material on the drawing. This is best done by including a note on the drawing that includes a picture of the pattern and the material that it is to represent. Figure 6-24 shows a drawing note for a hatch pattern used to represent SAE 1040 steel. The representation is unique for the drawing shown.

**Figure 6-24**

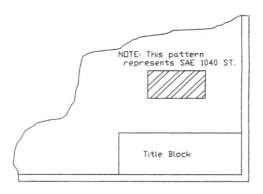

## 6-7 Sectional View Location

Sectional views should be located on a drawing behind the arrows. The arrows represent the viewing direction for the sectional view (Figure 6-25). If it is impossible to locate sectional views behind the arrows, they may be located above or below, but still behind, the arrowed portion of the cutting plane line. Sectional views should never be located in front of the arrows.

**Figure 6-25**

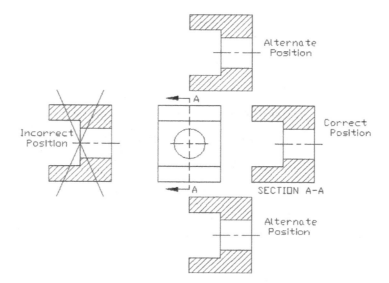

Sectional views located on a different drawing sheet from the cutting plane line must be cross-referenced to the appropriate cutting plane line (Figure 6-26). The boxed notation C/3 SHT2 next to the cutting plane line means that the sectional view may be found in zone C/3 on sheet 2 of the drawing.

**Figure 6-26**

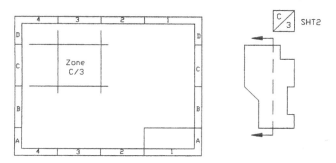

The reference numbers and letters are based on a drawing area charting system similar to that used for locating features on maps. A sectional view located at C/3 SHT2 can be found by going to sheet 2 of the drawing and then drawing a vertical line from the box marked 3 at the top or bottom of the drawing and a horizontal line from the box marked C on the left or right edge of the drawing. The sectional view should be located somewhere near the intersection of the two lines.

## 6-8 Holes in Sections

Figure 6-27 shows a sectional view of an object that contains three holes. As with orthographic views, a conical point must be included on holes that do not completely penetrate the object.

**Figure 6-27**

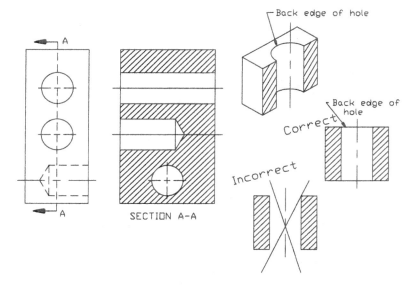

SECTION A-A

A common mistake is to omit the back edge of a hole when drawing a sectional view. Figure 6-27 shows a hole drilled through an object. Note that the sectional view includes a straight line across the top and bottom edges of the view that represents the back edges of the hole.

Figure 6-28 shows a counterbored hole, a countersunk hole, a spotface, and a hole through a boss. Remember that any hole that does not completely penetrate the object must include a conical point.

**Figure 6-28**

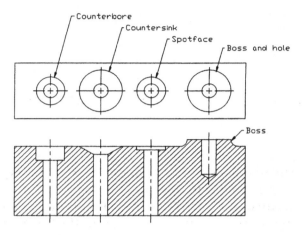

## 6-9 Gradients

In AutoCAD, a *gradient* is shading that varies in intensity. Figure 6-29 shows a rectangular shape with two internal circles. The figure also shows the same shape with various gradients added.

**Figure 6-29**

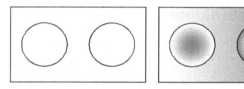

## Creating a Gradient

**1** Select the **Gradient** tool from the **Draw** panel.

The **Hatch Creation** contextual tab appears, with a default gradient selected and a number of additional patterns available (Figure 6-30).

**2** Click a point within the area to which to apply the gradient.

**3** Right-click and select the **Enter** option.

The gradient's pattern, color, angle, and density, among other properties, are controlled through the **Hatch Creation** contextual tab.

Figure 6-30

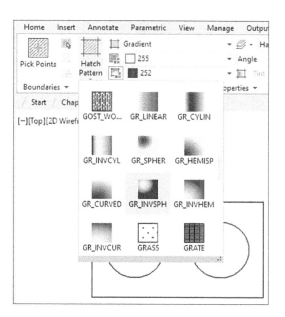

## 6-10 Offset Sections

Cutting plane lines need not be drawn as straight lines across the surface of an object. They may be stepped so that more features can be included in the sectional view. In the object shown in Figure 6-31, the cutting plane line crosses two holes and a directly visible open surface that contains a hole. There is no indication in the sectional view that the cutting plane line has been offset.

Figure 6-31

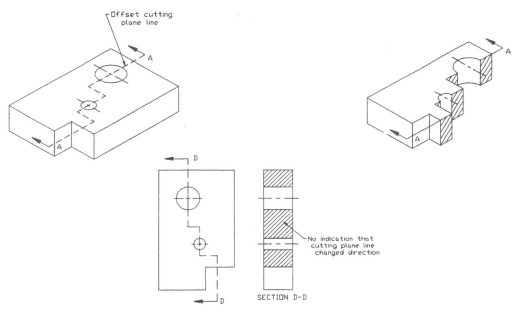

Cutting plane lines should be placed to include as many features as possible without causing confusion. The goal in using sectional views is to simplify views and to clarify the drawing. Several features can be included on the same cutting plane line so that fewer views are used, giving the drawing a less cluttered look and making it easier for the reader to understand the shape of the object's features.

Figure 6-32 shows another example of an offset cutting plane line.

Figure 6-32

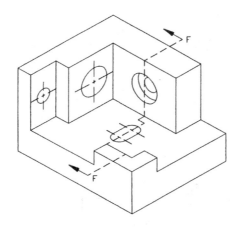

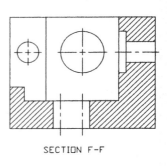

SECTION F-F

## 6-11 Multiple Sections

More than one sectional view may be taken from the same orthographic view. Figure 6-33 shows a drawing that includes three sectional views, all taken from a front view. Each cutting plane line is labeled with a letter. These letters are used to identify the appropriate sectional views. Identifying letters are also placed at the ends of the cutting plane lines, behind the arrowheads, and below the sectional view. They are written in the format SECTION A-A, SECTION B-B, and so on. The abbreviation SECT may also be used (that is, SECT A-A, SECT B-B, and so on).

Figure 6-33

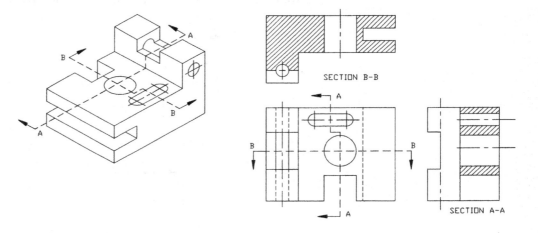

SECTION B-B

SECTION A-A

The letters I, O, and X are generally not used to identify sectional views because they can easily be misread. If more than 23 sectional views are used, the lettering starts again with double letters: AA-AA, BB-BB, and so on.

## 6-12 Aligned Sections

Cutting plane lines taken at angles on circular shapes may be aligned, as shown in Figure 6-34. Aligning the sectional views prevents the foreshortening that would result if the view were projected from the original cutting plane line location. A foreshortened view would not present an accurate picture of the object's surfaces.

**Figure 6-34**

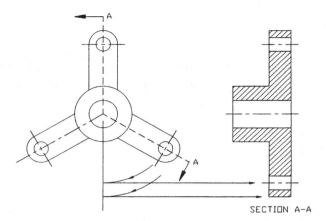

SECTION A-A

## 6-13 Drawing Conventions in Sections

Slots and small holes that penetrate cylindrical surfaces may be drawn as straight lines, as shown in Figure 6-35. Larger holes—that is, holes whose diameters are greater than the radii of their cylinders—should be drawn showing an elliptical curvature.

**Figure 6-35**

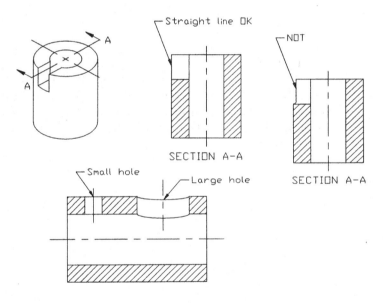

Intersecting holes are represented by crossed lines, as shown in Figure 6-36. The crossed lines are drawn from the intersecting corners of the holes.

**Figure 6-36**

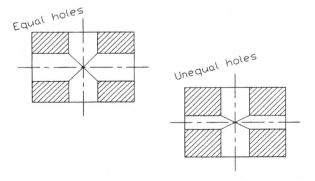

## 6-14 Half, Partial, and Broken-Out Sectional Views

Half and partial sectional views allow a designer to show an object by an orthographic view and a sectional view within one view. A half-sectional view is shown in Figure 6-37. Half of the view is a sectional view; the other half is a normal orthographic view, including hidden lines. The cutting plane line is drawn as shown and includes an arrowhead at only one end of the line.

**Figure 6-37**

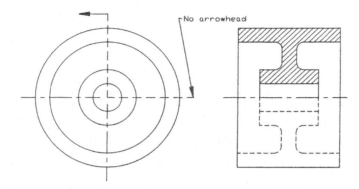

Figure 6-38 shows a partial sectional view. It is similar to a half-sectional view, but the sectional view is taken at a location other than directly on a centerline or one defined by a cutting plane line. A broken line is used to separate the sectional view from the orthographic view. A broken line is a freehand line drawn using the **Polyline** command.

**Figure 6-38**

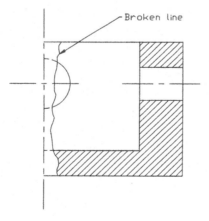

Broken-out sectional views are like small partial views. They are used to show only small internal portions of an object. Figure 6-39 shows a broken-out sectional view. Broken lines are used to separate the broken-out section from the rest of the orthographic views.

**Figure 6-39**

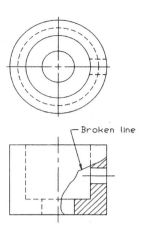

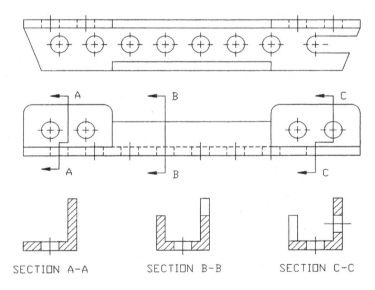

## 6-15 Removed Sectional Views

Removed sectional views are used to show how an object's shape changes over its length. Removed sectional views are most often used with long objects whose shape changes continuously over its length (Figure 6-40). The sectional views are not positioned behind the arrowheads but are positioned across the drawing as shown; however, the view orientation is the same as it would be if the view were projected from the arrowheads; it is simply located in a different position in the drawing.

**Figure 6-40**

It is good practice to identify the cutting plane lines and the sectional views in alphabetical order. This will make it easier for the drawing's readers to find the sectional views.

## 6-16 Breaks

It is often convenient to break long continuous shapes so that they take up less drawing space. There are two drawing conventions used to show breaks: *freehand lines*, which are used for rectangular shapes, and *S-breaks*, which are used for cylindrical shapes (Figure 6-41). Draw freehand break lines with the **Polyline** command, as explained in Section 6-14. Instructions for drawing S-breaks follow.

Figure 6-41

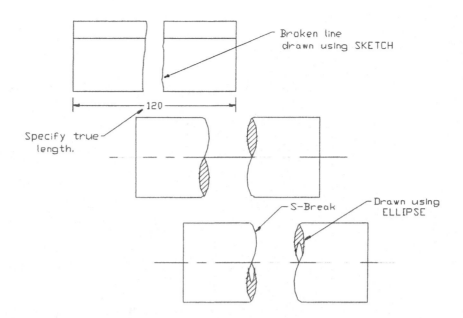

## Drawing an S-Break

**1** Draw a rectangular view of the cylindrical object and draw a construction line where the break is to be located. The rectangular view should include a centerline, as shown in Figure 6-42.

Figure 6-42

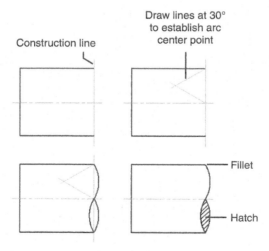

**2** Draw two **30°** lines: one from the intersection of the construction line and the outside edge line of the view and the other from the intersection of the construction line and the centerline, as shown.

**3** Draw an arc, using the intersection created in step 2 as the center point. Mirror the arc about the centerline and then about the construction line.

**4** Use **Fillet**, set to a small radius, to smooth the corners between the arc and the edge lines. Any small radius may be used for the fillet, provided that it produces a smooth visual transition between the arc and the edge lines.

5 Erase and trim any excess lines.

6 Hatch the area created by the two arcs and fillet as shown.

The **Copy**, **Mirror**, and **Move** commands may be used to create the opposing S-break shown in Figure 6-42. The internal shapes of the tubular S-breaks are created by using **Ellipse**. Position the end of the ellipse according to the thickness specifications and determine the elliptical shape by eye. Trim the sectional lines from the inside of the ellipse.

## 6-17 Sectional Views of Castings

Cast objects are usually designed to include a feature called a *rib* (Figure 6-43). Ribs add strength and rigidity to an object. Sectional views of ribs do not include complete section lines because they can be misleading to the reader. Ribs are usually narrow, and a large sectioned area gives the impression of a denser and stronger area than is actually on the casting.

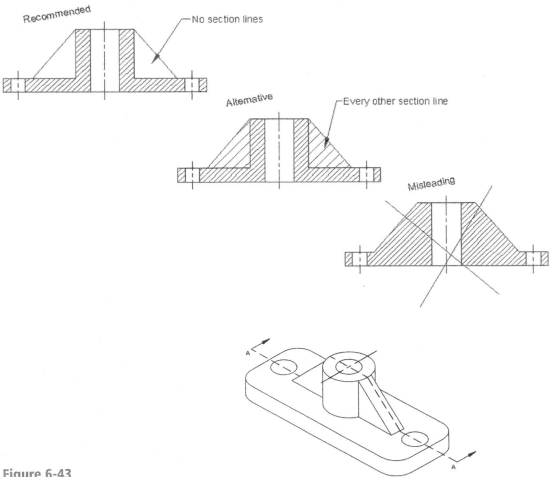

**Figure 6-43**

There are two conventions used to present sectional views of cast ribs: one that does not draw any section lines on the ribs and one that puts every other section line on the rib. Sectional views of castings that do not include section lines on ribs are created by using **Hatch** for those areas that are to be hatched.

# 6-18 EXERCISE PROBLEMS

Draw a complete front view and a sectional view of the objects in Exercise Problems EX6-1 through EX6-4. The cutting plane line is located on the vertical centerline of the object.

## EX6-1 Millimeters

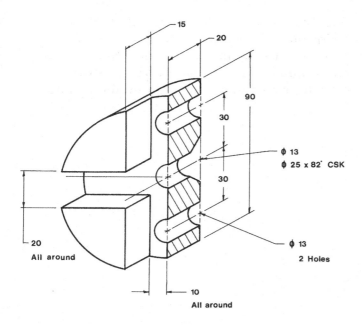

## EX6-2 Millimeters

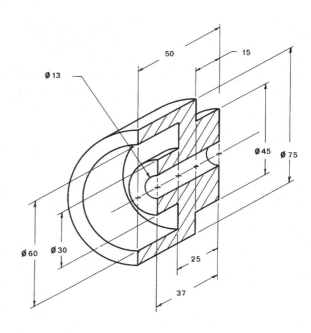

## EX6-3 Inches

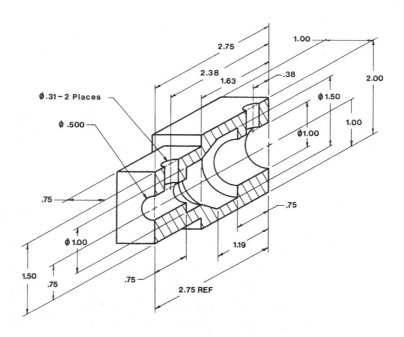

## EX6-4 Millimeters

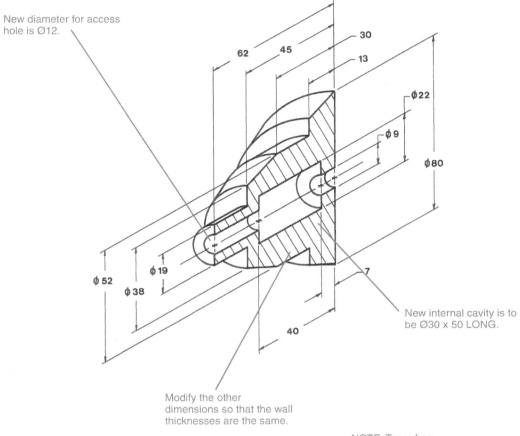

New diameter for access hole is Ø12.

30

62    45

13

Ø22

Ø9

Ø80

Ø52

Ø19

Ø38

7

40

New internal cavity is to be Ø30 x 50 LONG.

Modify the other dimensions so that the wall thicknesses are the same.

NOTE: Taper from Ø80 to Ø68 over 13.

## EX6-5

Draw the following sectional views, using the given dimensions.

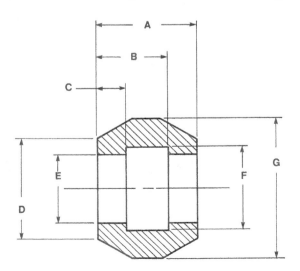

| DIMENSIONS | INCHES | mm |
|---|---|---|
| A | .50 | 12 |
| B | 1.25 | 32 |
| C | 1.75 | 44 |
| D | Ø1.75 | 44 |
| E | Ø1.25 | 32 |
| F | Ø1.50 | 38 |
| G | Ø2.50 | 64 |

## EX6-6

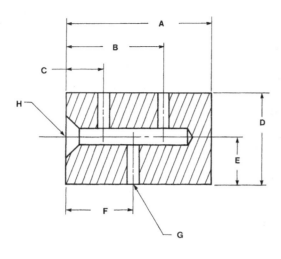

| DIMENSIONS | INCHES | mm |
|---|---|---|
| A | 3.00 | 72 |
| B | 2.00 | 48 |
| C | .75 | 18 |
| D | 2.00 | 48 |
| E | 1.00 | 24 |
| F | 1.38 | 33 |
| G | Ø.25 | 6 |
| H | Ø.375 X 2.50 DEEP<br>Ø.875 X 82° CSINK | Ø10 X 60 DEEP<br>Ø24 X 82° CSINK |

## EX6-7

Redraw the given top view and Section A-A; then sketch Sections B-B, C-C, and D-D.

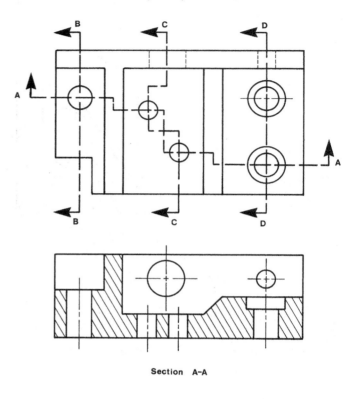

Section A-A

Redraw the given front views in Exercise Problems EX6-8 through EX6-11 and replace the given side orthographic view with the appropriate sectional view.

## EX6-8

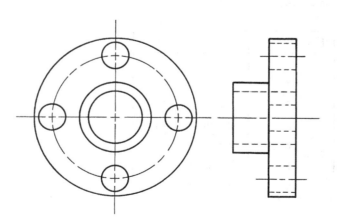

## EX6-9

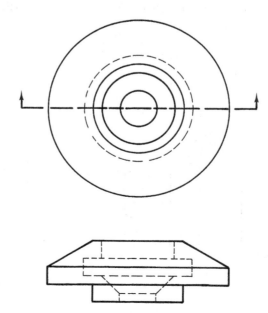

## EX6-10 Inches

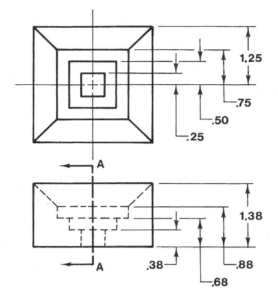

Object is symmetrical
about both
centerlines

## EX6-11

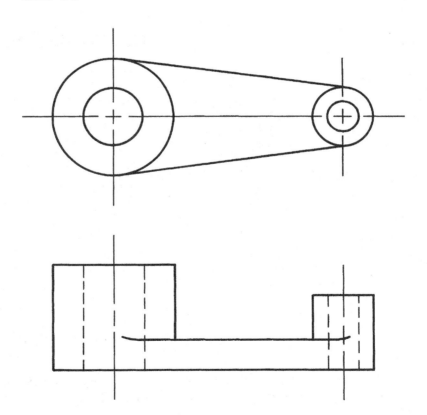

Redraw the given front views in Exercise Problems EX6-12 through EX6-15, and replace the given side orthographic view with the appropriate sectional view. The cutting plane is located on the vertical centerlines of the objects.

## EX6-12 Inches

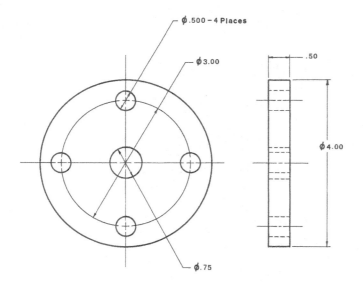

## EX6-13 Inches

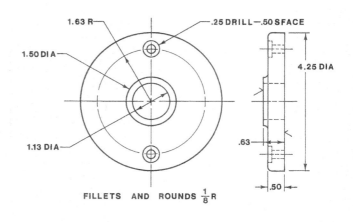

## EX6-14 Inches

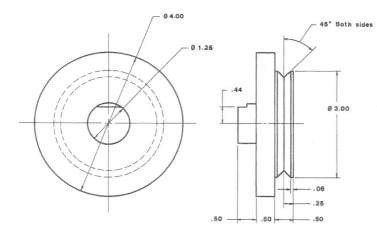

## EX6-15 Millimeters

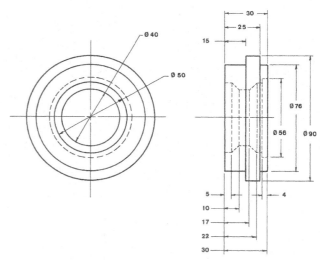

In Exercise Problems EX6-16 through EX6-19, draw the top orthographic view and the indicated sectional view.

## EX6-16 Millimeters

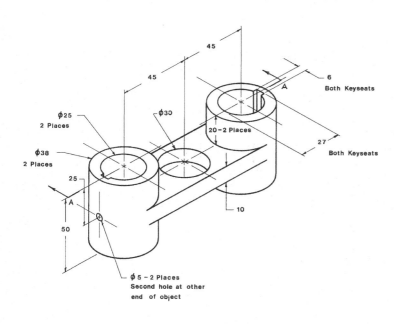

## EX6-17 Inches

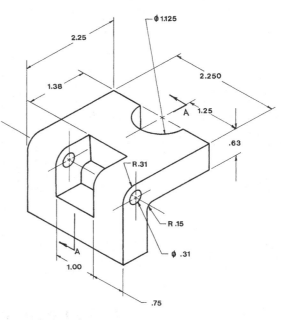

## EX6-18 Millimeters

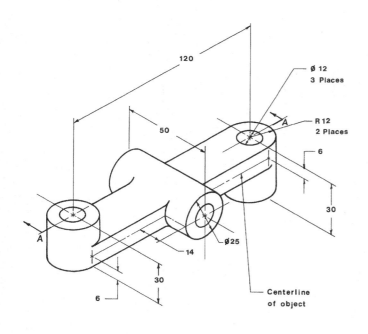

## EX6-19 Millimeters

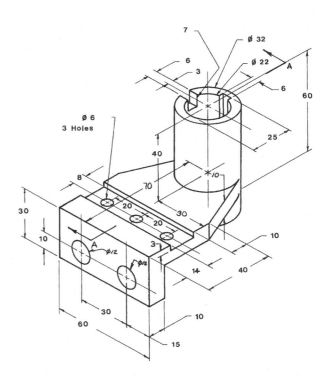

Redraw the given views and add the specified sectional views in Exercise Problems EX6-20 through EX6-34.

## EX6-20 Inches

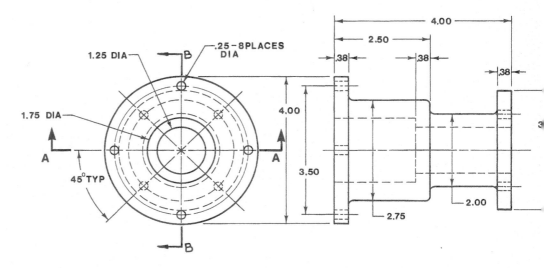

ALL FILLETS AND ROUNDS = R.125

## EX6-21 Inches

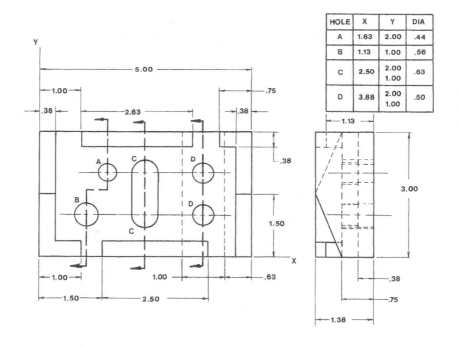

| HOLE | X | Y | DIA |
|------|------|-------------|------|
| A | 1.63 | 2.00 | .44 |
| B | 1.13 | 1.00 | .56 |
| C | 2.50 | 2.00 1.00 | .63 |
| D | 3.88 | 2.00 1.00 | .50 |

## EX6-22 Inches

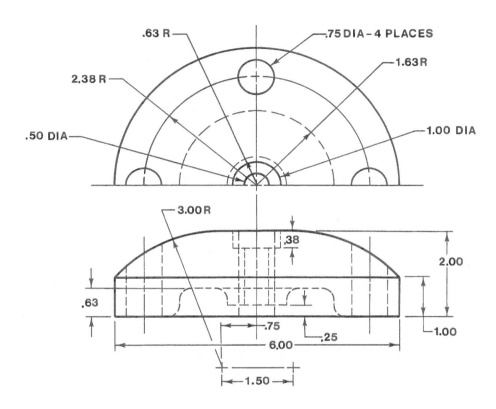

## EX6-23 Inches

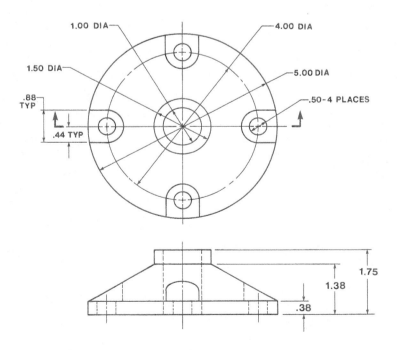

## EX6-24 Inches

Redraw the given front and top views and add Sections A-A, B-B, and C-C, as indicated.

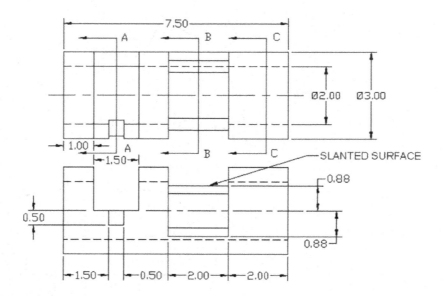

## EX6-25 Millimeters

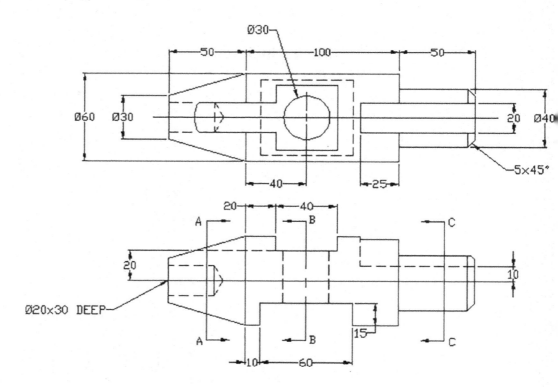

## EX6-26 Inches

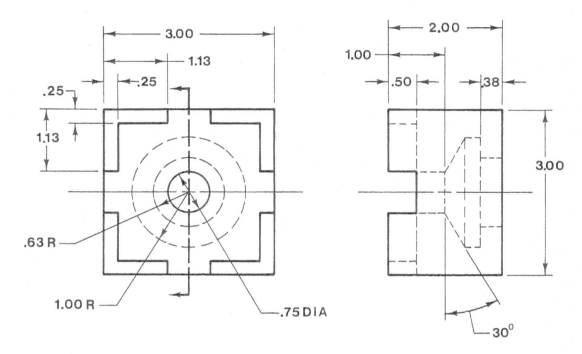

## EX6-27 Inches

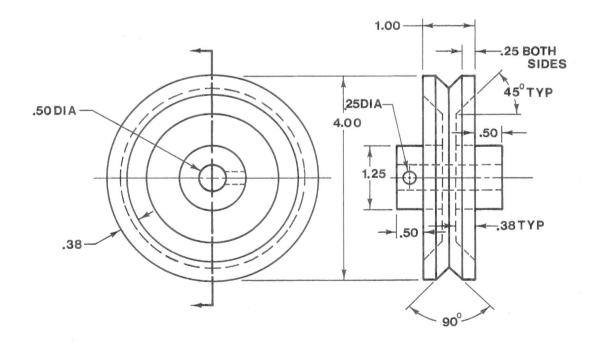

## EX6-28 Inches

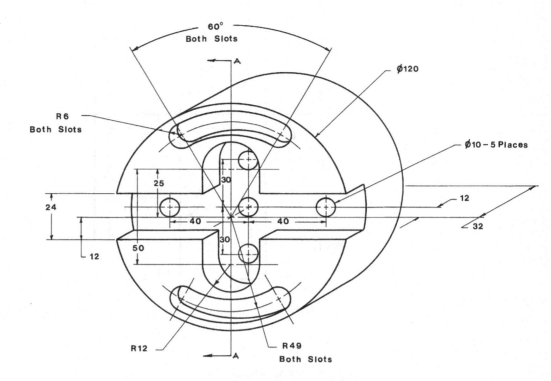

## EX6-29 Millimeters

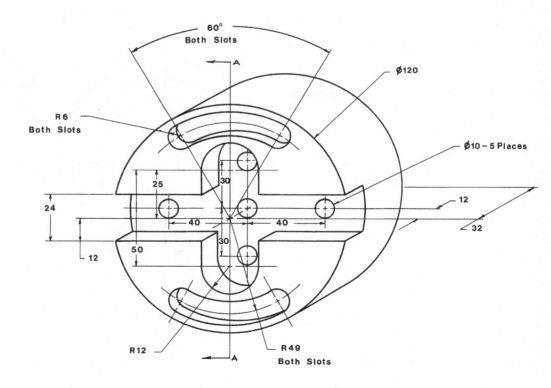

## EX6-30 Millimeters

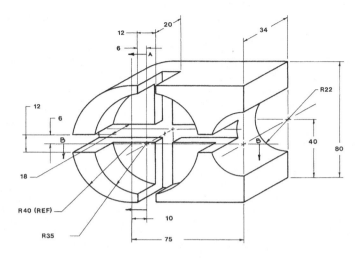

## EX6-31 Millimeters

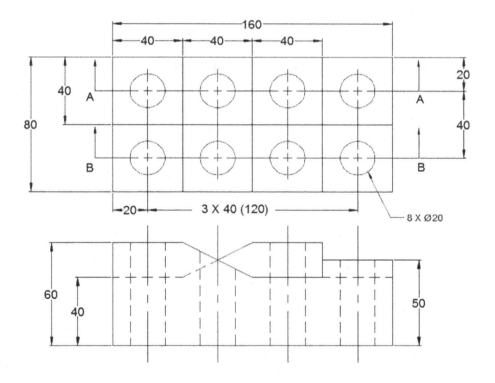

## EX6-32 Millimeters

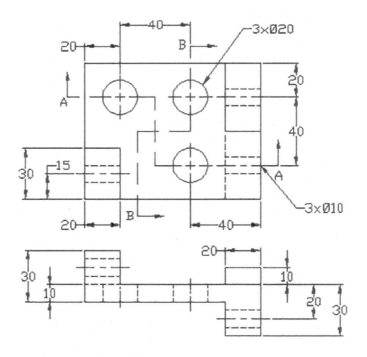

## EX6-33 Millimeters

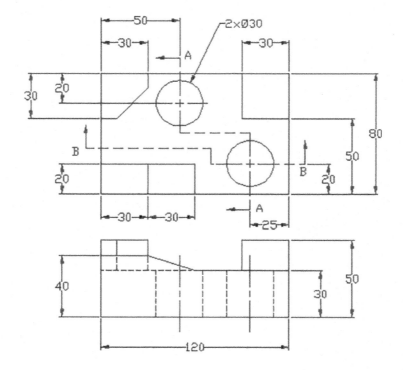

## EX6-34 Inches

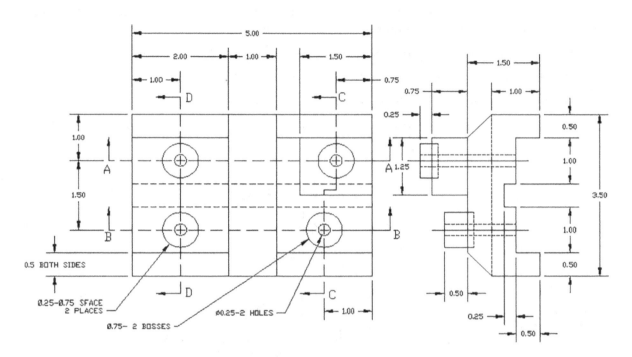

# EX6-35

New customer requirements dictate that a part be redesigned according to the given specifications. Draw a front view and a sectional view of the redesigned part.

**1** The diameters of the Ø9 internal access holes are to be increased to Ø12.

**2** The diameter of the internal cavity is to be increased to Ø30.

**3** The length of the internal cavity is to be increased from 33 to 50.

**4** All other sizes and distances are to be increased to maintain the same wall thickness.

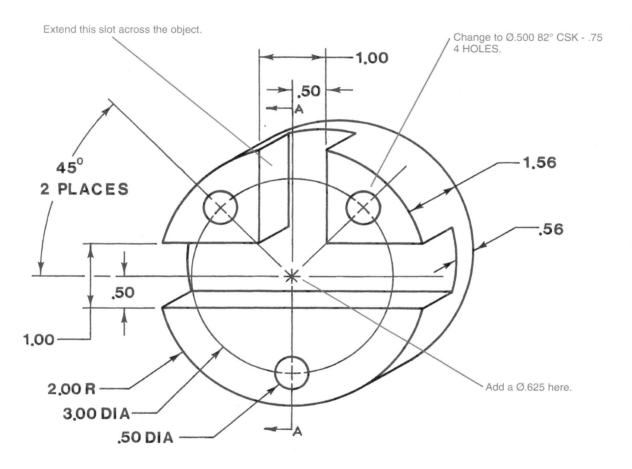

## EX6-36

An object is to be redesigned as follows:

**1** Extend the 1.00-inch vertical slot all the way through the object, creating four corner sections.

**2** Locate countersunk holes in each of the four corner sections. Note that two of the corner sections presently have Ø.50 holes. The countersink specifications are Ø.50 – 82°, Ø.75.

**3** Locate a Ø.625 hole in the center of the object.

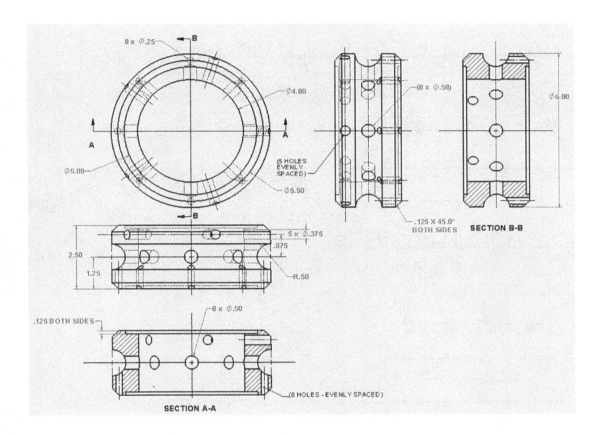

## EX6-37

Given the following front, top, and sectional views, create a 2D isometric drawing of the object.

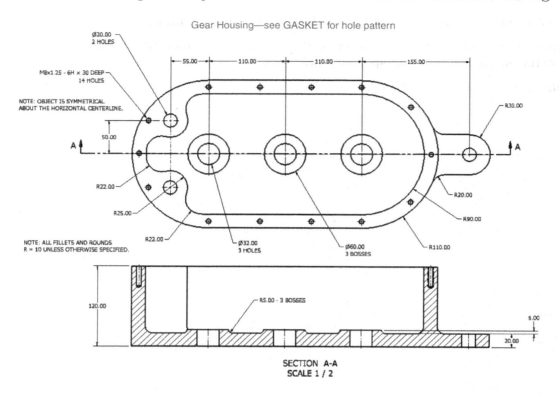

Gear Housing—see GASKET for hole pattern

SECTION A-A
SCALE 1 / 2

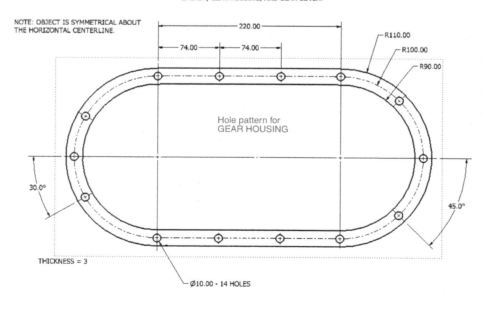

NOTE: HOLE PATTERN IS THE SAME FOR THE
GASKET, GEAR HOUSING, AND GEAR COVER.

NOTE: OBJECT IS SYMMETRICAL ABOUT
THE HORIZONTAL CENTERLINE.

Hole pattern for
GEAR HOUSING

## EX6-38

Given the following six views, create a 2D isometric drawing of the object.

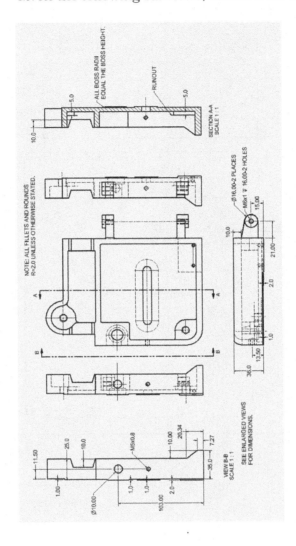

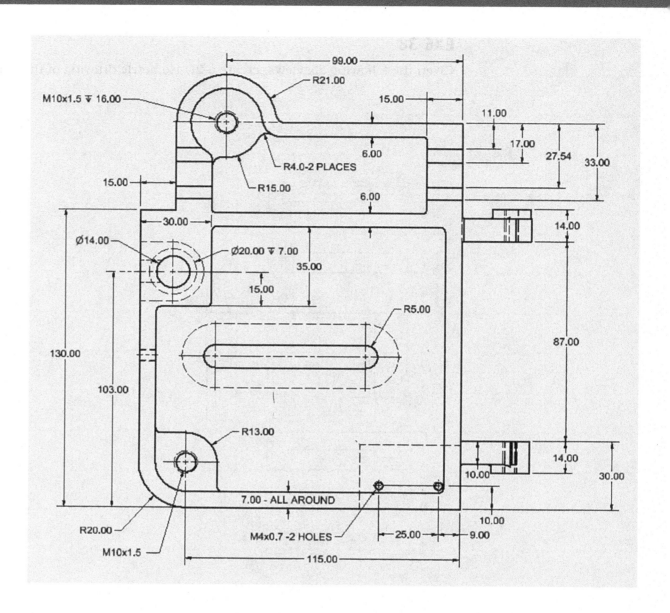

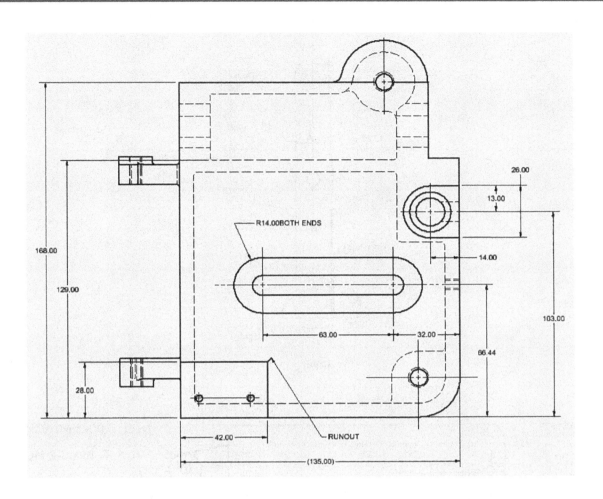

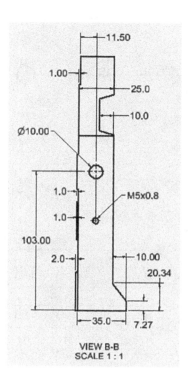

VIEW B-B
SCALE 1 : 1

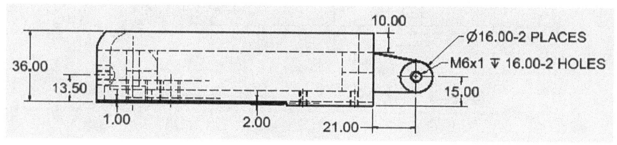

Ø16.00-2 PLACES

M6x1 ▼ 16.00-2 HOLES

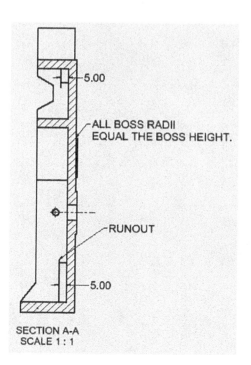

ALL BOSS RADII
EQUAL THE BOSS HEIGHT.

RUNOUT

SECTION A-A
SCALE 1 : 1

# 7 chapter seven

# Auxiliary Views

## 7-1 Introduction

*Auxiliary views* are orthographic views that are used to present true views of slanted and oblique surfaces. Slanted and oblique surfaces appear foreshortened or as edge views in normal orthographic views. Holes in the surfaces are elliptical, and other features are also distorted.

Figure 7-1 shows an object with a slanted surface that includes a hole drilled perpendicular to that surface. Note how the slanted surface is foreshortened in both the normal top and side views; also note that the hole appears as an ellipse in both of these views. The hole appears as an edge view with hidden lines in the front view, so none of the normal views show the hole as a circle.

**Figure 7-1**

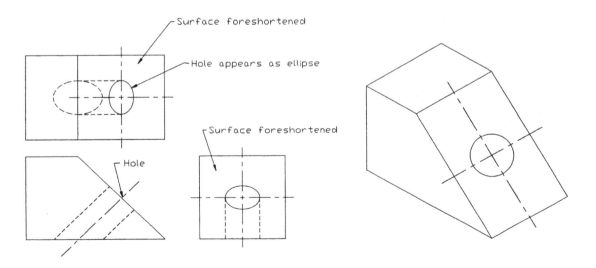

Figure 7-2 shows the same object shown in Figure 7-1. The front and side views are the same, but the top view is replaced with an auxiliary view. The auxiliary view shows the true shape of the slanted surface, and the hole appears as a circle.

**Figure 7-2**

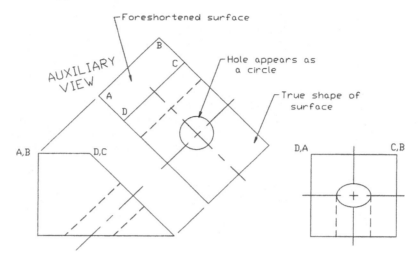

The auxiliary view in Figure 7-2 shows the true shape of the slanted surface but a foreshortened view of surface **A–B–C–D**. Positioning the auxiliary view to generate the true shape of the slanted surface foreshortened the other surfaces.

## 7-2 Projection Between Normal and Auxiliary Views

You can project information about an object's features between the normal views and any additional auxiliary views by establishing reference planes. A reference plane RPT is located between the top and front views of Figure 7-3. The plane appears as a horizontal line, and its location is arbitrary. In the example shown, the plane was located 10 millimeters from the top view.

**Figure 7-3**

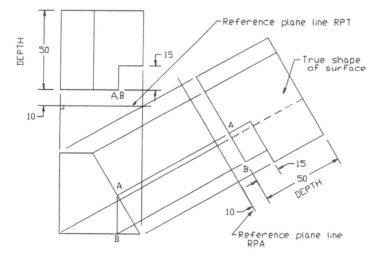
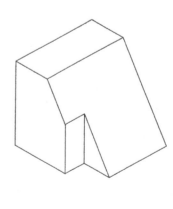

A second reference plane, RPA, is established parallel to the slanted surface at a location that prevents the auxiliary view from interfering with the top view. You can use the **Move** command to move the top view farther away from the front view, if necessary.

Information is projected from the front view into the auxiliary view with projection lines perpendicular to reference plane RPA.

The depth of the object is transferred from the top view to the auxiliary view. Figure 7-3 shows the 50-millimeter depth and 15-millimeter slot depth dimensioned in both the top and auxiliary views.

Figure 7-4 shows information projected from given front and side views into an auxiliary view. Reference planes RPS and RPA are located 10 millimeters from, and parallel to, the side and auxiliary views, and information is projected from the front view into the auxiliary view by lines perpendicular to plane RPA. The depth information is transferred from the side view to the auxiliary view.

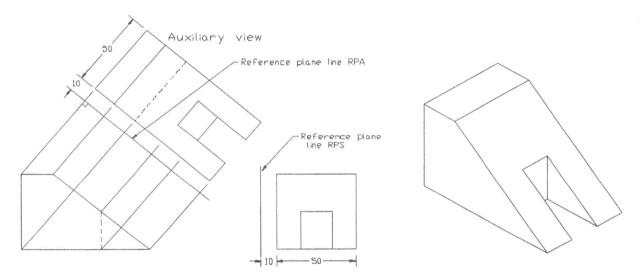

**Figure 7-4**

Figure 7-5 shows an object that has a slanted surface in the top view. The reference plane line, RPA, for the auxiliary view is located parallel to the slanted surface, and another reference plane, RPF (horizontal line), is established between the front and top views. Information is projected from the top view into the auxiliary view with lines perpendicular to RPA. The 30-millimeter height measurement is transferred from the front view into the auxiliary view.

Reference plane lines and projection lines drawn perpendicular to them are best drawn by rotating the drawing's axis system, indicated by the crosshairs, so that it is parallel to the slanted surface (Figure 7-6). You can create a separate layer for projection lines.

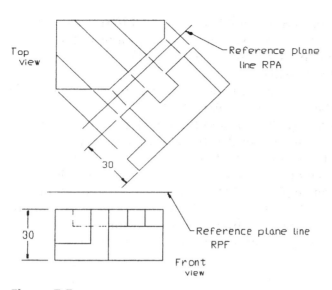
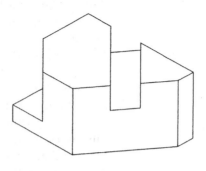

**Figure 7-5**

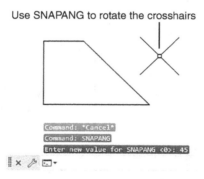

**Figure 7-6**

## Rotating the Drawing's Axis System

To enable easier drafting on a non-orthographic set of axes, you can use the **Snapang** (for *snap angle*) system variable to rotate the crosshairs.

**1** Type **Snapang** at the command prompt.

The command prompts are as follows:

```
Command: SNAPANG
Enter new value for SNAPANG <0>:
```

**2** Type **45** and press **Enter**.

The cursor rotates 45° counterclockwise (Figure 7-6). Any angle value, including negative values, may be used.

The grid also is rotated, and the **Snap** command limits the crosshairs to spacing aligned with the rotated axis. **Ortho** limits lines to horizontal and vertical relative to the rotated axis.

The angle value entered for **Snapang** is always interpreted as an absolute value. For example, if the procedure just described is repeated and a value of 60 is entered, the crosshairs advances only 15° from the present location or 60° from the system's absolute 0° axis system.

## 7-3 Drawing Problem

Figure 7-7 shows an object that includes a slanted surface. The front, top, and auxiliary views projected from the slanted surface were developed as follows (Figure 7-8):

**Figure 7-7**

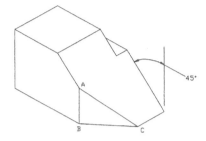

**Figure 7-8**

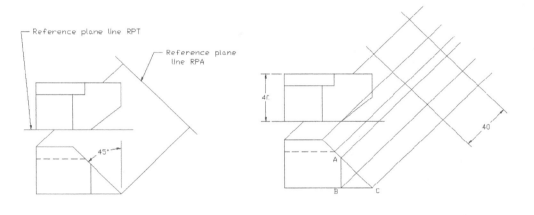

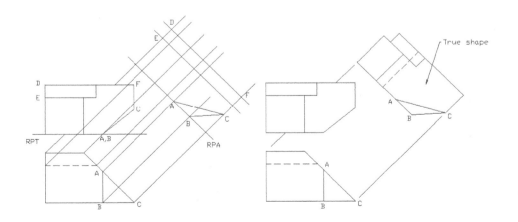

**1** Draw the front and top orthographic views as explained in Chapter 5.

Use the **Move** command to position the top view so that it does not interfere with the auxiliary view.

**2** Establish two reference plane lines: **RPT** parallel to the top view (horizontal line) and **RPA** parallel to the slanted surface (45° line).

In this example, the reference plane line for the top view is located along the lower edge of the view.

**3** Use **Snapang** to establish an axis system parallel to the slanted surface. The slanted surface is 45° to the horizontal.

**4** Turn on **Ortho** and draw a line parallel to the slanted surface.

Optionally create a layer for projection lines.

**5** Project lines perpendicular to RPA from the drawing's feature presented in the front view into the area of the auxiliary view. Use **Osnap Intersection** to ensure accuracy.

**6** Type **Dist** in response to a command prompt to determine the distance from the reference plane line, RPT, to the object's features.

**7** Use **Offset** to draw a line parallel to RPA at a distance equal to the distances of the object's features.

**8** Erase and trim any excess lines and save the drawing, if desired.

## 7-4 Transferring Lines Between Views

Objects are often measured so that only some of their edge lines are dimensioned. This means that **Offset** may not be used to transfer distances to auxiliary views until the line length is known. Three methods can be used to transfer an edge line of unknown length: Measure the line length by using **Dist**, and then use the determined distance with the **Offset** command; use grips, and rotate and move the line; or use **Copy**, **Modify**, and **Rotate** to relocate the line. The procedures are described next.

### Measuring the Length of a Line

**1** Type **Dist** at the command prompt.

The command prompts are as follows:
```
Command: Dist
Specify first point:
```

**2** Select one end of the line.

The **Osnap Endpoint** option helps identify the endpoint of the line. The intersection of one of the projection lines with a reference plane is usually used.
```
Specify second point:
```

**3** Select the other end of the line.

The following style display appears in the screen's prompt area:

```
Distance=40, Angle in X-Y Plane=45, Angle from the X-Y Plane=0
Delta X=28.2885, Delta Y=28.2885, Delta Z=0.0000
```

Figure 7-9 shows the meaning of the displayed distance information.

Record the distance and use it with the **Offset** command to locate the line's endpoints relative to a reference plane.

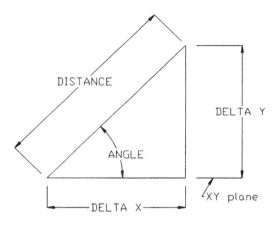

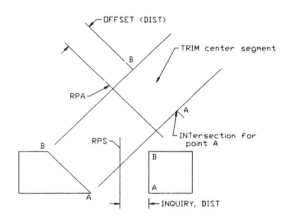

**Figure 7-9**

## Using Grips to Move a Line

**1** Copy the line and move the copy to an open area of the drawing.

**2** Click the line to display its grip points (refer to Section 3-15).

**3** Select the line's lower endpoint, right-click, and select **Rotate** (Figure 7-10).

**Figure 7-10**

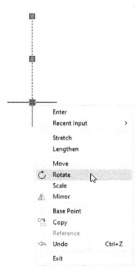

```
**ROTATE**
Specify rotation angle or [Base point Copy Undo Reference eXit]:
```

**4** Type **B** or click **Base point** at the command prompt. Select the lower endpoint as the base point.

**5** Type **45** and press **Enter**.

The **Dist** command can also be used to determine the angle of a slanted surface if it is not known. Note that the angle value returned depends on which of the endpoints is selected first.

**6** Select the line's lower endpoint again.

**7** Select **Move** from the right-click menu.

**8** Select the lower endpoint as the base point.

**9** Move the line to a new location or use dynamic input to define a new location.

## Rotating and Moving a Line

**1** Copy the line and move the copy to an open area of the drawing.

**2** Select **Rotate** from the **Modify** panel and rotate the line **45°** (refer to Section 3-15).

**3** Select **Move** from the **Modify** panel and relocate the line to the auxiliary view. Use **Osnap**, if necessary, to ensure accuracy.

## 7-5 Drawing Problem

Figure 7-11 shows an object that contains two slanted surfaces and two cutouts. Draw front and right-side orthographic views, as well as an auxiliary view (Figure 7-12).

**Figure 7-11**

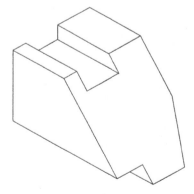

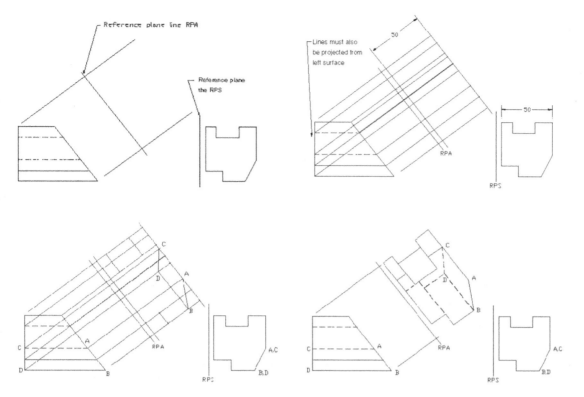

**Figure 7-12**

**1** Draw the front and side orthographic views as described in Chapter 5.

**2** Define a reference plane, **RPS**, between the front and side views.

**3** Use **Snapang (37.5)** to align the crosshairs with the slanted surface. The 37.5° value was determined by using the **Dist** command.

**4** Draw a reference plane line, **RPA**, parallel to the slanted surface, and project the features of the object into the auxiliary view area.

**5** Transfer the distance measurements from RPS and the side view into the auxiliary view. Label the various points as needed.

**6** Erase and trim any excess lines and save the drawing, if desired.

## 7-6 Projecting Rounded Surfaces

Rounded surfaces are projected into auxiliary views in the same way they are projected into the orthographic views as described in Chapter 5, Section 5-15. Additional lines are added to one of the orthographic views and then projected into the other orthographic view. The additional lines define a series of points that define the outside shape of the surface. The two views with the added lines project and transfer the points into the auxiliary view.

## 7-7 Drawing Problem

Figure 7-13 shows a cylindrical object that includes a slanted surface. Draw the front, side, and auxiliary views (Figure 7-14).

**1** Draw the front and side orthographic views.

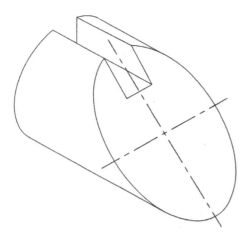

Figure 7-13

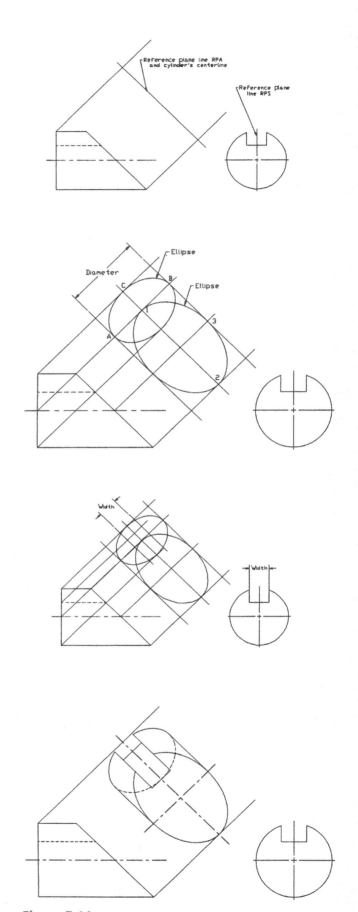

Figure 7-14

Draw a reference plane line, **RPS**.

In this example, the reference plane line is the side view's vertical centerline.

**3** Draw a reference plane line, **RPA**, parallel to the slanted surface. The reference plane line will also be used as the centerline for the auxiliary view.

In this example, the endpoints of both the major and minor axes of the projected elliptical auxiliary view are known, as is the angle of the auxiliary view. It is therefore not necessary to define points in the circular side view, as was done in Section 5-21. Enough information is present to draw the elliptical shape directly in the auxiliary view.

**4** Draw the elliptical surfaces in the auxiliary view, as shown.

**5** Transfer the width and location of the slot from the side view to the auxiliary view.

**6** Erase and trim any excess lines and save the drawing, if desired.

## 7-8 Projecting Irregular Surfaces

Auxiliary views of irregular surfaces are created by projecting information from given normal orthographic views into the auxiliary views in a manner similar to the way information is projected between orthographic views (refer to Section 5-9). The irregular surface is defined by a series of points along its edge line. The locations of the points are random, although more points should be used when the curve's shape is changing sharply than when the curve tends to be smoother.

## 7-9 Drawing Problem

Figure 7-15 shows an object that includes an irregular surface. Draw front and side orthographic and auxiliary views of the object (Figure 7-16). The procedure is described below.

**Figure 7-15**

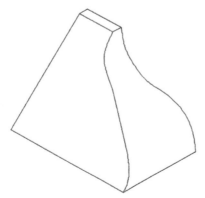

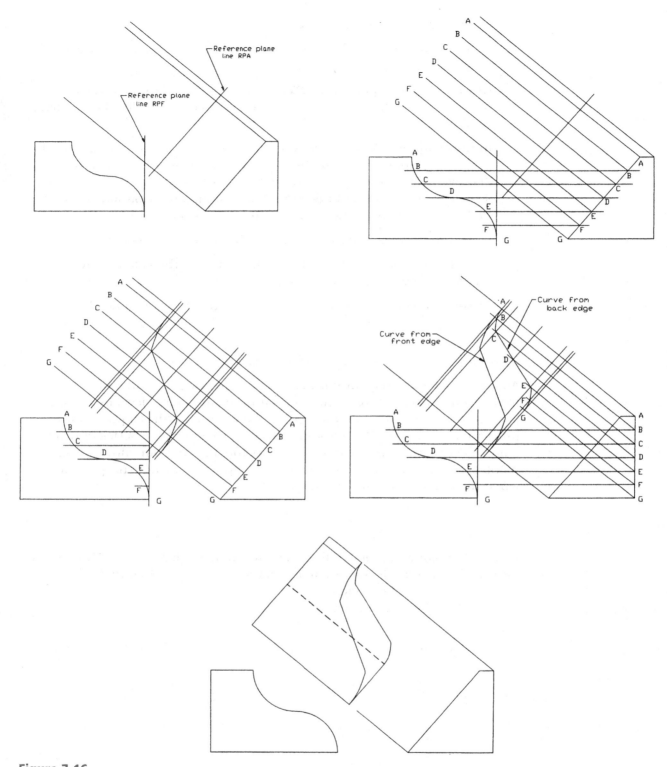

Figure 7-16

**1** Draw a front view and a side view.

**2** Draw two reference lines: **RPF** between the front and side views and **RPA** parallel to the slanted surface in the side view.

Use **Snapang** to align the crosshairs with the slanted surface.

**3** Define points along the irregular surface edge line in the front view and project the points into the side view by using horizontal lines.

**4** Project the points into the auxiliary view, using lines perpendicular to line RPA. Label the points and their projection lines.

**5** Transfer the depth measurements from RPS and the object's features, as well as the points defining the irregular curve, to the auxiliary view.

Type **Dist** in response to a command prompt to determine the distance from RPF to the points.

Use **Offset** to draw lines parallel to RPA.

**6** Use **Polyline**, **Edit Polyline**, and **Fit** to draw the irregular curve required in the auxiliary view. Use **Edit Vertex** to smooth the curve, if necessary.

**7** Project the points defined in the front view to the back surface (far-right vertical line) in the side view and project the points into the auxiliary view.

**8** Use **Polyline**, **Edit Polyline**, and **Fit** to draw the required irregular curve.

**9** Erase and trim any excess lines and save the drawing, if desired.

## 7-10 Drawing Problem

Figure 7-17 shows an isometric view of a block with a triangular notch. The notch depth is not consistent, and the notch is not parallel to any of the sides. Figure 7-18 shows a top view and an auxiliary view of the object. Redraw the given views and add the front and right-side views. The procedure is described as follows.

**1** Draw a reference plane line, **RPA**, parallel to the auxiliary view and a reference plane line, **RPT**, a horizontal line.

**Figure 7-17**

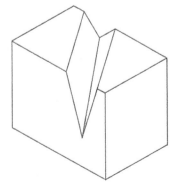

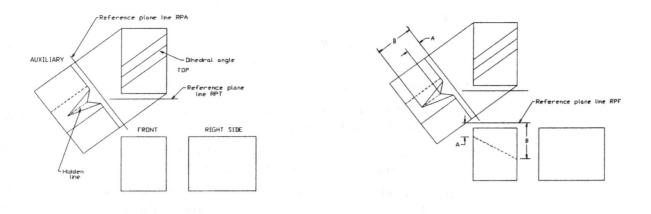

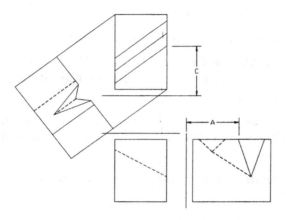

**Figure 7-18**

The object contains a dihedral angle (an angle between two planes), and the auxiliary view has been aligned with the vertex line of the angle. Reference plane RPA is perpendicular to the vertex of the dihedral angle's vertex.

**2** Project information from the top view and transfer information from the auxiliary view into the front view.

**3** Project information from the front view and transfer information from the top view into the side view.

**4** Erase and trim any excess lines and save the drawing, if desired.

## 7-11 Partial Auxiliary Views

Auxiliary views present true views of slanted and oblique surfaces, but in doing so, they generate foreshortened views of other surfaces. It is often clearer to create an auxiliary view of just the slanted surface and omit the surfaces that would be foreshortened. An auxiliary view that shows only one surface of an object is called a *partial auxiliary view*.

Figure 7-19 shows a front view and three partial views of the object: a partial top view and two partial auxiliary views. A broken line (refer to Section 6-14) may be used to show that the partial auxiliary view is part of a larger view that has been omitted. Likewise, hidden lines may or may not be included. Figure 7-20 shows a front view, a side view, and two partial auxiliary views of an object. Both the hidden lines and broken lines were omitted. If you are unsure about the interpretation of a view with hidden lines omitted, add a note to the drawing next to the partial views that says **ALL HIDDEN LINES OMITTED FOR CLARITY**.

**Figure 7-19**

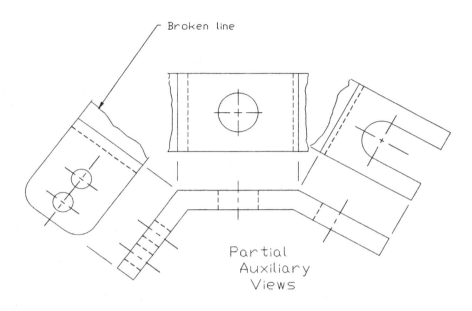

**Figure 7-20**

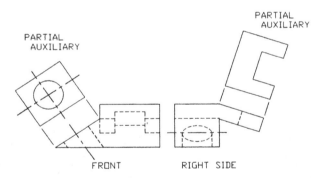

## 7-12 Sectional Auxiliary Views

Sectional views may also be drawn as auxiliary views. Figure 7-21 shows an auxiliary sectional view. The cutting plane line is positioned across the object. A reference plane line is drawn parallel to the cutting plane line, and information is projected into the auxiliary sectional view by use of lines perpendicular to the cutting plane line.

Figure 7-21

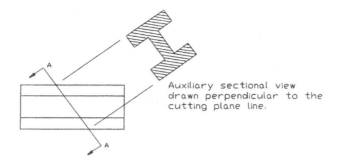

Auxiliary sectional view
drawn perpendicular to the
cutting plane line.

Figure 7-22 shows front, partial auxiliary, and auxiliary sectional views of an object. In this example, the partial sectional view was used to help clarify the shape of the object's feature that would appear vague in the normal top or side views.

**Figure 7-22**

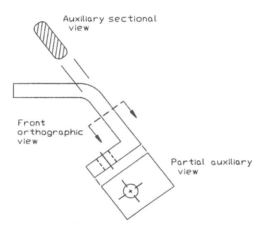

Auxiliary sectional view

Front orthographic view

Partial auxiliary view

## 7-13 Auxiliary Views of Oblique Surfaces

The true shape of an oblique surface cannot be determined by a single auxiliary view taken directly from the oblique surface. An auxiliary view shows the true shape of a surface only when it is taken at exactly 90° to the surface.

A *slanted surface* is a surface that is rotated about only one axis (Figure 7-23). One of the orthographic views must be an edge view of the surface (i.e., the surface appears as a line) for an auxiliary view created by projecting lines perpendicular to that view to show the true shape of the surface.

**Figure 7-23**

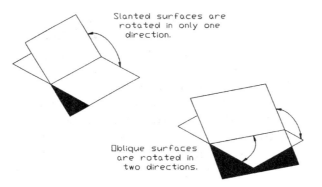

An *oblique surface* is a surface that is rotated about two axes (Figures 7-23 and 7-24). This means that none of the normal orthographic views will show the oblique surface as an edge view; there is no given end view of the surface. This, in turn, means that an auxiliary view taken directly from one of the given views will not be perpendicular to the surface and therefore will not show the true shape of the surface. An auxiliary view that shows an edge view of the surface must first be created; then a second auxiliary view taken perpendicular to one of the other normal orthographic views is needed to show the true shape of the surface.

**Figure 7-24**

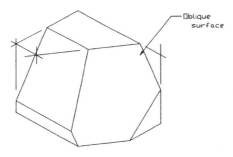

## 7-14 Secondary Auxiliary Views

Consider the object shown in Figure 7-25. What is the true shape of surface **A–B–C**? An auxiliary view taken perpendicular to the surface will show its true shape, but what is the angle for a plane perpendicular to the surface? Figure 7-26 shows the normal orthographic views of the object.

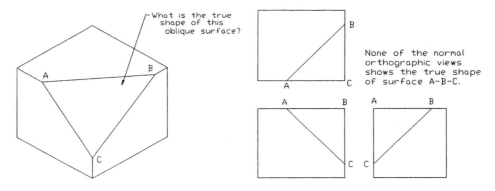

**Figure 7-25**          **Figure 7-26**

Start by choosing an edge line in the plane that is perpendicular to either the X or Y axis. Edge line **A–B** in the front view is a horizontal line, so it is parallel to the X axis. Take an auxiliary view aligned with the top view of the edge line (you're looking straight down the line). This auxiliary view will be perpendicular to the edge line and will generate an end view of the plane. A second auxiliary view can then be taken perpendicular to the end view that will show the true shape of the surface.

Figure 7-27 shows how a secondary auxiliary view is created for the object shown in Figure 7-25. The specific procedure is described next.

**Figure 7-27**

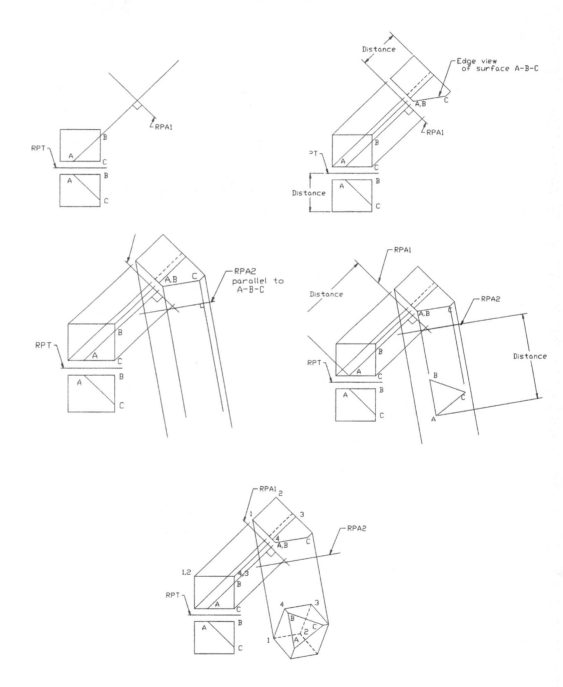

## Drawing the First Auxiliary View

**1** Draw the normal orthographic views of the object.

**2** Draw a reference plane, **RPT**, between the front and top views.

**3** Extend a line from the top view of line **A–B** in the area for the first auxiliary view.

Use the **Extend** command to draw a construction line slightly beyond the expected area of the first auxiliary view, then use the construction line as an **Extend** boundary line (refer to Section 2-23), and extend line **A–B** to the boundary. Erase the construction line.

**4** Draw a reference plane line, **RPA1**, perpendicular to the line **A–B** extension.

Use **Snapang** to align the crosshairs with the extension line. Use the **Dist** command to determine the line's angle if it is not known.

**5** Project the slanted surface of the object into the auxiliary view by using lines perpendicular to **RPA1**.

**6** Transfer the distance measurements from **RPT** and the front view as shown at top right in Figure 7-27.

**7** Erase and trim any excess lines and create the first auxiliary view.

The surface **A–B–C** should appear as a straight line. This is an edge view of surface **A–B–C**.

## Drawing the Secondary Auxiliary View

**1** Use **Snapang** and align the crosshairs with the end view of surface **A–B–C**. Use **Dist** to determine the angle of the edge view line.

**2** Draw a reference plane line, **RPA2**, parallel to the edge view of the surface (Figure 7-27, center left).

**3** Project the features of the object into the second auxiliary view, using lines perpendicular to **RPA2** (Figure 7-27, center right).

**4** Transfer the distance measurements from **RPA1** and the top view as shown in Figure 7-27, bottom.

**5** Erase and trim any excess lines and save the drawing, if desired.

The secondary auxiliary view shows the true shape of surface **A–B–C**. Figure 7-28 shows another example of a secondary auxiliary view used to show the true shape of an oblique surface. In this example, the first auxiliary view was taken from line **F–A** in the front view because it is a vertical line in the side view. The distance measurements came from the top view. The procedure used is the same as described previously.

Figure 7-28

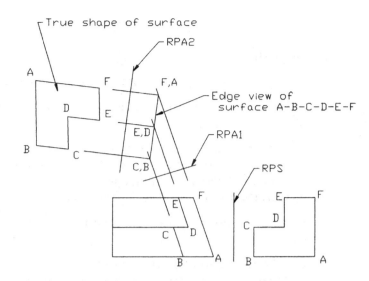

The auxiliary view shown in Figure 7-28 includes only the oblique surface. This is a partial auxiliary view. The purpose of the auxiliary view is to determine the true shape of the oblique surface. All of the other surfaces would be foreshortened, not showing their true shape, if included in the auxiliary views.

## 7-15 Drawing Problem

What is the true shape of the plane shown in Figure 7-29?

Figure 7-29

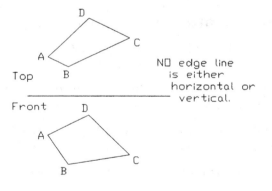

None of the edge lines are horizontal or vertical lines, so a line that is either horizontal or vertical must be added. In Figure 7-29, a horizontal line is added between the top and front views, and can then be used to generate the two auxiliary views needed to define the true shape of the plane.

The procedure is as follows (Figure 7-30):

**1** Draw a horizontal line from point **A** in the front view.

Use **Osnap Intersection** with **Ortho** on and draw the line across the view. Use **Trim** to remove the excess portion of the line.

**Figure 7-30**

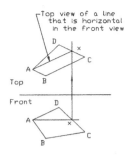

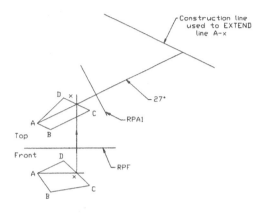

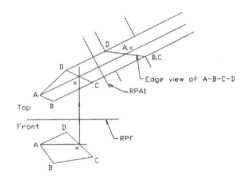

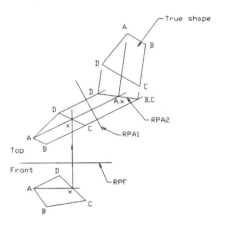

**2** Define the intersection of the new line with one of the plane's edge lines (**D–C**) as **x**.

**3** Project line **A–x** into the top view.

Optionally, create a layer for projection lines.

The location of point **A** is already known in the top view. The location of point **x** in the top view is found by drawing a vertical line from point **x** in the front view so that the line intersects line **D–C** in the top view. Use **Osnap Intersection** with **Ortho** on to ensure accuracy.

**4** Extend line **A–x** into the area for the first auxiliary view.

Draw a construction line to use as a boundary line for the **Extend** command.

**5** Draw two reference plane lines: **RPT** between the front and top views, and **RPA1**, perpendicular to the extension of line **A–x**.

Use **Snapang** to align the crosshairs with the extension of line **A–x**.

**6** Project the plane's corner points into the area of the first auxiliary view from the top view. Transfer the distance measurements from RPT and the front view.

Use **Dist** to determine the distance from **RPF** and the corner points of the surface. Use **Offset** to transfer the point distance from **RPF** to **RPA1**. Use **Trim** to remove the internal portion of the offset lines. This helps clarify the drawing by removing excess lines from the auxiliary view, but you can retain intersection points needed to draw lines by using **Osnap Intersection**.

The end view of the plane should appear as a straight line.

**7** Draw a third reference plane line, **RPA2**, parallel to the end view of the plane, and project the plane's corner points into the secondary auxiliary view area.

**8** Transfer the depth distances from **RPA1** and the top view to **RPA2** and the secondary auxiliary view.

**9** Erase and trim any excess lines and save the drawing. if desired.

The secondary auxiliary view shows the true shape of surface **A–B–C–D**.

## 7-16 Secondary Auxiliary View of an Ellipse

Figure 7-31 shows the front and side views of an oblique surface and includes a foreshortened view of a hole—that is, an ellipse. Also included are two auxiliary views, the second of which shows the hole as a circle.

**Figure 7-31**

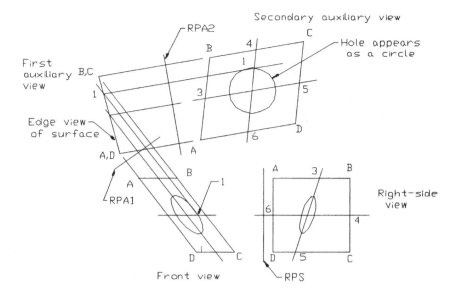

The ellipse is projected by first determining the correct projection angle that produces an edge view of surface **A–B–C–D**. In this example, line **B–C** appears as a vertical line in the side view, so its front view can be used to project the required edge view.

It is known that the secondary view of the surface shows the hole as a circle, so only a radius value need be carried between the views. In this example, point 1 in the front view was projected into the first auxiliary view and then into the second auxiliary view, thereby defining the radius of the circle.

The hole is located at the center of the surface, which means that its centerlines are located on the midpoints of the edge lines in the secondary auxiliary views. If the hole's center point were not in the center of the surface, the intersections of the hole's centerlines with the surface's edge lines would also have to be projected into the secondary auxiliary view to accurately locate the hole.

# 7-17 EXERCISE PROBLEMS

Given the outlines for front, side, and auxiliary views shown in Exercise Problem EX7-1, substitute one of the side views shown in Exercise Problems EX7-1A through EX7-1D and complete the front and auxiliary views. All dimensions are in millimeters.

## EX7-1

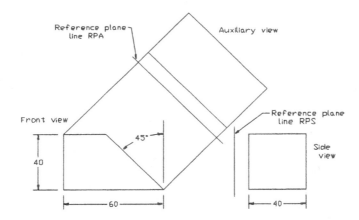

## EX7-1A

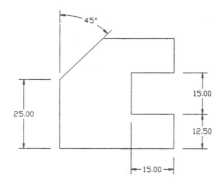

## EX7-1B

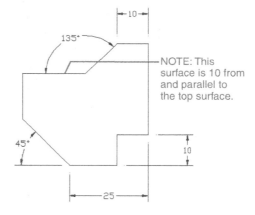

## EX7-1C

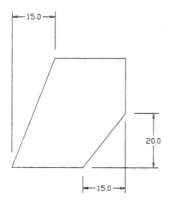

## EX7-1D

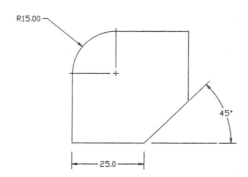

Given the outlines for front, side, and auxiliary views, as shown, substitute one of the side views shown in Exercise Problems EX7-2A through EX7-2D and complete the front and auxiliary views. All dimensions are in millimeters.

Draw two orthographic views and an auxiliary view for each of the objects shown.

## EX7-2

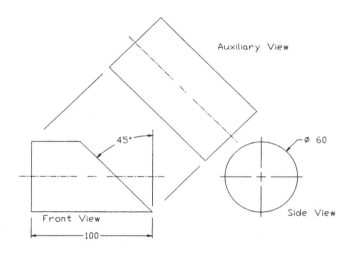

## EX7-2A

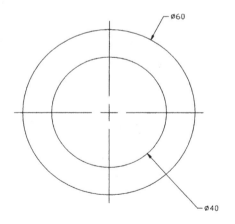

## EX7-2B

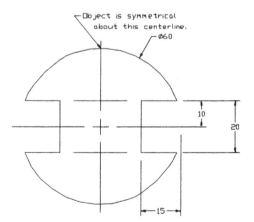

## EX7-2C

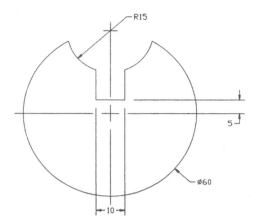

## EX7-2D

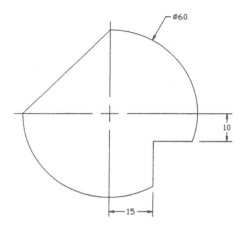

Draw two orthographic views and an auxiliary view for each of the objects in Exercise Problems EX7-3 through EX7-6.

## EX7-3 Millimeters

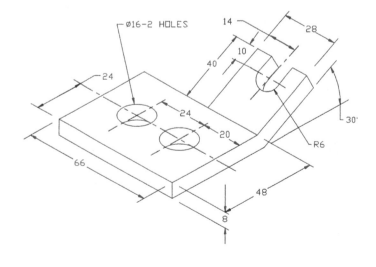

## EX7-4 Millimeters

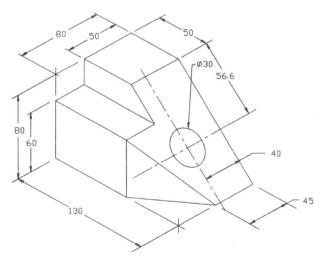

## EX7-5 Inches

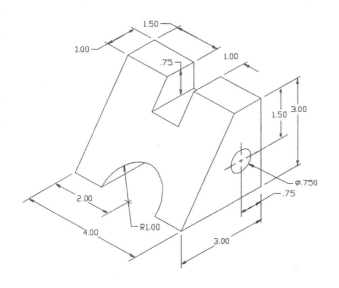

## EX7-6 Millimeters

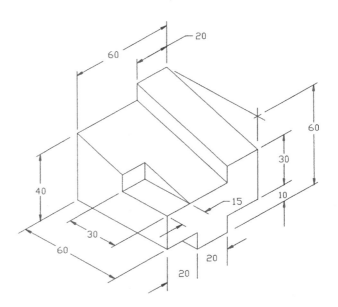

Redraw the given orthographic views in Exercise Problems EX7-7 through EX7-10 and add the appropriate auxiliary view.

## EX7-7 Millimeters

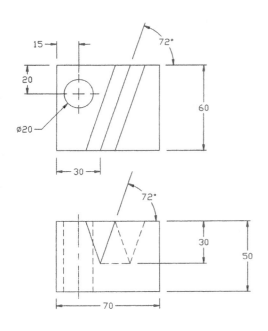

## EX7-8 Millimeters

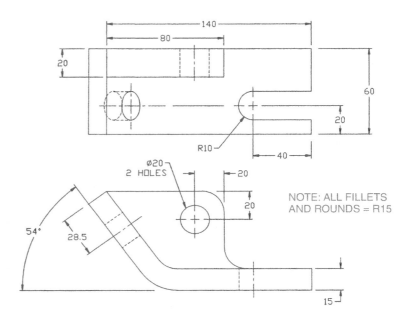

NOTE: ALL FILLETS AND ROUNDS = R15

## EX7-9 Inches

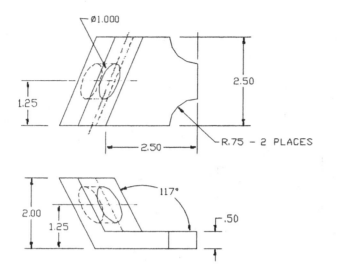

## EX7-10 Millimeters

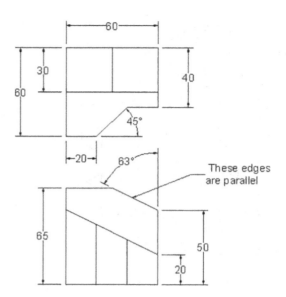

Draw two orthographic views and an auxiliary view for each of the objects in Exercise Problems EX7-11 through EX7-40.

## EX7-11 Millimeters

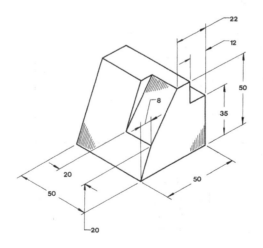

## EX7-12 Millimeters

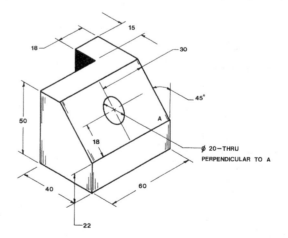

## EX7-13 Millimeters

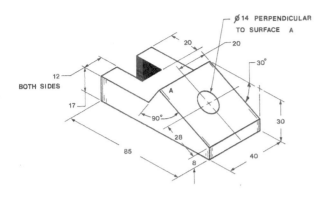

## EX7-14 Millimeters

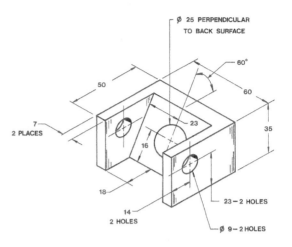

## EX7-15 Inches

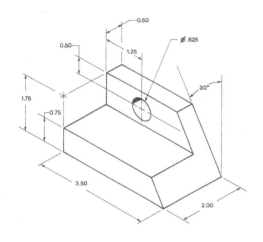

## EX7-16 Inches

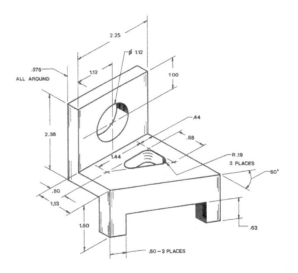

## EX7-17 Millimeters

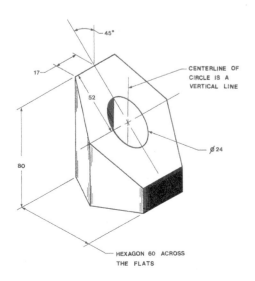

## EX7-18 Millimeters

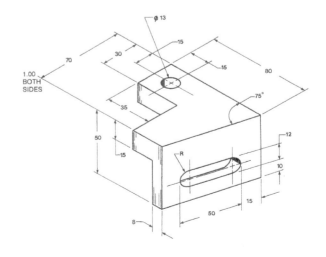

## EX7-19 Millimeters

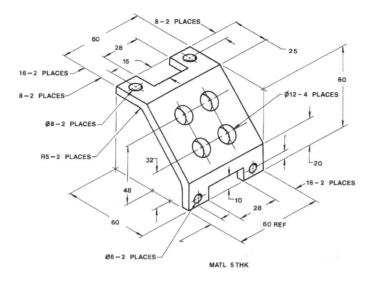

## EX7-20 Inches

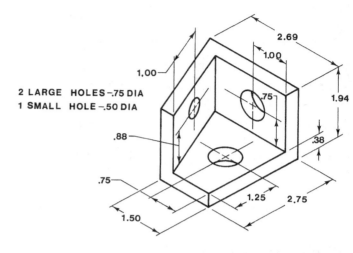

2 LARGE HOLES –.75 DIA
1 SMALL HOLE –.50 DIA

## EX7-21 Millimeters

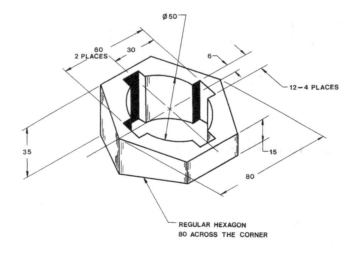

REGULAR HEXAGON
80 ACROSS THE CORNER

## EX7-22 Millimeters

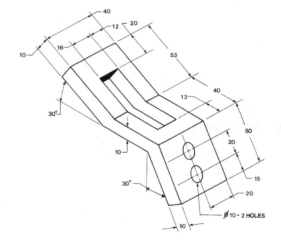

## EX7-23 Inches

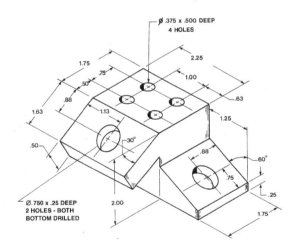

## EX7-24 Millimeters

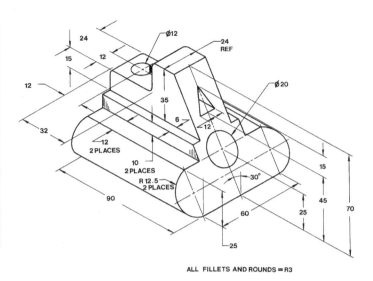

ALL FILLETS AND ROUNDS = R3

## EX7-25 Inches

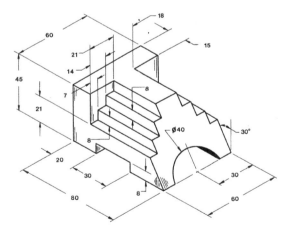

## EX7-26 Millimeters

## EX7-27 Millimeters

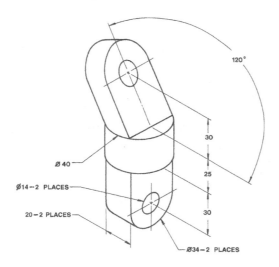

## EX7-28 Millimeters

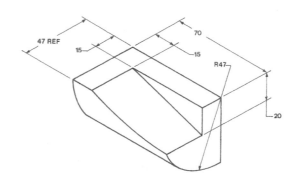

## EX7-29 Millimeters

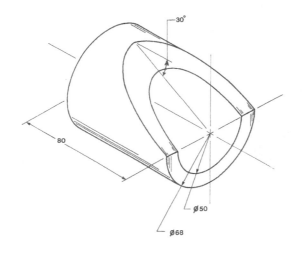

## EX7-30 Millimeters

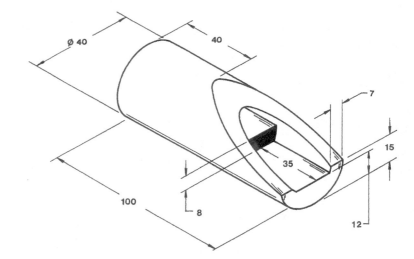

## EX7-31 Inches

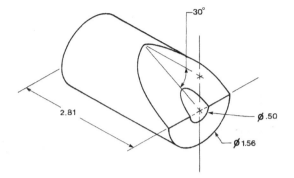

## EX7-32 Millimeters

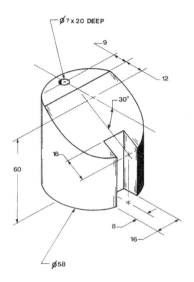

## EX7-33 Millimeters

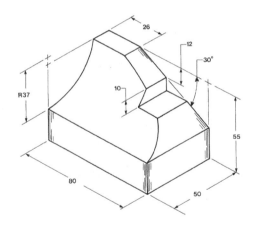

## EX7-34 Millimeters

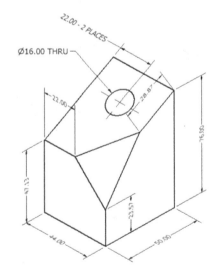

## EX7-35 Millimeters

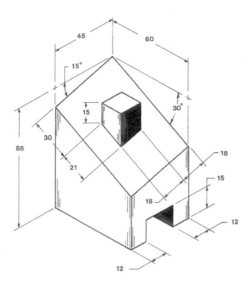

## EX7-36 Inches

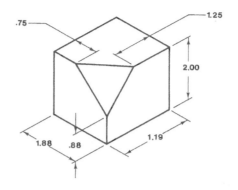

## EX7-37 Inches

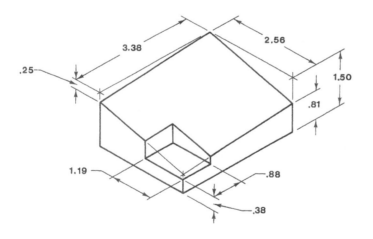

## EX7-38 Inches

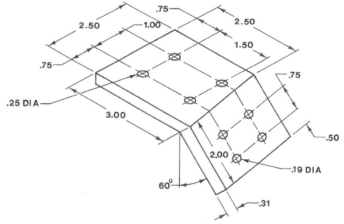

## EX7-39 Millimeters

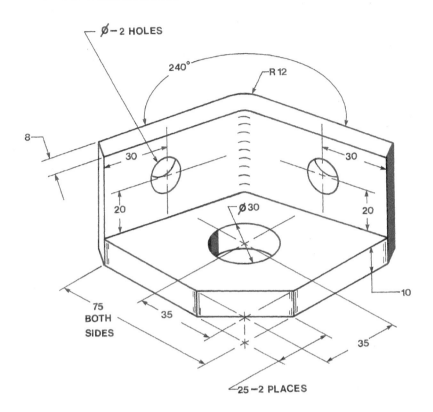

## EX7-40 Millimeters

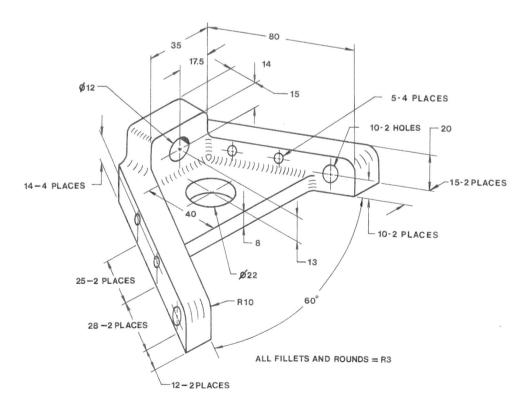

Draw at least two orthographic views and one auxiliary view for each of the objects in Exercise Problems EX7-41 through EX7-44.

## EX7-41 Inches

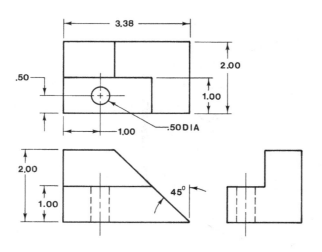

## EX7-42 Inches

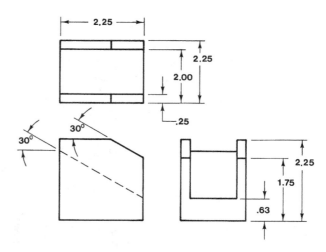

## EX7-43 Inches

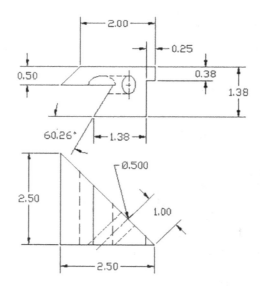

## EX7-44 Inches

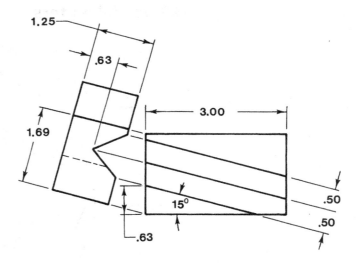

Use a secondary auxiliary view to find the true shape of the planes in Exercise Problems EX7-45 through EX7-50.

## EX7-45 Millimeters

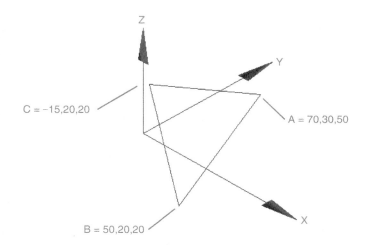

C = -15,20,20

A = 70,30,50

B = 50,20,20

## EX7-46 Millimeters

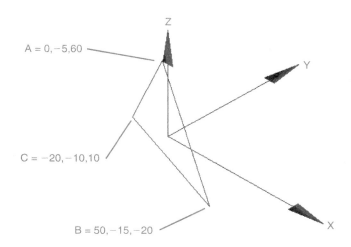

A = 0,-5,60

C = -20,-10,10

B = 50,-15,-20

## EX7-47 Millimeters

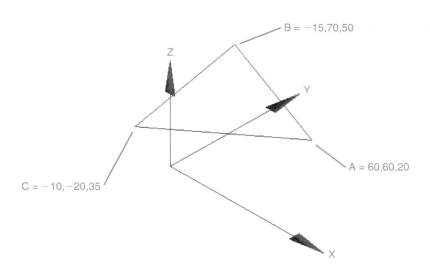

B = -15,70,50

A = 60,60,20

C = -10,-20,35

### EX7-48 Inches (Scale: 4:1)

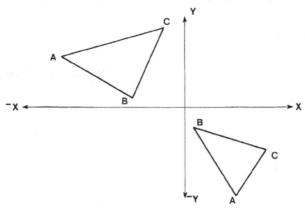

|   | TOP | | SIDE | |
|---|---|---|---|---|
|   | X | Y | X | Y |
| A | −2.30 | .96 | .96 | −1.68 |
| B | −.98 | .15 | .15 | −.40 |
| C | −.40 | 1.50 | 1.50 | −.80 |

### EX7-49 Millimeters (Scale: 2:1)

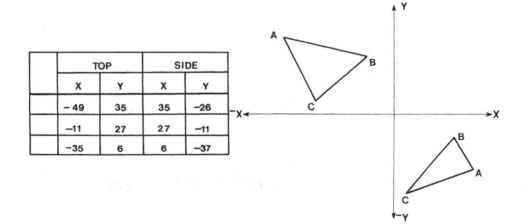

|   | TOP | | SIDE | |
|---|---|---|---|---|
|   | X | Y | X | Y |
|   | −49 | 35 | 35 | −26 |
|   | −11 | 27 | 27 | −11 |
|   | −35 | 6 | 6 | −37 |

### EX7-50 Inches (Scale: 3:1)

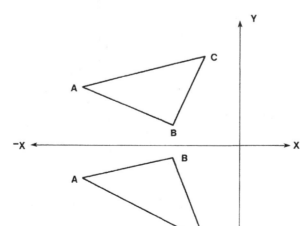

|   | FRONT | | TOP | |
|---|---|---|---|---|
|   | X | Y | X | Y |
| A | −2.80 | −.60 | −2.80 | 1.05 |
| B | −1.17 | −.20 | −1.17 | .35 |
| C | −.61 | −1.62 | −.61 | 1.62 |

## EX7-51 Millimeters

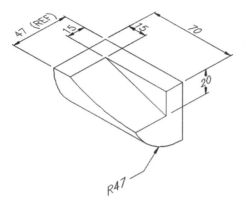

Redesign the given object to include two Ø10 holes in the slanted surface. The holes should be centered along the longitudinal axis, and spaced so that the distance between the holes' centers equals the distance from the holes' centers to the upper and lower edges of the slanted surface. The holes should be perpendicular to the slanted surface.

Draw the front, top, and side views of the object, plus an auxiliary view of the slanted surface. Include the new holes in the slanted surface.

## EX7-52 Millimeters

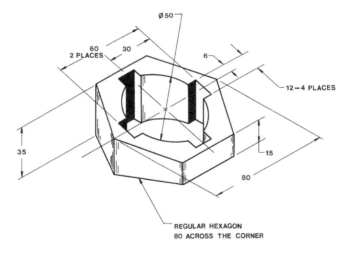

Redesign the given object so that the outside shape is a regular heptagon (seven-sided polygon) 80 across the flats, with the inside Ø50 hole intersected by six evenly spaced slots each 12 wide. Draw front and top orthographic views and an auxiliary view of the object.

## EX7-53 Millimeters

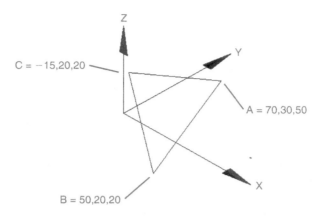

Calculate the area of the given plane. Redesign the plane so that the new plane is congruent to the original but has an area equal to 1.5 times that of the original area. Draw and label the true shape of the new plane relative to the X, Y, and Z axes.

# 8 chapter eight

# Dimensioning

## 8-1 Introduction

Adding dimensions to a drawing can be time-consuming, but dimensions are the most important part of any drawing because they are what is used to build the object being drawn. All the graphical elements are simply visual tools to help in reading the dimensions. AutoCAD provides a number of dimension types and enables users to document practically any component of an object. Figure 8-1 shows examples of the many dimension types you can create.

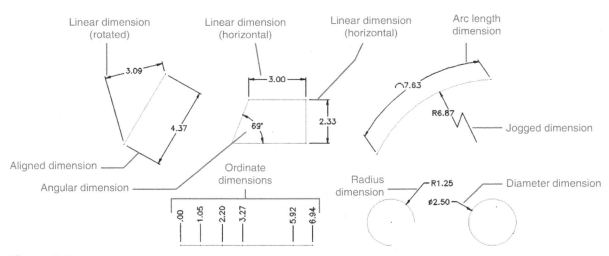

**Figure 8-1**

This chapter introduces the **Dimensions** panel of the **Annotate** tab (Figure 8-2). The chapter first explains dimensioning terminology and conventions and then presents an explanation of each tool available in the **Dimensions** panel. The chapter also demonstrates how dimensions are applied to drawings and gives examples of standard drawing conventions and practices.

Figure 8-2

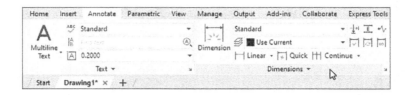

## 8-2 Terminology and Conventions

### Some Common Terms

Here are some commonly used terms related to dimensions (Figure 8-3):

- **Dimension lines:** On mechanical drawing, lines between extension lines that end with arrowheads and include numerical dimensional values located within the lines. On architectural drawings, lines between extension lines that end with tick marks and include numerical dimensional values above the lines. Dimension lines are normally parallel to the object or distance they describe.

Figure 8-3

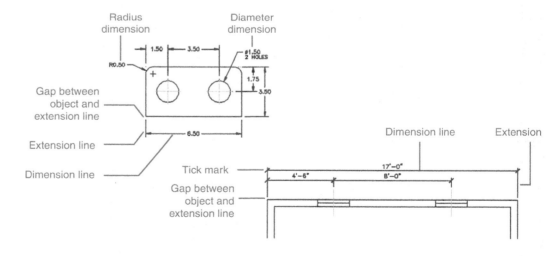

- **Extension lines:** Lines that extend away from an object and allow dimensions to be located off the surface of an object. Extension lines are normally perpendicular to the object or distance being dimensioned. There is a small gap between an extension line and an object, and an extension line usually extends slightly beyond the dimension line.

- **Leader lines:** Lines drawn at an angle, not horizontally or vertically, that are used to dimension specific shapes such as holes. The starting point of a leader line includes an arrowhead. Numerical values are drawn at the end opposite the arrowhead.

- **Linear dimensions:** Dimensions that define the straight-line distance between two points.

- **Angular dimensions:** Dimensions that define the angular value, measured in degrees, between two straight lines.

- **Radial dimensions:** Dimensions that define the radius or diameter of an arc or a circle.

## Some Dimensioning Conventions

Standard rules in drafting apply to dimensions as well as everything else. Standardization makes drawings easier to read by others and is essential in creating any kind of drafting documentation. Here are some conventions in dimensioning (see Figure 8-4):

- Dimension lines are drawn evenly spaced; that is, the distance between dimension lines is uniform. A general rule of thumb is to locate dimension lines about 1/2 inch, or 15 millimeters, apart.

**Figure 8-4**

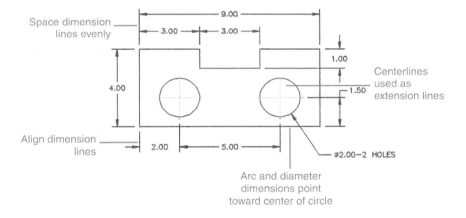

- There should be a noticeable gap between the edge of a part and the beginning of an extension line. This serves as a visual break between the object and the extension line. The visual difference between the linetypes is emphasized by using different lineweights for the two types of lines.

- A leader line in a radius or diameter dimension defines the size of a hole and should be positioned so that the arrowhead points toward the center of the hole.

- Centerlines may be used as extension lines. No gap is used when a centerline is extended beyond the edge lines of an object.

- Dimension lines should be aligned whenever possible to give a drawing a neat, organized appearance.

## Some Common Errors to Avoid

Dimensioning is complicated, and the rules can take some getting used to. Figure 8-5 shows a few common errors to avoid:

- Avoid crossing extension lines. Place longer dimensions farther away from the object than shorter dimensions.

Figure 8-5

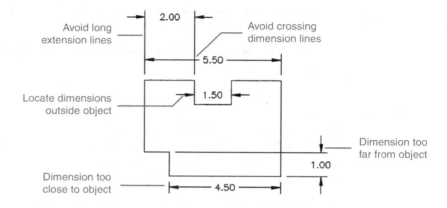

- Do not locate dimensions within cutouts; always use extension lines.

- Do not locate any dimension too close to an object. Dimension lines should be at least 1/2 inch, or 15 millimeters, from the edge of the object.

- Avoid long extension lines. Locate dimensions in the same general area as the feature being defined.

## 8-3 Linear Dimensions

The **Linear** dimension tool is used to create horizontal and vertical dimensions.

### Creating a Linear Dimension

Create basic linear dimensions with the **Linear** dimension tool. Linear dimensions can be horizontal or vertical, depending on where you drag the crosshairs to place the dimension line. Select the extension line locations or origins to create linear dimensions.

**1** Select **Linear** on the **Dimensions** panel of the **Annotate** tab (Figure 8.6).

    Command: _dimlinear

    Specify first extension line origin or <select object>:

**2** Select the starting point for the first extension line.

    Specify second extension line origin:

**Figure 8-6**

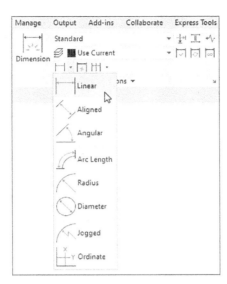

**3** Select the starting point for the second extension line.

`[MText Text Angle Horizontal Vertical Rotated]:`

**4** Locate the dimension line by moving the crosshairs to the desired location.

**5** Press the left mouse button to place the dimension.

The dimension text locations shown in Figure 8-7 are the default setting locations. The location and style can be changed using the **Dimension Style** command discussed in Section 8-4.

## Creating a Vertical Dimension

The vertical dimension shown in Figure 8-7 was created using the same procedure demonstrated for the horizontal dimension, except that different extension line origin points were selected. AutoCAD automatically switches from horizontal to vertical dimension lines as you move the cursor around an object.

If there is confusion between horizontal and vertical lines when adding dimensions—that is, if you don't seem to be able to generate a vertical line—type **V** and press **Enter** in response to the following prompt:

`[MText Text Angle Horizontal Vertical Rotated]:`

AutoCAD now draws vertical dimension lines.

## Creating a Horizontal Dimension by Selecting the Object to Be Dimensioned

If you are dimensioning a specific object rather than a distance between objects, you can select the object directly to dimension it (Figure 8-7).

**1** Select **Linear** from the **Dimensions** panel.

`Command: _dimlinear`

`Specify first extension line origin or <select object>:`

Figure 8-7

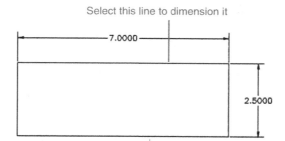

Select this line to dimension it

7.0000

2.5000

**2** Right-click.

```
Select object to Dimension:
```

**3** Select the line to be dimensioned.

This option allows you to select the distance to be dimensioned directly. The option applies only to horizontal and vertical lengths. Aligned dimensions, although linear, are created by using the **Aligned** tool.

## Changing the Default Dimension Text Using the Text Option

AutoCAD automatically creates a text value for a given linear distance. A different value or additional information can be added, as described next (Figure 8-8).

Figure 8-8

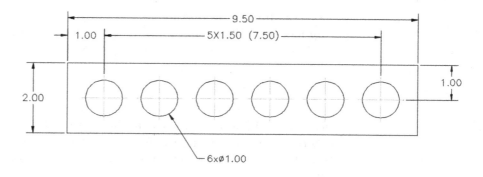

**1** Select **Linear** from the **Dimensions** panel.

```
Command: _dimlinear
Specify first extension line origin or <select object>:
```

**2** Select the starting point for the first extension line.

```
Specify second extension line origin:
```

**3** Select the starting point for the second extension line.

```
[MText Text Angle Horizontal Vertical Rotated]:
```

**4** Type **t** and press **Enter**.

```
Enter dimension text <7.50>:
```

The value given is the linear value of the distance selected. In this example, more information is required, so the default distance value must be modified. To retain the true distance in the dimension, type open and closed angle brackets (**<>**) where the true distance should go.

**5** Type **5 × 1.50 (<>)** and press **Enter**.

The additional information appears as part of the dimension text.

> **NOTE**
>
> AutoCAD uses a pair of closed angle brackets to indicate where the true text should go. If you do not add the angle brackets, the entire dimension value will be replaced with what you type. If you want a blank dimension with no text, enter **T** for the text option, press the **Spacebar**, and then place the dimension.

## Changing the Default Dimension Text with the Mtext Option

**1** Select **Linear** from the **Dimensions** panel.

```
Command: _dimlinear
Specify first extension line origin or <select object>:
```

**2** Select the starting point for the first extension line.

```
Specify second extension line origin:
```

**3** Select the starting point for the second extension line.

```
[MText Text Angle Horizontal Vertical Rotated]:
```

**4** Type **m** and press **Enter**.

The **Text Editor** contextual tab appears (Figure 8-9). The text value appears in a box below the **Text Editor** tab. To remove the existing text, highlight the text and press the **Delete** key. You can then type new text into the box. In the example shown, by typing **%%P<>**, the default value of 9.50 was replaced with a plus/minus symbol followed by the true distance value returned by the angle brackets.

**Figure 8-9**

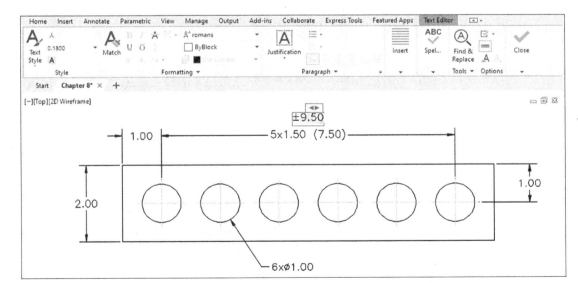

You can add information before or after the default text by placing the cursor in the appropriate place and typing the additional information.

You can edit the dimension text in the same way as you edited regular drawing text (refer to Section 2-15). Figure 8-10 shows the **Font** drop-down menu. To access the available fonts, double-click the dimension text to display the **Text Editor** contextual tab. In the **Formatting** panel, click the arrow next to the **Font** name.

**Figure 8-10**

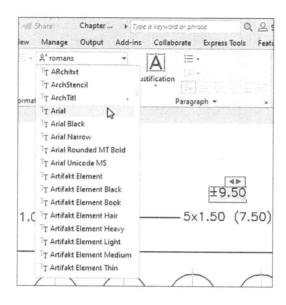

Figure 8-11 shows the text **Color** option that can be used to change the color of text.

**Figure 8-11**

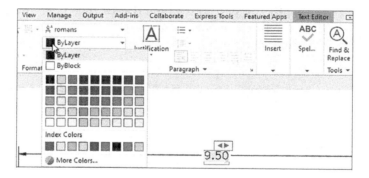

## Editing an Existing Dimension

Figure 8-12 shows a figure with an existing 7.00 - 2 PLACES dimension.

**1** Click the existing dimension.

Blue grips appear on the dimension text, the arrows, and the definition points of the dimension.

**Figure 8-12**

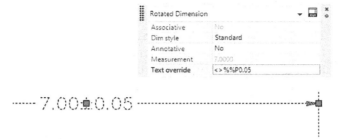

**2** Move the cursor away from the figure, right-click, and select **Quick Properties**.

The **Quick Properties** mini-palette appears.

**3** Click the **Text override** box and highlight the dimension text value **7.00 - 2 PLACES**.

**4** Enter the new text value. In this example, enter **<>%%P0.05**.

The closed angle brackets indicate the true distance value. The ± sign is created by typing two percent symbols and the letter P (**%%P**).

**5** Close the **Quick Properties** palette by pressing the **Esc** key.

Figure 8-13 shows the edited dimension.

**Figure 8-13**

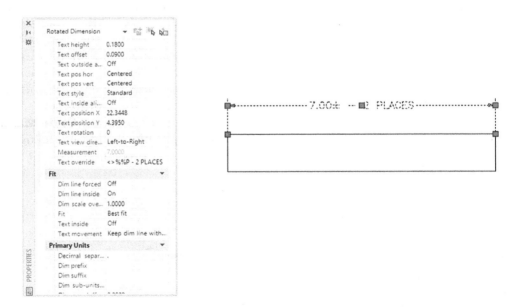

You can also edit dimension text in the **Properties** palette. Open the **Properties** palette by clicking a dimension, right-clicking one of the grips, and selecting **Properties**. Scroll down the palette to **Text override** and enter the new values (Figure 8-13).

> **NOTE**
> You can also access the **Text Editor** by double-clicking the existing dimension.

## 8-4 Dimension Styles

The **Dimension Style Manager** establishes the dimension styles that control the appearance and format of dimensions. Open the **Dimension Style Manager** by clicking the arrow in the lower-right corner of the **Dimensions** panel of the **Annotate** tab (Figure 8-14).

**Figure 8-14**

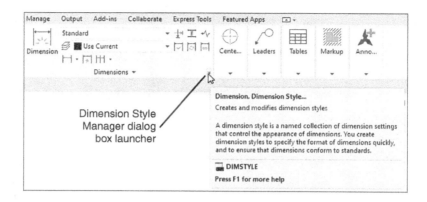

A great variety of dimension styles are used to create technical drawings. The differences in styles may be the result of different drawing conventions. For example, when following North American conventions, architects locate dimensions above the dimension lines, and mechanical engineers locate dimensions within the dimension lines. AutoCAD works in decimal units, whether millimeters or inches are assumed, so parameters set for inches are not usable for millimeter drawings. The **Dimension Style Manager** allows you to conveniently choose and set dimension parameters that suit your particular drawing requirements.

Figure 8-15 shows the **Dimension Style Manager** dialog box. Open the **Dimension Style Manager** by clicking its dialog box launcher, the arrow at the right end of the **Dimensions** panel title.

**Figure 8-15**

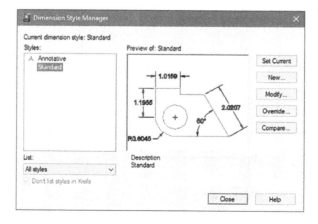

This section explains how to use the **Modify** option to change the **Standard** style settings to suit a specific drawing requirement. The **Set Current**, **New**, **Override**, and **Compare** options are used to create new custom dimension styles designed to meet specific applications. Click **Modify...**

on the first screen of the **Dimension Style Manager** to begin. Figure 8-16 shows the **Primary Units** tab of the **Modify Dimension Style: Standard** dialog box.

**Figure 8-16**

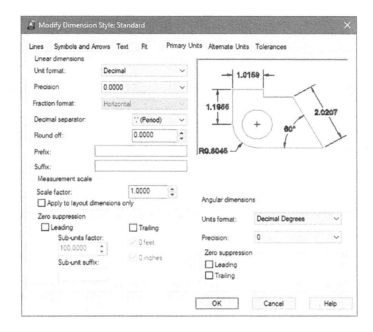

## Changing the Scale of a Drawing

Drawings are often drawn to scale because a part is either too big to fit on a sheet of drawing paper or too small to be seen. For example, a microchip circuit must be drawn at several thousand times its actual size in order to be seen.

Drawing scales are written according to the following formats:

- SCALE: 1 = 1
- SCALE: FULL
- SCALE: 1000 = 1
- SCALE: .25 = 1

In each example, the value on the left indicates the scale factor. A scale factor value greater than 1 indicates that the drawing is larger than actual size. A scale factor value less than 1 indicates that the drawing is smaller than actual size.

Regardless of the drawing scale selected, the dimension values must be the true measure. Figure 8-17 shows the same rectangle drawn at two different scales. The top rectangle is drawn at a scale of 1 = 1, or its true size. The bottom rectangle is drawn at a scale of 2 = 1, or twice its true size. In both examples, the 3.00 dimension remains the same.

Figure 8-17

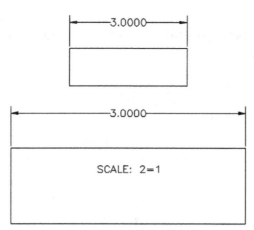

The **Scale factor** edit box on the **Primary Units** tab of the **Modify Dimension Style: Standard** dialog box is used to change the dimension values to match different drawing scales. Figure 8-18 shows the measurement scale set to a factor of 0.5000. If the drawing scale is 2 = 1, as shown in Figure 8-17, then the scale factor for **Measurement scale** must be 0.5000. Compare the preview in Figure 8-16 with the preview in Figure 8-18, in which the scale factor has been changed.

Figure 8-18

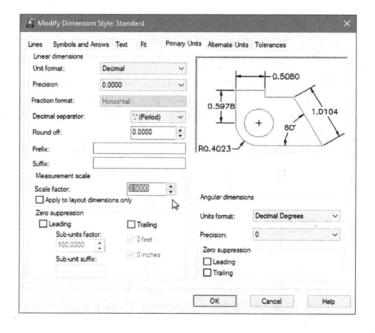

## Using the Text Tab

Figure 8-19 shows the **Text** tab of the **Modify Dimension Style: Standard** dialog box. You can use this tab to change the height of dimension text or the text placement. In Figure 8-20, the text height is changed from the default value of 0.1800 to the new value 0.3000. The preview box shows the resulting changes in both the text and how it will be positioned on the drawing.

**Figure 8-19**

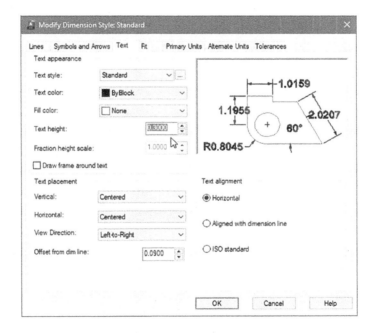

**Figure 8-20**

Figure 8-21 shows text located above the dimension. This change was created using the **Vertical** drop-down list in the **Text placement** area.

Figure 8-21

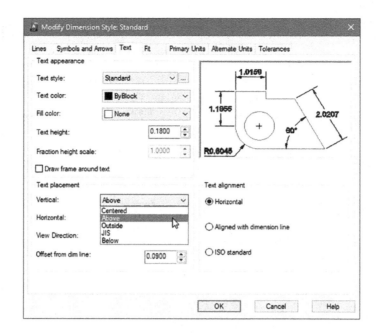

Figure 8-22 shows text aligned with the direction of the dimension lines in accordance with ISO (International Organization for Standardization) standards. This change was made by clicking the **ISO standard** radio button in the **Text alignment** area. Note that dimensions in this book are created in compliance with ANSI (American National Standards Institute) standards.

Figure 8-22

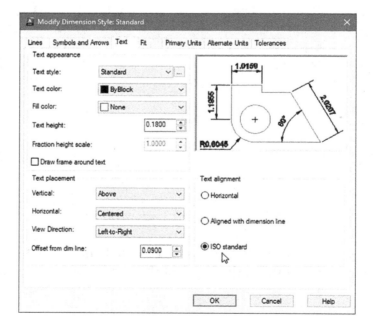

## 8-5 Units

It is important to understand that dimension values are not the same as the mathematical units defined in the **Drawing Units** dialog box (refer to

Section 1-7). Dimension values are manufacturing instructions and always include a tolerance, even if the tolerance value is not stated. Manufacturers use a predefined set of standard dimensions that are applied to any dimension value that does not include a written tolerance. Standard tolerance values vary from organization to organization.

Figure 8-23 shows a chart of standard tolerances.

**Figure 8-23**

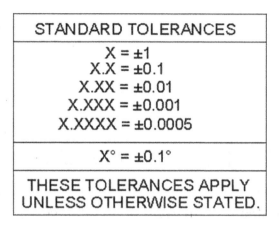

| STANDARD TOLERANCES |
|:---:|
| X = ±1 |
| X.X = ±0.1 |
| X.XX = ±0.01 |
| X.XXX = ±0.001 |
| X.XXXX = ±0.0005 |
| X° = ±0.1° |
| THESE TOLERANCES APPLY UNLESS OTHERWISE STATED. |

In Figure 8-24, a distance is dimensioned twice: once as 2.75 and a second time as 2.7500. Mathematically, these two values are equal, but they are not equal according to the same manufacturing instruction. The 2.75 value could, for example, have a standard tolerance of ±0.01, whereas the 2.7500 value could have a standard tolerance of ±0.0005. A tolerance of ±0.0005 is more difficult and therefore more expensive to manufacture than a tolerance of ±0.01.

**Figure 8-24**

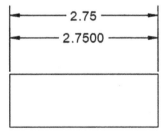

Figure 8-25 shows examples of units expressed in millimeters, decimal inches, and architectural units. A zero is not required to the left of the decimal point for decimal inch values less than one. Millimeter values do not require zeros to the right of the decimal point. Architectural units should always include the foot (') and inch (") symbols. Millimeter and decimal inch values never include symbols; the units are defined in the title block of a drawing.

Figure 8-25

MILLIMETERS
| 0.25 | 0.5 | 0.033 |
| 32 | 1.45 | 3 |

INCHES
| 25 | 5 | .003 |
| 32.00 | 145.0 | 3.000 |

ARCHITECTURAL UNITS
| 0'-0 1/2" | 8" | 2'-8" |

## Preventing a Zero from Appearing to the Left of the Decimal Point

**1** Open the **Dimension Style Manager** by clicking the arrow in the lower-right corner of the **Dimensions** panel of the **Annotate** tab.

**2** Click **Modify**.

The **Modify Dimension Style: Standard** dialog box appears.

**3** Select the **Primary Units** tab (Figure 8-26).

Figure 8-26

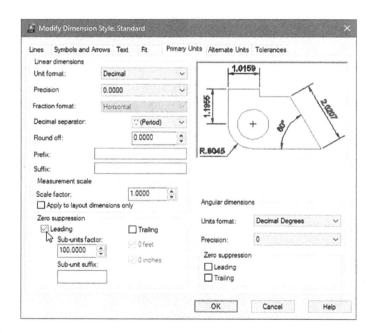

**4** Select the **Leading** checkbox in the **Zero suppression** area.

A check mark appears in the box, indicating that the function is on.

**5** Click **OK** and then **Close** to return to the drawing.

Save the change, if desired. You can now dimension using any of the dimension commands, and no zeros will appear to the left of the decimal points. Figure 8-27 shows the results.

Figure 8-27

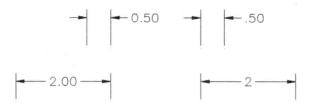

## Changing the Number of Decimal Places in a Dimension Value

**1** Open the **Dimension Style Manager** by clicking the arrow in the lower-right corner of the **Dimensions** panel of the **Annotate** tab.

**2** Click **Modify**.

The **Modify Dimension Style: Standard** dialog box appears.

**3** Select the **Primary Units** tab.

**4** Click the arrow to the right of the **Precision** drop-down list.

A list of precision options cascades down (Figure 8-28).

Figure 8-28

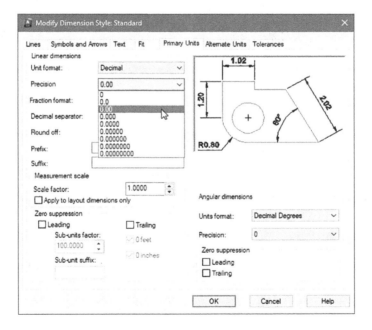

**5** Select the desired precision.

Save the changes, if desired. You can now dimension using any of the dimension commands, and the resulting values will be expressed with the selected precision.

## 8-6 Aligned Dimensions

*Aligned dimensions* are a particular form of linear dimensions that must be created with the **Aligned** dimension tool. Aligned dimensions are created by selecting an object or picking a distance. The resulting dimension line will be parallel with the object or selected points (Figures 8-29 and 8-30).

**Figure 8-29**

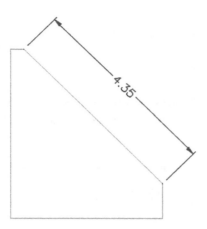

**Figure 8-30**

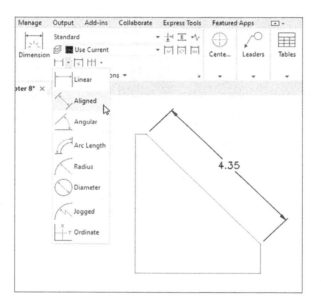

## Creating an Aligned Dimension

**1** On the **Dimensions** panel of the **Annotate** tab, click the down arrow beside the **Linear** tool and select **Aligned**.

Command: _dimaligned

Specify first extension line origin or <select object>:

**2** Select the first extension line origin point.

Specify second extension line origin:

**3** Select the second extension line origin point.

```
[Mtext Text Angle]:
```

**4** Select the location for the dimension line.

Figure 8-30 shows an aligned dimension with the dimension text aligned with the dimension line.

## Using Text Options

**1** Select **Aligned** from the **Linear** flyout on the **Dimensions** panel.

```
Command: _dimaligned
Specify first extension line origin or <select object>:
```

**2** Press **Enter**.

```
Select object to dimension:
```

**3** Select the line.

```
[Mtext Text Angle]:
```

**4** Select the dimension line location.

A response of **M** to the prompt line in step 3 activates the **Multiline Text** tool (refer to Section 2-15). The **Text** option can be used to replace or supplement the default text generated by AutoCAD.

A response of **A** to the prompt in step 3 activates the **Angle** option. The **Angle** option allows you to change the angle of the text within the dimension line.

## 8-7 Radius and Diameter Dimensions

Figure 8-31 shows an object that includes both arcs and circles. The general rule is to dimension arcs with radius dimensions and circles with diameter dimensions. This convention is consistent with the tooling required to produce the feature shape. Any arc greater than 180° is considered a circle and is dimensioned by using a diameter.

**Figure 8-31**

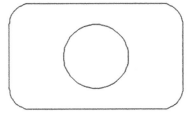

## Creating a Radius Dimension

**1** On the **Dimensions** panel of the **Annotate** tab, click the down arrow beside the **Linear** tool and select **Radius**.

```
Command: _dimradius
Select arc or circle:
```

**2** Select the arc to be dimensioned.

```
Specify dimension line location or [Mtext Text Angle]:
```

**3** Position the radius dimension so that its leader line is neither horizontal nor vertical.

Figure 8-32 shows the resulting dimension. The dimension text can be altered by clicking the text. The **Multiline Text Editor** appears (Figure 8-33). Highlight the existing text and type in the new text. Close the text editor and press the **Esc** key.

**Figure 8-32**

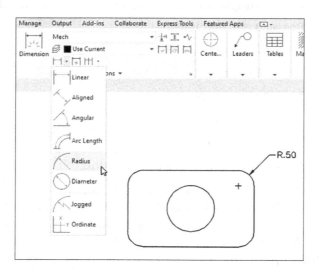

**Figure 8-33**

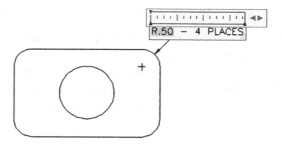

## Altering the Default Dimension

**1** Double-click the dimension.

The dimension is enclosed in a shaded box.

**2** Press the **Delete** key to remove the existing dimension.

**3** Add the desired text or type in the new dimension.

**4** Click the mouse.

Figure 8-34 shows the resulting dimension. The **Radius** dimension tool automatically includes a center mark with the dimension. The center mark can be excluded from the dimension as described next.

**Figure 8-34**

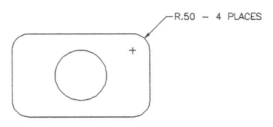

## Removing the Center Mark from a Radius Dimension

**1** Open the **Dimension Style Manager** by clicking the arrow in the lower-right corner of the **Dimensions** panel of the **Annotate** tab.

**2** Click **Modify**.

The **Modify Dimension Style: Standard** dialog box appears.

**3** Select the **Symbols and Arrows** tab.

**4** In the **Center marks** area, select the **None** radio button (Figure 8-35).

**Figure 8-35**

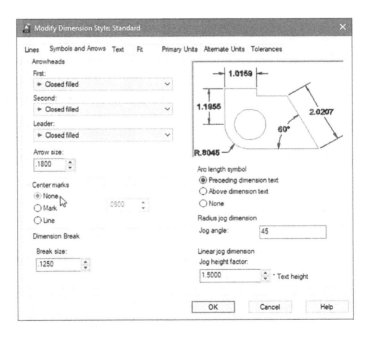

**5** Click **OK** to return to the drawing.

The radius dimension automatically updates to the new dimension style setting. Figure 8-36 shows the result.

Figure 8-36

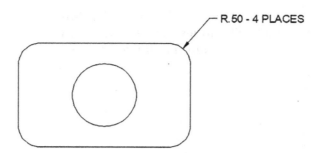

R.50 - 4 PLACES

## Creating a Diameter Dimension

You can create a dimension *substyle*—that is, a new style that applies to only one dimension type. In this case, you would like centerlines on diameter dimensions but no center marks at all on radius dimensions. Create the new dimension style for diameter dimensions only as follows (see Figure 8-37):

**1** Open the **Dimension Style Manager**.

Figure 8-37

**2** Click **New**.

The **Create New Dimension Style** dialog box appears.

**3** Leave **New Style Name** setting as is. Under **Use for**, click the down arrow and select **Diameter dimensions**. Click **Continue**.

AutoCAD creates a new substyle called **Diameter** under the **Standard** dimension style. The **New Dimension Style: Standard Diameter** dialog box appears.

**4** Select the **Symbols and Arrows** tab.

**5** In the **Center marks** area, select the **Line** radio button. Click **OK**.

The **Dimension Style Manager** lists **Diameter** as a new substyle within the Standard dimension style.

**6** Click **Close**.

## Creating Center Marks and Lines

The **Symbols and Arrows** tab of the **Modify Dimension Style** dialog box presents three options for indicating the center of an existing circle. You can specify **None** (no marks), **Mark** (a small cross at the center of the circle), or **Line** (the small cross plus horizontal and vertical lines that extend beyond the circumference of the circle).

You can configure AutoCAD to automatically add center marks or horizontal and vertical centerlines as follows:

**1** On the **Dimensions** panel of the **Annotate** tab, click the down arrow beside the **Linear** tool and select **Diameter**.

```
Command: _dimdiameter
Select arc or circle:
```

**2** Select the circle.

```
Specify dimension line location or [MText Text Angle]:
```

**3** Locate the dimension away from the object so that the leader line is neither horizontal nor vertical.

## Adding Linear Dimensions to Given Centerlines

**1** Select **Linear** from the **Dimension** tool on the **Dimensions** panel.

```
Command: _dimlinear
Specify first extension line origin or <select object>:
```

**2** Select the lower endpoint of the circle's vertical centerline.

```
Specify second extension line origin:
```

**3** Select the endpoint of the vertical edge line (the endpoint that joins with the corner arc).

Figure 8-38 shows the results.

Figure 8-38

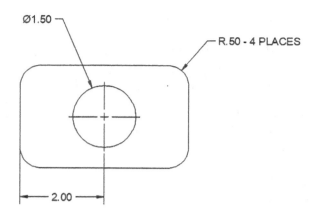

**4** Repeat steps 1–3 to add the vertical dimension needed to locate the circle's center point.

**5** Add the overall dimensions, using the **Linear** dimension tool.

Figure 8-39 shows the result. Radius and diameter dimensions are usually added to a drawing after the linear dimensions because they are less restricted in their locations. Linear dimensions are located close to the distance that they are defining, whereas radius and diameter dimensions can be located farther away and use leader lines to identify the appropriate arc or circle.

**Figure 8-39**

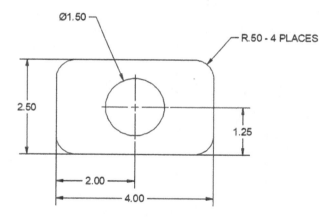

Avoid crossing extension and dimension lines with leader lines (Figure 8-40).

> **NOTE**
>
> The diameter symbol Ø can be added when creating text by typing **%%c**. The characters **%%c** start appearing in the **Text Editor** window but are converted to the diameter symbol Ø as soon as you type the letter **c**.

**Figure 8-40**

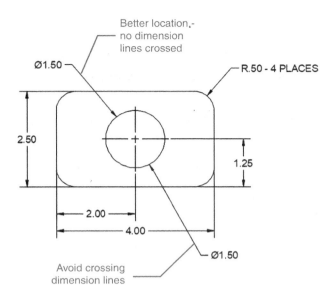

**8-8 Angular Dimensions**

Figure 8-41 shows four possible angular dimensions that you can create using the **Angular** dimension tool, which is a flyout from the **Dimension** tool on the **Dimensions** panel. The extension lines and degree symbol are added automatically.

**Figure 8-41**

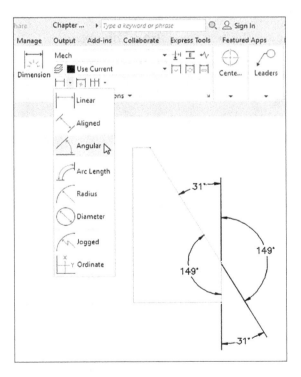

## Creating an Angular Dimension

Follow the steps below to dimension the object in Figure 8-42.

**1** Select **Angular** from the **Dimension** tool on the **Dimensions** panel.

Command: _dimangular

Select arc, circle, line, or <specify vertex>:

Figure 8-42

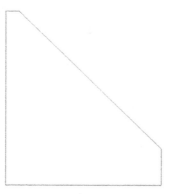

**2** Select the short vertical line on the lower-right side of the object.

Select second line:

**3** Select the slanted line.

Specify dimension arc line location [MText Text Angle]:

**4** Locate the text away from the object.

Figure 8-43 shows the result.

> **NOTE**
>
> It is considered best practice to use two extension lines for angular dimensions and to avoid having the arrowhead touch the surface of a part.

**Figure 8-43**

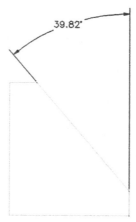

39.82°

**NOTE**

The degree symbol is added automatically when you create an angular dimension. You can add the degree symbol to regular text by typing **%%d**.

## Avoiding Overdimensioning

Figure 8-44 shows a shape dimensioned by using an angular dimension. The shape is completely defined. Any additional dimension would be an error. It is tempting, in an effort to make sure that a shape is completely defined, to add more dimensions, such as a horizontal dimension for the short horizontal edge at the top of the shape. This dimension is not needed, though, and adding it is considered double dimensioning (see Chapter 9, Section 9-10).

**Figure 8-44**

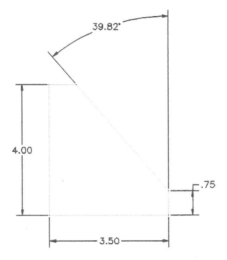

## 8-9 Ordinate Dimensions

*Ordinate dimensions* are dimensions based on an X,Y coordinate system. Ordinate dimensions do not include extension or dimension lines or arrowheads; they have simple horizontal and vertical leader lines drawn directly from the features of the object. While standard dimensions indicate the distances between points or objects, ordinate dimensions denote the distance *each* object is from the origin point. Ordinate dimensions are particularly useful when dimensioning an object that includes many small holes.

Figure 8-45 shows an object that is to be dimensioned using ordinate dimensions. Ordinate dimensions are automatically calculated from the X,Y origin or, in this example, the lower-left corner of the screen. If the object had been drawn with its lower-left corner on the origin, you could proceed directly to the **Ordinate** tool, which is a flyout from the **Dimension** tool on the **Dimensions** panel. However, the lower-left corner of the object in Figure 8-45 is not located on the origin.

Figure 8-45

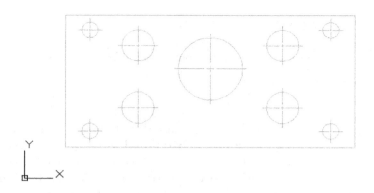

## Moving the Origin and the Origin Icon

To move the origin and the origin icon, you first move the origin to the corner of the object and then use the **Ordinate** dimension tool (Figure 8-46).

**Figure 8-46**

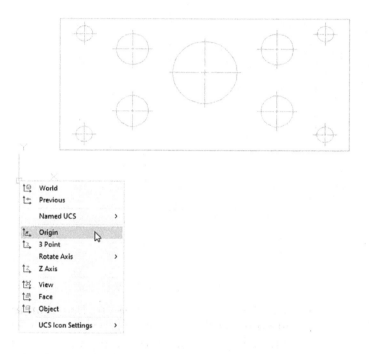

**1** Move the cursor onto the origin icon.

**2** Right-click and select the **Origin** option.

The cursor becomes attached to the origin.

**3** Move the origin to the desired location.

**4** Click the mouse (Figures 8-47 and 8-48).

Figure 8-47

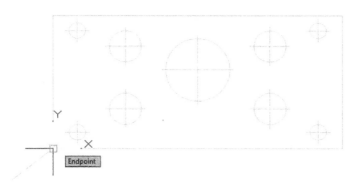

Figure 8-48

## Adding Ordinate Dimensions to an Object

The following procedure assumes that you have already used the **Dimension Style Manager** (refer to Section 8-4) to set the desired dimension style and that you have moved the origin to the lower-left corner of the object, as just described.

**1** Click the **Ortho Mode** button in the status bar at the bottom of the screen.

**2** Select the **Ordinate** tool flyout from the **Dimension** tool on the **Dimensions** panel (Figure 8-49).

```
Command: _dimordinate

Select feature location:
```

**3** Select the lower endpoint of the first circle's vertical centerline.

```
Specify leader endpoint or [Xdatum Ydatum MText Text Angle]:
```

**4** Select a point along the X axis directly below the vertical centerline of the circle.

The ordinate value of the point is added to the drawing. This point should have a **0.50** value. The text value may be modified by using either the **MText** or **Text** option or by using the **Dimension Style Manager** dialog box to define the precision of the text.

**5** Right-click to restart the command and dimension the object's other features.

Figure 8-49

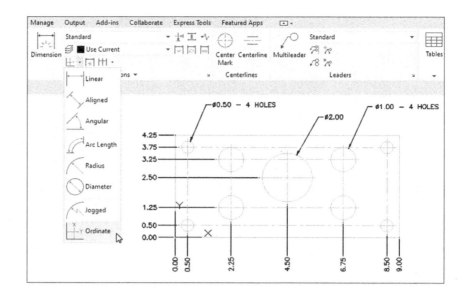

6 Extend the centerlines across the object and add the diameter dimensions for the holes.

Once the ordinate dimensioning is complete, you can return the UCS icon from the corner of the object to the origin of the drawing.

7 Click the UCS icon at the corner of the object to display the grips.

8 Hover the mouse over the intersection of the X and Y axes (do not click the grip) and, in the shortcut menu that appears, click **World**.

Figure 8-49 shows the completed drawing. The **Text** option of the prompt shown in step 3 can be used to modify or remove the default text value.

## 8-10 Baseline Dimensions

*Baseline dimensions* are a series of dimensions that originate from a common baseline or datum line. Baseline dimensions are very useful because they help eliminate tolerance buildup associated with chain-type dimensions.

The **Baseline** tool can be used only after an initial dimension has been drawn. AutoCAD defines the first extension line origin of the initial dimension selected as the baseline for all baseline dimensions.

### Using the Baseline Dimension Tool

Figure 8-50 shows the same object from Section 8-9, this time dimensioned using **Baseline** dimensions. You do not need to move the UCS as you do with ordinate dimensions. When you use baseline dimensions, the origin of the first point chosen is understood.

1 Select the **Linear** tool flyout from the **Linear** tool on the **Dimensions** panel.

Command: _dimlinear

Specify first extension line origin or <select object>:

Figure 8-50

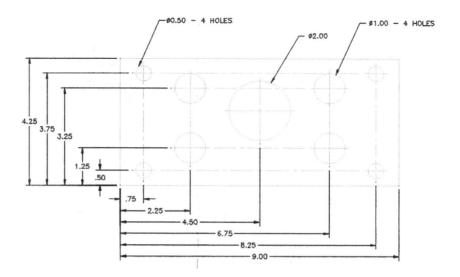

**2** Select the upper-left corner of the object.

This selection determines the baseline.

`Specify second extension line origin:`

**3** Select the endpoint of the first circle's vertical centerline.

`Specify dimension line location or [Text Angle Horizontal Vertical Rotated]:`

**4** Select a location for the dimension line.

`Command:`

**5** Select the **Baseline** tool from the **Dimensions** panel.

`Specify a second extension line origin or [Undo Select] <Select>:`

**6** Select the endpoint of the next circle's vertical centerline.

`Specify a second extension line origin or [Undo Select] <Select>:`

**7** Continue to select the circle centerlines until all circles are located.

`Specify a second extension line origin or [Undo Select] <Select>:`

**8** Select the upper-right corner of the object.

**9** Right-click and select the **Enter** option.

This ends the **Baseline** dimension command.

**10** Repeat steps 1–9 for the vertical baseline dimensions. Remember to start with an existing vertical dimension.

**11** Add the circles' diameter values.

Figure 8-50 shows the completed drawing. The **Baseline** dimension option can also be used with the **Angular** dimension option.

## 8-11 Continued Dimensions

The **Continue** tool on the **Dimensions** panel creates chain dimensions based on an initial linear, angular, or ordinate dimension.

The second extension line's origin becomes the first extension line origin for the continued dimension.

## Using the Continue Dimension Command

Figure 8-51 shows a continuous string of chain dimensions, created using **Continue**.

**1** Select the **Linear** tool flyout from the **Dimension** tool on the **Dimensions** panel.

```
Command: _dimcontinue

Specify first extension line origin or <select object>:
```

**Figure 8-51**

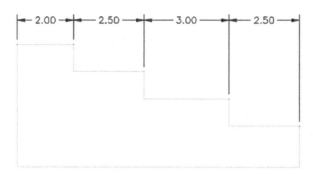

**2** Select the upper-left corner of the object.

```
Specify second extension line origin:
```

**3** Select the right endpoint of the uppermost horizontal line.

```
Dimension line location (Text Angle Horizontal Vertical Rotated):
```

**4** Select a dimension line location.

```
Command:
```

**5** Select the **Continue** tool from the **Dimensions** panel.

```
Command: _dimcontinue

Specify a second extension line origin or [Undo Select] <Select>:
```

**6** Select the next linear distance to be dimensioned.

```
Specify a second extension line origin or [Undo Select] <Select>:
```

**7** Continue selecting features to the dimension string until the object's horizontal edges are completely dimensioned.

AutoCAD automatically aligns the dimensions. Figure 8-52 shows how the **Continue** tool dimensions distances that are too small for both the arrowhead and dimension value to fit within the extension lines.

**Figure 8-52**

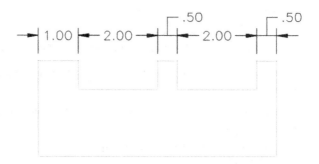

## 8-12 Quick Dimension

Use the **Quick** dimension tool to add a series of dimensions (Figure 8-53).

**Figure 8-53**

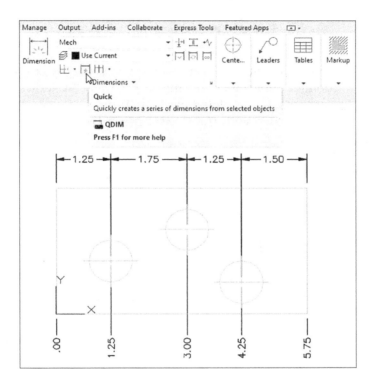

## Using the Quick Dimension Tool

**1** Select the **Quick** tool from the **Dimensions** panel.

```
Command: _qdim

Select geometry to dimension:
```

**2** Window select the entire object to be dimensioned—in this example, the rectangle and the three circles—and press **Enter**.

```
Specify dimension line position, or [Continuous Staggered Baseline
Ordinate Radius Diameter datumPoint Edit seTtings]<Baseline>:
```

**3** Right-click.

```
Specify dimension line position, or [Continuous Staggered Baseline
Ordinate Radius Diameter datumPoint Edit seTtings]<Baseline>:
```

**4** Choose a dimension type, such as **Continuous**, from the right-click menu.

In the example in Figure 8-53, the **Quick** dimension tool was run twice. **Continuous** was chosen for the top dimension string, and **Ordinate** was used for the bottom string (after the UCS icon was moved to the desired origin).

**5** Position the dimension lines, right-click, and enter the position.

Notice that the extension lines start from the centers of the circles. You can select the dimensions and drag their extension lines to the endpoints of the centerlines to make a drawing clearer.

## 8-13 Center Mark

When AutoCAD first draws a circle or an arc, a guideline appears from the center mark; however, as soon as you pick or enter a radius, the circle no longer shows a center mark. Figure 8-54 shows the **Circle** command in process, a completed circle with no center mark, and a circle with center-lines added with the **Center Mark** tool.

Figure 8-54

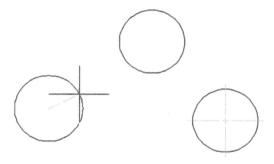

## Adding Centerlines to a Given Circle

**1** Open the **Dimension Style Manager** by clicking the arrow in the lower-right corner of the **Dimensions** panel of the **Annotate** tab.

**2** Click **Modify**.

The **Modify Dimension Style: Standard** dialog box appears.

**3** Select the **Symbols and Arrows** tab.

**4** In the **Center marks** area, select the **Line** radio button.

The preview display shows a horizontal centerline and a vertical centerline.

**5** Click **OK** and then **Close** to return to the drawing.

**6** Select the **Center Mark** tool from the **Dimensions** panel.

```
Select arc or circle:
```

**7** Select the circle.

Horizontal and vertical centerlines appear. The size of the center mark can be controlled by using the **Size** edit box in the **Center marks** area. If the centerline's size appears to be unacceptable, try different sizes until you get an acceptable size.

## 8-14 Mleader and Qleader

*Leader lines* are slanted lines that extend from notes or dimensions to specific features or locations on the surface of a drawing. A leader line usually ends with an arrowhead or a dot. The **Radius** and **Diameter** tools, which are flyouts from the **Dimension** tool on the **Dimensions** panel, automatically create leader lines. The **Multileader** and **Quick Leader** tools can add leader lines to drawing notations not associated with radius or diameter dimensions. **Quick Leader** creates two objects: a leader line and a text or multiline text object.

### Creating a Quick Leader

**1** Type **qleader** at the command prompt.

```
Command: _qleader
Specify first leader point, or [Settings]<Settings>:
```

**2** Select the starting point for the leader line.

This is the point at which the arrowhead appears. In the example shown in Figure 8-55, the upper-right corner of the object is selected.

```
Specify next point:
```

**Figure 8-55**

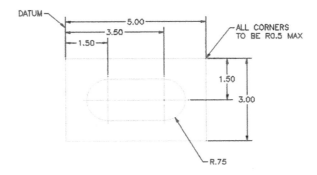

**3** Select the location of the endpoint of the slanted line segment.

```
Specify next point:
```

**4** Draw a short horizontal line segment and press **Enter**.

```
Specify text width <0.0000>:
```

**5** Press **Enter**.

```
Enter first line of annotation text <MText>:
```

**6** Press **Enter**.

**7** Use the cursor to extend the text box as needed.

**8** Type the desired text (Figure 8-56).

**Figure 8-56**

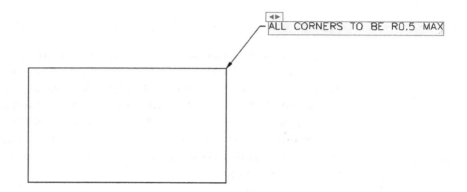

**9** Click **OK**.

The text appears next to the horizontal line segment of the leader line.

## Drawing a Curved Leader Line

The **Quick Leader** tool is used to draw curved leader lines and leader lines that end with dots (Figure 8-57).

**1** Type **qleader** in response to a command prompt.

```
Command: _qleader

Specify first leader point, or [Settings] <Settings>:
```

**Figure 8-57**

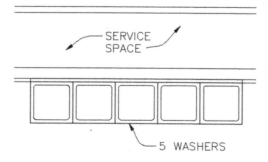

**2** Type **s** and press **Enter**.

The **Leader Settings** dialog box appears (Figure 8-58).

Figure 8-58

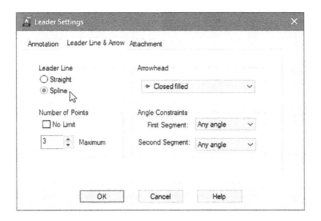

**3** Select the **Leader Line & Arrow** tab.

**4** Select the **Spline** option in the **Leader Line** area and then click **OK**.

```
Specify first leader point, or [Settings] <Settings>:
```

**5** Select the starting point for the leader line.

The arrowhead appears.

```
Specify next point:
```

**6** Select the next point.

```
Select next point:
```

AutoCAD shifts to **Drag** mode, allowing you to move the cursor around and watch the leader line change shape. You can select more than one point to define the shape.

**7** Complete the leader line, as explained previously.

## Drawing a Leader Line with a Dot at Its End

In this example, a leader is created with the **Multileader** command. The current multileader style is modified to use a dot rather than an arrowhead.

**1** Click the arrow in the lower-right corner of the **Leaders** panel of the **Annotate** tab.

The **Multileader Style Manager** dialog box appears (Figure 8-59).

**2** Click **Modify**.

The **Modify Multileader Style: Standard** dialog box appears (Figure 8-59).

**3** Click the arrow on the right end of the **Symbol** box in the **Arrowhead** area and select the **Dot** option.

**4** Click **OK**.

**5** Select **Multileader** on the **Leaders** panel of the **Annotate** tab.

Figure 8-59

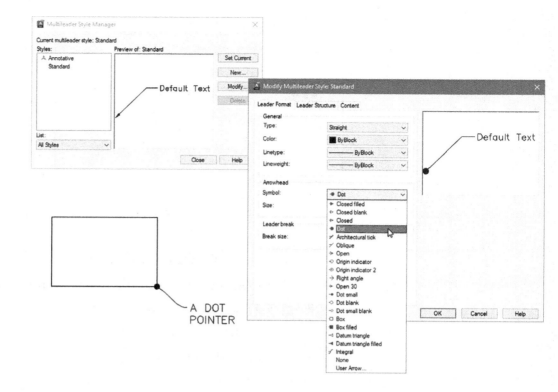

6   Select an arrowhead location and a leader landing location and then enter text in the **Text Editor** edit box.

7   Click anywhere in the drawing area to complete the multileader.

## 8-15 Text Angle

The **Text Angle** tool is used to change the angle of existing dimension text.

### Changing the Angle of Dimension Text

1   Select the **Text Angle** tool from the **Dimensions** panel.

```
Select dimension:
```

2   Select the dimension text.

```
Select new location for dimension or [Left Right Center Home
Angle]: _a
```

```
Specify angle for dimension text:
```

3   Type **90** and press **Enter** (Figure 8-60).

**Figure 8-60**

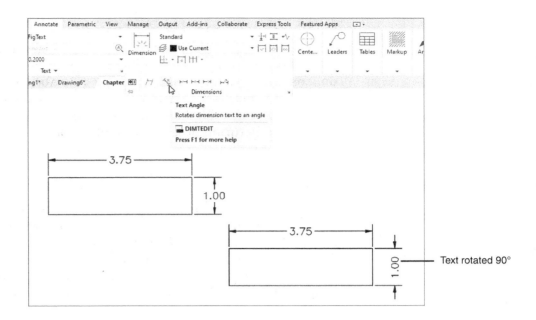

## 8-16 Tolerances

*Tolerances* are numerical values assigned with the dimensions that define the limits of manufacturing acceptability for a distance. AutoCAD can create four types of tolerances: symmetrical, deviation, limits, and basic (Figure 8-61). A company may also use a group of standard tolerances that are applied to any dimensional value that is not assigned a specific tolerance (refer to Figure 8-23). Tolerances for numerical values expressed in millimeters are applied using a convention different from the convention used for inches. (Tolerances are discussed in Chapters 9 and 10. The dimensioning tools are also covered in those chapters.)

**Figure 8-61**

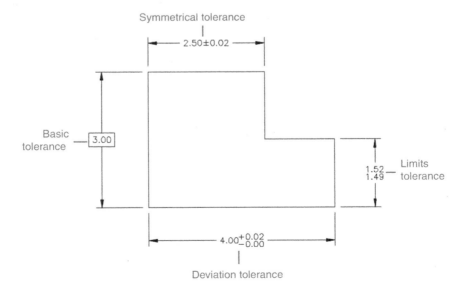

## 8-17 Dimensioning Holes

Holes are dimensioned by stating their diameter and depth, if any. The symbol ⌀ is used to represent diameter. It is considered good practice to dimension a hole by using a diameter value because the tooling used to produce the hole is also defined in terms of diameter values. A notation like 12 DRILL is considered less desirable because it specifies a machining process. Manufacturing processes should be left, whenever possible, to the discretion of the shop.

### Dimensioning Individual Holes

Figure 8-62 shows three different methods that can be used to dimension a hole that does not go completely through an object. If a hole goes completely through, only the diameter needs to be specified. The **Radius** and **Diameter** dimension tools are covered in Section 8-7. Depth values may be specified by modifying the default text using **Text override** in the **Properties** or **Quick Properties** palette, as described in Section 8-3.

**Figure 8-62**

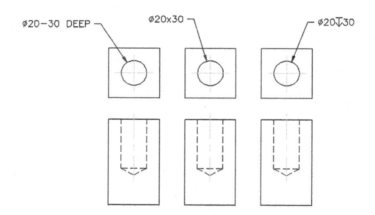

Figure 8-63 shows two methods of dimensioning holes in sectional views. The single-line note version on the left is the preferred method.

**Figure 8-63**

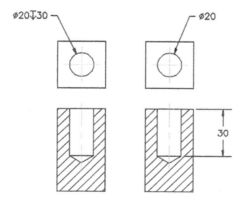

## Dimensioning Hole Patterns

Figure 8-64 shows two different hole patterns dimensioned. The circular pattern includes the note **ø10 – 4 HOLES**. This note serves to define all four holes within the object.

Figure 8-64

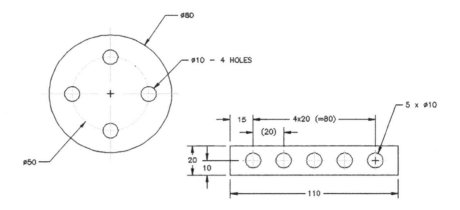

Figure 8-64 also shows a rectangular object that contains five holes of equal diameter, equally spaced from one another. The notation **5 × ø10** specifies five holes of 10 diameter. The notation **4×20 (=80)** means 4 equal spaces of 20. The notation **(=80)** is a reference dimension and is included for convenience. Reference dimensions are explained in Chapter 9, Section 9-10.

Figure 8-65 shows two additional methods for dimensioning repeating hole patterns. Figure 8-66 shows a circular hole pattern that includes two different hole diameters. The hole diameters are not noticeably different from one another and could be confused. One group is defined by indicating letter **A**; the other is dimensioned in a normal manner.

Figure 8-65

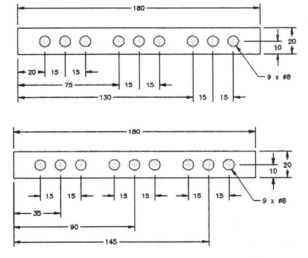

Figure 8-66

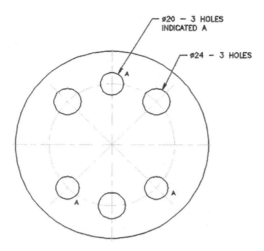

## 8-18 Placing Dimensions

There are several general rules concerning the placement of dimensions (Figure 8-67):

- Place dimensions near the features that they are defining.

- Do not place dimensions on the surface of an object.

- Align and group dimensions so that they are neat and easy to understand.

- Avoid crossing extension lines. Sometimes it is impossible not to cross extension lines because of the complex shape of the object, but whenever possible, avoid crossing extension lines.

- Place shorter dimensions closer to the object than longer ones.

- Always place overall dimensions the farthest away from the object.

- Do not dimension the same distance twice. Doing so is called *double dimensioning*. Double dimensioning is discussed in Chapter 9, Section 9-10.

Figure 8-67

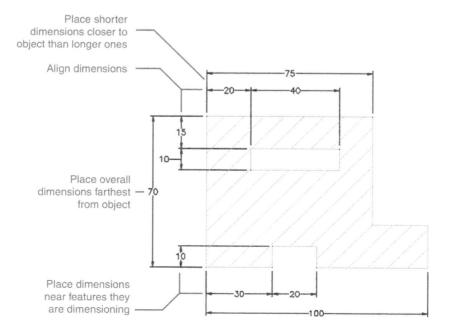

## 8-19 Fillets and Rounds

Fillets and rounds may be dimensioned individually or by using a note. In many design situations, all of the fillets and rounds are the same size, and a note like the one shown in Figure 8-68 is used. Any fillets or rounds that have a different radius from that specified by the note are dimensioned individually.

**Figure 8-68**

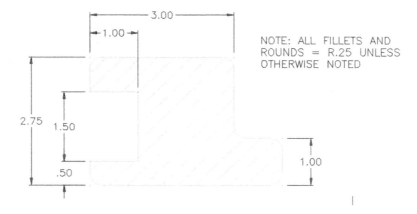

NOTE: ALL FILLETS AND ROUNDS = R.25 UNLESS OTHERWISE NOTED

See Section 2-26 in Chapter 2 for an explanation of how to draw fillets and rounds using the **Fillet** command.

## 8-20 Rounded Shapes—Internal

Internal rounded shapes are called *slots*. Figure 8-69 shows three different methods of dimensioning slots. The end radii are indicated by the note **R - 2 PLACES**, but no numerical value is given. The width of the slot is dimensioned, and it is assumed that the radius of the rounded ends is exactly half of the stated width.

**NOTE**
You can use AutoCAD's **Fillet** command to make a 180° arc by selecting two parallel lines. The arc radius will be precisely half the distance between the lines.

**Figure 8-69**

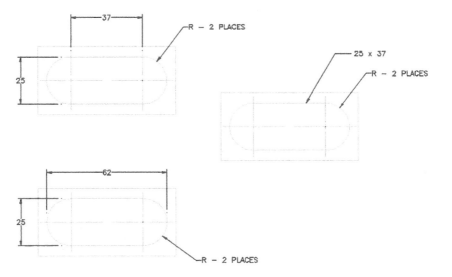

## 8-21 Rounded Shapes—External

Figure 8-70 shows three examples of shapes with external rounded ends. As with internal rounded shapes, the end radii are indicated, but no value is given. The width of the object is given, and the radius of the rounded end is assumed to be exactly half of the stated width.

**Figure 8-70**

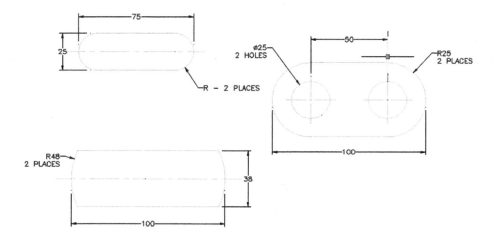

The second example in Figure 8-70 is an object dimensioned using the object's centerlines. This type of dimensioning is used when the distance between the holes is more important than the overall length of the object—that is, when the tolerance for the distance between the holes is more exact than the tolerance for the overall length of the object.

The overall length of the object is given as a reference dimension (100). This means that the object will be manufactured on the basis of other dimensions, and the 100 value will be used only for reference.

Objects with partially rounded edges should be dimensioned as shown in Figure 8-70. The radii of the end features are dimensioned. The center point of the radii is implied to be on the object centerline. The overall dimension is given; it is not referenced unless specific radius values are included.

## 8-22 Irregular Surfaces

There are three different methods for dimensioning irregular surfaces: tabular, baseline, and baseline with oblique extension lines. Figure 8-71A shows an irregular surface dimensioned using the tabular method. In Figure 8-71B, the curve points are defined using baseline dimensions with the extension lines of one dimension obliqued for clarity. The X,Y axes are defined by using the edges of the object. Points are then defined relative to the X,Y axes. The points are assigned reference numbers, and the reference numbers and X,Y coordinate values are listed in chart form, as shown.

**Figure 8-71**

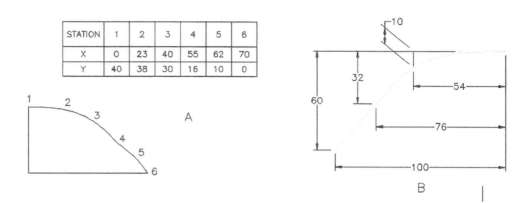

| STATION | 1 | 2 | 3 | 4 | 5 | 6 |
|---------|---|---|---|---|---|---|
| X | 0 | 23 | 40 | 55 | 62 | 70 |
| Y | 40 | 38 | 30 | 16 | 10 | 0 |

Figure 8-72 shows an irregular curve fully dimensioned with baseline dimensions. The baseline method references all dimensions back to specified baselines. There are usually two baselines: one horizontal and one vertical.

**Figure 8-72**

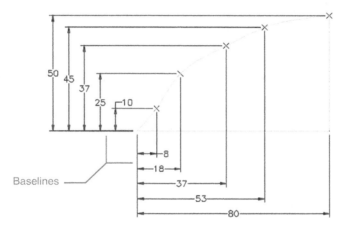

It is considered poor practice to use a centerline as a baseline. Centerlines are imaginary lines that do not exist on an actual object, and having a centerline as a baseline would make it more difficult to manufacture and inspect the finished objects.

Baseline dimensioning is very common because it helps eliminate tolerance buildup (see Section 9-11) and is easily adaptable to many manufacturing processes. AutoCAD has a special **Baseline** dimension tool for creating baseline dimensions.

## 8-23 Polar Dimensions

Polar dimensions are similar to polar coordinates. A location is defined by a radius (distance) and an angle. Figure 8-73 shows an object that includes polar dimensions. The holes are located on a circular centerline, and their positions from the vertical centerline are specified by angles.

Figure 8-73

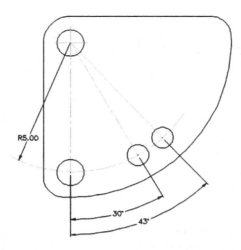

Figure 8-74 shows an example of a hole pattern dimensioned by using polar dimensions.

Figure 8-74

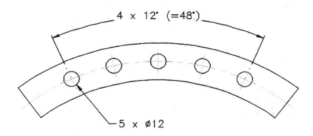

## 8-24 Chamfers

*Chamfers* are angular cuts made on the edges of objects. They are usually used to make it easier to fit two parts together. They are most often made at 45° angles but may be made at any angle. Figure 8-75 shows two objects with chamfers between surfaces 90° apart and two examples between surfaces that are not 90° apart. Either of the two types of dimensions shown for the 45° dimension can be used. If an angle other than 45° is used, the angle and setback distance must be specified.

Figure 8-75

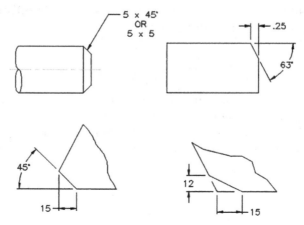

Figure 8-76 shows two examples of internal chamfers. Both of them define the chamfers by using an angle and a diameter. Internal chamfers are very similar to countersunk holes (refer to Chapter 5, Section 5-26).

**Figure 8-76**

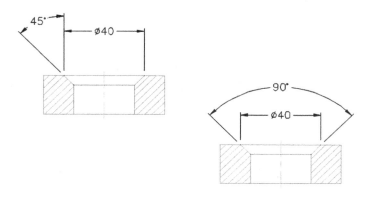

## 8-25 Knurling

*Knurls* are used to make it easier to grip a shaft or to roughen a surface before it is used in a press fit. There are two types of knurls: diamond and straight.

Knurls are defined by their pitch and diameter (Figure 8-77). The *pitch* of a knurl is the ratio of the number of grooves on the circumference to the diameter. Standard knurling tools sized to a variety of pitch sizes are used to manufacture knurls for both English and metric units.

**Figure 8-77**

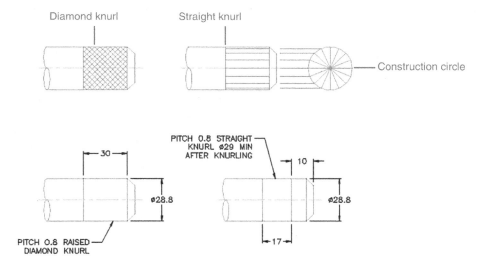

Diamond knurls may be represented by using a double-hatched pattern or by an open area with notes. Use the **Hatch** command with the **ANSI37** pattern to draw the double-hatched lines. (Hatching is covered in Section 6-4.)

Straight knurls may be represented using straight lines in the pattern shown in Figure 8-77 or using an open area with notes. The straight-line pattern is created by projecting lines from a construction circle. The construction points are evenly spaced on the circle. Once drawn, the straight-line knurl pattern can be wblocked for use on other drawings. See Section 3-22 for an explanation of **Wblock**.

## 8-26 Keys and Keyseats

*Keys* are small pieces of material used to transmit power. For example, Figure 8-78 shows how a key can be fitted between a shaft and a gear so that the rotary motion of the shaft can be transmitted to the gear.

**Figure 8-78**

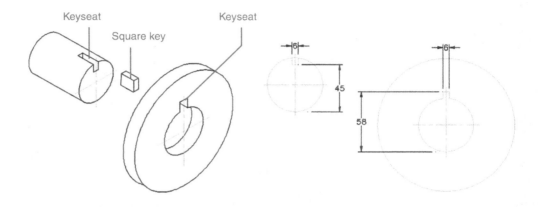

There are many different key styles. The key shown in Figure 8-78 has a rectangular cross section and is called a *square key*. Keys fit into grooves called *keyseats*, or *keyways*.

Keyseats are dimensioned from the bottom of the shaft, or hole, as shown.

## 8-27 Symbols and Abbreviations

Symbols in dimensioning help accurately display the meaning of each dimension. Symbols also help eliminate language barriers when reading drawings. Figure 8-79 lists a number of dimensioning symbols and their meanings. The height of a symbol should be the same as the text height.

**Figure 8-79**

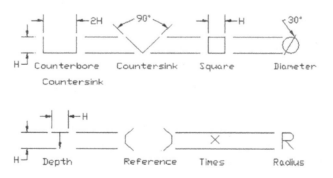

Abbreviations should be used on drawings very carefully. Whenever possible, write out the full word, including correct punctuation. Figure 8-80 shows several standard abbreviations used on technical drawings.

**Figure 8-80**

STANDARD ABBREVIATIONS FOR TECHNICAL DRAWINGS

| | | | |
|---|---|---|---|
| AL | Aluminum | MATL | Material |
| C'BORE | Counterbore | R | Radius |
| CRS | Cold Rolled Steel | SAE | Society of Automotive Engineers |
| CSK | Countersink | SFACE | Spotface |
| DIA | Diameter | ST | Steel |
| EQ | Equal | SQ | Square |
| HEX | Hexagon | REQD | Required |

## 8-28 Symmetry and Centerline

An object is symmetrical about an axis when one side is an exact mirror image of the other. Figure 8-81 shows a symmetrical object. The symbol comprising two short parallel lines or the note **OBJECT IS SYMMETRICAL ABOUT THIS AXIS** (centerline) can be used to designate symmetry.

**Figure 8-81**

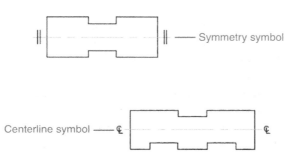

If an object is symmetrical, only half of the object needs to be dimensioned. The other dimensions are implied by the symmetry note or symbol.

A centerline is slightly different from the axis of symmetry. An object may or may not be symmetrical about its centerline (Figure 8-81). Centerlines are used to define the center of both individual features and entire objects. Use the centerline symbol when a line is a centerline but do not use it in place of the symmetry symbol.

## 8-29 Dimensioning to Points

Curved surfaces can be dimensioned by using theoretical points (Figure 8-82). There should be a small gap between the surface of an object and the lines used to define a theoretical point. The point should be defined by the intersection of at least two lines.

There should also be a small gap between the extension lines and the theoretical point used to locate the point.

Figure 8-82

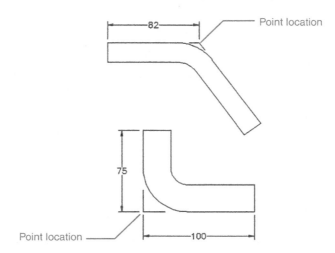

## 8-30 Coordinate Dimensions

Coordinate dimensions are used for objects that contain many holes. Baseline dimensions can also be used, but when there are many holes, baseline dimensions can create a confusing appearance and require a large area on the drawing. Coordinate dimensions use charts that simplify the appearance, use far less space on the drawing, and are easy to understand.

Figure 8-83 shows an object that has been dimensioned with coordinate dimensions rather than dimension lines. Holes are identified on the drawing by letters. Holes of equal diameter use the same letter. The hole diameters are presented in chart form.

Figure 8-83

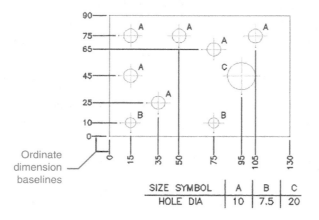

| SIZE SYMBOL | A | B | C |
|---|---|---|---|
| HOLE DIA | 10 | 7.5 | 20 |

Hole locations are defined by a series of centerlines referenced to baselines. The distance from the baseline to the centerline is written below the centerline, as shown.

Figure 8-84 shows an object that has been dimensioned using coordinate dimensions in tabular form. Each hole is assigned both a letter and a number. Holes of equal diameter are assigned the same letter. A chart defines the diameter values for the hole letters.

**Figure 8-84**

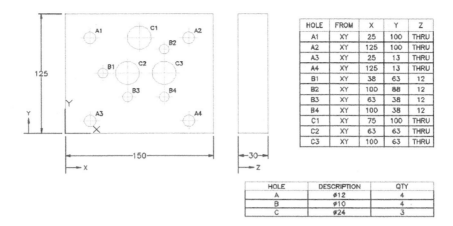

| HOLE | FROM | X | Y | Z |
|------|------|-----|-----|------|
| A1 | XY | 25 | 100 | THRU |
| A2 | XY | 125 | 100 | THRU |
| A3 | XY | 25 | 13 | THRU |
| A4 | XY | 125 | 13 | THRU |
| B1 | XY | 38 | 63 | 12 |
| B2 | XY | 100 | 88 | 12 |
| B3 | XY | 63 | 38 | 12 |
| B4 | XY | 100 | 38 | 12 |
| C1 | XY | 75 | 100 | THRU |
| C2 | XY | 63 | 63 | THRU |
| C3 | XY | 100 | 63 | THRU |

| HOLE | DESCRIPTION | QTY |
|------|-------------|-----|
| A | ⌀12 | 4 |
| B | ⌀10 | 4 |
| C | ⌀24 | 3 |

Hole locations are defined relative to X,Y axes. A Z axis is used for depth dimensions. A chart lists each hole by its letter – number designation and specifies its distance from the X, Y, or Z axis. The overall dimensions are given by using extension and dimension lines.

The side view in Figure 8-84 does not show any hidden lines because if all of the lines were shown, it would be too confusing to understand. A note such as **THIS VIEW LEFT BLANK FOR CLARITY** may be added to such a drawing.

## 8-31 Sectional Views

Sectional views are dimensioned (Figure 8-85). The sectional lines should be drawn at an angle that allows the viewer to clearly distinguish between sectional lines and extension lines.

**Figure 8-85**

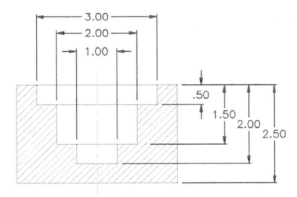

## 8-32 Orthographic Views

Like sectional views, orthographic views are also dimensioned. Add dimensions to orthographic views where the features appear in contour. Holes should be dimensioned in their circular views. Figure 8-86 shows three views of an object that has been fully dimensioned.

Figure 8-86

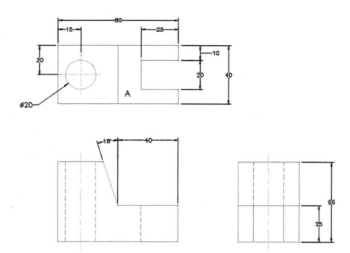

The hole dimensions are added to the top view, where the hole appears circular. The slot is also dimensioned in the top view because it appears in contour. The slanted surface is dimensioned in the front view.

The height of surface A is given in the side view rather than run along extension lines across the front view. The length of surface A is given in the front view. This is a contour view of the surface.

It is good practice to keep dimensions in groups. Doing so makes it easier for the viewer to find dimensions.

Be careful not to double dimension a distance. A distance should be dimensioned only once per view. If a 30 dimension were added above the 25 dimension on the right-side view, it would be an error. The distance would be double dimensioned: once with the 25 + 30 dimension and again with the 55 overall dimension. The 25 + 30 dimensions are mathematically equal to the 55 overall dimension, but there is a distinct difference in how they affect the manufacturing tolerances. Double dimensions are explained more fully in Chapter 9.

Figure 8-87 shows an object dimensioned from its centerline. This type of dimensioning is used when the distances between the holes relative to one another are critical.

Figure 8-87

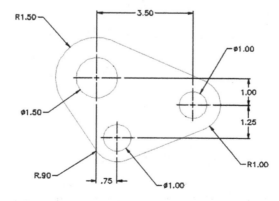

## 8-33 Very Large Radii

Some radii are so large that it is not practical to draw the leader for the radius dimension at full size. Figure 8-88 shows an example of an object that uses foreshortened leader lines.

**Figure 8-88**

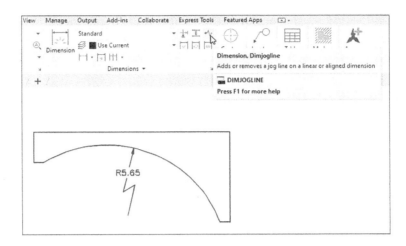

## Creating a Radius for Large Radii

**1** Click the **Jogged** tool on the **Dimensions** panel.

    Select arc or circle:

**2** Click the large arc.

    Specify center location override:

**3** Select a center point for the dimension.

The point selected is not the arc's true center point, as that is probably off the screen. The **Jogged** tool overrides the true center point location and substitutes the one selected (Figure 8-88).

**4** Right-click and select **Enter**.

**5** Select a text location by moving the cursor and then clicking the left mouse button.

Add a center mark to the end of the leader line.

 **chapter eight**

# 8-34 EXERCISE PROBLEMS

Redraw the shapes shown in Exercise Problems EX 8-1 through EX 8-6. Locate the dimensions and tolerances as shown.

## EX8-1 Inches

1. 3.00
2. 1.56
3. 46°
4. .750
5. 2.75
6. 3.625
7. 45°
8. 2.250

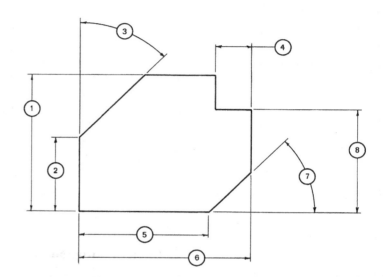

## EX8-2 Millimeters

1. 38
2. 10
3. 5
4. 45°
5. 40
6. 22
7. 12
8. 25
9. 51
10. 76

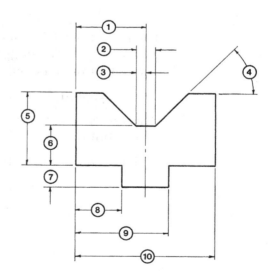

## EX8-3 Millimeters

1. 34.0
2. 17.0
3. 25.0
4. 15.00
5. 50.0
6. 80.0
7. R5 - 8 PLACES
8. 45
9. 60
10. Ø14 - 3 HOLES
11. 15.00
12. 30.00

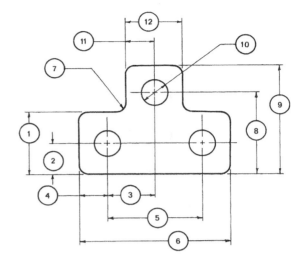

## EX8-4 Inches

1. 1.50
2. 1.50
3. .625
4. .750
5. .625
6. 2.250
7. ø.500

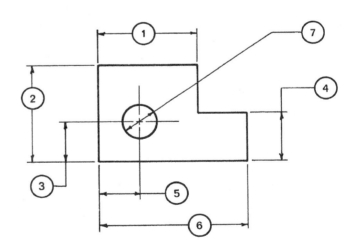

## EX8-5 Millimeters

1. ⌀30.0

2. ⌀15.00

3. 10.0

4. 20.0

5. 66.2

6. 15.1

7. 35.02

8. 70.00

NOTE: ALL FILLETS AND
ROUNDS = R5.0 UNLESS
OTHERWISE STATED.

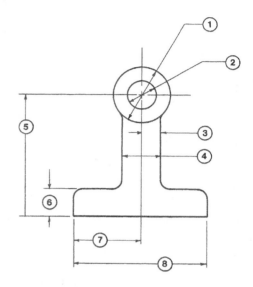

## EX8-6 Millimeters

| | | | |
|---|---|---|---|
| 1. 184.5 | 7. 28.0 | 13. 83.2 | 19. 120.0 |
| 2. 91.5 | 8. 16.00 | 14. 63.00 | 20. ⟨184.0⟩ |
| 3. 44.2 | 9. 16.00 | 15. 50.00 | 21. 12 × 31 |
| 4. 22.00 | 10. 28.0 | 16. 28.5 | R – 3 SLOTS |
| 5. 13.00 | 11. 12.5 | 17. 32.0 | 22. 6.00 |
| 6. 6.51 | 12. ⌀6.00 | 18. 76.0 | 23. 6.00 |

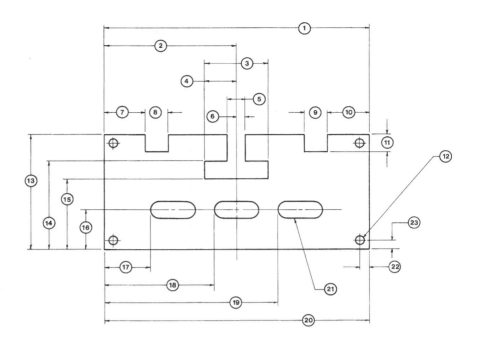

Measure and redraw the shapes in Exercise Problems EX 8-7 through EX 8-53. Add the appropriate dimensions. Specify the units and scale of the drawing. The dotted grid background has either 0.50-inch or 10-millimeter spacing.

## EX8-7

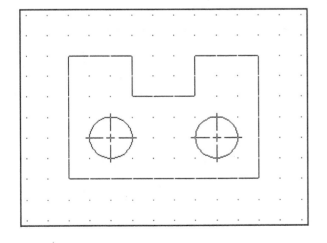

## EX8-8

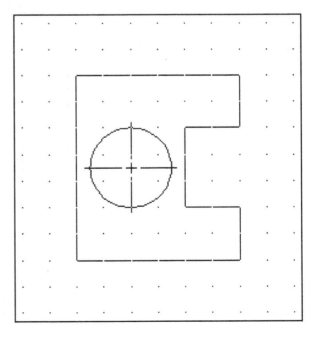

**EX8-9**

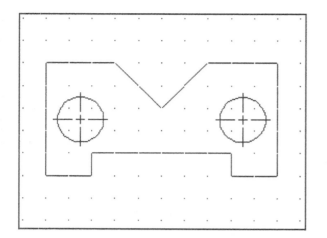

**EX8-10**

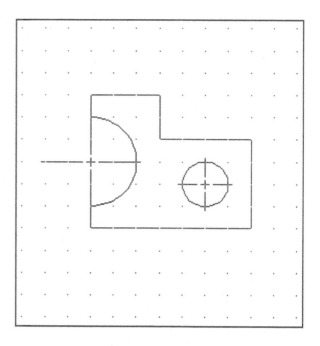

**EX8-11**

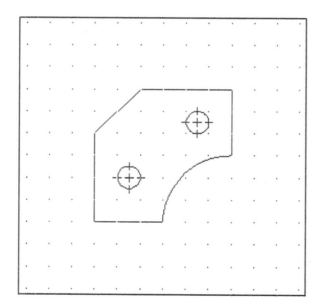

**EX8-12**

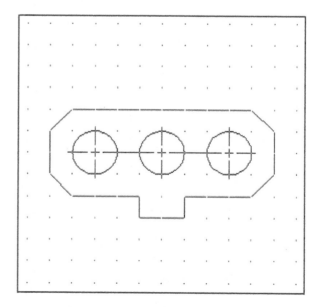

## EX8-13

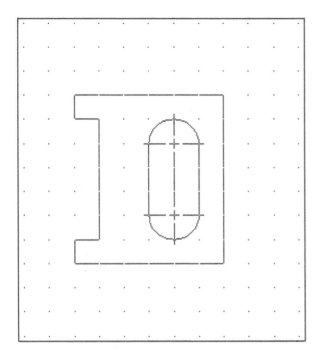

## EX8-14

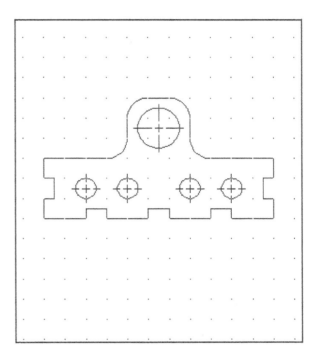

## EX8-15

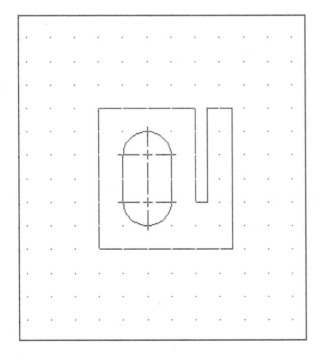

## EX8-16

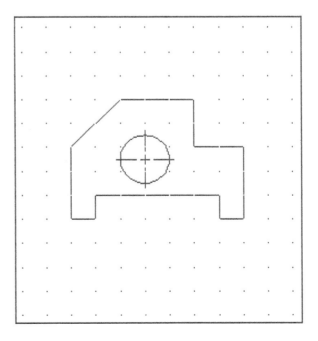

**EX8-17**

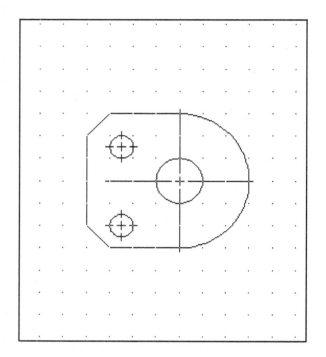

**EX8-18**

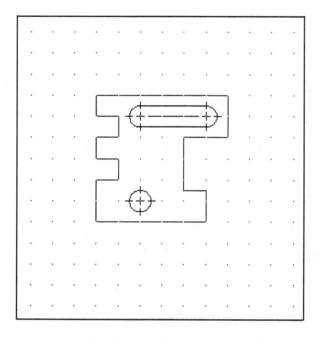

**EX8-19**

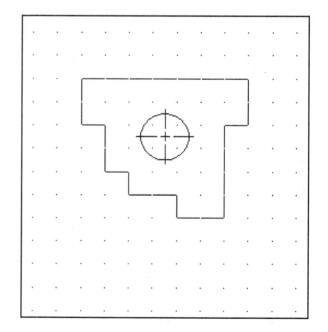

**EX8-20**

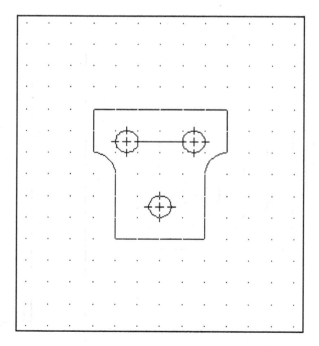

**EX8-21**

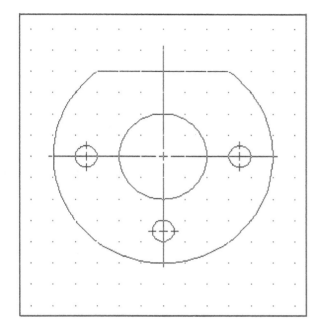

**EX8-22**

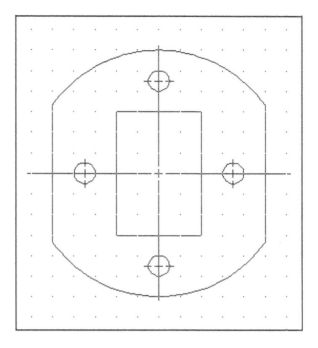

**EX8-23**

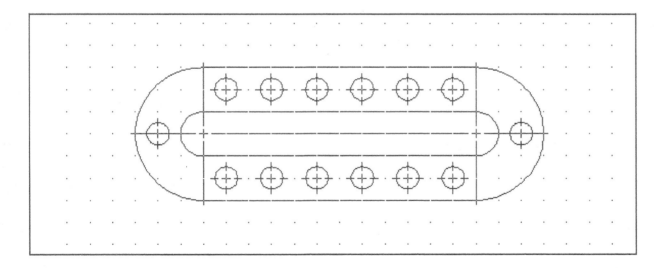

**EX8-24**

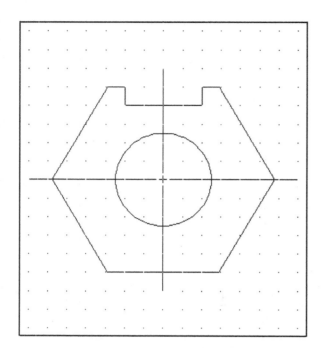

**EX8-25**

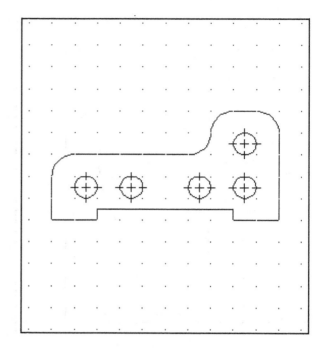

**EX8-26**

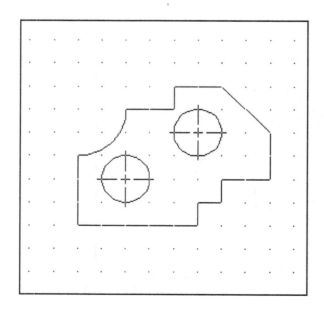

**EX8-27**

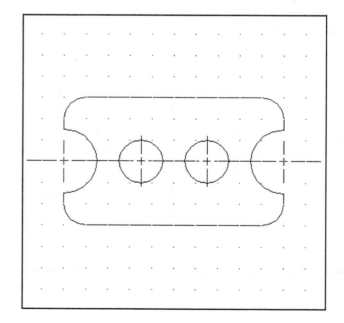

**EX8-28**

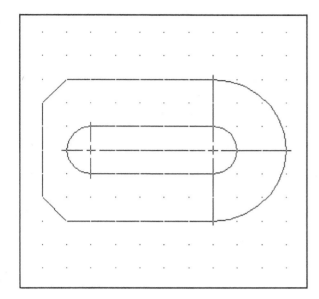

**EX8-29**

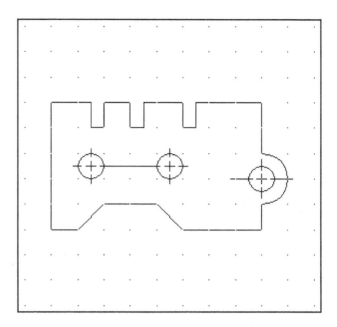

**EX8-30**

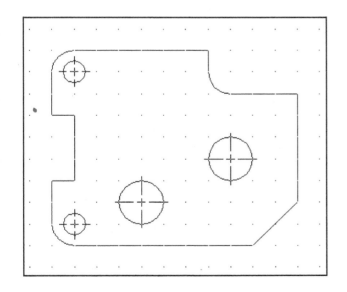

**EX8-31**

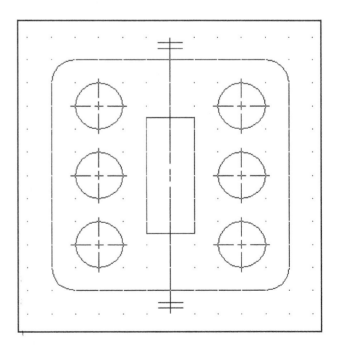

**EX8-32**

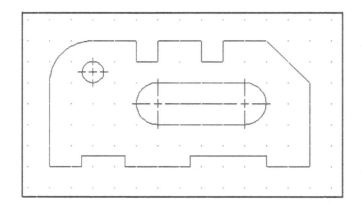

**EX8-33**

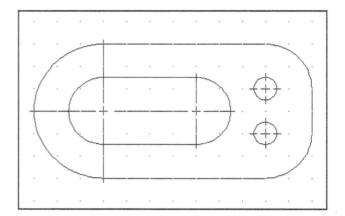

**EX8-34**

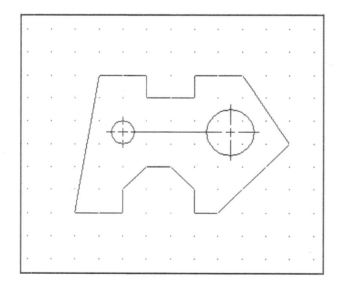

**EX8-35**

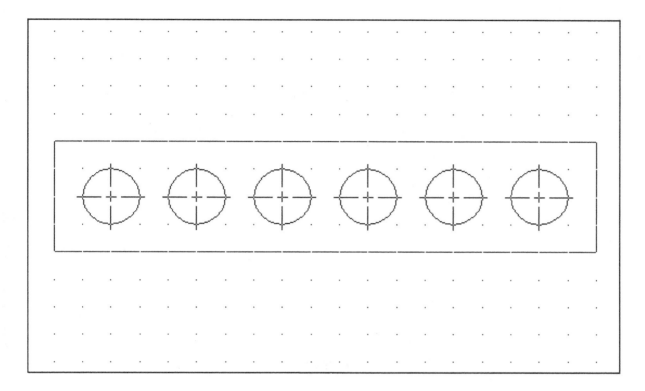

**EX8-36**

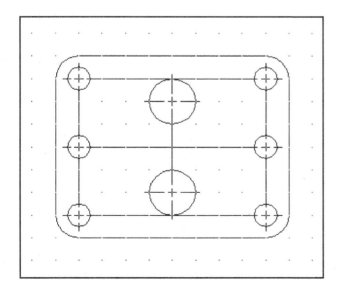

**EX8-37**

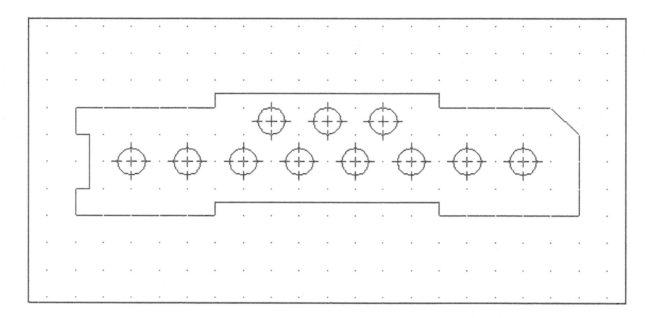

**EX8-38**

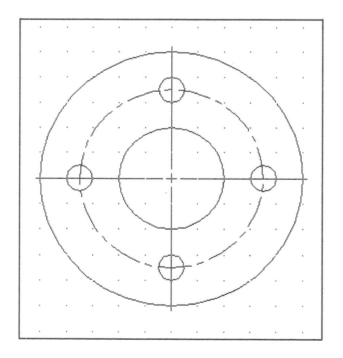

**EX8-39**

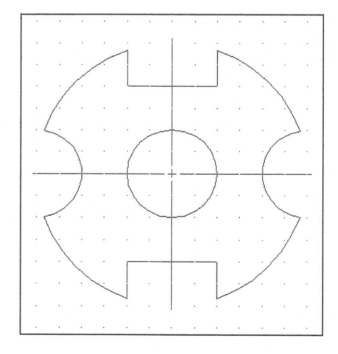

**EX8-40**

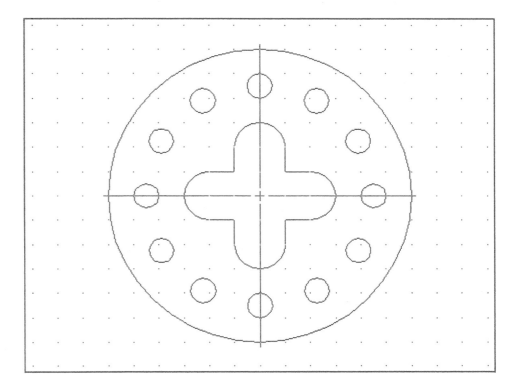

**EX8-41**

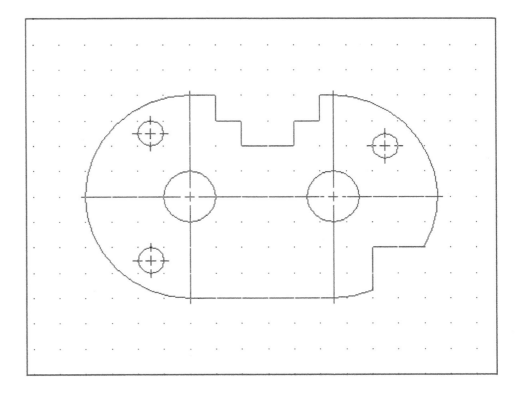

**EX8-42**

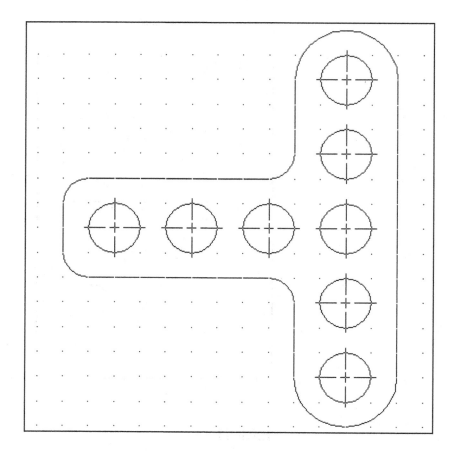

**EX8-43**

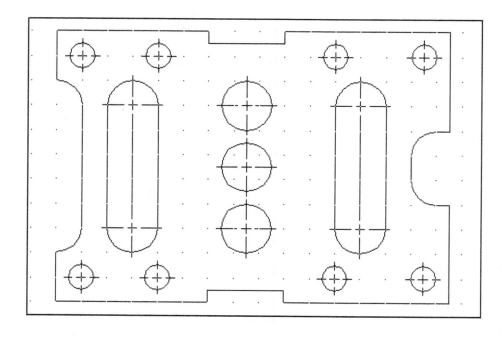

**EX8-44**

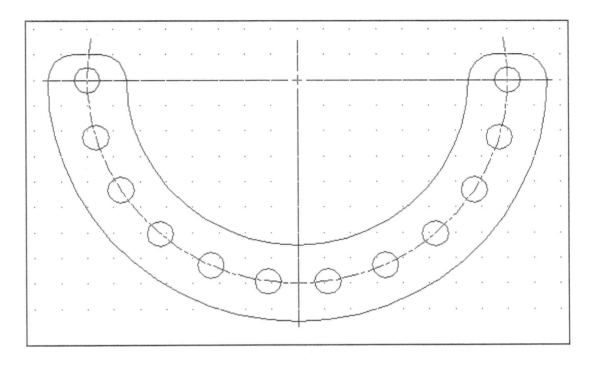

**EX8-45**

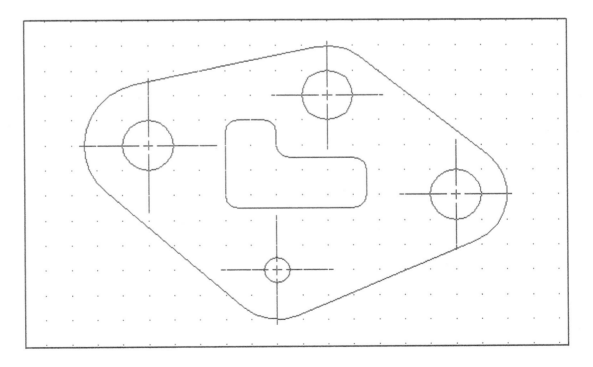

**EX8-46**

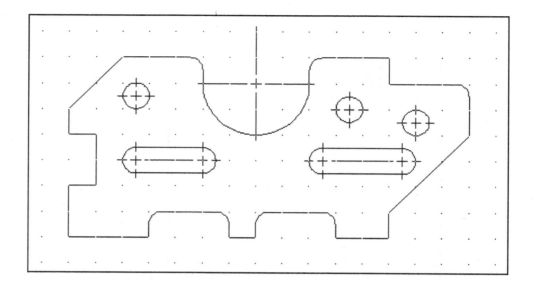

**EX8-47**

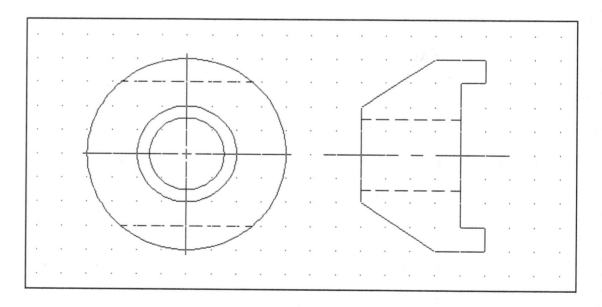

**EX8-48**

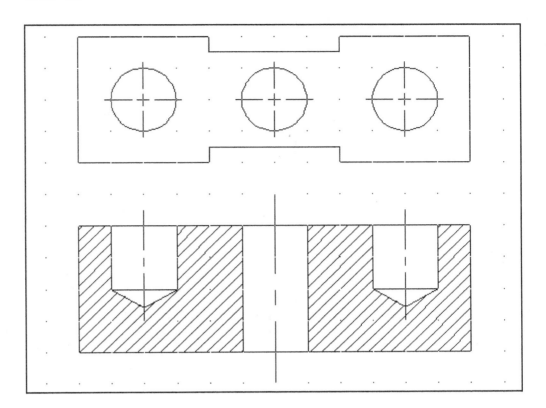

**EX8-49**

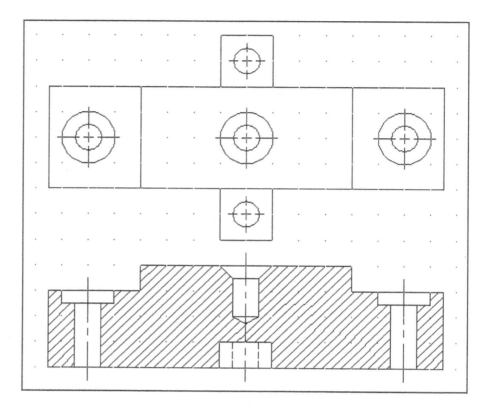

**EX8-50**

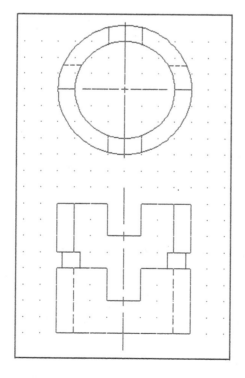

**EX8-51**

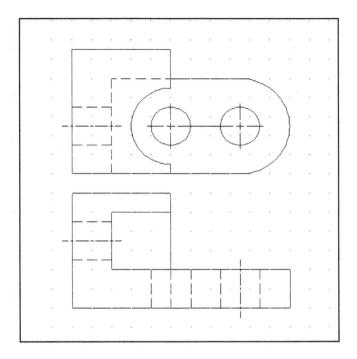

**EX8-52**

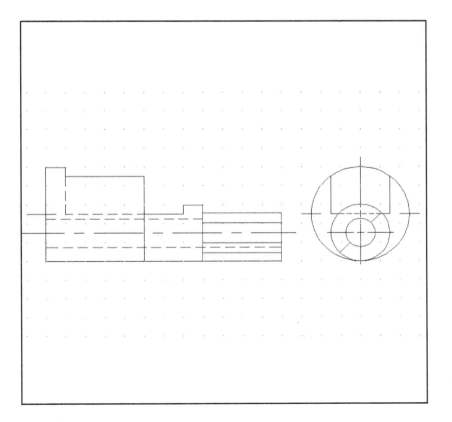

**EX8-53**

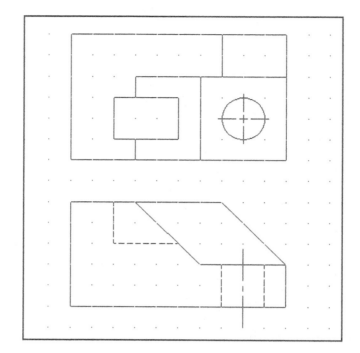

# chapter nine
## Tolerancing

### 9-1 Introduction

*Tolerances* define the manufacturing limits for dimensions. All dimensions have tolerances either written directly on a drawing as part of the dimension or implied by a predefined set of standard tolerances that apply to any dimension that does not have a stated tolerance.

This chapter explains general tolerance conventions and how they are applied using AutoCAD. It includes a sample tolerance study and an explanation of standard fits and surface finishes.

Chapter 10 explains geometric tolerances.

### 9-2 Direct Tolerance Methods

Two methods can be used to include tolerances as part of a dimension: plus and minus, and limits. Plus and minus tolerances can be expressed in either bilateral form or unilateral form.

A *bilateral tolerance* has both a plus value and a minus value. A *unilateral tolerance* has either the plus or minus value equal to 0. Figure 9-1 shows a horizontal dimension of 60 millimeters that includes a bilateral tolerance of plus or minus 1 and another dimension of 60 millimeters that includes a bilateral tolerance of plus .20 or minus .10. Figure 9-1 also shows a dimension of 65 millimeters that includes a unilateral tolerance of plus 1 or 0 in the minus position.

*Plus or minus tolerances* define a range for manufacturing. If inspection shows that all dimensioned distances on an object fall within their specified tolerance range, the object is considered acceptable; that is, it has been manufactured correctly.

The dimension and tolerance 60 ± 1 means that the distance must be manufactured within a range no greater than 61 nor less than 59. The dimension and tolerance 60.00 + 0.20/–0.10 defines the tolerance range as 60.20 to 59.90. The dimension and tolerance 60 + 2/0 defines the tolerance range as 62 to 60.

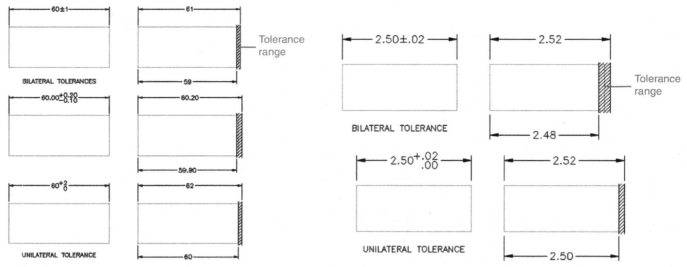

**Figure 9-1**

**Figure 9-2**

Figure 9-2 shows some bilateral and unilateral tolerances applied using decimal inch values. Inch dimensions and tolerances are written in a slightly different format from that used for millimeter dimensions and tolerances, but they also define manufacturing ranges for dimension values. The horizontal bilateral dimension and tolerance 2.50 ± .02 defines the longest acceptable distance as 2.52 inches and the shortest as 2.48. The unilateral dimension 2.50 + .02/–.00 defines the longest acceptable distance as 2.52 and the shortest as 2.50.

## 9-3 Tolerance Expressions

Dimension and tolerance values are written differently for inch and millimeter values (Figure 9-3). Unilateral dimensions for millimeter values specify a zero limit with a single 0. A zero limit for inch values must include the same number of decimal places given for the dimension value. In the example shown in Figure 9-3, the dimension value .500 has a unilateral tolerance with minus zero tolerance. The zero limit is written as .000, with three decimal places for both the dimension and the tolerance.

**Figure 9-3**

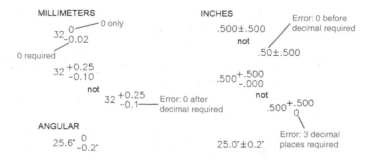

Both values in a bilateral tolerance must contain the same number of decimal places, although for millimeter values the tolerance values need not include the same number of decimal places as the dimension value. In Figure 9-3, the dimension value 32 is accompanied by tolerances of +0.25 and –0.10. This form is not acceptable for inch dimensions and tolerances. An equivalent inch dimension and tolerance would be written as 32.00 + 0.25/–0.10.

Degree values must include the same number of decimal places in both the dimension value and the tolerance values for bilateral tolerances. A single 0 may be used for a unilateral tolerance.

## 9-4 Understanding Plus and Minus Tolerances

A millimeter dimension and tolerance of 12.0 + 0.2/–0.1 means that the longest acceptable distance is 12.2000…0 and the shortest is 11.9000…0. The total range is 0.3000…0.

After an object is manufactured, it is inspected to ensure that the object has been manufactured correctly. Each dimensioned distance is measured and, if it is within the specified tolerance, is accepted. If the measured distance is not within the specified tolerance, the part is rejected. Some rejected objects may be reworked to bring them into the specified tolerance range, whereas others are simply scrapped.

Figure 9-4 shows a dimension with a tolerance. Assume that five objects were manufactured by using the same 12 + 0.2/–0.1 dimension and tolerance. The objects were then inspected, and the results were as listed in the figure. Inspected measurements usually have at least one more decimal place than specified in the tolerance. Which objects are acceptable, and which are not? In this case, object 3 is too long, and object 5 is too short because their measured distances are not within the specified tolerances.

Figure 9-5 shows a dimension and tolerance of 3.50 ± 0.02 inches. Object 3 is not acceptable because it is too short, and object 4 is not acceptable because it is too long.

GIVEN (mm)

$12^{+0.2}_{-0.1}$

MEANS
Maximum Tolerance = 12.2
Minimum Tolerance = 11.9

Total Tolerance = 0.3

| OBJECT | AS MEASURED | ACCEPTABLE |
|--------|-------------|------------|
| 1 | 12.160 | OK |
| 2 | 12.020 | OK |
| 3 | 12.203 | TOO LONG |
| 4 | 11.920 | OK |
| 5 | 11.895 | TOO SHORT |

**Figure 9-4**

GIVEN (Inches)

3.50±.02

MEANS
Maximum Tolerance = 3.52
Minimum Tolerance = 3.48

Total Tolerance = 0.04

| OBJECT | AS MEASURED | ACCEPTABLE |
|--------|-------------|------------|
| 1 | 3.520 | OK |
| 2 | 3.486 | OK |
| 3 | 3.470 | TOO SHORT |
| 4 | 3.521 | TOO LONG |
| 5 | 3.515 | OK |

**Figure 9-5**

## 9-5 Creating Plus and Minus Tolerances with AutoCAD

You can create plus and minus tolerances using AutoCAD in one of four ways: using the **Text** option or the **Mtext** option, using the **Text Override** tool, typing the tolerances directly using **Dtext**, or setting the plus and minus values by using the **Dimension Style** tool.

### Creating Plus and Minus Tolerances Using the Text Option

The example given is for a horizontal dimension, but the procedure is the same for any linear or radial dimension.

**1** Select the **Linear** tool from the **Dimensions** panel.

**2** Select the extension line origins, as explained in Section 8-3. Drag the dimension line to its location but don't click to place it.

```
Specify dimension line location or
[Mtext Text Angle Horizontal Vertical Rotated]:
```

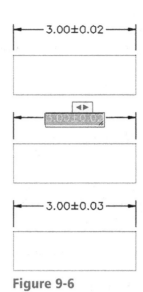

**Figure 9-6**

**3** Type **t** and press **Enter**.

`Dimension text <x.xxxx>:`

**4** Type the appropriate text value and press **Enter**.

Type **<>** (open and closed angle bracket to retain the measured value), then **%%p**, then the tolerance value.

`Dimension text <x.xxxx><>%%p.02.`

In this example, the resulting dimension shows the real dimension value followed by ± 0.02 (Figure 9-6, top dimension).

## Creating Plus and Minus Tolerances with the Text Override Tool

Any existing text can be changed by using the **Text Override** tool. Figure 9-6 shows a 3.00 ± .02 dimension. Say that you want to change that tolerance to ±.03.

**1** Double-click the dimension value.

A box with a shaded background appears around the dimension value.

**2** Delete the existing text by pressing the **Delete** key.

The value disappears.

**3** Type in the new value and press **Enter**.

> **NOTE**
>
> The symbol ± can also be created with the Windows character map: Hold down the Alt key and type 0177.

## Using Dtext to Create a Plus and Minus Tolerance

**1** Type **Dtext** in response to a command prompt.

**2** Place the starting point for the text and then define the appropriate height and angle.

**3** Type **5.00%%p.02** and press **Enter**.

In the example shown, the resulting dimension is 5.00 ± .02. The symbol initially appears on the screen as %%p but changes to ± when the last text line is entered.

## Using the Dimension Style Manager

**1** Access the **Dimension Style Manager** from the **Dimensions** panel.

**2** Select the **Modify** option and then select the **Tolerances** tab.

**3** Click the arrow to the right of the **Method** box.

A list of available tolerancing methods appears (Figure 9-7). AutoCAD offers two options for plus and minus tolerancing: **Symmetrical** and **Deviation**.

Figure 9-7

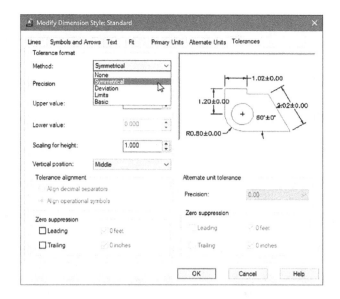

Note that the steps below are not all to be taken together. If you are creating symmetrical tolerances, follow steps 4a through 6a. If you are creating deviation tolerances, follow steps 4b through 6b.

## Symmetrical Tolerances

**4a** Select **Symmetrical** from the **Method** drop-down (Figure 9-8).

Figure 9-8

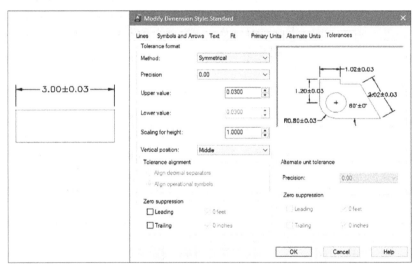

**5a** In the **Upper value** box, type the value **0.0300**.

Only an upper value needs to be entered here because the tolerance value is symmetrical.

**6a** Return to the drawing screen.

Dimensions created by using the **Dimensions** panel now automatically include a ±0.0300 tolerance.

## Deviation Tolerances

**4b** Select **Deviation** from the **Method** drop-down (Figure 9-9).

Figure 9-9

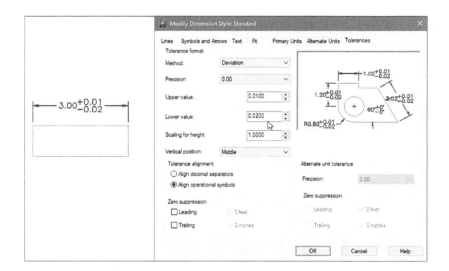

**5b** In the **Upper value** and **Lower value** boxes, enter the values **0.0100** and **0.0200**, respectively.

**6b** Return to the drawing screen.

Dimensions created by using the **Dimensions** panel now automatically include a –0.0100, –0.0300 tolerance.

You can also use the **Dimension Style Manager** to change the precision of the initial AutoCAD-selected dimension values. (The default value is four places: 1.0000.) If, for example, two decimal places are desired, use the **Precision** box on the **Primary Units** tab on the **Dimension Style Manager** dialog box to reset the system for two decimal places (see Section 8-5).

## 9-6 Limit Tolerances

Figure 9-10 shows examples of limit tolerances. Limit tolerances replace dimension values. Two values are given: the upper and lower limits for the dimension value. The limit tolerance 62.1 and 59.9 is mathematically equal to 62 ± 0.1, but the stated limit tolerance is considered easier to read and understand.

Figure 9-10

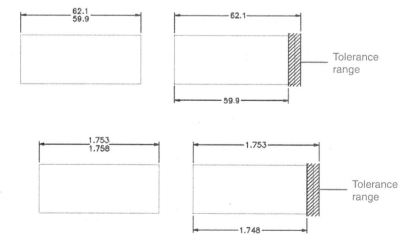

Limit tolerances define a range for manufacture. Final distances on an object must fall within the specified range in order to be acceptable.

## 9-7 Creating Limit Tolerances in AutoCAD

Limit tolerances are created by using AutoCAD in one of two ways: by using the **Dimension Style Manager** or by modifying a given dimension using the **Dimension Edit** tool.

### Creating a Limit Tolerance Using the Dimension Style Manager

**1** Access the **Dimension Style Manager** from the **Dimensions** panel.

**2** Select **Modify** and then select the **Tolerances** tab. The **Modify Dimension Style: Standard** dialog box appears.

**3** Click the arrow to the right of the **Method** drop-down.

A list of available tolerance methods appears (Figure 9-7).

**4** Select **Limits**.

The **Tolerance format** area reappears with the headings **Upper value** and **Lower value** now in black letters, meaning that they can be accessed.

**5** Type in the upper and lower values—in this case, **0.0100** and **0.0300** (Figure 9-11).

**6** Return to the drawing screen.

**Figure 9-11**

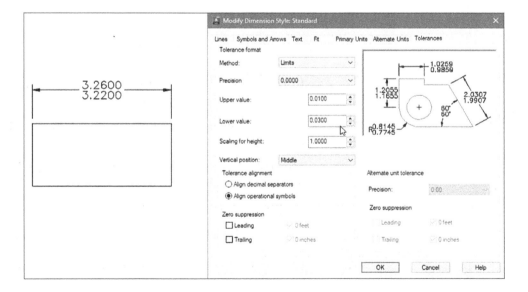

Every dimension created with the **Linear** dimension tool now automatically creates a limit tolerance on the basis of the selected distance and the selected upper and lower values. Figure 9-11 shows the results of the **Linear** dimension tool applied to the distance 3.2500. The upper limit is 3.2500+0.0100, and the lower limit is 3.2500–0.0300.

## Using the Properties Palette to Change an Existing Dimension to a Limit Tolerance Dimension

**1** Open the **Properties** palette by pressing **Ctrl+1**. Select the dimension (Figure 9-12).

**Figure 9-12**

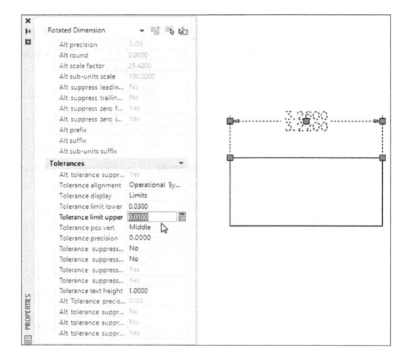

**2** In the **Properties** palette, scroll to the **Tolerances** section at the bottom of the list of properties.

**3** On the **Tolerance display** row, click **None**. From the drop-down, select **Limits**.

The Tolerance limit lower and Tolerance limit upper boxes become active.

**4** Highlight the text in the box and type in the new text.

**5** Click the drawing screen.

Figure 9-12 shows the resulting changed dimension.

## 9-8 Angular Tolerances

Figure 9-13 shows an example of an angular dimension with a tolerance. The procedure explained for plus and minus tolerances applies to angular, as well as to linear, dimensions and tolerances.

Figure 9-13

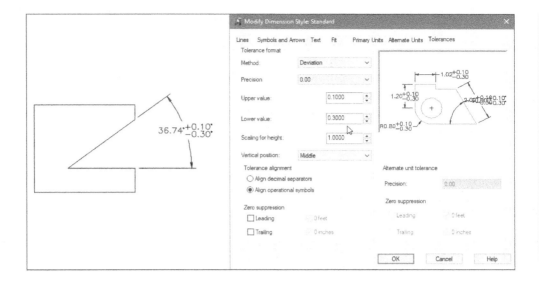

The precision of angular dimensions is set using the **Primary Units** dialog box. In the example that follows, a deviation tolerance of +0.10, –0.30 was also specified.

## Setting the Precision for Angular Dimensions and Tolerances

**1** Access the **Dimension Style Manager**, select **Modify**, and then select the **Primary Units** tab.

**2** Click the arrow to the right of **Precision**.

A list of available precision factors appears.

**3** Select two significant figures for both **Dimension** and **Tolerance** and then return to the drawing screen.

The precision for the angular value can be changed by using the **Precision** option under **Angular Dimensions**.

## Creating an Angular Dimension and Tolerance

**1** Select **Angular** from the **Dimension** tool on the **Dimensions** panel.

`Select arc, circle, line, or <specify vertex>:`

**2** Select one of the lines that define the angle.

`Select second line:`

**3** Select the second line.

`Specify dimension arc line location or [Mtext Text Angle]:`

**4** Select a location for the dimension and press **Enter**.

The **Mtext** and **Text** options are used as explained for linear dimensions and tolerance in Section 9-5. Symmetrical, deviation, and limit tolerances can be applied to angular tolerances in the same way that they are applied to linear tolerances.

## 9-9 Standard Tolerances

A manufacturer is likely to establish a set of standard tolerances that are applied to any dimension that does not include a specific tolerance. Figure 9-14 shows some possible standard tolerances. Standard tolerances vary from company to company. Standard tolerances are usually listed on the first page of a drawing to the left of the title block, but this location may vary.

**Figure 9-14**

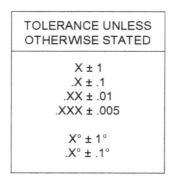

TOLERANCE UNLESS
OTHERWISE STATED

X ± 1
.X ± .1
.XX ± .01
.XXX ± .005

X° ± 1°
.X° ± .1°

The X value used when specifying standard tolerances means any X stated in that format. The dimension value 52.00 has an implied tolerance of ± .01. This is because the stated standard tolerance is .XX ± .01, so any dimension value with two decimal places has a standard implied tolerance of ± .01. The dimension value 52.000 has an implied tolerance of ± .005.

## 9-10 Double Dimensioning

It is an error, called *double dimensioning*, to dimension the same distance twice. Double dimensioning is an error because it does not allow for tolerance buildup across a distance.

Figure 9-15 shows an object that has been dimensioned twice across its horizontal length: once by using three 30-millimeter dimensions and a second time by using the 90-millimeter overall dimension. The two dimensions are mathematically equal, but they are not equal when tolerances are considered. Assume that each dimension has a standard tolerance of ±1 millimeter. The three 30-millimeter dimensions could create an acceptable distance of 90 ± 3 millimeters, or a maximum distance of 93 and a minimum distance of 87. The overall dimension of 90 millimeters allows a maximum distance of 91 and a minimum distance of 89. The two dimensions yield different results when tolerances are considered.

**Figure 9-15**

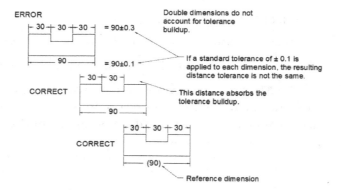

The size and location of a tolerance depends on the design objectives for the object, how the object will be manufactured, and how it will be inspected. Even objects that have similar shapes may be dimensioned and toleranced very differently.

One possible solution to the double dimensioning shown in Figure 9-15 is to remove one of the 30-millimeter dimensions and to allow that distance to "float"—that is, absorb the cumulated tolerances. The choice of which 30-millimeter dimension to eliminate depends on the design objectives for the part. For this example, the far-right dimension was eliminated to remove the double dimensioning error.

Another possible solution to the double dimensioning error is to retain the three 30-millimeter dimensions and to change the 90-millimeter overall dimension to a reference dimension. A reference dimension is used only for mathematical convenience. It is not used during the manufacturing or inspection process. A reference dimension is designated on a drawing with parentheses: (90).

If the 90-millimeter dimension were referenced, then only the three 30-millimeter dimensions would be used to manufacture and inspect the object. This would eliminate the double dimensioning error.

## 9-11 Chain Dimensions and Baseline Dimensions

Two systems are used to apply dimensions and tolerances to a drawing: *chain* and *baseline*. Figure 9-16 shows examples of both systems. Chain dimensions relate each feature to the feature next to it; baseline dimensions relate all features to a single baseline or datum.

**Figure 9-16**

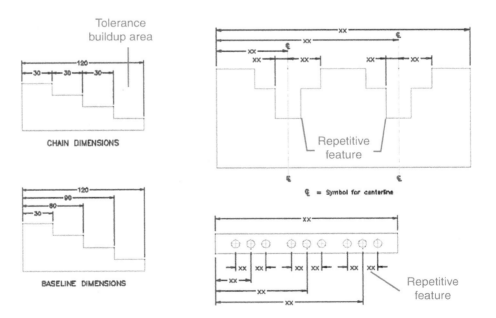

Chain and baseline dimensions may be used together. Figure 9-16 also shows two objects with repetitive features: one object includes two slots, and the other object includes three sets of three holes. In each example, the center of the repetitive feature is dimensioned to the left side of the object, which serves as a baseline. The sizes of the individual features are dimensioned by using chain dimensions referenced to centerlines.

Baseline dimensions eliminate tolerance buildup and can be related directly to the reference axis of many machines. They tend to take up much more area on a drawing than do chain dimensions.

Chain dimensions are useful in relating one feature to another, such as the repetitive hole pattern shown in Figure 9-16. In this example, the distance between the holes is more important than the distance of the individual hole from the baseline.

Figure 9-17 shows the same object dimensioned twice, once using chain dimensions and once using baseline dimensions. All distances are assigned a tolerance range of 2 millimeters, stated in terms of limit tolerances. The maximum distance for line A is 28 millimeters by the chain system and 27 millimeters by the baseline system. The 1-millimeter difference comes from the elimination of the first 26 – 24 limit dimension found on the chain example but not on the baseline.

**Figure 9-17**

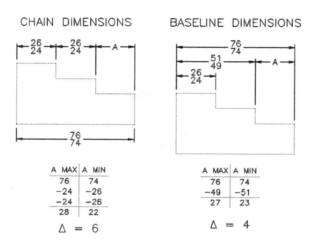

The total tolerance difference is 6 millimeters for the chain and 4 millimeters for the baseline. The baseline reduces the tolerance variations for the object simply because it applies the tolerances and dimensions differently. So why not always use baseline dimensions? For most applications, the baseline system is probably better, but if the distance between the individual features is more critical than the distance from the feature to the baseline, it is advisable to use the chain system.

## Creating Baseline Dimensions

The **Baseline** tool can be applied only after a linear dimension has been created. The object shown in Figure 9-18 was dimensioned by first creating the 1.00 dimension by use of the **Linear** dimension tool and then by using the **Baseline** tool, as follows:

**1** Create a linear dimension with the **Linear** tool from the **Dimensions** panel.

**Figure 9-18**

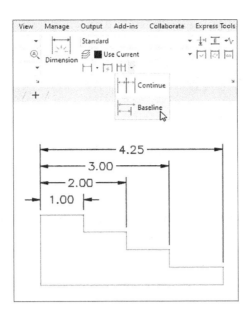

The point selected as the origin for the first extension line becomes the origin of the baseline.

**2** Select the **Baseline** tool from the **Dimensions** panel.

```
Specify a second extension line origin or [Undo Select] <Select>:
```

**3** Select the origin for the second extension line of the baseline dimension.

```
Specify a second extension line origin or [Undo Select] <Select>:
```

**4** Repeat the process until the baseline dimensioning is complete.

**5** Right-click and press **Enter**.

When you create a series of baseline dimensions, the spacing between dimension lines is often too close. You can use the **Dimspace** command to equally space the dimension lines a more suitable distance apart, as described in the following steps.

**6** Type **Dimspace** and press **Enter** or click the **Adjust Space** button on the **Dimensions** panel.

```
Select base dimension:
```

**7** Select the first dimension you created.

```
Select dimensions to space:
```

**8** Select the remaining baseline dimensions and press **Enter**.

```
Enter value of [Auto] <Auto>:
```

**9** Press **Enter** to automatically space the baseline dimensions or enter a specific value.

## 9-12 Tolerance Studies

The term *tolerance study* is used when analyzing the effects of a group of tolerances on each other and on an object. Figure 9-19 shows an object on the left with two horizontal dimensions. The horizontal distance A is not dimensioned. Its length depends on the tolerances of the two horizontal dimensions.

Figure 9-19

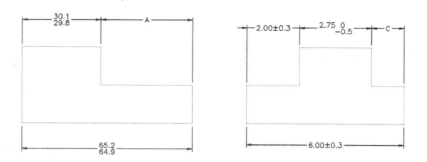

## Calculating A's Maximum Length

Distance A is longest when the overall distance is at its longest and the other distance is at its shortest:

$$
\begin{array}{r}
65.2 \\
-29.8 \\
\hline
35.4
\end{array}
$$

## Calculating A's Minimum Length

Distance A is shortest when the overall length is at its shortest and the other length is at its longest:

$$
\begin{array}{r}
64.9 \\
-30.1 \\
\hline
34.8
\end{array}
$$

Figure 9-19 shows a second figure that includes three horizontal dimensions. Distance C is at its maximum length when the overall dimension is at its longest and the other dimensions are at their shortest. Distance C is at its minimum length when the overall length is at its shortest and the other dimensions are at their longest.

## 9-13 Rectangular Dimensions

Figure 9-20 shows an example of rectangular dimensions referenced to baselines. Figure 9-21 shows a circular object for which dimensions are referenced to a circle's centerlines. Dimensioning to a circle's centerline is critical to accurate hole location.

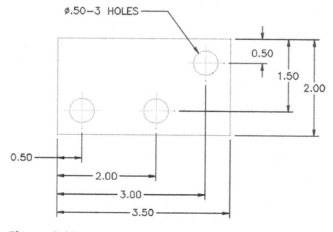

**Figure 9-20**

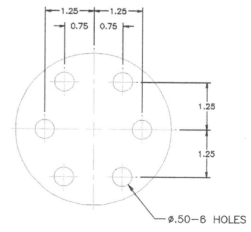

**Figure 9-21**

## 9-14 Hole Locations

When rectangular dimensions are used, the location of a hole's center point is defined by two linear dimensions. The result is a rectangular tolerance zone whose size is based on the linear dimension's tolerances. The shape of the center point's tolerance zone may be changed to circular by positional tolerancing, as described in Section 10-16.

Figure 9-22 shows the location and size dimensions for a hole. Also shown are the resulting tolerance zone and the overall possible hole shape. The center point's tolerance is ± 0.2 by ± 0.3, based on the given linear locating tolerances.

**Figure 9-22**

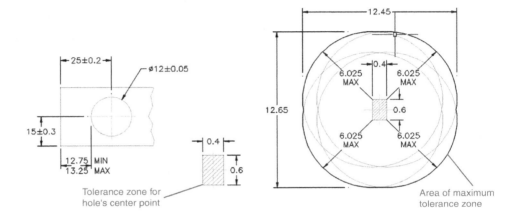

Tolerance zone for hole's center point

Area of maximum tolerance zone

The hole diameter has a tolerance of ± 0.05. This value must be added to the center point location tolerances to define the maximum possible overall shape of the hole. The maximum possible hole shape is determined by drawing the maximum radius from the four corner points of the tolerance zone. This means that the left edge of the hole could be as close to the vertical baseline as 12.75 or as far as 13.25. The 12.75 value was derived by subtracting the maximum hole diameter value, 12.05, from the minimum linear distance, 24.80 (24.80 – 12.05 = 12.75). The 13.25 value was derived by subtracting the minimum hole diameter, 11.95, from the maximum linear distance, 25.20 (25.20 – 11.95 = 13.25).

Figure 9-23 shows a hole's tolerance zone based on polar dimensions. The zone has a sector shape, and the possible hole shape is determined by locating the maximum radius at the four corner points of the tolerance zone.

**Figure 9-23**

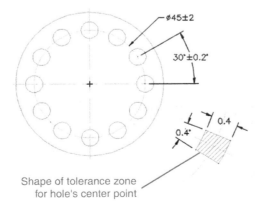

Shape of tolerance zone for hole's center point

## 9-15 Choosing a Shaft for a Toleranced Hole

Given the hole location and size shown in Figure 9-23, what is the largest-diameter shaft that will always fit into the hole?

Figure 9-24 shows the hole's center point tolerance zone based on the given linear locating tolerances. Four circles drawn centered at the four corners of the linear tolerance zone represent the smallest possible hole diameter. The circles define an area that represents the maximum shaft size that will always fit into the hole, regardless of how the given dimensions are applied.

**Figure 9-24**

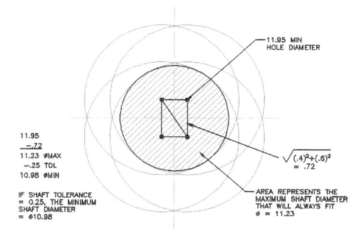

```
11.95
 −.72
11.23 ∅MAX
 −.25 TOL
10.98 ∅MIN

IF  SHAFT  TOLERANCE
=  0.25,  THE  MINIMUM
SHAFT  DIAMETER
=  ∅10.98
```

11.95 MIN
HOLE  DIAMETER

$\sqrt{(.4)^2 + (.6)^2}$
= .72

AREA  REPRESENTS  THE
MAXIMUM  SHAFT  DIAMETER
THAT  WILL  ALWAYS  FIT
∅ = 11.23

The diameter of this circular area can be calculated by subtracting the maximum diagonal distance across the linear tolerance zone (corner to corner) from the minimum hole diameter.

The results can be expressed as a formula.

## For Linear Dimensions and Tolerances

$$S_{max} = H_{min} - DTZ$$

where

$S_{max}$ = Maximum shaft diameter

$H_{min}$ = Minimum hole diameter

DTZ = Diagonal distance across the tolerance zone

In the example shown, the diagonal distance is determined by using the Pythagorean theorem:

$$DTZ = \sqrt{(.4)^2 + (.6)^2}$$
$$= \sqrt{.16 + .36}$$
$$DTZ = .72$$

This means that the maximum shaft diameter that will always fit into the given hole is 11.23.

$$S_{max} = H_{min} - DTZ$$
$$= 11.95 - .72$$
$$S_{max} = 11.23$$

This procedure represents a restricted application of the general formula for positional tolerances presented in Chapter 10. For a more complete discussion, see Section 10-16. Once the maximum shaft size has been established, a tolerance can be applied to the shaft. If the shaft had a total tolerance of 0.25, the minimum shaft diameter would be 11.23 – 0.25, or 10.98. Figure 9-24 shows a shaft dimensioned and toleranced according to these values.

The formula presented is based on the assumption that the shaft is perfectly placed on the hole's center point. This assumption is reasonable if two objects are joined by a fastener and both objects are free to move. When both objects are free to move about a common fastener, they are called *floating objects*.

## 9-16 Drawing Problem

Parts A and B in Figure 9-25 are to be joined by a common shaft. The total tolerance for the shaft is to be 0.05. What are the maximum and minimum shaft diameters?

**Figure 9-25**

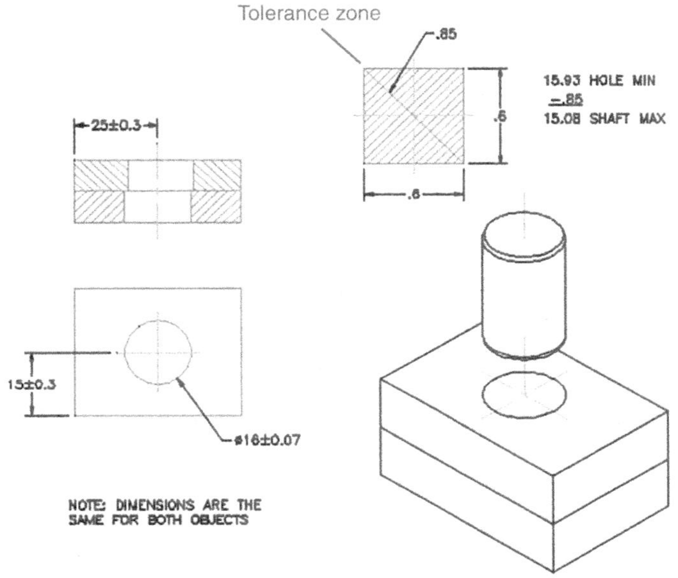

Both objects have the same dimensions and tolerances and are floating relative to each other.

$$S_{max} = H_{min} - DTZ$$

$$= 15.93 - .85$$

$$S_{max} = 15.08$$

The shaft's minimum diameter is found by subtracting the total tolerance requirement from the calculated maximum diameter.

$$15.08 - .05 = 15.03$$

Therefore,

Shaft max = 15.08

Shaft min = 15.03

## 9-17 Drawing Problem

The procedure presented in the drawing problem in Section 9-16 can be worked in reverse to determine the maximum and minimum hole sizes, according to a given shaft size.

Objects AA and BB in Figure 9-26 are to be joined by a bolt whose maximum diameter is 0.248. What is the minimum hole size for the objects that will always accept the bolt? What is the maximum hole size if the total hole tolerance is 0.007?

$$S_{max} = H_{min} - DTZ$$

**Figure 9-26**

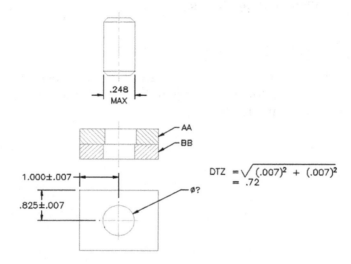

In this example, $H_{min}$ is the unknown factor, so the equation is rewritten:

$$H_{min} = S_{max} + DTZ$$

$$= .248 + .010$$

$$H_{min} = .258$$

This is the minimum hole diameter, so the total tolerance requirement is added to this value:

$$.258 + .007 = .265$$

Therefore,

Hole max = .265

Hole min = .258

## 9-18 Standard Fits (Metric Values)

Calculating tolerances between holes and shafts that fit together is so common in engineering design that a group of standard values and notations has been established.

There are three possible types of fits between a shaft and a hole: clearance, interference, and transition (Figure 9-27). There are several subclassifications within each of these categories.

Figure 9-27

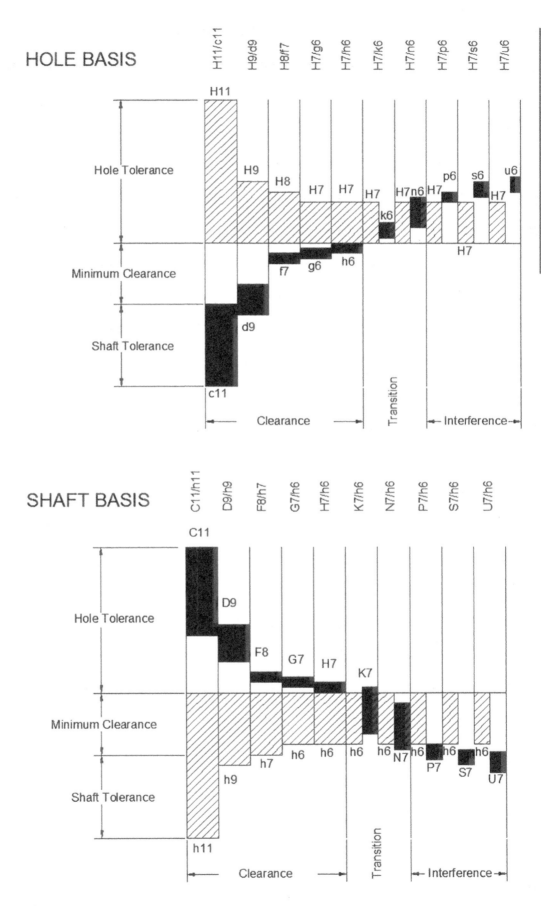

A *clearance fit* always defines the maximum shaft diameter as smaller than the minimum hole diameter. The difference between the two diameters is the amount of clearance. It is possible for a clearance fit to be defined with zero clearance; this means that the maximum shaft diameter is equal to the minimum hole diameter.

An *interference fit* always defines the minimum shaft diameter as larger than the maximum hole diameter; that is, the shaft is always bigger than the hole. An interference fit is the converse of a clearance fit. The difference between the diameter of the shaft and the hole is the amount of interference.

An interference fit is primarily used to assemble objects together. Interference fits eliminate the need for threads, welds, or other joining methods. Using an interference fit for joining two objects is generally limited to light-load applications.

It is sometimes difficult to visualize how a shaft can be assembled into a hole with a diameter smaller than that of the shaft. It is sometimes done by a hydraulic press that slowly forces the two parts together. The joining process can be augmented by the use of lubricants or heat. The hole is heated, causing it to expand, the shaft is inserted, and the hole is allowed to cool and shrink around the shaft.

A *transition fit* may be either a clearance fit or an interference fit. There may be a clearance between the shaft and the hole, or there may be an interference.

Figure 9-27 shows two graphic representations of 20 different standard hole/shaft tolerance ranges. The figure shows ranges for hole tolerances, shaft tolerances, and the amount of clearance or interference for each classification. The notations are based on Standard International Tolerance values. A specific description for each category of fit follows.

## Clearance Fits

H11/c11 or C11/h11 = Loose running fit

H9/d9 or D9/h9 = Free running fit

H8/f7 or F8/h7 = Close running fit

H7/g6 or G7/h6 = Sliding fit

H7/h6 = Locational clearance fit

## Transition Fits

H7/k6 or K7/h6 = Locational transition fit

H7/n6 or N7/h6 = Locational transition fit

## Interference Fits

H7/p6 or P7/h6 = Locational transition fit

H7/s6 or S7/h6 = Medium drive fit

H7/u6 or U7/h6 = Force fit

Not all possible sizes can be listed in this book. See the online Appendix, which lists preferred sizes. Tolerances for sizes between the stated sizes are derived by going to the next nearest given size. The values are not interpolated. A basic size of 27 would use the tolerance values listed for 25. Sizes that are exactly halfway between two stated sizes may use either set of values, depending on the design requirements.

## 9-19 Nominal Sizes

The term *nominal* refers to the approximate size of an object that matches a common fraction or whole number. A shaft with dimension 1.500 ± 0.003 is said to have a nominal size of "one and a half inches." The dimension 1.500 + 0.000/–0.005 is also said to have a nominal size of "one and a half inches." In both examples, 1.5 is the closest common fraction.

## 9-20 Hole and Shaft Basis

One of the charts shown in Figure 9-27 applies tolerances starting with the nominal hole sizes, called *hole basis tolerances*; the other applies tolerances starting with the shaft nominal sizes, called *shaft basis tolerances*. The choice of which set of values to use depends on the design application. In general, hole basis numbers are used more often because it is more difficult to vary hole diameters manufactured by the use of specific drill sizes than shaft sizes manufactured by the use of a lathe. Shaft sizes may be used when a specific fastener diameter is used to assemble several objects.

Figure 9-28 shows a hole, a shaft, and a set of values taken from tables in the online Appendix. One set of values is for hole basis tolerance, and the other set is for shaft basis tolerance. The fit values are the same for both sets of values. The hole basis values were derived starting with a nominal hole size of 20.000, whereas the shaft basis values were derived starting with a shaft nominal size of 20.000. The letters used to identify holes are always written in capital letters, and the letters for shaft values are lowercase.

**Figure 9-28**

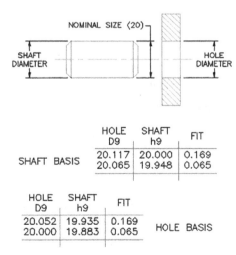

| SHAFT BASIS | HOLE D9 | SHAFT h9 | FIT |
|---|---|---|---|
| | 20.117 | 20.000 | 0.169 |
| | 20.065 | 19.948 | 0.065 |

| HOLE D9 | SHAFT h9 | FIT | |
|---|---|---|---|
| 20.052 | 19.935 | 0.169 | HOLE BASIS |
| 20.000 | 19.883 | 0.065 | |

Additional fit tolerances can be found on the Web. Search for fits and tolerances.

## 9-21 Drawing Problem

Dimension a hole and a shaft that are to fit together, using a preferred clearance fit. Use hole basis values based on a nominal size of 12 mm.

Figure 9-29 shows values taken from the appropriate table in the online Appendix. The values may be applied directly to the shaft and hole as shown.

**Figure 9-29**

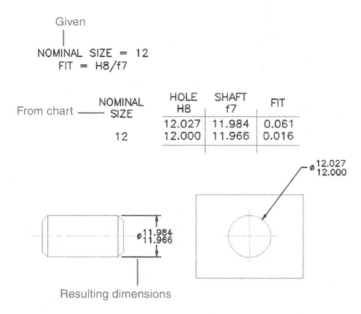

Resulting dimensions

## 9-22 Standard Fits (Inch Values)

The online Appendix includes tables of standard fit tolerances for inch values. The tables for inches are presented for a range of nominal values and are not for specific values, as are the metric value tables. The values may be on a hole or shaft basis.

### Fits Defined by Inch Values

Fits defined by inch values are classified as follows:

RC = Running and sliding fits

LC = Clearance locational fits

LT = Transitional locational fits

LN = Interference fits

FN = Force fits

Each of these general categories has several subclassifications within it, defined by a number—for example, Class RC1, Class RC2, and so on through Class RC9. The letter designations are based on International Tolerance Standards, as are metric designations.

The values are listed in thousandths of an inch. A table value of 1.1 means 0.0011 inch. A table value of 0.5 means 0.0005 inch.

Figure 9-30 shows a set of values for a Class RC3 clearance fit hole basis taken from the online Appendix. If the values are applied to a nominal size of 0.5 inch, the resulting hole and shaft sizes are as shown. Plus table values are added to the nominal value; minus values are subtracted from the nominal value.

**Figure 9-30**

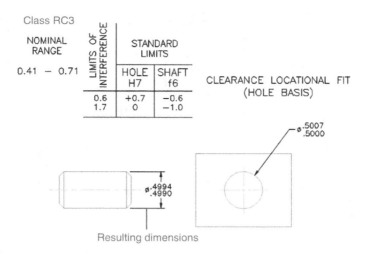

Nominal values that are common to two nominal ranges (such as 0.71) may use values from either range.

## 9-23 Drawing Problem

Dimension a hole and shaft for a Class LN1 interference fit based on a nominal diameter of 0.25 inches. Use hole basis values.

Figure 9-31 shows the values for the 0.24 – 0.40 nominal range as listed in the online Appendix. The values are in thousandths of an inch. Plus values are added to the nominal size. The resulting shaft and hole dimensions are as shown. The diameter of the shaft is larger than that of the hole because this example calls for an interference fit.

**Figure 9-31**

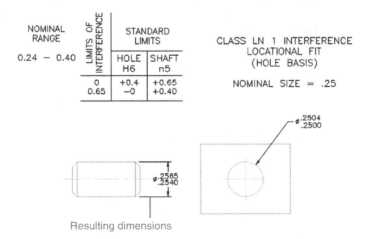

## 9-24 Preferred and Standard Sizes

It is important that designers always consider preferred and standard sizes when selecting sizes for designs. Most tooling is set up to match these sizes, so manufacturing is greatly simplified when preferred and standard sizes are specified. Figure 9-32 shows a list of preferred sizes for metric values.

Figure 9-32

| PREFERRED SIZES (mm) | | | |
|---|---|---|---|
| First Choice | Second Choice | First Choice | Second Choice |
| 1 | 1.1 | 12 | 14 |
| 1.2 | 1.4 | 16 | 18 |
| 1.6 | 1.8 | 20 | 22 |
| 2 | 2.2 | 25 | 28 |
| 2.5 | 2.8 | 30 | 35 |
| 3 | 3.5 | 40 | 45 |
| 4 | 4.5 | 50 | 55 |
| 5 | 5.5 | 60 | 70 |
| 6 | 7 | 80 | 90 |
| 8 | 9 | 100 | 110 |
| 10 | 11 | 120 | 140 |

Consider the case of design calculations that call for a 42-mm-diameter hole. A 42-mm-diameter hole is not a preferred size. A diameter of 40 mm is the closest preferred size, and a 45-mm diameter is a second choice. A 42-mm hole could be manufactured but would require an unusual drill size that may not be available. It would be wise to reconsider the design to see whether a 40-mm-diameter hole could be used, and if not, then a 45-mm-diameter hole possibly could be used.

A very large-quantity production run could possibly justify the cost of special tooling, but for smaller runs, it is probably better to use preferred sizes. Machinists have the required drills, and maintenance people have the appropriate tools for these sizes.

Figure 9-33 lists standard fractional drill sizes. Most companies now specify metric units or decimal inches; however, many standard items are still available in fractional sizes, and many older objects may still require fractional-sized tools and replacement parts. A more complete list is available in the online Appendix.

Figure 9-33

| Fraction | Decimal Equivalent | Fraction | Decimal Equivalent | Fraction | Decimal Equivalent |
|---|---|---|---|---|---|
| 7/64 | .1094 | 21/64 | .3281 | 11/16 | .6875 |
| 1/8 | .1250 | 11/32 | .3438 | 3/4 | .7500 |
| 9/64 | .1406 | 23/64 | .3594 | 13/16 | .8125 |
| 5/32 | .1562 | 3/8 | .3750 | 7/8 | .8750 |
| 11/64 | .1719 | 25/64 | .3906 | 15/16 | .9375 |
| 3/16 | .1875 | 13/32 | .4062 | 1 | 1.0000 |
| 13/64 | .2031 | 27/64 | .4219 | Partial List of standard Twist Drill Sizes (Fractional sizes) | |
| 7/32 | .2188 | 7/16 | .4375 | | |
| 1/4 | .2500 | 29/64 | .4531 | | |
| 17/64 | .2656 | 15/32 | .4688 | | |
| 9/32 | .2812 | 1/2 | .5000 | | |
| 19/64 | .2969 | 9/16 | .5625 | | |
| 5/16 | .3125 | 5/8 | .6250 | | |

# 9-25 Surface Finishes

The term *surface finish* refers to the accuracy (flatness) of a surface. Metric values are measured in micrometers (μm), and inch values are measured in microinches (μin).

The accuracy of a surface depends on the manufacturing process used to produce the surface. Figure 9-34 lists several manufacturing processes and the quality of the surface finish each can be expected to produce.

**Figure 9-34**

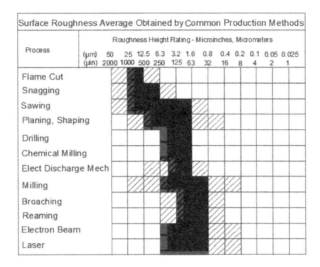

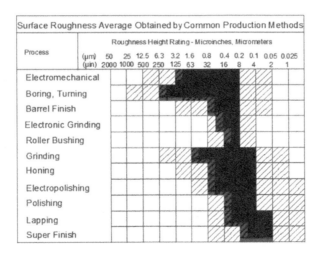

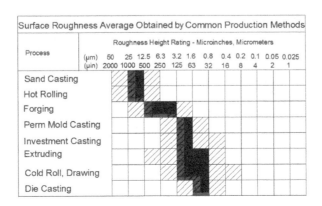

Surface finishes have several design applications. *Datum surfaces*, or surfaces used for baseline dimensioning, should have fairly accurate surface finishes to help ensure accurate measurements; bearing surfaces should have good-quality surface finishes for better load distribution; and parts that operate at high speeds should have smooth finishes to help reduce friction.

Figure 9-35 shows a screw head sitting on a very wavy surface. Note that the head of the screw is in contact with only two wave peaks, meaning that the entire bearing load is concentrated on the two peaks. This situation could cause stress cracks, which could greatly weaken the surface. A better-quality surface finish would increase the bearing contact area.

Figure 9-35 also shows two very rough surfaces moving in contact with each other. The result will be excess wear to both surfaces because the surfaces touch only on the peaks, and these peaks will tend to wear faster than flatter areas. Excess vibration can also result when interfacing surfaces are too rough.

Surface finishes are classified into three categories: surface texture, roughness, and lay. *Surface texture* is a general term that refers to the overall quality and accuracy of a surface.

*Roughness* is a measure of the average deviation of a surface's peaks and valleys (Figure 9-36).

*Lay* refers to the direction of machine marks on a surface. See Figure 9-37. The lay of a surface is particularly important when two moving objects are in contact with each other, especially at high speeds.

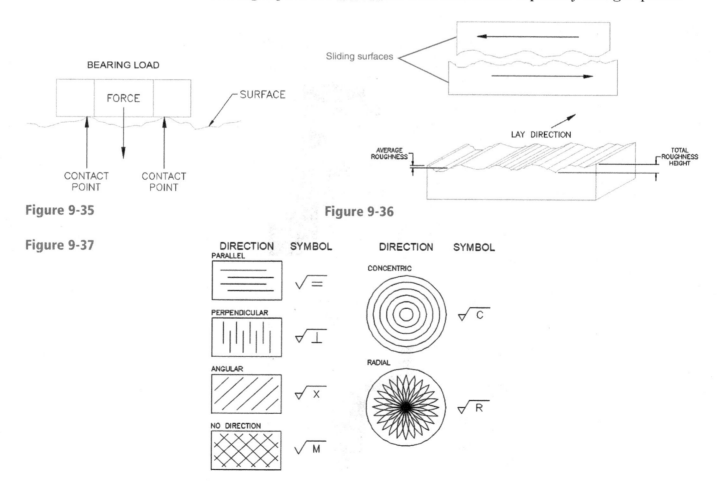

**Figure 9-35**

**Figure 9-36**

**Figure 9-37**

## 9-26 Surface Control Symbols

Surface finishes are indicated on a drawing with surface control symbols (Figure 9-38). The general surface control symbol looks like a check mark. Roughness values may be included with the symbol to specify the required accuracy. Surface control symbols can also be used to specify the manufacturing process that may or may not be used to produce a surface.

Figure 9-39 shows two applications of surface control symbols. In the first example, a 0.8-μm (32-μin) surface finish is specified on the surface that serves as a datum for several horizontal dimensions. A 0.8-μm surface finish is generally considered the minimum acceptable finish for a datum.

A second finish mark with a value of 0.4 μm is located on an extension line that refers to a surface that will be in contact with a moving object. The extra flatness will help prevent wear between the two surfaces.

It is suggested that a general finish mark be drawn and saved as a drawing file with the **Wblock** command so that it can be inserted as needed on future drawings.

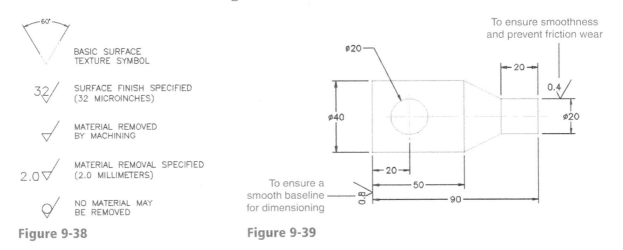

**Figure 9-38**

**Figure 9-39**

## 9-27 Drawing Problem

Figure 9-40 shows two objects that are to be fitted together using a fastener such as a screw-and-nut combination. For this example, a cylinder will be used to represent a fastener. Only two nominal dimensions are given. The dimensions and tolerances were derived as follows.

**Figure 9-40**

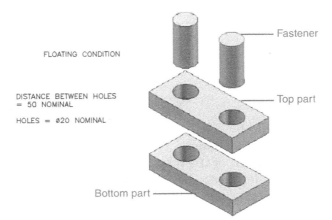

The distance between the centers of the holes is given as 50 nominal. The term *nominal* means that the stated value is only a starting point. The final dimensions will be close to the given value but do not have to equal it.

Assigning tolerances is an iteration process; that is, a tolerance is selected, and other tolerance values are calculated from the selected initial values. If the results are not satisfactory, go back and modify the initial value and calculate the other values again. As your experience grows, you will become better at selecting realistic initial values.

In the example shown in Figure 9-40, start by assigning a tolerance of ± 0.01 to both the top and bottom parts for both the horizontal and vertical dimensions used to locate the holes. This means that there is a possible center point variation of 0.02 for both parts. The parts must always fit together, so tolerances must be assigned on the basis of a worst-case condition, or when the parts are made at the extreme ends of the assigned tolerances.

Figure 9-41 shows a greatly enlarged picture of the worst-case condition created by a tolerance of ± 0.01. The center points of the two holes could be as much as 0.028 apart if they were located at opposite corners of the tolerance zones. This means that the minimum hole diameter must always be at least 0.028 larger than the maximum stud diameter (see Section 9-15). In addition, there should be a clearance tolerance assigned so that the hole and stud are never exactly the same size.

Figure 9-42 shows the resulting tolerances. The 19.96 value includes a 0.1 clearance allowance, and the 19.94 value is the result of an assigned feature tolerance of .02.

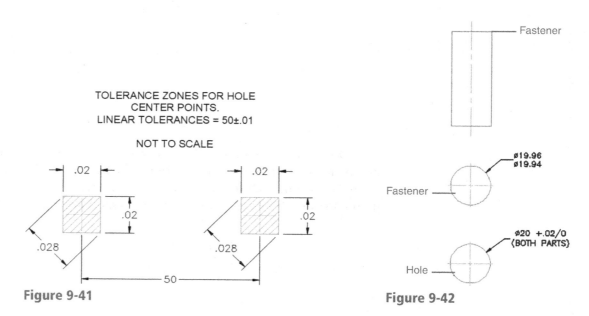

Figure 9-41

Figure 9-42

## Floating Condition

The top and bottom parts shown in Figure 9-40 are to be joined by two independent fasteners; that is, the location of one fastener does not depend on the location of the other. This is called a *floating condition*. This means that the tolerance zones for both the top and bottom parts can be assigned the same values and that a fastener diameter selected to fit one part will also fit the other part.

The final tolerances are developed by first defining a minimum hole size of 20.00. An arbitrary tolerance of 0.02 is assigned to the hole and is expressed as 20.00 + 0.02/–0 so that the hole can never be any smaller than 20.00.

The 20.00 minimum hole diameter dictates that the maximum fastener diameter can be no greater than 19.97, or 0.03 (i.e., the rounded-off diagonal distance across the tolerance zone—0.028) less than the minimum hole diameter. A 0.01 clearance is assigned. The clearance ensures that the hole and fastener are never exactly the same diameter. The resulting maximum allowable diameter for the fastener is 19.96. Again, an arbitrary tolerance of 0.02 is assigned to the fastener. The final fastener dimensions are, therefore, 19.96 to 19.94.

The assigned tolerances ensure that there will always be at least 0.01 clearance between the fastener and the hole. The other extreme condition occurs when the hole is at its largest possible size (10.02) and the fastener is at its smallest (19.94). This means that there could be as much as 0.08 clearance between the parts. If this much clearance is not acceptable, then the assigned tolerances will have to be reevaluated.

Figure 9-43 shows the top and bottom parts dimensioned and toleranced. Any dimensions that do not have assigned tolerances are assumed to have standard tolerances (refer to Figure 9-14).

**Figure 9-43**

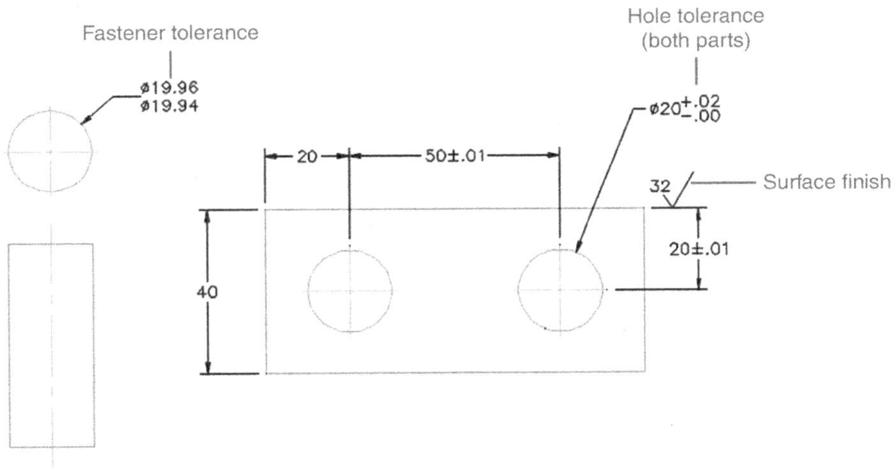

Note in Figure 9-43 that the top edge of each part was assigned a surface finish. This was done to help ensure the accuracy of the 20 ± 0.01 dimension. If this edge surface were rough, it could affect the tolerance measurements.

This example will be repeated in Chapter 10 with geometric tolerances. Geometric tolerance zones are circular rather than rectangular.

## Fixed Condition

Figure 9-44 shows the same nominal conditions presented in Figure 9-40, but the fasteners are now fixed to the top part. This is called a *fixed condition*. In analyzing the tolerance zones for the fixed condition, you must consider two positional tolerances: the positional tolerances for the holes in the bottom part and the positional tolerances for the fixed fasteners in the top part. This may be expressed in an equation as follows:

$$S_{max} + DTSZ = H_{min} - DTZ$$

where

$S_{max}$ = Maximum shaft (fastener) diameter

$H_{min}$ = Minimum hole diameter

DTSZ = Diagonal distance across the shaft's center point tolerance zone

DTZ = Diagonal distance across the hole's center point tolerance zone

If a dimension and tolerance of 50 ± 0.01 and 20 ± 0.01 are assigned to both the center distance between the holes and the center distance between the fixed fasteners, the values for DTSZ and DTZ will be equal. The formula can then be simplified as follows:

$$S_{max} = H_{min} - 2(DTZ)$$

Here, DTZ equals the diagonal distance across the tolerance zone. If a hole tolerance of 20.00 + 0.02/–0 is also defined, the resulting maximum shaft size can be determined, assuming that the calculated distance of 0.028 is rounded to 0.03 (Figure 9-45).

$$S_{max} = 20.00 - 2(.03)$$

$$= 19.94$$

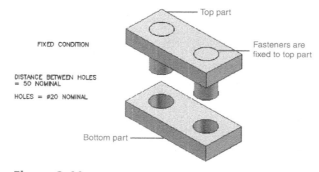

FIXED CONDITION

DISTANCE BETWEEN HOLES
= 50 NOMINAL

HOLES = ⌀20 NOMINAL

**Figure 9-44**

**Figure 9-45**

This means that the largest possible shaft diameter that will just fit equals 19.94. If a clearance tolerance of 0.01 is assumed to ensure that the shaft and hole are never exactly the same size, the maximum shaft diameter becomes 19.93 (Figure 9-46).

**Figure 9-46**

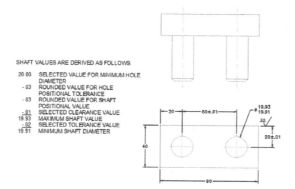

SHAFT VALUES ARE DERIVED AS FOLLOWS:

| | |
|---|---|
| 20.00 | SELECTED VALUE FOR MINIMUM HOLE DIAMETER |
| - .03 | ROUNDED VALUE FOR HOLE POSITIONAL TOLERANCE |
| - .03 | ROUNDED VALUE FOR SHAFT POSITIONAL VALUE |
| - .01 | SELECTED CLEARANCE VALUE |
| 19.93 | MAXIMUM SHAFT VALUE |
| - .02 | SELECTED TOLERANCE VALUE |
| 19.91 | MINIMUM SHAFT DIAMETER |

A feature tolerance of 0.02 on the shaft will result in a minimum shaft diameter of 19.91. Note that the 0.01 clearance tolerance and the 0.02 feature tolerance were arbitrarily chosen. Other possible values could have been used.

### Designing a Hole Given a Fastener Size

The previous two examples started by selecting a minimum hole diameter and then calculating the resulting fastener size. Figure 9-47 shows a situation in which the fastener size is defined and the problem is to determine the appropriate hole sizes. Figure 9-48 shows the dimensions and tolerances for both top and bottom parts.

**Figure 9-47**

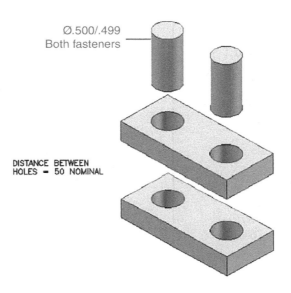

**Figure 9-48**

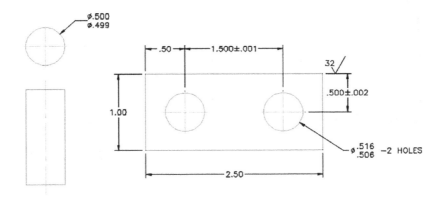

Requirements:

Clearance, minimum = 0.003

Hole tolerances = 0.005

Positional tolerance = 0.002

# 9-28 EXERCISE PROBLEMS

Redraw the objects shown in Exercise Problems EX9-1 through EX9-4, using the given dimensions. Include the listed tolerances.

## EX9-1 Millimeters

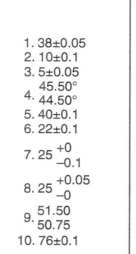

1. 38±0.05
2. 10±0.1
3. 5±0.05
4. 45.50°
   44.50°
5. 40±0.1
6. 22±0.1
7. $25 \begin{array}{c}+0\\-0.1\end{array}$
8. $25 \begin{array}{c}+0.05\\-0\end{array}$
9. 51.50
   50.75
10. 76±0.1

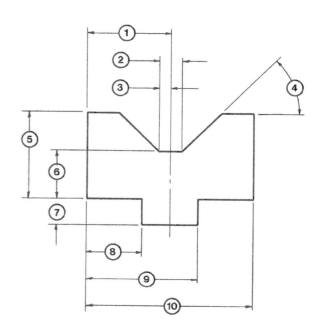

## EX9-2 Millimeters

1. 34±0.25
2. 17±0.25
3. 25±0.05
4. 15.00
   14.80
5. 50±0.05
6. 80±0.1
7. R5±0.1-8 PLACES
8. 45±0.25
9. 60±0.1
10. Ø14-3 HOLES
11. 15.00
    14.80
12. 30.00
    29.80

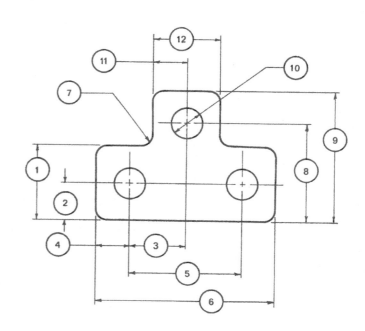

## EX9-3 Inches

1. 3.00±0.1
2. 1.56±.01
3. 46.50
   45.50
4. .750±.005
5. 2.75
   2.70
6. 3.625±.010
7. 45°±.5°
8. 2.250±.005

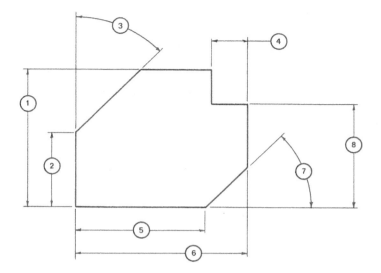

## EX9-4 Inches

1. 50 $^{+.2}_{0}$
2. R45±.1-2 PLACES
3. 63.5 $^{0}_{0.2}$
4. 76±.1
5. 38±.1
6. Ø12.00 $^{+.05}_{0}$ -3 HOLES
7. 30±.03
8. 30±.03
9. 100 $^{+.4}_{0}$

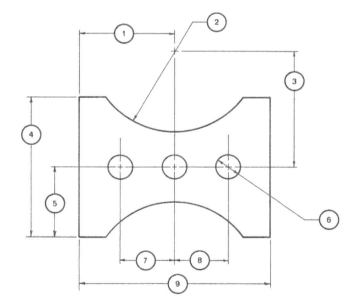

## EX9-5 Millimeters

Redraw the following object, including the given dimensions and tolerances. Calculate and list the maximum and minimum distances for surface A.

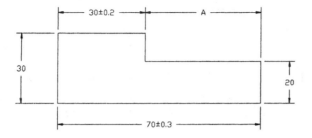

## EX9-6 Inches

- Redraw the following object, including the dimensions and tolerances. Calculate and list the maximum and minimum distances for surface A.

- Redraw the given object and dimension it, using baseline dimensions. Calculate and list the maximum and minimum distances for surface A.

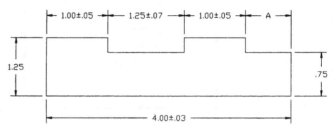

## EX9-7 Millimeters

Redraw the following object, including the dimensions and tolerances. Calculate and list the maximum and minimum distances for surfaces D and E.

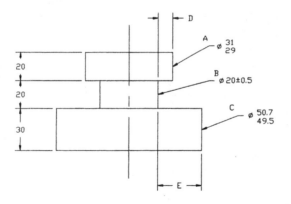

## EX9-8 Millimeters

Dimension the following object twice: once using chain dimensions and once using baseline dimensions. Calculate and list the maximum and minimum distances for surface D for both chain and baseline dimensions. Compare the results.

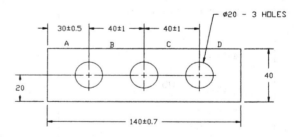

## EX9-9 Inches

Redraw the following shapes, including the dimensions and tolerances. Also list the required minimum and maximum values for the specified distances.

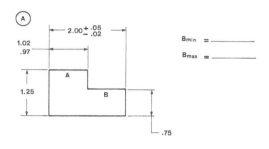

$B_{min}$ = _____

$B_{max}$ = _____

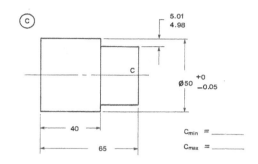

$C_{min}$ = _____

$C_{max}$ = _____

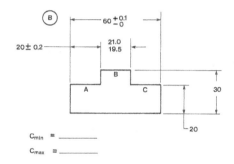

$C_{min}$ = _____

$C_{max}$ = _____

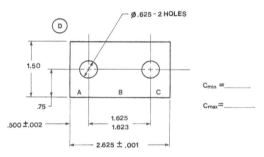

$C_{min}$ = _____

$C_{max}$ = _____

## EX9-10

Redraw and complete the inspection report that follows. Under the Results column classify each "AS MEASURED" value as OK if the value is within the stated tolerances, REWORK if the value indicates that the measured value is beyond the stated tolerance but can be reworked to bring it into the acceptable range, or SCRAP if the value is not within the tolerance range and cannot be reworked to make it acceptable.

### INSPECTION REPORT

PART NAME AND NO: 1073500 2

INSPECTOR:

DATE:

1.00 3 PLACES

| BASE DIMENSION | TOLERANCES | | AS MEASURED | RESULTS |
|---|---|---|---|---|
| | MAX | MIN | | |
| (1) $100 \pm 0.5$ | | | 99.8 | |
| (2) $\phi ^{57}_{56}$ | | | 57.01 | |
| (3) $22 \pm 0.3$ | | | 21.72 | |
| (4) $^{40.05}_{39.95}$ | | | 39.98 | |
| (5) $22 \pm 0.3$ | | | 21.68 | |
| (6) $R52 ^{0}_{-0.2}$ | | | 51.99 | |
| (7) $35 ^{+0.2}_{-0.3}$ | | | 35.20 | |
| (8) $30 ^{+0.4}_{0}$ | | | 30.27 | |
| (9) $6.0 ^{+.1}_{-.2}$ | | | 5.85 | |
| (10) $12.0 \pm 0.2$ | | | 11.90 | |

.50 – 10 PLACES

## EX9-11 Millimeters

Redraw the following charts and complete them on the basis of the following information:

A.  Nominal = 16, Fit = H9/d9
B.  Nominal = 30, Fit = H11/c11
C.  Nominal = 22, Fit = H7/g6
D.  Nominal = 10, Fit = C11/h11
E.  Nominal = 25, Fit = F8/h7
F.  Nominal = 12, Fit = H7/k6
G.  Nominal = 3, Fit = H7/p6
H.  Nominal = 19, Fit = H7/s6
I.  Nominal = 27, Fit = H7/u6
J.  Nominal = 30, Fit = N7/h6

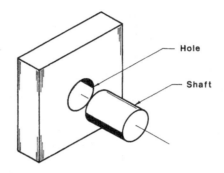

half space

3.75
6 equal
spaces

| NOMINAL | HOLE | | SHAFT | | CLEARANCE | |
|---|---|---|---|---|---|---|
| | MAX | MIN | MAX | MIN | MAX | MIN |
| A | | | | | | |
| B | | | | | | |
| C | | | | | | |
| D | | | | | | |
| E | | | | | | |

|← 1.5 →|← 6.0 – 6 equal spaces →|

| NOMINAL | HOLE | | SHAFT | | INTERFERENCE | |
|---|---|---|---|---|---|---|
| | MAX | MIN | MAX | MIN | MAX | MIN |
| F | | | | | | |
| G | | | | | | |
| H | | | | | | |
| I | | | | | | |
| J | | | | | | |

Use the same dimensions given above

## EX9-12 Inches

Redraw the following charts and complete them on the basis of the following information:

A. Nominal = 0.25, Fit = Class LC5
B. Nominal = 1.00, Fit = Class LC7
C. Nominal = 1.50, Fit = Class LC10
D. Nominal = 0.75, Fit = Class RC3
E. Nominal = 2.50, Fit = Class RC6
F. Nominal = 0.500, Fit = Class LT2
G. Nominal = 1.25, Fit = Class LT5
H. Nominal = 3.00, Fit = Class LN3
I. Nominal = 1.625, Fit = Class FN1
J. Nominal = 2.00, Fit = Class FN4

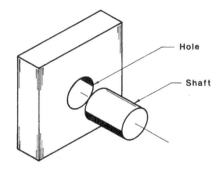

half space

| NOMINAL | HOLE | | SHAFT | | CLEARANCE | |
|---|---|---|---|---|---|---|
| | MAX | MIN | MAX | MIN | MAX | MIN |
| A | | | | | | |
| B | | | | | | |
| C | | | | | | |
| D | | | | | | |
| E | | | | | | |

3.75
6 equal
spaces

1.5 — 6.0 – 6 equal spaces

| NOMINAL | HOLE | | SHAFT | | INTERFERENCE | |
|---|---|---|---|---|---|---|
| | MAX | MIN | MAX | MIN | MAX | MIN |
| F | | | | | | |
| G | | | | | | |
| H | | | | | | |
| I | | | | | | |
| J | | | | | | |

Use the same dimensions given above

Draw the chart shown in EX9-13 and add the appropriate values according to the dimensions and tolerances given in Exercise Problems EX9-13 through EX9-16.

### EX9-13 Millimeters

```
PART NO: 9-M53A
   A.  20±0.1
   B.  30±0.2
   C.  Ø20±0.05
   D.  40
   E.  60
```

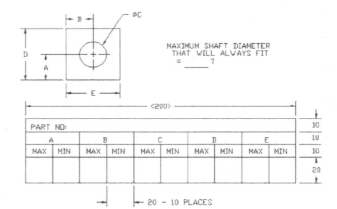

### EX9-14 Millimeters

```
PART NO: 9-M53B
   A.  32.02
       31.97
   B.  47.52
       47.50
   C.  Ø18 +0.05
            0
   D.  64±0.05
   E.  100±0.05
```

### EX9-15 Millimeters

```
PART NO: 9-M53B
   A.  32.02
       31.97
   B.  47.52
       47.50
   C.  Ø18 +0.05
            0
   D.  64±0.05
   E.  100±0.05
```

### EX9-16 Millimeters

```
PART NO: 9-E47B
   A.  18 +0
         -0.02
   B.  26 +0
         -0.04
   C.  Ø  24.03
          23.99
   D.  52±0.04
   E.  36±0.02
```

## EX9-17 Millimeters

Prepare front and top views of parts 4A and 4B on the basis of the given dimensions. Add tolerances to produce the stated clearances.

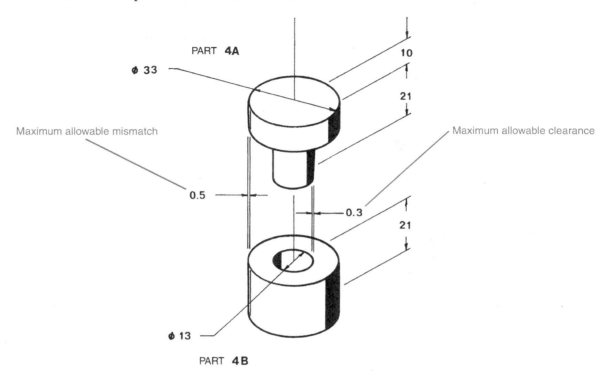

PART **4A**

ø 33

Maximum allowable mismatch

Maximum allowable clearance

0.5

0.3

10

21

21

ø 13

PART **4B**

Material is 1.00 thick.

Nominal sizes

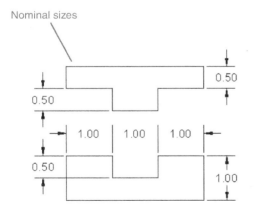

0.50

0.50

1.00   1.00   1.00

0.50

0.50

1.00

The UPON ASSEMBLED requirements.

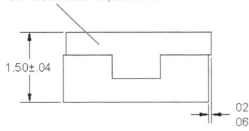

1.50±.04

.02
.06

## EX9-18 Inches

Redraw parts A and B and add dimensions and tolerances to meet the "UPON ASSEMBLED" requirements.

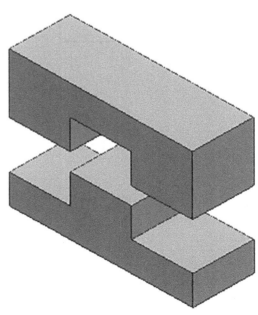

## EX9-19 Millimeters

Draw a front and a top view of each given object. Add dimensions and tolerances to meet the "FINAL CONDITION" requirements.

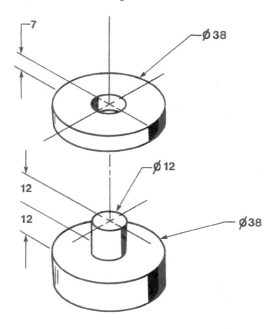

FINAL CONDITION

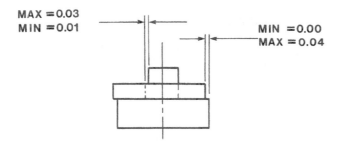

MAX = 0.03
MIN = 0.01

MIN = 0.00
MAX = 0.04

## EX9-20 Inches

Given the nominal sizes that follow, dimension tolerance parts AM311 and AM312 so that they always fit together, regardless of orientation. Further, dimension the overall lengths of each part so that, in the assembled condition, they will always pass through a clearance gauge with an opening of 90.00 ± 0.02.

In the assembled condition, both parts must always pass through the clearance gauge.

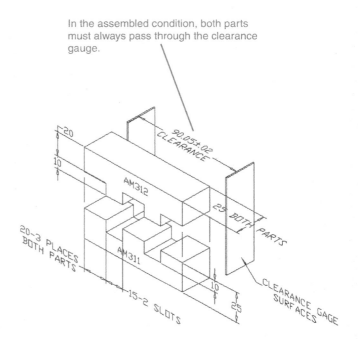

All given dimensions, except for the clearance gauge, are nominal.

## EX9-21 Millimeters

Design a bracket that supports the three Ø100 wheels shown. The wheels should use three Ø5.00 ± 0.01 shafts attached to the bracket. The bottom of the bracket must have a minimum of 10 millimeters from the ground. The wall thickness of the bracket must always be at least 5 millimeters, and the minimum bracket opening must be at least 15 millimeters.

**1** Prepare front and side views of the bracket.

**2** Draw the wheels in their relative positions, using phantom lines.

**3** Add all appropriate dimensions and tolerances.

ALL SIZES ARE NOMINAL, UNLESS
OTHERWISE STATED.

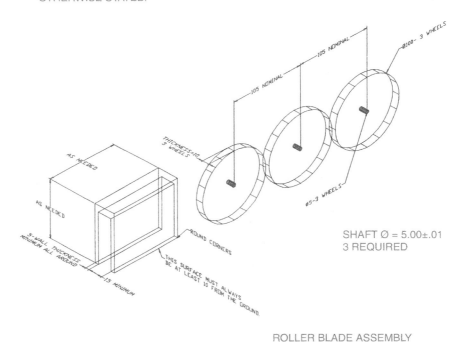

SHAFT Ø = 5.00±.01
3 REQUIRED

ROLLER BLADE ASSEMBLY
PART NUMBER  BU110-44

Given a top and bottom part in the floating condition, as shown in Figure EX9-22, add dimensions and tolerances to satisfy the given conditions. Size the top and bottom parts and fastener length as needed.

## EX9-22 Inches–Clearance Fit

- The distance between the holes is 2.00 nominal.
- The diameter of the fasteners is Ø.375 nominal.
- The fasteners have a total tolerance of 0.001.1.
- The holes have a tolerance of 0.002.
- The minimum allowable clearance between the fastener and the holes is 0.003.
- The material is 0.375 inch thick.

## EX9-23 Millimeters–Clearance Fit

- The distance between the holes is 80 nominal.
- The nominal diameter of the fasteners is Ø12.
- The fasteners have a total tolerance of 0.05.
- The holes have a tolerance of 0.03.
- The minimum allowable clearance between the fastener and the holes is 0.02.
- The material is 12 millimeters thick.

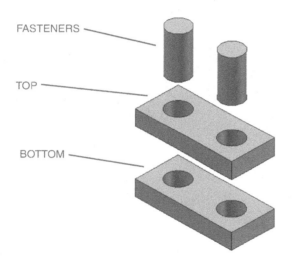

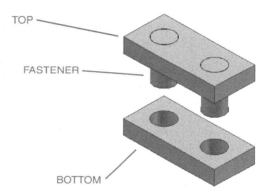

## EX9-24 Inches–Clearance Fit

- The distance between the holes is 3.50 nominal.
- The diameter of the fasteners is Ø.625.
- The fasteners have a total tolerance of 0.005.
- The holes have a tolerance of 0.003.
- The minimum allowable clearance between the fastener and the holes is 0.002.
- The material is 0.500 inch thick.

## EX9-25 Millimeters–Clearance Fit

- The distance between the holes is 120 nominal.
- The diameter of the fasteners is Ø24 nominal.
- The fasteners have a total tolerance of 0.01.
- The holes have a tolerance of 0.02.
- The minimum allowable clearance between the fastener and the holes is 0.04.
- The material is 20 millimeters thick.

## EX9-26 Inches–Interference Fit

- The distance between the holes is 2.00 nominal.
- The diameter of the fasteners is Ø.250 nominal.
- The fasteners have a total tolerance of 0.001.
- The holes have a tolerance of 0.002.
- The maximum allowable interference between the fastener and the holes is 0.0065.
- The material is 0.438 inch thick.

## EX9-27 Millimeters–Interference Fit

- The distance between the holes is 80 nominal.
- The diameter of the fasteners is Ø10 nominal.
- The fasteners have a total tolerance of 0.01.

- The holes have a tolerance of 0.02.
- The maximum allowable interference between the fastener and the holes is 0.032.
- The material is 14 millimeters thick.

## EX9-28 Inches–Locational Fit

- The distance between the holes is 2.25 nominal.
- The diameter of the fasteners is Ø.50 nominal.
- The fasteners have a total tolerance of 0.001.
- The holes have a tolerance of 0.002.
- The minimum allowable clearance between the fastener and the holes is 0.0010.
- The material is 0.370 inch thick.

## EX9-29 Millimeters–Transitional Fit

- The distance between the holes is 100 nominal.
- The diameter of the fasteners is Ø16 nominal.
- The fasteners have a total tolerance of 0.01.
- The holes have a tolerance of 0.02.
- The minimum allowable clearance between the fastener and the holes is 0.01.
- The material is 20 millimeters thick.

Given a top part and a bottom part in the fixed condition, as shown in Figure EX9-23, add dimensions and tolerances to satisfy the given conditions. Size the top and bottom parts and fastener length as needed.

## EX9-30 Inches–Clearance Fit

- The distance between the holes is 2.00 nominal.
- The diameter of the fasteners is Ø.375 nominal.
- The fasteners have a total tolerance of 0.001.
- The holes have a tolerance of 0.002.

- The minimum allowable clearance between the fastener and the holes is 0.003.
- The material is 0.375 inch thick.

## EX9-31 Millimeters–Clearance Fit

- The distance between the holes is 80 nominal.
- The nominal diameter of the fasteners is Ø12.
- The fasteners have a total tolerance of 0.05.
- The holes have a tolerance of 0.03.
- The minimum allowable clearance between the fastener and the holes is 0.02.
- The material is 12 millimeters thick.

## EX9-32 Inches–Clearance Fit

- The distance between the holes is 3.50 nominal.
- The diameter of the fasteners is Ø.625.
- The fasteners have a total tolerance of 0.005.
- The holes have a tolerance of 0.003.
- The minimum allowable clearance between the fastener and the holes is 0.002.
- The material is 0.500 inch thick.

## EX9-33 Millimeters–Clearance Fit

- The distance between the holes is 120 nominal.
- The diameter of the fasteners is Ø24 nominal.
- The fasteners have a total tolerance of 0.01.
- The holes have a tolerance of 0.02.
- The minimum allowable clearance between the fastener and the holes is 0.04.
- The material is 20 millimeters thick.

## EX9-34 Inches–Interference Fit

- The distance between the holes is 2.00 nominal.
- The diameter of the fasteners is Ø.250 nominal.

- The fasteners have a total tolerance of 0.001.
- The holes have a tolerance of 0.002.
- The maximum allowable interference between the fastener and the holes is 0.0065.
- The material is 0.438 inch thick.

## EX9-35 Millimeters–Interference Fit

- The distance between the holes is 80 nominal.
- The diameter of the fasteners is Ø10 nominal.
- The fasteners have a total tolerance of 0.01.
- The holes have a tolerance of 0.02.
- The maximum allowable interference between the fastener and the holes is 0.032.
- The material is 14 millimeters thick.

## EX9-36 Inches–Locational Fit

- The distance between the holes is 2.25 nominal.
- The diameter of the fasteners is Ø.50 nominal.
- The fasteners have a total tolerance of 0.001.
- The holes have a tolerance of 0.002.
- The minimum allowable clearance between the fastener and the holes is 0.0010.
- The material is 0.370 inch thick.

## EX9-37 Millimeters–Transitional Fit

- The distance between the holes is 100 nominal.
- The diameter of the fasteners is Ø16 nominal.
- The fasteners have a total tolerance of 0.01.
- The holes have a tolerance of 0.02.
- The minimum allowable clearance between the fastener and the holes is 0.01.
- The material is 20 millimeters thick.

## EX9-38 Millimeters

Given the following two assemblies, size the individual parts so that they always fit together. Create a drawing for each part, including dimensions and tolerances.

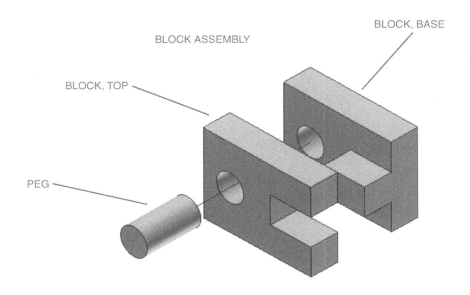

BLOCK ASSEMBLY

BLOCK, BASE

BLOCK, TOP

PEG

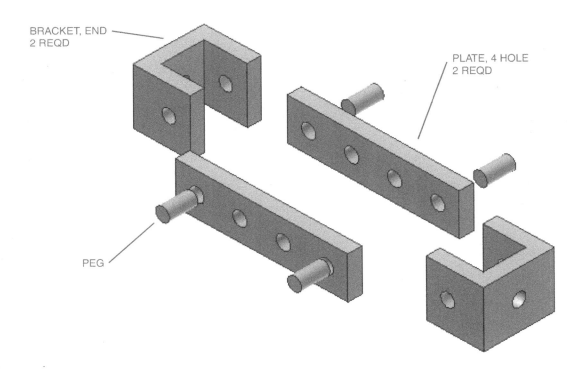

SUPPORT ASSEMBLY

BRACKET, END
2 REQD

PLATE, 4 HOLE
2 REQD

PEG

# Geometric Tolerances

## 10-1 Introduction

*Geometric tolerancing* is a dimensioning and tolerancing system based on the geometric shape of an object. Surfaces may be defined in terms of their flatness or roundness or in terms of how perpendicular or parallel they are to other surfaces (Figure 10-1, right).

Geometric tolerances allow a more exact definition of the shape of an object than do conventional coordinate-type tolerances. Objects can be toleranced in a manner more closely related to their design function or so that their features and surfaces are more directly related to each other.

Figure 10-1 (left) shows a square shape dimensioned and toleranced according to plus and minus tolerances. The resulting tolerance zone has an outside length of 51 square and an inside length of 49 square. The defined tolerance zone allows any shape that falls within it to be deemed acceptable, or correctly manufactured. Figure 10-1 (center) shows an exaggerated shape that fits within the defined tolerance zone and is not square, yet would be acceptable under the specified dimensions and tolerances. Geometric tolerancing can be used to more precisely define the tolerance zone when a more nearly square shape is required.

**Figure 10-1**

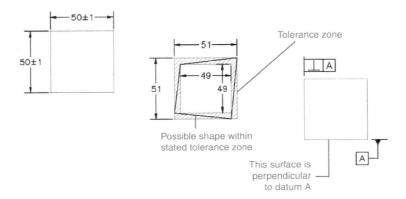

It should be pointed out that geometric tolerancing is not a panacea for all dimensioning and tolerancing problems. In many cases, coordinate tolerancing, as presented in Chapter 9, is sufficient to accurately define an object. Unnecessary or excessive use of geometric tolerances can increase production costs. Most objects are toleranced by using a combination of coordinate and geometric tolerances, depending on the design function of the object.

The key to using tolerances and selecting types of tolerances may be simply stated as, "Decimal points cost money." Every tolerance should be made as loose as possible while still maintaining the design integrity of the object. If a surface flatness is critical to the correct functioning of the object, then, of course, it will require a very close tolerance. But every tolerance should be considered individually and loosened wherever possible to make the object's manufacture easier and, therefore, less expensive.

## 10-2 Tolerances of Form

*Tolerances of form* are used to define the shape of a surface relative to itself. There are four classifications: flatness, straightness, roundness, and cylindricity. Tolerances of form are not related to other surfaces but apply only to an individual surface.

## 10-3 Flatness

*Flatness tolerances* are used to define the amount of variation permitted in an individual surface. The surface is thought of as a plane not related to the rest of the object.

Figure 10-2 shows a rectangular object. How flat is the top surface? The given plus or minus tolerances allow a variation of ±0.5 across the surface. Without additional tolerances, the surface could look like a series of waves that vary between 30.5 and 29.5.

If the example in Figure 10-2 is assigned a flatness tolerance of 0.3, the height of the object, the feature tolerance could continue to vary according to the 30 ± 0.5 tolerance, but the surface itself could not vary by more than 0.3. In the most extreme condition, one end of the surface could be 30.5 above the bottom surface and the other end 29.5, but the surface would still be limited to within two parallel planes 0.3 apart, as shown.

To better understand the meaning of flatness, consider how the surface would be inspected. The surface would be acceptable if a gauge could be moved all around the surface and never varied by more than 0.3 (Figure 10-3). Every point in the plane must be within the specified tolerance.

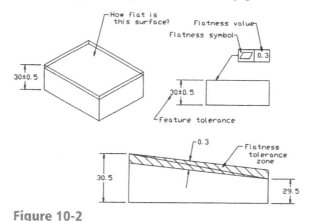

**Figure 10-2**

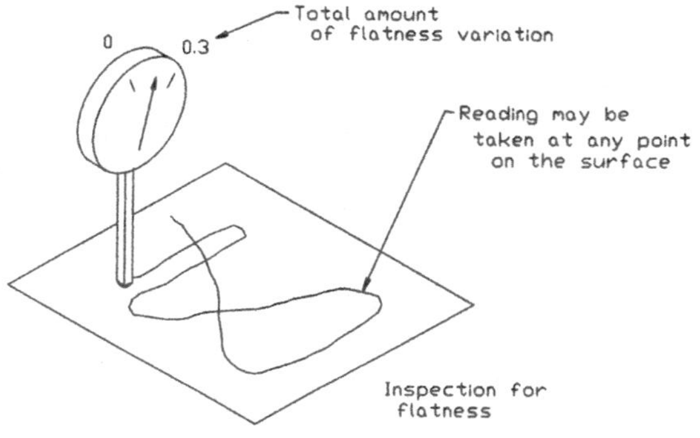

**Figure 10-3**

## 10-4 Straightness

*Straightness tolerances* are used to measure the variation of an individual feature along a straight line in a specified direction. Figure 10-4 shows an object with a straightness tolerance applied to its top surface. Straightness differs from flatness in that straightness measurements are checked by moving a gauge directly across the surface in a single direction. The gauge is not moved randomly about the surface, as is required with flatness.

Straightness tolerances are most often applied to circular or matching objects to help ensure that the parts are not barreled or warped within the given feature tolerance range and therefore not fitted together well. Figure 10-5 shows a cylindrical object dimensioned and toleranced by the use of a standard feature tolerance. The surface of the cylinder may vary within the specified tolerance range, as shown.

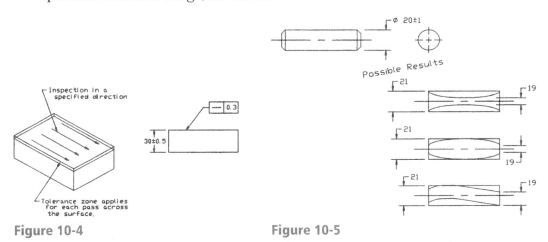

**Figure 10-4**

**Figure 10-5**

Figure 10-6 shows the same object shown in Figure 10-5, dimensioned and toleranced by use of the same feature tolerance but also including a 0.05 straightness tolerance. The straightness tolerance limits the surface variation to 0.05, as shown.

**Figure 10-6**

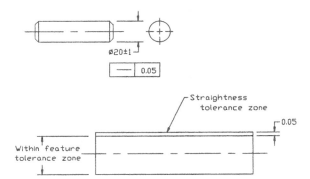

## 10-5 Straightness (RFS and MMC)

Figure 10-7 again shows the same cylinder shown in Figures 10-5 and 10-6. This time, the straightness tolerance is applied about the cylinder's centerline. This type of tolerance permits the feature tolerance and geometric tolerance to be used together to define a virtual condition. A virtual condition is used to determine the maximum possible size variation of the cylinder or the smallest diameter hole that will always accept the cylinder (see Section 10-17).

Figure 10-7

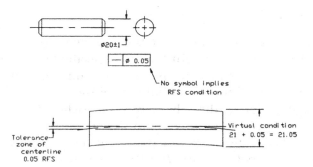

The geometric tolerance specified in Figure 10-7 is applied to any circular segment along the cylinder, regardless of the cylinder's diameter. This means that the 0.05 tolerance is applied equally when the cylinder's diameter measures 19 or when it measures 21. This application is called *RFS*, which stands for *regardless of feature size*. RFS conditions are specified in a tolerance either by an S with a circle around it or implied tacitly when no other symbol is used. In Figure 10-7, no symbol is listed after the 0.05 value, so it is assumed to be applied RFS.

Figure 10-8 shows the cylinder dimensioned with an *MMC* condition applied to the straightness tolerance. *MMC* stands for *maximum material condition* and means that the specified straightness tolerance (0.05) is applied only at the MMC condition or when the cylinder is at its maximum diameter size (21).

**Figure 10-8**

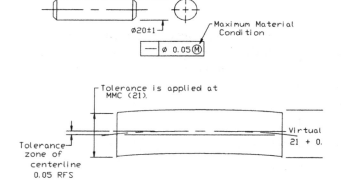

| Measured Size | Allowable Tolerance Zone | Virtual Condition |
|---|---|---|
| 21.0 | 0.05 | 21.05 |
| 20.9 | 0.15 | 21.15 |
| 20.8 | 0.25 | 21.25 |
| . | . | . |
| . | . | . |
| . | . | . |
| 20.0 | 1.05 | 22.05 |
| . | . | . |
| . | . | . |
| . | . | . |
| 19.0 | 2.05 | 23.05 |

A shaft is an external feature, so its largest possible size, or MMC, occurs when it is at its maximum diameter. A hole is an internal feature. A hole's MMC condition occurs when it is at its smallest diameter. The MMC condition for holes is discussed later in the chapter, along with positional tolerances.

Applying a straightness tolerance at MMC allows for a variation in the resulting tolerance zone. Because the 0.05 flatness tolerance is applied at MMC, the virtual condition is still 21.05, the same as with the RFS condition; however, the tolerance is applied only at MMC. As the cylinder's diameter varies within the specified feature tolerance range, the acceptable tolerance zone may vary to maintain the same virtual condition.

Figure 10-8 lists ways in which the tolerance zone varies as the cylinder's diameter varies. When the cylinder is at its largest size, or MMC, the tolerance zone equals 0.05, or the specified flatness variation. When the cylinder is at its smallest diameter, the tolerance zone equals 2.05, or the total feature size plus the total flatness size. In all variations, the virtual size remains the same, so at any given cylinder diameter value, the size of the tolerance zone can be determined by subtracting the cylinder's diameter value from the virtual condition.

Figure 10-9 shows a comparison between different methods used to dimension and tolerance a .750 shaft. The first example uses only a feature tolerance. This tolerance sets an upper limit of .755 and a lower limit of .745. Any variations within that range are acceptable.

**Figure 10-9**

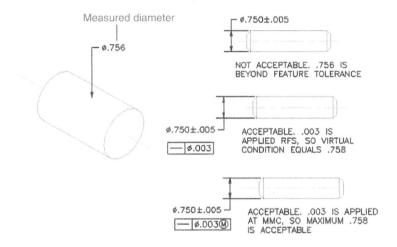

The second example in Figure 10-9 sets a straightness tolerance of .003 about the cylinder's centerline. No conditions are defined, so the tolerance is applied RFS. This limits the variations in straightness to .003 at all feature sizes. For example, when the shaft is at its smallest possible feature size, .745, the .003 still applies. This means that a shaft measuring .745 that had a straightness variation greater than .003 would be rejected. If the tolerance has been applied at MMC, the part would be accepted. This does not mean that straightness tolerances should always be applied at MMC. If straightness is critical to the design integrity or function of the part, then straightness should be applied in the RFS condition.

The third example in Figure 10-9 applies the straightness tolerance about the centerline at MMC. This tolerance creates a virtual condition of .758. The MMC condition allows the tolerance to vary as the feature tolerance varies, so when the shaft is at its smallest feature size, .745, a straightness tolerance of .013 is acceptable (.010 feature tolerance + .003 straightness tolerance).

If the tolerance specification for the cylinder shown in Figure 10-9 were to have a 0.000 tolerance applied at MMC, it would mean that the shaft would have to be perfectly straight at MMC, or when the shaft was at its maximum value (.755); however, the straightness tolerance could vary as the feature size varied, as discussed for the other tolerance conditions. A 0.000 tolerance means that the MMC and the virtual conditions are equal.

Figure 10-10 shows a very long .750-diameter shaft. Its straightness tolerance includes a length qualifier that serves to limit the straightness variations over each inch of the shaft length and prevents excess waviness over the full length. The tolerance Ø.002/1.000 means that the total straightness may vary over the entire length of the shaft by .003 but that the variation is limited to .002 per 1.000 of shaft length.

Figure 10-10

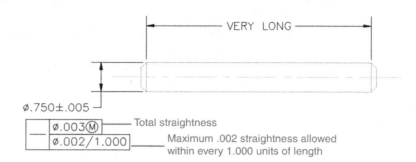

## 10-6 Circularity

*Circularity tolerances* are used to limit the amount of variation in the roundness of a surface of revolution and are measured at individual cross sections along the length of the object. The measurements are limited to the individual cross sections and are not related to other cross sections. This means that in extreme conditions, the shaft shown in Figure 10-11 could actually taper from a diameter of 21 to a diameter of 19 and never violate the circularity requirement. It also means that qualifications such as MMC could not be applied.

Figure 10-11 shows a shaft that includes a feature tolerance and a circularity tolerance of 0.07. To understand circularity tolerances, consider an individual cross section, or slice, of the cylinder. The shape of the outside edge of the slice varies around the slice. The difference between the maximum diameter and the minimum diameter of the slice can never exceed the stated circularity tolerance.

Circularity tolerances can be applied to tapered sections and spheres, as shown in Figure 10-12. In both applications, circularity is measured around individual cross sections, as it was for the shaft shown in Figure 10-11.

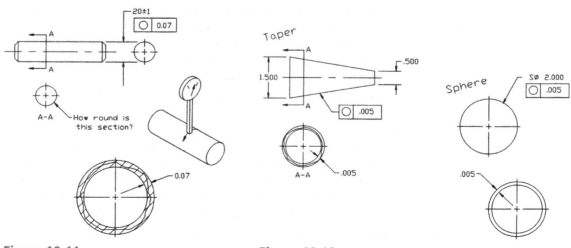

Figure 10-11

Figure 10-12

## 10-7 Cylindricity

*Cylindricity tolerances* are used to define a tolerance zone both around individual circular cross sections of an object and also along its length. The resulting tolerance zone looks like two concentric cylinders.

Figure 10-13 shows a shaft that includes a cylindricity tolerance that establishes a tolerance zone of .007. This means that if the maximum measured diameter is determined to be .755, the minimum diameter cannot be less than .748 anywhere on the cylindrical surface. Figure 10-14 shows how to draw the feature control frames that surround the tolerance symbol and size specifications.

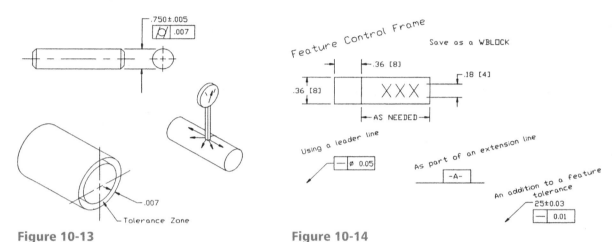

**Figure 10-13**  **Figure 10-14**

Cylindricity and circularity are somewhat analogous to flatness and straightness. Flatness and cylindricity are concerned with variations across an entire surface or plane. In the case of cylindricity, the plane is shaped like a cylinder. Straightness and circularity are concerned with variations of a single element of a surface—that is, a straight line across the plane in a specified direction for straightness and a path around a single cross section for circularity.

## 10-8 Creating Geometric Tolerances in AutoCAD

Geometric tolerances are tolerances that limit dimensional variations on the basis of geometric properties of an object. Figure 10-15 shows a list of

| | TYPE OF TOLERANCE | CHARACTERISTIC | SYMBOL |
|---|---|---|---|
| FOR INDIVIDUAL FEATURES | FORM | STRAIGHTNESS | — |
| | | FLATNESS | ▱ |
| | | CIRCULARITY | O |
| | | CYLINDRICITY | ⌀ |
| INDIVIDUAL OR RELATED FEATURES | PROFILE | PROFILE OF A LINE | ⌒ |
| | | PROFILE OF A SURFACE | ⌓ |
| RELATED FEATURES | ORIENTATION | ANGULARITY | ∠ |
| | | PERPENDICULARITY | ⊥ |
| | | PARALLELISM | // |
| | LOCATION | POSITION | ⌖ |
| | | CONCENTRICITY | ◎ |
| | RUNOUT | CIRCULAR RUNOUT | ↗ |
| | | TOTAL RUNOUT | ⫽ |

**Figure 10-15**

| TERM | SYMBOL |
|---|---|
| AT MAXIMUM MATERIAL CONDITION | Ⓜ |
| REGARDLESS OF FEATURE SIZE | Ⓢ |
| AT LEAST MATERIAL CONDITION | Ⓛ |
| PROJECTED TOLERANCE ZONE | Ⓟ |
| DIAMETER | ⌀ |
| SPHERICAL DIAMETER | S⌀ |
| RADIUS | R |
| SPHERICAL RADIUS | SR |
| REFERENCE | ( ) |
| ARC LENGTH | ⌒ |

geometric tolerance symbols. Figure 10-16 shows an object dimensioned by the use of geometric tolerances. The geometric tolerances were created as follows.

**Figure 10-16**

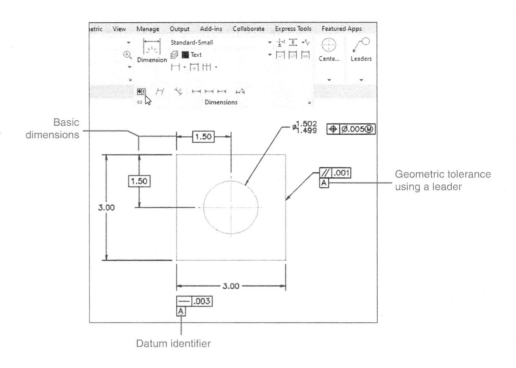

Basic dimensions

Geometric tolerance using a leader

Datum identifier

## Defining a Datum

**1** Select the **Tolerance** tool from the **Dimensions** panel.

The **Geometric Tolerance** dialog box appears (Figure 10-17).

**Figure 10-17**

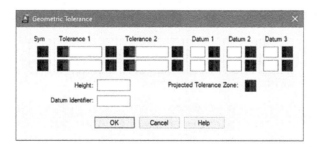

**2** Click the **Datum Identifier** box, and type **A**, and then click **OK**.

```
Command: _tolerance
Enter tolerance location:
```

**3** Position the datum identifier and press the left mouse button (refer to Figure 10-16).

## Defining a Straightness Value

**1** Select the **Tolerance** tool from the **Dimensions** panel.

The **Geometric Tolerance** dialog box appears.

**2** Select the top open box under the heading **Sym**.

The **Symbol** dialog box appears (Figure 10-18).

**Figure 10-18**

Straightness value

Straightness symbol

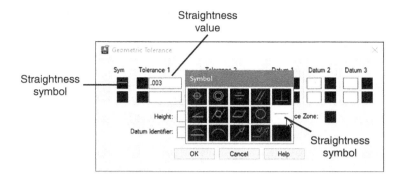

Straightness symbol

**3** Select the straightness symbol and click **OK**.

The **Geometric Tolerance** dialog box reappears with the straightness symbol in the first box under the heading **Sym**.

**4** Click the open **Tolerance 1** edit box, type **.003**, and click **OK**.

```
Command: _tolerance
Enter tolerance location:
```

**5** Position the straightness tolerance as shown in Figure 10-19 and press the left mouse button.

Use **Move** and **Object Snap**, if necessary, to reposition the tolerance box (refer to Figure 10-16).

**Figure 10-19**

A straightness tolerance

## Creating a Positional Tolerance

A *positional tolerance* is used to locate and tolerance a hole in an object. Positional tolerances require base locating dimensions for the hole's center point. Positional tolerances also require a feature tolerance to define the diameter tolerances of the hole and a geometric tolerance to define the position tolerance for the hole's center point.

## Creating a Basic Dimension

See the two 1.50 dimensions in Figure 10-16 used to locate the center position of the hole.

**1** Access the **Dimension Style Manager** or type **DDIM** at a command prompt.

**2** Select **Modify**.

The **Modify Dimension Style: Standard** dialog box appears (refer to Figure 9-7).

**3** On the **Tolerances** tab, select **Basic** next to the heading **Method** in the **Tolerance format** area (Figure 10-20).

**Figure 10-20**

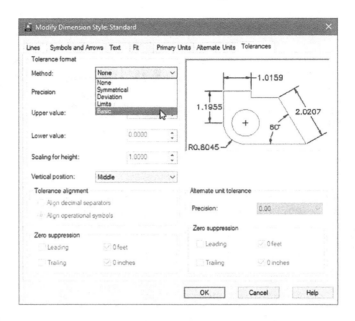

**4** Click **OK**, click **Close**, and return to the drawing screen.

**5** Choose **Linear** from the **Dimensions** panel and add the appropriate dimensions.

Refer to Figure 10-16 for examples.

## Creating Basic Dimensions from Existing Dimensions

Figure 10-21 shows a shape that includes dimensions. The designer has decided to change two of the dimensions to basic dimensions. The procedure is as follows.

**Figure 10-21**

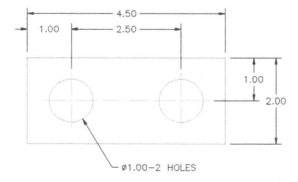

**1** Click on the **2.50** dimension.

Grips appear on the dimension.

**2** Right-click and select **Properties**.

The **Properties** palette appears (Figure 10-22).

**Figure 10-22**

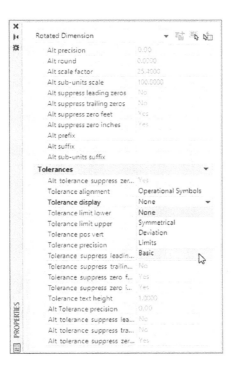

■ Scroll down to the **Tolerance** settings.

■ Click next to **Tolerance display** and select **Basic** (Figure 10-22).

■ Scroll down the options and select the **Basic** option; then click the close **X** and press the **Esc** key.

■ Repeat steps 1–5 for the vertical 1.00 dimension.

Figure 10-23 shows the final result.

**Figure 10-23**

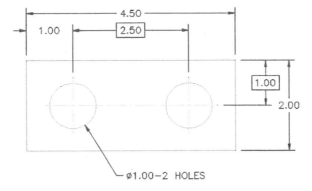

## Adding a Limit Feature Tolerance to a Hole

■ Access the **Dimension Style Manager** or type **DDIM** in response to a command prompt.

■ Select **Modify**.

The **Modify Dimension Style: Standard** dialog box appears.

■ On the **Tolerances** tab, select **Limits** in the **Method** edit box located in the **Tolerance format** area (Figure 10-24).

Figure 10-24

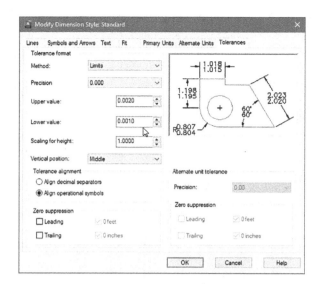

**4** Change the upper value to **0.002** by typing in the new value.

**5** Change the lower value to **0.001** by typing in the new value.

**6** Click the arrow to the right of the **Precision** box in the **Tolerance Format** area.

**7** Change the precision to three decimal places (**0.000**).

AutoCAD truncates any input according to the number of decimal places allowed by the precision settings. If the precision settings were two decimal places (0.00), the resulting limit dimensions would both be 1.50. The values defined in the third decimal place would be ignored.

**8** Click **OK**, click **Close**, and return to the drawing screen.

**9** Select **Diameter** on the **Dimensions** panel.

```
Select arc or circle:
```

**10** Select the hole.

```
Dimension line location (Text Angle):
```

**11** Locate the diameter dimension.

## Adding a Positional Tolerance to the Hole's Feature Tolerance

**1** Select **Tolerance** on the **Dimensions** panel.

The **Geometric Tolerance** dialog box appears.

**2** Select the top open box under the heading **Sym**.

The **Symbol** dialog box appears, with the positional tolerance symbol highlighted (Figure 10-25).

Figure 10-25

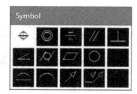

**3** Select the top-left edit box under the heading **Tolerance 1**.

A diameter symbol appears.

**4** Click inside the **Value** edit box and type **0.0005**.

The numbers appear in the box.

**5** Select the top far-right open box under the heading **Tolerance 1**.

The **Material Condition** dialog box appears.

**6** Select the maximum material condition (MMC) symbol (the circle with an M in it) (Figure 10-26).

**Figure 10-26**

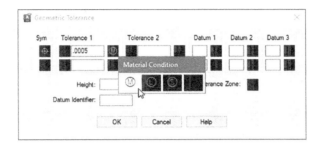

**7** Click **OK**.

**8** Click **OK**.

```
Enter tolerance location:
```

**9** Locate the tolerance box (Figure 10-27).

Use **Move** to position the box, if necessary.

**Figure 10-27**

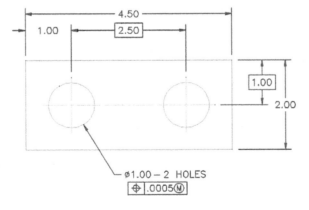

## Adding a Geometric Tolerance with a Leader Line

**1** Type **qleader** at the command prompt.

```
Specify first leader point, or [Settings] <Settings>:
```

**2** Select **Settings** by pressing **Enter**.

The **Leader Settings** dialog box appears (Figure 10-28).

Figure 10-28

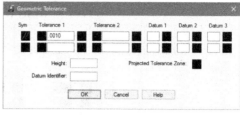

**3** Select **Tolerance** in the **Annotation Type** area and click **OK**.

```
Specify first leader point, or [Settings] <Settings>:
```

**4** Select a starting point for the leader line.

```
Specify next point:
```

**5** Draw a short horizontal segment.

The **Geometric Tolerance** dialog box appears (Figure 10-28).

**6** Select the top **Sym** box for **Tolerance 1**.

The **Symbol** dialog box appears.

**7** Select **Parallel**.

**8** Select the edit box under the heading **Tolerance 1**, type **0.0010**, and click **OK**.

## 10-9 Tolerances of Orientation

*Tolerances of orientation* are used to relate a feature or surface to another feature or surface. Tolerances of orientation include perpendicularity, parallelism, and angularity. They may be applied under RFS or MMC conditions, but they cannot be applied to individual features by themselves. Defining a surface as parallel to another surface is very much like assigning a flatness value to the surface. The difference is that flatness applies only within the surface; every point on the surface is related to a defined set of limiting parallel planes. Parallelism defines every point in the surface relative to another surface. The two surfaces are therefore directly related to each other, and the condition of one affects the other.

Orientation tolerances are used with locational tolerances. A feature is first located, and then it is oriented within the locational tolerances. This means that the orientation tolerance must always be less than the locational tolerances. The next four sections further explain this requirement.

## 10-10 Datums

A *datum* is a point, an axis, or a surface that is used as a starting reference point for dimensions and tolerances. Figure 10-29 shows a rectangular object with three datum planes labeled A, B, and C. The three datum planes are called the primary, secondary, and tertiary datums, respectively. The three datum planes are, by definition, oriented exactly 90° to one another. A datum surface is defined by placing a filled datum triangle at the end of a leader line.

**Figure 10-29**

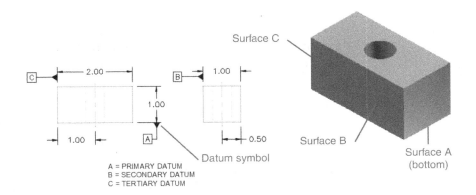

A = PRIMARY DATUM
B = SECONDARY DATUM
C = TERTIARY DATUM

Figure 10-30 shows the A datum symbol. Create it as follows.

**Figure 10-30**

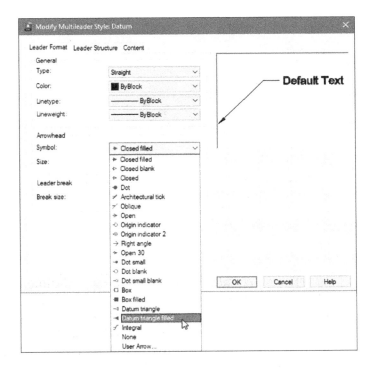

**1** Access the **Multileader Style Manager** by clicking the arrowhead in the lower-right corner of the **Leaders** panel under the **Annotate** tab.

**2** Click **New** to create a new multileader style. Name it **Datum** and click **Continue**.

**3** On the **Leader Format** tab, in the **Arrowhead** area, click the down arrow next to **Symbol**. Scroll down the symbols options and select **Datum triangle filled**.

**4** Click **OK** and then click **Close**.

> **NOTE**
>
> In step 3, either **Datum triangle filled** or **Datum triangle** is acceptable.

Datum planes are assumed to be perfectly flat. When assigning a datum status to a surface, be sure that the surface is reasonably flat. This means that datum surfaces should be toleranced by using surface finishes or created by using machine techniques that produce flat surfaces.

## 10-11 Perpendicularity

*Perpendicularity tolerances* are used to limit the amount of variation for a surface or feature within two planes perpendicular to a specified datum. Figure 10-31 shows a rectangular object. The bottom surface is assigned as datum A, and the right vertical edge is toleranced so that it must be perpendicular within a limit of 0.05 to datum A. The perpendicularity tolerance defines a tolerance zone 0.05 wide between two parallel planes that are perpendicular to datum A.

**Figure 10-31**

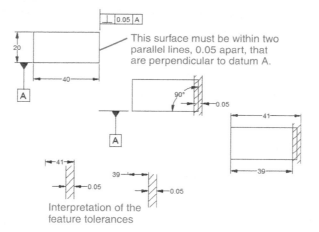

The object also includes a horizontal dimension and tolerance of 40 ± 1. This tolerance is called a *locational tolerance* because it serves to locate the right edge of the object. As with rectangular tolerances discussed in Chapter 9, the 40 ± 1 controls the location of the edge—that is, how far away or how close it can be to the left edge—but does not directly control the shape of the edge. Any shape that falls within the specified tolerance range is acceptable. This may, in fact, be sufficient for a given design, but if a more controlled shape is required, a perpendicularity tolerance must be added. The perpendicularity tolerance works within the locational tolerance to ensure that the edge is not only within the locational tolerance but also is perpendicular to datum A.

Figure 10-31 shows the two extreme conditions for the 40 ± 1 locational tolerance. The perpendicularity tolerance is applied by first measuring the surface and determining its maximum and minimum lengths. The difference between these two measurements must be less than 0.05. Thus, if the measured maximum distance is 41, then no other part of the surface may be less than 41 – 0.05 = 40.95.

Tolerances of perpendicularity serve to complement locational tolerances, to make the shape more exact, so that tolerances of perpendicularity must always be smaller than tolerances of location. It would be of little use, for example, to assign a perpendicularity tolerance of 1.5 for the object shown in Figure 10-31. The locational tolerance would prevent the variation from ever reaching the limits specified by such a large perpendicularity tolerance.

Figure 10-32 shows a perpendicularity tolerance applied to cylindrical features: a shaft and a hole. The figure includes examples of both RFS and MMC applications. As with straightness tolerances applied at MMC, perpendicularity tolerances applied about a hole or shaft's centerline allow the tolerance zone to vary as the feature size varies.

The inclusion of the Ø symbol in a geometric tolerance is critical to its interpretation (Figure 10-33). If the Ø symbol is not included, the tolerance applies only to the view in which it is written. This means that the tolerance zone is shaped like a rectangular slice, not a cylinder, as would be the case if the Ø symbol were included. In general, it is better always to include the Ø symbol for cylindrical features because it generates a tolerance zone more like that used in positional tolerancing.

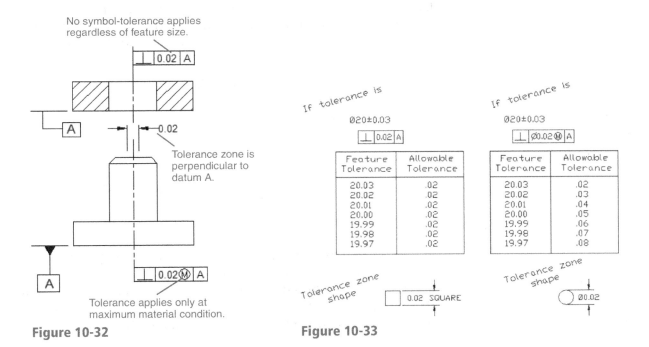

**Figure 10-32**

**Figure 10-33**

Figure 10-34 shows a perpendicularity tolerance applied to a slot, which is a noncylindrical feature. The MMC specification is for variations in the tolerance zone.

Figure 10-34

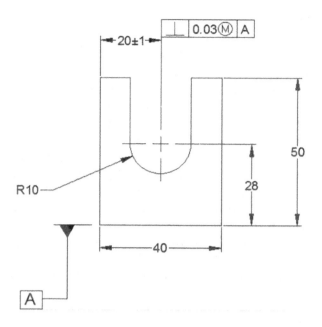

## 10-12 Parallelism

*Parallelism* is used to ensure that all points within a plane are within two parallel planes that are parallel to a referenced datum plane. Figure 10-35 shows a rectangular object that is toleranced so that its top surface is parallel to the bottom surface within 0.02. This means that every point on the top surface must be within a set of parallel planes 0.02 apart. These parallel tolerancing planes are located by determining the maximum and minimum distances from the datum surface. The difference between the maximum and minimum values may not exceed the stated 0.02 tolerance.

Figure 10-35

In the extreme condition of maximum feature size, the top surface is located 40.5 above the datum plane. The parallelism tolerance is then applied, meaning that no point on the surface may be closer than 40.3 to the datum. This is an RFS condition. The MMC condition may also be applied, thereby allowing the tolerance zone to vary as the feature size varies.

## 10-13 Angularism

*Angularism tolerances* are used to limit the variance of surfaces and axes that are at an angle relative to a datum. Angularism tolerances are applied, like perpendicularity and parallelism tolerances, as a way to better control the shape of locational tolerances.

Figure 10-36 shows an angularism tolerance and several ways in which it is interpreted at extreme conditions.

**Figure 10-36**

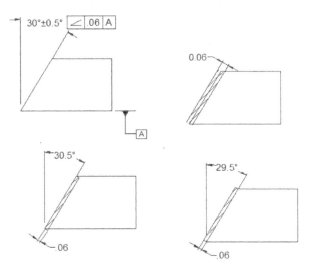

## 10-14 Profiles

*Profile tolerances* are used to limit the variations of irregular surfaces. They may be assigned as either bilateral or unilateral tolerances. There are two types of profile tolerances: surface and line. *Surface profile tolerances* limit the variation of an entire surface, whereas a *line profile tolerance* limits the variations along a single line across a surface.

Figure 10-37 shows an object that includes a surface profile tolerance referenced to an irregular surface. The tolerance is considered a bilateral tolerance because no other specification is given. This means that all points on the surface must be located between two parallel planes 0.08 apart that are centered about the irregular surface. The measurements are taken perpendicular to the surface.

**Figure 10-37**

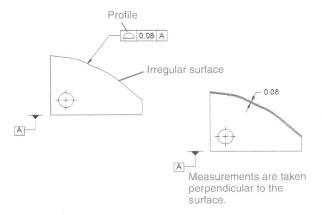

Unilateral applications of surface profile tolerances must be indicated on the drawing via phantom lines. A phantom line indicates on which side of the true profile line of the irregular surface the tolerance is to be applied. A phantom line above the irregular surface indicates that the tolerance is to be applied by making the true profile line 0 and then adding a specified tolerance range above that line (Figures 10-38 and 10-39).

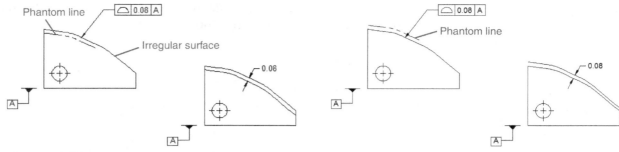

**Figure 10-38**

**Figure 10-39**

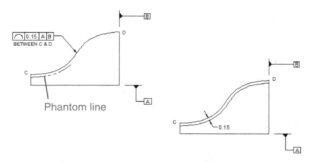

Profiles of line tolerances are applied to irregular surfaces, as shown in Figure 10-38. Profiles of line tolerances are particularly helpful for tolerancing an irregular surface that is constantly changing, such as the surface of an airplane wing.

Surface and line profile tolerances are somewhat analogous to flatness and straightness tolerances. Flatness and surface profile tolerances are applied across an entire surface; straightness and line profile tolerances are applied only along a single line across the surface.

## 10-15 Runouts

A *runout tolerance* is used to limit the variations between features of an object and a datum. More specifically, runout tolerances are applied to surfaces around a datum axis such as a cylinder or to a surface constructed perpendicular to a datum axis. There are two types of runout tolerances: circular and total.

Figure 10-40 shows a cylinder that includes a circular runout tolerance. The runout requirements are checked by rotating the object about its longitudinal axis or datum axis while holding an indicator gauge in a fixed position on the surface of the object.

**Figure 10-40**

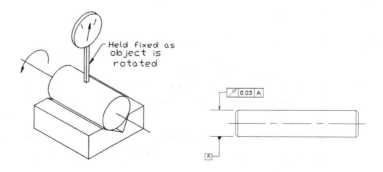

Runout tolerances may be either bilateral or unilateral. A runout tolerance is assumed to be bilateral unless otherwise indicated. If a runout tolerance is to be unilateral, a phantom line is used to indicate to which side
of the object's true surface the tolerance is to be applied (Figure 10-41).

Runout tolerances may be applied to tapered areas of cylindrical
objects, as shown in Figure 10-42. The tolerance is checked by rotating the
object about a datum axis while holding an indicator gauge in place.

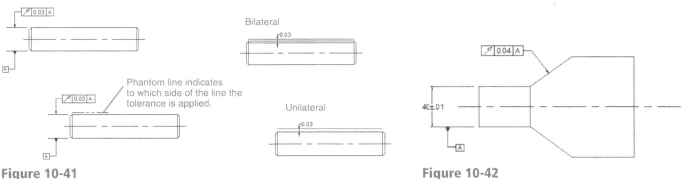

**Figure 10-41**

**Figure 10-42**

A total runout tolerance limits the variation across an entire surface
(Figure 10-43). An indicator gauge is not held in place while the object is
rotated, as it is for circular runout tolerances, but is moved about the rotating surface.

**Figure 10-43**

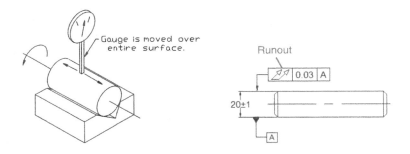

Figure 10-44 shows a circular runout tolerance that references two
datums. The two datums serve as one datum. The object can be rotated
about both datums simultaneously as the runout tolerances are checked.

**Figure 10-44**

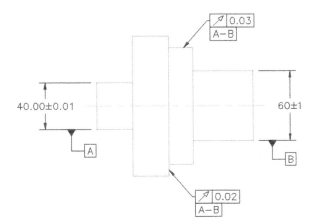

## 10-16 Positional Tolerances

*Positional tolerances* are used to locate and tolerance holes. Positional tolerances create a circular tolerance zone for hole center point locations that differs from the rectangular-shaped tolerance zone created by linear coordinate dimensions (Figure 10-45).

The circular tolerance zone allows for an increase in acceptable tolerance variation without compromising the design integrity of the object. Note that some of the possible hole center points fall in an area outside the rectangular tolerance zone but are still within the circular tolerance zone.

If the hole had been located according to linear coordinate dimensions, center points located beyond the rectangular tolerance zone would have been rejected as being beyond tolerance, and yet holes produced according to these locations would function correctly, from a design standpoint. The center point locations would be acceptable if positional tolerances had been specified. The finished hole is round, so a round tolerance zone is appropriate. The rectangular tolerance zone rejects some holes unnecessarily.

Holes are dimensioned and toleranced by the use of geometric tolerances with a combination of locating dimensions, feature dimensions and tolerances, and positional tolerances (Figure 10-46). The locating dimensions, which are enclosed in rectangular boxes, are called *basic dimensions*. Basic dimensions are assumed to be exact.

The feature tolerances for the hole are as presented in Chapter 9. They can be presented by using plus or minus, or limit-type, tolerances. In the example shown in Figure 10-46, the diameter of the hole is toleranced by a ±0.05 tolerance.

The basic locating dimensions of 45 and 50 are assumed to be exact. The tolerances that would normally accompany linear locational dimensions are replaced by the positional tolerance. The positional tolerance also specifies that the tolerance be applied at the centerline at maximum material condition. The resulting tolerance zones are as shown in Figure 10-46.

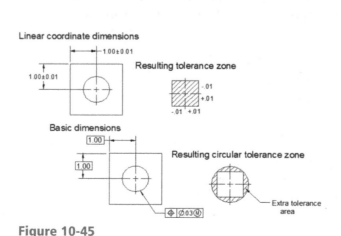

**Figure 10-45**

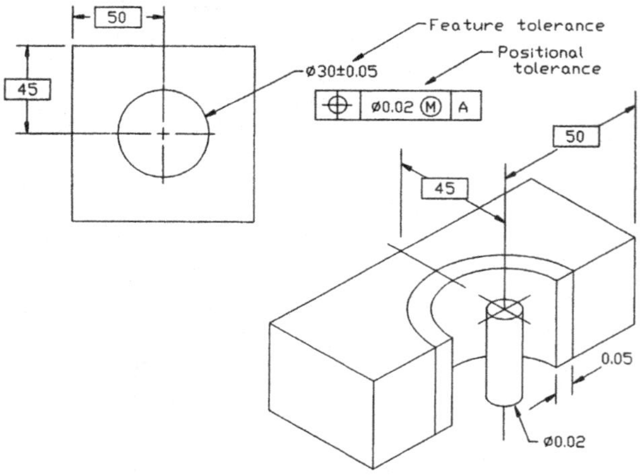

**Figure 10-46**

Figure 10-47 shows an object containing two holes that are dimensioned and toleranced by using positional tolerances. There are two consecutive horizontal basic dimensions. Because basic dimensions are exact, they do not have tolerances that accumulate; that is, there is no tolerance buildup.

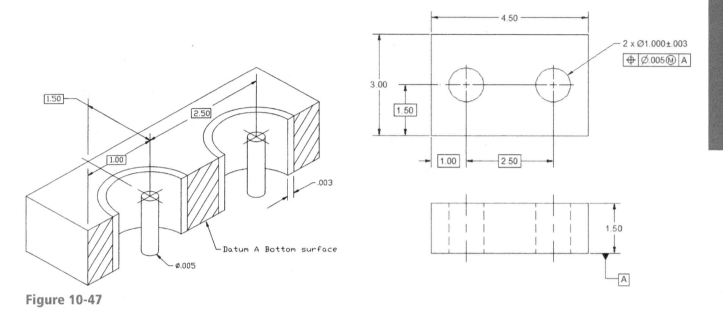

**Figure 10-47**

## 10-17 Virtual Condition

*Virtual condition* is a combination of a feature's MMC and its geometric tolerance. For external features (shafts), it is the MMC plus the geometric tolerance; for internal features (holes), it is the MMC minus the geometric tolerance.

The following calculations are based on the dimensions shown in Figure 10-48. (The symbol –A– is an older datum plane symbol.)

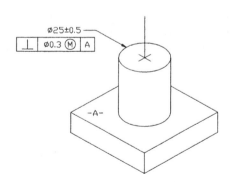

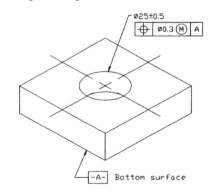

**Figure 10-48**

### Calculating the Virtual Condition for a Shaft

    25.5   MMC for shaft—maximum diameter

  +0.3   Geometric tolerance

    25.8   Virtual condition

## Calculating the Virtual Condition for a Hole

24.5 MMC for hole—minimum diameter

−0.3 Geometric tolerance

24.2 Virtual condition

## 10-18 Floating Fasteners

Positional tolerances are particularly helpful when dimensioning matching parts. Because basic locating dimensions are considered exact, the sizing of mating parts is dependent only on the MMC of the hole and shaft and the geometric tolerance between them.

The relationship for floating fasteners and holes in objects may be expressed as the formula

$$H - T = F$$

where

$H$ = Hole at MMC

$T$ = Geometric tolerance

$F$ = Shaft at MMC

A *floating fastener* is a fastener that is free to move in either object. It is not attached to either object, and it does not screw into either object. Figure 10-49 shows two objects that are to be joined by a common floating shaft, such as a bolt or screw. The feature size and tolerance and the positional geometric tolerance are both given. The minimum size hole that will always just fit is determined by the following formula:

$$H - T = F$$

$$11.97 - 0.02 = 11.95$$

Therefore, the shaft's diameter at MMC, the shaft's maximum diameter, equals 11.95. Any required tolerance would have to be subtracted from this shaft size.

The 0.02 geometric tolerance is applied at the hole's MMC. Thus, as the hole's size expands within its feature tolerance, the tolerance zone for the acceptable matching parts also expands (see the table in Figure 10-49).

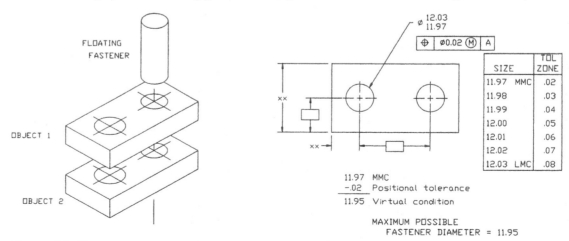

**Figure 10-49**

# 10-19 Drawing Problem

The situation presented in Figure 10-49 can be worked in reverse; that is, hole sizes can be derived from given shaft sizes.

The two objects shown in Figure 10-50 are to be joined by a .250-inch bolt. The parts are floating; that is, they are both free to move, and the fastener is not joined to either object. What is the MMC of the holes if the positional tolerance is to be .030?

A manufacturer's catalog specifies that the tolerance for a .250 bolt is .2500 to .2600.

Rewriting the formula

$$H - T = F$$

to isolate the $H$, we have

$$H = F + T$$

$$= 0.260 + 0.030$$

$$= 0.290$$

The 0.290 value represents the minimum hole diameter, MMC, for all four holes, that will always accept the 0.250 bolt. Figure 10-51 shows the resulting drawing callout.

Any clearance requirements or tolerances for the hole would have to be added to the 0.290 value.

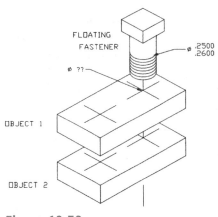

**Figure 10-50**

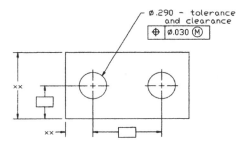

**Figure 10-51**

# 10-20 Drawing Problem

Repeat the problem presented in Drawing Problem 10-19 but be sure that there is always a minimum clearance of .002 between the hole and the shaft and assign a hole tolerance of .0010.

Drawing Problem 10-19 determined that the maximum hole diameter that would always accept the .250 bolt was .290, according to the .030 positional tolerance. If the minimum clearance is to be .002, the maximum hole diameter is found as follows:

    .290   Minimum hole diameter that will always accept the bolt (0 clearance at MMC)

   <u>+.002</u>  Minimum clearance

    .292   Minimum hole diameter including clearance

Now assign the tolerance to the hole:

.292   Minimum hole diameter

+.001   Tolerance

.293   Minimum hole diameter

Figure 10-52 shows the appropriate drawing callout. The choice of clearance size and hole tolerance varies with the design requirements for the objects.

**Figure 10-52**

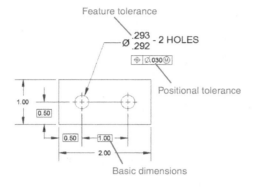

**10-21 Fixed Fasteners**

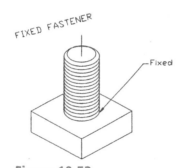

**Figure 10-53**

A *fixed fastener* is a fastener that is attached to one of the mating objects (Figure 10-53). Because the fastener is fixed to one of the objects, the geometric tolerance zone must be smaller than that used for floating fasteners. The fixed fastener cannot move without moving the object to which it is attached. The relationship between fixed fasteners and holes in mating objects is defined by the following formula:

$$H - 2T = F$$

The tolerance zone is cut in half, as can be demonstrated by the objects shown in Figure 10-54. The same feature sizes that were used in Figure 10-49 are assigned, but in this example, the fasteners are fixed. Solving for the geometric tolerance, we obtain the following value:

$$H - F = 2T$$

$$11.97 - 11.95 = 2T$$

$$.02 = 2T$$

$$.01 = T$$

**Figure 10-54**

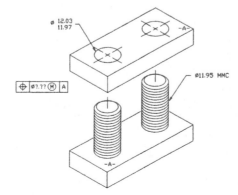

The resulting positional tolerance is half that obtained for floating fasteners.

## 10-22 Drawing Problem

This problem is similar to Drawing Problem 10-19, but the given conditions are applied to fixed fasteners rather than to floating fasteners. Compare the resulting shaft diameters for the two problems (Figure 10-55).

A. What is the minimum-diameter hole that will always accept the fixed fasteners?

B. If the minimum clearance is .005 and the hole is to have a tolerance of .002, what are the maximum and minimum diameters of the hole?

$$H - 2T = F$$

$$H = F + 2T$$

$$= .260 + 2(.030)$$

$$= .260 + .060$$

$$= .320 \text{ Minimum diameter that will always accept the fixed fastener}$$

If the minimum clearance is .005 and the hole tolerance is .002,

| .320 | Virtual condition |
| +.005 | Clearance |
| .325 | Minimum hole diameter |
| +.002 | Tolerance |
| .327 | Maximum hole diameter |

The maximum and minimum values for the hole's diameter can then be added to the drawing of the object that fits over the fixed fasteners (Figure 10-56).

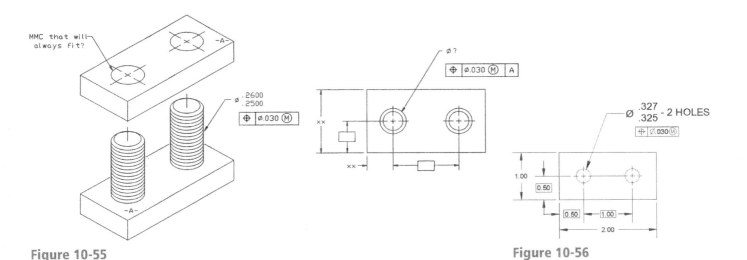

**Figure 10-55**

**Figure 10-56**

## 10-23 Design Problems

This problem was originally done in Section 9-27 using rectangular tolerances. It is done in this section using positional geometric tolerances so that the two systems can be compared. It is suggested that you review Section 9-27 before reading this section.

Figure 10-57 shows top and bottom parts that are to be joined in the floating condition. A nominal distance of 50 between hole centers and 20 for the holes has been assigned. In Section 9-27, a rectangular tolerance of ±0.01 was selected, and there was a minimum hole diameter of 20.00. Figure 10-58 shows the resulting tolerance zones.

**Figure 10-57**

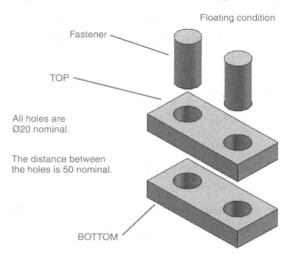

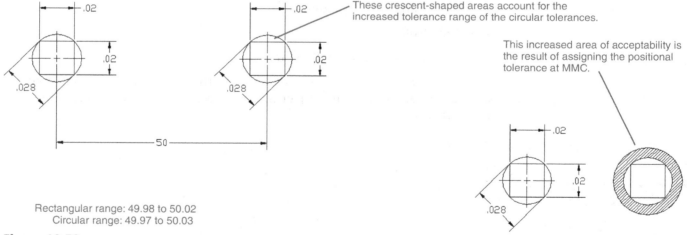

Rectangular range: 49.98 to 50.02
Circular range: 49.97 to 50.03

**Figure 10-58**

The diagonal distance across the rectangular tolerance zone is .028 and was rounded to .03 to yield a maximum possible fastener diameter of 19.97. If the same .03 value is used to calculate the fastener diameter by using positional tolerance, the results are as follows:

$$H - T = F$$

$$20.00 - 0.03 = 19.97$$

The results seem to be the same, but because of the circular shape of the positional tolerance zone, the manufactured results are not the same. The minimum distance between the inside edges of the rectangular zones is

49.98, or .01 from the center point of each hole. The minimum distance from the innermost points of the circular tolerance zones is 49.97, or .015 (half of the rounded .03 value) from the center point of each hole.

The same value difference also occurs for the maximum distance between center points, where 50.02 is the maximum distance for the rectangular tolerances and 50.03 is the maximum distance for the circular tolerances. The size of the circular tolerance zone increased more because the hole tolerances are assigned at MMC. Figure 10-58 shows a comparison between the tolerance zones, and Figure 10-59 shows how the positional tolerances would be presented on a drawing of either the top or bottom part.

Figure 10-60 shows the same top and bottom parts joined together in the fixed condition. The initial nominal values are the same. If the same .03 diagonal value is assigned as a positional tolerance, the results are as follows:

$$H - 2T = F$$

$$20.00 - .06 = 19.94$$

**Figure 10-59**

**Figure 10-60**

These results appear to be the same as those generated by the rectangular tolerance zone, but the circular tolerance zone allows a greater variance in acceptable manufactured parts. Figure 10-61 shows how the positional tolerance would be presented on a drawing.

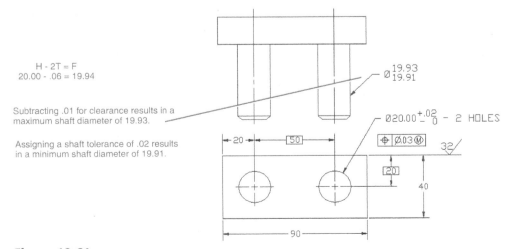

**Figure 10-61**

# 10-24 EXERCISE PROBLEMS

## EX10-1

Redraw the object shown. Include all dimensions and tolerances.

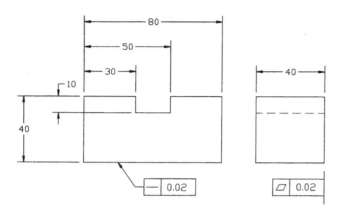

## EX10-2

Redraw the following shaft and add a feature dimension and tolerance of 36 ± 0.1 and a straightness tolerance of 0.07 about the centerline at MMC.

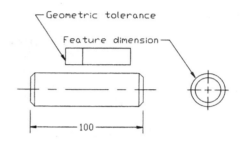

## EX10-3

- Given the shaft shown, what is the minimum hole diameter that will always accept the shaft?

- If the minimum clearance between the shaft and a hole is equal to 0.02 and the tolerance on the hole is to be 0.6, what are the maximum and minimum diameters for the hole?

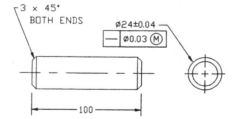

## EX10-4

- Given the shaft shown, what is the minimum hole diameter that will always accept the shaft?

- If the minimum clearance between the shaft and a hole is equal to .005 and the tolerance on the hole is to be .007, what are the maximum and minimum diameters for the hole?

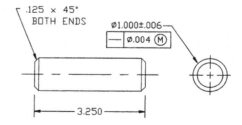

## EX10-5

Draw front and right-side views of the object shown and add the appropriate dimensions and tolerances on the basis of the information that follows. Numbers located next to an edge line indicate the length of the edge.

- Define surfaces A, B, and C as primary, secondary, and tertiary datums, respectively.

- Assign a tolerance of ±0.5 to all linear dimensions.

- Assign a feature tolerance of 12.07 – 12.00 to the protruding shaft.

- Assign a flatness tolerance of 0.01 to surface A.

- Assign a straightness tolerance of 0.03 to the protruding shaft.

- Assign a perpendicularity tolerance of 0.02 to the centerline of the protruding shaft at MMC relative to datum A.

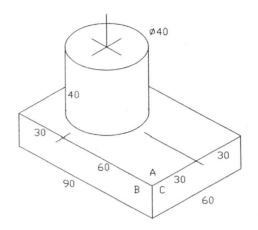

## EX10-6

Draw front and right-side views of the object shown, and add the following dimensions and tolerances:

- Define the bottom surface as datum A.

- Assign a perpendicularity tolerance of 0.4 to both sides of the slot relative to datum A.

- Assign a perpendicularity tolerance of 0.2 to the centerline of the 30-diameter hole centerline at MMC relative to datum A.

- Assign a feature tolerance of ±0.8 to all three holes.

- Assign a parallelism tolerance of 0.2 to the common centerline between the two 20-diameter holes relative to datum A.

- Assign a tolerance of ±0.5 to all linear dimensions.

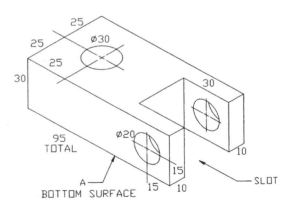

## EX10-7

Draw a circular front and the appropriate right-side view of the object shown and add the following dimensions and tolerances:

- Assign datum A as indicated.

- Assign the object's longitudinal axis as datum B.

- Assign the object's centerline through the slot as datum C.

- Assign a tolerance of ±0.5 to all linear tolerances.

- Assign a tolerance of ±0.5 to all circular-shaped features.

- Assign a parallelism tolerance of 0.01 to both edges of the slot.

- Assign a perpendicularity tolerance of 0.01 to the outside edge of the protruding shaft.

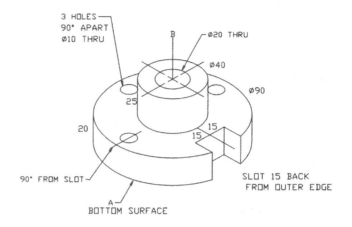

## EX10-8

Given the two objects shown, draw a front view and a side view of each. Assign a tolerance of ±0.5 to all linear dimensions. Assign a feature tolerance of ±0.4 to the shaft and also assign a straightness tolerance of 0.2 to the shaft's centerline at MMC.

    Tolerance the hole so that it will always accept the shaft with a minimum clearance of 0.1 and a feature tolerance of 0.2. Assign a perpendicularity tolerance of 0.05 to the centerline of the hole at MMC.

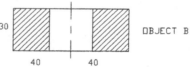

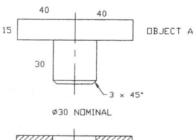

## EX10-9

Given the two objects shown, draw a front view and a side view of each. Assign a tolerance of ±.005 to all linear dimensions. Assign a feature tolerance of ±.004 to the shaft and also assign a straightness tolerance of .002 to the shaft's centerline at MMC.

    Tolerance the hole so that it will always accept the shaft with a minimum clearance of .001 and a feature tolerance of .002.

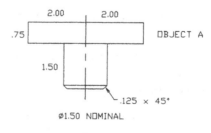

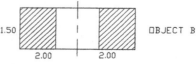

## EX10-10

Refer to parts A through G for this exercise problem. Use the format shown and redraw the given geometric tolerance symbols and frame as shown in the sample. Express in words (use **Mtext**) the meaning of each tolerance callout.

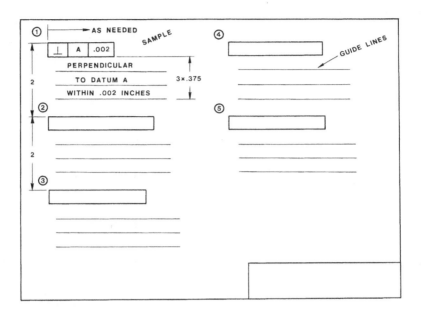

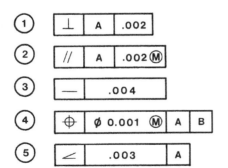

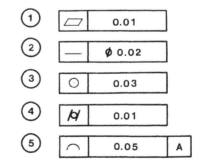

# EX10-10, continued

**(1)** ↗ | .015 | A | B

**(2)** ⌒ | .008 | A | B Ⓜ

**(3)** — | Ø 0.000 Ⓜ | Ø 0.002MAX

**(4)** ◎ | Ø 0.005 | A

**(5)** ↗↗ | .004 | A-B
TOTAL

---

**(1)** ⊕ | 0.25 Ⓜ | A | B | C

**(2)** ⊕ | 0.8 Ⓜ | A | B Ⓜ

**(3)** ⊕ | Ø 0.4 Ⓜ | A | B | C

**(4)** ⊕ | Ø 0.3 Ⓜ | A | B Ⓜ | C Ⓜ

**(5)** ⊕ | Ø 0.1 Ⓜ

---

**(1)** ⊕ | Ø 0.06 Ⓜ | A Ⓜ

**(2)** — | Ø 0.02 Ⓜ | Ø 0.05MAX

**(3)** ⊕ | Ø 0.0 Ⓜ | A | Ø .05MAX

**(4)** ↗↗ | .002 | A | B
TOTAL

**(5)** ⌒ | .003 | A | B | C
ALL AROUND

---

**(1)** ∠ | 0.04 Ⓜ | C | A Ⓜ | B Ⓜ

**(2)** ↗ | 0.02 | A

**(3)** ⊥ | 0.03 | A | B

**(4)** // | Ø 0.01 | A | B Ⓜ

**(5)** ⌒ | 0.03 | A | B
ALL AROUND

---

**(1)** ⊕ | Ø .002 Ⓜ

**(2)** ⊕ | .005 Ⓜ | A | B | C

**(3)** ⊕ | .002 | A | B Ⓜ

**(4)** ⊕ | Ø .003 Ⓜ | A | B Ⓜ | C Ⓜ

**(5)** ⊕ | Ø .015 Ⓜ | A | B

## EX10-11 Millimeters

Draw front, top, and right-side views of the object shown, including dimensions. Add the following tolerances and specifications to the drawing:

**1** Surface 1 is datum A.

**2** Surface 2 is datum B and is perpendicular to datum A within 0.1 millimeter.

**3** Surface 3 is datum C and is parallel to datum A within 0.3 millimeter.

**4** Locate a 16-millimeter-diameter hole in the center of the front surface that goes completely through the object. Use positional tolerances to locate the hole. Assign a positional tolerance of 0.02 at MMC perpendicular to datum A.

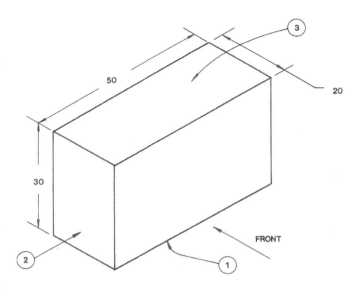

## EX10-12 Inches

Draw front, top, and right-side views of the object shown, including dimensions. Add the following tolerances and specifications to the drawing:

**1** Surface 1 is datum A.

**2** Surface 2 is datum B and is perpendicular to datum A within .003 inch.

**3** Surface 3 is parallel to datum A within .005 inch.

**4** The cylinder's longitudinal centerline is to be straight within .001 inch at MMC.

**5** Surface 2 is to have circular accuracy within .002 inch.

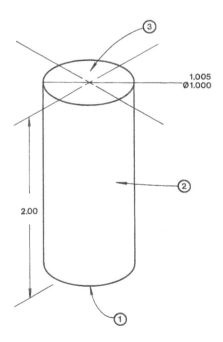

## EX10-13 Millimeters

Draw front, top, and right-side views of the object shown, including dimensions. Add the following tolerances and specifications to the drawing:

- Surface 1 is datum A.

- Surface 4 is datum B and is perpendicular to datum A within .08 millimeter.

- Surface 3 is flat within .03 millimeter.

- Surface 5 is parallel to datum A within .01 millimeter.

- Surface 2 has a runout tolerance of .2 millimeter relative to surface 4.

- Surface 1 is flat within .02 millimeter.

- The longitudinal centerline is to be straight within .02 millimeter at MMC and perpendicular to datum A.

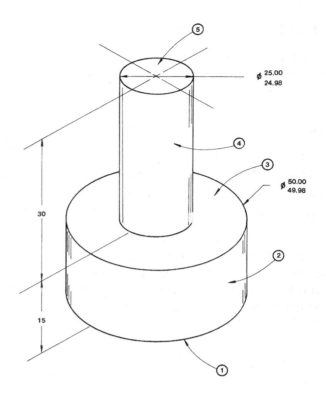

## EX10-14 Inches

Draw front, top, and right-side views of the object shown, including dimensions. Add the following tolerances and specifications to the drawing:

- Surface 2 is datum A.

- Surface 6 is perpendicular to datum A with .000 allowable variance at MMC but with a .002-inch MAX variance limit beyond MMC.

- Surface 1 is parallel to datum A within .005 inch.

- Surface 4 is perpendicular to datum A within .004 inch.

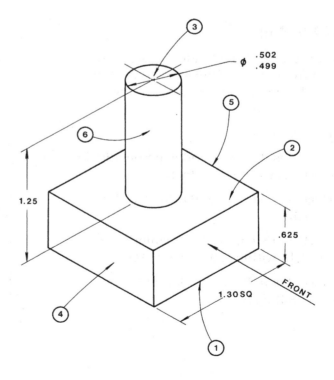

## EX10-15 Millimeters

Draw front, top, and right-side views of the object shown, including dimensions. Add the following tolerances and specifications to the drawing:

- Surface 1 is datum A.

- Surface 2 is datum B.

- The hole is located using a true position tolerance value of 0.13 millimeter at MMC. The true position tolerance is referenced to datums A and B.

- Surface 1 is to be straight within 0.02 millimeter.

- The bottom surface is to be parallel to datum A within 0.03 millimeter.

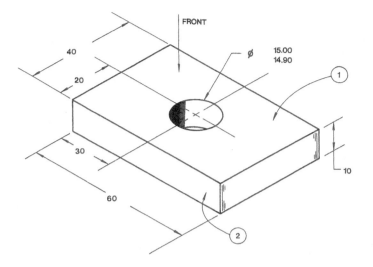

## EX10-16 Millimeters

Draw front, top, and right-side views of the object shown, including dimensions. Add the following tolerances and specifications to the drawing:

- Surface 1 is datum A.

- Surface 2 is datum B.

- Surface 3 is perpendicular to surface 2 within 0.02 millimeter.

- The four holes are to be located by using a positional tolerance of 0.07 millimeter at MMC referenced to datums A and B.

- The centerlines of the holes are to be straight within 0.01 millimeter at MMC.

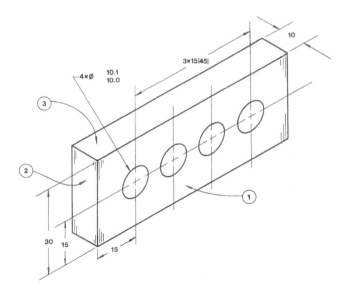

## EX10-17 Inches

Draw front, top, and right-side views of the object shown, including dimensions. Add the following tolerances and specifications to the drawing:

- Surface 1 has a dimension of .378 – .375 inch and is datum A. The surface has a dual primary runout with datum B to within .005 inch. The runout is total.

- Surface 2 has a dimension of 1.505 – 1.495 inch. Its runout relative to the dual primary datums A and B is .008 inch. The runout is total.

- Surface 3 has a dimension of 1.000 ± .005 and has no geometric tolerance.

- Surface 4 has no circular dimension but has a total runout tolerance of .006 inch relative to the dual datums A and B.

- Surface 5 has a dimension of .500 – .495 inch and is datum B. It has a dual primary runout with datum A within .005 inch. The runout is total.

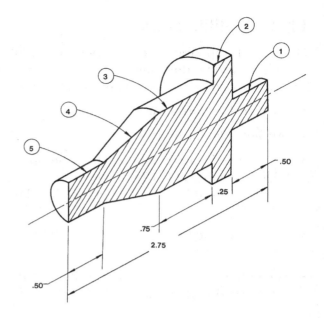

## EX10-18 Millimeters

Draw front, top, and right-side views of the object shown, including dimensions. Add the following tolerances and specifications to the drawing:

- Hole 1 is datum A.

- Hole 2 is to have its circular centerline parallel to datum A within 0.2 millimeter at MMC when datum A is at MMC.

- Assign a positional tolerance of 0.01 to each hole's centerline at MMC.

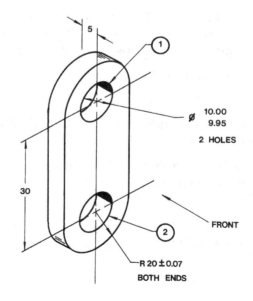

## EX10-19 Inches

Draw front, top, and right-side views of the object shown, including dimensions. Add the following tolerances and specifications to the drawing:

- Surface 1 is datum A.

- Surface 2 is datum B.

- The six holes have a diameter range of .500 – .499 inch and are to be located by using positional tolerances so that their centerlines are within .005 inch at MMC relative to datums A and B.

The back surface is to be parallel to datum A within .002 inch.

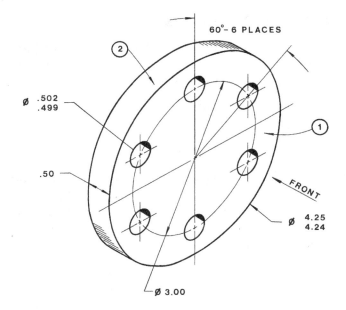

## EX10-20 Millimeters

Draw front, top, and right-side views of the object shown, including dimensions. Add the following tolerances and specifications to the drawing:

- Surface 1 is datum A.

- Hole 2 is datum B.

- The eight holes labeled 3 have diameters of 8.4 – 8.3 millimeters, with a positional tolerance of 0.15 millimeter at MMC relative to datums A and B. Also, the eight holes are to be counter-bored to a diameter of 14.6 – 14.4 millimeters and to a depth of 5.0 millimeters.

- The large center hole is to have a straightness tolerance of 0.2 at MMC about its centerline.

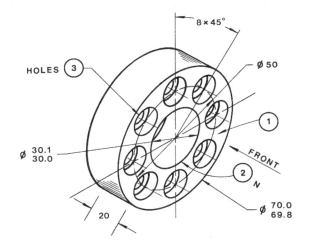

## EX10-21 Millimeters

Draw front, top, and right-side views of the object shown, including dimensions. Add the following tolerances and specifications to the drawing:

- Surface 1 is datum A.

- Surface 2 is datum B.

- Surface 3 is datum C.

- The four holes labeled 4 have a dimension and tolerance of 8 + 0.3, –0 millimeters. The holes are to be located by using a positional tolerance of 0.05 millimeter at MMC relative to datums A, B, and C.

- The six holes labeled 5 have a dimension and tolerance of 6 + 0.2, –0 millimeters. The holes are to be located by using a positional tolerance of 0.01 millimeter at MMC relative to datums A, B, and C.

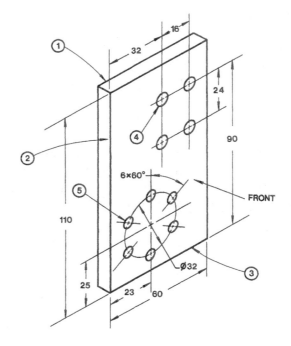

## EX10-22

The objects on the next page labeled A and B are to be toleranced by four different tolerances, as shown. Redraw the charts shown and list the appropriate allowable tolerance for "as measured" increments of 0.1 millimeter or .001 inch. Also include the appropriate geometric tolerance drawing called out above each chart.

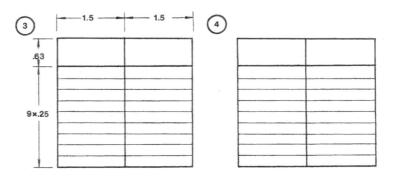

# EX10-22, continued

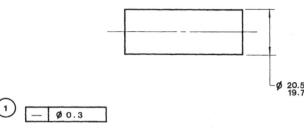

Ø 20.5 / 19.7

① ─ | Ø 0.3

② ─ | Ø 0.3 Ⓜ

③ ─ | Ø 0.0 Ⓜ

④ ─ | Ø 0.0 Ⓜ | Ø0.04 MAX

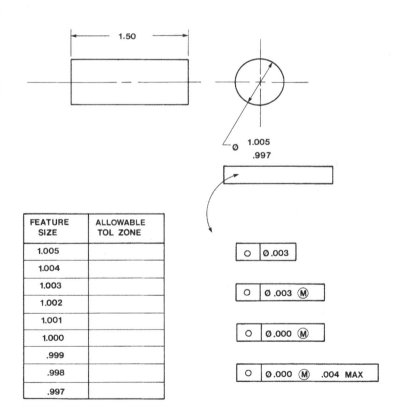

1.50

Ø 1.005 / .997

| FEATURE SIZE | ALLOWABLE TOL ZONE |
|---|---|
| 1.005 | |
| 1.004 | |
| 1.003 | |
| 1.002 | |
| 1.001 | |
| 1.000 | |
| .999 | |
| .998 | |
| .997 | |

○ | Ø .003

○ | Ø .003 Ⓜ

○ | Ø .000 Ⓜ

○ | Ø .000 Ⓜ | .004 MAX

## EX10-23

Dimension and tolerance parts 1 and 2 so that part 1 always fits into part 2 with a minimum clearance of .005 inch. The tolerance for part 1's outer matching surface is .006 inch.

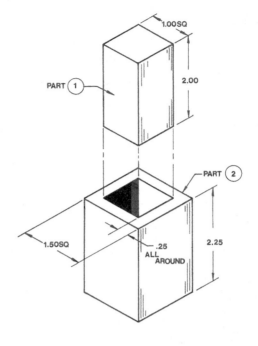

## EX10-24

Dimension and tolerance parts 1 and 2 so that part 1 always fits into part 2 with a minimum clearance of 0.03 millimeter. The tolerance for part 1's diameter is 0.05 millimeter. Take into account the fact that the interface is long relative to the diameters.

## EX10-25

Prepare front and top views of parts 4A and 4B according to the given dimensions. Add geometric tolerances to produce the stated maximum clearance and mismatch.

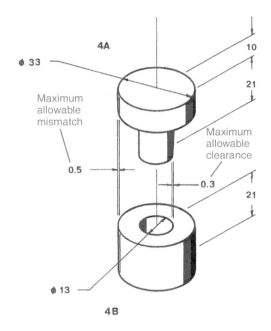

## EX10-26 Inches–Clearance Fit

- The distance between the holes is 2.00 nominal.
- The diameter of the fasteners is Ø.375 nominal.
- The fasteners have a total tolerance of .001.
- The holes have a tolerance of .002.
- The minimum allowable clearance between the fastener and the holes is .003.
- The material is .375 inch thick.

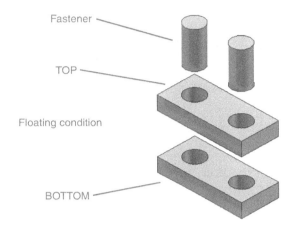

## EX10-27 Millimeters–Clearance Fit

- The distance between the holes is 80 nominal.
- The nominal diameter of the fasteners is Ø12.
- The fasteners have a total tolerance of 0.05.
- The holes have a tolerance of 0.03.
- The minimum allowable clearance between the fastener and the holes is 0.02.
- The material is 12 millimeters thick.

## EX10-28 Inches–Clearance Fit

- The distance between the holes is 3.50 nominal.
- The diameter of the fasteners is Ø.625.
- The fasteners have a total tolerance of 0.005.
- The holes have a tolerance of 0.003.
- The minimum allowable clearance between the fastener and the holes is 0.002.
- The material is 0.500 inch thick.

## EX10-29 Millimeters–Clearance Fit

- The distance between the holes is 120 nominal.
- The diameter of the fasteners is Ø24 nominal.
- The fasteners have a total tolerance of 0.01.
- The holes have a tolerance of 0.02.
- The minimum allowable clearance between the fastener and the holes is 0.04.
- The material is 20 millimeters thick.

## EX10-30 Inches–Interference Fit

- The distance between the holes is 2.00 nominal.
- The diameter of the fasteners is Ø.250 nominal.
- The fasteners have a total tolerance of .001.
- The holes have a tolerance of .002.
- The maximum allowable interference between the fastener and the holes is .0065.
- The material is .438 inch thick.

### EX10-31 Millimeters–Interference Fit

- The distance between the holes is 80 nominal.
- The diameter of the fasteners is Ø10 nominal.
- The fasteners have a total tolerance of 0.01.
- The holes have a tolerance of 0.02.
- The maximum allowable interference between the fastener and the holes is 0.032.
- The material is 14 millimeters thick.

### EX10-33 Millimeters–Transitional Fit

- The distance between the holes is 100 nominal.
- The diameter of the fasteners is Ø16 nominal.
- The fasteners have a total tolerance of 0.01.
- The holes are to have a tolerance of 0.02.
- The minimum allowable clearance between the fastener and the holes is 0.01.
- The material is 20 millimeters thick.

Given a top part and a bottom part in the fixed condition, as shown, add dimensions and tolerances to satisfy the given conditions in Practice Exercises EX10-34 through EX10-41. Size the top and bottom parts and fastener length as needed. Use geometric and positional tolerances.

### EX10-32 Inches–Locational Fit

- The distance between the holes is 2.25 nominal.
- The diameter of the fasteners is Ø.50 nominal.
- The fasteners have a total tolerance of .001.
- The holes have a tolerance of .002.
- The minimum allowable clearance between the fastener and the holes is .0010.
- The material is .370 inch thick.

### EX10-34 Inches–Clearance Fit

- The distance between the holes is 2.00 nominal.
- The diameter of the fasteners is Ø.375 nominal.
- The fasteners have a total tolerance of .001.
- The holes have a tolerance of .002.
- The minimum allowable clearance between the fastener and the holes is .003.
- The material is .375 inch thick.

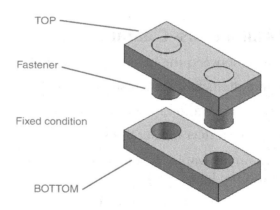

### EX10-35 Millimeters–Clearance Fit

- The distance between the holes is 80 nominal.
- The nominal diameter of the fasteners is Ø12.
- The fasteners have a total tolerance of 0.05.
- The holes have a tolerance of 0.03.
- The minimum allowable clearance between the fastener and the holes is 0.02.
- The material is 12 millimeters thick.

### EX10-36 Inches–Clearance Fit

- The distance between the holes is 3.50 nominal.
- The diameter of the fasteners is Ø.625.
- The fasteners have a total tolerance of .005.
- The holes have a tolerance of .003.
- The minimum allowable clearance between the fastener and the holes is .002.
- The material is .500 inch thick.

## EX10-37 Millimeters–Clearance Fit

- The distance between the holes is 120 nominal.
- The diameter of the fasteners is Ø24 nominal.
- The fasteners have a total tolerance of 0.01.
- The holes have a tolerance of 0.02.
- The minimum allowable clearance between the fastener and the holes is 0.04.
- The material is 20 millimeters thick.

## EX10-38 Inches–Interference Fit

- The distance between the holes is 2.00 nominal.
- The diameter of the fasteners is Ø.250 nominal.
- The fasteners have a total tolerance of .001.
- The holes have a tolerance of .002.
- The maximum allowable interference between the fastener and the holes is .0065.
- The material is .438 inch thick.

## EX10-39 Millimeters–Interference Fit

- The distance between the holes is 80 nominal.
- The diameter of the fasteners is Ø10 nominal.
- The fasteners have a total tolerance of 0.01.
- The holes have a tolerance of 0.02.
- The maximum allowable interference between the fastener and the holes is 0.032.
- The material is 14 millimeters thick.

## EX10-40 Inches–Locational Fit

- The distance between the holes is 2.25 nominal.
- The diameter of the fasteners is Ø.50 nominal.
- The fasteners have a total tolerance of .001.
- The holes have a tolerance of .002.
- The minimum allowable clearance between the fastener and the holes is .0010.
- The material is .370 inch thick.

## EX10-41 Millimeters–Transitional Fit

- The distance between the holes is 100 nominal.
- The diameter of the fasteners is Ø16 nominal.
- The fasteners have a total tolerance of 0.01.
- The holes are to have a tolerance of 0.02.
- The minimum allowable clearance between the fastener and the holes is 0.001.
- The material is 20 millimeters thick.

## EX10-42

Given the two assemblies that follow, size the parts so that they always fit together. Create individual drawings of each part, including dimensions and tolerances. Use geometric and positional tolerances.

SUPPORT ASSEMBLY

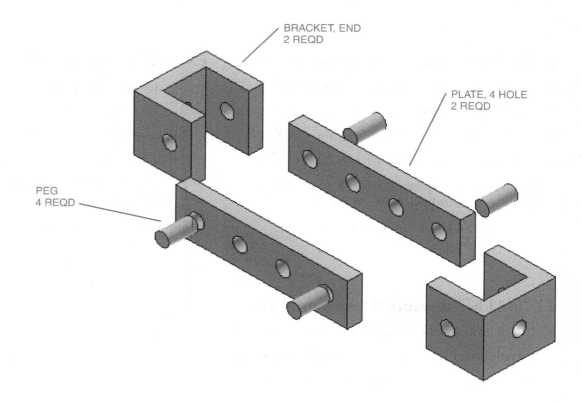

BRACKET, END
2 REQD

PLATE, 4 HOLE
2 REQD

PEG
4 REQD

## EX10-43

Assume that there are two copies of the part shown and that these parts are to be joined together by four fasteners in the floating condition. Draw front and top views of the object, including dimensions and tolerances. Add the given tolerances and specifications to the drawing and then draw front and top views of a shaft that can be used to join the two objects. The shaft should be able to fit into any of the four holes.

- Surface 1 is datum A.

- Surface 2 is datum B.

- Surface 3 is perpendicular to surface 2 within 0.02 millimeter.

- Specify the positional tolerance for the four holes applied at MMC.

- The centerlines of the holes are to be straight within 0.01 millimeter at MMC.

- The clearance between the shafts and the holes is to be 0.05 minimum and 0.10 maximum.

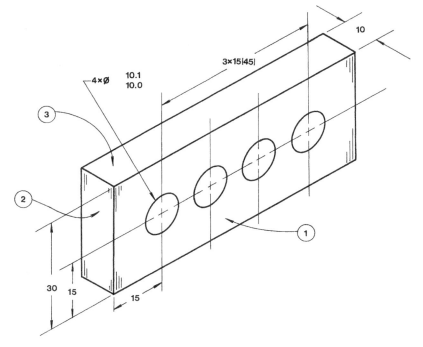

## EX10-44

Assume that there are two copies of the part shown and that these parts are to be joined together by six fasteners in the floating condition. Draw front and top views of the object, including dimensions and tolerances. Add the given tolerances and specifications to the drawing and then draw front and top views of a shaft that can be used to join the two objects. The shaft should be able to fit into any of the six holes.

- Surface 1 is datum A.

- Surface 2 is round within .003.

- Specify the positional tolerance for the six holes applied at MMC.

- The clearance between the shafts and the holes is to be .001 minimum and .003 maximum.

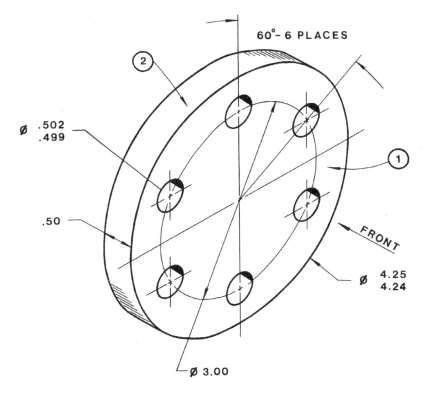

# chapter eleven

# Threads and Fasteners

## 11-1 Introduction

This chapter explains how to draw threads, washers, keys, and springs. It explains how to use fasteners to join parts together and describes the design uses for washers, keys, and springs.

This chapter suggests in many places that you create blocks and wblocked drawings of the various thread and fastener shapes. Thread representations, fastener head shapes, set screws, and both internal and external thread representations for orthographic views and sectional views are so common in technical drawings that it is good practice to create a set of blocks and drawings that can be used on future drawings in order to avoid having to redraw a thread shape every time it is needed.

See Chapter 3 for an explanation of the **Block** and **Wblock** commands.

## 11-2 Thread Terminology

Figure 11-1 shows a detailed representation of a thread. The peak of a thread is called the *crest*, and the valley portion is called the *root*. The *major diameter* of a thread is the distance across the thread from crest to crest. The *minor diameter* is the distance across the thread from root to root.

**Figure 11-1**

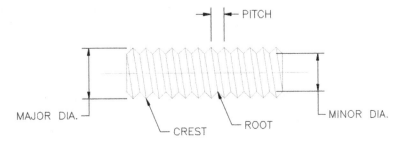

The *pitch* of a thread is the linear distance along the thread from crest to crest. Thread pitch is usually referred to in terms of a unit of length, such as 20 threads per inch or 1.5 threads per millimeter.

## 11-3 Thread Callouts—Metric Units

Threads on a drawing are specified by drawing callouts (Figure 11-2). The M preceding a drawing callout specifies that the callout is for a metric thread. Holes that are not threaded use the ø symbol.

**Figure 11-2**

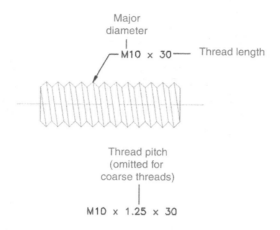

Major diameter

M10 × 30 —— Thread length

Thread pitch
(omitted for
coarse threads)

M10 × 1.25 × 30

The number following the M is the major diameter of the thread; for example, an M10 thread has a major diameter of 10 millimeters. The pitch of a metric thread is assumed to be a coarse thread unless otherwise stated. The callout M10 × 30 assumes a coarse thread, or 1.5 threads per millimeter. In this case, the number 30 is the thread length in millimeters. The × is read as "by," so the thread is called a "ten by thirty."

The callout M10 × 1.25 × 30 specifies a pitch of 1.25 threads per millimeter. This is not a standard coarse thread size, so the pitch must be specified.

Figure 11-3 shows a list of preferred thread sizes. These sizes are similar to the standard sizes shown in Figure 9-32. A list of other metric thread sizes is included in the online Appendix.

Whenever possible, use preferred thread sizes for designing. Preferred thread sizes are readily available and are usually cheaper than nonstandard sizes. In addition, tooling such as wrenches is readily available for preferred sizes.

| Major Dia | Coarse | | Fine | |
|---|---|---|---|---|
| | Pitch | Tap Drill Dia | Pitch | Tap Drill Dia |
| 1.6 | 0.35 | 1.25 | | |
| 2 | 0.4 | 1.6 | | |
| 2.5 | 0.45 | 2.05 | | |
| 3 | 0.5 | 2.5 | | |
| 4 | .7 | 3.3 | | |
| 5 | 0.8 | 4.2 | | |
| 6 | 1 | 5.0 | | |
| 8 | 1.25 | 6.7 | 1 | 7.0 |
| 10 | 1.5 | 8.5 | 1.25 | 8.7 |
| 12 | 1.75 | 10.2 | 1.25 | 10.8 |
| 16 | 2 | 14 | 1.5 | 14.5 |
| 20 | 2.5 | 17.5 | 1.5 | 18.5 |
| 24 | 3 | 21 | 2 | 22 |
| 30 | 3.5 | 26.5 | 2 | 28 |
| 36 | 4 | 32 | 3 | 33 |
| 42 | 4.5 | 37.5 | 3 | 39 |
| 48 | 5 | 43 | 3 | 45 |

**Figure 11-3**

## 11-4 Thread Callouts—English Units

English unit threads always include a thread form specification. Thread form specifications are designated by capital letters, as shown in Figure 11-4, and are defined as follows:

UNC—Unified National Coarse

UNF—Unified National Fine

UNEF—Unified National Extra Fine

UN—Unified National, or constant pitch threads

**Figure 11-4**

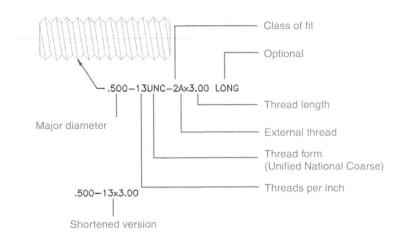

An English unit thread callout starts by defining the major diameter of the thread, followed by the pitch specification. The callout .500 – 13 UNC means a thread whose major diameter is .500 inch, with 13 threads per inch, manufactured to the Unified National Coarse standards.

There are three possible classes of fit for a thread: 1, 2, and 3. The different classes specify sets of manufacturing tolerances. A class 1 thread is the loosest, and a class 3 is the most exact. A class 2 fit is the most common.

The letter A designates an external thread, B an internal thread. The symbol × means "by," as in 2 × 4, or "two by four." The thread length (e.g., 3.00) may be followed by the word LONG to prevent confusion about which value represents the length.

Drawing callouts for English unit threads are sometimes shortened, as shown in Figure 11-4. The callout .500 – 13UNC – 2A × 3.00 LONG is shortened to .500 – 13 × 3.00. Only a coarse thread has 13 threads per inch, and it should be obvious whether a thread is internal or external, so these specifications may be dropped. Most threads are class 2, so it is tacitly accepted that all threads are class 2 unless otherwise specified. The shortened callout form is not universally accepted. When in doubt, use a complete thread callout.

A partial list of standard English unit threads is shown in Figure 11-5. A more complete list is included in the online Appendix. Some of the drill sizes listed use numbers and letters. The decimal equivalents to the numbers and letters are listed in the online Appendix.

**Figure 11-5**

| Major Dia | Decimal | UNC | | UNF | | UNEF | |
|---|---|---|---|---|---|---|---|
| | | Thread/in | Tap drill Dia. | Thread/in | Tap drill Dia. | Thread/in | Tap drill Dia. |
| #6 | .138 | 40 | #38 | 44 | #37 | | |
| #8 | .164 | 32 | #29 | 36 | #29 | | |
| #10 | .190 | 24 | #25 | 32 | #21 | | |
| 1/4 | .250 | 20 | 7 | 28 | 3 | 32 | .219 |
| 5/16 | .312 | 18 | F | 24 | 1 | 32 | .281 |
| 3/8 | .375 | 16 | .312 | 24 | Q | 32 | .344 |
| 7/16 | .438 | 14 | U | 20 | .391 | 28 | Y |
| 1/2 | .500 | 13 | .422 | 20 | .453 | 28 | .469 |
| 9/16 | .562 | 12 | .484 | 18 | .516 | 24 | .516 |
| 5/8 | .625 | 11 | .531 | 18 | .578 | 24 | .578 |
| 3/4 | .750 | 10 | .656 | 16 | .688 | 20 | .703 |
| 7/8 | .875 | 9 | .766 | 14 | .812 | 20 | .828 |
| 1 | 1.000 | 8 | .875 | 12 | .922 | 20 | .953 |
| 1 1/4 | 1.250 | 7 | 1.109 | 12 | 1.172 | 18 | 1.188 |
| 1 1/2 | 1.500 | 6 | 1.344 | 12 | 1.422 | 18 | 1.438 |

UNC = Unified National Coarse

UNF = Unified National Fine

UNEF = Unified National Extra Fine

## 11-5 Thread Representations

There are three ways to graphically represent threads on a drawing: detailed, schematic, and simplified. Figure 11-6 shows the three representations.

**Figure 11-6**

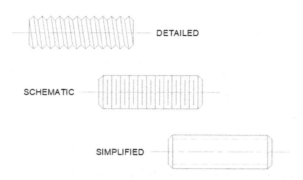

DETAILED

SCHEMATIC

SIMPLIFIED

Detailed representations look the most like actual threads but drawing them is time-consuming. Using **Wblock** to create a drawing file of a detailed shape helps eliminate this time constraint.

Schematic and simplified thread representations are created by drawing a series of straight lines. The simplified representation uses only two hidden lines and can be mistaken for an internal hole if it is not accompanied by a thread specification callout. The choice of which representation to use depends on individual preferences. The resulting drawing should be clear and easy to understand. All three representations may be used on the same drawing, but in general, only very large threads (those over 1.00 in., or 25 mm) are drawn for detailed representations.

Ideally, thread representations should be drawn with each thread equal to the actual pitch size. This is not practical for smaller threads and not necessary for larger ones. Thread representations are not meant to be exact duplications of the threads but representations, so convenient drawing distances are acceptable.

### Drawing a Detailed Thread Representation

Draw a detailed thread representation for a 1.00-inch-diameter thread that is 3.00 inches long (Figure 11-7).

**1** Set **Grid** to **.5** and **Snap** to **.125**.

**Figure 11-7**

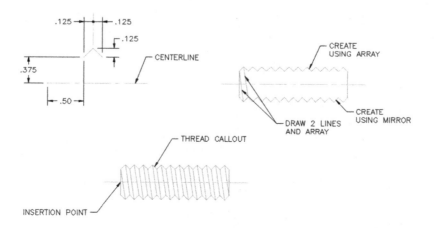

**2** Draw a **4.00-inch** centerline near the center of the screen.

**3** Zoom the area around the centerline.

**4** Draw a single zigzag pattern **.375** above the centerline using the 0.125 snap points. Start the zigzag line **.50** from the left end of the centerline.

**5** Access Rectangular **Array**.

**6** Select the zigzag pattern.

**7** Set the **Rows** values to **1** and the distance between rows to **0**.

**8** Set the **Columns** value to **12**.

**9** Set the distance between columns to **0.25** and then press **Enter**.

**10** Mirror the arrayed zigzag line about the centerline.

**11** Draw vertical lines at both ends of the thread and two slanted lines between the thread's roots and crests, as shown.

**12** Array both slanted lines, using the same array parameters used for the zigzag line: **12** columns **.25** apart.

**13** Use **Wblock** to save the thread representation as a block and drawing named **DETLIN**. Define the insertion point as shown. Creating blocks is explained in Chapter 3.

Another technique for drawing a detailed thread representation is to draw a single thread completely and then use the **Copy** command or the **Array** command to generate as many additional threads as are necessary.

It is recommended that you use **Wblock** to save all thread blocks in a dedicated file folder. This folder will become a reference folder that you can use when creating other drawings that require threads.

Figure 11-8 shows a metric unit detailed thread representation. It was created by using the procedure just outlined. **Grid** is set to **10**, **Snap** is set to **2.5**, and the distance from the end of the centerline to the zigzag pattern is **10**. Draw and save the metric detailed thread representation shown in Figure 11-8 as a block named **DETLMM**.

**Figure 11-8**

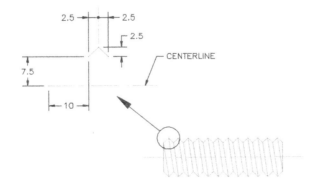

## Creating an Internal Detailed Thread Representation in a Sectional View

Figure 11-9 shows how to create a 1.00-inch internal detailed thread representation from the block **DETLIN** of the external detailed thread created previously.

Figure 11-9

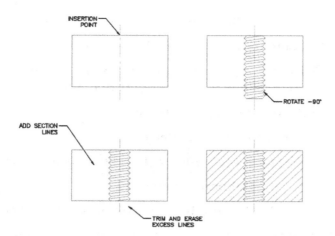

**1** Use **Insert** and locate the detailed block on the drawing screen at the indicated insertion point. In this example, the thread is to be drawn in a vertical orientation, so the block is rotated **–90°** when it is inserted. The same scale size is used for the block as was used for a 1.00-inch diameter thread.

**2** The thread created from the block **DETLIN** is longer than needed, so explode the block and then trim and erase the excess lines.

**3** Use the **ANSI31** hatch pattern and apply hatching to the areas outside the thread, as shown.

## Creating a Schematic Thread Representation

Draw a schematic representation of a 1.00-inch-diameter thread (Figure 11-10).

Figure 11-10

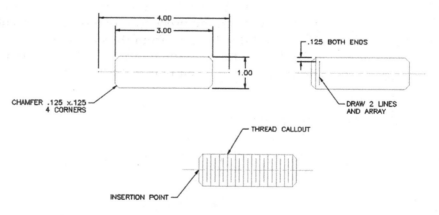

**1** Set **Grid** to **.50** and **Snap** to **.125**.

**2** Draw a **4.00-inch** centerline near the middle of the drawing screen.

**3** Draw the outline of the thread, including a chamfer, using the dimensions shown.

The chamfer was drawn in this example by using the 0.125 snap points, but the **Chamfer** command could also be used.

The 1.00 diameter was chosen because it makes it easier to determine scale factors for the block when inserting the representation into other drawings.

**4** Draw three vertical lines, as shown.

**5** Use the **Array, Rectangular** command to draw **11** vertical lines across the thread. The distance between the 11 lines (**COLUMNS**) is **.25**.

A distance of –.25 would create lines to the left of the original line.

**6** Save the representation as a block named **SCHMINCH**. Define the insertion point as shown and then use **Wblock** to write the block to your hard disk.

Figure 11-11 shows a metric unit version of a schematic thread representation in a sectional view. The procedure used to create the representation is the same as that explained previously but with different drawing limits and different values. The major diameter is **20**, and the spacing between lines is **2.5** and **5**, as shown. Draw and save the representation as a block named **SCHMMM**.

**Figure 11-11**

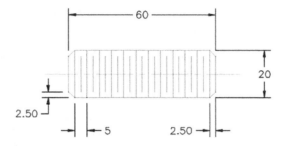

## Creating an Internal Schematic Thread Representation

Figure 11-12 shows a 36-millimeter-diameter internal schematic thread representation. It was developed from the block **SCHMMM** created previously.

**Figure 11-12**

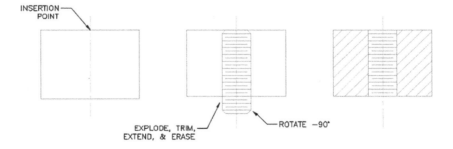

**1** Set **Grid** to **10**, **Snap** to **5**, **Limits** to **297,210**, and **Zoom** to **ALL**.

**2** Insert the block **SCHMMM** at the indicated insertion point.

The required thread diameter is **36** millimeters. The block **SCHMMM** was drawn with a diameter of **20** millimeters. This means that the block must be enlarged by using a scale factor. The scale factor is determined by dividing the desired diameter by the block's diameter: 36/20 = 1.8.

Ensure that the block is rotated **–90°** to give it the correct orientation.

**3** The inserted thread shape is longer than desired, so first explode the block and then use the **Erase**, **Trim**, and **Extend** commands as needed.

**4** Draw the sectional lines by using the **ANSI31** hatch pattern.

**5** Save the block and wblock, if desired.

## Creating a Simplified Thread Representation

The simplified representation looks very similar to the orthographic view of an internal hole, so it is important to always include a thread callout with the representation. In the example shown in Figure 11-13, a leader line is included with the representation. The leader serves as a reminder to add the appropriate drawing callout. If the leader line is in an inconvenient location when the block is inserted, the leader line can be moved or simply erased.

**1** Set **Grid** to **.5** and **Snap** to **.125**.

**2** Draw a **4.00** centerline near the center of the screen.

**3** Draw the thread outline, using the given dimensions.

**4** Draw the hidden lines, using the given dimensions.

**5** Save the thread representation as a block named **SIMPIN**. Define the insertion point as shown.

Figure 11-14 shows an internal simplified thread representation in a sectional view. Note how hidden lines that cross over the sectional lines are used. The hatch must be drawn first and the hidden lines added over the pattern. If the hidden lines are drawn first, the **Hatch** command may not add section lines to the portion between the hidden line and the solid line that represents the edge of the threaded hole.

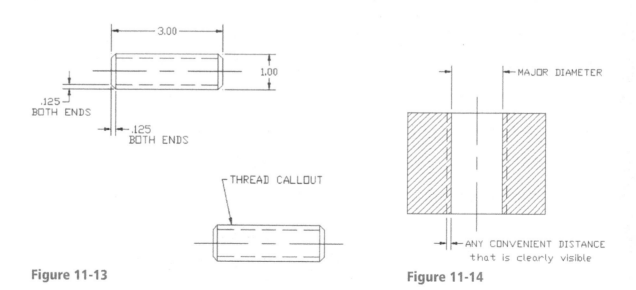

**Figure 11-13**

**Figure 11-14**

## 11-6 Orthographic Views of Internal Threads

Figure 11-15 shows top and front orthographic views of internal threads. One thread goes completely through the object, and the other goes only partially through the object.

**Figure 11-15**

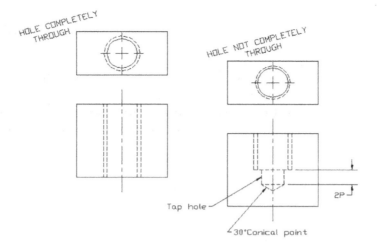

Internal threads are represented in orthographic views by parallel hidden lines. The distance between the lines should be large enough so that there is a clear distinction between the lines; that is, the lines should not appear to blend together or become a single, very thick line.

Circular orthographic views of threaded holes are represented by two circles: one drawn by using a continuous linetype and the other drawn by using a hidden line. The distance between the circles should be large enough to be visually distinctive. The two circles shown should both be clearly visible.

Threaded holes are created by first drilling a tap hole and then tapping (cutting) the threads with a tapping bit. Tapping bits have cutting surfaces on their side surfaces, not on the bottom. This means that if the tapping bit were forced all the way to the bottom of the tap hole, the bit could be damaged or broken. It is good design practice to make the tap hole deep enough so that a distance equivalent to at least two thread lengths ($2P$) extends beyond the tapped portion of the hole.

Threaded holes that do not go completely through an object must always show the unused portion of the tap hole. The unused portion should also include the conical point (see Section 5-17 in Chapter 5).

If an internal 0.500 – 13 UNC thread does not go completely through an object, the length of the unused portion of the tap hole is determined as follows:

Pitch length = Inches/Thread = 1.00/13

$$= .077 \text{ inch}$$

Therefore,

$2P = 2(.077) = .15$ inch

The distance .15 represents a minimum. It would be acceptable to specify a pilot hole depth greater than .15, depending on the specific design requirements.

If an internal M12 × 1.75 thread does not go completely through an object, the length of the unused portion of the tap hole is determined as follows:

2(Pitch length) = 2(1.75) = 3.50 mm

## 11-7 Sectional Views of Internal Thread Representations

Figure 11-16 shows sectional views of internal threads that do not go completely through an object. Each example was created from blocks of the representations. The hatch pattern used is ANSI31. Each example includes both a threaded portion and an untapped pilot hole that extends approximately 2P beyond the end of the tapped portion of the hole.

**Figure 11-16**

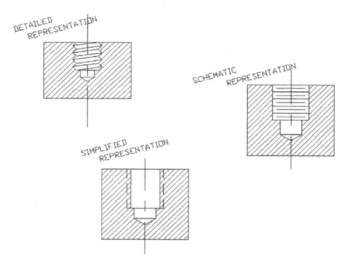

When drawing a simplified representation in a sectional view, draw the hidden lines that represent the outside edges of the threads after the section lines have been added. If the lines are drawn before the section lines are added, the section lines stop at the outside line. Section lines should be drawn up to the solid line, as shown.

## 11-8 Types of Threads

Figure 11-17 shows the profiles of four different types of threads: American National, square, acme, and knuckle. There are many other types of threads. In general, square and acme threads are used when heavy loading is involved. A knuckle thread can be manufactured from sheet metal and is most commonly found on a lightbulb.

**Figure 11-17**

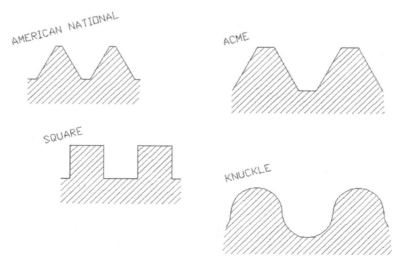

The American National thread is the thread shape most often used in mechanical design work. All threads in this chapter are assumed to be American National threads unless otherwise stated.

## 11-9 How to Draw an External Square Thread

Figure 11-18 shows how to draw a 4.00-inch-long external square thread that has a major diameter of 5.25 and 2 threads per inch. The procedure is as follows:

**1** Set **Grid** to **.50** and **Snap** to **.125**.

**2** Draw a **4.50** centerline.

**3** Draw a rhomboid centered about the centerline according to the given dimensions.

In this example, $P = .5$, so $.5P = .25$.

**4** Use the **Array, Rectangular** command to create eight columns (2 threads per inch) **.50** apart.

**5** Draw slanted lines 1–2 and 3–4.

**6** Zoom the upper-right portion of the thread as needed.

**7** Draw a horizontal line **.25** (.5*P*) from the outside edge of the thread as shown.

**8** Draw line 5–6 from the intersection of the horizontal line drawn in step 7 with line 1–2, labeled point 5, to the intersection of the toothline 1–6 and the thread's centerline.

**9** Trim the horizontal line to create line 5–7 and trim line 1–2 below point 5.

**10** Array lines 1–5, 5–6, and 5–7 by using **Array, Rectangular** with eight columns **–.25** apart.

**Figure 11-18**

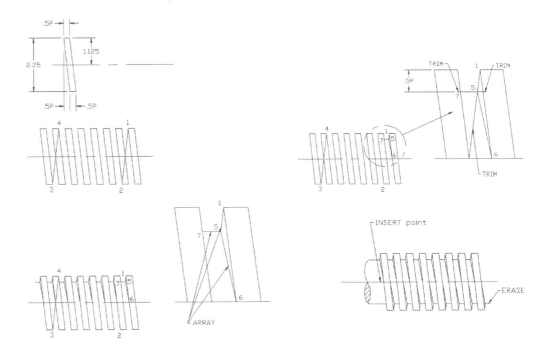

The minus sign generates a right-to-left array.

**11** Repeat steps 7 through 10 for the lower portion of the thread. Array eight columns **+.25** apart. The plus sign generates a left-to-right array.

**12** Erase any excess lines and add any necessary shaft information to the drawing.

**13** Save the square thread pattern as a block named **SQIN**, using the indicated insertion point (Figure 11-18).

## 11-10 How to Draw an Internal Square Thread

Figure 11-19 shows an internal 2.25 × 2 square thread. The drawing is developed from the block **SQIN** created in Section 11-9. The block is rotated to the correct orientation. **Erase** and **Trim** are used to fit the thread within the required depth. No scale factor is needed.

**Figure 11-19**

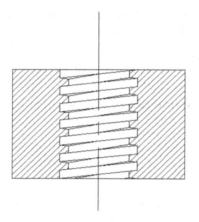

## 11-11 How to Draw an External Acme Thread

Draw a 2.25 × 2 × 4.00-long external acme thread (Figure 11-20). The procedure is as follows:

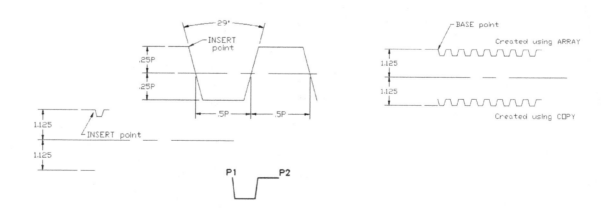

**Figure 11-20, Part 1**

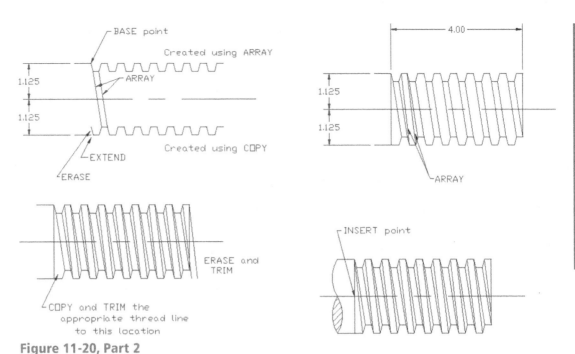

**Figure 11-20, Part 2**

**1** Set **Grid** to **.5** and **Snap** to **.125**.

**2** Draw a **5.00**-long horizontal centerline.

**3** Draw two **.5**-long horizontal lines **1.125** above and below.

These lines establish the major diameter of the thread.

**4** Draw a single acme thread, using the given dimensions. Use **Zoom** to help create an enlarged working area. The first thread should start at the right end of the short horizontal line above the centerline.

The width dimensions are taken along the horizontal centerline of the individual thread. Each side of the thread is slanted at **14.5°** [.5(29)]. In this example, $P = .5$, so $.5P = .25$, and $.25P = .125$.

**5** Use the **Array** command and draw eight columns (two threads per inch). When prompted to specify the distance between columns, pick the top of the leftmost angled line (P1 in Figure 11-20, Part 1) and the end of the short horizontal line (P2).

**6** Copy and move the top portion of the thread to create the lower portion.

Do not use **Mirror**. The lower portion of the thread is not a mirror image of the upper portion.

**7** Erase and extend lines as necessary along the lower-left portion of the thread to blend the thread into the shaft.

**8** Draw two slanted lines between the thread's root lines at the left end of the thread.

**9** Array the lines drawn in step 8 so that there are eight columns. Use Points P1 and P2 to specify the distance apart.

**10** Draw two slanted lines across the thread's crest lines at the left end of the thread.

**11** Array the lines drawn in step 10 so that there are eight columns, distanced apart as in previous steps.

**12** Draw a vertical line at each end of the thread to establish the thread's 4.00-inch length.

**13** Erase and trim the excess lines from the left end of the thread.

**14** Copy and trim a crest-to-crest line to complete the left end of the thread.

**15** Save the drawing as a block named **ACMEIN**, using the indicated insertion point. Use **Wblock** to create a drawing of **ACMEIN** on your hard disk.

## 11-12 Bolts and Nuts

A *bolt* is a fastener that passes through a clearance hole in an object and is joined to a nut. There are no threads in the object (Figure 11-21). Note that there are no hidden lines within the nut to indicate that the bolt is passing through. Drawing convention allows for nuts to be drawn without hidden lines.

**Figure 11-21**

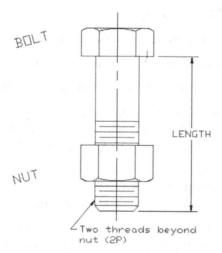

Threads on a bolt are usually made just long enough to correctly accept a nut. This is done to minimize the amount of contact between the edges of threads and the inside surfaces of the clearance holes. The sharp, knifelike thread edges could cut into the object, particularly if the application involves vibrations.

It is considered good design practice to specify a bolt length long enough to allow at least two threads to extend beyond the end of the nut. This ensures that the nut is fully attached to the bolt.

Bolt drawings can be created from drawings of threads. Remember that blocks are usually exploded before they can be edited.

> **NOTE**
> AutoCAD can create dynamic blocks, which can be edited after they have been inserted. You can also edit blocks without exploding them in AutoCAD's Block Editor. Neither dynamic blocks nor the Block Editor are covered in this book.

## 11-13 Screws

A *screw* is a fastener that assembles into an object. It does not use a nut. The joining threads are cut into the assembling object (Figure 11-22).

**Figure 11-22**

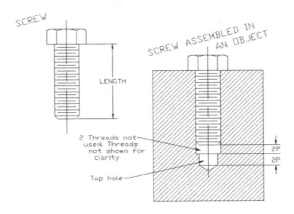

Screws may or may not be threaded over their entire length. If a screw passes through a clearance hole in an object before it assembles into another object, it is good design practice to minimize the number of threads that contact the sides of the clearance hole.

It is also considered good design practice to allow a few (at least two) unused threads in the threaded hole beyond the end of an assembled screw. If a screw were forced to the bottom of a tapped hole, it might not assemble correctly or could possibly be damaged.

Figure 11-22 shows a schematic thread representation of a screw correctly mounted in a threaded hole. In this example, there is a distance of 2*P* (two threads) between the end of the screw and the end of the threaded portion of the hole. There should also be a 2*P* distance between the end of the threaded hole and the end of the pilot hole, plus the conical point of the tap hole, as described in Section 11-6.

Threads are usually not drawn in a threaded hole beyond the end of an assembling screw. This makes it easier to visually distinguish the end of the screw.

Figure 11-23 shows a screw assembled into a hole drawn by using the detailed, schematic, and simplified representations in a sectional view. An orthographic view of a screw in a threaded hole is also shown.

The top view shown in Figure 11-23 applies to all three representations and the orthographic view.

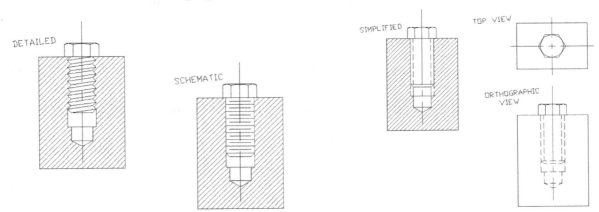

**Figure 11-23**

## 11-14 Studs

A *stud* is a threaded fastener that both screws into an object and accepts a nut (Figure 11-24). The thread callouts and representations for studs are the same as the ones for bolts and screws.

**Figure 11-24**

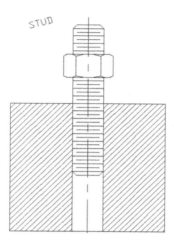

STUD

## 11-15 Head Shapes

Bolts and screws are manufactured with a variety of different head shapes, but hexagon (hex) and square head shapes are the most common. There are many different head sizes available for different applications. Extra-thick heads are used for heavy-load applications, and very thin heads are used for applications where space is limited. The exact head size specifications are available from fastener manufacturers.

This section shows how to draw hex and square heads according to accepted average sizes that are functions of the major diameters of both the bolt and the screw. It is suggested that hexagon and square head drawings be saved as blocks for both inch and millimeter values so that they can be combined with the thread blocks to form fasteners.

### Drawing a Hexagon-Shaped (Hex) Head

Draw front and top orthographic views of a hex head based on a thread with an M24 major diameter (Figure 11-25).

**1** Set **Limits** to **297,210**, **Grid** to **10**, and **Snap** to **5**.

**2** Draw a vertical line and two horizontal lines according to the given dimensions.

Use the two horizontal lines to locate the center of the head in the top view and the bottom of the head in the front view.

**3** Use **Polygon** to draw a hexagon distance across the flats equal to **1.5D**, where *D* is the major diameter of the thread.

In this example, a radius of **18** is used to draw the hexagon. $1.5D = 1.5(24) = 36$ is the distance across the flats of the hexagon. Use the **Polygon** command to circumscribe a six-sided polygon around a circle of radius 18.

**4** Offset a line **.67D** from the lower horizontal.

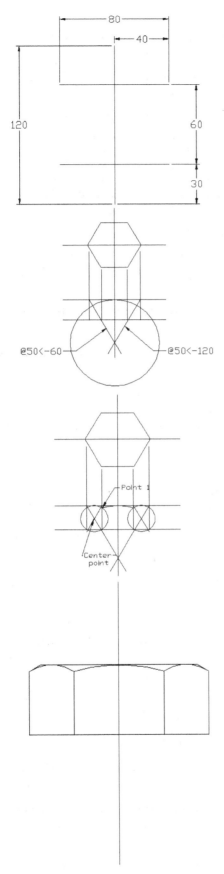

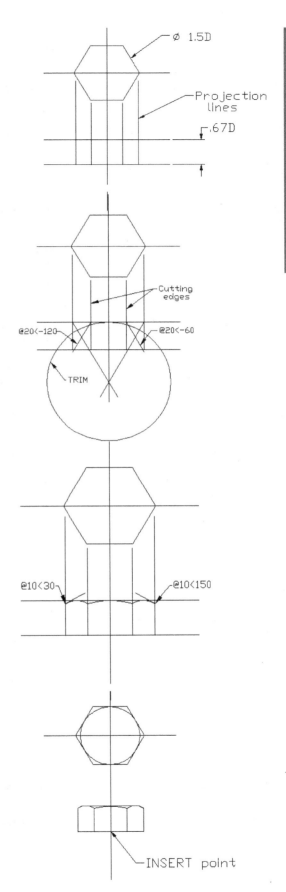

**Figure 11-25**

This line defines the thickness of the head. The head thickness is 0.67D, where D is the major diameter of the thread. In this example, D = 24, so 0.67D = 0.67(24) = 16.08, which can be rounded off to 16.

**5** Draw projection lines from the corners of the hexagon in the top view into the front view.

**6** Zoom in the front view portion of the drawing if necessary. Draw two **60°** lines from the corners of the front view as shown so that they intersect on the vertical centerline.

Use **Osnap Intersection** to accurately locate the corner points. The line from the left corner uses the input **@50<–60**; the line from the right corner uses the input **@50<–120**.

**7** Draw a circle whose center point is the intersection of the two 60° lines drawn in step 6 and the vertical centerline and whose radius equals the distance from the center point to the line at the top of the front view.

**8** Trim the circle so that only the arc between the inside projection lines remains.

**9** Draw two **60°** lines as shown, using the inputs **@20<–120** and **@20<–60**.

**10** Draw two circles centered about the intersection of the slanted lines drawn in steps 6 and 8. The radius of each circle equals the distance from the center point to the intersection of the circle drawn in step 7 and the inside projection lines labeled point 1.

**11** Trim and erase as needed.

**12** Draw two lines from the intersections of the smaller arcs with the outside edge of the head. The input for the lines is **@10<30** and **@10<150**.

These lines could have been generated by the **Chamfer** command.

**13** Trim the chamfer lines to the top of the head.

**14** Use **Zoom All** and draw a circle that is circumscribed within the hexagon, as shown.

**15** Save the drawing as a block named **HEXHEAD**, using the indicated insertion point. Wblock it to a folder on your hard disk if you wish.

## Drawing a Square-Shaped Head

Draw front and top orthographic views of a square head on the basis of a thread with a 1.00-inch major diameter (Figure 11-26).

**1** Set **Grid** to **.50** and **Snap** to **.25**.

**2** Draw two horizontal lines and a vertical line, using the given dimensions.

The intersection of the top horizontal line and the vertical line is the center point of the top view, and the lower horizontal line is the bottom edge of the head.

**3** Use **Draw, Polygon** and **Modify, Rotate (45°)** to create a square oriented as shown.

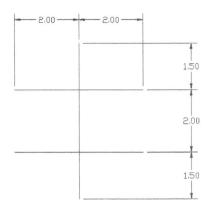

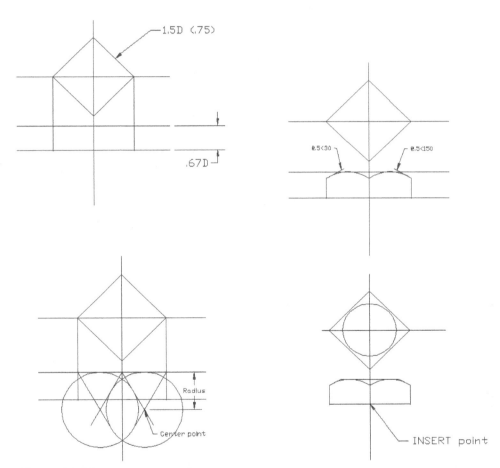

**Figure 11-26**

The distance across the square equals 1.50*D*, or 1.50 inches. This means that the radius for the polygon is **.75**.

**4** Offset a line **.67D** from the lower horizontal line.

The offset distance is equal to the thickness of the head.

**5** Project the corners of the square in the top view into the front view.

**6** Zoom the front view and draw four **60°** lines from the head's upper corners and the intersection of the centerline and the top surface of the head, as shown. The inputs for the lines are **@1.5<–120** and **@1.5<–60**. Use **Osnap Intersection** to ensure accuracy.

**7** Use **Draw, Circle, Center, Radius** and draw two circles about the center points created in step 6. Trim the excess portions of the circle.

**8** Trim and erase any excess lines.

**9** Add the **30°** chamfer lines as shown. The line inputs are **@.5<150** and **@.5<30**. Use **Osnap Intersection** to accurately locate the intersection between the arc and the vertical side line of the head.

**10** Trim any excess lines.

**11** Zoom the drawing back to its original size and draw a circle in the top view tangent to the inside edges of the square.

**12** Save the drawing as a block named **SQHEAD**, using the insertion point indicated. Wblock it to a folder on your hard disk if you wish.


## 11-16 Nuts

This section explains how to draw hexagon- and square-shaped nuts. Both construction methods are based on the hex and square head shape blocks created in Section 11-15.

There are many different styles of nuts. A *finished nut* has a flat surface on one side that acts as a bearing surface when the nut is tightened against an object. A finished nut has a thickness equal to .88*D*, where *D* is the major diameter of the nut's thread size.

A *locknut* is symmetrical, with the top and bottom surfaces identical. A locknut has a thickness equal to .5*D*, where *D* is the major diameter of the nut's thread size.

### Drawing a Hexagon-Shaped Finished Nut

Draw a hexagon-shaped finished nut for an M36 thread (Figure 11-27).

**1** Set **Limits** to **297,210**, **Grid** to **10**, and **Snap** to **2.5**.

**2** Construct a vertical line that is intersected by two horizontal lines **32** millimeters apart.

The thickness of a finished nut is 0.88*D*. In this example, 0.88(36) = 31.68, or 32.

**3** Use **Insert** and insert the **HEXHEAD** block created in Section 11-15.

The block **HEXHEAD** was created for an M24 thread, so the X and Y scale factors must be increased to accommodate the larger thread size. The scale factor is determined by dividing the desired size by the block size. In this example, 36/24 = 1.5. The scale factor is **1.5**. Respond to the command prompts as follows:

Command: INSERT

The **Blocks** palette appears.

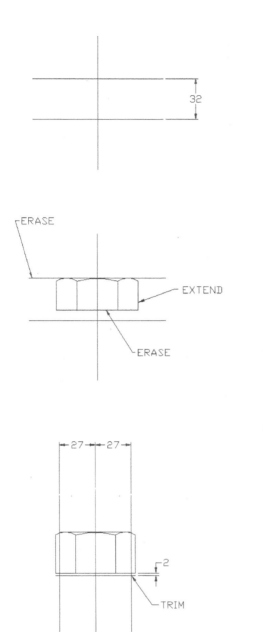

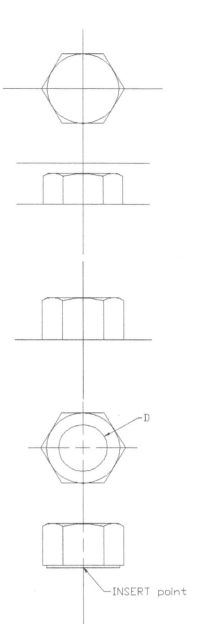

**Figure 11-27**

**4** Highlight **HEXHEAD** in the **Recent Blocks** area. In the **Options** area, click the **Scale** button and select **Uniform Scale**. In the adjacent edit box, enter **1.5**. Confirm that **Rotation Angle** is set to **0**.

**5** Drag the block from the **Blocks** palette into the drawing area.

The **Hexhead** block is placed in the drawing. If you have not created a block, refer to Section 11-15 and draw a hexagon-shaped head.

**6** Explode the block.

**7** Move the front view of the nut so that the top surface aligns with the top parallel horizontal line.

**8** Erase the bottom line of the front view of the nut and extend the vertical line to the lower horizontal line. Erase the top horizontal line in the front view.

**9** Use **Offset** to draw a horizontal line **2** millimeters below the bottom of the nut.

This line defines the shoulder surface of the nut. Any offset distance may be used as long as the line is clearly visible. The actual shoulder surface is less than 1 millimeter deep and would not appear clearly on the drawing.

The shoulder surface has a diameter equal to 1.5*D* [1.5(36) = 54] or, in this example, 54.

**10** Offset the centerline **27** (half of 54) to each side and trim the excess lines.

**11** Save the drawing as a block named **FNUTHEX**. Define the insertion point as shown. Wblock it to a folder on your hard disk if you wish.

## Drawing a Locking Nut

Draw a locking nut for an M24 thread (Figure 11-28). The **HEXHEAD** block was originally drawn for an M24 thread, so no scale factor is needed.

**1** Set **Limits** to **297,210**, **Grid** to **10**, and **Snap** to **5**.

**2** Draw a vertical line and two horizontal lines according to the given dimensions.

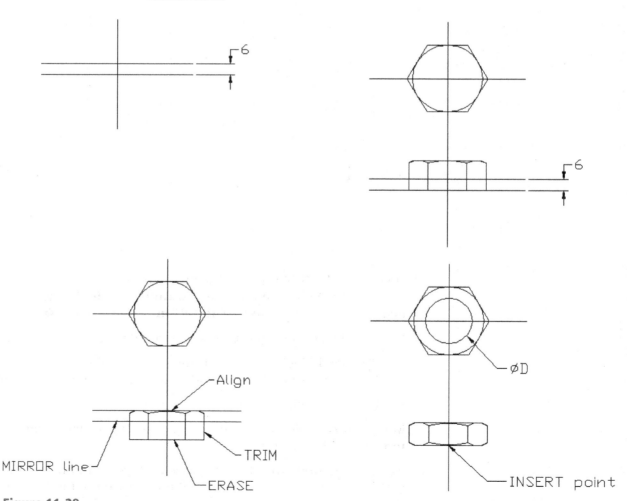

**Figure 11-28**

The 6 distance is half the 0.5$D$ [0.5(24) = 12] thickness distance recommended for locknuts. Locknuts are symmetrical, so half of the nut is drawn and then mirrored.

**3** Insert the **HEXHEAD** block at the indicated insertion point.

**4** Explode the block.

**5** Move the front view of the hex head so that it aligns with the horizontal line, as shown.

**6** Trim and erase the lines that extend beyond the lower horizontal line.

**7** Mirror the remaining portion of the front view about the lower horizontal line and then erase the horizontal line.

**8** Draw a circle of diameter $D$ in the top view, as shown.

**9** Save the drawing as a block named **LNUTHEX**, using the indicated insertion point.

The procedure explained previously for hexagon-shaped finish nuts and locknuts is the same as that for square-shaped nuts. Use the block **SQHEAD** in place of the **HEXHEAD** block.

## 11-17 Drawing Problem

Draw and specify the minimum threaded hole depth and pilot hole depth for an M12 × 1.75 × 50 hex head screw. Assemble the screw into the object shown in Figure 11-29. Use the schematic thread representation and a sectional view.

**Figure 11-29**

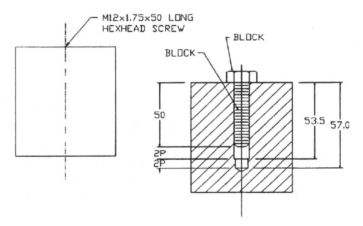

The **SCHMMM** block was originally drawn for an M20 thread, so a scale factor is needed. The scale factor to reduce an M20 diameter to an M12 is 12/20 = 0.6.

**1** Insert the **SCHMMM** block and insert it at the indicated point. Use an X and Y scale factor of **.6**.

**2** Explode the block and trim any excess threads.

**3** Insert the **HEXHEAD** block as indicated. The **HEXHEAD** block was also created for an M20 thread, so the scale factor is again **.6**.

The thread pitch equals 1.75, so $2P$ = 3.5. This means that the threaded hole should be at least 50 + 3.5, or 53.5 deep to allow for two unused threads beyond the end of the screw.

The unused portion of the pilot hole should also extend 2P beyond the end of the threaded portion of the hole, so the minimum pilot hole depth equals 53.5 + 3.5 = 57.

The diameter of the tap hole for the thread is given in a table in the online Appendix as 10.3. For this example, a diameter of 10 was used for drawing purposes. If required, the value 10.3 would be given in the hole's drawing callout.

**4** Draw the unused portion of the thread hole and pilot hole, as shown. Omit the thread representation in the portion of the threaded hole beyond the end of the screw for clarity.

## 11-18 Drawing Problem

Determine the length of a .750 – 10UNC square head bolt needed to pass through objects 1 and 2, as shown in Figure 11-30. Include a hexagon-shaped locknut on the end of the bolt. Allow at least two threads beyond the end of the nut. Use the closest standard bolt length and draw a schematic representation as a sectional view.

**Figure 11-30**

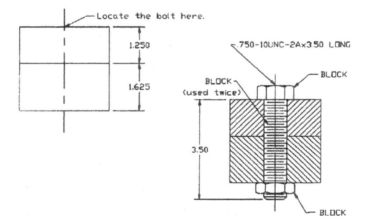

This construction is based on the blocks **SCHMINCH**, **HEXHEAD**, and **LNUTHEX** created in Sections 11-5, 11-15, and 11-16. If you did not use **Wblock** to create new drawing files from those blocks earlier in the chapter, refer to those sections for an explanation of how to create the required shapes.

The blocks **SCHMINCH**, **HEXHEAD**, and **LNUTHEX** were created for a major diameter of 1.00 inch, so the scale factor needed to create a major diameter of .750 is **.75**.

**1** Insert the **SCHMINCH** block at the indicated point. Use an X and Y scale factor of **.75**. Rotate the block **–90°** to the correct orientation.

**2** Repeat step 1 to insert another copy of **SCHMINCH** below the first one.

The block **SCHMINCH** is not long enough to go completely through the objects, so a second block is inserted below the first.

**3** Insert the **SQHEAD** block at the indicated point. Use an X and Y scale factor of **.75**.

**4** Insert the block **LNUTHEX** at the indicated point. Use an X and Y scale factor of **.75**.

**5** Explode the blocks.

6 Trim the excess lines within the nut.

7 Calculate the minimum length for the bolt.

The total depth of objects 1 and 2 equals 1.250 + 1.625 = 2.875.

The thickness of the nut equals .88D, or .88(.75) = .375.

The pitch length of the thread equals 1.00/10 = .1, so 2P = .2.

The minimum bolt length equals 2.875 + .375 + .200 = 3.450.

From the table of standard bolt lengths in the online Appendix, the standard bolt length that is greater than 3.45 is 3.50, so the bolt callout can now be completed:

0.750 – 10 UNC-2 A × 3.50 LONG

The completed drawing with the appropriate bolt callout is shown in Figure 11-30.

## 11-19 Standard Screws

Figure 11-31 shows a group of standard screw shapes. The proportions given in Figure 11-30 are acceptable for general drawing purposes and represent average values. The exact dimensions for specific screws are available from manufacturers' catalogs. A partial listing of standard screw sizes is included in the online Appendix.

The given head shape dimensions are all in terms of D, the major diameter of the screw's thread. Information about the available standard major diameters and lengths is included in the online Appendix.

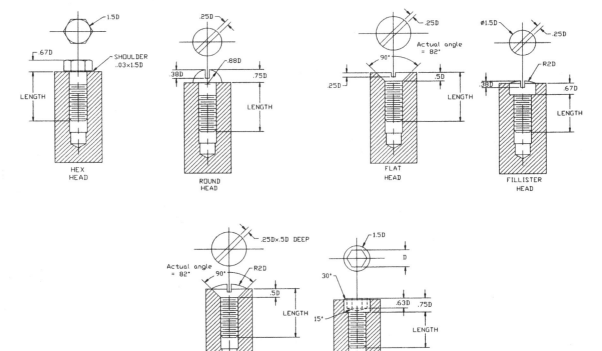

**Figure 11-31**

The choice of head shape is determined by the specific design requirements. For example, a flat head mounted flush with the top surface is a good choice when space is critical, when two parts butt against each other, or when aerodynamic considerations are involved. A round head can be assembled by using a common blade screwdriver, but it is more susceptible to damage than a hex head. The hex head, however, requires a specific wrench for assembly.

## 11-20 Set screws

*Set screws* are fasteners used to hold parts like gears and pulleys to rotating shafts or other objects in order to prevent slippage between the two objects (Figure 11-32).

**Figure 11-32**

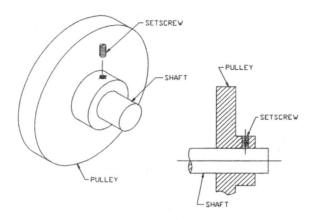

Most set screws have recessed heads to help prevent interference with other parts. Many different head styles and point styles are available (Figure 11-33).

**Figure 11-33**

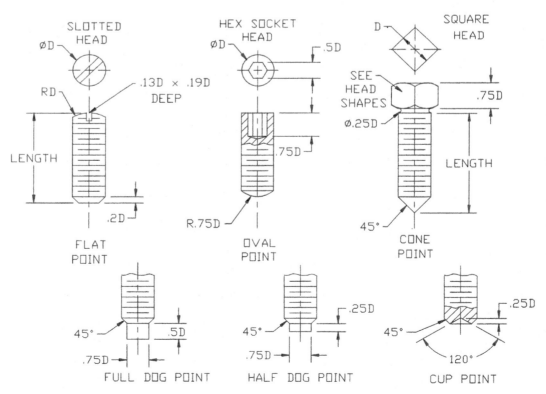

Set screws are referenced on a drawing using the following format:

THREAD SPECIFICATION

HEAD SPECIFICATION POINT SPECIFICATION

SET SCREW

.250 – 20 UNC-2 A 1.00 LONG

SLOT HEAD FLAT POINT

SET SCREW

The words "LONG," "HEAD," and "POINT" are optional.

## 11-21 Washers

There are many different styles of washers available for different design applications. The three most common types of washers are *plain*, *lock*, and *star* washers. Plain washers can be used to help distribute the bearing load of a fastener or used as a spacer to help align and assemble objects. Lock and star washers help absorb vibrations and prevent fasteners from loosening prematurely. All washers are identified as follows:

*Inside diameter × Outside diameter × Thickness*

Examples of plain washers and their callouts are shown in Figure 11-34. A list of standard washer sizes is included in the online Appendix.

**Figure 11-34**

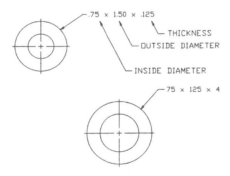

## Drawing a Plain Washer

The following steps show how to construct a plain washer (Figure 11-35).

**1** Draw concentric circles for the inside and outside diameters.

**2** Project lines from the circular view and draw a line that defines the width of the washer.

**3** Use **Offset** to define the thickness.

**Figure 11-35**

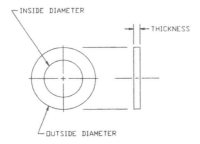

Figure 11-36 shows two views of a lock washer. As the lock washer is compressed during assembly, it tends to flatten so that the slanted end portions are not usually included on the drawing. The drawing callout should include the words "LOCK WASHER."

Figure 11-37 shows internal and external tooth lock-type washers. These types of washers may also be called *star washers.*

These washers are best drawn by first drawing an individual tooth and then using **Array** to draw a total of 12 teeth. Because there are 12 teeth, each tooth and the space between it and the next tooth requires 30°—that is, 15° for the tooth and 15° for the space between the tooth and the next one.

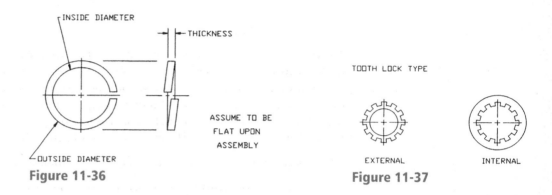

**Figure 11-36**

**Figure 11-37**

## 11-22 Keys

*Keys* are used to help prevent slippage in power transmission between parts—for example, a gear and a drive shaft. Grooves called *keyways*, or *keyseats*, are cut into both the gear and the drive shaft, and a key is inserted between, as shown in Figure 11-38.

There are four common types of keys: *square, Pratt & Whitney, Woodruff,* and *gib head* (Figure 11-39). Each type has design advantages and disadvantages. A list of standard key sizes is included in the online Appendix.

Square keys are called out on a drawing by specifying the length of one side of the square cross section and the overall length. Pratt & Whitney and Woodruff keys are specified by numbers. Gib head keys are defined by a

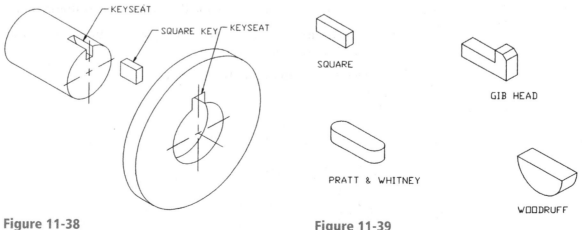

**Figure 11-38**

**Figure 11-39**

group of dimensions. See the online Appendix for the appropriate tables and charts of standard key sizes.

Keyways are dimensioned as shown in Figure 8-78. Note that the depth of a keyway in a shaft is dimensioned from the bottom of the shaft. Because material has been cut away, the intersection between the shaft's centerline and top outside edge does not exist. It is better to dimension from a real surface than from a theoretical one. The same dimensioning technique also applies to the gear.

## 11-23 Rivets

*Rivets* are fasteners that hold adjoining or overlapping objects together. A rivet starts with a head at one end and a straight shaft at the other. The rivet is then inserted into the object, and the headless end is "bucked" or otherwise forced into place. A force is applied to the headless end that changes its shape so that another head is formed, holding the objects together.

There are many different shapes and styles of rivets. Figure 11-40 shows five common head shapes for rivets. Aircraft use hollow rivets because they are very lightweight. A design advantage for the use of rivets is that they can be drilled out, and removed or replaced, without damaging the objects that they hold together.

**Figure 11-40**

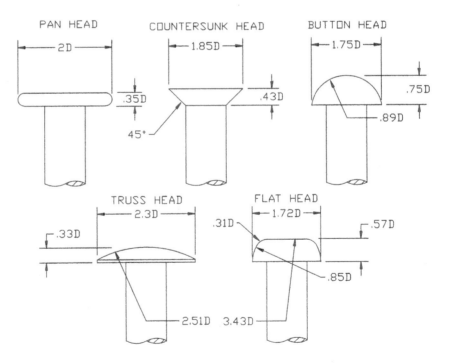

Rivet types are represented on technical drawings using a coding system (Figure 11-41). The lines used to code a rivet must be clearly visible on the drawing. Because rivets are sometimes so small and the material that they hold together so thin that it is difficult to clearly draw the rivets, companies draw only the rivet's centerline in the side view and identify the rivet by a drawing callout.

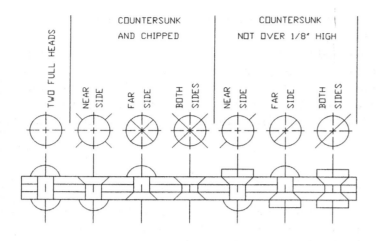

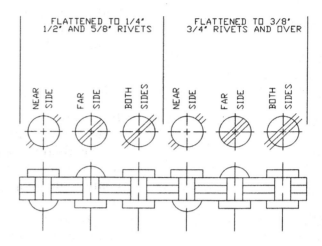

**Figure 11-41**

## 11-24 Springs

The most common types of springs used on technical drawings are compression, extension, and torsional. This section explains how to draw detailed and schematic representations of springs. Springs are drawn in their relaxed position (not expanded or compressed). Phantom lines may be used to show several different positions for springs as they are expanded or compressed.

Springs are defined by the diameter of their wire, the direction of their coils, their outside diameter, their total number of coils, and their total relaxed length. Information about their loading properties may also be included. The pitch of a spring equals the distance from the center of one coil to the center of the next coil.

As with threads, the detailed representations of springs are difficult and time-consuming to draw, but the **Array** command shortens the drawing time considerably. Using **Wblock** to save a representation as a drawing file also helps avoid the necessity of having to redraw the representation for each new drawing.

Ideally, the distance between coils should be exactly equal to the pitch of the spring, but this is not always practical for smaller springs. Any convenient distance between coils may be used, as long as it presents a clear, easy-to-understand representation of the spring.

### Drawing a Detailed Representation of an Extension Spring

Draw an extension spring 2.00 inches in diameter with right-hand coils made from 0.250-inch wire. The spring's pitch equals .25, and the total length of the coils is 3.00 inches (Figure 11-42). Because the pitch of the spring equals the wire diameter, the coils will touch each other.

**1** Set **Grid** to **.5** and **Snap** to **.25**.

**2** Draw the rounded shape of one of the coils.

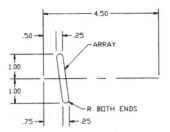

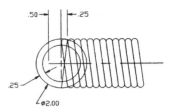

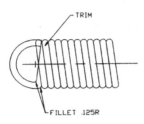

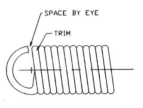

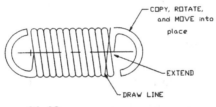

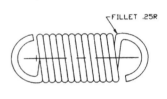

**Figure 11-42**

The distance between the lines equals the diameter of the spring wire. The diameter of the rounded ends also equals the diameter of the wire. The coil's offset equals the spring's pitch.

**3** Array the coil shape.

Create a rectangular array of one row, with 12 columns **.25** apart.

**4** Draw two concentric circles at the left end of the spring so that the larger circle's diameter equals the spring's diameter. The vertical centerline of the circles is tangent to the left edge of the first coil.

**5** Draw a line across the spring offset a distance equal to one pitch. The endpoints of the line are on snap points.

**6** Trim the excess portion of the circles and fillet the circles as shown.

**7** Trim the excess portion of the slanted line and cut back the end of the circles so that there is a noticeable gap between the first coil and the end of the circles. Determine the gap distance by eye.

**8** Copy, rotate, and move the circular end portion to the right end of the spring.

**9** Draw a slanted line across the farthest right coil, as shown.

**10** Trim and extend the lines as necessary and add the **FILLET .25R** as shown.

**11** Save the drawing as a block named **EXTSPRNG**. You can also use **Wblock** to save the block as a drawing file to your hard disk.

## Drawing a Detailed Representation of a Compression Spring

Draw a compression spring with six right-hand coils made from .25-inch-diameter wire. The pitch of the spring equals .50 inch. The diameter of the spring is 2.00 inches (Figure 11-43).

**1** Set **Grid** to **.50** and **Snap** to **.25**.

**2** Draw the rounded shape of the first left coil, as shown. The diameter of the rounded ends of the coil equals the diameter of the spring's wire.

**3** Array the coil shape.

In this example, a rectangular array was used to draw one row, with six columns **.50** inch apart.

**4** Draw two slanted lines, as shown.

These lines represent the back portion of the coil. They are most easily drawn from a snap point next to the rounded portion of the coil shape (the point that would be the corner point of the coil if the coil were not rounded) to a point tangent to the opposite rounded end of the coil.

**5** Trim and array the slanted lines as shown.

Use a rectangular array with one row and with six columns **.50** inch apart.

**6** Draw the right end of the spring so that it appears to end just short of the spring's centerline. Any convenient distance may be used.

**7** Draw the left end of the spring using **Copy** and copy one of the existing slanted lines. Use **Zoom**, if necessary, to align the copied line with the coil. Draw the left end of the spring so that it appears to end just short of the centerline.

**8** Save the drawing as a block named **COMPSPNG**.

Figure 11-44 shows schematic representations of a compression spring and an extension spring. The distance between the peaks of the slanted lines should equal the pitch of the spring.

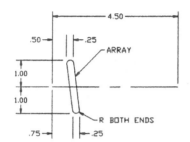

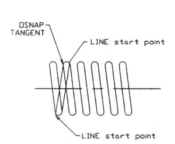

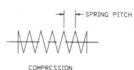

**Figure 11-43**

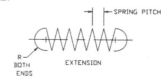

**Figure 11-44**

## 11-25 Tool Palettes

AutoCAD includes a *tool palette* that has, among other features, a set of fastener blocks. (See Section 3-21 for an explanation of blocks.) Access the tool palettes by selecting **Tool Palettes** on the **Palettes** panel of the **View** tab (Figure 11-45).

**Figure 11-45**

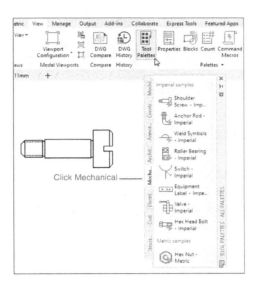

### Creating a Shoulder Screw

Use the **Mechanical** tool palette to insert a shoulder screw.

**1** Click **Tool Palettes** on the **Palettes** panel of the **View** tab.

The **Tool Palettes – All Palettes** palette appears.

**2** Select the **Mechanical** tab.

A list of available blocks appears.

**3** Click **Shoulder Screw – Imperial**.

The shoulder screw block appears on the screen. Use the mouse wheel to increase the viewing size of the screw. The shoulder screw is automatically saved as a block.

Close the **Tool Palettes** by clicking the large **X** in the upper-right corner.

**4** **Erase** the shoulder screw block.

Like any other block, the shoulder screw block can be scaled or edited.

### Changing the Scale of a Tool Palette Block

**1** Click the **Insert** tool on the **Block** panel of the **Home** tab. Select **Recent Blocks**.

The **Blocks** palette opens, with the **Recent** tab active (Figure 11-46).

**2** In the **Options** area, change the X and Y scale factor to **2.00** and the rotation angle to **90°**.

The Z scale need not be changed, as this is a 2D (two-dimensional) drawing; that is, only the X and Y axes are being used.

**3** Click anywhere in the drawing area to leave the **Blocks** palette.

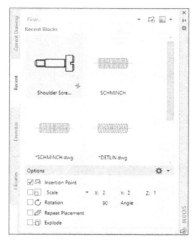

**Figure 11-46**

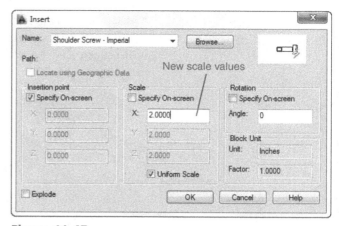

**Figure 11-47**

Figure 11-47 shows the original shoulder screw next to the scaled one. Centerlines are added using **Midpoint** object snap. You can use the **Blocks** palette to change the screw's proportions—that is, to scale the X direction to one value and the Y direction to a different value.

## Modifying the Block

You can modify the shoulder screw block by first exploding it.

**1** Access **Explode** and click the shoulder screw block.

There is no visible change in the block's appearance, but it is now composed of individual lines that can be erased or edited.

**2** Use **Move** to relocate the threaded portion of the screw (Figure 11-48).

**Figure 11-48**

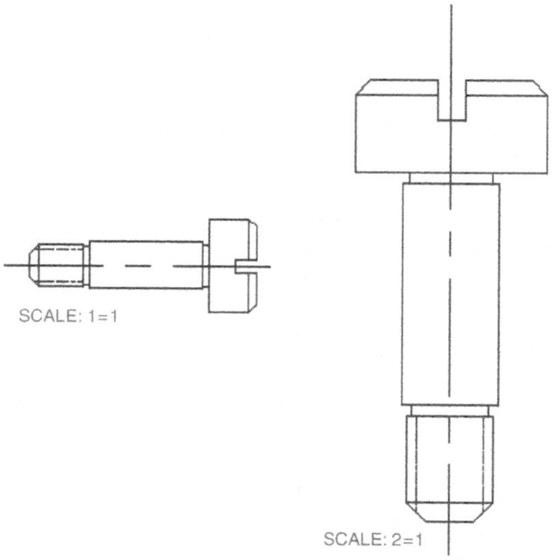

SCALE: 1=1

SCALE: 2=1

**3** Using **Extend**, increase the thread length of the screw. Extend the centerline by adding a vertical line to the left and beyond the end of the screw. Extend the center to the vertical line and erase the vertical line.

The revised shoulder screw now shows a longer thread.

You can change the proportions of the screw by using either the scale values on the **Blocks** palette or the **Explode** tool and then reproportioning the screw.

# 11-26 EXERCISE PROBLEMS

## EX11-1

Create blocks for the following thread major diameters:

- 1.00-in. detailed representation
- 1.00-in. schematic thread representation
- 1.00-in. simplified thread representation
- 100-mm detailed representation
- 100-mm schematic thread representation
- 100-mm simplified thread representation

## EX11-2

Draw a .750 – 10UNC – 2_ × ____ LONG thread. Include the thread callout.

- External –3.00 LONG.
- Internal to fit into the object shown in Figure EX11-2.
- Use a detailed representation.
- Use a schematic representation.
- Use a simplified representation.

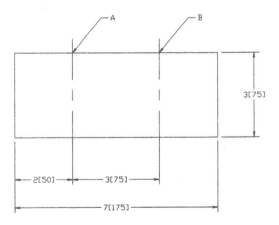

## EX11-3

Draw a .250 – 28UNF – 2_ × ____ LONG thread. Include the thread callout.

- External –1.50 LONG.
- Internal to fit into the object shown in Figure EX11-2.

- Use a detailed representation.
- Use a schematic representation.
- Use a simplified representation.

## EX11-4

Draw an M36 × 4 × ____ LONG thread. Include the thread callout.

- External –100 LONG.
- Internal to fit into the object shown in Figure EX11-2.
- Use a detailed representation.
- Use a schematic representation.
- Use a simplified representation.

## EX11-5

Draw an M12 × 1.75 × ____ LONG thread. Include the thread callout.

- External –40 LONG.
- Internal to fit into the object shown in Figure EX11-2.
- Use a detailed representation.
- Use a schematic representation.
- Use a simplified representation.

## EX11-6

Draw a 2.75 × 2 × 5.00 inch-long external square thread.

## EX11-7

Draw a 50 × 2 × 100 millimeter-long external square thread.

## EX11-8

Draw a 3 × 1.5 × 6 inch-long external acme thread.

## EX11-9

Draw an 80 × 1.5 × 200 millimeter-long external acme thread.

For Exercise Problems EX11-10 through EX11-13, draw the bolts, nuts, and screws assembled into the object shown in Figure EX11-2. If not given, determine the lengths of the fasteners, using the tables given in this chapter or in the online Appendix. Include the appropriate drawing callout.

## EX11-10

- .500 – 13UNC × ____ LONG HEX HEAD BOLT. Include a finished nut on the end of the bolt.

- 5/8(.625) – 18UNF × 1.5 LONG HEX HEAD SCREW. Specify the diameter and length of the tap hole.

- Draw a detailed representation.

- Draw a schematic representation.

- Draw a simplified representation.

- Draw an orthographic view.

- Draw a sectional view.

## EX11-11

- M24 – ____ LONG HEX HEAD BOLT. Include a finished nut on the end of the bolt.

- M16 – 30 LONG HEX HEAD SCREW. Specify the diameter and length of the tap hole.

- Draw a detailed representation.

- Draw a schematic representation.

- Draw a simplified representation.

- Draw an orthographic view.

- Draw a sectional view.

## EX11-12

- M30 × ____ LONG SQUARE HEAD BOLT. Include two locknuts on the end of the bolt.

- M12 × 1.4 × 24 LONG SQUARE HEAD SCREW. Specify the diameter and length of the tap hole.

- Draw a detailed representation.

- Draw a schematic representation.

- Draw a simplified representation.

- Draw an orthographic view.

- Draw a sectional view.

## EX11-13

- 1.25 – 7UNC × ____ LONG SQUARE HEAD BOLT. Include two locknuts on the end of the bolt.

- .375 – 32UNEF × 1.5 LONG SQUARE HEAD SCREW. Specify the diameter and length of the tap hole.

- Draw a detailed representation.

- Draw a schematic representation.

- Draw a simplified representation.

- Draw an orthographic view.

- Draw a sectional view.

## EX11-14

Redraw the sectional view shown here. Include a drawing callout that defines the threads as M12. Specify the depth of the threaded hole and the diameter and depth of the tap hole.

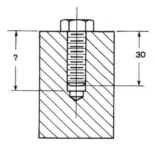

## EX11-15

Redraw the drawing shown here. Add a drawing callout for the bolt and nut according to the given thread major diameters. Use only standard bolt lengths, as defined in the online Appendix.

- .375 – 24UNF – 2A × _____ LONG

- M16 × 2 × _____ LONG

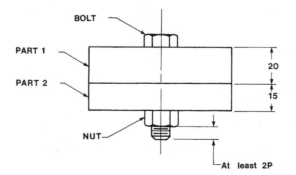

## EX11-16

Draw a front sectional view and a top orthographic view according to the given drawing and table information. Include the set screws in the indicated holes. Include the appropriate drawing callout for each set screw.

For inch values:

- 0.250 – 20UNC – 2A × 1.00
  - SLOT HEAD, FLAT POINT
  - SET SCREW
- .375 – 24UNF – 2A × .750
  - HEX SOCKET, FULL DOG
  - SET SCREW
- #10 – 28UNF – 2A × .625
  - SQUARE, OVAL
  - SET SCREW
- #6 – 32UNC – 2A × .50
  - SLOT, CONE POINT
  - SET SCREW

For millimeter values:

- M12 × 20
  - SLOT HEAD, FLAT POINT
  - SET SCREW
- M16 × 2 × 30
  - SQUARE HEAD, HALF DOG
  - SET SCREW
- M6 × 20
  - HEX SOCKET, CONE
  - SET SCREW
- M10 × 1.5 × 20
  - CUP, SLOT
  - SET SCREW

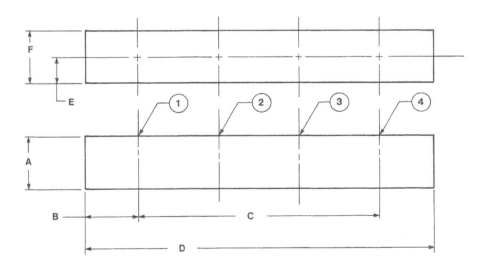

| DIMENSION | INCHES | mm |
|-----------|--------|-----|
| A | 2.00 | 50 |
| B | 1.00 | 25 |
| C | 3 X 1.00 | 3 X 40 |
| D | 6.5 | 170 |
| E | .75 | 20 |
| F | 1.50 | 40 |

## EX11-17

Draw a front sectional view and a top orthographic view according to the following drawing and table information:

- Use inch values.
- Use millimeter values.

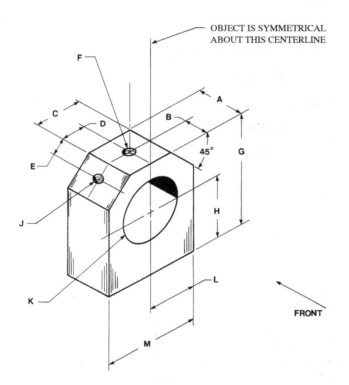

| DIMENSION | INCHES | mm |
|---|---|---|
| A | 1.00 | 26 |
| B | .50 | 13 |
| C | 1.00 | 26 |
| D | .50 | 13 |
| E | .38 | 10 |
| F | .190–32 UNF | M8 X 1 |
| G | 2.38 | 60 |
| H | 1.38 | 34 |
| J | .164–36 UNF | M6 |
| K | Ø1.25 | Ø30 |
| L | 1.00 | 26 |
| M | 2.00 | 52 |

## EX11-18

Redraw the drawing that follows as a sectional view. Include the drawing callouts for the nut and washer according to the given bolts. Specify the bolt lengths according to standard lengths listed in the online Appendix.

- .625 – 11UNC – 2A × ____ LONG HEX HEAD BOLT

- M16 × 2 × ____ LONG HEX HEAD

- .500 – 20 UNF × ____ LONG SQUARE HEAD

- M20 × ____ SQUARE HEAD

- .438-28 UNEF × ____ LONG HEX HEAD

- M12 × 1.25 × ____ LONG HEX HEAD

- .750 – 10 UNC × ____ LONG HEX HEAD

- M24 × 3 × ____ LONG HEX HEAD

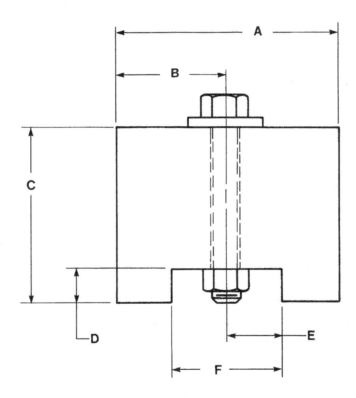

| DIMENSION | INCHES | mm |
|-----------|--------|-----|
| A | 3.00 | 76 |
| B | 1.50 | 38 |
| C | 2.50 | 64 |
| D | .50 | 13 |
| E | .75 | 19 |
| F | 1.50 | 38 |

## EX11-19

Draw a front sectional view and a top orthographic view according to the given drawing and table information. Add fasteners to the labeled holes according to the information here. Include the appropriate drawing callouts. Use only standard sizes, as listed in the online Appendix.

For inch values:

- Nominal diameter = .250, UNC
  - Square head bolt and nut
  - A washer between the bolt head and part 23
  - A washer between the nut and part 24
- .375 – 24UNF – 2A × 1.00
  - SLOT, OVAL
  - SET SCREW

- Nominal diameter = .375, UNF
  - Flat head screw, 1.25 LONG

For millimeter values:

- Nominal diameter = 12, coarse
  - Square head bolt and nut
  - A washer between the bolt head and part 23
  - A washer between the nut and part 24
- M10 × .5 × 20
  - SQUARE HEAD, FULL DOG
  - SET SCREW
- Nominal diameter = 12, fine
  - Flat head screw, 20 LONG

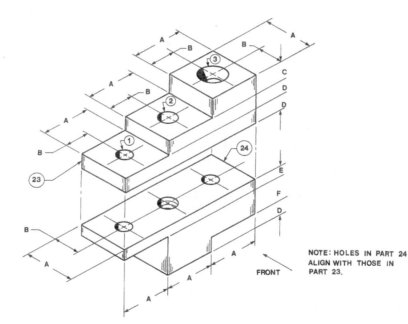

NOTE: HOLES IN PART 24 ALIGN WITH THOSE IN PART 23.

FRONT

| DIMENSION | INCHES | mm |
|-----------|--------|----|
| A | 1.25 | 32 |
| B | .63 | 16 |
| C | .50 | 13 |
| D | .38 | 10 |
| E | .25 | 7 |
| F | .63 | 16 |

## EX11-20

Redraw the sectional view that follows and include the appropriate bolts and nuts at locations W, X, Y, and Z so that the selected bolt heads sit flat on their bearing surfaces. Select the bolts from the standard sizes listed in the online Appendix.

Ⓦ Ⓧ Ⓨ Ⓩ  INDICATES FASTENER LOCATIONS

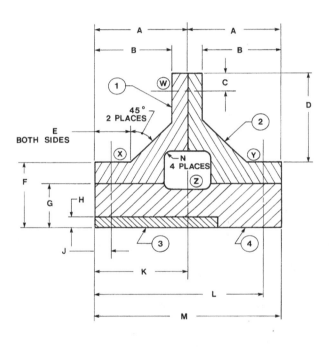

| DIMENSION | INCHES | mm |
|-----------|--------|-----|
| A | 1.00 | 50 |
| B | 1.63 | 41 |
| C | .38 | 10 |
| D | 2.00 | 50 |
| E | .75 | 19 |
| F | 1.50 | 38 |
| G | 1.00 | 25 |
| H | .25 | 6 |
| J | .38 | 10 |
| K | 2.00 | 50 |
| L | 3.63 | 92 |
| M | 4.00 | 100 |
| N | R.13 | 3 |

## EX11-21

Redraw the given drawing based on the information that follows. Include all bolt, nut, washer, and spring callouts. Use only standard sizes as listed in the online Appendix.

For inch values:

- Major diameter of bolt = .375 coarse thread.
- Add the appropriate nut.
- Washer is .125 thick and allows a minimum clearance from the bolt of at least .125.
- Compression springs are made from .125-diameter wire and are 1.00 long. They have an inside diameter that always clears the bolt by at least .125.
- Parts 1 and 2 are 1.00 high and 4.00 wide.
- Locate the bolts at least 1.00 from each end.

For millimeter values:

- Major diameter of bolt = 12 coarse thread.
- Add the appropriate nut.
- Washer is 3 thick and allows a minimum clearance from the bolt of at least 2.
- Compression springs are made from 4-diameter wire and are 24 long. They have an inside diameter that always clears the bolt by at least 3.
- Parts 1 and 2 are 25 high and 100 wide.
- Locate the bolts at least 25 from each end.

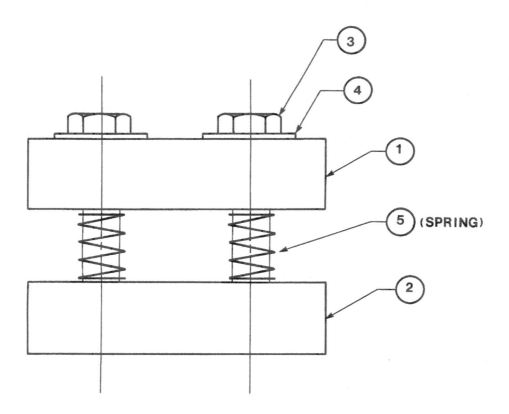

## EX11-22

As shown here, two identical blocks are to be held together by a bolt and a nut. Two washers are also used. Specify the appropriate fastener, nut, and washer for the following block sizes:

Block and nominal hole sizes:

- 1.50 × 1.50 × 0.75 inches; ø.375 inch

- 20 × 20 × 12 mm; ø8 mm

- 2.00 × 2.00 × 0.625 inches; ø.500 inch

- 30 × 30 × 15 mm; ø10 mm

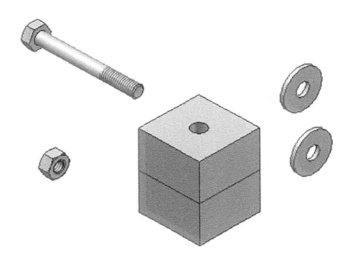

# EX11-23

As shown here, three parts are to be held together by six screws. Given the part sizes, specify the six fasteners needed to assemble the parts.

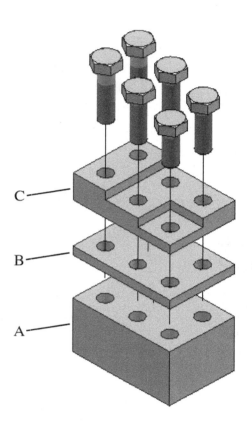

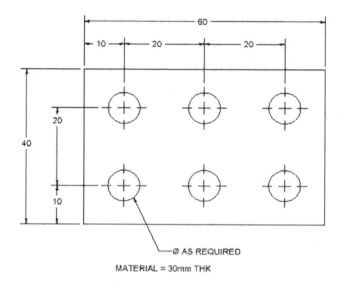

Ø AS REQUIRED

MATERIAL = 30mm THK

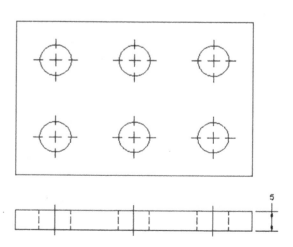

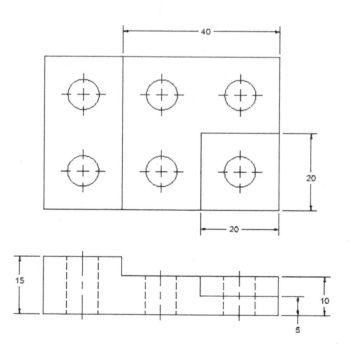

# chapter twelve

# Working Drawings

## 12-1 Introduction

This chapter explains how to create assembly drawings, parts lists, and detail drawings. It includes guidelines for titles, revisions, tolerances, and release blocks. This chapter shows how to create a design layout and then use the design layout to create assembly and detail drawings with the **Layer** command.

## 12-2 Assembly Drawings

An *assembly drawing* shows how objects fit together (Figure 12-1). All information necessary to complete an assembly must be included on the assembly drawing. This information may include specific assembly dimensions, torque requirements for bolts, finishing and shipping instructions, and any other appropriate company or customer specifications.

**Figure 12-1**

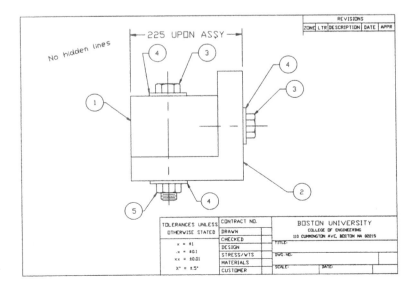

An assembly drawing may be called a *top drawing* because it is the first of a series of drawings used to define a group of parts that are to be assembled together. Such a group of drawings, referred to as a *family of drawings*, may include subassemblies, modification drawings, detail drawings, and a parts list (Figure 12-2).

Figure 12-2

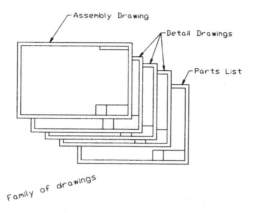

Assembly drawings do *not* contain hidden lines. A sectional view may be used to show internal areas that are critical to the assembly. Specific information about the internal surfaces of objects that make up the assembly can be found on the detail drawings of the individual objects (Figure 12-3).

Figure 12-3

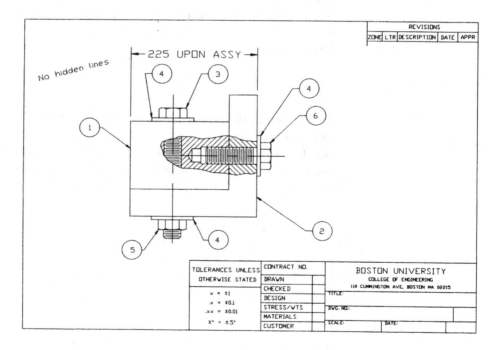

Each part of an assembly is identified by an assembly, or item, number. An assembly number is enclosed in a circle or an ellipse, and a leader line is drawn between the assembly number and the part. Assembly numbers are unique to each assembly drawing; that is, a part that is used in several different assemblies may have a different assembly number on each assembly drawing.

If several of the same part are used in the same assembly, each part should be assigned the same assembly number. A leader line should be used to identify each part unless the differences between the parts are obvious. In Figure 12-4, the difference between head sizes for the fasteners is obvious, so all parts need not be identified.

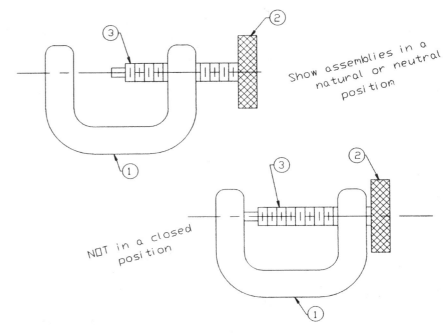

**Figure 12-4**

**Figure 12-5**

Assemblies should be shown in their natural, or neutral, positions. Figure 12-5 shows a clamp in a slightly open position. It is best to show the clamp jaws partially open rather than fully closed or fully open. In general, a drawing should show an assembly in its most common position.

The range of motion for an assembly is shown by the use of phantom lines. In Figure 12-6, note how the range of motion for the hinged top piece is displayed by using phantom lines.

**Figure 12-6**

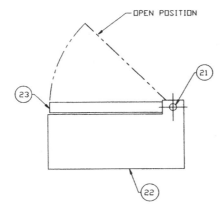

## 12-3 Drawing Formats (Templates)

Figure 12-7 shows a general format for an assembly drawing. The format varies from company to company and with the size of the drawing paper.

**Figure 12-7**

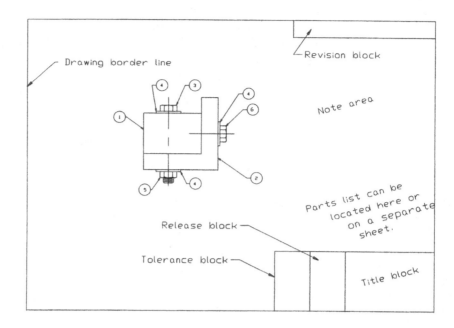

## Adding a Drawing Template

AutoCAD includes many different drawing templates that conform to ANSI and ISO standards. A template automatically includes a drawing border, a title block, a revision block, and a partial release block.

**1** Click the **Application Menu** button in the top-left corner of the AutoCAD window, click **New**, and click **Drawing**.

The **Select template** dialog box appears (Figure 12-8).

**2** Select the **Tutorial-iMfg** template and click **Open**.

**Figure 12-8**

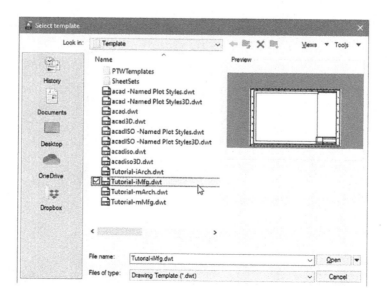

A new, unsaved drawing using the selected template appears on the screen (Figure 12-9). Drawing geometry in previous chapters has been created in **model space**, the infinitely large, three-dimensional drawing and modeling environment. When you need to create a drawing, you switch to **paper space** and create your drawing layout.

**Figure 12-9**

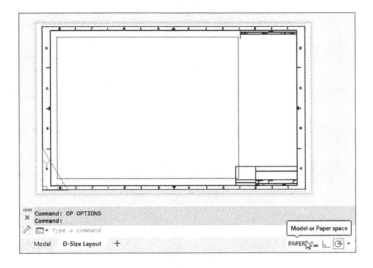

Figure 12-9 shows identifiers for the current space. The triangular UCS icon in the lower-left corner of the drawing area indicates paper space, and represents 2D space only.

At the left end of the status bar, tabs let you select model space or a paper space drawing layout. When you start a new drawing with **acad.dwt** or **acadiso.dwt**, there are two layout tabs: **Layout1** and **Layout2**. In the drawing template **Tutorial-iMfg**, one layout tab has been deleted, and the other has been renamed **D-Size Layout**. Finally, the **MODEL/PAPER** status bar button tells you which space you are in.

Figure 12-10 shows a completed title block for an iMfg template. It was completed using the **Text** tool, located on the **Annotate** tab. An A-size drawing sheet is 8.5 × 11 inches. If an A-size template is selected, the screen units are automatically fitted to the sheet size and are in inches. (A list of standard drawing sheet sizes is included in Section 1-8. Standard metric drawing sheet sizes are also listed in Section 1-8.)

**Figure 12-10**

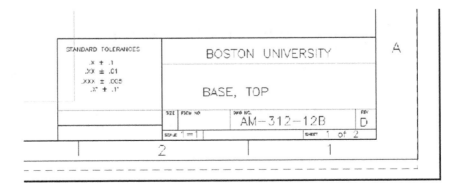

The closest equivalent to an A-size inch drawing is an A4-size drawing, which is $210 \times 297$ millimeters. Figure 12-11 shows the **Select template** dialog box set to select a **Tutorial-mMfg** template. The screen units are millimeters.

**Figure 12-11**

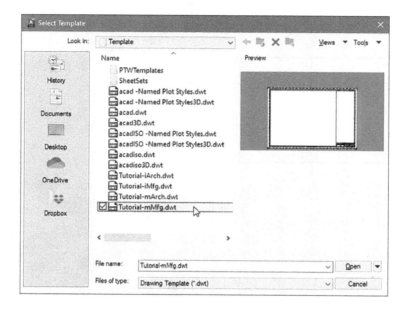

## 12-4 Title Block

A title block is located in the lower-right corner of a drawing and includes the drawing's name and number, the company's name, the drawing scale, the release date of the drawing, and the sheet number of the drawing. Other information may be included as well. Figure 12-12 shows a sample title block created from an iMfg template. The text was added using the **Multiline Text** tool and positioned using the **Move** tool.

**Figure 12-12**

Figure 12-13 shows the title block from an mMfg template. The title block appears with a series of XXX inputs. Use the **Explode** command located on the **Modify** panel of the **Home** tab to explode the title block.

**Figure 12-13**

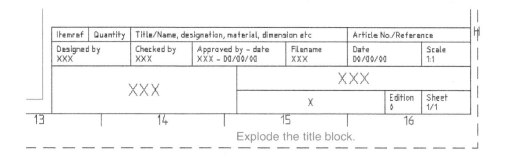

| Itemref | Quantity | Title/Name, designation, material, dimension etc | | Article No./Reference | | H |
|---|---|---|---|---|---|---|
| Designed by<br>XXX | Checked by<br>XXX | Approved by – date<br>XXX – DD/MM/YY | Filename<br>XXX | Date<br>DD/MM/YY | Scale<br>1:1 | |
| XXX | | XXX | | | | |
| | | X | | | Edition<br>0 | Sheet<br>1/1 |

13     14     15     16

Explode the title block.

| Itemref | Quantity | Title/Name, designation, material, dimension etc | | Article No./Reference | | H |
|---|---|---|---|---|---|---|
| Designed by<br>DESIGNED_BY | Checked by<br>CHECKED_BY | Approved by – date<br>APPROVED_BY_DATE | Filename<br>FILENAME | Date<br>DATE | Scale<br>SCALE | |
| OWNER | | TITLE | | | | |
| | | DRAWING_NUMBER | | | Edition<br>EDITION | Sheet<br>SHEET |

14     15     16

Erase unwanted words and type in new text.

| Itemref | Quantity | Title/Name, designation, material, dimension etc | | Article No./Reference | | H |
|---|---|---|---|---|---|---|
| Designed by<br>BETHUNE,J | Checked by<br>KELLEY,C | Approved by – date<br>4-15-10 | Filename<br>ME311-1 | Date | Scale<br>1 = 1 | |
| Boston University | | BRACKET, GUIDE | | | | |
| | | ME311-1 | | | | Sheet<br>1 of 3 |

14     15     16

Revised title block

To replace the **XXX** inputs with words, erase the **XXX** and replace them with the appropriate names and numbers.

## Drawing Titles (Names)

A drawing title should clearly define the function of the part. It should be presented using the following word sequence:

*Noun, modifier, modifying phrase (optional)*

For example:

SHAFT, HIGH SPEED, LEFT HAND

GASKET, LOWER

The noun in a title may consist of two words if normal usage includes the two words. For example:

GEAR BOX, COMPOSITE

SHOCK ABSORBER, LEFT

## Drawing Numbers

Drawing numbers are assigned by companies according to their usage requirement. Numbering systems vary greatly. Drawing numbers are usually recorded in a log book or an online register to prevent duplication of numbers.

## Company Name

The company's name and logo are preprinted on drawing paper or are included as a block so that they can be inserted on each drawing.

## Scale

Define the scale of the drawing.

When the drawing size is the same as the object size, define the scale as follows:

SCALE: FULL, or 1 = 1

When the drawing size is twice as large as the object size, the scale is defined like this:

SCALE: 2 = 1

When the drawing size is half as large as the object size, the scale is defined as follows:

SCALE: 1 = 2

## Release Date

A drawing is released only after all persons required by the company's policy to review it have reviewed it and added their signatures to the release block. Once released, a drawing becomes a legal document. Drawings that have not been officially released are often stamped with a statement such as "NOT RELEASED" or "FOR REFERENCE ONLY." Stamps are usually created in AutoCAD and saved to a hard drive or network drive so they can be reused in other drawings. Stamps would be removed when a drawing is released.

## Sheet

The number of the sheet relative to the total number of sheets that make up the drawing should be stated clearly. For example:

SHEET 2 OF 3

or

SH 2 OF 3

## 12-5 Revision Block

Drawings used in industry are constantly being changed. Products are improved or corrected, and drawings must be changed to reflect and document these changes. Figure 12-14 shows a sample revision block.

Figure 12-14

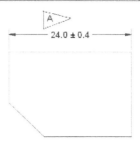

| REV. | DESCRIPTION | DATE | APPROVED |
|---|---|---|---|
| A | WAS 22.0 ± 0.5, NOW 24.0 ± 0.4 | 4/12/10 | JDB |

Drawing changes are listed in the revision block by letter. A revision block is located in the upper-right corner of a drawing (refer to Figure 12-7). Figure 12-15 shows a revision block from an mMfg template. The text was added with **Mtext**, and the lines were added with **Line**.

Figure 12-15

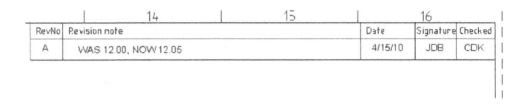

| RevNo | Revision note | Date | Signature | Checked |
|---|---|---|---|---|
| A | WAS 12.00, NOW 12.05 | 4/15/10 | JDB | CDK |

Each drawing revision is listed by letter in the revision block. A brief description of the change is also included. It is important that the description be as accurate and complete as possible. Revisions are often used to check drawing requirements on parts manufactured before the revisions were introduced.

The revision letter is also added to the field of the drawing in the area where the change was made. The letter is located within a "flag" to distinguish it from dimensions and drawing notes. The flag serves to notify anyone reading the drawing that revisions have been made.

Most companies have systems in place that allow engineers and designers to quickly make changes to drawings. These change orders are called *engineering change orders* (*ECOs*), *change orders* (*COs*), or *engineering orders* (*EOs*), depending on the company's preference. Change orders are documented on special drawing sheets that are usually stapled to a print of the drawing. Figure 12-16 shows a change order attached to a drawing.

After a group of change orders accumulates, the change orders are incorporated into the drawing. This process, called a *drawing revision*, is different from a revision to the drawing. A drawing revision is usually indicated by a letter located somewhere in the title block. Revision letters may be included as part of the drawing number or in a separate box in the title block. Whenever you are working on a drawing, make sure that you have the latest revision and all appropriate change orders. Companies have recording and referencing systems for listing all drawing revisions and drawing changes.

Figure 12-16

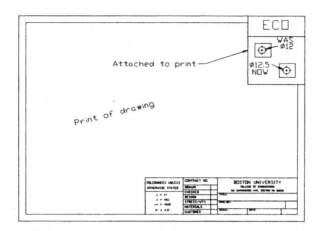

## 12-6 Tolerance Block

Most drawings include a *tolerance block* next to the title block, which lists the standard tolerances that apply to the dimensions on the drawing. A dimension that does not include a specific tolerance is assumed to have the appropriate standard tolerance.

Figure 12-17 shows a sample tolerance block for inch values, and Figure 12-18 shows a sample tolerance block for millimeter values. In Figure 12-17, the dimension 2.00 has an implied tolerance of ±.01. In Figure 12-18, the 20.0 dimension has an implied tolerance of ±0.1.

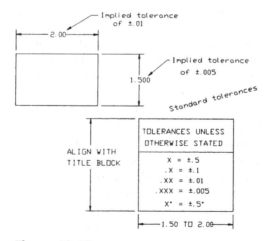

**Figure 12-17**

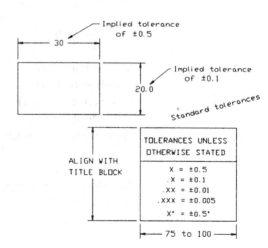

**Figure 12-18**

## 12-7 Release Block

A *release block* contains a list of approval signatures or initials required before a drawing can be released for production (Figure 12-19). The required signatures are generally as follows:

**Figure 12-19**

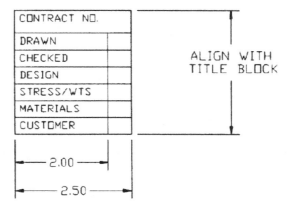

- *Drawn*—The person who created the drawing.

- *Checked*—The person or department that checked the drawing. Drawings are checked for errors and compliance with company procedures and conventions. Some large companies have checking departments, whereas smaller companies have drawings checked by a senior person or the drafting supervisor.

- *Design*—The engineer in charge of the design project. The designer and the drafter may be the same person.

- *Stress/Wts*—The department or person responsible for the stress analysis of the design.

- *Materials*—Usually, a person in the production department checks the design and makes sure that the necessary materials and the machine times for the design are available. This person may also schedule production time.

- *Customer*—The customer for the design may have a representative on site at the production facility to check that its design requirements are being met. For example, it is not unusual for the Air Force to assign an officer to a plant that manufactures its fighter aircraft.

## 12-8 Parts List (Bill of Materials [BOM])

A *parts list* is a list of all parts used on an assembly. The parts list in Figure 12-20 was created using the **Table** tool (see Section 2-27). The terms *parts list* and *bill of materials* are interchangeable (Figure 12-21).

**Figure 12-20**

| PARTS LIST | | | | | |
|---|---|---|---|---|---|
| NO. | DESCRIPTION | PART NO. | MATL | NOTE | QTY |
| 1 | BLOCK, TOP | BU311S1 | SAE 1020 | | 1 |
| 2 | BLOCK, BOTTOM | BU311S2 | SAE 1020 | | 1 |
| 3 | M16×24 HEX HEAD BOLT | SPM16H | STEEL | 2 | 1 |
| 4 | 20×40×3 PLAIN WASHER | | STEEL | | 3 |
| 5 | M16 HEX NUT | 2P M16N | STEEL | | 1 |
| 6 | M16×20 HEX HEAD SCREW | | STEEL | | 1 |

Figure 12-21

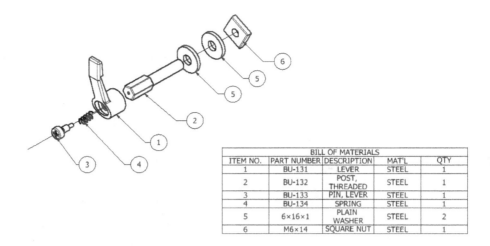

| BILL OF MATERIALS | | | | |
|---|---|---|---|---|
| ITEM NO. | PART NUMBER | DESCRIPTION | MAT'L | QTY |
| 1 | BU-131 | LEVER | STEEL | 1 |
| 2 | BU-132 | POST, THREADED | STEEL | 1 |
| 3 | BU-133 | PIN, LEVER | STEEL | 1 |
| 4 | BU-134 | SPRING | STEEL | 1 |
| 5 | 6×16×1 | PLAIN WASHER | STEEL | 2 |
| 6 | M6×14 | SQUARE NUT | STEEL | 1 |

A parts lists may be located on an assembly drawing above the title block or on a separate drawing sheet. An assembly drawing made with AutoCAD may include the parts list on a separate layer within the drawing. Use only uppercase letters on a parts list.

Figure 12-22 shows two sample parts list formats, including dimensions. Parts list formats vary greatly from company to company. The dimensions are given in inches. They may be converted to millimeters by the conversion factor 1.00 inch = 25.4 millimeters. The AutoCAD template includes a parts list format that is automatically sized to the sheet size.

Figure 12-22

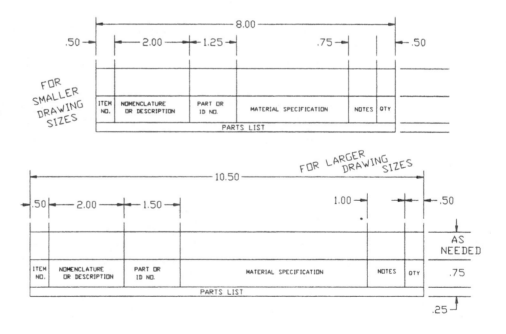

A parts list provides a way to cross-reference detail drawing numbers to assembly item numbers. It also provides a list of the materials needed for production and is very helpful for scheduling and materials purchasing.

Parts purchased from a vendor and used exactly as they are supplied, without any modification, do not have detail drawings but are included on the parts list. The washers, bolts, and screws listed on the parts list shown in Figure 12-21 would not have detail drawings. This means that the information on the parts list must be sufficient for a purchaser to know exactly what size washers, bolts, and screws to buy. The information used to define an object on the drawing, the drawing callout, is also used on the parts list. See Chapter 11 for an explanation of drawing callouts for fasteners.

## 12-9 Detail Drawings

A *detail drawing* is a drawing of a single part. The drawing should include all information necessary to accurately manufacture the part, including orthographic views with all appropriate hidden lines, dimensions, tolerances, material requirements, and any special manufacturing requirements. Figure 12-23 shows a sample detail drawing.

**Figure 12-23**

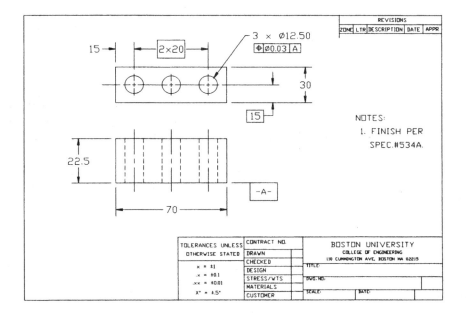

Detail drawings include title, release, tolerance, and revision blocks located on the drawing in the same places they are found on assembly drawings.

## 12-10 First-Angle Projection

The instructions for the creation of orthographic views as presented in this book are based on third-angle projection (see Section 5-36 in Chapter 5). Third-angle projection is used in the United States, Canada, and Great Britain, among other countries. Many other countries such as Japan use first-angle projection to create orthographic views.

Figure 12-24 shows an object and the orthographic views of the object created in first-angle projection. Note that the top view in the first-angle projection is the same as the top view in the third-angle projection, but it is located below the front view rather than above the front view, as in the third-angle projection. Right-side views are also the same but are located to the left of the front view in first-angle projections and to the right in third-angle projections.

Figure 12-24

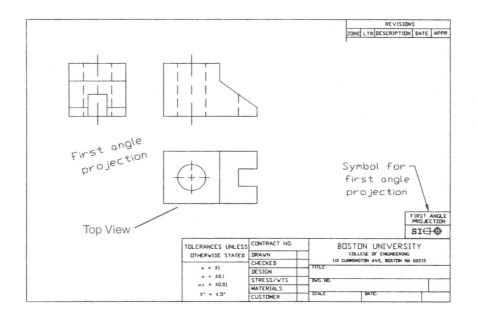

Many companies now do business internationally. A company may have manufacturing plants in one country and assembly plants in another. Drawings can be prepared in several different countries. It is important to indicate on a drawing whether first-angle or third-angle projections are being used. Figure 12-25 shows the SI (International System of Units) symbols for first-angle projections. The SI symbol is included on a drawing in the lower-right corner above the title block, as shown in Figure 12-24.

Figure 12-25

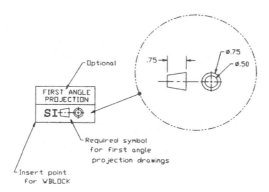

## 12-11 Drawing Notes

Drawing notes are used to provide manufacturing information that is not visual—for example, finishing instructions, torque requirements for bolts, and shipping instructions.

Drawing notes are usually located above the title block on the right side of the drawing (Figure 12-26). Drawing notes are listed by number. If a note applies to a specific part of the drawing, the note number is enclosed in a triangle. The note numbers enclosed in triangles are also drawn next to the corresponding areas of the drawing.

Figure 12-26

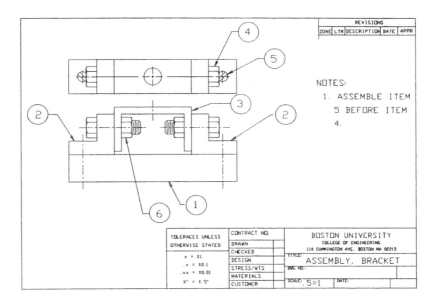

NOTES:
1. ASSEMBLE ITEM
   5 BEFORE ITEM
   4.

| TOLERANCES UNLESS OTHERWISE STATED | | CONTRACT NO. | | BOSTON UNIVERSITY COLLEGE OF ENGINEERING 110 CUMMINGTON AVE. BOSTON MA 02215 | |
| --- | --- | --- | --- | --- | --- |
| | | DRAWN | | | |
| | | CHECKED | | TITLE: ASSEMBLY, BRACKET | |
| x = ±1 | | DESIGN | | | |
| .x = ±0.1 | | STRESS/WTS | | DWG NO: | |
| .xx = ±0.01 | | MATERIALS | | | |
| X° = ±.5° | | CUSTOMER | | SCALE: .5=1 | DATE: |

## 12-12 Design Layouts

A *design layout* is not the same as a drawing layout. It is like a visual calculation sheet used to size and locate parts as a design is developed. A design layout allows you to "build the assembly" on paper.

When drawings are created on a drawing board, an initial design layout is made to locate and size the parts. Then the individual detail drawings and the assembly drawing are created from the layout.

The same procedure can be followed with AutoCAD. First, create a design layout on one layer and then either transfer the individual parts and assembly drawing to other layers or create a new drawing from the design layout drawing by using the **Save As** command.

The drawing problem in the next section demonstrates how to create a design layout and then use it to create the required detail and assembly drawings.

## 12-13 Drawing Problem

Figure 12-27 shows an engineer's sketch for a design problem. Prepare an assembly drawing and a detail drawing of the PN123 base and PN124 center plate on the basis of the following information:

Figure 12-27

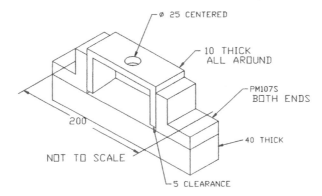

Ø 25 CENTERED

10 THICK
ALL AROUND

PM107S
BOTH ENDS

200

40 THICK

NOT TO SCALE

5 CLEARANCE

The part PM107S end brackets are existing parts and can be used as is. Figure 12-28 shows a detail drawing of PM107S.

Figure 12-28

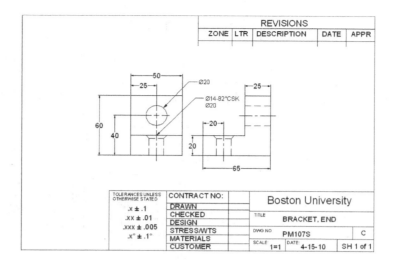

1. Place the mounting holes for the two end brackets 200 millimeters apart, as shown in the engineer's sketch in Figure 12-28.

2. Establish the size of the base so that it aligns with the end brackets and is 40 millimeters thick.

3. Determine the size for the center bracket so that it just fits between the end plates and has a 25-millimeter-diameter hole centered in its top surface. The center bracket should extend 10 millimeters above the end brackets and 5 millimeters above the base. The center bracket should be 10 millimeters thick all around.

4. Mount the end brackets to the base, using M12 flat head screws, and attach the end brackets to the center bracket by M20 bolts with appropriate nuts.

5. Use only standard-length fasteners.

## Creating the Design Layout

Follow the steps below and refer to Figure 12-29 to create the design layout of the part.

1. Draw horizontal and vertical lines that define the top of the base and the distance between the mounting holes in the end brackets.

2. Draw front and top views of the end brackets, using the vertical lines drawn in step 1. The vertical lines should align with the centerlines of the mounting holes.

3. Draw the base 40 millimeters thick.

4. Size the center brackets.

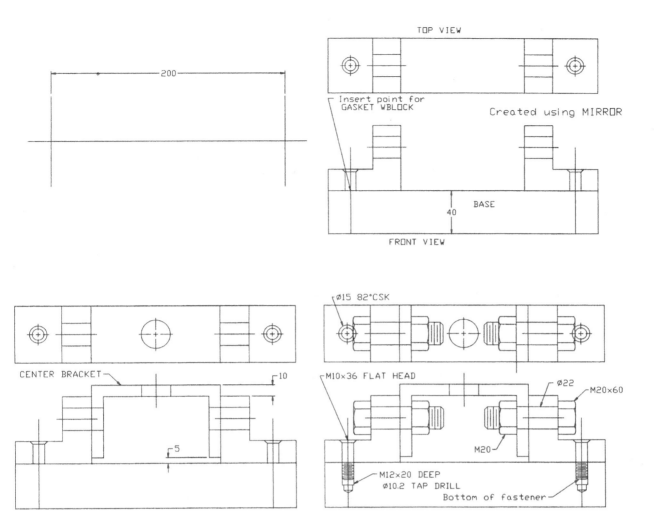

**Figure 12-29**

Note that at this stage of the design layout, all lines are drawn according to the same pattern. Lines can be changed to hidden lines or centerlines when the detail and assembly drawings are created.

**5** Add the M12 flat head screws. A length of 20 millimeters is chosen from the tables in the online Appendix. The threaded holes in the base are M12 to match the screws. The tap drill size is included on the layout for reference.

**6** Add the M20 × 60 bolts and nuts.

The bolt length is determined by adding 25 (end bracket) + 10 (center bracket) + 15 (nut thickness = .75D) + 2 thread pitches = 52 millimeters. The next-largest standard bolt length, as listed in the online Appendix, is 60, so an M20 × 60 bolt is specified.

**7** The diameter of the clearance holes is chosen as 14 and 22 and is listed on the design layout.

The design layout is complete. It may be used to create the required assembly drawing and detail drawings in one of two ways: by using the **Layer** command and including all of the drawings under one file name or by using the **Save As** command to create separate drawings.

## Creating a Drawing Using Layers

Depending on the visibility setting of each layer, when lines are moved from one layer to another, the lines are removed from the original layer. The design layout may be preserved by first making a copy of it, or that part of the design layout that you wish to transfer, and then using the copy for the transfers.

To make a copy of the layout, use the **Copy** command. Select all the drawing geometry and then select a base point. Select exactly the same point as the second point of displacement, and AutoCAD copies the layout exactly over itself. You can then move the appropriate lines to different layers.

Create a detail drawing of the base by transferring the base from the design layout. Respond to the prompts as follows.

**1** Copy the layout onto itself.

```
COMMAND:_Copy
Select objects:
```

**2** Window the entire layout and press **Enter**.

```
<Base point or displacement>/Multiple:
```

**3** Select a point on the screen.

```
Second point of displacement:
```

**4** Type @ and press **Enter**.

You must select exactly the same point as in step 3. Entering the @ symbol tells AutoCAD to use the previous point.

**5** Create the following layers (see Section 3-23):

ASSEMBLY

END

END-DIM

BASE

BASE-DIM

CENTER

CENTER-DIM

PARTSLIST

The "DIM" layers will be used for the dimensions for the detail drawings. This will allow the dimensions to be shut off if they are not needed.

**6** Transfer the base to a layer called **BASE**. Turn off all of the other layers. The resulting transfer should look like Figure 12-30.

It is difficult to make a perfectly clean transfer—that is, a transfer of only the lines of the base. If other lines appear on the transferred base, erase and trim them as necessary.

**7** Move the views closer together, if necessary.

**8** Turn on the **BASE-DIM** layer and make it the current layer. Add the appropriate dimensions, tolerances, and callouts.

**9** Create the drawing format and add the necessary information (drawing title, etc.).

The title block and so forth may be saved as a block or as part of a prototype drawing. Figure 12-31 shows the resulting drawing.

**Figure 12-30**

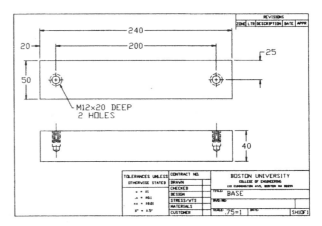

**Figure 12-31**

## Creating a Drawing from a Layout

Figure 12-32 shows an assembly drawing that was created from the design layout. The procedure is as follows:

**1** Save the design layout.

**Figure 12-32**

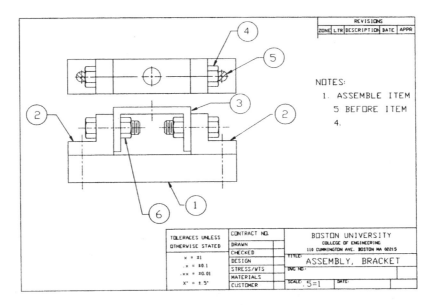

**2** Create the assembly drawing from the design layout drawing but use the **Save As** command to save it under a different drawing name.

**3** Add the appropriate drawing sheet format and notes.

**4** Save the assembly drawing, using its new name.

Figure 12-33 shows a parts list for the assembly.

**Figure 12-33**

| ITEM NO | DESCRIPTION | MATL | QTY |
|---|---|---|---|
| 1 | BASE | STEEL | 1 |
| 2 | END BRACKET - PM107S | STEEL | 2 |
| 3 | CENTER PLATE | STEEL | 1 |
| 4 | M20×60 HEX HEAD BOLT | STEEL | 2 |
| 5 | M12×36 FLAT HEAD SCREW | STEEL | 2 |
| 6 | M20 NUT | STEEL | 2 |

*PARTS LIST*

## 12-14 Drawing Problem

Figure 12-34 shows an assembly made from four different parts: a plate, a bracket, and two posts. The detail drawings of the parts are shown in Figure 12-35 on this and the following page.

**Figure 12-34**

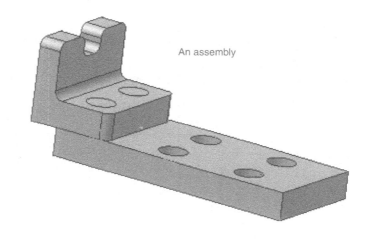

An assembly

**Figure 12-35**

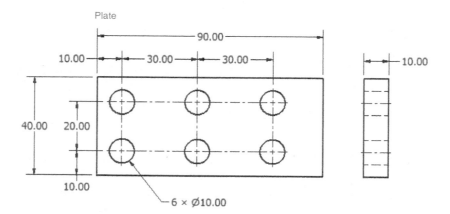

Plate

Bracket

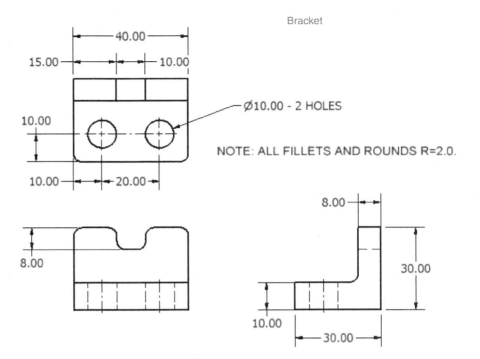

∅10.00 - 2 HOLES

NOTE: ALL FILLETS AND ROUNDS R=2.0.

Post

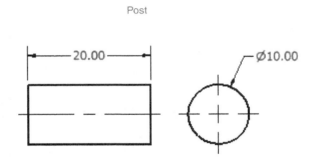

## Creating an Assembly Drawing

**1** Draw orthographic views of the parts in their assembled position (Figure 12-36).

In this example, only a front view and a top view were drawn, as these views are sufficient to define the assembly. The front view orientation was selected to display the profile of the assembled parts. Note that there are no hidden lines in assembly drawings.

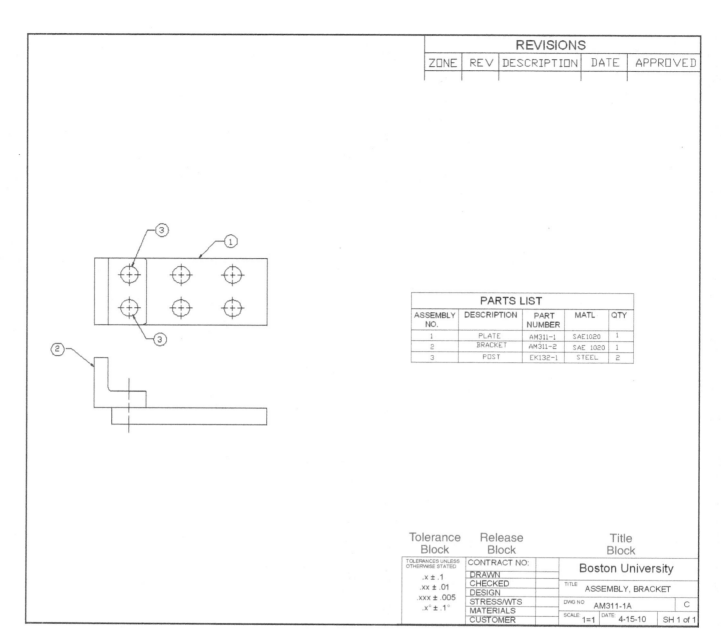

**Figure 12-36**

**2** Add assembly numbers to the drawing.

Remember that assembly numbers are different from part numbers. A part number is a number assigned to an individual part and remains with that part regardless of what assembly uses the part. An assembly number is unique to each assembly and does not transfer to other assemblies.

**3** Create a parts list for the assembly.

As stated earlier, there is no standard format for parts lists. The example shown represents an average approach. Note the use of assembly numbers and part numbers.

**4** Add a title block, a release block, and a tolerance block.

## 12-15 Drawing Problem

Figure 12-37 shows another example of an assembly drawing. In this example, a front view, a right-side view, and a bottom view were used to define the assembly. The parts list is located on a second sheet. In general, drawings should not be overcrowded. Parts lists, sectional views, and other drawing information are often located on second or third sheets.

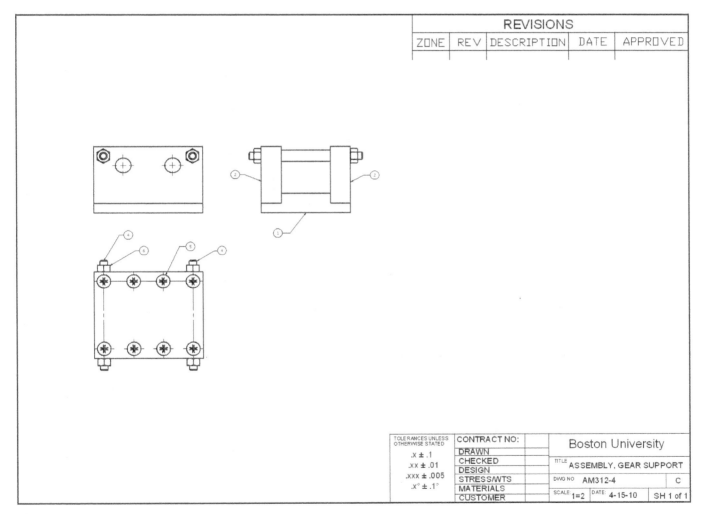

| REVISIONS | | | | |
|---|---|---|---|---|
| ZONE | REV | DESCRIPTION | DATE | APPROVED |
| | | | | |

| TOLERANCES UNLESS OTHERWISE STATED | CONTRACT NO: | Boston University | |
|---|---|---|---|
| .X ± .1 | DRAWN | | |
| .XX ± .01 | CHECKED | TITLE ASSEMBLY, GEAR SUPPORT | |
| | DESIGN | | |
| .XXX ± .005 | STRESS/WTS | DWG NO AM312-4 | C |
| .X° ± .1° | MATERIALS | SCALE 1=2  DATE 4-15-10 | SH 1 of 1 |
| | CUSTOMER | | |

**Figure 12-37**

| ZONE | REV | DESCRIPTION | DATE | APPROVED |
|------|-----|-------------|------|----------|
|      |     |             |      |          |

| Parts List | | | | |
|------|-------------|-------------|----------|-----|
| ITEM | DESCRIPTION | PART NUMBER | MATERIAL | QTY |
| 1 | PLATE, BASE | BU-311-A | Plexiglas | 1 |
| 2 | PLATE, SIDE | BU-311-B | Plexiglas | 2 |
| 3 | POST, GUIDE | BU-311-C | Steel | 2 |
| 4 | POST, THREADED | BU-311-D | Steel | 2 |
| 5 | Pozidriv ISO metric machine screws | AS 1427 - M8 x 20 | Steel, Mild | 8 |
| 6 | Metric Hex Nuts Styles 2 | ANSI B18.2.4.2M - M8x1.25 | Steel, Mild | 4 |

TOLERANCES UNLESS OTHERWISE STATED

.x ± .1
.xx ± .01
.xxx ± .005
.x° ± .1°

| CONTRACT NO: | |
|--------------|--|
| DRAWN | |
| CHECKED | |
| DESIGN | |
| STRESS/WTS | |
| MATERIALS | |
| CUSTOMER | |

Boston University

TITLE ASSEMBLY, GEAR SUPPORT

DWG NO AM312-4          C

SCALE: 1=2   DATE: 4-15-10   SH 1 of 1

**Figure 12-37 continued**

# 12-16 EXERCISE PROBLEMS

## EX12-1 Millimeters

**1** Draw an assembly drawing of the given objects.

**2** Draw detail drawings for all nonstandard parts.

**3** Prepare a parts list. Specify the length for the M10 hex head screw.

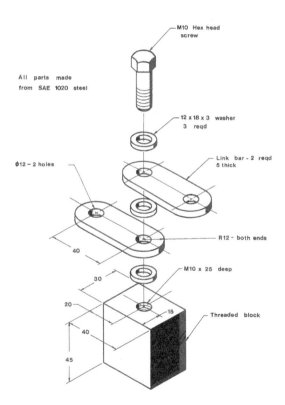

## EX12-2 Millimeters

**1** Draw an assembly drawing of the given objects.

**2** Draw detail drawings for all nonstandard parts.

**3** Prepare a parts list.

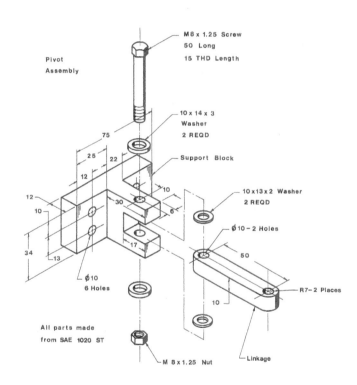

## EX12-3 Millimeters

**1** Draw an assembly drawing of the given objects.

**2** Draw detail drawings for all nonstandard parts.

**3** Prepare a parts list.

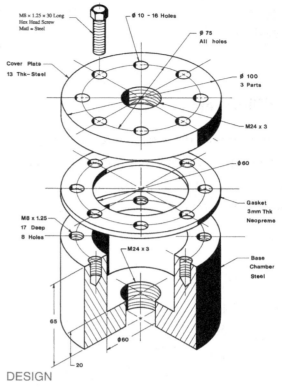

## EX12-4 Millimeters

**1** Draw an assembly drawing of the given objects.

**2** Draw detail drawings for all nonstandard parts.

**3** Prepare a parts list.

**4** Replace part 3 with a bolt and an appropriate nut. Add four washers.

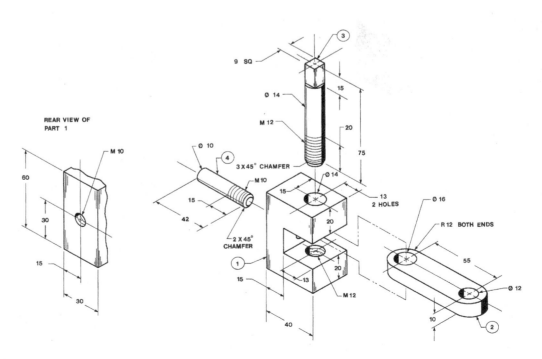

## EX12-5 Millimeters

**1** Draw an assembly drawing of the given objects.

**2** Draw detail drawings for all nonstandard parts.

**3** Prepare a parts list.

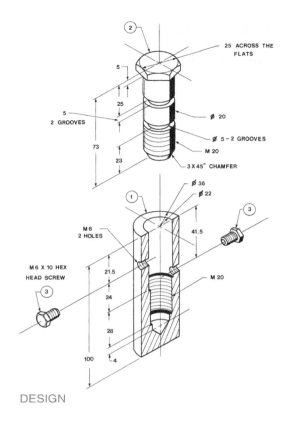

DESIGN

## EX12-6 Millimeters

**1** Draw an assembly drawing of the given objects.

**2** Draw detail drawings for all nonstandard parts.

**3** Prepare a parts list.

**4** Replace the rivets with the appropriate screws and nuts.

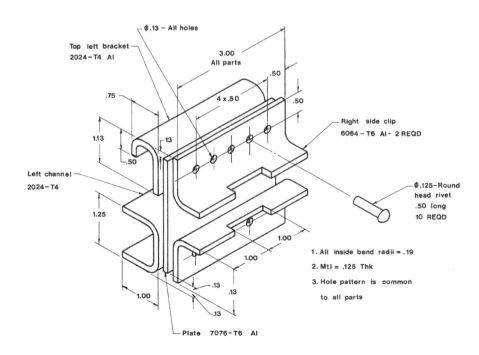

# EX12-7 Millimeters

**1** Draw an assembly drawing of the given objects.

**2** Prepare a parts list.

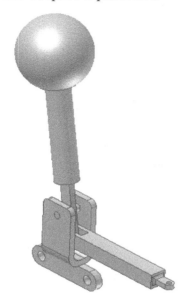

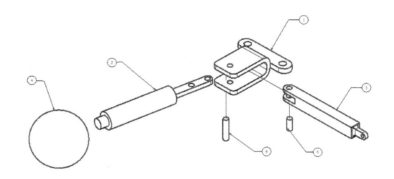

| Parts List | | | | |
|---|---|---|---|---|
| ITEM | PART NUMBER | DESCRIPTION | MATERIAL | QTY |
| 1 | ENG-A43 | BOX,PIVOT | SAE1020 | 1 |
| 2 | ENG-A44 | POST,HANDLE | SAE1020 | 1 |
| 3 | ENG-A45 | LINK | SAE1020 | 1 |
| 4 | AM300-1 | HANDLE | STEEL | 1 |
| 5 | EK-132 | POST-Ø6x14 | STEEL | 1 |
| 6 | EK-131 | POST-Ø6x26 | STEEL | 1 |

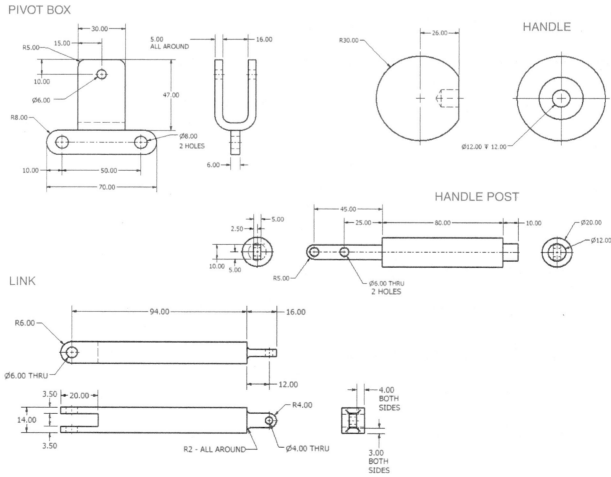

PIVOT BOX

HANDLE

HANDLE POST

LINK

# EX12-8 Inches

Draw an assembly drawing and parts list for the guide assembly.

## ADJUSTABLE ASSEMBLY

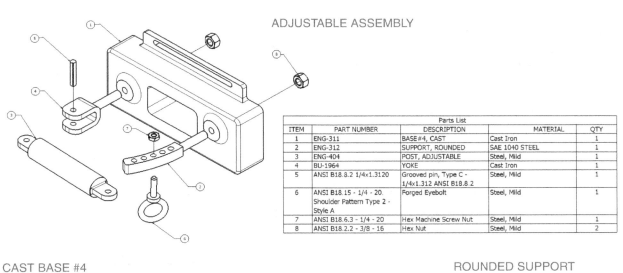

| Parts List | | | | |
|---|---|---|---|---|
| ITEM | PART NUMBER | DESCRIPTION | MATERIAL | QTY |
| 1 | ENG-311 | BASE #4, CAST | Cast Iron | 1 |
| 2 | ENG-312 | SUPPORT, ROUNDED | SAE 1040 STEEL | 1 |
| 3 | ENG-404 | POST, ADJUSTABLE | Steel, Mild | 1 |
| 4 | BU-1964 | YOKE | Cast Iron | 1 |
| 5 | ANSI B18.8.2 1/4x1.3120 | Grooved pin, Type C - 1/4x1.312 ANSI B18.8.2 | Steel, Mild | 1 |
| 6 | ANSI B18.15 - 1/4 - 20. Shoulder Pattern Type 2 - Style A | Forged Eyebolt | Steel, Mild | 1 |
| 7 | ANSI B18.6.3 - 1/4 - 20 | Hex Machine Screw Nut | Steel, Mild | 1 |
| 8 | ANSI B18.2.2 - 3/8 - 16 | Hex Nut | Steel, Mild | 2 |

## CAST BASE #4

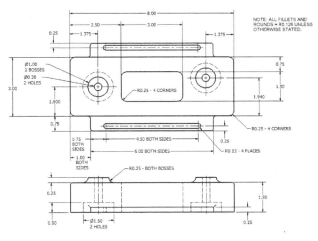

## ROUNDED SUPPORT

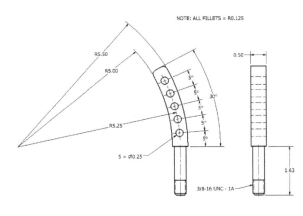

## ADJUSTABLE POST

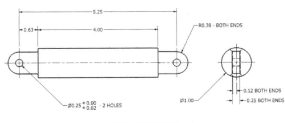

## YOKE

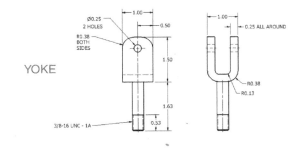

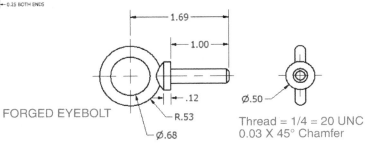

FORGED EYEBOLT

# EX12-9

Redraw the given objects as an assembly drawing and add bolts with the appropriate nuts at the L and H holes. Add the appropriate drawing call-outs. Specify standard bolt lengths.

**1** Use inch values.

**2** Draw the front assembly view, using a sectional view.

**3** Draw the fasteners, using schematic representations.

**4** Draw the fasteners, using simplified representations.

**5** Prepare a parts list.

**6** Prepare detail drawings for the parts.

**7** Repeat steps 2 through 6 using millimeter values.

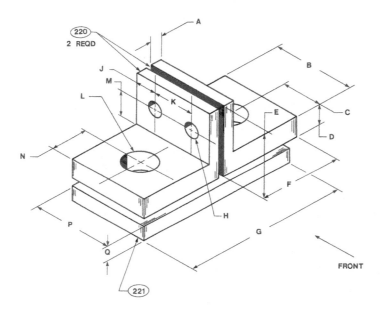

| DIMENSION | INCHES | mm |
|-----------|--------|-----|
| A | .25 | 6 |
| B | 2.00 | 50 |
| C | 1.00 | 25 |
| D | .50 | 13 |
| E | 1.75 | 45 |
| F | 2.00 | 50 |
| G | 4.00 | 100 |
| H | Ø.438 | Ø11 |
| J | .50 | 12.5 |
| K | 1.00 | 25 |
| L | Ø.781 | Ø19 |
| M | .63 | 16 |
| N | .88 | 22 |
| P | 2.00 | 50 |
| Q | .25 | 6 |

# EX12-10

Redraw the given views and add the appropriate hex head machine screws at M and N. Use standard length screws and allow at least two unused threads at the bottom of each threaded hole. Add a bolt with the appropriate nut at hole P.

**1** Use inch values.

**2** Draw the front assembly view, using a sectional view.

**3** Draw the fasteners, using schematic representations.

**4** Draw the fasteners, using simplified representations.

**5** Prepare a parts list.

**6** Prepare detail drawings for the parts.

**7** Repeat steps 2 through 6 using millimeter values.

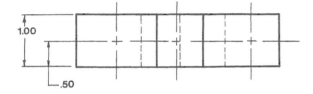

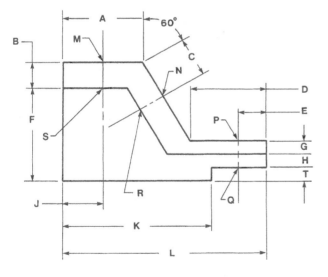

| DIMENSION | INCHES | mm |
|---|---|---|
| A | 1.50 | 38 |
| B | .50 | 13 |
| C | .75 | 19 |
| D | 1.38 | 35 |
| E | .50 | 13 |
| F | 1.75 | 44 |
| G | .25 | 6 |
| H | .25 | 6 |
| J | .75 | 19 |
| K | 2.75 | 70 |
| L | 3.75 | 96 |
| M | Ø.31 | Ø8 |
| N | Ø.25 | Ø6 |
| P | Ø.41 | Ø12 |
| Q | Ø.41 | Ø12 |
| R | .164–32 UNF X .50 DEEP | M4 X 14 DEEP |
| S | .250–20 UNC X 1.63 DEEP | M6 X 14 DEEP |
| T | .25 | 6 |

# EX12-11 Millimeters

Draw an assembly drawing and parts list for the circular damper assembly shown.

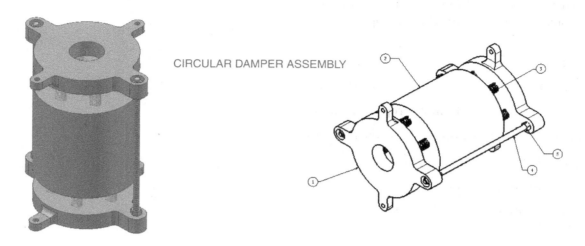

CIRCULAR DAMPER ASSEMBLY

| Parts List | | | | |
|---|---|---|---|---|
| ITEM | PART NUMBER | DESCRIPTION | MATERIAL | QTY |
| 1 | BU2008-1 | BASE, HOLDER | Steel | 2 |
| 2 | BU2008-2 | SPRING, COMPRESSION | Steel, Mild | 12 |
| 3 | BU2008-3 | COUNTERWEIGHT | Steel | 1 |
| 4 | AM312-12 | POST, THREADED | Steel | 2 |
| 5 | AS 1112 - M18  Type | HEX NUT | Steel, Mild | 8 |

Note: AM-312-12 Threaded Post is M18 x 560 long with 1 x 45° chamfers at each end

COUNTERWEIGHT

HOLDER BASE

R20.00

Ø16.00
2 HOLES

Ø30.00 - 6 HOLES

R150.00

Ø100.00

Ø200.00

Ø30.00 ▼ 5.00
6 HOLES

Ø200.01

R30.00

Ø20.00
⌴H0▼25 - BACK SIDE
2 HOLES

Ø100.00 THRU

R16.00
ALL AROUND

200.00

200.00

300.00

Ø300.00

25.00

50.00

SPRING
Wire Ø = 3.0
Outside Ø = 28.0
Number of Coils = 16
Coil Direction = Right
Grind both ends

## EX12-12 Inches

The objects shown on the pages that follow are to be assembled as indicated. Select sizes for the parts that make the assembly possible. (Choose dimensions for the end blocks and then determine the screw and stud lengths.) The hex head screws (5) have a major diameter of either 0.375 inch or M10. The studs (3) are to have the same thread sizes as the screws and are to be screwed into the top part (2). The holes in the lower part (1) that accept the studs are to be clearance holes.

**1** Draw an assembly drawing.

**2** Draw a detail drawing of each nonstandard part. Include positional tolerances for all holes.

**3** Prepare a parts list.

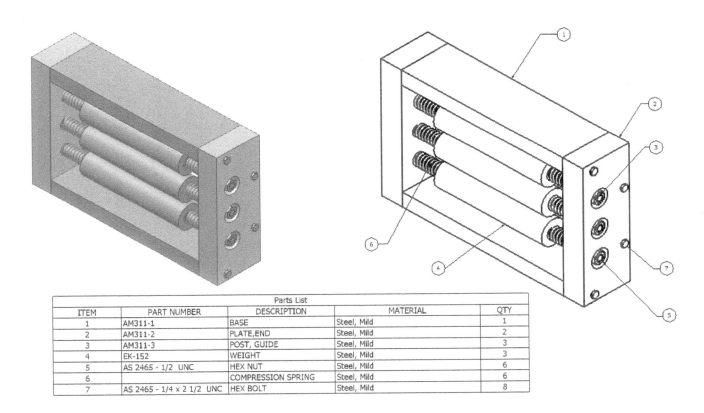

| Parts List | | | | |
|---|---|---|---|---|
| ITEM | PART NUMBER | DESCRIPTION | MATERIAL | QTY |
| 1 | AM311-1 | BASE | Steel, Mild | 1 |
| 2 | AM311-2 | PLATE,END | Steel, Mild | 2 |
| 3 | AM311-3 | POST, GUIDE | Steel, Mild | 3 |
| 4 | EK-152 | WEIGHT | Steel, Mild | 3 |
| 5 | AS 2465 - 1/2  UNC | HEX NUT | Steel, Mild | 6 |
| 6 |  | COMPRESSION SPRING | Steel, Mild | 6 |
| 7 | AS 2465 - 1/4 x 2 1/2  UNC | HEX BOLT | Steel, Mild | 8 |

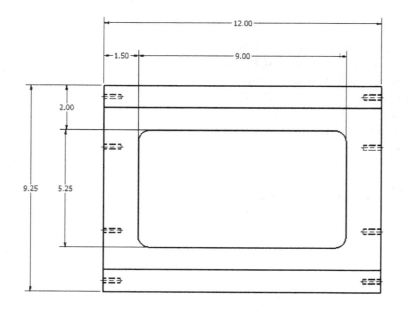

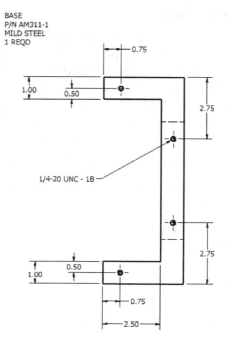

BASE
P/N AM311-1
MILD STEEL
1 REQD

1/4-20 UNC - 1B

WEIGHT
P/N EK-152
MILD STEEL
3 REQD

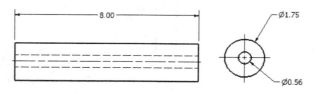

END

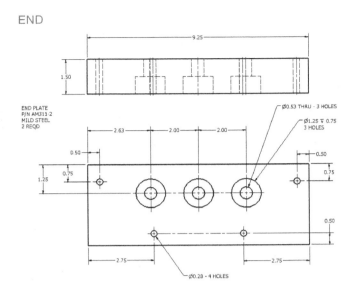

END PLATE
P/N AM311-2
MILD STEEL
2 REQD

Ø0.53 THRU - 3 HOLES

Ø1.25 ∇ 0.75
3 HOLES

Ø0.28 - 4 HOLES

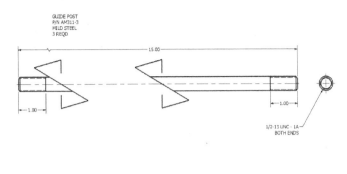

GUIDE POST
P/N AM311-3
MILD STEEL
3 REQD

1/2-13 UNC - 1A
BOTH ENDS

SPRING
Wire Ø = 0.125
Outside Ø = 1.000
Length = 2.00
Coil direction = light
Number of coils = 10
Grind both ends

# EX12-13 Inches

Draw an assembly drawing and parts list for the winding assembly.

WINDING ASSEMBLY

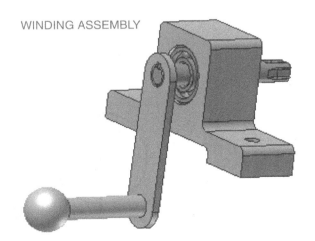

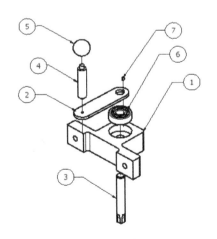

| Parts List | | | | |
|---|---|---|---|---|
| ITEM | PART NUMBER | DESCRIPTION | MATERIAL | QTY |
| 1 | EK131-1 | SUPPORT | STEEL | 1 |
| 2 | EK131-2 | LINK | STEEL | 1 |
| 3 | EK131-3 | SHAFT,DRIVE | STEEL | 1 |
| 4 | EK131-4 | POST, THREADED | STEEL | 1 |
| 5 | EK131-5 | BALL | STEEL | 1 |
| 6 | BS 292 - BRM 3/4 | Deep Groove Ball Bearings | STEEL,MILD | 1 |
| 7 | 3/16x1/8x1/4 | RECTANGULAR KEY | STEEL | 1 |

SUPPORT

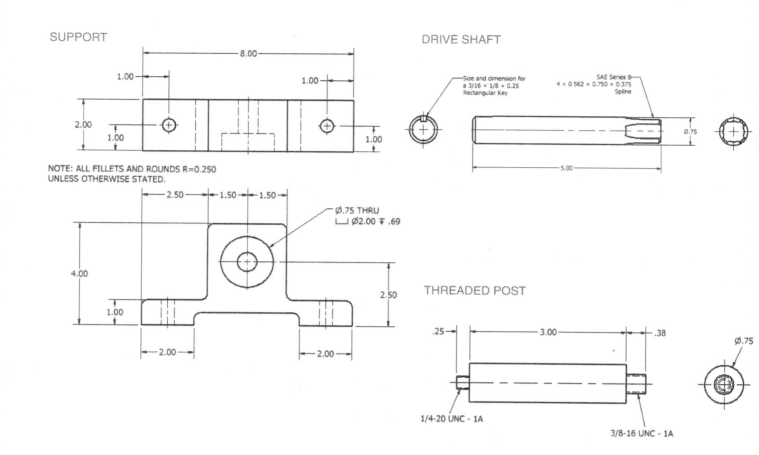

NOTE: ALL FILLETS AND ROUNDS R=0.250
UNLESS OTHERWISE STATED.

DRIVE SHAFT

THREADED POST

LINK

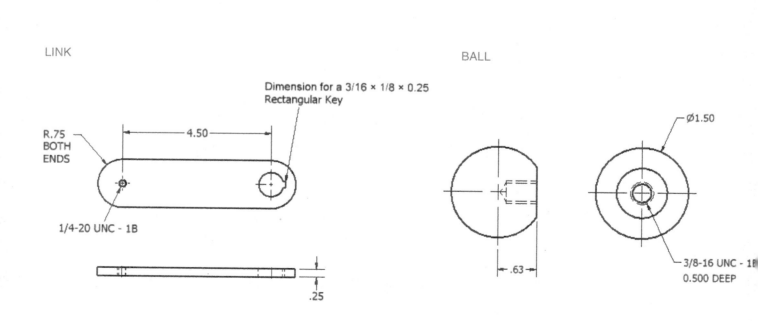

BALL

## EX12-14 Inches

Design a hand-operated grinding wheel specifically for sharpening a chisel. The chisel is to be located on an adjustable rest while it is being sharpened. The mechanism should be able to be clamped to a table during operation via two thumbscrews.

A standard grinding wheel is ⌀6.00 inch and 1/2 inch thick and has an internal mounting hole with a 50 ± 0.03-millimeter bore.

**1** Draw an assembly drawing.

**2** Draw a detail drawing of each non-standard part. Include positional tolerances for all holes.

**3** Prepare a parts list.

This is a nominal setup. It may be improved. Consider how the spacers rub against the stationary support and consider using double nuts at each end of the shaft.

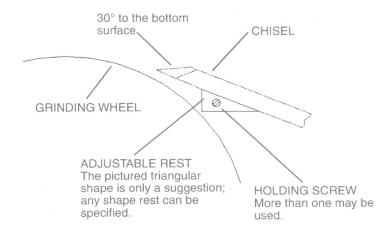

30° to the bottom surface

CHISEL

GRINDING WHEEL

ADJUSTABLE REST
The pictured triangular shape is only a suggestion; any shape rest can be specified.

HOLDING SCREW
More than one may be used.

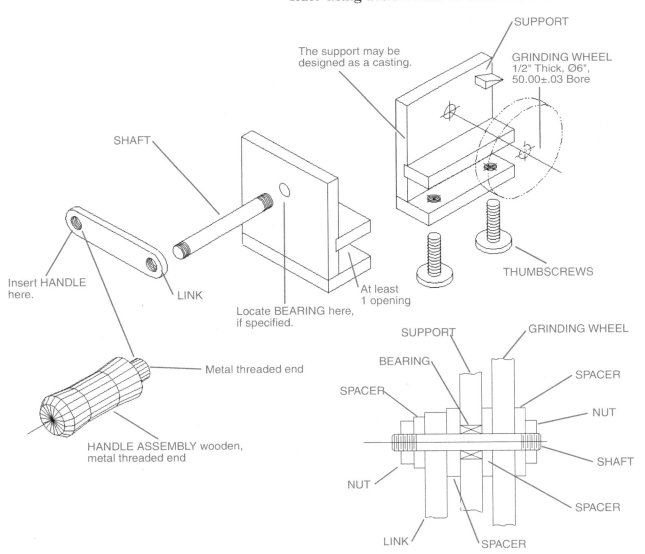

The support may be designed as a casting.

SUPPORT

GRINDING WHEEL
1/2" Thick, Ø6", 50.00±.03 Bore

SHAFT

Insert HANDLE here.

LINK

Metal threaded end

HANDLE ASSEMBLY wooden, metal threaded end

Locate BEARING here, if specified.

At least 1 opening

THUMBSCREWS

SUPPORT

GRINDING WHEEL

BEARING

SPACER

SPACER

NUT

NUT

SHAFT

SPACER

LINK

SPACER

## EX12-15 Millimeters

1 Draw an assembly drawing of the given object.

2 Prepare a parts list.

3 Select appropriate fasteners to hold the object together.

4 Define the appropriate tolerances.

5 Define an assembly sequence, considering the size of any screw heads and nuts, and the tooling required for assembly.

BRACKET ASSEMBLY

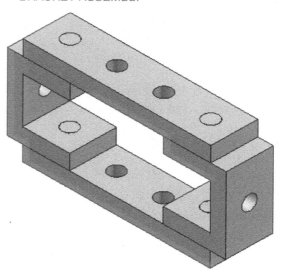

C-BRACKET, SAE1020 STEEL, 2 REQD
Part Number: AM311-1

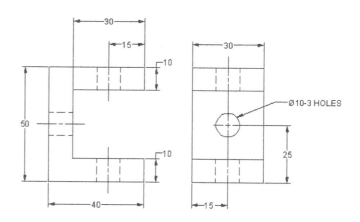

QUAD SPACER, SAE 1020 STEEL
2 REQD, Part Number: AM311-2

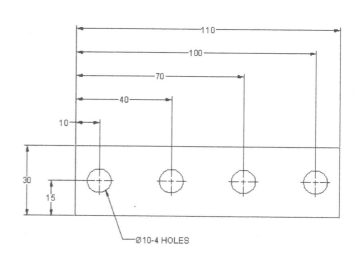

# EX12-16 Millimeters

**1** Draw an assembly drawing of the given object.

**2** Prepare a parts list.

**3** Select appropriate fasteners to hold the object together.

**4** Define the appropriate tolerances.

**5** Define an assembly sequence, considering the size of any screw heads and nuts, and the tooling required for assembly.

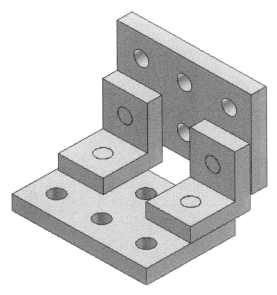

CLIP ASSEMBLY

SUPPORT PLATE
SAE 1040 STEEL, 2 REQD
Part Number: AM312-3

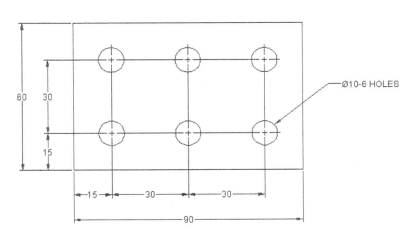

L-CLIP
SAE 1040 STEEL, 2 REQD
Part Number: AM312-4

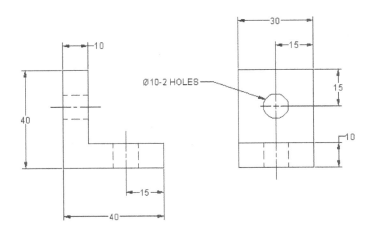

# EX12-17 Millimeters

**1** Draw an assembly drawing of the given object.

**2** Prepare a parts list.

**3** Select appropriate fasteners to hold the object together.

**4** Define the appropriate tolerances.

**5** Define an assembly sequence, considering the size of any screw heads and nuts, and the tooling required for assembly.

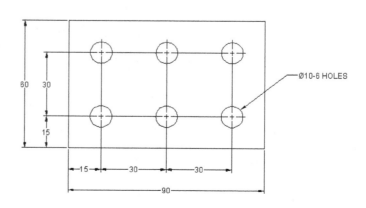

GUIDE ASSEMBLY

C-BRACKET
SAE 1020 STEEL, 4 REQD
Part Number: AM311-1

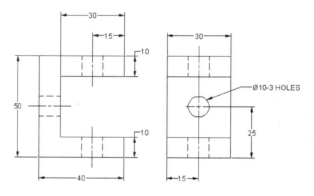

L-CLIP
SAE 1040 STEEL, 2 REQD
Part Number: AM312-4

SUPPORT PLATE
SAE 1040 STEEL, 2 REQD
Part Number: AM312-3

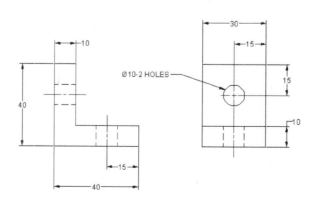

# EX12-18 Millimeters

**1** Draw an assembly drawing of the given object.

**2** Prepare a parts list.

**3** Select appropriate fasteners to hold the object together. Note that the fastener used to join the center link and the drive link passes over the web plate as the drive link rotates.

**4** Define the appropriate tolerances.

**5** Use phantom lines and define the motion of the center link and the rocker link if the drive link rotates 360°.

ROCKER ASSEMBLY

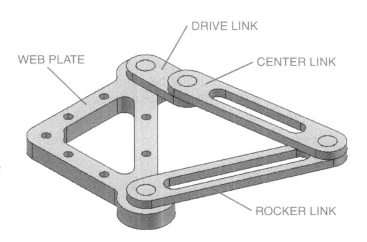

WEB PLATE
DRIVE LINK
CENTER LINK
ROCKER LINK

DRIVE LINK
Part Number:
AM311-22A

SAE 1040 STEEL
5mm THK

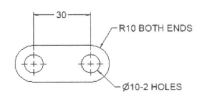

30

R10 BOTH ENDS

Ø10-2 HOLES

ROCKER LINK
Part Number: AM311-2C
SAE 1040 STEEL
5mm THK

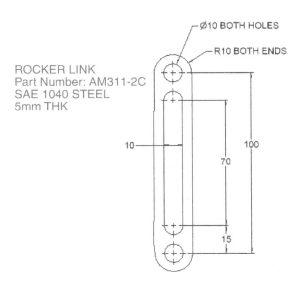

Ø10 BOTH HOLES

R10 BOTH ENDS

10    100

70

15

ALL FILLETS AND ROUNDS = R3

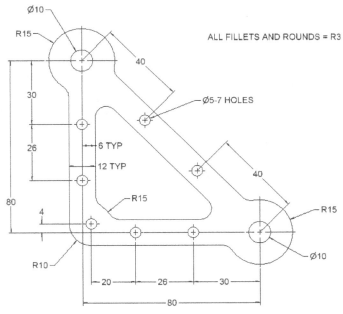

Ø10

R15

40

Ø5-7 HOLES

30

26

6 TYP

12 TYP

40

R15

80

4

R15

Ø10

R10

20    26    30

80

WEB PLATE
Part Number: AM311-22B
SAE 1040 STEEL
10mm THK

CENTER LINK
Part Number: AM311-22D
SAE 1040 STEEL
5mm THK

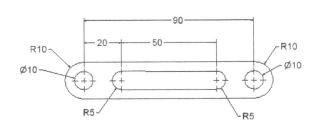

90

20    50

R10

R10

Ø10

Ø10

R5    R5

# EX12-19 Millimeters

**1** Draw an assembly drawing of the given object.

**2** Prepare a parts list.

**3** Select appropriate fasteners to hold the object together. Note that the fasteners used to join the side links to the holder arm pass over the holder base.

**4** Define the appropriate tolerances. Use an H7/p6 tolerance between bushing-A and the holder base.

**5** Use phantom lines to define the motion of the holder arm, side links, and cross link if the holder arm rotates between +30° and −30°.

LINK ASSEMBLY

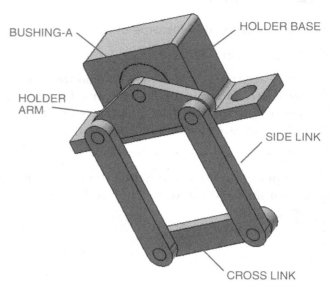

HOLDER BASE

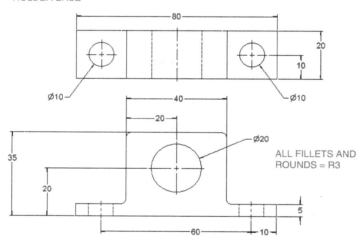

ALL FILLETS AND
ROUNDS = R3

SIDE LINK
BU100-4
7075-T6 AL
5mm THK
2 REQD

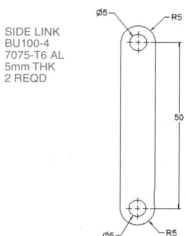

CROSS LINK, BU100-3, 7075-T6, AL, 5mm THK

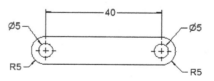

HOLDER ARM, BU100-2, 7075-T6, AL, 5mm THK

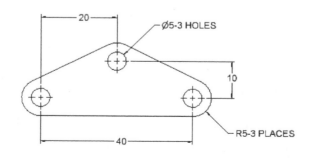

BUSHING-A
A/M CORP - B20-AD
TEFLON

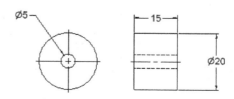

## EX12-20 Millimeters

**1** Draw an assembly drawing of the minivise.

**2** Prepare a parts list.

**3** Select the appropriate fasteners to hold the vise together.

**4** Redesign the interface between the drive screw and the holder plate.

## Minivise (Assembled View)

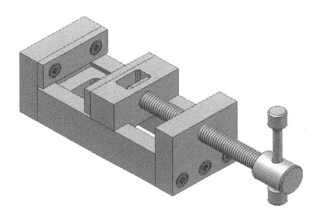

## Minivise (Exploded View)

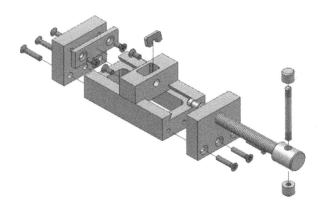

BASE

SAE 1040 STEEL

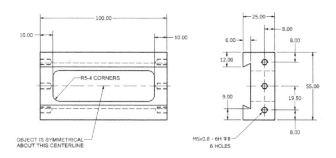

DRIVE SCREW

SAE 1040 STEEL

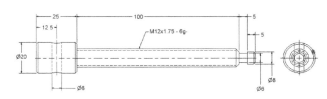

END PLATE

SAE 1040 STEEL

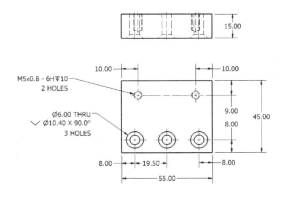

SLIDER

SAE 1040 STEEL

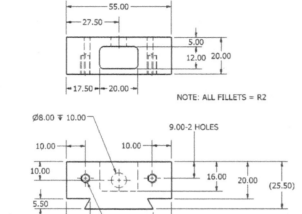

NOTE: ALL FILLETS = R2

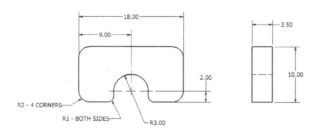

HOLDER PLATE

SAE 1040 STEEL

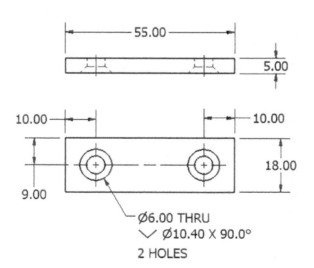

FACE PLATE

SAE 1040 STEEL

HANDLE

SAE 1040 STEEL

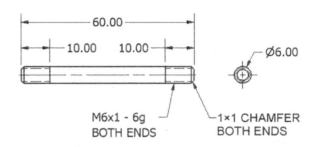

M6x1 - 6g
BOTH ENDS

1×1 CHAMFER
BOTH ENDS

END CAP

SAE 1040 STEEL

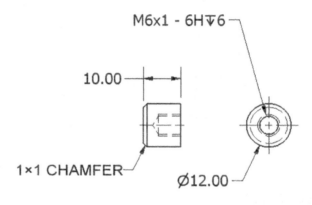

M6x1 - 6H▼6

10.00

1×1 CHAMFER

Ø12.00

DRIVE PLATE

SAE 1040 STEEL

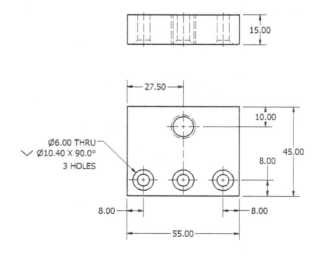

M5 × 10 RECESSED COUNTERSUNK

HEAD STEEL

M5 × 22 RECESSED COUNTERSUNK

HEAD STEEL

## EX12-21 Inches

**1** Draw an assembly drawing of the rocker assembly.

**2** Prepare a parts list that includes all parts used in the assembly.

**3** Draw a detailed 2D drawing with dimensions of each manufactured part used in the assembly.

Do not create drawings of purchased parts, screws, nuts, washers, or bearings.

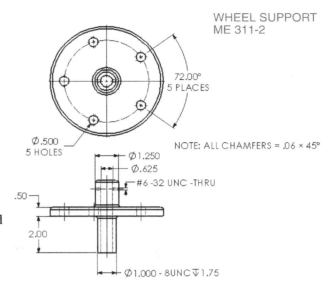

WHEEL SUPPORT
ME 311-2

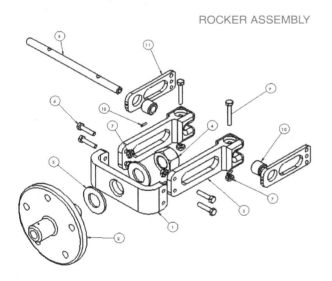

ROCKER ASSEMBLY

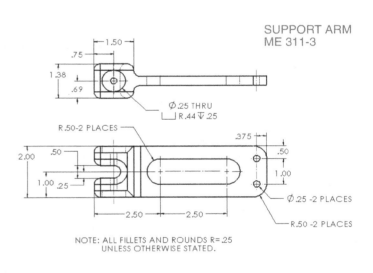

SUPPORT ARM
ME 311-3

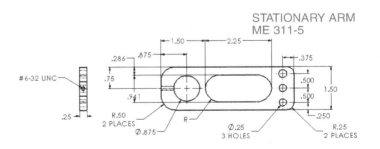

STATIONARY ARM
ME 311-5

| ITEM NO. | PART NUMBER | DESCRIPTION | QTY. |
|---|---|---|---|
| 1 | ME 311-1 | WHEEL BRACKET | 1 |
| 2 | ME 311-2 | WHEEL SUPPORT | 1 |
| 3 | | 1.00 × 1.75 × .06 PLAIN WASHER | 2 |
| 4 | | 1 × 8 UNC HEX NUT | 1 |
| 5 | ME 311-3 | SUPPORT ARM | 2 |
| 6 | | 1/4 - 28 UNF × 1.25 HEX HEAD | 4 |
| 7 | | 1/4 - 28 UNF × 1.75 HEX HEAD | 2 |
| 8 | | 1/4 - 28 UNF HEX NUT | 6 |
| 9 | ME 311-4 | PIVOT SHAFT | 1 |
| 10 | | .500 × .875 .750 BEARING | 2 |
| 11 | ME 311-5 | STATIONARY ARM | 2 |
| 12 | | #6-32 × .560 UNC SET SCREW CONE POINT | 2 |

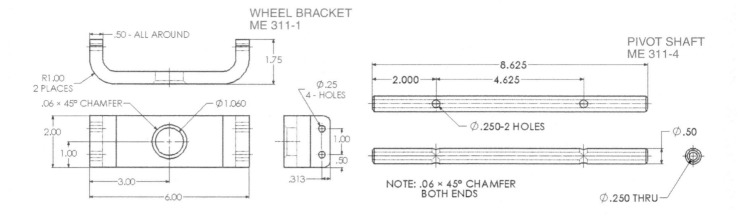

WHEEL BRACKET
ME 311-1

PIVOT SHAFT
ME 311-4

## EX12-22 Millimeters

**1** Draw an assembly drawing of the dome assembly.

**2** Prepare a parts list that includes all parts used in the assembly.

**3** Draw a detailed 2D drawing with dimensions of the semisphere. Include section views as shown.

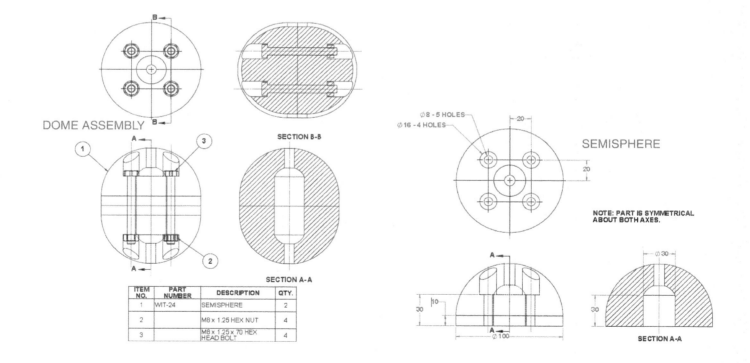

DOME ASSEMBLY

SECTION B-B

SECTION A-A

| ITEM NO. | PART NUMBER | DESCRIPTION | QTY. |
|---|---|---|---|
| 1 | WIT-24 | SEMISPHERE | 2 |
| 2 | | M8 x 1.25 HEX NUT | 4 |
| 3 | | M8 x 1.25 x 70 HEX HEAD BOLT | 4 |

SEMISPHERE

NOTE: PART IS SYMMETRICAL ABOUT BOTH AXES.

SECTION A-A

## 13-1 Introduction

This chapter explains how to draw and design with gears and bearings. The chapter does not discuss how to design specific gears and bearings; instead, it covers how to design by using existing parts selected from manufacturers' catalogs. Various gear terms are defined, and design applications are demonstrated.

This chapter also discusses how to design and draw a cam according to a displacement diagram. Different types of follower motion are explained, as are different types of followers.

## 13-2 Types of Gears

There are many types of gears, including spur, bevel, worm, helical, and rack gears (Figure 13-1). Each type has its own terminology, drawing requirements, and design considerations.

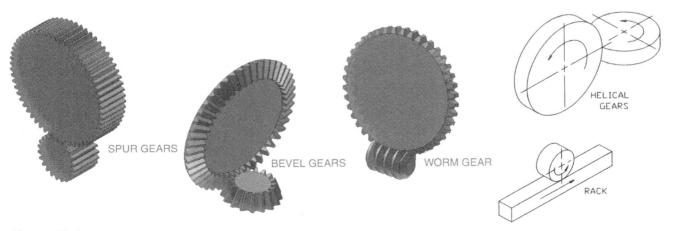

SPUR GEARS  BEVEL GEARS  WORM GEAR  HELICAL GEARS  RACK

**Figure 13-1**

## 13-3 Gear Terminology—Spur

Following is a list of common spur gear terms and their meanings. Figure 13-2 illustrates the terms, and Figure 13-3 shows a list of relevant formulas. Manufacturers' catalogs are online and are updated frequently. To check catalogs, use your browser's search engine to search on gears, bearings, and other relevant topics.

**Figure 13-2**

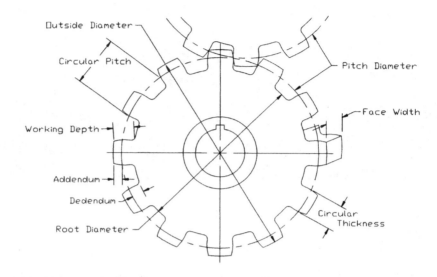

**Figure 13-3**

| | |
|---|---|
| Pitch Diameter (PD) | See catalog |
| Circular Pitch (CP) | $CP = \dfrac{\pi}{DP}$ |
| Diametral Pitch (DP) | $DP = \dfrac{\pi}{CP}$ |
| Number of Teeth (N) | $N = (PD)(DP)$ |
| Outside Diameter (OD) | See catalog |
| Addendum (a) | $a = \dfrac{1}{DP}$ |
| Dedendum (d) | $d = a + .125$ (For drawing purposes ONLY) |
| Root Diameter (RD) | $RD = PD - d$ |
| Circular Thickness (CT) | $CT = \dfrac{PD}{2N}$ |
| Face Width (F) | See catalogs |

*Pitch diameter (PD)*—The diameter used to define the spacing of gears.

*Diametral pitch (DP)*—The number of teeth per inch or millimeter.

*Circular pitch (CP)*—The circular distance from a fixed point on one tooth to the same position on the next tooth, as measured along the pitch diameter. The circumference of the pitch diameter divided by the number of teeth.

*Preferred pitches*—The standard sizes available from gear manufacturers. Whenever possible, use preferred gear sizes.

*Center distance (CD)*—The distance between the center points of two meshing gears.

*Backlash*—The difference between a tooth width and the engaging space on a meshing gear.

*Addendum (a)*—The height of a tooth above the pitch diameter.

*Dedendum (d)*—The depth of a tooth below the pitch diameter.

*Whole depth*—The total depth of a tooth. The addendum plus the dedendum.

*Working depth*—The depth of engagement of one gear into another. Equal to the sum of the two gear addendums.

*Circular thickness (CT)*—The distance across a tooth as measured along the pitch diameter.

*Face width (FW)*—The distance from front to back along a tooth, as measured perpendicular to the pitch diameter.

*Outside diameter (OD)*—The largest diameter of the gear. Equals the pitch diameter plus the addendum.

*Root diameter (RD)*—The diameter of the base of the teeth. The pitch diameter minus the dedendum.

*Clearance*—The distance between the addendum of a meshing gear and the dedendum of the mating gears.

*Pressure angle*—The angle between the line of action and a line tangent to the pitch diameter. Most gears have pressure angles of either 14.5° or 20°.

## English and Metric Units for Spur Gears

The preceding definitions apply to both English unit and metric unit spur gears, with the exception of pitch. For English unit gears, pitch is defined as the number of teeth per inch relative to the pitch diameter and is expressed using the formula shown in Figure 13-4. Gears made to metric specifications are defined in terms of the amount of pitch diameter per tooth, called the gear's *module*. Figure 13-4 shows the formula for calculating a gear's module. Metric gears also have a slightly different tooth shape that makes them incompatible with English unit gears.

**Figure 13-4**

ENGLISH UNITS

$$\text{Pitch} = \frac{\text{Number of Teeth (N)}}{\text{Pitch Diameter (PD)}} = \frac{N}{PD}$$

METRIC UNITS

$$\text{Module} = \frac{\text{Pitch Diameter (PD)}}{\text{Number of Teeth (N)}} = \frac{PD}{N}$$

## 13-4 Spur Gear Drawings

Figure 13-5 shows a representation of spur gears. The individual teeth are not included in the front view but are represented by three phantom lines. The diameters of the three lines represent the outside diameter, the pitch diameter, and the root diameter.

**Figure 13-5**

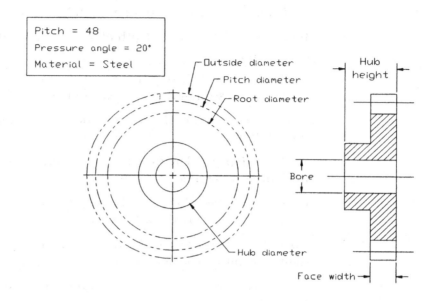

The outside diameter and the pitch diameter are usually given in manufacturers' catalogs. The root diameter can be calculated from the pitch diameter using the formula presented in Figure 13-3.

The side view of the gear is drawn as a sectional view taken along the vertical centerline. The gear size is defined by using the manufacturer's stock number and dimensions, as well as a list of appropriate design information.

Figure 13-6 shows the front representation view of three meshing gears. The gears are positioned so that the pitch circle diameters are tangent. Ideally, mating gears should always mesh exactly tangent to their pitch circles.

**Figure 13-6**

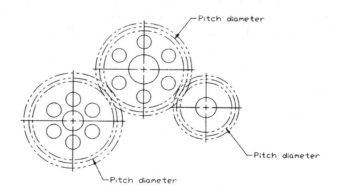

Gear representations were developed because it was both difficult and time-consuming to accurately draw individual teeth when creating drawings on a drawing board. The AutoCAD **Array** and **Block** commands, among others, can be used to create detailed gear drawings that include all teeth; however, it is usually sufficient to show a few meshing teeth and use the representative centerlines for the remaining portions of both gears (Figure 13-7).

**Figure 13-7**

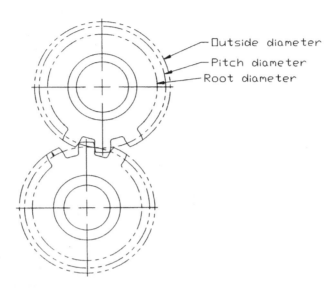

Most gear tooth shapes are based on an involute curve. Involute-based teeth fit together well, transfer forces smoothly, and can use one cutter to generate all gear tooth variations within the same pitch. Standards for tooth proportions have been established by the American National Standards Institute (ANSI) and the American Gear Manufacturers Association (AGMA).

## 13-5 Drawing Problem

Draw a front view of a spur gear that has an outside diameter of 6.50 inches, a pitch diameter of 6.00 inches, and a root diameter of 5.25 inches. The gear has 12 teeth.

The method presented here is a simplified method that creates an acceptable representation for most drawing applications (Figure 13-8).

**Figure 13-8**

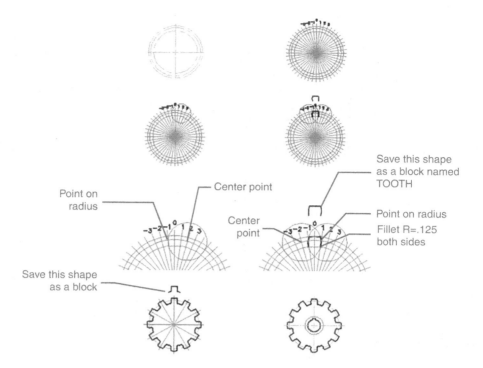

**1** Draw three concentric circles with diameters **6.50**, **6.00**, and **5.25**. Use the **Center Mark** tool to draw a centerline for the circles.

**2** Use the **Array** command to create **48** radiating lines, as shown. Label three lines on each side of the top vertical centerline as shown. Zoom in to the labeled area.

The number of lines should equal four times the number of teeth to be drawn. Two adjoining sectors define the width of a tooth, and the next two adjacent sectors define the space between teeth.

**3** Draw a circle whose center point is at the intersection of the pitch diameter and the line labeled **2** and whose radius is determined by the distance from the center point to the intersection of the pitch diameter and the line labeled **–1**.

**4** Repeat step 3, using the intersection of the pitch diameter and the line labeled **–2** as the center point.

**5** Use the **Fillet** command to draw a radius at the base of the tooth. Select the side of the tooth as one of the lines for the fillet and the root diameter as the other line.

Both the circle and radial line appear to be selected, but AutoCAD uses the last entity drawn, so the diameter is selected.

The tooth shape can be saved as a block named **TOOTH** and used when drawing other gears. Only the lines that represent the top of the gear and the two side sections need to be saved. A different-sized gear will have a different root diameter, and new fillets can be drawn that align with the new root diameter.

**6** Use the **Trim** and **Erase** commands to remove excess lines and create the tooth shape between lines **–2** and **2**, as shown.

This tooth shape may be saved as a block and used when drawing other gears.

**7** Array the tooth shape about the gear's center point.

**8** Erase the excess ray lines and change the pitch diameter to a centerline.

**9** Draw the gear's bore hole or center hole and hub, as required.

## 13-6 Drawing Problem

Figure 13-9 shows two meshing gears and their construction in AutoCAD. In the example shown, the larger gear has a diameter of 6.00 inches and 24 teeth; the smaller gear has a diameter of 3.00 inches and 12 teeth. The drawing utilizes the wblocked block created in Drawing Problem 13.5.

**Figure 13-9**

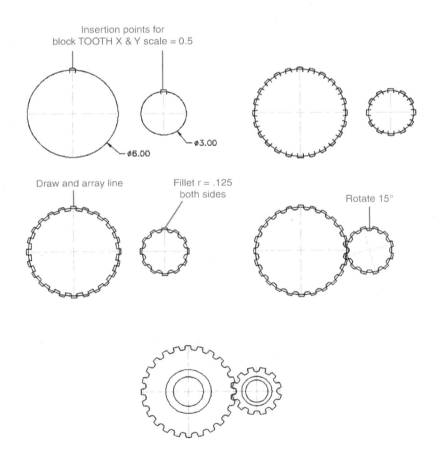

The circular thickness of the block tooth as measured along the pitch diameter equals 1/12 the circumference of the pitch diameter:

(1/12)($\phi$ PD)

For the gear in Drawing Problem 13-5, where PD = 6:

(1/12)($\phi$ 6) = $\phi$/2

= 1.57 inches

The large gear requires 24 teeth on a pitch diameter of 6, or twice as many teeth as the gear used to create the block. The teeth on the 24-tooth gear must be half the size of the tooth created in the block. The teeth on the smaller gear must be the same size as the teeth on the larger gear.

## Drawing Meshing Spur Gears

**1** Draw two circles with diameters **6.00** and **3.00** inches. Include the circles' centerlines by using the **Center Mark** tool.

The gears will be drawn separately and then meshed.

**2** Insert the **TOOTH** block on both gears as shown on the pitch diameter. Use an X and Y scale factor of **.5**. Explode the block.

**3** Use the **Array** command to create the required 24 and 12 teeth.

**4** Draw a line between the roots of two of the teeth as shown. Use the **Array** command to create the root circle. Add the fillet to each tooth base.

The line in this example is a straight line acceptable for smaller gears. If more accuracy of shape is required, draw a complete root circle and then trim all of it away except the portion between two tooth roots. Array this sector between all of the other teeth.

**5** Use the **Rotate** command to orient the small gear with the large gear.

Each tooth on the large gear requires 360/24 = 15°, so rotate the smaller gear **15°**.

**6** Use the **Move** command to position the small gear.

The pitch circles of the two gears should be tangent.

**7** Rotate the smaller gear **–15°**.

**8** Add the center hubs to both gears, as shown.

**9** Change the linetype of the pitch diameter circle to **Center**.

## 13-7 Drawing Problem

Figure 13-10 shows a gear that has a pitch diameter of 4.00 and 18 teeth. Use the **TOOTH** block as follows.

**Figure 13-10**

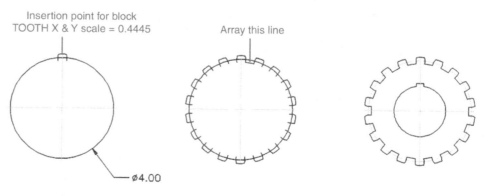

The block is first scaled to accommodate the smaller diameter.

**1** Draw a circle with a **4.00**-inch diameter. Include centerlines.

**2** Insert the block **TOOTH**, using an X and Y scale factor of **.4445**.

The scale factor was derived by considering the ratio between the number of teeth on the gear used to create the **TOOTH** block (12) and the number of teeth on the desired gear, 18, or 12/18 = .6667. The ratio between the diameters is also considered: 4.00/6.00 = .6667. The two ratios are multiplied together: (.6667)(.6667) = .4445.

**3** Use the **Array** command to create the required 18 teeth.

**4** Draw a line between the end lines of two of the teeth and array the line **18** times around the gear.

The line may be drawn as a straight line for small gears or as an arc for larger gears. The arc may be created by drawing a circle and then using the **Trim** command to create the desired length.

**5** Add the center hub as required.

The same block can be used for metric gears, using the conversion factor 1.00 inch = 25.4 millimeters. It is probably easier to create a separate block for a metric tooth.

## 13-8 Selecting Spur Gears

When two spur gears are engaged, the smaller gear is called the *pinion gear*, and the larger gear is called simply the *gear*. The relationship between the relative speeds of two mating gears is directly proportional to the gears' pitch diameters. Also, the number of teeth on a gear is proportional to the gear's pitch diameter. This means that the ratio of speed between two meshing gears is equal to the ratio of the number of teeth on the two gears. If one gear has 40 teeth and the other 20, the speed ratio between the two gears is 2:1.

For gears to mesh properly, they must have the same pitch and pressure angle. Gear manufacturers present their gears in charts that include a selection of gears with common pitches and pressure angles. Figure 13-11 shows a sample spur gear listing from the website of Stock Drive Products. The site allows you to select a diametral pitch and all other appropriate product details. Once a gear is selected, the gear information is displayed. You may be able to generate an AutoCAD drawing of the gear if you have a compatible setup. Many manufacturers offer free product catalogs.

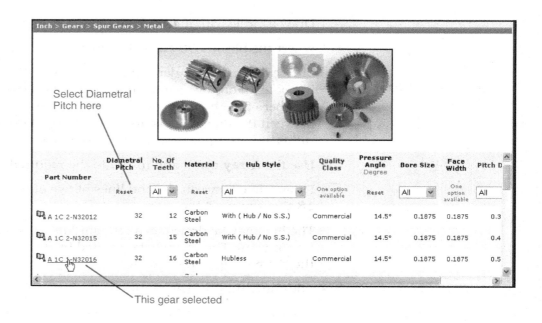

Select Diametral Pitch here

This gear selected

Selected gear

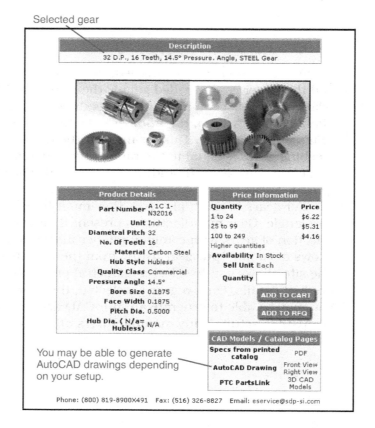

Figure 13-11

Courtesy of Stock Drive Products/Sterling Instrument, a division of Designatronics, Inc., sdp-si.com

## 13-9 Center Distance Between Gears

The center distance between meshing spur gears is needed to align the gears properly. Ideally, gears mesh exactly on their pitch diameters, so the ideal center distance between two meshing gears is equal to the sum of the two pitch radii, or the sum of the two diameters divided by 2:

CD1 = (PD1 + PD2)/2

If two gears were chosen from the table in Figure 13-11, and one had 30 teeth and a pitch diameter of .9375 and the other had 60 teeth and a pitch diameter of 1.8750, the center distance between the gears would be

CD1 = (.9375 + 1.8750)/2 = 1.4062

The center distance of gears is dependent on the tolerance of the gears' bores, the tolerance of the supporting shafts, and the feature and positional tolerance of the holes in the shaft's supporting structure. The following drawing problem shows how these tolerances are considered and applied when matching two spur gears.

## 13-10 Drawing Problem

An electric motor generates power at 1750 rpm. Reduce this speed by a factor of 2, using steel metric gears with a module of 1.5 and a pressure angle of 20°. Figure 13-12 shows a list of gears. Determine the center distance between the gears and specify the shaft sizes required for the two gears.

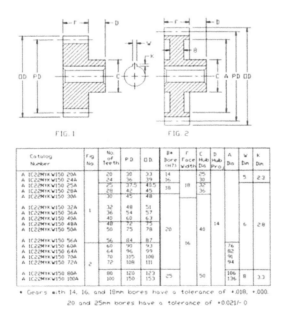

FIG. 1          FIG. 2

| Catalog Number | Fig No. | No. of Teeth | P.D. | O.D. | B* Bore (H7) | Face Width | C Hub Dia | D Hub Proj. | A Dia | W Dim | K Dim |
|---|---|---|---|---|---|---|---|---|---|---|---|
| A 1C22MYKW150 20A | | 20 | 30 | 33 | 14 | | 25 | | | | |
| A 1C22MYKW150 24A | | 24 | 36 | 39 | 16 | | 30 | | | 5 | 23 |
| A 1C22MYKW150 25A | | 25 | 37.5 | 40.5 | | 18 | 32 | | | | |
| A 1C22MYKW150 28A | | 28 | 42 | 45 | 18 | | 36 | | | | |
| A 1C22MYKW150 30A | | 30 | 45 | 48 | | | | | | | |
| A 1C22MYKW150 32A | | 32 | 48 | 51 | | | | | | | |
| A 1C22MYKW150 36A | 1 | 36 | 54 | 57 | | | | | | | |
| A 1C22MYKW150 40A | | 40 | 60 | 63 | | | | 14 | | | |
| A 1C22MYKW150 48A | | 48 | 72 | 75 | | | | | | 6 | 28 |
| A 1C22MYKW150 50A | | 50 | 75 | 78 | 20 | | 40 | | | | |
| A 1C22MYKW150 56A | | 56 | 84 | 87 | | | | | | | |
| A 1C22MYKW150 60A | | 60 | 90 | 93 | | 16 | | | 76 | | |
| A 1C22MYKW150 64A | | 64 | 96 | 99 | | | | | 82 | | |
| A 1C22MYKW150 70A | | 70 | 105 | 108 | | | | | 91 | | |
| A 1C22MYKW150 72A | 2 | 72 | 108 | 111 | | | | | 94 | | |
| A 1C22MYKW150 80A | | 80 | 120 | 123 | 25 | | 50 | | 106 | 8 | 33 |
| A 1C22MYKW150 100A | | 100 | 150 | 153 | | | | | 136 | | |

* Gears with 14, 16, and 18mm bores have a tolerance of +.018, +.000.
20 and 25mm bores have a tolerance of +0.021/- 0

**Figure 13-12**
Courtesy of Stock Drive Products/Sterling Instrument, a division of Designatronics, Inc., sdp-si.com

Gears number A 1C22MYKW150 50A and number A 1C22MKYW150 100A were selected from the table shown in Figure 13-12. The pinion gear has 50 teeth, and the large gear has 100, so if the pinion gear is mounted on the motor shaft, the larger gear will turn at 875 rpm, or half of the 1750 rpm motor speed.

$$\frac{1}{2} = \frac{x}{1750}$$

$$x = \frac{1750}{2} = 875 \text{ rpm}$$

The specific design information for the selected gears is as follows:

PINION GEAR

PD = 75

OD = 78

N = 50

Bore = $20^{+0.021}_{-0.000}$

Tolerance = H7

LARGE GEAR

PD = 150

OD = 153

N = 100

Bore = $25^{+0.021}_{-0.000}$

Tolerance = H7

The center distance between the gears is equal to the sum of the two pitch diameters divided by 2:

$$\frac{PD1 + PD2}{2} =$$

$$\frac{75 + 150}{2} = 112.5$$

The manufacturer's catalog lists the bore tolerance as an H7. One gear has a nominal bore diameter of 20, and the other has a nominal bore diameter of 25. Standard fit tolerances for metric values are discussed in Chapter 9, and appropriate tables are included in the online Appendix.

Tolerance values for a sliding fit (H7/g6) hole basis were selected for this design application. This means that the shaft tolerances are 19.993 and 19.980 for the pinion gear and 24.993 and 24.980 for the large gear.

## 13-11 Combining Spur Gears

Gears may be mounted on the same shaft. Gears on a common shaft have the same turning speed. Combining gears on the same shaft enables the designer to develop larger gear ratios within a smaller space.

Combining gears can also be used to help reduce the size of gear ratios between individual gears and the amount of space needed to create the reductions. Figure 13-13 shows a four-gear setup. Gears B and C are mounted on the same shaft. Gear A is the driver gear and is turning at a speed of 1750 rpm. The speed of gear D is determined as follows.

The ratio between gears A and B is

$$\frac{48}{72} = 0.6667$$

The speed of gear B is therefore

1750 × .6667 = 1166.7 rpm

Gears B and C are on the same shaft, so they have the same speed. Gear C is turning at
1166.7 rpm.

The ratio between gears C and D is

$$\frac{24}{48} = 0.5000$$

The speed of gear D is therefore

1166.7 × .5000 = 583 rpm

The ratio between gears A and D is 3:1.

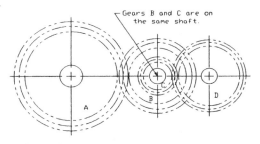

**Figure 13-13**

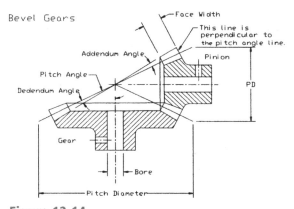

**Figure 13-14**
Courtesy of Stock Drive Products/Sterling Instrument, a division of Designatronics, Inc., sdp-si.com.

## 13-12 Gear Terminology—Bevel

*Bevel gears* align at an angle with each other. An angle of 90° is most common. Bevel gears use much of the same terminology as spur gears, but with the addition of several terms related to the angles between the gears and the shape and position of the teeth. Figure 13-14 defines the related terminology.

Bevel gears must have the same pitch or module value and have the same pressure angle in order to mesh properly. Manufacturers' catalogs usually list bevel gears in matched sets designated by ratios that have been predetermined to fit together correctly. Figure 13-15 shows a sample list of matched set bevel gears with millimeter values, and Figure 13-16 shows a list with inch values.

**Figure 13-15**
Courtesy of Stock Drive Products/Sterling Instrument, a division of Designatronics, Inc., sdp-si.com

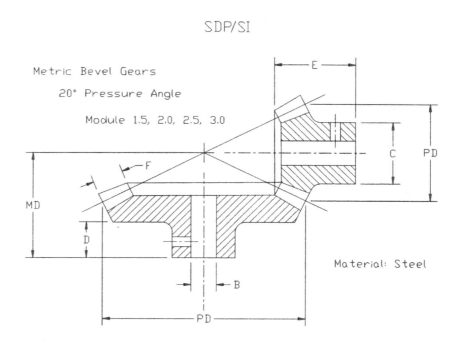

SDP/SI

Metric Bevel Gears

20° Pressure Angle

Module 1.5, 2.0, 2.5, 3.0

Material: Steel

| Catalog Number | Module | No. of Teeth | Ratio | PD | OD | B* Bore (H8) | F Face Width | E Length | C Hub Dia | D Hub Proj | MD Dim |
|---|---|---|---|---|---|---|---|---|---|---|---|
| A 1C 3MYK 15018 | 1.5 | 18 | | 27 | 29.7 | 8 | 9.8 | 23 | 22 | 12.5 | 40.74 |
| A 1C 3MYK 15036 | | 36 | | 54 | 55.4 | 10 | | 18.5 | 30 | 10 | 26.75 |
| A 1C 3MYK 20018 | 2.0 | 18 | | 36 | 39.6 | 9 | 12.6 | 29 | 28 | 15 | 53.12 |
| A 1C 3MYK 20036 | | 36 | 1:2 | 72 | 73.8 | 12 | | 24 | 36 | 13 | 35.21 |
| A 1C 3MYK 25018 | 2.5 | 18 | | 45 | 49.5 | 12 | 16.7 | 35 | 36 | 17 | 64.29 |
| A 1C 3MYK 25036H | | 36 | | 90 | 92.2 | 14 | | 29 | 50 | 15 | 42.55 |
| A 1C 3MYK 30018 | 3.0 | 18 | | 54 | 59.4 | 12 | 20 | 40 | 41 | 18 | 75.27 |
| A 1C 3MYK 30036H | | 36 | | 108 | 110.7 | 16 | | 36 | 60 | 19 | 52.32 |

\* Gears with 8, 9, 10mm bores have a tolerance of +0.022/-0
12, 14, 16mm bores have a tolerance of +0.027/-0

Courtesy of Stock Drive Products/Sterling Instrument, a division of Designatronics, Inc., sdp-si.com

**Figure 13-16**
Courtesy of Stock Drive Products/
Sterling Instrument, a division of
Designatronics, Inc., sdp-si.com

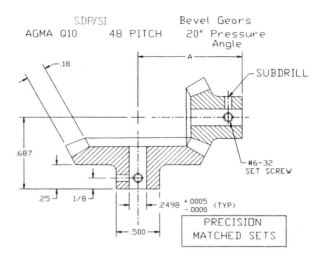

| Catalog Number | Ratio | No. of Teeth | PD | A | Material |
|---|---|---|---|---|---|
| S1346Z-48S30A030 | 1:1 | 30 30 | .625 | .687 | St Steel Aluminum |
| S1346Z-48S30S030 | 1:1 | 30 30 | .625 | .687 | St Steel |
| S1346Z-48A30A030 | 1:1 | 30 30 | .625 | .687 | Aluminum |
| S1346Z-48S30A045 | 1:1-1/2 | 30 45 | .625 .937 | .812 | St Steel Aluminum |
| S1346Z-48S30S045 | 1:1-1/2 | 30 45 | .625 .937 | .812 | St Steel |
| S1346Z-48A30A045 | 1:1-1/2 | 30 45 | .625 .937 | .812 | Aluminum |
| S1346Z-48S30A060 | 1:2 | 30 60 | .625 1.250 | .937 | St Steel Aluminum |
| S1346Z-48S30S060 | 1:2 | 30 60 | .625 1.250 | .937 | St Steel |
| S1346Z-48A30A060 | 1:2 | 30 60 | .625 1.250 | .937 | Aluminum |
| S1346Z-48S30A090 | 1:3 | 30 90 | .625 1.875 | 1.250 | St Steel Aluminum |
| S1346Z-48S30S090 | 1:3 | 30 90 | .625 1.875 | 1.250 | St Steel |
| S1346Z-48S30A090 | 1:3 | 30 90 | .625 1.875 | 1.250 | Aluminum |
| S1346Z-48S30A120 | 1:4 | 30 120 | .625 2.500 | 1.531 | St Steel Aluminum |
| S1346Z-48S30S120 | 1:4 | 30 120 | .625 2.500 | 1.531 | St Steel |
| S1346Z-48A30A120 | 1:4 | 30 120 | .625 2.500 | 1.531 | Aluminum |

## 13-13 How to Draw Bevel Gears

Bevel gears are usually drawn by working from dimensions listed in manufacturers' catalogs for specific matching sets. Draw the gears using either a sectional view or a half-sectional view that shows the profiles of the two gears. Figure 13-17 shows a matching set of bevel gears that were drawn from the information given in Figure 13-15.

The procedure used to draw the gears, based on information given in manufacturers' catalogs, is as follows.

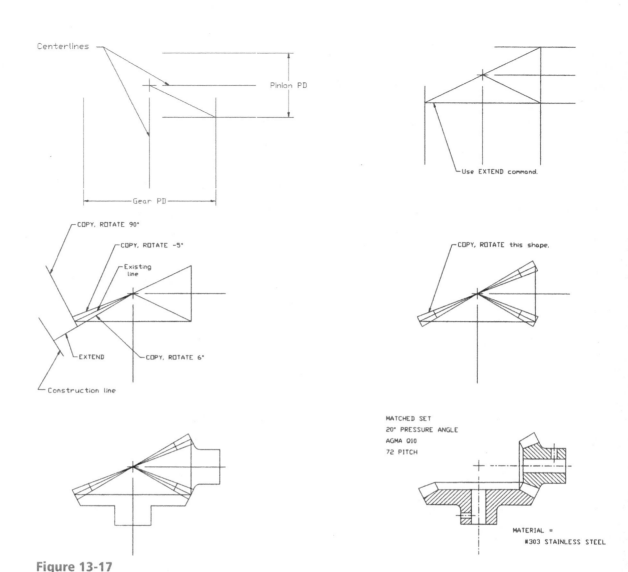

**Figure 13-17**

## Drawing a Matched Set of Beveled Gears

**1** Draw a perpendicular centerline pattern and use **Offset** to define the pitch diameters of the pinion and gear.

**2** Extend the pitch diameter lines and draw lines from the center point to the intersections, as shown.

These lines are called the *face angle lines.* The ends of beveled gears are drawn perpendicular to the face angle lines. Gear manufacturers do not always include the outside diameter values with matching sets of gears. The values are sometimes listed, with data for the individual gears elsewhere in the catalog. If the outside diameter values are not given, they can be conservatively estimated by drawing the addendum angle approximately –5.0° from the face angle and the dedendum 6.0° from the face angle.

The perpendicular end lines may be constructed by using the **Copy** and **Rotate** commands. Copy the existing face angle line directly over the existing line and rotate the line 90° from the face angle line.

Use **Extend** to extend the rotated lines as needed. Add a construction line to help define an intersection between the dedendum ray line and the face line perpendicular to the face angle line. Trim and erase any excess lines.

**3** Use **Copy** and **Rotate** to copy the face shape and rotate it into the two other positions shown.

**4** Use the given dimensions to complete the profiles. Erase and trim lines as necessary.

**5** Draw the bore holes and holes for the set screws according to the manufacturer's specifications.

**6** Use **Hatch** to draw the appropriate hatch lines.

The two gears should have hatch patterns at different angles. In this example, the hatch pattern on the pinion is at 90° to the pattern on the gear.

## 13-14 Worm Gears

A worm gear setup is created by using a cylindrical gear called a *worm* and a circular matching gear called a *worm gear* (Figure 13-18). As with other types of gears, worm gears must have the same pitch and pressure angle in order to mesh correctly. Manufacturers list matching worms and worm gears together in their catalogs. (Later, in Figure 13-20, you will see a gear manufacturer's listing for a worm gear and the appropriate worms.)

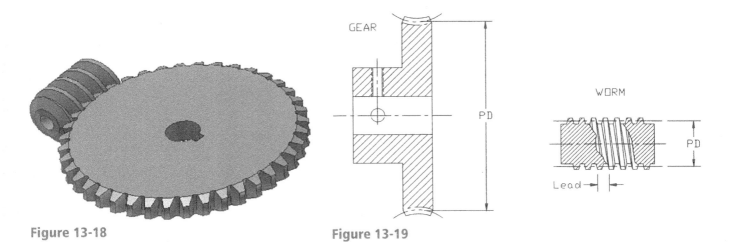

**Figure 13-18**

**Figure 13-19**

Worm gears are drawn using sectional views, as shown in Figure 13-19, or according to the representation shown in Figure 13-20. The worm teeth shown can be drawn by using the procedure for acme threads explained in Chapter 11.

**Figure 13-20**

Courtesy of WM Berg Inc.
Copyright © 2019 WM Berg.
Berg is a division of Rexnord.

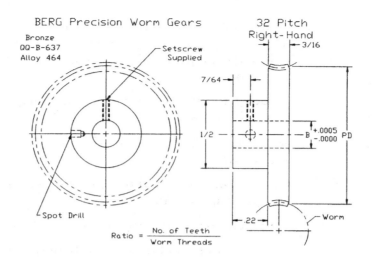

BERG Precision Worm Gears

| FOR SINGLE THREAD WORM | | FOR DOUBLE THREAD WORM | | NO. OF TEETH | PITCH DIA |
|---|---|---|---|---|---|
| CIRCULAR PITCH | .0982 | CIRCULAR PITCH | .1963 | | |
| HELIX ANGLE | 4° – 5′ | HELIX ANGLE | 8° – 8′ | | |
| PRESSURE ANGLE | 14-1/2° | PRESSURE ANGLE | 20° | | |
| STOCK NUMBER | | STOCK NUMBER | | | |
| W32B29-S20 | | W32B29-D20 | | 20 | .625 |
| W32B29-S30 | | W32B29-D30 | | 30 | .938 |
| W32B29-S40 | | W32B29-D40 | | 40 | 1.250 |
| W32B29-S50 | | W32B29-D50 | | 50 | 1.562 |
| W32B29-S60 | | W32B29-D60 | | 60 | 1.875 |
| W32B29-S80 | | W32B29-D80 | | 80 | 2.500 |
| W32B29-S96 | | W32B29-D96 | | 96 | 3.000 |
| W32B29-S100 | | W32B29-D100 | | 100 | 3.125 |
| W32B29-S120 | | W32B29-D120 | | 120 | 3.750 |
| W32B29-S180 | | W32B29-D180 | | 180 | 5.625 |

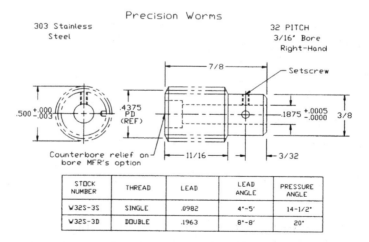

Precision Worms

| STOCK NUMBER | THREAD | LEAD | LEAD ANGLE | PRESSURE ANGLE |
|---|---|---|---|---|
| W32S-3S | SINGLE | .0982 | 4°-5′ | 14-1/2° |
| W32S-3D | DOUBLE | .1963 | 8°-8′ | 20° |

The relationship between worm gears is determined by the *lead* of the worm thread. The lead of a worm thread is similar to the pitch of a thread discussed in Chapter 11. Worm threads may be single, double, or quadruple. If a worm has a double thread, it will advance the gear twice as fast as a worm with a single thread.

## 13-15 Helical Gears

Helical gears work as shown in Figure 13-21. The two gears are called the *driver* and the *driven*, as indicated. Figure 13-22 shows a manufacturer's listing of compatible helical gears.

**Figure 13-21**
Courtesy of Stock Drive Products/Sterling Instrument, a division of Designatronics, Inc., sdp-si.com

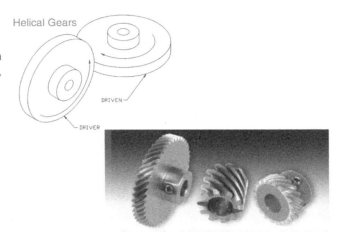

**Figure 13-22**
Courtesy of WM Berg Inc. Copyright © 2019 WM Berg. Berg is a division of Rexnord.

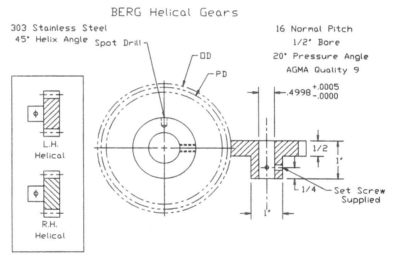

| STOCK NUMBER | | NO. OF TEETH | PITCH DIAMETER | OUTSIDE DIAMETER |
|---|---|---|---|---|
| RIGHT-HAND | LEFT-HAND | | | |
| H16S38-R 12 | H16S38-L 12 | 12 | 1.060 | 1.185 |
| H16S38-R 16 | H16S38-L 16 | 16 | 1.4142 | 1.539 |
| H16S38-R 20 | H16S38-L 20 | 20 | 1.7677 | 1.892 |
| H16S38-R 24 | H16S38-L 24 | 24 | 2.1213 | 2.246 |
| H16S38-R 32 | H16S38-L 32 | 32 | 2.8284 | 2.953 |
| H16S38-R 40 | H16S38-L 40 | 40 | 3.5355 | 3.660 |
| H16S38-R 48 | H16S38-L 48 | 48 | 4.2426 | 4.367 |

Helical gears may be manufactured with either left- or right-hand threads. Left- and right-hand threads determine the relative rotation direction of the gears.

## 13-16 Racks

*Racks* are gears whose teeth are in a straight row. Racks are used to change rotary motion into linear motion (Figure 13-23). Racks are usually driven by a spur gear called a *pinion*.

**Figure 13-23**
Courtesy of Stock Drive Products/Sterling Instrument, a division of Designatronics, Inc., sdp-si.com

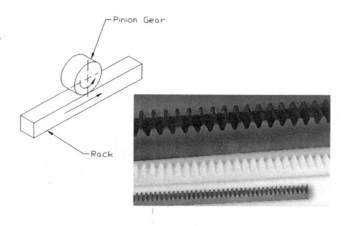

**Figure 13-24**
Courtesy of WM Berg Inc. Copyright © 2019 WM Berg. Berg is a division of Rexnord.

BERG Precision Racks

416 ST. Steel &
2024T4 Aluminum
Anodized

24 to 120 Pitch
20° Pressure Angle
AGMA Quality 10

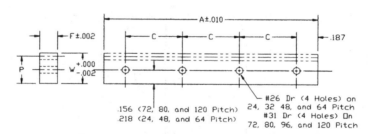

| STOCK NUMBER | MATERIAL | PITCH | A | P | W | F | C |
|---|---|---|---|---|---|---|---|
| R4-5 R4-6 | STAINLESS ST ALUMINUM | 24 | 10° | .4383 | .480 | .230 | 3.208 |
| R4-9 R4-10 | STAINLESS ST ALUMINUM | 32 | 10° | .4487 | .480 | .230 | 3.208 |
| R4-11 R4-12 | STAINLESS ST ALUMINUM | 48 | 9° | .4592 | .480 | .230 | 2.879 |
| R4-15 R4-16 | STAINLESS ST ALUMINUM | 64 | 7° | .4644 | .480 | .230 | 2.208 |
| R4-17 R4-18 | STAINLESS ST ALUMINUM | 72 | 5° | .3411 | .355 | .167 | 1.541 |
| R4-19 R4-20 | STAINLESS ST ALUMINUM | 80 | 5° | .3425 | .355 | .167 | 1.541 |
| R4-21 R4-22 | STAINLESS ST ALUMINUM | 96 | 3° | .3446 | .355 | .167 | .875 |
| R4-23 R4-24 | STAINLESS ST ALUMINUM | 120 | 3° | .3467 | .355 | .167 | .875 |

One of the most common applications of gear racks is the steering mechanism of an automobile. Rack-and-pinion steering helps create a more positive relationship between the rotation of the steering wheel and the linear input to the car's wheel than did the mechanical linkages used on older-model cars.

Figure 13-24 shows a manufacturer's list for racks. The rack and pinions must have the same pitch and pressure angle to mesh correctly.

## 13-17 Ball Bearings

*Ball bearings* are used to help eliminate friction between moving and stationary parts. The moving and stationary parts are separated by a series of balls that ride in a *race*.

Figure 13-25 shows a listing from the Stock Drive Products website for ball bearings that includes applicable dimensions and tolerances. There are many other types and sizes of ball bearings available.

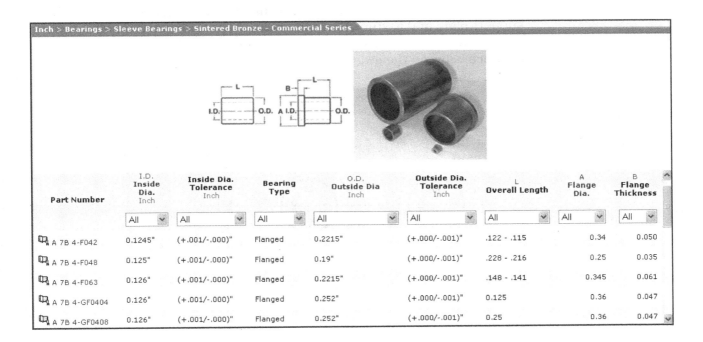

**Figure 13-25**
Courtesy of Stock Drive Products/Sterling Instrument, a division of Designatronics, Inc., sdp-si.com

Ball bearings may be drawn as shown in Figure 13-25 or by using one of the representations shown in Figure 13-26. Representations should be drawn and saved as blocks for use on future drawings.

The outside diameter of the bearings listed in Figure 13-25 has a tolerance of +.0000/−.0002. The same tolerance range applies to the center hole. These tight tolerances are manufactured because this type of ball bearing is usually assembled by using a force fit. See Chapter 9 for an explanation of fits. Ball bearings that do not assemble by the use of force fits are also available.

Figure 13-26

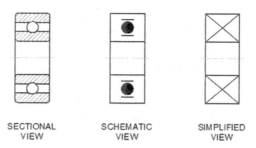

SECTIONAL VIEW　　SCHEMATIC VIEW　　SIMPLIFIED VIEW

The following drawing problem shows how ball bearings can be used to support a gear's shafts.

## 13-18 Drawing Problem

Figure 13-27 shows two spur gears and a dimensioned drawing of a shaft used to support both gears. Design a support plate for the shafts. Use ball bearings to support the shafts. Specify dimensions and tolerances for the support plate and assume that the bearings are to be fitted into the support plate by the use of an LN2 medium press fit. The tolerance for the center distance between the gears is to be +.001/−.000.

**Figure 13-27**
Courtesy of WM Berg Inc. Copyright © 2019 WM Berg. Berg is a division of Rexnord.

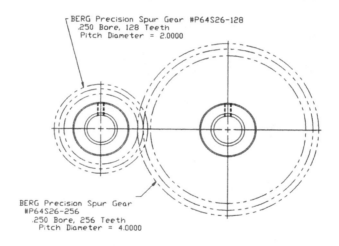

BERG Precision Spur Gear #P64S26-128
.250 Bore, 128 Teeth
Pitch Diameter = 2.0000

BERG Precision Spur Gear
#P64S26-256
.250 Bore, 256 Teeth
Pitch Diameter = 4.0000

BERG Ground Shaft
S4-30  303 Stainless Steel

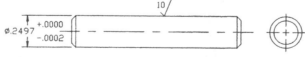

ø.2497 +.0000 / −.0002

The maximum interference permitted for an LN2 medium press fit is .0011 (see the fits tables in the online Appendix). For purposes of calculation, the bearing is considered to be the combination of the shaft and the holes in the support plate.

Maximum interference occurs when the shaft (bearing) is at its maximum diameter and the hole (support plate) is at its minimum. The maximum shaft diameter, the maximum diameter of the bearing, is .5000, as defined in the manufacturer's listing. This means that the minimum hole diameter should be .5000 − .0011 = .4989. An LN2 fit has a hole tolerance of +.0007, so the maximum hole size should be .4989 + .0007 = .4996.

The minimum interference, or the difference between the minimum shaft diameter and the maximum hole diameter, is .4998 − .4996 = .0002. There will always be at least .0002 interference between the ball bearing and the hole.

The bore of the selected bearing, listed in Figure 13-25, has a limit tolerance of .2500 − .2498. The shafts specified in Figure 13-27 have a limit tolerance of .2497 − .2495. This means that there will always be a slight clearance between the shaft and the bore hole.

The nominal center distance between the two gears is 3.000 inches. The given tolerance for the center distance is +.001/−.000. This tolerance can be ensured by assigning a positional tolerance of .0005 to each of the two holes applied at maximum material condition at the centerline. The base distance between the two holes is defined as 3.0000. The maximum center distance, including the positional tolerance, is 3.0000 + .0005 = 3.0005, and the minimum is 3.0000 − .0005 = 2.9995, or a total maximum tolerance of .001.

Figure 13-28 shows a detail drawing of the support plate.

**Figure 13-28**

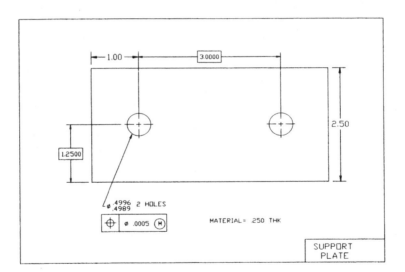

## 13-19 Bushings

A *bushing* is a cylindrically shaped bearing that helps reduce friction between a moving part and a stationary part. Bushings, unlike ball bearings, have no moving parts. Bushings are usually made from oil-impregnated bronze or Teflon. Figure 13-29 shows a manufacturer's list of bronze bushings, and Figure 13-30 shows a list of Teflon bushings.

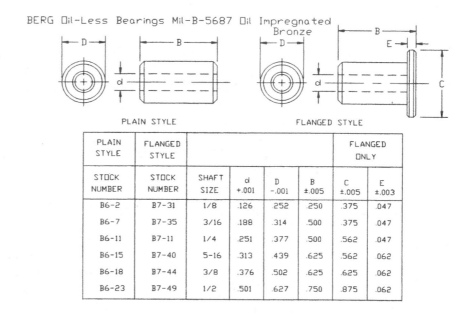

**Figure 13-29**
Courtesy of WM Berg Inc. Copyright © 2019 WM Berg. Berg is a division of Rexnord.

BERG Oil-Less Bearings Mil-B-5687 Oil Impregnated Bronze

PLAIN STYLE          FLANGED STYLE

| PLAIN STYLE | FLANGED STYLE | | | | | FLANGED ONLY | |
|---|---|---|---|---|---|---|---|
| STOCK NUMBER | STOCK NUMBER | SHAFT SIZE | d +.001 | D -.001 | B ±.005 | C ±.005 | E ±.003 |
| B6-2 | B7-31 | 1/8 | .126 | .252 | .250 | .375 | .047 |
| B6-7 | B7-35 | 3/16 | .188 | .314 | .500 | .375 | .047 |
| B6-11 | B7-11 | 1/4 | .251 | .377 | .500 | .562 | .047 |
| B6-15 | B7-40 | 5-16 | .313 | .439 | .625 | .562 | .062 |
| B6-18 | B7-44 | 3/8 | .376 | .502 | .625 | .625 | .062 |
| B6-23 | B7-49 | 1/2 | .501 | .627 | .750 | .875 | .062 |

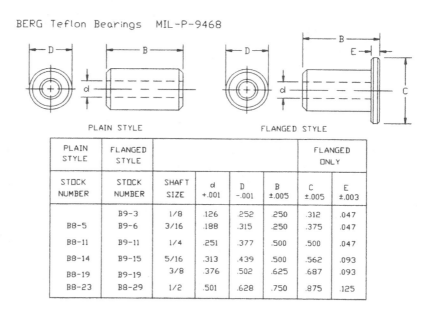

**Figure 13-30**
Courtesy of WM Berg Inc. Copyright © 2019 WM Berg. Berg is a division of Rexnord.

BERG Teflon Bearings  MIL-P-9468

PLAIN STYLE          FLANGED STYLE

| PLAIN STYLE | FLANGED STYLE | | | | | FLANGED ONLY | |
|---|---|---|---|---|---|---|---|
| STOCK NUMBER | STOCK NUMBER | SHAFT SIZE | d +.001 | D -.001 | B ±.005 | C ±.005 | E ±.003 |
| | B9-3 | 1/8 | .126 | .252 | .250 | .312 | .047 |
| B8-5 | B9-6 | 3/16 | .188 | .315 | .250 | .375 | .047 |
| B8-11 | B9-11 | 1/4 | .251 | .377 | .500 | .500 | .047 |
| B8-14 | B9-15 | 5/16 | .313 | .439 | .500 | .562 | .093 |
| B8-19 | B9-19 | 3/8 | .376 | .502 | .625 | .687 | .093 |
| B8-23 | B8-29 | 1/2 | .501 | .628 | .750 | .875 | .125 |

Bushings are cheaper than ball bearings, but they wear over time, particularly if the application is high speed or involves heavy loading. Bushings are usually pressed into a supporting plate. Gear shafts must always have clearance from the inside diameters of bushings.

## 13-20 Drawing Problem

The drawing problem is to design a support system for two bevel gears. Figure 13-31 shows two support plates used to support and align a matched set of bevel gears. The gears selected are numbered S1346Z–48S30S60 in the list presented in Figure 13-16. The calculations are similar to those presented earlier for Drawing Problem 13-18 but with the addition of tolerances for the holes and machine screws used to join the two perpendicular support plates together.

**Figure 13-31**

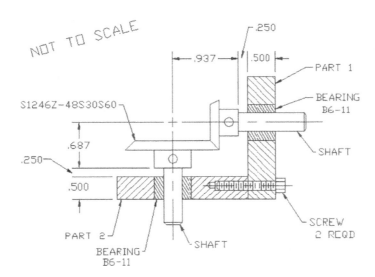

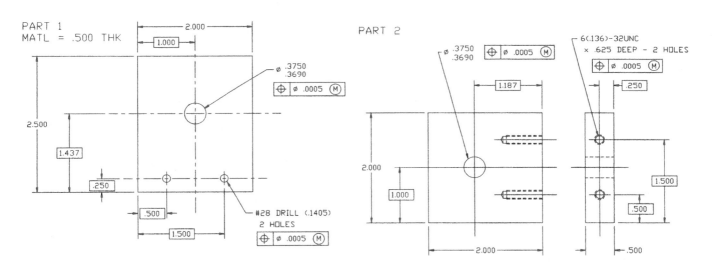

Figure 13-31 shows an assembly drawing of the two gears along with appropriate bushings, stock number B6 11 from Figure 13-29, and shafts and supporting parts 1 and 2. The figure also shows detail drawings of the two support plates with appropriate dimensions and tolerances.

The bushings are fitted into the support plates by the use of an FN1 fit. The fit tables in the online Appendix define the maximum interference for an FN1 fit as .0075 and the minimum interference as .0001. The outside diameter of the bushing has a tolerance of .3770 – .3760, per Figure 13-29. The feature tolerances for the holes in the support parts are found as follows:

Shaft max – Hole min = Interference max

Shaft min – Hole max = Interference min

The feature tolerance for the hole is therefore .3750 – .3695.

The positional tolerance is determined as described in the drawing problem in Section 13-18 and is based on a tolerance of 0.001 between gear centers.

## 13-21 Cam Displacement Diagrams

A *displacement diagram* is used to define the motion of a cam follower. Displacement diagrams are set up as shown in Figure 13-32. The horizontal axis is marked off in 12 equal spaces that represent 30° on the cam. The vertical axis is used to define the linear displacement of the follower and is defined either in inches or in millimeters.

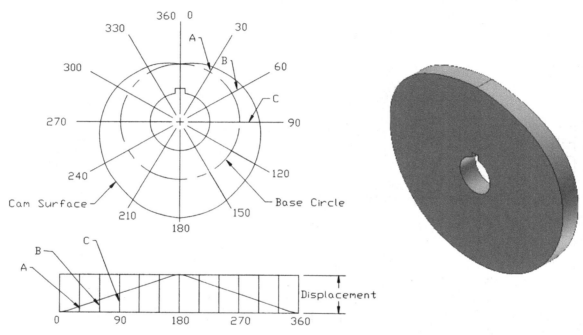

**Figure 13-32**

The vertical axis of a displacement diagram must be drawn to scale because, once defined, the vertical distances are transferred to the cam's base circle to define the cam's shape. Figure 13-32 shows distances A, B, and C on both the displacement diagram and cam. The distances define the follower displacement at the 30°, 60°, and 90° marks, respectively.

The horizontal axis may use any equal spacing to indicate the angle because the vertical distances will be transferred to the cam along ray lines. The lower horizontal line represents the circumference of the base circle.

Figure 13-33 shows a second displacement diagram. Note how the distance between the 30° and 90° lines has been further subdivided. The additional lines are used to more accurately define the cam motion. Additional degree lines are often added when the follower is undergoing a rapid change of motion.

Figure 13-33

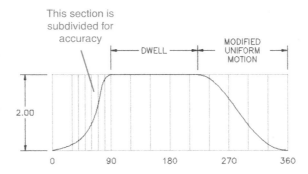

The term *dwell* means that the cam follower does not move either up or down as the cam turns. Dwells are drawn as straight horizontal lines on a displacement diagram. Note the horizontal line between the 90° and 210° lines on the displacement diagram shown in Figure 13-33. Dwells are drawn as sectors of constant radius on the cam.

## Setting Up a Displacement Diagram

In the diagram in Figure 13-34, the dimensions are given in inches, with millimeter equivalents in brackets, [ ].

**1** Set **Grid** to **.5 [10]** and **Snap** to **.25 [5]**.

**2** Draw a horizontal line **6 [120]** long.

**3** Draw a vertical line **2 [40]** from the left end of the horizontal line, as shown.

Figure 13-34

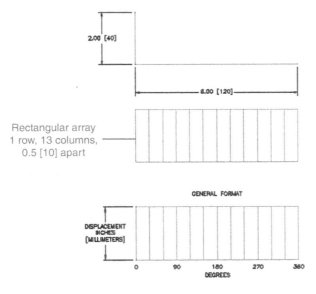

The length 2 [40] was chosen arbitrarily for this example. The vertical distance should be equal to the total displacement of the follower.

**4** Use the **Array** command to create a rectangular array with **12** columns **.5 [10]** apart. Draw a horizontal line across the top of the diagram.

**5** Label the horizontal axis in degrees, with each vertical line representing **30°** and the vertical axis in inches [millimeters] of displacement.

## 13-22 Cam Motions

The shape of a cam surface is designed to move a follower through a specific distance. The surface also determines the acceleration, deceleration, and smoothness of motion of the follower. It is important that a cam surface be shaped to maintain continuous contact with the follower. Several standard cam motions are defined next.

## Uniform Motion

Uniform motion is drawn as a straight line on a displacement diagram (Figure 13-35). The follower rises the same distance for each degree of rotation by the cam.

**Figure 13-35**

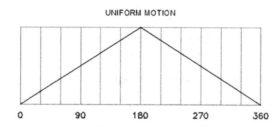

## Modified Uniform Motion

Modified uniform motion is similar to uniform motion but has a curved radius shape added to each end of the line to facilitate a smooth transition from the uniform motion to another type of motion or to a dwell section.

Figure 13-36 shows how to create a modified uniform motion on a displacement diagram. The procedure is as follows:

**1** Set up a displacement diagram, as presented in the preceding section.

**Figure 13-36**

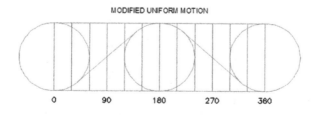

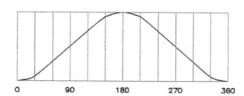

**2** Draw two arcs or circles of radius no greater than half of the required displacement.

Any radius value can be used. In general, the larger the radius, the smoother the transition will be. In the example shown, a radius equal to half of the total displacement was used.

**3** Use **Tangent** object snap and draw a line between the two arcs.

**4** Erase and trim any excess lines.

## Harmonic Motion

Figure 13-37 shows how to create a harmonic cam motion. The procedure is as follows:

**1** Set up a displacement diagram as presented in Section 13-21.

**Figure 13-37**

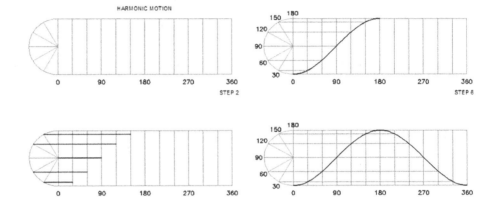

**2** Draw a semicircle aligned with the left side of the displacement diagram. The diameter of the semicircle equals the total height of the displacement.

**3** Use the **Array** command or the **Line** command with relative coordinate inputs and draw lines every **30°** on the semicircle, as shown. Label the lines from 0° to 180° in 30° segments.

**4** Using **Intersection** object snap with **Ortho** on, press **F8** and draw projection lines from the intersections of the radial lines with the circumference of the semicircle across the displacement diagram.

**5** Draw a spline that starts at the lower-left corner of the diagram and connects the intersections of like angle lines.

```
Enter next point or [start Tangency toLerance]:
Specify start tangent:
```

**6** Enter **T** to set the starting tangency and pick a point along the bottom line of the displacement diagram. Then pick the intersections of the projection lines with the vertical diagram lines. For this example, the horizontal line from the semicircle's 30° increment intersects with the vertical line from the 30° mark on the displacement diagram.

```
Enter next point or [end Tangency toLerance Undo]:
Specify end tangent:
```

**7** After you pick the last point at the top of the 180° line, enter **T** to set the ending tangency and pick a point on the top line of the diagram.

**8** Project the same lines to the far side of the diagram to define the deceleration harmonic motion path.

## Uniform Acceleration and Deceleration

Uniform acceleration and deceleration are based on the knowledge that acceleration is related to distance by the square of the distance. Acceleration is measured in distance per second squared. Distances of units 1, 2, and 3 may be expressed as 1, 4, and 9, respectively.

Uniform acceleration and deceleration motions create smooth transitions between various displacement heights and are often used in high-speed applications.

Figure 13-38 shows how to create a uniform acceleration cam motion. The procedure is as follows:

**1** Set up a displacement diagram as presented in Section 13-21.

**Figure 13-38**

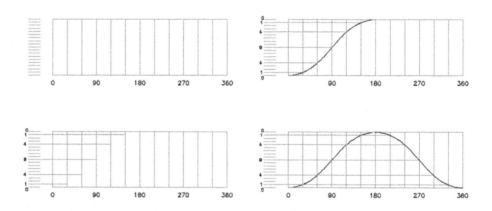

**2** Draw a horizontal construction line to the left and align it with the bottom horizontal line of the displacement diagram.

**3** Use the **Array** command and create **1** column and **19** rows that are **.1111** apart.

The 19 rows create 18 spaces. The uniform motion shape is created by combining six horizontal steps (30°, 60°, 90°, 120°, 150°, 180°) and the squares of six vertical steps (1, 4, 9, 4, 1, 0).

The vertical spacing is symmetrical about the centerline of the displacement diagram, so the original spacing is 1, 2, 3, 2, 1. The square of these values is used to create the uniform acceleration and deceleration.

The .1111 value was derived by dividing the displacement distance by the number of spaces, 2.00/18 = .1111.

**4** Label the stack of vertical construction lines as shown.

5. Use **Extend** to extend the horizontal construction lines so that they intersect with the appropriate vertical degree line.

6. Use **Spline Fit** to create a smooth, continuous curve between the 0° and 180° lines.

The same line may be used to create a deceleration curve, as shown.

## 13-23 Cam Followers

There are two basic types of cam followers: those that roll as they follow the cam's surface and those that have a fixed surface which slides in contact with the cam surface. Figure 13-39 shows an example of a roller follower and a fixed- or flat-surface follower. The flat-surface-type followers are limited to slow-moving cams with low force requirements.

**Figure 13-39**

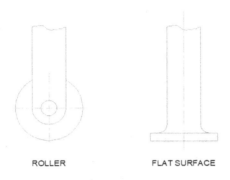

ROLLER          FLAT SURFACE

Followers are usually spring loaded to keep them in contact with the cam surface during operation. Springs are discussed in Section 11-24.

## 13-24 Drawing Problem

Design a cam that rises 2.00 inches over 180° by harmonic motion, dwells for 60°, descends 2.00 inches in 90° by modified uniform motion, and dwells the remaining 30°. The base circle for the cam is 3.00 inches in diameter, and the follower is a roller type with a 1.00-inch diameter. The cam will rotate in a counterclockwise direction. The center hole is .75 inch in diameter with a .125 × .875 keyway (Figures 13-40 and 13-41).

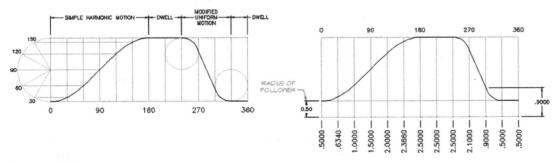

**Figure 13-40**

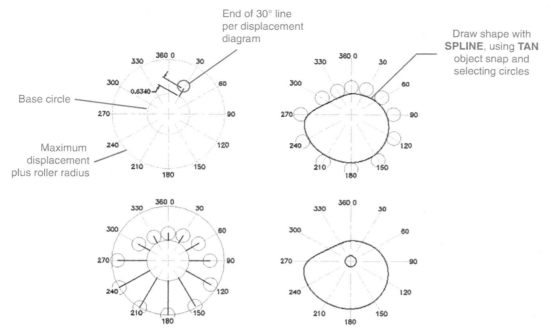

**Figure 13-41**

1. Set up a displacement diagram as described in Section 13-21.

2. Define a path between the 0° and 180° vertical lines, using the method described for harmonic motion. Draw the required semicircle on the left end of the diagram as shown.

3. Draw a horizontal line from the 180° line to the 240° line.

   This line defines the follower's dwell.

4. Using **Circle Ttr**, draw two circles of **.50** radius, one tangent to the top horizontal line of the displacement diagram and the second tangent to the bottom line.

   Draw one circle on the 240° line and the other on the 330° line as shown. In this example, the circles have a radius equal to .25 of the total displacement. Any convenient radius value may be used.

5. Use **Tangent** object snap, and draw a line tangent to the two arcs.

6. Erase and trim any excess lines and constructions.

   This completes the displacement diagram. The follower distances are now transferred to the cam's base circle to define the surface shape (Figure 13-41).

7. Draw two concentric circles of **3.00** diameter and **8.00** diameter, respectively.

   The 3.00 diameter is the base circle. The 8.00-diameter-circle value is derived from the radius of the base circle, plus the maximum displacement, plus the radius of the follower: 1.50 + 2 + .5 = 4.00 radius, or 8.00 diameter.

**8** Use the **Center Mark** tool to draw the centerlines for the 8.00 circle. Explode the center mark.

You will array the upper vertical line of the center mark, so you must explode the mark into its individual lines.

**9** Using **Polar Array**, array the top portion of the vertical centerline **12** times around the full 360°.

**10** Label the radial lines as shown.

Note that the top vertical line is labeled as both 0 and 360.

**11** Transfer the follower distances from the displacement diagram to the cam drawing.

In this example, the measured distance values are listed below the displacement diagram in Figure 13-40. The .50 addition to the bottom of the diagram accounts for the .50 follower radius. Note how the distance of 2.1000 was measured on the displacement diagram (Figure 13-40).

Use the distance values to draw lines from the base circle along the appropriate radial line on the cam drawing using relative coordinate values. The values for this example are as follows:

| | |
|---|---|
| .5000-(0) | @.5000 < 90 |
| .6340-(30) | @.6340 < 60 |
| 1.0000-(60) | @1.0000 < 30 |
| 1.5000-(90) | @1.5000 < 0 |
| 2.0000-(120) | @2.0000 < –30 |
| 2.3660-(150) | @2.3660 < –60 |
| 2.5000-(180) | @2.5000 < –90 |
| 2.5000-(210) | @2.5000 < –120 |
| 2.5000-(240) | @2.5000 < –150 |
| 2.1000-(270) | @2.1000 < 180 |
| .9000-(300) | @.9000 < 150 |
| .5000-(330) | @.5000 < 120 |

**12** Draw circles of diameter **.50**, representing the roller follower, with their center points on the ends of the lines created in step 11.

Note that these lines and their endpoints are not visible on the screen because they are drawn directly over the existing radial lines. **Endpoint** object snap should be used to locate the circle's center point.

**13** Using the **Spline** command, draw a line tangent to the follower at each radial line.

The tangent point for each line may not be exactly on the line due to rounding in the calculations used to create the spline.

**14** Draw the center hole and keyway according to the given dimensions.

**15** Save the drawings, if desired.

# 13-25 EXERCISE PROBLEMS

## EX13-1 Inches

Draw a spur gear with 24 teeth on a 4.00-pitch circle. The fillets at the base of each tooth have a radius of .0625. Locate a 1.00-diameter mounting hole in the center of the gear.

## EX13-2 Millimeters

Draw a spur gear with 36 teeth on a 100-pitch circle. The fillets at the base of each tooth have a radius of 3. Locate a 20-diameter mounting hole in the center of the gear.

## EX13-3

Using the information presented in Figure 13-12, draw front and side sectional views of gear number A 1C22MYKW150 32A.

## EX13-4

Using the information presented in Figure 13-12, draw front and side sectional views of gear number A 1C22MYKW150 64A.

## EX13-5

Using the information presented in Figure 13-15, draw a sectional view of bevel gears A 1C3MYK 30018 and A 1C3MYK 30036H.

## EX13-6

Using the information presented in Figure 13-15, draw a sectional view of bevel gears A 1C3MYK 15018 and A 1C3MYK 15036.

## EX13-7

Using the information presented in Figure 13-16, draw a sectional view of the matched set of bevel gears S1346Z–48S30A120.

## EX13-8

Using the information presented in Figure 13-20, draw front and side views of a set of worm gears.

## EX13-9

Using the information presented in Figure 13-22, draw a front view of a matched set of helical gears.

## EX13-10

Using the information presented in Figure 13-24, draw a front view of a set of rack-and-pinion gears. Select a pinion gear from Figure 13-12.

## EX13-11 Inches

Draw a displacement diagram and appropriate cam on the basis of the following information:

- Dwell for 60°, rise 1.00 inch by harmonic motion over 180°, dwell for 30°, then descend 1.00 inch by harmonic motion over 90°.

- The cam's base circle is 4.00 inches in diameter. Include a 1.25-inch center mounting hole.

## EX13-12 Millimeters

Draw a displacement diagram and appropriate cam on the basis of the following information:

- Dwell for 60°, rise 30 millimeters by harmonic motion over 180°, dwell for 30°, and then descend 30 millimeters by harmonic motion over 90°.

- The cam's base circle is 120 millimeters in diameter. Include a 20-millimeter center mounting hole.

## EX13-13 Inches

Draw a displacement diagram and appropriate cam on the basis of the following information:

- Rise 1.25 inches over 180° by uniform acceleration motion, dwell for 60°, descend 1.25 inches over 90° by modified uniform motion, dwell for 30°.

- The cam's base circle is 3.25 inches in diameter. Include a .75-inch-diameter center mounting hole.

## EX13-15 Inches

Draw a displacement diagram and appropriate cam on the basis of the following information:

- Rise 0.60 inch in 90° by harmonic motion, dwell for 30°, rise .60 inch in 60° by modified uniform motion, dwell 60°, descend 1.20 inches by uniform deceleration in 120°.

- The cam's base circle is 3.20 inches in diameter. Include a 1.75-inch-diameter center mounting hole.

## EX13-17 Inches

Draw a displacement diagram and appropriate cam on the basis of the following information:

- The cam's base circle is 2.00 inches.

- Include a Ø0.625 center mounting hole.

- Rise 0.375 inch in 90° by harmonic motion, dwell for 90°, rise 0.375 inch in 90° by harmonic motion, descend 0.750 inch by harmonic motion in 90°.

## EX13-19 Inches

Draw a displacement diagram and appropriate cam on the basis of the following information:

- The cam's base circle is 2.00 inches.

- Include a Ø0.625 center mounting hole.

- Rise 0.375 inch in 90° by uniform acceleration and deceleration motion, dwell for 90°, rise 0.375 inch in 90° by uniform acceleration and deceleration motion, descend 0.750 inch by harmonic motion in 90°.

## EX13-14 Millimeters

Draw a displacement diagram and appropriate cam on the basis of the following information:

- Rise 20 millimeters over 180° by uniform acceleration motion, dwell for 60°, descend 20 millimeters over 90° by modified uniform motion, dwell for 30°.

- The cam's base circle is 80 millimeters in diameter. Include a 16-millimeter-diameter center mounting hole.

## EX13-16 Millimeters

Draw a displacement diagram and appropriate cam on the basis of the following information:

- Rise 16 millimeters in 90° by harmonic motion, dwell for 30°, rise 16 millimeters in 60° by modified uniform motion, dwell 60°, descend 32 millimeters by uniform deceleration in 120°.

- The cam's base circle is 84 millimeters in diameter. Include a 20-millimeter-diameter center mounting hole.

## EX13-18 Millimeters

Draw a displacement diagram and appropriate cam on the basis of the following information:

- The cam's base circle is 98 millimeters.

- Include a Ø18 center mounting hole.

- Rise 15 millimeters in 90° by harmonic motion, dwell for 90°, rise 15 millimeters in 90° by harmonic motion, descend 30 millimeters by harmonic motion in 90°.

## EX13-20 Millimeters

Draw a displacement diagram and appropriate cam on the basis of the following information:

- The cam's base circle is 98 millimeters.

- Include a Ø18 millimeter center mounting hole.

- Rise 15 millimeters in 90° by uniform acceleration and deceleration motion, dwell for 90°, rise 15 millimeters in 90° by uniform acceleration and deceleration motion, descend 30 millimeters by harmonic motion in 90°.

# EX13-21 Inches

Draw an assembly drawing and parts list for the two-gear assembly shown.

2-GEAR ASSEMBLY

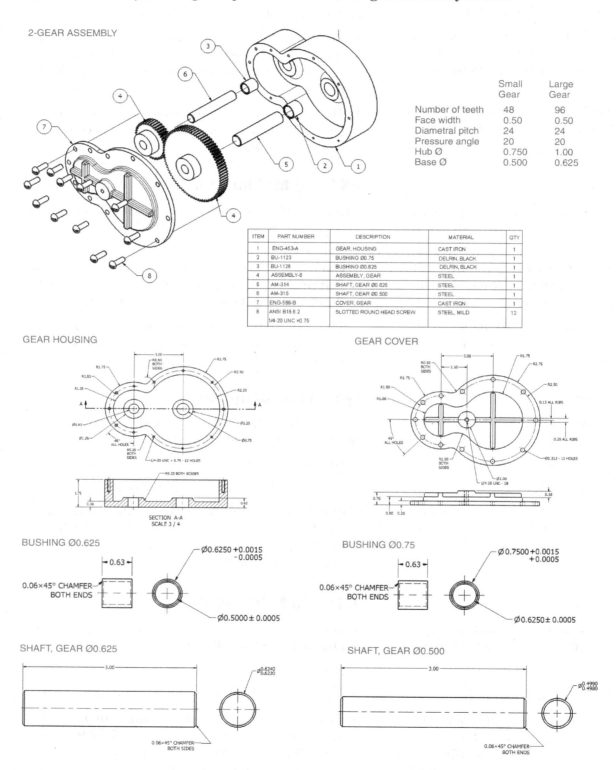

|  | Small Gear | Large Gear |
|---|---|---|
| Number of teeth | 48 | 96 |
| Face width | 0.50 | 0.50 |
| Diametral pitch | 24 | 24 |
| Pressure angle | 20 | 20 |
| Hub Ø | 0.750 | 1.00 |
| Base Ø | 0.500 | 0.625 |

| ITEM | PART NUMBER | DESCRIPTION | MATERIAL | QTY |
|---|---|---|---|---|
| 1 | ENG-453-A | GEAR, HOUSING | CAST IRON | 1 |
| 2 | BU-1123 | BUSHING Ø0.75 | DELRIN, BLACK | 1 |
| 3 | BU-1126 | BUSHING Ø0.825 | DELRIN, BLACK | 1 |
| 4 | ASSEMBLY-8 | ASSEMBLY, GEAR | STEEL | 1 |
| 5 | AM-314 | SHAFT, GEAR Ø0.825 | STEEL | 1 |
| 6 | AM-315 | SHAFT, GEAR Ø0.500 | STEEL | 1 |
| 7 | ENG-588-B | COVER, GEAR | CAST IRON | 1 |
| 8 | ANSI B18.6.2 | SLOTTED ROUND HEAD SCREW | STEEL, MILD | 12 |
|  | 1/4-20 UNC ×0.75 |  |  |  |

GEAR HOUSING

SECTION A-A
SCALE 3 / 4

GEAR COVER

BUSHING Ø0.625

BUSHING Ø0.75

SHAFT, GEAR Ø0.625

SHAFT, GEAR Ø0.500

## EX13-22

An electric motor operates at 3600 rpm. Design a gear that includes at least four spur gears (or more, if needed) and reduces the motor speed to 200 rpm. Select gears and bearings from the tables in this book or from manufacturers' websites. Design each shaft as needed.

Enclose the gears in a box made from .50-inch [12-millimeter] plates, assembled using flat head screws. There should be at least three screws per edge on the box.

Extend the shafts for the input and output, at least .50 [12] outside of the box. The other shafts should end at the edge of the box. Mount each shaft by using two ball bearings, one mounted in each support plate.

Assume that the center distances have tolerances of +.001/−.000 and the support shafts have tolerances of +.0000/−.0002, or their respective metric equivalents.

**1** Draw an assembly drawing, showing the gears in their assembled positions.

**2** Support the gear shafts with ball bearings press-fitted into the support plate. The support plate is to be .50 inch, or 12 millimeters, thick. The length and width dimensions are arbitrary, but there should be at least .25 [6] clearance between the gears and the support plate.

**3** Draw detail drawings of the required support plates and shafts. Include dimensions and tolerances. Locate all support holes by using positional tolerances.

Suggested websites:

www.wmberg.com

www.bostongear.com

www.newmantools.com

Do your own search for gears and bearings.

Top and end pieces omitted for clarity

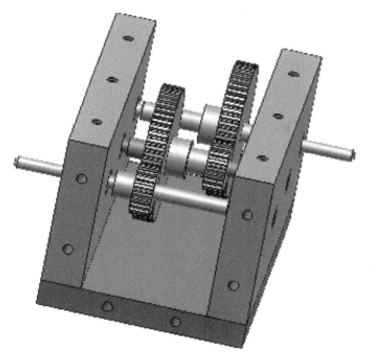

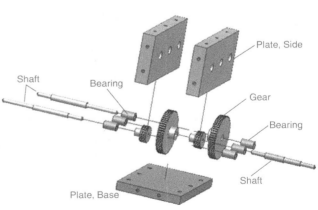

## EX13-23

The accompanying figure shows a general setup for matched bevel gears. Complete the design for a gear box with a ratio of 3:1 between the two gears. Select appropriate bearings and fasteners. Dimension and tolerance the shaft sizes and each of the six supporting plates. Extend the input and output shafts by at least 1.00 inch [24 millimeters] beyond the surface of the box.

Assume that the center distances have tolerances of +.001/−.000 and the support shafts have tolerances of +.0000/−.0002, or their respective metric equivalents.

The figure shown represents half of the gear box. The other half includes another three plates without the holes for the shafts. There should be at least three screws in each edge of the box.

**1** Draw an assembly drawing that shows the gears in their assembled positions.

**2** Support the gear shafts with ball bearings press-fitted into the support plate. The support plate is to be .50 inch, or 12 millimeters, thick. The length and width dimensions are arbitrary, but there should be at least .375 [10] clearance between the gears and the support plates.

**3** Draw detail drawings of the required support plates. Include dimensions and tolerances. Locate all support holes, using positional tolerances.

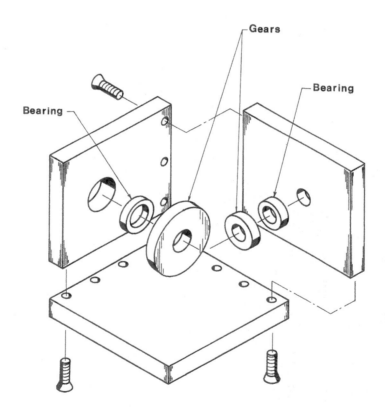

Gears

Bearing

Bearing

# EX13-24 Millimeters

Draw an assembly drawing and parts list for the four-gear assembly shown.

4-GEAR ASSEMBLY

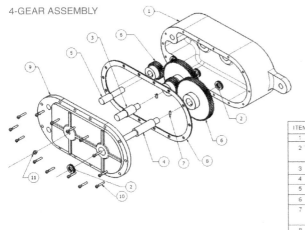

| ITEM | PART NUMBER | DESCRIPTION | MATERIAL | QTY |
|------|-------------|-------------|----------|-----|
| 1 | ENG-311-1 | HOUSING, 4 GEAR | CAST IRON | 1 |
| 2 | BS 5989, PART 1 010 - 20×32×8 | BALL BEARING, THRUST | STEEL, MILD | 4 |
| 3 | SH-4002 | SHAFT, NEUTRAL | STEEL | 1 |
| 4 | SH-4003 | SHAFT, OUTPUT | STEEL | 1 |
| 5 | SH-4004A | SHAFT, INPUT | STEEL | 1 |
| 6 | | ASSEMBLY, 4-GEAR | STEEL | 2 |
| 7 | CSN 02 1181 M6 × 16 | SET SCREW, SLOTTED HEADLESS - FLAT POINT | STEEL, MILD | 2 |
| 8 | ENG-312-1 | GASKET | BRASS, SOFT YELLOW | 1 |
| 9 | ENG-312-2 | COVER | CAST IRON | 1 |
| 10 | CNS 4355-M6×35 | SCREW, SLOTTED CHEESE HEAD | STEEL, MILD | 14 |
| 11 | CSN 02 7421- M10 × 1 coned short | NIPPLE, LUBRICATING, CONED TYPE A | STEEL, MILD | 1 |

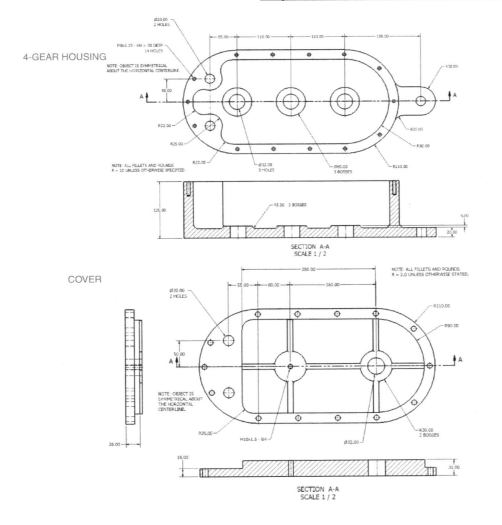

4-GEAR HOUSING

COVER

## GASKET

NOTE: HOLE PATTERN IS THE SAME FOR THE
GASKET, GEAR HOUSING, AND GEAR COVER.

NOTE: OBJECT IS SYMMETRICAL ABOUT
THE HORIZONTAL CENTERLINE.

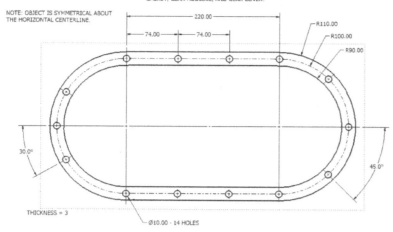

220.00

74.00    74.00

R110.00
R100.00
R90.00

30.0°

45.0°

THICKNESS = 3

Ø10.00 - 14 HOLES

## GEAR ASSEMBLY

Large Gear
Module = 2
Pitch Ø = 160
Number of teeth = 80

Small Gear
Module = 2
Pitch Ø = 60
Number of teeth = 30

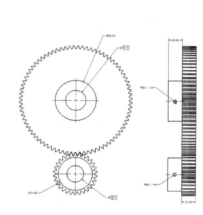

## INPUT SHAFT

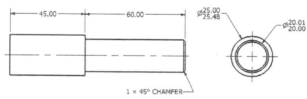

45.00    60.00

Ø25.00 / 25.48

Ø20.01 / 20.00

1 × 45° CHAMFER

## OUTPUT SHAFT

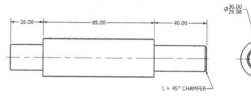

25.00    85.00    40.00

Ø30.00 / 29.98

Ø20.01 / 20.00 BOTH ENDS

1 × 45° CHAMFER

## NEUTRAL SHAFT

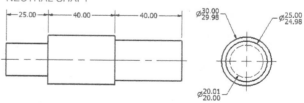

25.00    40.00    40.00

Ø30.00 / 29.98

Ø25.00 / 24.98

Ø20.01 / 20.00

## LUBRICATING NIPPLE

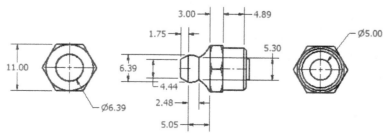

3.00    4.89

1.75

5.30

11.00

6.39

4.44

2.48

5.05

Ø5.00

Ø6.39

## EX13-25

Perform the following functions for the slider assembly shown:

**1** Select the appropriate fasteners.

**2** Create an assembly drawing.

**3** Create a parts list.

**4** Specify the tolerance for the guide shaft/bearings interface.

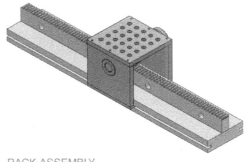

RACK ASSEMBLY

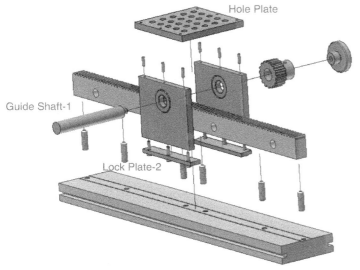

Guide Shaft-1

Lock Plate-2

RACK ASSEMBLY - 1

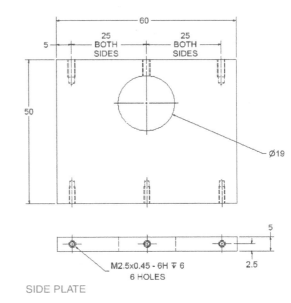

Ø19

M2.5x0.45 - 6H ⍌ 6
6 HOLES

SIDE PLATE

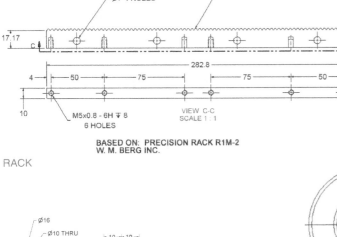

Ø7-4 HOLES

1.25 MODULE, 20° PRESSURE ANGLE

17.17

282.8

4 — 50 — 75 — 75 — 50 — 4

10

M5x0.8 - 6H ⍌ 8
6 HOLES

VIEW C-C
SCALE 1 : 1

5

BASED ON: PRECISION RACK R1M-2
W. M. BERG INC.

RACK

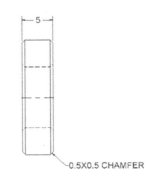

Ø19

Ø10

5

BALL BEARING
W. M. BERG INC.
PART NUMBER: B1M-11

0.5X0.5 CHAMFER

Ø16

Ø10 THRU

M3.5x0.6 - 6H ⍌ 4

10 — 10

PITCH Ø = 20.00

1.25 MODULE

PRECISION SPUR GEAR
W. M. BERG INC.
PART NUMBER: PBS86-16

GEAR 16

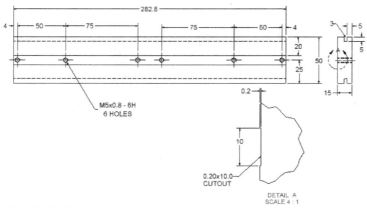

M5x0.8 - 6H
6 HOLES

0.20x10.0
CUTOUT

DETAIL A
SCALE 4 : 1

BASE SLIDER

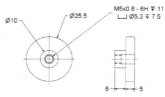

M5x0.8 - 6H ⍋ 11
⊔ Ø5.3 ⍋ 7.5

Ø10        Ø25.5

KNURLED THUMB NUT
W. M. BERG INC.
STOCK NUMBER: PD1M-15
THUMB NUT

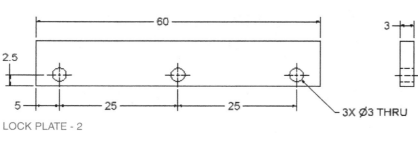

3X Ø3 THRU

LOCK PLATE - 2

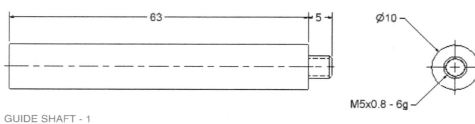

Ø10

M5x0.8 - 6g

GUIDE SHAFT - 1

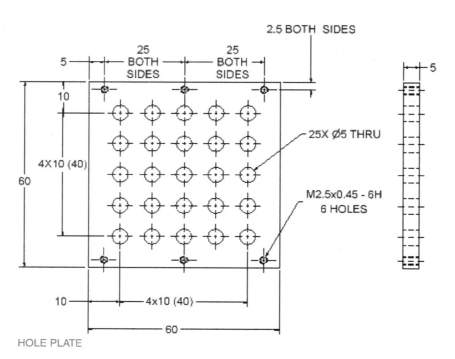

2.5 BOTH SIDES

25
BOTH
SIDES

25
BOTH
SIDES

4X10 (40)

25X Ø5 THRU

M2.5x0.45 - 6H
6 HOLES

4x10 (40)

HOLE PLATE

# EX13-26 Millimeters

Draw an assembly drawing and parts list for the cam assembly shown.

### Cam parameters:

Base circle = Ø146

Face width = 16

Motion: rise 10 by harmonic motion in 90°, dwell for 180°, fall 10 in 90°

Bore = Ø 16.0

Keyway = 2.3 × 5 × 16

Follower Ø = 16

Follower width = 4

Square key = 5 × 5 × 16

### Bearing overall dimensions:

DIN625-SKF 6203 (ID × OD × THK) 17 × 40 × 10

DIN625-SKF 634 4 × 13 × 4

GB 2273.2-87-7/70 8 × 18 × 5

### Spring parameters:

Wire Ø = 1.5

Inside Ø = 9.0

Length = 20

Coil direction = Right

Active coils = 10

Grind both ends

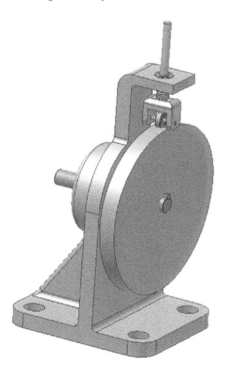

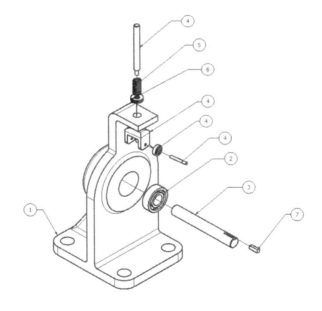

| Parts List | | | |
|---|---|---|---|
| ITEM | QTY | PART NUMBER | DESCRIPTION |
| 1 | 1 | ENG-2008-A | BASE, CAST |
| 2 | 1 | DIN625 - SKF 6203 | Single row ball bearings |
| 3 | 1 | SHF-4004-16 | SHAFT: Ø16×120, WITH 2.3×5×16 KEYWAY |
| 4 | 1 | | SUBASSEMBLY, FOLLOWER |
| 5 | 1 | SPR-C22 | SPRING, COMPRESSION |
| 6 | 1 | GB 273.2-87 - 7/70 - 8 x 18 x 5 | Rolling bearings - Thrust bearings - Plan of boundary dimensions |
| 7 | 1 | IS 2048 - 1983 - Specification for Parallel Keys and Keyways B 5 x 5 x 16 | Specification for Parallel Keys and Keyways |

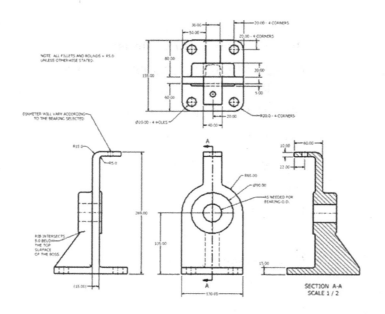

NOTE: ALL FILLETS AND ROUNDS + R5.0 UNLESS OTHERWISE STATED.

DIAMETER WILL VARY ACCORDING TO THE BEARING SELECTED.

AS NEEDED FOR BEARING O.D.

RIB INTERSECTS 5.0 BELOW THE TOP SURFACE OF THE BOSS

SECTION A-A
SCALE 1 / 2

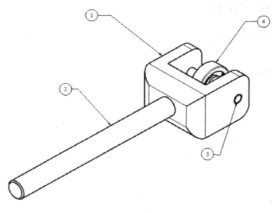

| Parts List | | | | |
|------|-------------|-------------|------------|-----|
| ITEM | PART NUMBER | DESCRIPTION | MATERIAL | QTY |
| 1 | AM-232 | HOLDER | STEEL | 1 |
| 2 | AM-256 | POST, FOLLOWER | STEEL | 1 |
| 3 | BS 1804-2 - 4 x 30 | Parallel steel dowel pins - metric series | Steel, Mild | 1 |
| 4 | DIN625- SKF 634 | Single row ball bearings | Steel, Mild | 1 |

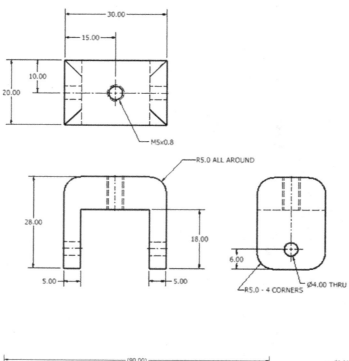

30.00

15.00

10.00

20.00

M5x0.8

R5.0 ALL AROUND

28.00

18.00

5.00

5.00

6.00

R5.0 - 4 CORNERS

Ø4.00 THRU

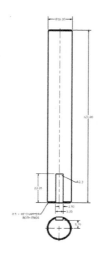

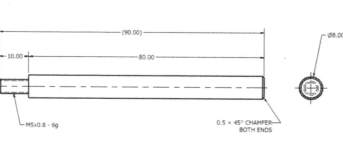

(90.00)

10.00

80.00

Ø8.00

M5x0.8 - 6g

0.5 × 45° CHAMFER BOTH ENDS

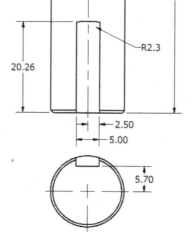

20.26

R2.3

2.50

5.00

5.70

# chapter fourteen
# Fundamentals of 3D Modeling

## 14-1 Introduction

This chapter introduces the fundamental concepts needed to produce 3D models in AutoCAD using the 3D Modeling tools with the **acad3D** and **acad-iso3D** templates. You will make the **3D Modeling** *workspace* current. This workspace presents many additional tools that are absent from the **Drawing & Annotation** workspace you have used up until now. This chapter also shows how to change viewpoints and how to create, save, and work with user-defined coordinate systems called *user coordinate systems*, or *UCSs*.

> **NOTE**
>
> A *workspace* is a collection of menus and tools that you use to make relevant settings and select 3D commands. You can access workspaces by using the **Quick Access Toolbar** or by clicking the **Workspace Switching** button in the status bar.

This chapter demonstrates how to use both the **Model Viewports** and **Coordinates** panels on the **Visualize** tab of the **3D Modeling** ribbon. It also shows how to create orthographic views from given 3D objects by using the **View** panel tools.

## 14-2 The World Coordinate System

AutoCAD's absolute coordinate system is called the *world coordinate system (WCS)*. The default setting for the WCS is a viewing position located so that you are looking at the system 90° to its XY plane (Figure 14-1).

Figure 14-1

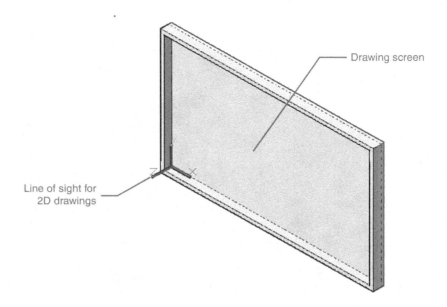

Drawing screen

Line of sight for
2D drawings

The Z axis is perpendicular to the XY plane, or directly aligned with your viewpoint. This setup is ideal for 2D drawings and is called a *plan view*. All of your drawings up to now have been done in this orientation.

Figure 14-2 shows a standard drawing screen created with the **acad. dwt** template. The display is oriented so that you are looking directly down on the XY plane of the world coordinate system. By default, the XY icon in the lower-left corner of the screen is located at the origin of the WCS. The WCS is a fixed coordinate system and is the basic system of AutoCAD. The *User Coordinate System (UCS)* is a movable coordinate system. The icon indicating the directions of the X and Y coordinates is called the **UCS Icon**, and it appears in paper space as well as model space (see Section 12-3).

For purposes of clarity, the background color is set to white.

Figure 14-2

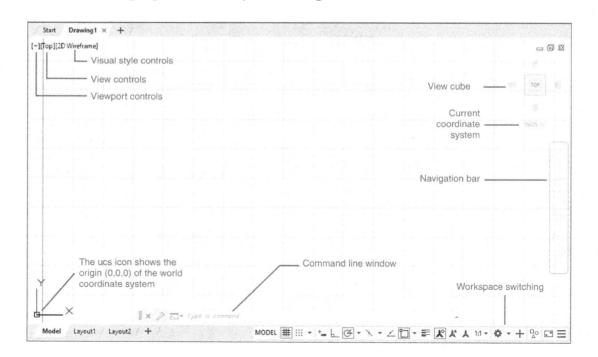

## Changing the Background Color to White

**1** With the crosshairs in the drawing area, right-click the mouse.

**2** Click **Options**.

The **Options** dialog box appears (Figure 14-3).

**Figure 14-3**

**3** Click the **Display** tab and then click **Colors**. In the **Drawing Window Colors** dialog box, click **2D model space**, click **Uniform background**, and set the color to **White** (Figure 14-4).

The preview box displays the white color.

**Figure 14-4**

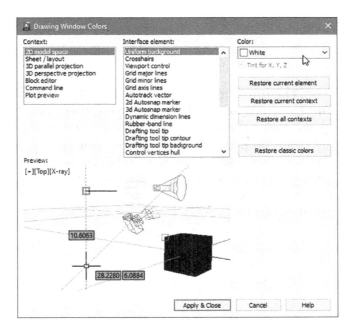

**4** Click **Apply & Close**, and then click **OK** to close the **Options** dialog box.

## 14-3 Viewpoints

The orientation of the WCS may be changed by changing a drawing's viewpoint. There are three ways to change the viewpoint:

**1** Type the word **view** at a command prompt to display the **View Manager** dialog box.

**2** Manipulate the **View Cube** located in the upper-right corner of the drawing screen.

**3** Click **View Manager** on the **Named Views** panel on the **Visualize** tab.

The following exercise assumes that the screen displays a grid. The grid serves to help define a visual orientation.

### Changing the Viewpoint by Using the View Command

**1** Type the word **view** at the command prompt and press **Enter**.

The **View Manager** dialog box appears (Figure 14-5).

**2** Click **Preset Views**, select **SE Isometric**, click **Set Current**, click **Apply**, and click **OK**.

**Figure 14-5**

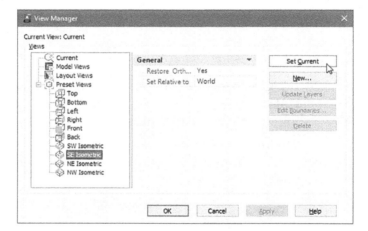

The drawing is now oriented as shown in Figure 14-6. Note the change in the crosshairs and the **UCS** icon; they now display the Z axis. It is important to remember that you are still in the world coordinate system (WCS). The Z axis is always there, but you are looking at it from a different perspective, and it becomes visible in the icon and crosshairs. This concept can be verified by drawing some simple shapes. Figure 14-7 shows a shape created using **Line** and a circle created using **Circle**. These shapes are 2D shapes drawn in the WCS.

**Figure 14-6**

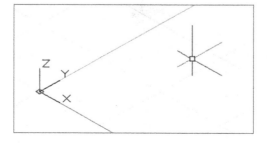

**Figure 14-7**

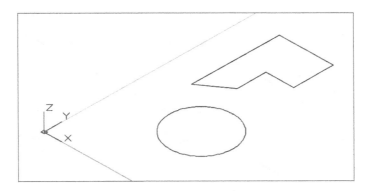

## Returning to the Original WCS Orientation

To return to the standard 2D plan view of the WCS, click **Top** on the **View Cube** (Figure 14-8).

**Figure 14-8**

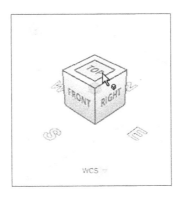

The drawing's orientation returns to the original top view of the XY plane (Figure 14-9).

**Figure 14-9**

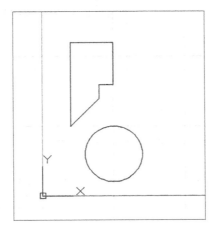

## 14-4 Perspective and Parallel Grids

Figures 14-10 and 14-11 show a box on a parallel isometric grid background and a box on a perspective grid background. Note the differences in the shape of the box shown against the two backgrounds. The top back corner of the box on the parallel grid appears higher than the same corner of the box on the perspective grid. Parallel grids are generated by selecting one of the preset isometric views listed in the **View Manager** dialog box (refer to Figure 14-5).

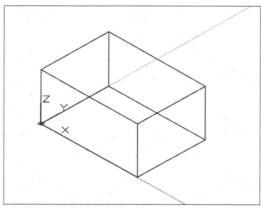

**Figure 14-10**                                    **Figure 14-11**

Perspective grid lines appear to recede to a vanishing point or a series of vanishing points. Parallel grid lines always appear parallel. AutoCAD uses a three-point perspective system. Perspective grids are generated by the **acad3D** and **acadiso3D** templates. (See Section 4-12 for an explanation of perspective drawings.)

## Creating a Drawing with a Perspective Grid

**1** Click **New** on the **Quick Access Toolbar**.

The **Select template** dialog box appears (Figure 14-12).

**Figure 14-12**

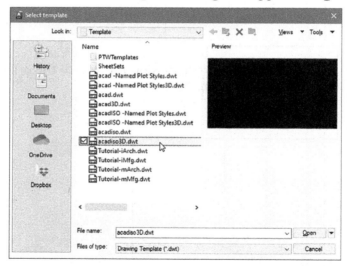

**2** Select the **acadiso3D** template and click **Open**.

**3** Right-click the house-like icon next to the **View Cube** and select **Perspective** (Figure 14-13).

**Figure 14-13**

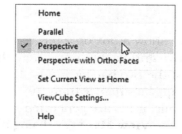

A perspective grid appears on the screen (Figure 14-14). This template has a default setting of millimeter values. The **acad3D** template has a default setting of inch values.

**Figure 14-14**

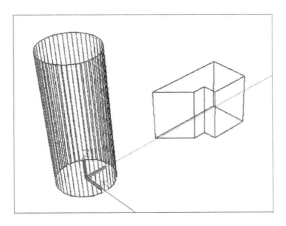

Figure 14-14 shows two figures drawn using the **Line** and **Circle** tools from the **Draw** panel on the **Home** tab. Using the **Properties** panel, their thickness was set to **20** and **50**, respectively, to give the figures 3D shapes. Note that the cylinder is centered on the XYZ origin.

## Returning to the 2D WCS

**1** Click **Top** on the **View Cube**.

**2** Use the mouse wheel to zoom the drawing as necessary.

Figure 14-15 shows the resulting top view. Although the **Top** view is set, the perspective grid is still active, so the thickened circle no longer appears as a 2D circle. Note that the Z axis does not appear as perpendicular to the XY plane. This is because the shapes are viewed on a perspective grid.

**Figure 14-15**

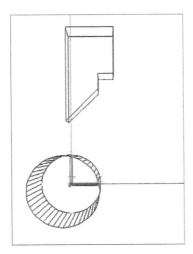

Lines on a perspective grid recede to a vanishing point, so they appear closer together as they get farther away from the viewer. When looking down on the shape, the bottom surface appears smaller than the top surface. Note that the top edge of the cylinder has a larger diameter than the base diameter. For this reason, it is better to use 3D parallel projection to create technical shapes in 3D space.

## 14-5 Setting the 3D Modeling Workspace

Notice the current ribbon tabs. In the **Drawing & Annotation** workspace that you've used up until now, 11 tabs appear by default, from **Home** to **Featured Apps**. The panels on these 11 tabs include nearly all the commands you need to create two-dimensional drawings.

Follow these steps to change the current workspace from the 2D setup in the **Drafting & Annotation** workspace to the **3D Modeling** workspace:

**1** On the status bar, click **Workspace Switching** (the icon looks like a gear wheel).

The menu shown in Figure 14-16 appears.

**Figure 14-16**

**2** Click **3D Modeling**.

The ribbon resets and displays four new panels between Home and Insert:

- Solid
- Surface
- Mesh
- Visualize

You can now find the solid modeling tools you use on the panels of the **Solid** tab. You are also likely to use tools on the **Visualize** tab, but the **Surface** and **Mesh** tabs are not covered in this book.

### Accessing the 3D Modeling Mode

**1** Start a new drawing and select an **acad3D** template.
You see the parallel projection grid shown in Figure 14-17.

**Figure 14-17**

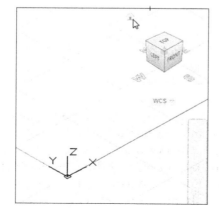

**2** Click the house-like icon next to the **View Cube**.

The grid background changes to a 3D parallel grid and is now a 3D workspace. You can verify this by clicking the gear-like icon in the status bar at the bottom of the screen.

In the remainder of this book, you will use the **3D Modeling** workspace.

## 14-6 User Coordinate Systems

A user coordinate system is a coordinate system you define relative to the WCS. Drawings often contain several UCSs, which can be saved and recalled.

AutoCAD drawings can be created only on one plane at a time. So, if you had a box whose bottom surface was drawn on the XY plane of the WCS and you wished to draw a circle on the top surface of the box, you would have to create a new XY plane and a new UCS on the box's top surface.

This section shows how to create new UCSs. You will draw a solid box and then use it to see how to create and use new UCSs.

### Drawing a Solid Box

**1** Create a new drawing by using the **acad3D.dwt** template, the **3D Modeling** workspace, an **SE Isometric** view orientation, and a parallel grid.

**2** Use the mouse wheel to fit the grid to the screen as needed.

The **3D Modeling** workspace is active because you switched to it in Section 14-5. The workspace remains active across sessions until you switch to a different workspace.

**3** Click **Box** on the **Primitive** panel of the **Solid** tab (Figure 14-18).

Command:_box

Specify first corner or [Center]:

**Figure 14-18**

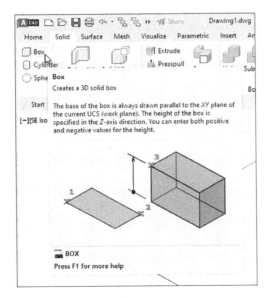

**4** Type **0,0,0** and press **Enter**.

```
Specify other corner or [Cube Length]:
```

These coordinates locate the box's corner on the XYZ origin. The corner could, however, be located anywhere on the grid.

**5** Type **5,5,0** or use the **Snap** tool with dynamic coordinates and press **Enter**.

```
Specify height:
```

**6** Type **2.0** and press **Enter**.

A box appears on the screen (Figure 14-19). The corner of the box is located on the WCS origin. The **Conceptual** viewing style is used for this example. You can set the visual style by clicking the **Visual Style Controls** at the top-left corner of the drawing area and choosing **Conceptual** from the menu.

**Figure 14-19**

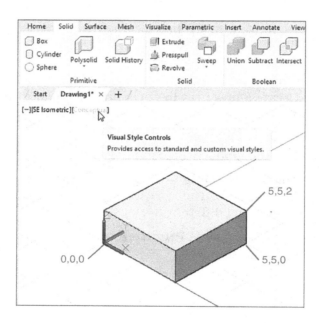

Clicking the box displays a series of dynamic grips (Figure 14-20). You can change the shape of a box by clicking and dragging any of the arrows or rectangles that appear.

**Figure 14-20**

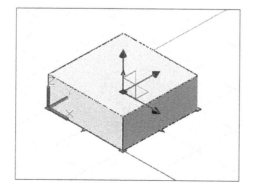

## Creating a UCS on the Top Surface

**1** Click **Origin** on the **Coordinates** panel of the **Visualize** tab (Figure 14-21). **Origin** can also be accessed using the **Coordinates** panel of the **Home** tab.

```
Specify new origin point <0,0,0>:
```

**Figure 14-21**

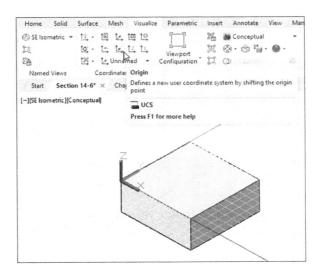

**2** Specify the top-left corner of the box as the new origin.

Use **Endpoint** object snap to define the corner. (It may already be activated. If it isn't, press **Shift** and right-click.) The cursor moves only in the XY plane. If you locate the cursor on the corner without using the **Endpoint** option, the cursor may appear to be on the corner, but, in fact, it is located on the XY plane, at a point behind the corner point.

The origin is now located on the top-left corner of the box. This is a new UCS.

**3** Use the **Cylinder** tool to draw a cylinder on the top surface of the box. **Cylinder** is located near the **Box** tool on the **Home** tab. Locate the cylinder's center point at **2.5,2.5,0**. Set the diameter to **4.00** and the height to **1.00**.

AutoCAD automatically locates the surface's center point. Click **Cylinder** and move the cursor onto the top surface. The center point appears.

## Saving a UCS

You can save the UCS created in Figure 14-21 and then later restore it without having to redefine it.

**1** Click **UCS, Named UCS** on the **Coordinates** panel of the **Visualize** tab.

The **UCS** dialog box appears (Figure 14-22), showing the current UCS as **Unnamed**.

Figure 14-22

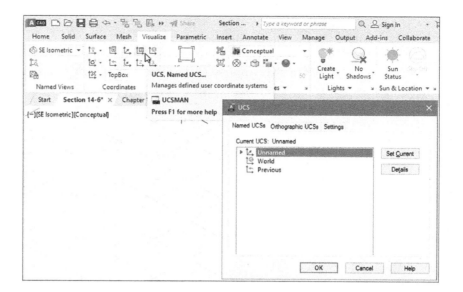

**2** Click **Unnamed** to activate the edit box and enter **TopBox**.

**3** Click **OK**.

The UCS is now saved, and the name of the new UCS now appears on the **Coordinates** panel of the **Visualize** tab.

## Returning to the WCS

Click **World** on the **Coordinates** panel of the **Visualize** tab.
The origin shifts to the original WCS axis (Figure 14-23).

Figure 14-23

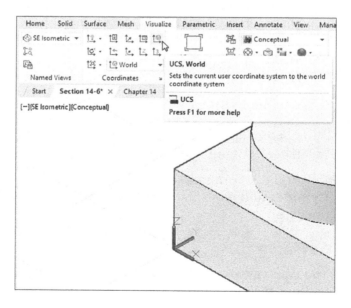

## Restoring a Saved UCS

**1** Click the **Named UCS** combo control on the **Coordinates** panel, which should currently read **World** (Figure 14-24).

Figure 14-24

**2** Scroll down and select **TopBox**.

The **TopBox** UCS is restored.

## Defining a UCS by Selecting Three Points

To use **3 Point** to define a UCS on the front right surface of the box, follow these steps:

**1** Click the **3 Point** tool on the **Coordinates** panel of the **Visualize** tab (Figure 14-25).

```
Specify new origin point <0,0,0>:
```

**Figure 14-25**

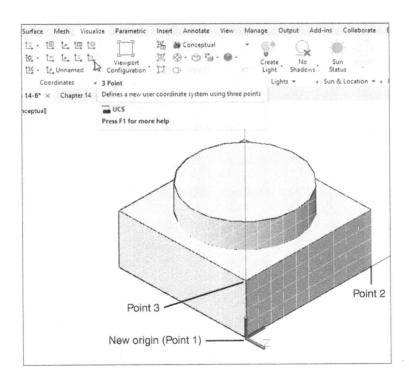

**2** Click the lower corner of the box.

This step assumes that **Snap** is on and set to match the grid. (To turn on **Snap**, press the **F9** key, and to turn on **Grid**, press **F7**.) Also, you can use **object snap** settings to ensure that you are grabbing endpoints. Press **Shift** and right-click to access the object snap menu.

```
Specify point on the positive portion of the X-axis <x,x,x>:
```

**3** Click the far-right lower corner of the box.

```
Specify point on the positive portion of the Y-axis <x,x,x>:
```

Use an object snap and pick the upper-front corner of the box, just above the new origin. You must use an object snap because the corner is not on the current XY plane.

**4** Use **Endpoint** object snap, click the corner, and use the **Cylinder** command on the **Primitive** panel to draw a **Ø2.00 × 1.00** cylinder centered about the **2.5,1,0** point on the new UCS.

**5** Select **Cylinder** and move the cursor onto the XY plane. Select the center point of the UCS surface (Figure 14-26). The center point can also be defined using coordinate values.

**Figure 14-26**

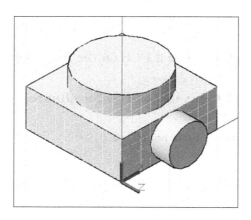

**6** Return to the WCS.

## 14-7 Editing a Solid Model

Solid models can be edited—that is, their shapes can be changed after they have been created. Figure 14-27 shows a view of the 5 × 5 × 2 solid model created in Section 14-6, with the farther left corner at the origin of the WCS.

**Figure 14-27**

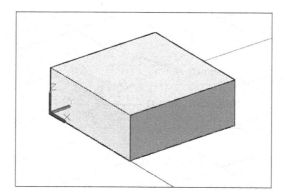

## Changing the Size of a Solid Model

**1** Click the box created in Section 14-6.

Blue arrows and grips appear on the base plane of the box (Figure 14-28). You can drag the corner grips to resize the box or drag an arrow to extend one side.

**Figure 14-28**

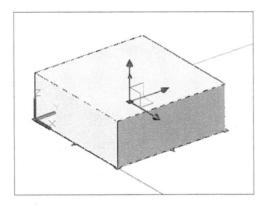

**2** Locate the cursor on the **5,5,0** corner of the box and then click and hold the mouse button.

**3** Move the cursor so that the corner has coordinate values **7,7,0**. Click the left mouse button.

Using **Snap**, locate the new corner point or enter the new values for the corner (**7,7,0**) (Figure 14-29).

**4** Press the **Esc** key.

**Figure 14-29**

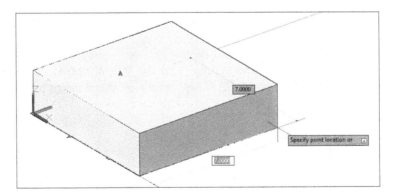

## 14-8 Visual Styles

Figure 14-30 shows the same 5 × 5 × 2 solid model from Figure 14-19 drawn on a parallel grid. The box was created using the **Box** tool from the **Primitive** panel on the **Solid** tab and the **acad3D** template with an **SE Isometric** view orientation and a **Conceptual** visual style.

**Figure 14-30**

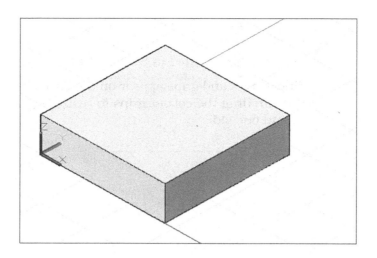

## Changing Visual Styles

In Section 14-6, you used the **Visual Style Controls** at the upper-left corner of the drawing area to set the visual style to **Conceptual**. You can also set the visual style on the **Visual Styles** panel of the **Visualize** tab.

On the **Visualize** tab, click the **Visual Styles** drop-down on the **Visual Styles** panel of the **Visualize** tab and select **2D Wireframe**, which is the default option (Figure 14-31).

**Figure 14-31**

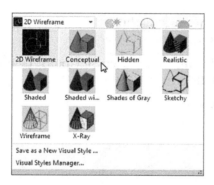

The model changes to the **2D Wireframe** visual style.

Figure 14-32 shows the box displaying four of the available styles.

**Figure 14-32**

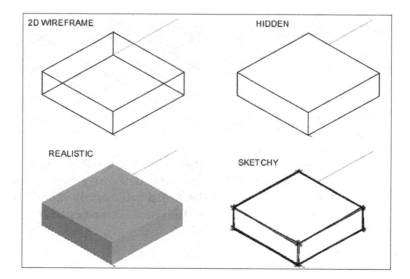

## 14-9 Rotating a UCS Axis

Figure 14-33 shows a 5 × 5 × 2 box drawn on the WCS axis with its origin on the 0,0,0 point. It is displayed in the **Conceptual** visual style and uses the **SW Isometric** view orientation.

**Figure 14-33**

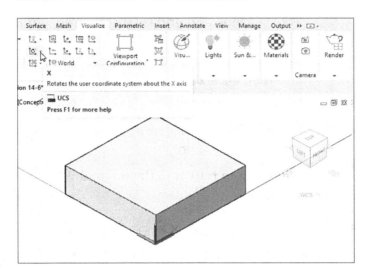

You can create a new UCS by rotating the coordinates about one of the major axes.

**1** Click **UCS, X** on the **Coordinates** panel.

```
Specify rotation axis about the X-axis <90>:
```

90° is the default value.

**2** Press **Enter** to accept the default value.

The axis and grid rotate 90° about the X axis. You can now draw on the new XY plane, which has the positive Y axis in the vertical direction. Note the orientation of the background grid (Figure 14-34).

**Figure 14-34**

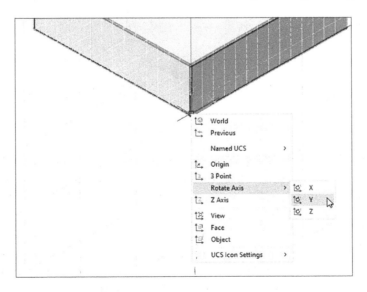

Axis rotation can be done dynamically by right-clicking the **UCS Icon** and selecting an axis. In this example the Y axis is rotated. Click the mouse to select an angle of rotation.

**3** Hover over the **UCS Icon** and right-click to display the **UCS** right-click menu. Click **Rotate Axis** and then click **Y**.

```
Specify rotation axis about the Y-axis <90°>:
```

**4** Press **Enter**.

The XZ plane and grid rotate 90°. You can now draw on the back plane of the box.

**5** Repeat step 3 to display the **UCS** right-click menu. Click **Rotate Axis** and then click **Z**.

```
Specify rotation angle about the Z-axis <90°>:
```

**6** Press **Enter**.

The axis rotates 90°.

**7** Use **Undo** to return to the original WCS orientation.

## 14-10 Drawing Problem

Draw an L-shaped bracket that will be used to demonstrate how to use UCSs.

**1** Start a new drawing using the **acad3D** template with a parallel grid. Make the **SE Isometric** view the active view.

**2** Use **Box** on the **Primitive** panel and draw a 5 × 5 × 2 box in the **Conceptual** visual style (Figure 14-35).

Figure 14-35

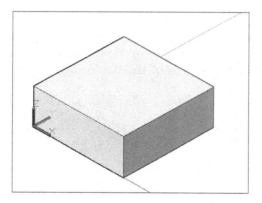

The **UCS Icon** is at the origin—0,0,0 in the WCS. You can change the UCS by selecting the **UCS Icon** and moving it to a different location. In the next steps, you will move the UCS straight up, to the top-left corner of the box.

**3** Click the **UCS Icon** to display its grips. Pick the grip at the origin and move the icon to the top surface of the box (Figure 14-36). Use **Endpoint** object snap (by pressing and holding the **Shift** key and right-clicking) to locate the new origin.

**Figure 14-36**

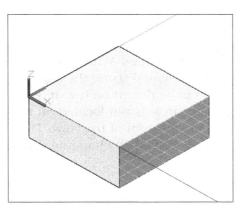

**4** Using the new origin, create a box whose base is located from the new origin (0,0,0) to a new corner (2.5,5.0,0). Make the height **2.5** (Figure 14-37).

**Figure 14-37**

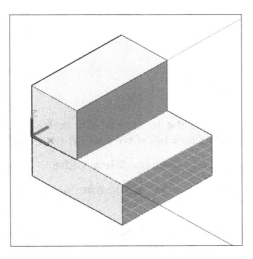

**5** Click the **Solid** tab and then click **Union** on the **Boolean** panel.

**6** Click both boxes.

**7** Return to the WCS.

As shown in Figure 14-38, the **Union** tool joins the two boxes together to form one object. Notice which lines are removed by the **Union** tool.

**Figure 14-38**

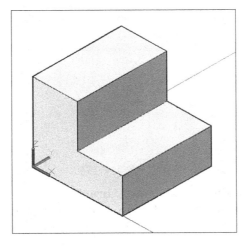

## 14-11 Visual Errors

When working in 3D, it is important to remember that you cannot rely on visual inputs to locate shapes. What you see may be misleading. For example, Figure 14-39, presented using the 3D wireframe visual style, shows a circle that appears to be drawn on the upper-right surface of an L-shaped bracket. In fact, the circle is not located on the surface. This visual distortion is due to the line of sight of the view. The fact that the circle is on the back surface can be verified by changing the object's orientation.

**Figure 14-39**

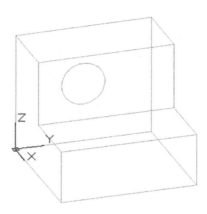

Use the **View Cube** to look at the bracket from different viewpoints. (Note that the grid has been turned off for clarity.)

**1** Move the mouse over the **View Cube**.

**2** Hover over the corner at the intersection of the **Top**, **Front**, and **Right** planes.

**3** When the corner is highlighted, press the left mouse button and gently drag to rotate the **View Cube** and your viewpoint until you can see the true location of the circle.

The new viewpoint is shown in Figure 14-40. This view clearly shows that the circle is drawn on the back surface.

**Figure 14-40**

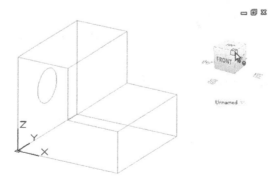

## 14-12 Drawing Problem

Figure 14-41 shows the same L-bracket drawn for Figure 14-38, this time displayed in the **2D Wireframe** visual style. This section uses different UCSs to draw 2D shapes on three of the surfaces of the L-bracket.

**Figure 14-41**

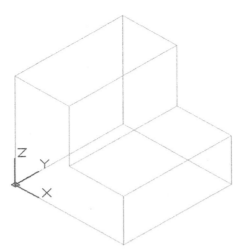

## Drawing a Circle on the Upper Front Surface

**1** Use the **3 Point** tool on the **Coordinates** panel and locate the origin and axis system as shown in Figure 14-42.

**Figure 14-42**

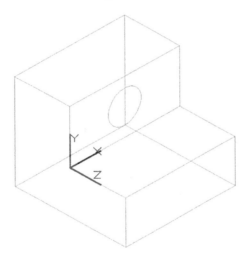

Remember that you can draw on only one plane at a time. Use the object snap options to ensure that the correct origin location is selected.

**2** Draw a circle on the front upper surface, as shown.

In this example, the circle is Ø1.50 and is located on the plane's center point.

## Adding a Rectangle on the Top Surface

**1** Return to the WCS and use the **Origin** tool on the **Coordinates** panel to move the axis to the top surface.

**2** Use **Rectangle** to draw a rectangle on the top surface.

If necessary, turn off the **3D Vertex** snap option on the **3D Object Snap** tab of the **Drafting Settings** dialog box.

In this example, a 1 × 3 rectangle is drawn (Figure 14-43).

Figure 14-43

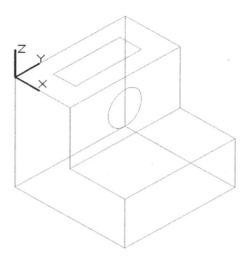

## Adding an Ellipse on the Left Vertical Surface

**1** Return to the WCS and use **UCS, X** on the **Coordinates** panel to rotate the axis system **90°** about the X axis.

As shown in Figure 14-44, the XY axis is now aligned with the left vertical axis.

**Figure 14-44**

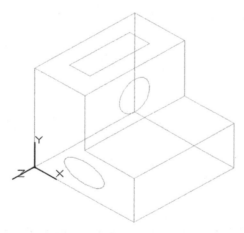

**2** Draw an ellipse on the left vertical surface.

**3** Save the L-bracket.

## 14-13 Orthographic Views

After a 3D object has been created, orthographic views can be taken directly from the object. The screen is first split into four viewports, each showing the 3D object. The viewpoints of three of the viewports are changed to create the front, top, and right-side views of the object.

For this example, the L-bracket is redrawn, using the same dimensions as presented in Drawing Problem 14-10 but using the **acad3D** template.

Create four equal viewports by following these steps:

**1** On the **Model Viewports** panel of the **Visualize** tab, click **Viewport Configuration**.

**2** Select the **Four: Equal** option (Figure 14-45).

Figure 14-45

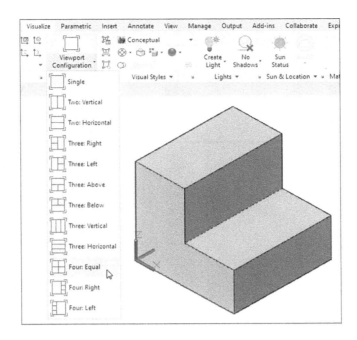

You can also create model space viewports by using the **Viewports** dialog box (see Figure 14-46). To create four equal viewports this way, follow these steps:

**1** Type **vports** at the command prompt.

**2** Select the **Four: Equal** option.

**Figure 14-46**

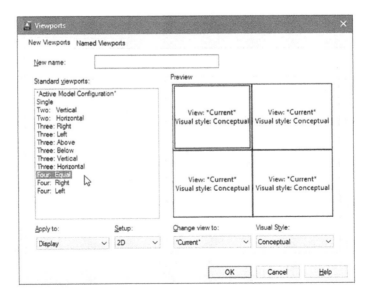

Figure 14-47 shows the L-bracket in four equal viewports. Note that the bold viewport border is a visual reminder that only one viewport can be active at a time. To make a different viewport active, move the cursor into that viewport and click the mouse.

Figure 14-47

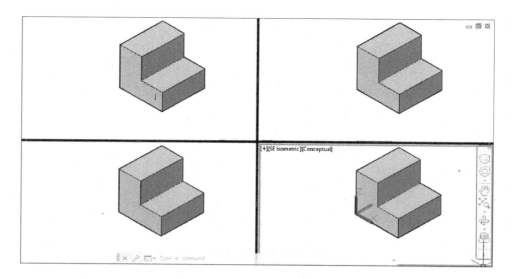

## Creating Orthographic Views

**1** Move the cursor into the top-left viewport and click the mouse.

This viewport is now the current viewport, and the cursor appears in the viewport.

**2** Click **View Control** at the top left of the active viewport (it should say **SE Isometric**) and set the view to **TOP** (Figure 14-48).

Figure 14-48

A top view of the object appears in the viewport.

**3** Pan and zoom the view as shown in Figure 14-48.

**4** Move the cursor into the lower-left viewport and click the mouse to make this viewport the current viewport.

**5** Use **View Controls** at the top left of the viewport to set the view to **FRONT**.

**6** Make the lower-right viewport active and set the view to **RIGHT**.

Figure 14-49 shows the three orthographic views—TOP, FRONT, and SIDE—as well as the original SE Isometric view in the fourth viewport.

**Figure 14-49**

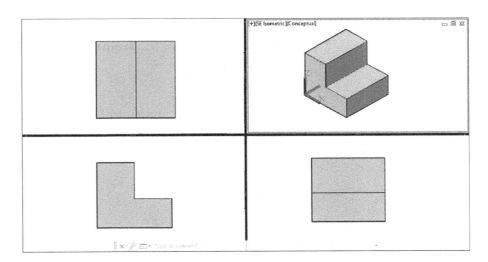

## 14-14 Line Thickness

The **Thickness** system variable is used to create 3D surfaces from 2D drawing objects. Figure 14-50 shows a line and a circle drawn as normal 2D entities and then drawn a second time with **Thickness** set for **2** and **3**, respectively. The figures are drawn with a 3D parallel grid background. The **Line** command generates a plane perpendicular to the plane of the original line, and the **Circle** command generates a cylinder perpendicular to the plane of the base circle.

**Figure 14-50**

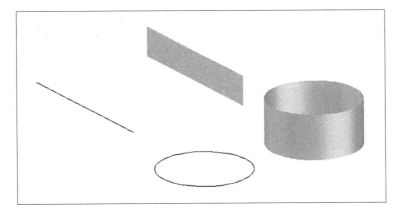

> **NOTE**
>
> *System variables* are settings in AutoCAD that govern how specific commands work. For example, **Line** is the command that draws a straight line segment, whereas **Thickness** is the system variable that tells AutoCAD how thick the line should be. The **Thickness** system variable is used with 2D drawing commands like **Line, Circle, Arc, Polygon**, and so on. System variables are defined in the online help, and you enter them at the command prompt the same way you enter commands.

### Using the Thickness Variable

In this example, you will create a new drawing using the **acad3D** template. Grid and snap spacing are **.5**, with decimal units, and the viewpoint is **SE Isometric**.

**1** Type the word **thickness** at the command prompt.

```
Enter new value for THICKNESS <0.0000>:
```

▣ Type **2** and press **Enter**.

▣ On the **Draw** panel of the **Home** tab, select **Line**.

```
Command: _line
From point:
```

▣ Draw the box shape shown in Figure 14-51.

▣ Right-click and select **Enter**.

**Figure 14-51**

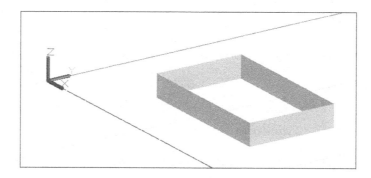

The shape shown in the figure is not a box but is four perpendicular surfaces. There is no top or bottom surface.

The default thickness value may also be defined using the **Properties** palette. Access the **Properties** palette by windowing the four surfaces, right-clicking the mouse, and selecting **Properties**. The **Properties** palette appears (Figure 14-52). Change the thickness value to **3.0000**.

**Figure 14-52**

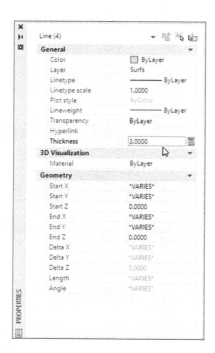

Figure 14-53 shows a hexagon and an arc drawn with the **Thickness** setting at values of 2 and 4, respectively.

**Figure 14-53**

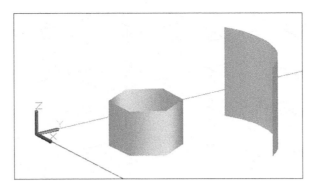

## Drawing a Curve with Thickness

Follow these steps to create a curved polyline with thickness:

**1** Start a new drawing using the **acad3D** template. Select the **Conceptual** visual style and the **SE Isometric** view.

**2** Type **thickness** at the command prompt.

```
Enter new value for THICKNESS <0.0000>:
```

**3** Type **3.5** and press **Enter**.

**4** Select **Polyline** from the **Draw** panel.

```
Command: _pline
Specify start point:
```

**5** Draw a polyline approximately like the one shown in Figure 14-54.

**Figure 14-54**

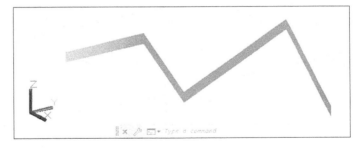

**6** Select **Edit Polyline** from the **Modify** panel.

```
Command: _pedit
Select polyline or [Multiple]:
```

**7** Select the polyline.

```
Enter an option [Close Join Width Edit vertex Fit Spline Decurve
Ltype gen Undo]:
```

**8** Select the **Fit** option.

Figure 14-55 shows the result.

Figure 14-55

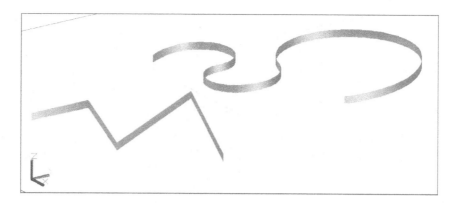

**9** Right-click and select **Enter**.

## 14-15 Using the Thickness Variable to Create Objects

The **Thickness** system variable can be used with different UCSs to create simulated 3D objects. The objects are actually open-ended plane structures. The procedure that follows shows how to create the object shown in Figure 14-56. The drawing was created with **Grid** and **Snap** set to **.5**, with decimal units, and with an **SE Isometric** viewpoint.

Figure 14-56

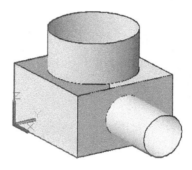

### Drawing the Box

**1** Type the word **thickness** at the command prompt.

Enter new value for THICKNESS <3.5000>:

**2** Type **6**.

**3** Select **Line** and draw a **10 × 10** box like the one shown in Figure 14-57. Place the starting point of the box shape at the origin, **0,0,0**.

Figure 14-57

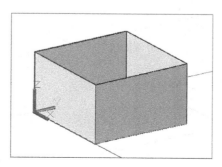

## Creating a New UCS

**1** Click the **3 Point** UCS tool on the **Coordinates** panel of the **View** tab.

```
Specify new origin point <0,0,0>:
```

**2** Select the lower-left corner of the box, as shown in Figure 14-58. Use an **Endpoint** object snap to pick the corner point.

```
Specify point on the positive portion of X-axis:
```

**Figure 14-58**

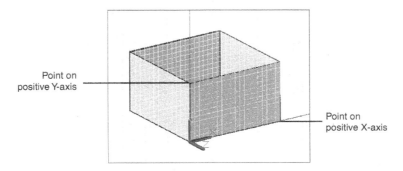

Point on positive Y-axis

Point on positive X-axis

**3** Click the lower-right corner, as shown.

```
Specify point on the positive portion of Y-axis:
```

**4** Pick the corner on the Y axis above the origin.

## Drawing the Right Cylinder

This cylinder will be 6 units long, so there is no need to change the thickness setting.

Select **Circle** and draw a cylinder centered on the right face of the box.

The coordinate value for the cylinder's center point is **5,3**, and the radius value is **2.00** (Figure 14-59).

**Figure 14-59**

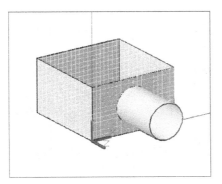

## Drawing the Top Cylinder

Return the drawing to the original WCS X,Y axes and then change the location of the XY plane so that the top cylinder can be drawn in the correct position.

**1** Type **UCS**, press **Enter**, and press **Enter** again.

The fastest way to return to the **WCS** from any **UCS** is to press **Enter** twice. The first **Enter** confirms the command, and the second **Enter** accepts the default value, which is **<World>**.

**2** Click **Origin** on the **Coordinates** panel and locate a new origin on the left corner of the top surface of the box.

**3** Type **thickness** at the command prompt.

```
Enter new value for THICKNESS <0.0000>:
```

**4** Type **4** and press **Enter**.

**5** Select **Circle** and draw the cylinder as shown in Figure 14-60.

The cylinder's center point is at **5,5**, and its radius is **4**.

Figure 14-60

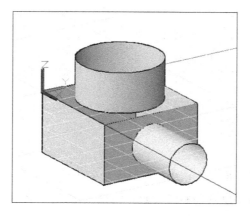

## Returning the Drawing to Its Original Settings

**1** Click **World** on the **Coordinates** panel.

**2** Type **thickness** at the command prompt.

```
Enter new value for THICKNESS <0.0000>:
```

**3** Type **0** and press **Enter**.

**4** Turn off the grid.

The object should look like the one shown in Figure 14-61.

Figure 14-61

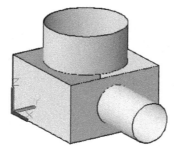

# 14-16 EXERCISE PROBLEMS

Exercise Problems EX14-1 through EX14-4 require you to draw 2D shapes on various surfaces of 3D objects created using the **Thickness** system variable. All 2D shapes should be drawn at the center of the surfaces on which they appear. Either the **acad** or the **acad3D** template can be used.

**1** Draw the 2D shapes as shown.

**2** Divide the screen into four viewports and create front, top, and right-side orthographic views for each object.

## EX14-1 Inches

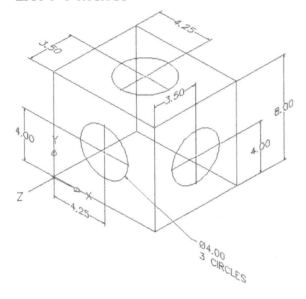

## EX14-2 Millimeters

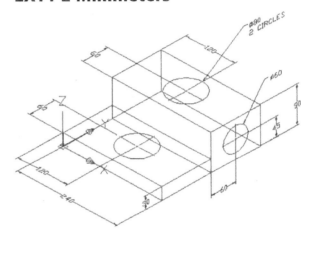

## EX14-3 Millimeters

Both cylinders are centered on the top surfaces as shown.

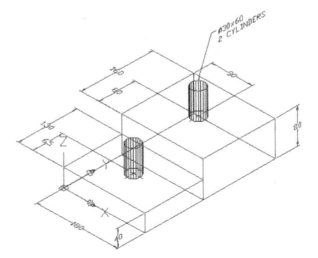

## EX14-4 Millimeters

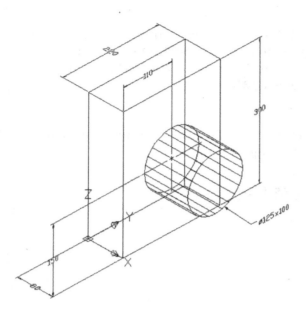

Redraw the figures presented in Exercise Problems EX14-5 through EX14-17 as wireframe models, using the **Thickness** variable. Divide the screen into four viewports and create front, top, and right-side orthographic views and one isometric view, as shown earlier in Figure 14-49.

## EX14-5 Inches

Box a: X = 6, Y = 5, Z = 2
Box b: X = 4, Y = 4, Z = 4
Box c: X = 5, Y = 2, Z = 1
*Hint:* Consider a modified version of the **NE Isometric** viewpoint.

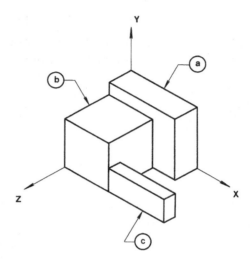

## EX14-6 Inches

Box a: X = 8, Y = 8, Z = 1
Box b: X = 6, Y = 6, Z = 2
Box c: X = 2, Y = 2, Z = 6

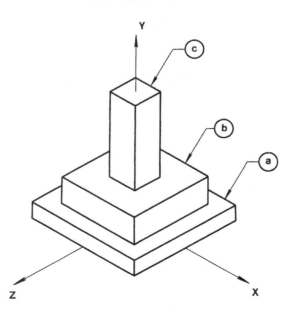

## EX14-7 Millimeters

Each box is 2 × 2 × 5.

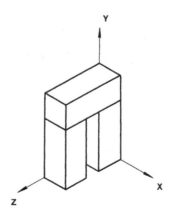

## EX14-8 Millimeters

Cylinder a: Ø10 × 30 LONG
Cylinder b: Ø20 × 8 LONG
Cylinder c: Ø35 × 18 LONG

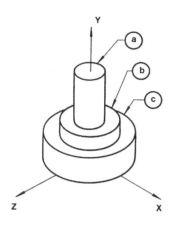

## EX14-9 Millimeters

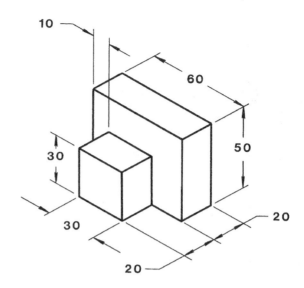

## EX14-10 Millimeters

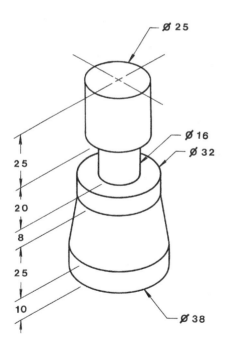

## EX14-11 Millimeters

Cylinders are 30 LONG.

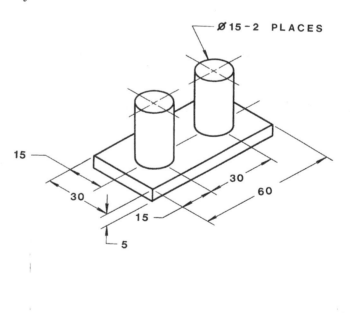

## EX14-12 Millimeters

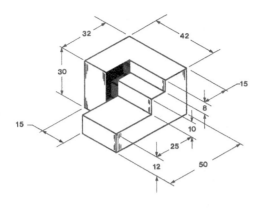

## EX14-13 Millimeters

The Ø12 cylinder is 20 LONG.
The Ø20 cylinder is 12 LONG.

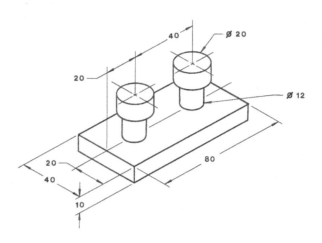

## EX14-14 Millimeters

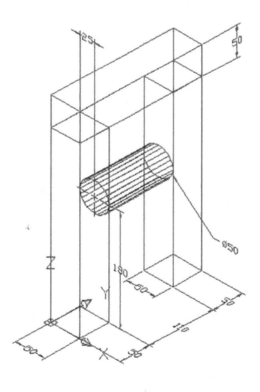

## EX14-15 Millimeters

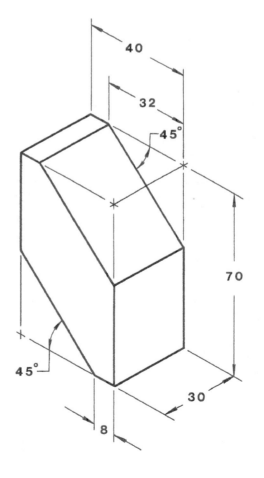

## EX14-16 Millimeters

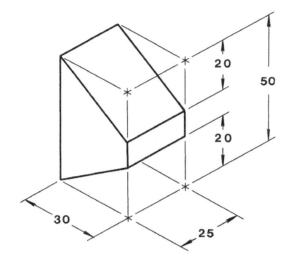

20

50

20

30

25

## EX14-17 Millimeters

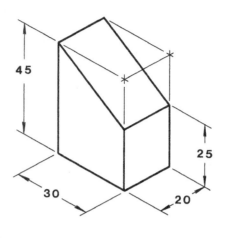

45

25

30

20

## 15-1 Introduction

This chapter furthers your knowledge of solid modeling. The solid modeling commands can be accessed through the **3D Modeling** workspace or the **3D Basics** workspace. Figure 15-1 shows the panels and tabs associated with both workspaces. Chapter 14 introduced the **3D Modeling** workspace. This chapter builds on that introduction.

**Figure 15-1**

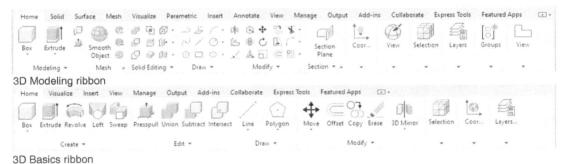

3D Modeling ribbon

3D Basics ribbon

Solid modeling enables you to create objects as solid entities. Solid models differ from surface models in that solid models have density and are not merely joined surfaces.

You create solid models by joining together, or *unioning*, basic primitive shapes—boxes, cylinders, wedges, and so on—or by defining a shape as a polyline and extruding it into a solid shape. Solid primitives can also be subtracted from one another. For example, to create a hole in a solid box, draw a solid cylinder and then subtract the cylinder from the box. The result is an open volume in the shape of a hole.

The first part of this chapter deals with the individual tools on the **Modeling** panel of the **Home** tab when the **3D Modeling** workspace is activated. The second part gives examples of how to create solid objects by joining primitive shapes and changing UCSs. The chapter ends with a discussion of the **Solid Editing** panel.

Drawings created with the **acad3D** template set to an **SE Isometric** view and a parallel grid are used throughout the chapter. The **Workspace Switching** tool (which looks like a gear) is located at the bottom of the drawing screen.

## 15-2 Box

The **Box** tool on the **Modeling** panel of the **Home** tab has two options that you see at the command prompt when you click the tool button: **Center** and **Corner**. **Corner** is the default option. The **Center** option is used to draw a box by first locating its center point. The **Corner** option draws a box by first locating one of its corner points.

### Drawing a Box (Corner Option)

Use the **acad3D** template, access the **3D Modeling** workspace, and set the drawing for an **SE Isometric** 3D view and a parallel grid. Access the **View Manager** dialog box by typing **View** at the command prompt.

 Select **Box** from the **Modeling** panel of the **Home** tab.

```
Command: _box
Specify corner of box or [Center]:
```

**2** Type **0,0,0** and press **Enter**.

The corner of the box is now located at the 0,0,0 (origin) point of the XY plane.

```
Specify other corner or [Cube Length]:
```

**3** Move the cursor in the positive X direction, type **10,10,0**, and press **Enter**.

```
Specify height or [2 points] <0.9396>:
```

**4** Move the cursor in the positive Z direction, type **6**, and press **Enter**.

### Changing the Visual Style

Figure 15-2 shows the box just created using the **Conceptual** visual style. The **Visual Styles Manager** is located on the **Visualize** tab and on the **View** panel of the **Home** tab (Figure 15-3). To change the visual style of the drawing, click on the desired new style.

**Figure 15-2**

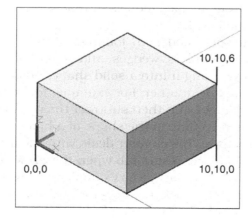

**NOTE**

You can quickly change visual styles by using the **Visual Styles Control** drop-down at the top-left corner of the drawing area.

**Figure 15-3**

## Drawing a Box from Given Dimensions

Draw a box with a length of **10**, a width of **8**, and a height of **4**, with its corner at the **2,2,0** point. Use the **SE Isometric** view orientation (see Figure 15-4).

**Figure 15-4**

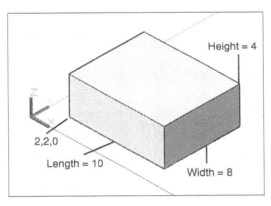

1. Select **Box** from the **Modeling** panel of the **Home** tab.

   Command: _box

   Specify corner or [Center]:

2. Type **2,2,0** and press **Enter**.

   Specify corner or [Cube Length]:

   There are three different ways to define the next point for the box: Enter coordinate values (e.g., **10,0**); activate the **Snap** command and use the dynamic screen coordinate display to select the point; or activate **Ortho** (by pressing **F8**) and enter a length value, as shown in this example.

3. Type **L** and click **Ortho** on the status bar at the bottom of the screen. Move the cursor in a positive **X** direction and press **Enter**.

   Specify length:

4. Type **10** and press **Enter**.

   Specify width:

**5** Move the cursor in a positive **Y** direction, type **8**, and press **Enter**.

Specify height:

**6** Move the cursor in a positive **Z** direction, type **4**, and press **Enter**.

## Drawing a Cube

**1** Select **Box** from the **Modeling** panel of the **Home** tab.

Command: _box

Specify corner of [Center]:

**2** Type **0,0,0** and press **Enter**.

Specify corner or [Cube Length]:

**3** Type **c** and press **Enter**.

Specify length:

**4** Move the cursor in a positive **X** direction, type **7.5**, and press **Enter**.

AutoCAD automatically makes all three edges of the box 7.5 units long (Figure 15-5).

> **NOTE**
> Use the **Ortho** tool to align the edge of the cube with the X axis.

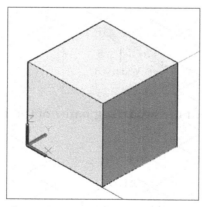

**Figure 15-5**

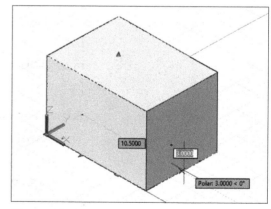

**Figure 15-6**

## Using Dynamic Grips

This example uses the 7.5 × 7.5 × 7.5 cube that was just drawn.

**1** Click any part of the box.

Blue arrows and grips appear on the XY plane of the box (Figure 15-6).

**2** Click and hold one of the arrowheads and drag the cursor away from the box.

Note how the box changes shape. Try moving different arrows to see how the cube responds. Click the mouse to establish a new edge location.

## 15-3 Sphere

### Drawing a Sphere

Follow these steps to create a sphere:

**1** Select **Sphere** from the **Box** drop-down on the **Modeling** panel of the **Home** tab (Figure 15-7).

```
Specify center of sphere or [3P 2P Ttr]:
```

**Figure 15-7**

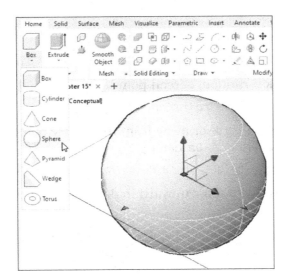

**2** Type **5,5,0** and press **Enter**.

```
Specify radius or [Diameter]:
```

**3** Type **4** and press **Enter**.

```
The sphere shown in Figure 15-7 uses the Conceptual visual style.
```

## 15-4 Cylinder

The **Cylinder** command has two options: circular and elliptical. This means that cylinders may be drawn with either elliptical or circular base planes. The base elliptical shape is drawn by using the same procedure as outlined for the **Ellipse** command in Chapter 2.

### Drawing a Cylinder with a Circular Base

The **Cylinder** tool is available under the **Box** drop-down on the **Modeling** panel of the **Home** tab (Figure 15-8).

Figure 15-8

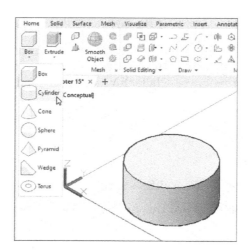

**1** Select **Cylinder** from the **Box** drop-down on the **Modeling** panel of the **Home** tab.

```
Command: _cylinder

Specify center point or base or [3P 2P Ttr Elliptical] <0,0,0>:
```

**2** Click a random screen point.

```
Specify base radius or [Diameter]:
```

**3** Move the cursor away from the center point and pick a point to define the cylinder's diameter.

```
Specify height or [2 Point/Axis endpoint] <0,0000>:
```

**4** Move the cursor upward to define the cylinder's height.

## Drawing a Cylinder with an Elliptical Base

The sequence that follows uses coordinate value input. The same points could also be selected by moving the crosshairs and pressing the left mouse button (Figure 15-9).

Figure 15-9

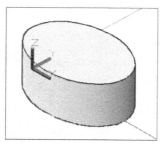

**1** Select **Cylinder** from the **Box** drop-down on the **Modeling** panel of the **Home** tab.

```
Command: _cylinder

Specify center point or base or [3P 2P Ttr Elliptical] <0,0,0>:
```

**2** Type **e** and press **Enter**.

```
Specify endpoint of first axis or [center]:
```

**3** Type **0,0,0** and press **Enter**.

One end of the base axis is now located on the 0,0,0 point of the XY plane.

```
Specify other endpoint of first axis:
```

Type **10,0,0** and press **Enter**.

The axis line is not located along the X axis. Use the **Ortho** tool, if necessary.

```
Specify endpoint of second axis:
```

Note that the line you are dragging from the crosshairs has one end centered on the axis just defined.

 Type **5,3.5,0** and press **Enter**.

```
Specify height or [2 Point Axis endpoint]:
```

 Type **4** and press **Enter**.

You can also define an elliptical base by first defining a center point for the ellipse and then defining the length of the radii of the major and minor axes.

## 15-5 Cone

There are two options associated with the **Cone** tool: circular and elliptical. This means that cones can be drawn with either an elliptical or circular base.

### Drawing a Cone with an Elliptical Base

The base elliptical shape is drawn using the same procedure as was outlined for the **Ellipse** command in Chapter 2 (Figure 15-10).

**Figure 15-10**

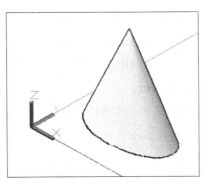

 Select **Cone** from the **Box** drop-down on the **Modeling** panel of the **Home** tab.

```
Command: _cone

Specify center point or base or [3P 2P Ttr Elliptical] <0,0,0>:
```

 Type **e** and press **Enter**.

```
Specify endpoint of first axis or [Center]:
```

 Pick a random point.

```
Specify other endpoint of first axis:
```

 Move the cursor away from the center point and select a second point.

```
Specify endpoint of second axis:
```

**5** Move the cursor, creating an elliptical shape, and pick a point.

    Specify height or [2 Point Axis endpoint Top radius]:

**6** Move the cursor in a positive Z direction, pick a point, and press **Enter**.

A response of **A** to the *Apex/<Height>:* prompt allows you to define the height of the cone using numerical values.

## Drawing a Cone with a Circular Base

The first steps in executing the **Cone** command are similar to those to draw a circle. Figure 15-11 shows a basic cone.

**Figure 15-11**

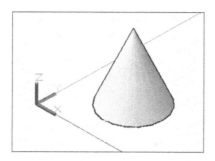

**1** Select **Cone** from the **Box** drop-down on the **Modeling** panel of the **Home** tab.

    Command: _cone

    Specify center point [3P 2P Ttr Elliptical] <0,0,0>:

**2** Type **5,5,0** and press **Enter**.

    Specify base radius or [Diameter]:

**3** Type **3** and press **Enter**.

    Specify height or [2 Point Axis endpoint Top radius]:

**4** Move the cursor in a positive **Z** direction, type **7**, and press **Enter**.

Figure 15-12 shows a cone with a top radius of 2.00 and height of 5.00. To create a top radius on the cone, type **T** in response to the *Specify height* prompt and enter a radius value.

**Figure 15-12**

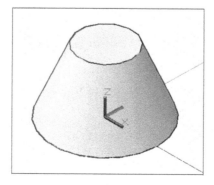

## 15-6 Wedge

There are two options associated with the **Wedge** command: center and corner.

### Drawing a Wedge by Defining Its Corner Point

You begin creating a wedge primitive solid as if it were a 2D rectangle. After the corner points are specified, enter a height value or simply drag the edge in the Z direction (Figure 15-13).

**Figure 15-13**

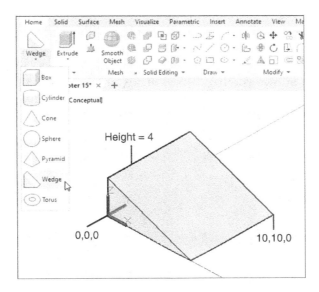

**1** Select **Wedge** from the **Box** drop-down on the **Modeling** panel of the **Home** tab.

```
Command: _wedge
Specify first corner or [Center]:
```

**2** Type **0,0,0** and press **Enter**.

The corner of the wedge is now located at the origin of the XY plane.

```
Specify other corner or [Cube Length]:
```

The default response to this command defines the diagonal corner of the wedge's base.

**3** Type **10,10,0** and press **Enter**.

```
Specify height:
```

**4** Move the cursor in a positive **Z** direction, type **4**, and press **Enter**.

You can also draw a wedge shape by picking random points.

### Drawing a Wedge by Defining Its Center Point

**1** Select **Wedge** from the **Box** drop-down on the **Modeling** panel of the **Home** tab.

```
Command: _wedge
Specify first corner or [Center] <0,0,0>
```

**2** Type **c** and press **Enter**.

Specify center:

**3** Type **5,5,0** and press **Enter**.

Specify corner or [Cube Length]:

**4** Type **10,10,0** and press **Enter**.

Specify height or [2 Point] <4.000>:

**5** Move the cursor in a positive **Z** direction, type **4**, and press **Enter**.

The wedge shown in Figure 15-14 is centered about the XY plane; that is, part of the wedge is above the plane and part is below. This is not easy to see even with the grid shown. The far-right corner of the wedge is actually located below the grid at the 10,10 point on the XY plane. Figure 15-14 also shows the front view of the same wedge. Note how the line bisects the height line of the wedge.

**Figure 15-14**

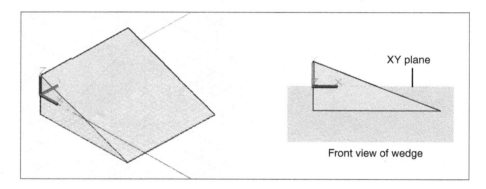

## Aligning a Wedge with an Existing Wedge

This example illustrates how you can use different inputs to position a wedge. Figure 15-15 shows a 10 × 8 × 4 wedge. The problem is to draw another wedge with its back surface aligned with the back surface of the existing wedge.

**Figure 15-15**

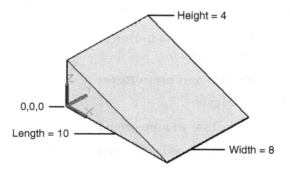

**1** Select **Wedge** from the **Box** drop-down on the **Modeling** panel of the **Home** tab.

Command: _wedge

Specify first corner or [Center]:

**2** Type **0,0,0** and press **Enter**.

```
Specify other corner or [Cube Length]:
```

**3** Specify the length. Type **L** and press **Enter**.

Move the cursor in a negative X direction.

**4** Type = **–10** and press **Enter**.

```
Specify width:
```

**5** Move the cursor in a positive **Y** direction, type **8.00**, and press **Enter**.

```
Specify height or [2 Point] <4.0000>:
```

**6** Use the **Endpoint** object snap and select the Z axis corner point of the existing wedge.

Figure 15-16 shows the finished model. The model could also have been constructed using the **Copy** command to create a second wedge, the **Rotate** command to rotate the new wedge 180°, and the **Move** command to align the wedge with the existing wedge. Using an **Endpoint** object snap allows you to ensure exact alignment.

**Figure 15-16**

Width = 8     Height = 4

Length = 10

0,0,0

## 15-7 Torus

A *torus* is a donutlike shape, defined by a circle that's rotated around an axis. In AutoCAD, a torus is a primitive solid, like a box or a cone (Figure 15-17).

**Figure 15-17**

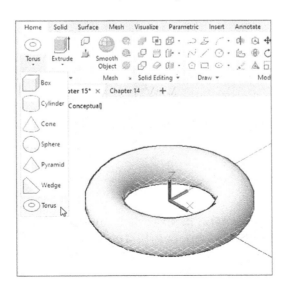

## Drawing a Torus

**1** Select **Torus** from the **Box** drop-down on the **Modeling** panel of the **Home** tab.

```
Command: _torus

Specify center point or [3P 2P Ttr]:
```

**2** Type **0,0,0** and press **Enter**.

The center of the torus is now located at the 0,0,0 point on the XY plane.

```
Specify radius or [Diameter] <3.0000>:
```

**3** Type **5** and press **Enter**.

```
Specify tube radius or [2 Point Diameter]:
```

**4** Type **1.5** and press **Enter**.

The finished torus is shown in Figure 15-17.

## 15-8 Extrude

The **Extrude** command extends existing 2D shapes into 3D shapes. **Extrude** can create a 3D solid from any closed single object.

### Extruding a 2D Polyline

Figure 15-18 shows a circumscribed hexagon drawn using the **Polygon** command (located on the **Draw** panel of the **Home** tab), centered about the origin. All shapes drawn using the **Polygon** command are automatically drawn as polylines, so the hexagon can be extruded. (How to draw a polygon is discussed in Chapter 2.)

**Figure 15-18**

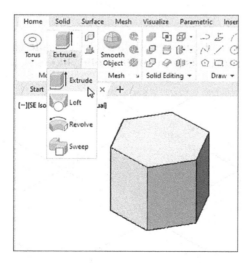

**1** Draw a hexagon (a six-sided polygon) and select the **Extrude** tool from the **Modeling** panel of the **Home** tab.

```
Command: _extrude

Select objects to extrude:
```

**2** Select the hexagon.

```
Select objects:
```

**3** Press **Enter**.

```
Specify height of extrusion or [Direction Path Taper angle] <4.0000>:
```

**4** Move the cursor in a positive Z direction, type **6**, and press **Enter**.

The dynamic mode is automatically activated and can be used to approximate the extrusion's height.

```
Specify angle of taper for extrusion <0>:
```

**5** Press **Enter**.

Figure 15-19 shows a closed spline created using **Spline**. The **Extrude** command was applied, and a height of **5** was specified.

**Figure 15-19**

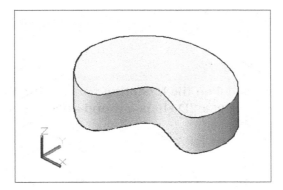

## Creating a Polyline from Line Segments

Figure 15-20 shows a 2D shape that was created using the **Line** tool. When you create such a shape, before the lines are joined into a single polyline, each line is extruded separately, so the shape is not a solid (Figure 15-20, left). Once the linework becomes a single polyline, the shape is extruded as a solid (Figure 15-20, right).

**Figure 15-20**

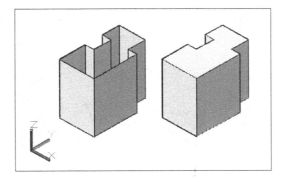

**1** Select **Edit Polyline** from the **Modify** panel of the **Home** tab.

```
Select polyline or [Multiple]:
```

**2** Select any one of the lines in the 2D shape.

```
Object selected is not a polyline
Do you want to turn it into one? <Y>:
```

**3** Press **Enter**.

```
Enter an option [Close Join Width Edit vertex Fit Spline Decurve
Ltype gen Undo]:
```

**4** Select the **Join** option.

The polyline is defined by joining together all of the line segments to form a polyline. A curve is considered to be a line segment.

```
Select objects:
```

**5** Window the entire shape.

```
Enter an option [Close Join Width Edit vertex Fit Spline Decurve
Ltype gen Undo]:
```

**6** Right-click twice and press **Enter**.

**7** Select **Extrude** from the **Modeling** panel of the **Home** tab and create an extrusion **5** units high.

## 15-9 Revolve

The **Revolve** tool on the **Modeling** panel of the **Home** tab creates a 3D solid object by rotating a 2D shape around an axis of revolution.

### Creating a Revolved Solid Object

This procedure assumes that the objects to be revolved and the line that will be used as the axis of revolution already exist on the drawing. If you revolved the 2D shapes 360°, a torus-like object would be created. In this example, the object is revolved 270°.

**1** Select **Revolve** from the **Extrude** drop-down on the **Modeling** panel of the **Home** tab (Figure 15-21).

**Figure 15-21**

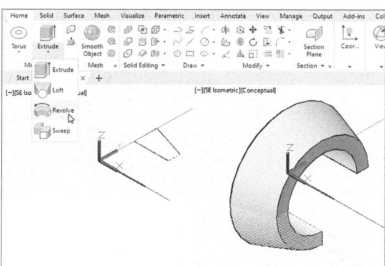

```
Command: _revolve
Select objects to revolve:
```

**2** Select the object to be revolved.

```
Select objects to revolve:
```

**3** Press **Enter**.

```
Specify start point for axis of revolution or define axis by [Object
X Y Z] <object>:
```

**4** Select one end of the line to be used as the axis of revolution. Use an **Endpoint** object snap if necessary.

```
Specify axis endpoint:
```

**5** Select the other end of the axis line.

```
Specify angle of revolution or [Start angle] <360>:
```

**6** Type **270** and press **Enter**.

## 15-10 Helix

In AutoCAD, a *helix* is an open or closed 2D or 3D spiral (Figure 15-22).

**Figure 15-22**

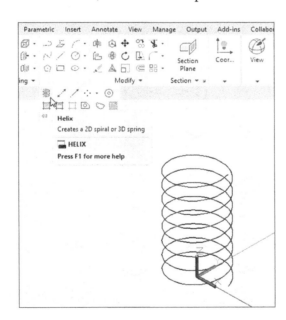

**1** From the **Draw** panel's extended menu, select **Helix**.

```
Number of turns = 3, Twist = CCW Specify center point of base:
```

In this example, the origin (0,0,0) was selected.

**2** Type **0,0,0** and press **Enter**.

```
Specify base radius or [Diameter] <1.0000>:
```

**3** Type **2** and press **Enter**.

```
Specify top radius or [Diameter] <2.0000>:
```

**4** Press **Enter**.

```
Specify helix height or [Axis endpoint Turns turn Height tWist]
<6.3885>:
```

**5** Type **t** and press **Enter**.

```
Enter number of turns <3.0000>:
```

**6** Type **8** and press **Enter**.

```
Specify helix height or [Axis endpoint Turns turn Height tWist]
<1.0000>:
```

**7** Use the dynamic input option and select a helix height by moving the cursor or by entering a number.

**8** Press the left mouse button.

The helical object created here will be used in the next section.

## 15-11 Sweep

A *sweep* is a 3D object created by "sweeping" a 2D object such as a circle along a 3D path (Figure 15-23). The following steps assume that both a circle and a helix exist in the drawing; the circle is known as the *profile*, and the helix is called the *path*.

**Figure 15-23**

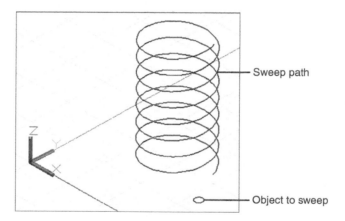

Sweep path

Object to sweep

**1** Select **Sweep** from the **Modeling** panel of the **Home** tab.

```
Current wire frame density: ISOLINES=4, Closed profiles creation
mode = Solid
```

```
Select object to sweep or [Mode]:
```

**2** Select the profile to sweep—in this case, the small circle.

```
Select sweep path or [Arc Close Undo]:
```

**3** Click anywhere on the sweep path—in this case, the helix.

AutoCAD generates the sweep (Figure 15-24).

**Figure 15-24**

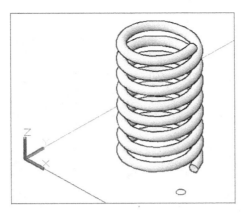

## 15-12 Loft

*Lofting* means creating a solid shape between profiles. A loft uses at least two profiles but may include more to fully define the loft. Figure 15-25 shows a simple loft between two profiles.

**Figure 15-25**

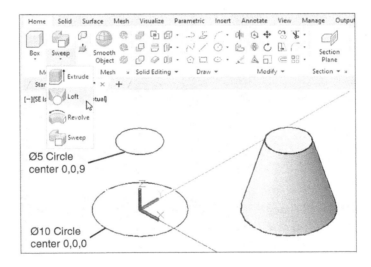

1. Draw a **ø10** circle centered about the 0,0,0 origin.

2. Draw a second circle, **ø5**, centered about 0,0,9.

   The Z value **12** locates the ø5 circle's center point above the ø10 circle's center point.

3. Select **Loft** from the **Modeling** panel of the **Solid** tab.

   ```
   Select the cross sections in lofting order or [POint Join multiple
   edges MOde]:
   ```

4. Select the **ø10** circle.

   ```
   Select the cross sections in lofting order:
   ```

5. Select the **ø5** circle.

   ```
   Select the cross sections in lofting order:
   ```

**6** Right-click and select **Enter**.

```
Enter an option [Guides Path Cross sections only Settings] <Cross
sections only>:
```

**7** Press **Enter** to confirm the loft.

AutoCAD generates the loft (Figure 15-25).

## 15-13 Union and Subtract

You can combine solid objects to form more complex objects by using *Boolean* operations. Objects can be added together with the **Union** command and subtracted from each other with the **Subtract** command. A volume common to two or more objects may be defined by using the **Intersect** command. The tools for these three commands are located on the **Solid Editing** panel of the **Home** tab in the **3D Modeling** workspace and on the **Edit** panel of the **Home** tab in the **3D Basics** workspace. This section uses the **3D Basics** workspace (Figure 15-26).

**Figure 15-26**

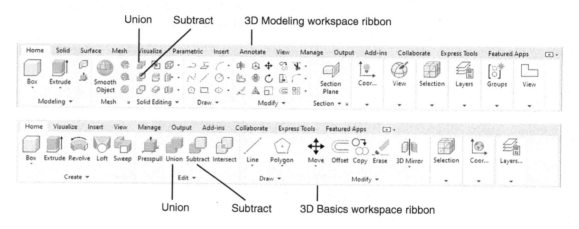

To access the **3D Basics** workspace, click the **Workspace Switching** tool on the ribbon at the bottom of the drawing screen.

## Unioning Two Objects

Figure 15-27 shows two $10 \times 10 \times 3$ solid boxes drawn with adjoining surfaces. Both are shown using the **Conceptual** visual style.

**Figure 15-27**

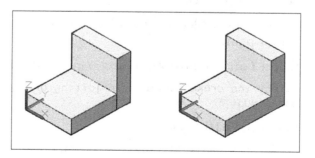

**1** Select **Union** from the **Edit** panel of the **Home** tab.

```
Command: _union
Select objects:
```

**2** Select a box.

```
Select objects:
```

**3** Select the other box.

```
Select objects:
```

**4** Press **Enter**.

Note the changes in the boxes after they have been unioned. The solid object is no longer two boxes; it is now an L-shaped object.

## Subtracting an Object

This exercise adds a hole to the front surface of the L-shaped bracket formed in Figure 15-27. Holes are created in solid objects by subtracting solid cylinders from the existing objects.

Using the **3D Basics** workspace, complete these steps:

**1** Select **Cylinder** from the **Box** drop-down on the **Create** panel of the **Home** tab.

```
Command: _cylinder

Specify center point of base or [3P 2P Ttr Elliptical]:
```

**2** Type **5,5,0** and press **Enter**.

Remember that you are still working on the XY plane.

```
Specify base radius or [2 Point Axis endpoint] <5.0000>:
```

**3** Type **3** and press **Enter**.

```
Specify height or [2 Point Axis endpoint] <10.0000>:
```

**4** Type **5** and press **Enter**.

The height of the cylinder is deliberately drawn higher than the top surface of the bracket to illustrate that the two heights need not be equal for the **Subtract** command to work. The only requirement is that the cylinder be equal to or greater than the height of the box surface (Figure 15-28).

**Figure 15-28**

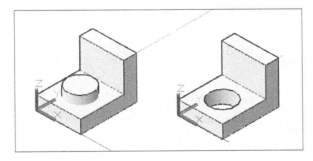

**5** Select the **Subtract** tool from the **Edit** panel of the **Home** tab.

```
Command: _subtract

Select solids and regions to subtract from . . .

Select objects:
```

This prompt is asking you to define the main object—that is, the object that you want to remain after the subtraction.

**6** Select the L-shaped bracket.

```
Select objects:
```

**7** Press **Enter**.

```
Select solids and regions to subtract . . .
Select objects:
```

This prompt is asking you to define the object that you want removed in the subtraction.

**8** Select the cylinder.

```
Select objects:
```

**9** Press **Enter**.

## 15-14 Intersect

The **Intersect** command is used to define a volume common to two or more existing solid objects. Figure 15-29 shows a ø12 × 12 cylinder centered about the 0,0,0 point and a 20 × 20 × 5 box with one of its corners located on the 0,0,0 point. They were both drawn on the XY plane. The following procedure defines the volume common to both of them:

**1** Select the **Intersect** tool from the **Solid Editing** panel of the **Home** tab.

```
Command: _intersect
Select objects:
```

**Figure 15-29**

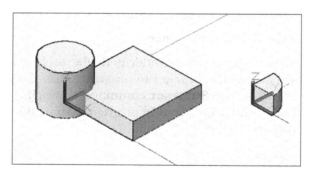

**2** Select the box.

```
Select objects:
```

**3** Select the cylinder.

```
Select objects:
```

**4** Press **Enter**.

Figure 15-29 shows the resulting common volume on the right.

## 15-15 Solid Modeling and UCSs

In this section, you will again work with the L-shaped bracket shown in Figure 15-27; this time, you will add a hole to the upper surface. To do so, you need to create a new UCS with its origin at the left intersection of the two perpendicular surfaces (Figure 15-30) and then create and subtract a cylinder.

**Figure 15-30**

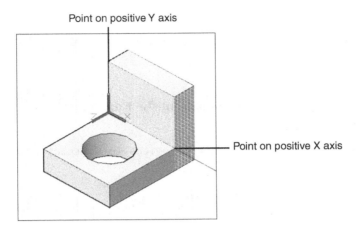

Point on positive Y axis

Point on positive X axis

**1** Select **3 Point** from the **Coordinates** panel of the **Home** tab.

```
Specify new origin point <0.0000>:
```

**2** Using **Endpoint** object snap, pick the corner as shown.

The coordinate system moves to the new location.

```
UCS Specify point on positive portion of X = Axis <1.0000, 0.0000,
0,0000>:
```

**3** Using **Endpoint** object snap, select the corner, as shown.

```
UCS Specify point on positive -1 portion of the USC XY plan
<1.0000, 0.0000, 0.0000>:
```

**4** Use **Endpoint** object snap and select the top corner, as shown.

**5** Select **Cylinder** from the **Create** panel of the **Home** tab.

```
Specify center point of the base or [3P 2P Ttr Elliptical]:
```

**6** Type **5,3.5,0** and press **Enter**.

You are now drawing on the new UCS.

```
Specify base radius or [Diameter] <1.5000>:
```

**7** Type **2.50** and press **Enter**.

```
Specify height or [2 Point Axis endpoint] <5.0000>:
```

**8** Use the dynamic input options and move the cursor in the negative **Z** direction.

```
The cylinder height increases as the cursor is moved.
```

**9** Define the cylinder height at any distance greater than 3, the thickness of the L-bracket, and press **Enter** (Figure 15-31).

Figure 15-31

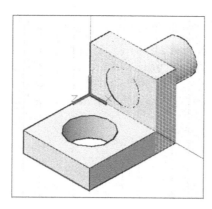

**10** Select **Subtract** from the **Edit** panel of the **Home** tab.

```
Command: _subtract
Select solids and regions to subtract from . . .
Select objects:
```

**11** Select the L-shaped bracket.

```
Select objects:
```

**12** Press **Enter**.

```
Select solids and regions to subtract . . .
Select objects:
```

**13** Select the cylinder.

```
Select objects:
```

**14** Press **Enter**.

**15** Type **UCS** and press **Enter** and then press **Enter** again to return to the WCS.

Figure 15-32 shows the resulting solid object.

Figure 15-32

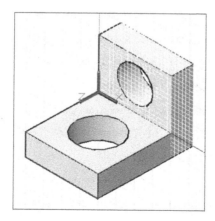

# 15-16 Combining Solid Objects

Figure 15-33 shows a dimensioned object. The following section explains how to create the object as a solid model. There are many different ways to create a solid model. The sequence presented here was selected to demonstrate several different input options.

**Figure 15-33**

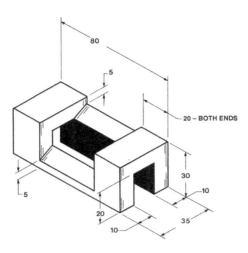

## Setting Up the Drawing

Set up the drawing as follows:

**Acadiso3D** template

**Units = Decimal** (millimeters)

**Drawing Limits = 297,210**

**Grid = 10 × 10 parallel**

**Snap = 5**

**View = SE Isometric**

**Workspace = 3D Basics**

**Visual Style = Conceptual**

The object is relatively small, so use the mouse wheel or the **Zoom** tool to create a size that you find visually comfortable.

## Drawing the First Box

The size specifications for this box are based on the given dimensions.

**1** Select **Box** from the **Create** panel.

    Command: _box

    Specify first corner or [Center]:

**2** Enter **0,0,0** and press **Enter**.

    Specify other or [Cube Length]:

**3** Type **L** and press **Enter**.

    Specify length:

**4** Move the cursor in the positive **X** direction, type **80**, and press **Enter**. Turn on **Ortho**, if needed.

Specify width:

**5** Move the cursor in the positive **Y** direction, type **36**, and press **Enter**.

Specify height:

**6** Move the cursor in the positive **Z** direction, type **30**, and press **Enter**. Figure 15-34 shows the first box.

**Figure 15-34**

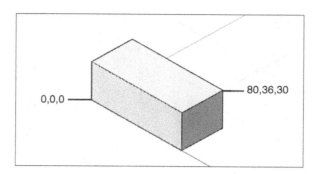

## Creating the Internal Open Volume

The volume is created by subtracting a second box from the first box.

**1** Select **Box** from the **Create** panel of the **Home** tab.

Command: _box

Specify corner of box or [Center]:

**2** Select the **0,10,0** point on the WCS.

The point 0,10,0 was selected on the basis of the given 10-millimeter dimension. The point can be selected using the crosshairs because it is on the grid located on the XY plane.

Specify corner or [Cube Length]:

**3** Type **L** and press **Enter**.

Specify length:

**4** Move the cursor in the positive **X** direction, type **80**, and press **Enter**.

Specify width:

**5** Move the cursor in the positive **Y** direction, type **15**, and press **Enter**.

Specify height:

**6** Move the cursor in the positive **Z** direction, type **20**, and press **Enter**. Figure 15-35 shows the second box within the first box.

**Figure 15-35**

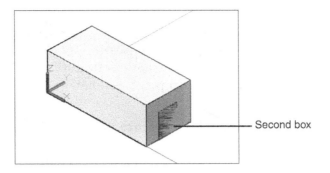

Second box

7  Select the **Subtract** tool from the **Edit** panel of the **Home** tab.

```
Command: _subtract
Select solids and regions to subtract from . . .
Select objects:
```

8  Select the first box.

```
Select objects:
```

9  Press **Enter**.

```
Select solids and regions to subtract . . .
Select objects:
```

10  Press **Enter**.

Figure 15-36 shows the second box subtracted from the first box.

**Figure 15-36**

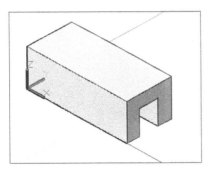

## Creating the Top Cutout

The cutout is created by drawing a box and wedge and subtracting them from the existing object (Figure 15-37).

**Figure 15-37**

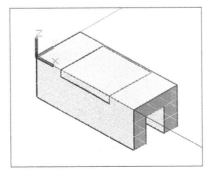

## Creating a Box

**1** Move the origin to the top surface of the box by selecting **3 Point** from the **Coordinates** panel of the **Home** tab. Define the origin, the second point, and the third point, as shown. Use the **Endpoint** object snap to define the point.

**2** Select **Box** from the **Create** panel of the **Home** tab.

```
Specify first corner or [Center]:
```

**3** Type **20,0,0** and press **Enter**.

```
Specify other corner or [Cube Length]:
```

**4** Move the cursor in the positive **X** and **Y** direction, type **60,36,0**, and press **Enter**.

```
Specify height or [2 Point]<0.0000>:
```

**5** Move the cursor in the negative **Z** direction, type **–5**, and press **Enter**.

**6** Select **Subtract** from the **Edit** panel of the **Home** tab and subtract the box from the existing object.

Figure 15-38 shows the first part of the cutout.

**Figure 15-38**

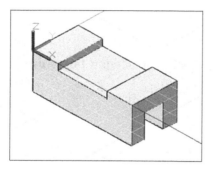

## Creating a Wedge

Next, a wedge is added to complete the cutout (Figure 15-39).

**Figure 15-39**

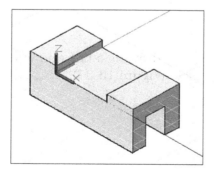

**1** Use **3 Point** to define a new UCS, as shown in Figure 15-39.

**2** Select the **Z** tool from the **Coordinates** panel of the **Home** tab and rotate the axis **–90°** around the Z axis (Figure 15-40).

**Figure 15-40**

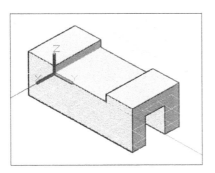

**3** Select **Wedge** from the **Create** panel of the **Home** tab.

```
Specify first corner or (Center):
```

**4** Select the **0,0,0** point of the current UCS.

```
Specify other corner or [Cube Length]:
```

**5** Use **Endpoint** object snap and select the opposite diagonal corner of the box cutout, as shown.

```
Specify height or [2 Point]<0.0000>:
```

**6** Move the cursor in the negative **Z** direction, type **–20**, and press **Enter** (Figure 15-41).

**Figure 15-41**

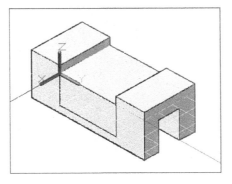

**7** Select **Subtract** from the **Edit** panel of the **Home** tab and subtract the wedge from the existing object.

**8** Use **World** from the **Coordinates** panel of the **Home** tab and return the axis system to the original location (Figure 15-42).

**Figure 15-42**

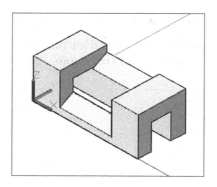

## 15-17 Intersecting Solids

Figure 15-43 shows an incomplete 3D drawing of a cone and a cylinder. The problem is to complete the drawing in 3D and show the front, top, and right-side orthographic views of the intersecting objects. In this example, the workspace is set to **3D Modeling**.

**Figure 15-43**

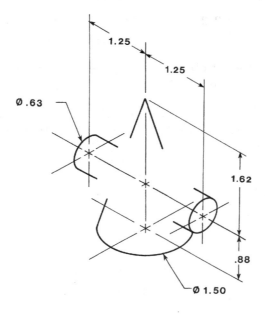

## Setting Up the Drawing

Set up the drawing screen as follows:

**Grid = 0.50 × 0.50**

**Snap = .25**

**Units = Decimal**

**View = SE Isometric**

**Template = acad3D**

**3D Modeling** workspace

The objects are small, so use the mouse wheel or the **Zoom** command to create a comfortable visual size.

## Drawing the Cone

**1** Select **Cone** from the **Box** drop-down on the **Modeling** panel of the **Home** tab (Figure 15-44).

```
Command: _cone
Specify center point of base or [3P 2P Ttr Elliptical]
```

**Figure 15-44**

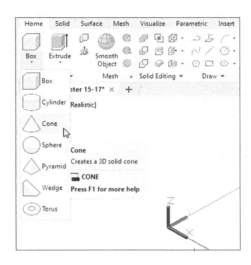

**2** Type **0,0,0** and press **Enter**.

The center point of the cone is located on the origin of the WCS.

```
Specify base radius or [Diameter] <0,0000>:
```

**3** Type **d** and press **Enter**.

```
Specify diameter:
```

**4** Type **1.50** and press **Enter**.

```
Specify height or [2 Point Axis endpoint Top radius]<1.0000>:
```

**5** Move the cursor in the positive **Z** direction, type **2.50**, and press **Enter**. (Figure 15-45).

**Figure 15-45**

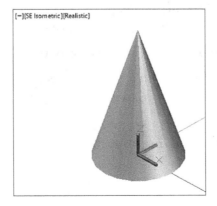

**6** Click **Realistic** in the **Visual Styles Controls** at the top left of the drawing area and change the style to **Conceptual**.

## Drawing the Cylinder

**1** Select the **Origin** UCS tool from the **Coordinates** panel on the **3D Modeling** workspace.

```
Command: _ucs

Specify new origin point <0,0,0>:
```

To change the workspace, click the **Workspace Switching** tool on the ribbon at the bottom of the drawing screen and select the **3D Modeling** workspace.

**2** Type **1.25,0,0** and press **Enter**.

The origin is now located in the same plane as the end of the cylinder (Figure 15-46).

**Figure 15-46**

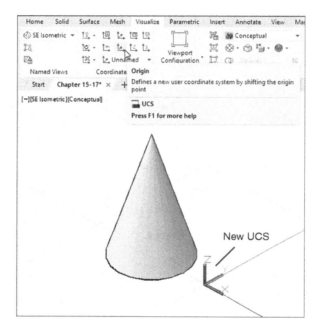

**3** Select **X Axis Rotate UCS** from the **Coordinates** panel of the **Home** tab and press **Enter** to accept the 90° default value. Then select **Y Axis Rotate UCS**, type **290**, and press **Enter**.

**4** Select **Cylinder** from the **Modeling** panel of the **Home** tab.

```
Command: _cylinder

Specify center point of base or [3P 2P Elliptical]:
```

**5** Type **0,.88,0**.

```
Specify base radius or [Diameter] <0.0000>:
```

**6** Type **d** and press **Enter**.

```
Specify diameter <1.0000>:
```

**7** Type **.63** and press **Enter**.

```
Specify height or [2Point Axis endpoint] <1.0000>:
```

**8** Move the cursor in the positive **Z** direction, type **2.50**, and press **Enter** (Figure 15-47).

**Figure 15-47**

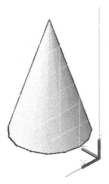

## Completing the 3D Model

**1** Select the **Union** tool from the **Solid Editing** panel of the **Home** tab.

```
Command: _union
Select objects:
```

**2** Select the cone.

```
Select objects:
```

**3** Select the cylinder.

```
Select objects:
```

**4** Press **Enter**.

```
Command:
```

**5** Select the **World** tool from the **Coordinates** panel of the **Home** tab.

**6** Turn off **Grid** (Figure 15-48).

**Figure 15-48**

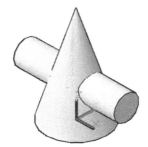

## Creating Viewports for the Orthographic Views

Click the **Visualize** tab in the **3D Modeling** workspace, access the **Viewport Configuration** panel, and select the **Four: Equal** option (Figure 15-49).

**Figure 15-49**

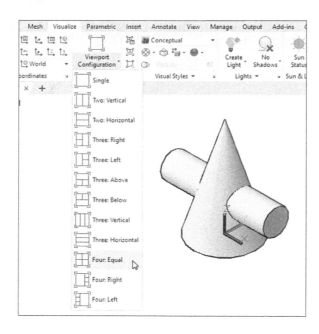

AutoCAD creates four equal viewports. These views can then be modified, as explained in Section 14-13, to show front, top, and right-side orthographic views of the object (Figure 15-50).

**Figure 15-50**

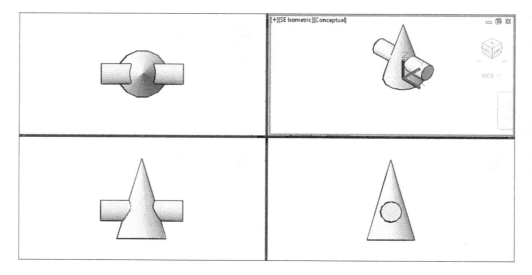

## 15-18 Solid Models of Castings

Figure 15-51 shows a casting. Note that the object includes rounded edges. These rounded edges can be created on a solid model by using the **Fillet** command. (The **Fillet** command is explained in Chapter 2.)

Decimal inches are used for all dimensions in this model.

**Figure 15-51**

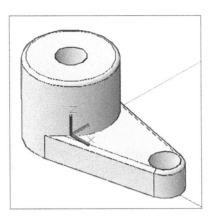

### Drawing the Basic Shape

The basic shape is first drawn in 2D and then extruded into a 3D solid.

**1** Set up the drawing screen as needed.

In this example, the **acad3D** template was used, and a top view was set by clicking the word **Top** on the **View** cube or by clicking **View Controls** in the top-left corner of the drawing area.

**2** Draw the basic shape by using first the **Circle** tool and then the **Line** tool along with the **Tangent** object snap (which you activate by pressing **Ctrl** and right-clicking) mode (Figure 15-52).

**Figure 15-52**

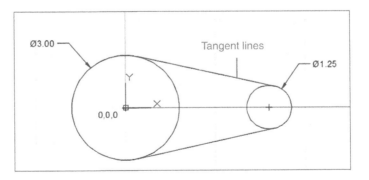

It is important to know the center point locations for the two circles in terms of their X,Y components. In this example, the center point location for the large circle is 0,0, and the location for the small circle is 4,0. The large circle's diameter equals 3.00 inches, and the small circle's diameter equals 1.25 inches. The circles are 4.0 inches apart.

**3** Trim the smaller circle so the inner portion is removed (Figure 15-53).

Figure 15-53

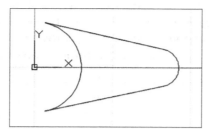

## Creating a Polyline from the Basic Shape

Because only closed objects can be extruded as solids, some of the lines in the basic shape must be formed into a polyline. The large circle can be extruded, so it need not be included as part of the polyline; however, the polyline must be a closed area, so it needs part of the circle. The needed circular segment can be created by drawing a second large circle directly over the existing circle and then using the **Trim** command to remove the excess portion. Remember that two lines can occupy the same space in AutoCAD drawings. If you have difficulty working with the two large circles, trim the circles and then add another larger circle, if needed.

Figure 15-53 shows the resulting shape that will be joined to form a polyline.

**1** Select the **Edit Polyline** tool from the **Modify** panel of the **Home** tab.

```
Command: _pedit

Select polyline or [Multiple]:
```

**2** Select the remaining portion of the small circle.

```
Object selected is not a polyline
Do you want to turn it into one? <Y>
```

**3** Press **Enter**.

```
Enter an option [Close Join Width Edit vertex Fit/Spline Decurve
Ltype gen Undo eXit] <X>:
```

**4** Select the **Join** option and press **Enter**.

```
Select objects:
```

**5** Window the object and press **Enter**.

```
Select objects:
```

**6** Press **Enter** twice.

There are no visible changes to the lines, but the lines are combined to form a single polyline.

## Extruding the Shape

**1** Select **SE Isometric** from the **Visualize** panel of the **Home** tab and make it the current view.

**2** Use the **Zoom** tool, if needed, to present the figure at a comfortable visual size (Figure 15-54).

**Figure 15-54**

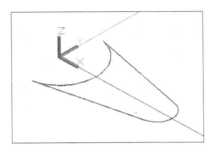

**3** Select **Extrude** from the **Modeling** panel of the **Home** tab.

```
Command: _extrude

Select objects to extrude:
```

**4** Select the polyline and assign a height of **1.00** (Figure 15-55).

```
Command:
```

The shape is presented in the **Conceptual** visual style.

**Figure 15-55**

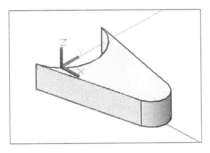

**5** Select **Cylinder** from the **Modeling** panel of the **Home** tab and create a cylinder whose diameter equals the original large-circle diameter (ø**3.00**) and whose height is **3**, with a center point of **0,0,0** (Figure 15-56).

**Figure 15-56**

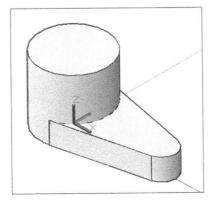

## Adding the Holes

Create the holes by subtracting cylinders from the object.

**1** Select **Cylinder** from the **Modeling** panel of the **Home** tab.

```
Command: _cylinder
Specify center point for base of cylinder or [Elliptical] <0,0,0>:
```

**2** Type **0,0,0** and press **Enter**.

This value came from the original circle's center point location.

**3** Enter the appropriate diameter and height values.

In this example, a radius of **0.50** inch and a height of **3.5** were selected.

```
Command:
```

**4** Repeat the **Cylinder** command.

```
Specify center point for base of cylinder or [Elliptical] <0,0,0>:
```

**5** Type **4,0,0**.

**6** Draw a **ø1.00 × 1.25** cylinder (Figure 15-57).

**Figure 15-57**

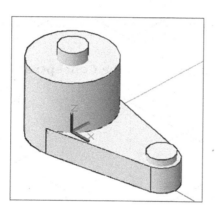

**7** Select **Union** from the **Solid Editing** panel of the **Home** tab and join the large cylinder portion of the object to the polyline portion.

**8** Select **Subtract** from the **Solid Editing** panel of the **Home** tab and subtract the cylinders from the basic shape (Figure 15-58).

**Figure 15-58**

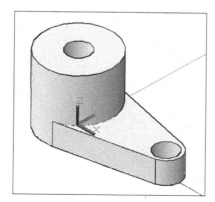

## Creating the Rounded Edges

**1** Select Fillet from the Modify panel of the Home tab.

Command: _fillet

Current settings: Mode = TRIM, Radius = 0.5000.

Select first object or [Undo Polyline Radius Trim Multiple]:

**2** Type **r** and enter the value **.125**.

**3** Repeat the **Fillet** command and select the outside edge of the top surface of the large cylindrical portion of the object.

Enter fillet radius <0.1250>:

**4** Press **Enter**.

Select first object or [Undo Polyline Radius Trim Multiple]:

**5** Press **Enter** (Figure 15-59).

**Figure 15-59**

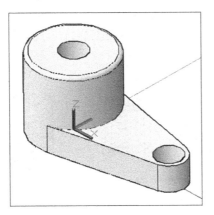

**6** Use the **Fillet** tool to create a fillet along the top edges of the object, as shown in Figure 15-60.

**Figure 15-60**

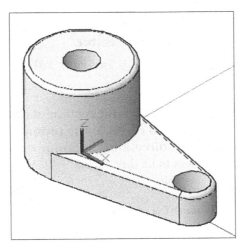

Note that the arc edge line between the large cylindrical portion of the object and the extended flat area cannot be filleted.

## 15-19 Thread Representations in Solid Models

This section explains how to draw thread representations for solid models. The procedure presented here only broadly represents a thread. It is not an actual detailed solid drawing of a thread. As with the thread representations presented in Chapter 11 for 2D drawings, 3D representations are acceptable for most applications.

**1** Select **Cylinder** from the **Modeling** panel of the **Home** tab and draw a cylinder.

In the example shown in Figure 15-61, a cylinder of diameter **3** and a height of **6** was drawn centered about the **0,0,0** point of the WCS. It is presented on the **acad3D** template with a **2D Wireframe** visual style, which displays the cylinder in its simplest wireframe form: circles at top and bottom and two lines to represent the diameter.

**Figure 15-61**

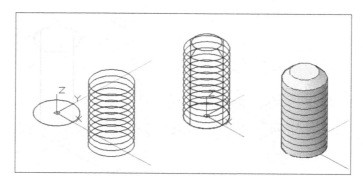

**2** Draw a circle with a diameter equal to the diameter of the cylinder. In this example, use ⌀**3.00**.

**3** Select the **Array** command from the **Modify** panel of the **Home** tab.

```
Select object:
```

**4** Select the circle and press **Enter**.

```
Enter array type [Rectangular Path Polar] <Polar>:
```

**5** Type **R**.

AutoCAD displays the default rectangular array pattern of three rows and four columns. Go through the prompts for the array by picking the number of rows (X direction), the number of columns (Y direction), and the number of levels (Z direction).

**6** Type **R** again.

```
Enter the number of rows or [Expression] <3>:
```

**7** Type **1** and press **Enter**.

```
Specify the distance between rows or [Total Expression] <4.5000>:
```

There is only one row, so the distance between is ignored.

**8** Press **Enter** to go to the next prompt, and click the word **COLumns** in the command prompt.

```
Enter the number of columns or [Expression] <4>:
```

**9** Type **1** and press **Enter**.

There is only one column, so the distance between is ignored.

**10** Press **Enter** to go to the next prompt, and type **L** or click **Levels** in the command prompt.

```
Enter the number of levels or [Expression]: <1>
```

**11** Type **11** and press **Enter**.

The number 11 is used because the cylinder is 6 units high, and in this example, circles representing threads are spaced 0.5 apart. The top edge of the thread is chamfered.

```
Specify the distance between levels or [Total Expression] <1.0000>:
```

**12** Type **.5** and press **Enter**.

**13** Select the **Move** tool from the **Modify** panel of the **Home** tab and move the arrayed circles' center points to the **0,0,0** origin.

**14** Select the **Chamfer** tool from the **Modify** panel of the **Home** tab and draw a **.5 × .5** chamfer around the top edge of the cylinder.

Figure 15-61 shows the completed simple thread representation in **2D Wireframe** and **Conceptual** visual styles.

## 15-20 List

Use the **List** command to display database information for a drawn solid object. Figure 15-62 shows a list for the cone-cylinder object shown in Figure 15-48. There is no icon for the **List** command. Type **list** in response to a command prompt and select the object.

**Figure 15-62**

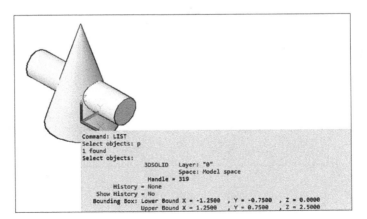

## 15-21 Massprop

Use the **Massprop** command to display information about the structural characteristics of an object. Figure 15-63 shows **Massprop** information for the object shown in Figure 15-48. To access the **Massprop** command, type **massprop** at the command prompt and select the object.

**Figure 15-63**

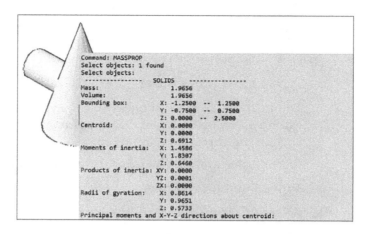

## 15-22 Face and Edge Editing

AutoCAD enables you to edit faces and edges of existing solids. The **Solid Editing** tools are located on the **Solid Editing** panel of the **Home** tab in the **3D Modeling** workspace (Figure 15-64). The following examples are based on a solid box with dimensions $4 \times 2 \times 3$ drawn in the **Shaded with edges** visual style.

**Figure 15-64**

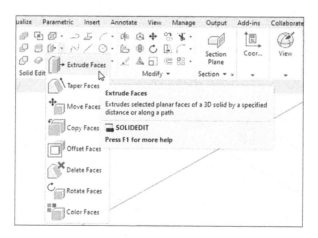

## Extruding a Face

In Figure 15-65, the right side face of the box has been extruded by two units.

**Figure 15-65**

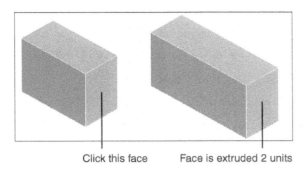

Click this face     Face is extruded 2 units

**1** Select **Extrude Faces** from the **Solid Editing** panel of the **Home** tab.

`Select faces or [Undo Remove]:`

**2** Select the right face by moving the cursor to the center of that face and clicking.

`Select faces or [Undo Remove ALL]:`

**3** Right-click and select **Enter**.

`Specify height of extrusion or [Path]:`

**4** Type **2** and press **Enter**.

`Specify angle of taper for extrusion or [Path] :`

**5** Press **Enter**.

**6** Select the **eXit** option or a new command.

## Extruding a Face Along a Path

In Figure 15-66, a line has been drawn from the right corner of the box 3 units long, at 30°. This line serves as the extrusion path.

**Figure 15-66**

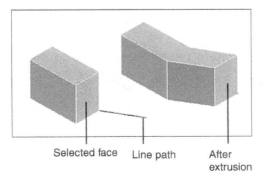

Selected face    Line path    After
extrusion

**1** Select **Extrude Faces** from the **Solid Editing** panel of the **Home** tab.

```
Select faces or [Undo Remove]:
```

**2** Click the right face.

```
Select faces or [Undo Remove]:
```

**3** Right-click and select **Enter**.

```
Specify height of extrusion or [Path]:
```

**4** Type **p** and press **Enter**.

```
Select extrusion path:
```

**5** Select the line.

```
[Extrude Move Rotate Offset Taper Delete Copy coLor mAterial Undo
eXit] <eXit>:
```

**6** Type **X** to exit the prompt.

A second set of options appears under the same heading.

```
Enter a solids editing option [Face Edge Body Undo eXit] <eXit>:
```

**7** Type **X** again to exit the command.

## Extruding Two Faces at the Same Time

In this example, two faces of a box are extruded at the same time (Figure 15-67).

**Figure 15-67**

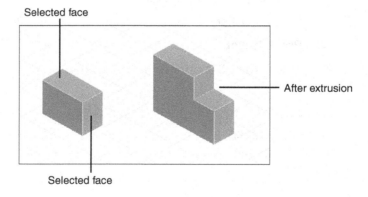

Selected face

After extrusion

Selected face

**1** Select **Extrude Faces** from the **Solid Editing** panel of the **Home** tab.

```
Select faces or [Undo Remove]:
```

**2** Select the right face and then select the top face.

```
Select faces or [Undo Remove ALL]:
```

**3** Right-click and select **Enter**.

```
Specify height of extrusion or [Path]:
```

**4** Type **2** and press **Enter**.

```
Specify angle of taper for extrusion <0>:
```

**5** Press **Enter**.

```
[Extrude Move Rotate Offset Taper Delete Copy coLor mAterial Undo
eXit] <eXit>:
```

**6** Type **X** to exit the prompt.

A second set of options appears under the same heading.

```
Enter a solids editing option [Face Edge Body Undo eXit] <eXit>:
```

**7** Type **X** to exit the command.

## Moving a Face

The process of moving a face is similar to the process of extruding a face (Figure 15-68). You might want to move a face when making minor adjustments.

**Figure 15-68**

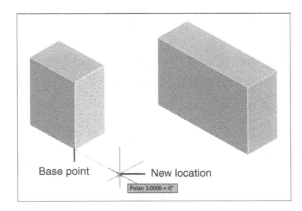

Base point    New location

Polar: 3.0000 < 0°

**1** Select **Move Faces** from the **Solid Editing** panel of the **Home** tab.

```
Select faces or [Undo Remove]:
```

**2** Select the right face and press **Enter**.

```
Select faces or [Undo Remove ALL]:
Specify a base point or displacement:
```

**3** Select the corner of the box, as shown.

Use **Endpoint** object snap to pick the corner.

```
Specify a second point of displacement:
```

**4** Select a second point along the X axis.

**5** Press **Enter**.

**6** Type **X** to exit the prompt.

A second set of options appears under the same heading.

```
Enter a solids editing option [Face Edge Body Undo eXit] <eXit>:
```

**7** Type **X** to exit the command.

## Offsetting Faces

The following steps show how to edit a solid box by offsetting its faces (Figure 15-69).

Figure 15-69

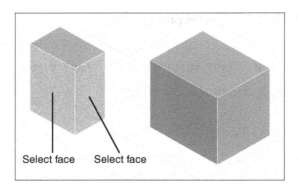

1. Select **Offset Faces** from the **Solid Editing** panel of the **Home** tab.

   ```
   Select faces or [Undo Remove]:
   ```

2. Select the right and front faces, right-click, and select **Enter**.

   ```
   Specify the offset distance:
   ```

3. Type **1.5** and press **Enter**.

4. Select the **eXit** option or a new command.

   A second set of options appears under the same heading.

5. Select the **eXit** option or a new command.

## Rotating a Face

The following steps show how to edit a solid box by rotating a face (Figure 15-70).

Figure 15-70

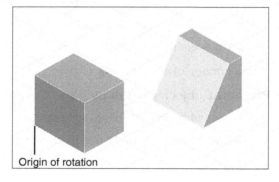

1. Select the **Rotate Faces** tool from the **Solid Editing** panel of the **Home** tab.

   ```
   Select faces or [Undo Remove]:
   ```

2. Select the front face, right-click, and select **Enter**.

   ```
   Specify an axis point or [Axis by object View Xaxis Yaxis Zaxis]
   <2 points>:
   ```

3. Type **x** and press **Enter**.

   ```
   Specify the origin of the rotation <0,0,0>:
   ```

**4** Pick the lower-left corner of the box.

```
Specify a rotation angle or [Reference]:
```

**5** Type **–30** and press **Enter**.

An input of **30** would rotate the face in the opposite direction.

```
[Extrude Move Rotate Offset Taper Delete Copy coLor mAterial Undo
eXit] <eXit>:
```

**6** Type **X** to exit the command prompt.

A second set of options appears under the same heading.

```
Enter a solids editing option [Face Edge Body Undo eXit] <eXit>:
```

**7** Type **X** to exit the command.

## Tapering a Face

The following steps show how to edit a solid box by tapering a face (Figure 15-71).

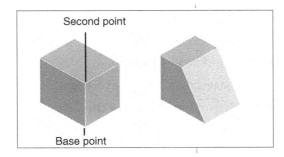

**1** Select **Taper Faces** from the **Solid Editing** panel of the **Home** tab.

```
Select faces or [Undo Remove]:
```

**2** Select the right front face.

```
Select faces or [Undo Remove]:
```

**3** Right-click and select **Enter**.

```
Specify the base point:
```

**4** Select the lower-right corner of the right face (Figure 15-71).

```
Specify another point along the axis of tapering:
```

**5** Use an **Endpoint** object snap and pick the lower-left corner of the front face, as shown in Figure 15-71.

```
Specify the taper angle:
```

**6** Type **30** and press **Enter**.

```
[Extrude Move Rotate Offset Taper Delete Copy coLor Undo eXit]<eXit>:
```

**7** Type **X** to exit the command prompt.

A second set of options appears under the same heading.

```
Enter a solids editing option [Face Edge Body Undo eXit] <eXit>:
```

**8** Type **X** to exit the command.

## Copying a Face

The following steps show how to edit a solid box by copying a face (Figure 15-72) as a 2D surface or region.

Figure 15-72

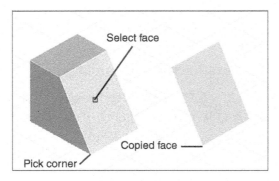

**1** Select **Copy Faces** from the **Solid Editing** panel of the **Home** tab.

    Select faces or [Undo Remove]:

**2** Select the tapered face.

    Select faces or [Undo Remove]:

**3** Right-click and select **Enter**.

    Specify a base point or displacement:

**4** Select the lower-left corner of the box.

    Specify a second point of displacement:

**5** Select the location for the copied face.

    [Extrude Move Rotate Offset Taper Delete Copy coLor Undo eXit]<eXit>:

**6** Type **X** to exit the command prompt.

    A second set of options appears under the same heading.

    Enter a solids editing option [Face Edge Body Undo eXit] <eXit>:

**7** Type **X** to exit the command.

## Copying Edges

The following steps show how to edit a solid box by tapering a face (Figure 15-73).

Figure 15-73

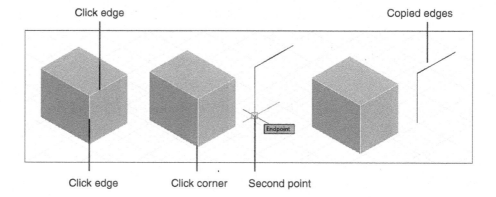

**1** Select **Copy Edges** from the **Extract Edges** drop-down on the **Solid Editing** panel of the **Home** tab.

```
Select edges or [Undo Remove]:
```

**2** Select two edges.

```
Select edges or [Undo Remove]:
```

**3** Right-click and select **Enter**.

```
Specify a base point or displacement:
```

**4** Select the lower endpoint of the vertical line.

```
Specify a second point of displacement:
```

**5** Select a second point.

```
Enter an edge editing option [Copy coLor Undo eXit] <eXit>:
```

**6** Type **x** and press **Enter**.

## Imprinting an Object

The following steps show how to edit a solid box by imprinting an object onto the solid (Figure 15-74).

**Figure 15-74**

2D circle to be imprinted          Circle imprinted on solid box

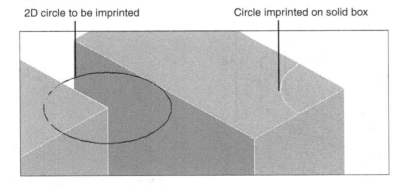

**1** Draw a solid box (**4 × 2 × 3**) and then draw a **ø2.00** circle with its center point on the upper-right corner of the box, as shown.

**2** Select **Imprint** from the **Extract Edges** drop-down on the **Solid Editing** panel of the **Home** tab.

```
Select a 3D solid:
```

**3** Select the box.

```
Select an object to imprint:
```

**4** Select the circle.

```
Select the source object <N>:
```

**5** Type **y** and press **Enter** twice.

# 15-23 EXERCISE PROBLEMS

Draw the objects in Exercise Problems EX15-1 through EX15-43 as follows:

**1** Draw each as a solid model.

**2** Create front, top, and right-side orthographic views from the solid models.

**3** Dimension the orthographic views.

## EX15-1 Inches

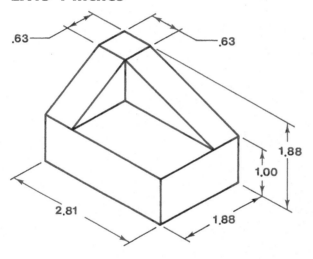

## EX15-2 Inches

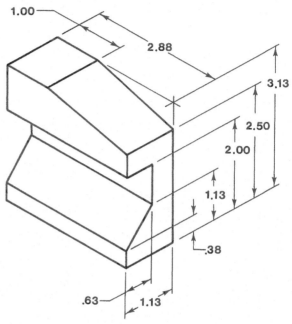

## EX15-3 Millimeters

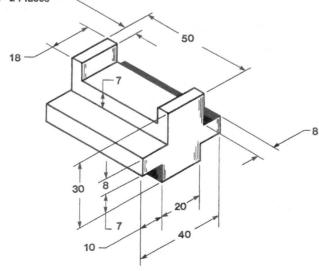

## EX15-4 Millimeters

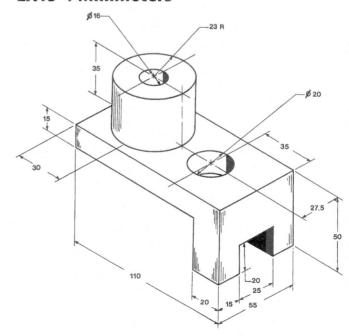

## EX15-5 Inches

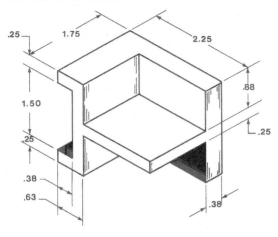

## EX15-6 Millimeters

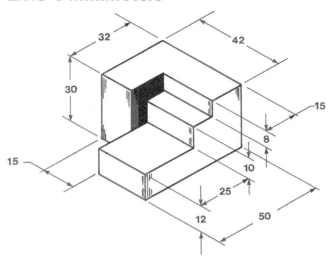

## EX15-7 Millimeters

Slot is 15 deep

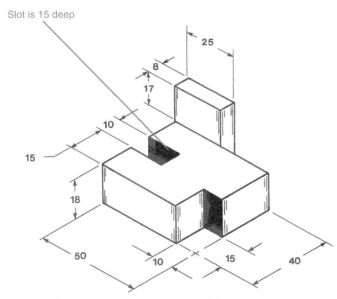

## EX15-8 Millimeters

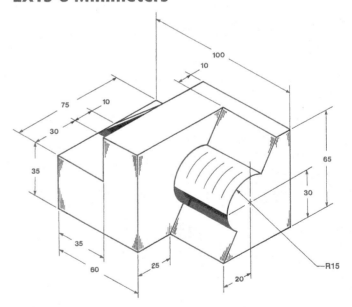

# EX15-9 Inches

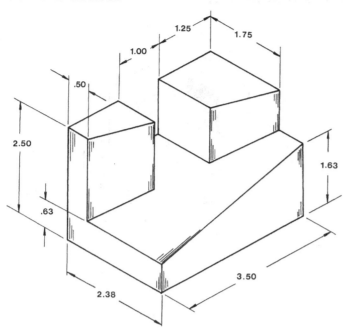

# EX15-10 Millimeters

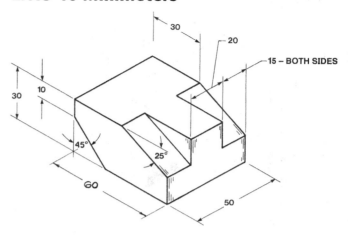

# EX15-12 Inches

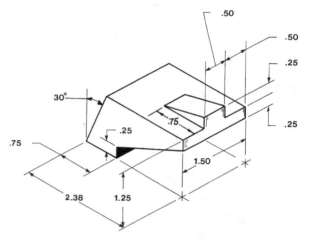

# EX15-11 Millimeters

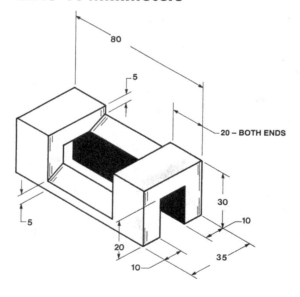

# EX15-13 Millimeters

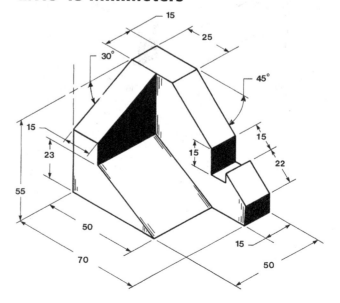

## EX15-14 Inches

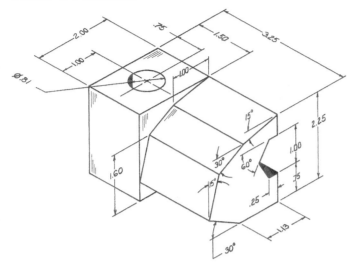

## EX15-15 Millimeters

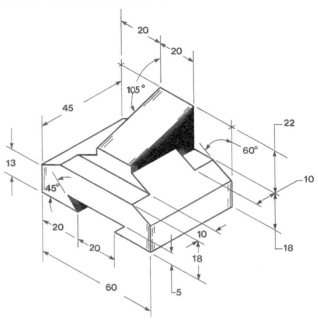

## EX15-16 Millimeters

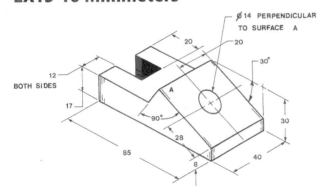

## EX15-17 Inches

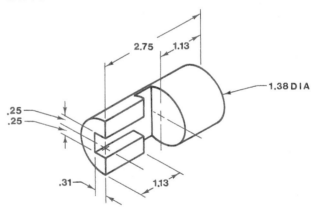

## EX15-18 Millimeters

Note: Slot is 12 deep
from centerline

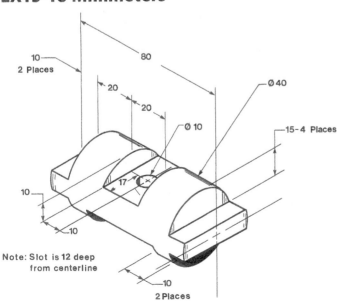

## EX15-19 Millimeters

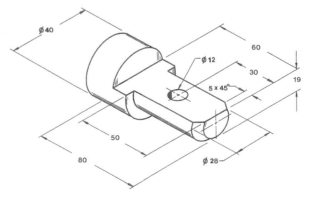

## EX15-20 Millimeters

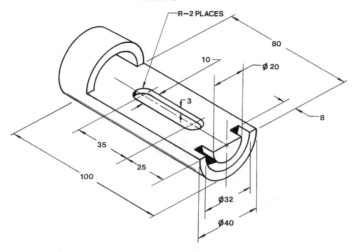

## EX15-21 Inches

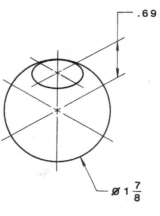

## EX15-22 Millimeters

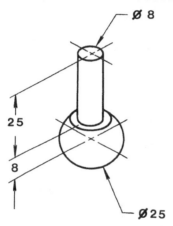

## EX15-23 Millimeters

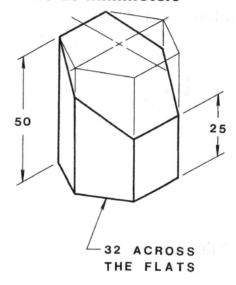

## EX15-24 Millimeters

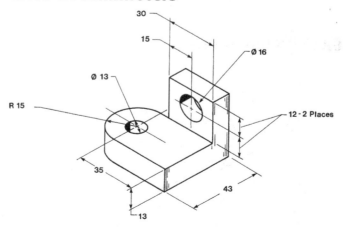

## EX15-25 Millimeters

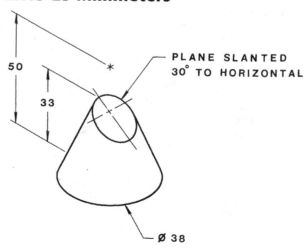

## EX15-26 Millimeters (Scale 2:1)

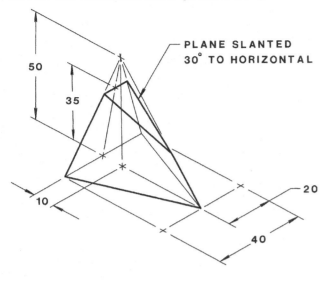

PLANE SLANTED
30° TO HORIZONTAL

50

35

10

20

40

## EX15-27 Millimeters

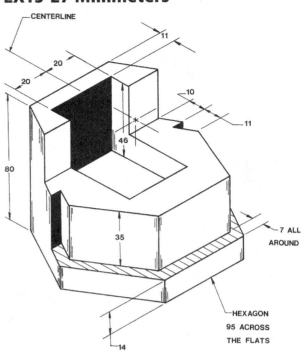

CENTERLINE

11

20

20

10

11

46

80

35

7 ALL
AROUND

14

HEXAGON
95 ACROSS
THE FLATS

## EX15-28 Inches

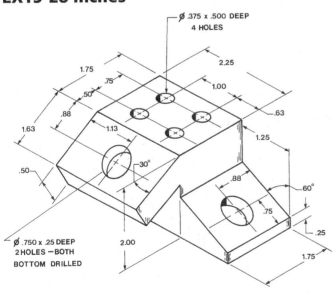

Ø .375 x .500 DEEP
4 HOLES

1.75

2.25

.75

.50

1.00

.88

.63

1.63

1.13

1.25

.50

30°

.88

60°

.75

.25

Ø .750 x .25 DEEP
2 HOLES — BOTH
BOTTOM DRILLED

2.00

1.75

## EX15-29 Millimeters

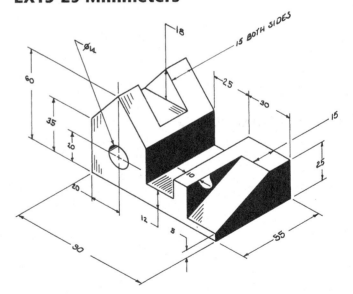

Ø 14

18

15 BOTH SIDES

60

35

20

25

30

15

20

25

10

12

8

90

55

## EX15-30 Inches (Scale 2:1)

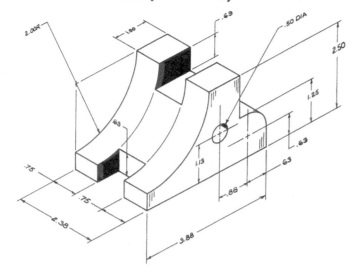

## EX15-31 Millimeters

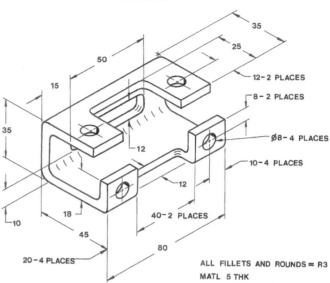

12- 2 PLACES
8- 2 PLACES
Ø8- 4 PLACES
10- 4 PLACES
40- 2 PLACES
20- 4 PLACES

ALL FILLETS AND ROUNDS = R3
MATL 5 THK

## EX15-32 Millimeters (Scale 2:1)

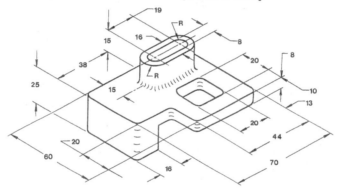

ALL FILLETS AND ROUNDS= R3

## EX15-33 Millimeters

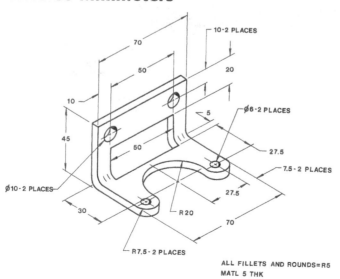

10- 2 PLACES
Ø6- 2 PLACES
7.5- 2 PLACES
Ø10- 2 PLACES
R 20
R7.5- 2 PLACES

ALL FILLETS AND ROUNDS=R5
MATL 5 THK

## EX15-34 Millimeters

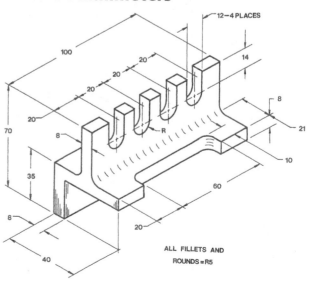

12—4 PLACES

ALL FILLETS AND
ROUNDS = R5

## EX15-35 Inches (Scale 2:1)

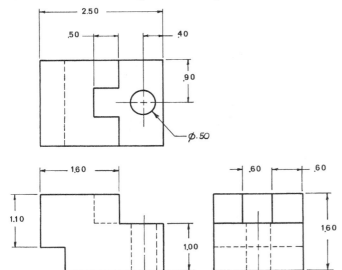

## EX15-36 Inches (Scale 4:1)

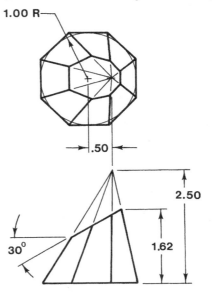

## EX15-37 Inches

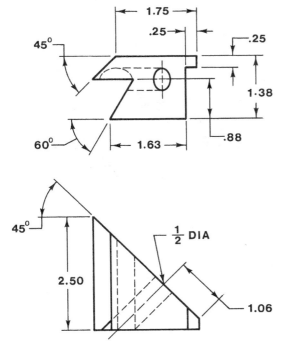

## EX15-38 Inches

TOP

ALL FILLETS AND ROUNDS $= \frac{1}{8}$ R

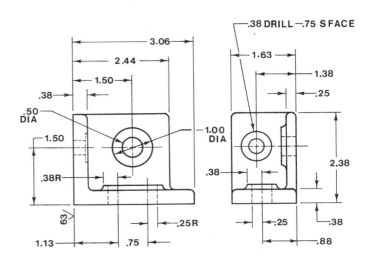

## EX15-39 Millimeters

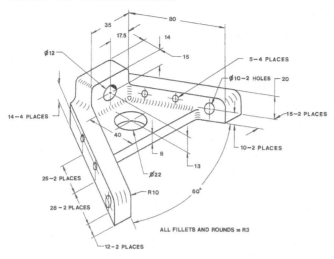

## EX15-40 Millimeters

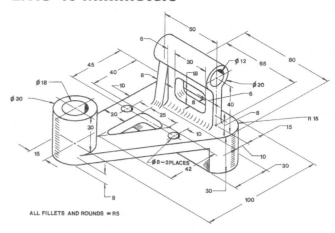

ALL FILLETS AND ROUNDS = R5

## EX15-41 Millimeters

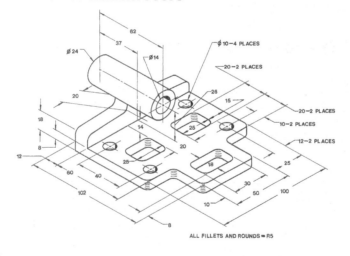

ALL FILLETS AND ROUNDS = R5

## EX15-42 Millimeters

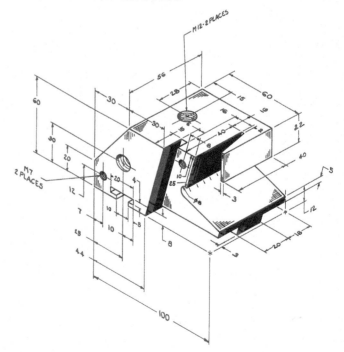

## EX15-43 Millimeters

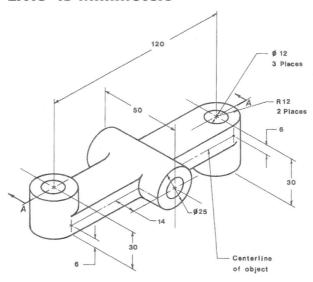

## EX15-44 Inches

Draw a solid model of the object and then create the three indicated sectional views from the model.

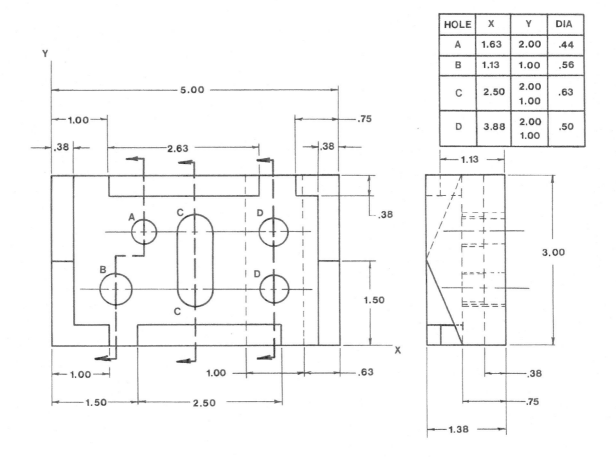

| HOLE | X | Y | DIA |
|------|------|-----------|------|
| A | 1.63 | 2.00 | .44 |
| B | 1.13 | 1.00 | .56 |
| C | 2.50 | 2.00<br>1.00 | .63 |
| D | 3.88 | 2.00<br>1.00 | .50 |

## EX15-45 Millimeters

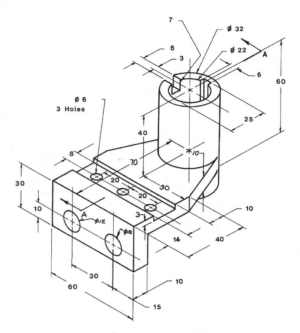

Redraw the assemblies in Exercise Problems EX 15-46 through EX 15-48 as exploded solid models with the individual parts located in approximately the positions shown.

## EX15-46 Millimeters

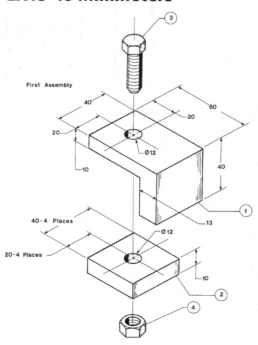

## EX15-47 Millimeters

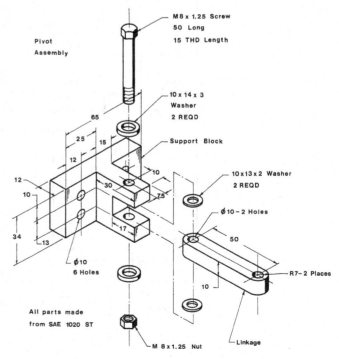

## EX15-48 Millimeters

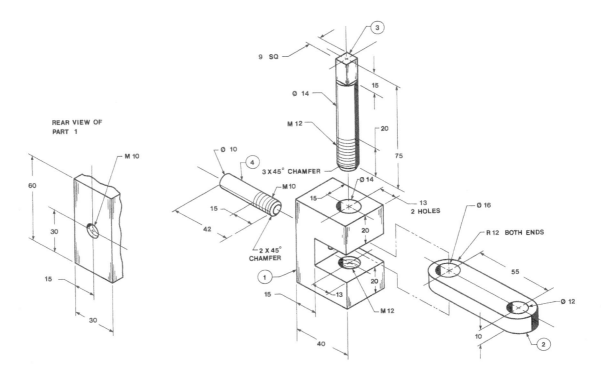

Prepare solid models and 3D orthographic views of the intersecting objects in Exercise Problems EX15-49 through EX15-54.

## EX15-49 Inches

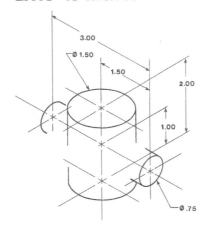

## EX15-50 Millimeters

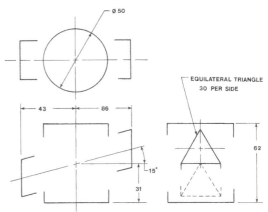

## EX15-51 Millimeters

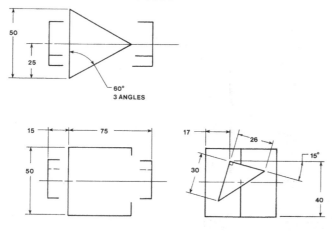

## EX15-52 Millimeters

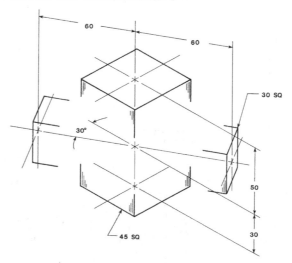

## EX15-53 Millimeters

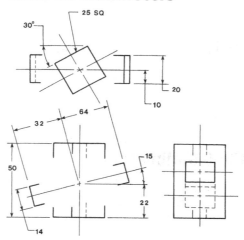

## EX15-54 Inches

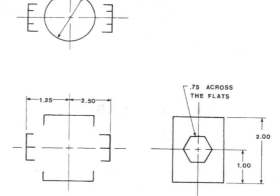

Prepare solid models and 3D orthographic views of the assemblies in Exercise Problems EX15-55 through EX15-59.

# EX15-55 Millimeters

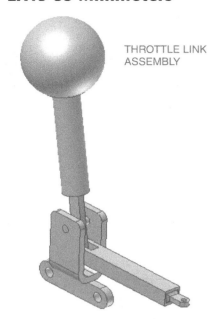

THROTTLE LINK
ASSEMBLY

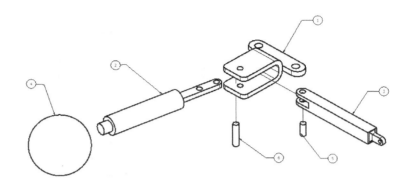

| Parts List | | | | |
|---|---|---|---|---|
| ITEM | PART NUMBER | DESCRIPTION | MATERIAL | QTY |
| 1 | ENG-A43 | BOX,PIVOT | SAE1020 | 1 |
| 2 | ENG-A44 | POST,HANDLE | SAE1020 | 1 |
| 3 | ENG-A45 | LINK | SAE1020 | 1 |
| 4 | AM300-1 | HANDLE | STEEL | 1 |
| 5 | EK-132 | POST-Ø6x14 | STEEL | 1 |
| 6 | EK-131 | POST-Ø6x26 | STEEL | 1 |

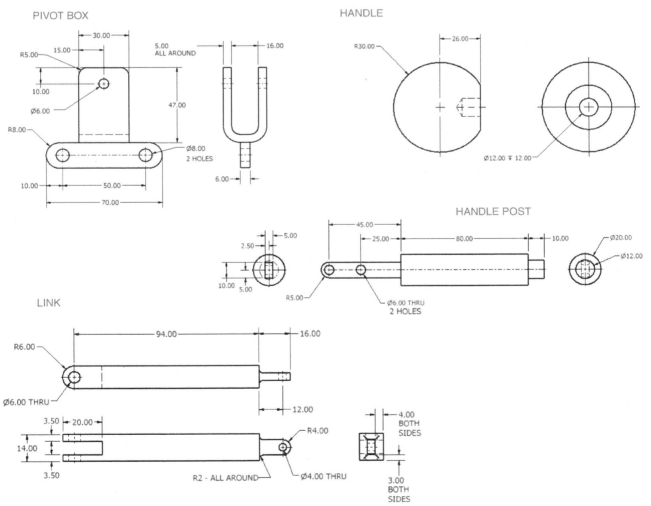

PIVOT BOX

HANDLE

HANDLE POST

LINK

# EX15-56

ADJUSTABLE ASSEMBLY

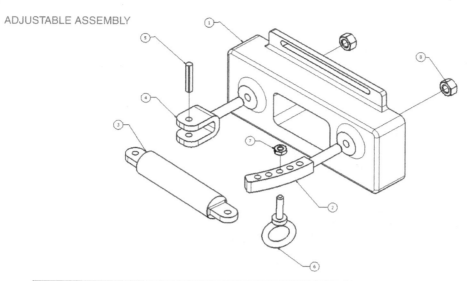

| Parts List | | | | |
|---|---|---|---|---|
| ITEM | PART NUMBER | DESCRIPTION | MATERIAL | QTY |
| 1 | ENG-311 | BASE#4, CAST | Cast Iron | 1 |
| 2 | ENG-312 | SUPPORT, ROUNDED | SAE 1040 STEEL | 1 |
| 3 | ENG-404 | POST, ADJUSTABLE | Steel, Mild | 1 |
| 4 | BU-1964 | YOKE | Cast Iron | 1 |
| 5 | ANSI B18.8.2 1/4x1.3120 | Grooved pin, Type C - 1/4x1.312 ANSI B18.8.2 | Steel, Mild | 1 |
| 6 | ANSI B18.15 - 1/4 - 20. Shoulder Pattern Type 2 - Style A | Forged Eyebolt | Steel, Mild | 1 |
| 7 | ANSI B18.6.3 - 1/4 - 20 | Hex Machine Screw Nut | Steel, Mild | 1 |
| 8 | ANSI B18.2.2 - 3/8 - 16 | Hex Nut | Steel, Mild | 2 |

CAST BASE #4

ROUNDED SUPPORT

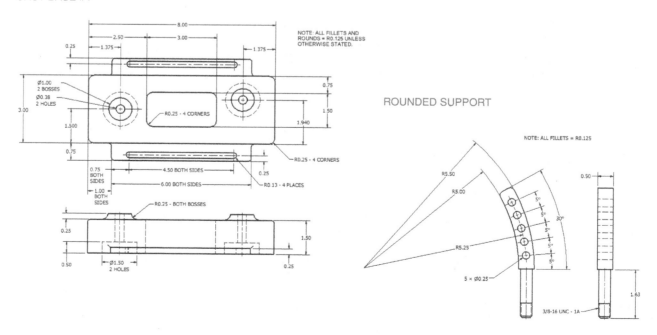

# EX15-56, continued

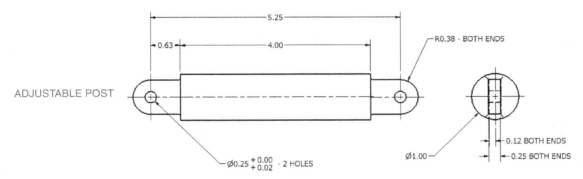

ADJUSTABLE POST

5.25
0.63
4.00
R0.38 - BOTH ENDS
Ø0.25 $^{+0.00}_{+0.02}$ - 2 HOLES
Ø1.00
0.12 BOTH ENDS
0.25 BOTH ENDS

NOTE: ALL FILLETS = R 0.125

YOKE

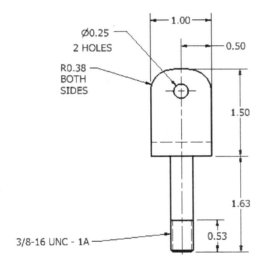

Ø0.25
2 HOLES
R0.38
BOTH
SIDES
1.00
0.50
1.50
1.63
0.53
3/8-16 UNC - 1A

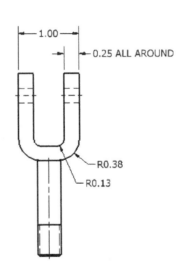

1.00
0.25 ALL AROUND
R0.38
R0.13

FORGED EYEBOLT

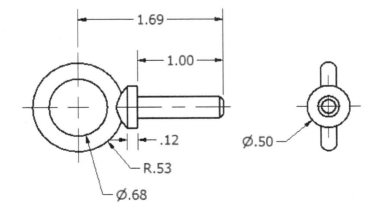

1.69
1.00
.12
R.53
Ø.68
Ø.50

# EX15-57

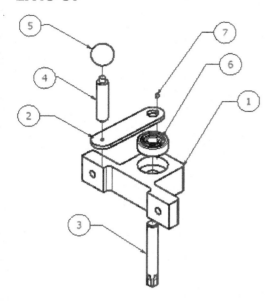

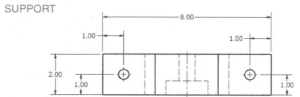

SUPPORT

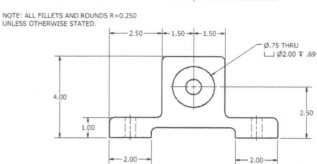

NOTE: ALL FILLETS AND ROUNDS R=0.250
UNLESS OTHERWISE STATED.

| Parts List | | | | |
|---|---|---|---|---|
| ITEM | PART NUMBER | DESCRIPTION | MATERIAL | QTY |
| 1 | EK131-1 | SUPPORT | STEEL | 1 |
| 2 | EK131-2 | LINK | STEEL | 1 |
| 3 | EK131-3 | SHAFT,DRIVE | STEEL | 1 |
| 4 | EK131-4 | POST, THREADED | STEEL | 1 |
| 5 | EK131-5 | BALL | STEEL | 1 |
| 6 | BS 292 - BRM 3/4 | Deep Groove Ball Bearings | STEEL,MILD | 1 |
| 7 | 3/16x1/8x1/4 | RECTANGULAR KEY | STEEL | 1 |

LINK

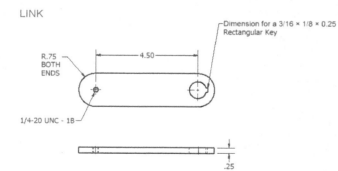

DRIVE SHAFT

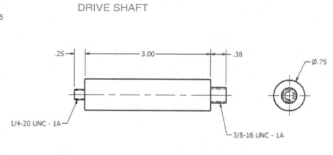

BALL

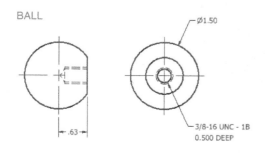

THREADED POST

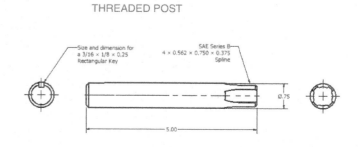

# EX15-58

| | | Parts List | |
|---|---|---|---|
| ITEM | QTY | PART NUMBER | DESCRIPTION |
| 1 | 1 | ENG-2008-A | BASE, CAST |
| 2 | 1 | DIN625 - SKF 6203 | Single row ball bearings |
| 3 | 1 | SHF--4004-16 | SHAFT: Ø16×120, WITH 2.3×5×16 KEYWAY |
| 4 | 1 | | SUB-ASSEMBLY, FOLLOWER |
| 5 | 1 | SPR-C22 | SPRING, COMPRESSION |
| 6 | 1 | GB 273.2-87 - 7/70 - 8 x 18 x 5 | Rolling bearings - Thrust bearings - Plan of boundary dimensions |
| 7 | 1 | IS 2048 - 1983 - Specification for Parallel Keys and Keyways B 5 x 5 x 16 | KEY, SQUARE |

## FOLLOWER SUBASSEMBLY

| | | Parts List | | |
|---|---|---|---|---|
| ITEM | PART NUMBER | DESCRIPTION | MATERIAL | QTY |
| 1 | AM-232 | HOLDER | STEEL | 1 |
| 2 | AM-256 | POST, FOLLOWER | STEEL | 1 |
| 3 | BS 1804-2 - 4 x 30 | Parallel steel dowel pins - metric series | Steel, Mild | 1 |
| 4 | DIN625- SKF 634 | Single row ball bearings | Steel, Mild | 1 |

## CAST BASE

NOTE: ALL FILLETS AND ROUNDS = R5.0 UNLESS OTHERWISE STATED.

SECTION A-A
SCALE 1 / 2

## FOLLOWER POST

## SHAFT

## HOLDER

## ENLARGED VIEW OF KEYWAY
## ON SHAFT SHF = 4004 = 16

## EX15-59

2-GEAR ASSEMBLY

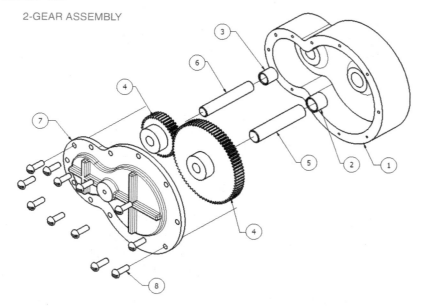

|  | Small Gear | Large Gear |
|---|---|---|
| Number of teeth | 48 | 96 |
| Face width | 0.50 | 0.50 |
| Diametral pitch | 24 | 24 |
| Pressure angle | 20 | 20 |
| Hub Ø | 0.750 | 1.00 |
| Base Ø | 0.500 | 0.625 |

| ITEM | PART NUMBER | DESCRIPTION | MATERIAL | QTY |
|---|---|---|---|---|
| 1 | ENG-453-A | GEAR, HOUSING | CAST IRON | 1 |
| 2 | BU-1123 | BUSHING Ø0.75 | DELRIN, BLACK | 1 |
| 3 | BU-1128 | BUSHING Ø0.625 | DELRIN, BLACK | 1 |
| 4 | ASSEMBLY-8 | ASSEMBLY, GEAR | STEEL | 1 |
| 5 | AM-314 | SHAFT, GEAR Ø0.625 | STEEL | 1 |
| 6 | AM-315 | SHAFT, GEAR Ø0.500 | STEEL | 1 |
| 7 | ENG-586-B | COVER, GEAR | CAST IRON | 1 |
| 8 | ANSI B18.6.2 1/4-20 UNC ×0.75 | SLOTTED ROUND HEAD SCREW | STEEL, MILD | 12 |

GEAR HOUSING

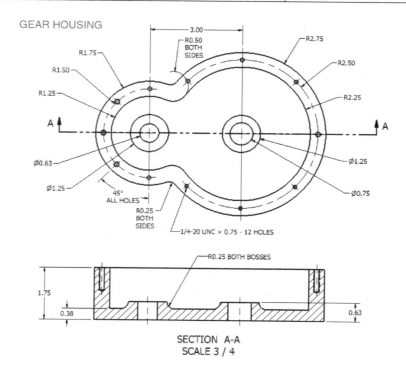

SECTION A-A
SCALE 3 / 4

## EX15-59, continued

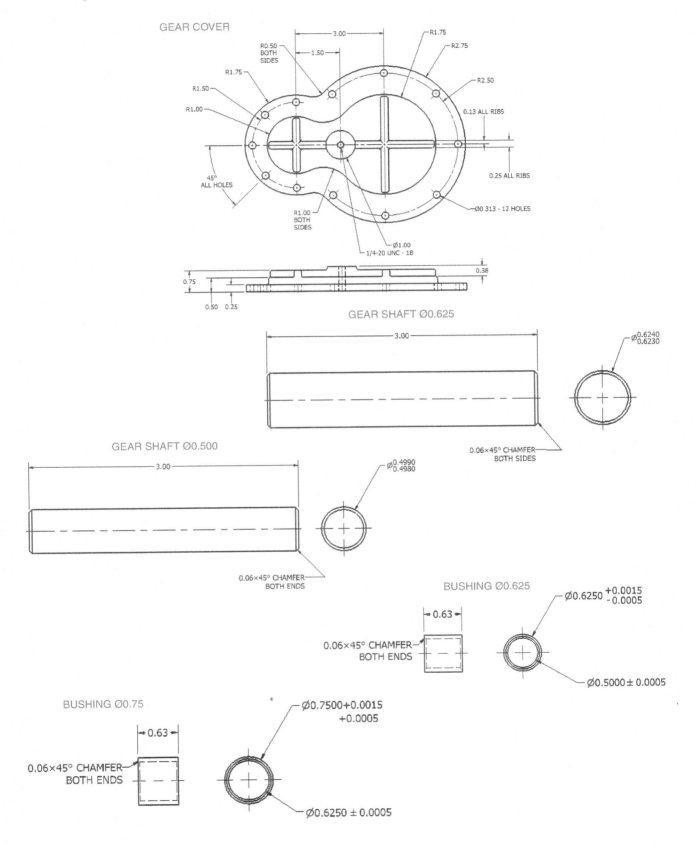

GEAR COVER

R0.50 BOTH SIDES

3.00

1.50

R1.75
R2.75
R1.75
R1.50
R1.00
R2.50

0.13 ALL RIBS

45° ALL HOLES

0.25 ALL RIBS

R1.00 BOTH SIDES

Ø0.313 - 12 HOLES

Ø1.00

1/4-20 UNC - 1B

0.38

0.75

0.50  0.25

GEAR SHAFT Ø0.625

3.00

Ø0.6240 / 0.6230

0.06×45° CHAMFER BOTH SIDES

GEAR SHAFT Ø0.500

3.00

Ø0.4990 / 0.4980

0.06×45° CHAMFER BOTH ENDS

BUSHING Ø0.625

0.63

0.06×45° CHAMFER BOTH ENDS

Ø0.6250 +0.0015 / -0.0005

Ø0.5000 ± 0.0005

BUSHING Ø0.75

0.63

0.06×45° CHAMFER BOTH ENDS

Ø0.7500 +0.0015 / +0.0005

Ø0.6250 ± 0.0005

## EX15-60

Design an access controller according to the information given. The controller works by moving an internal cylinder up and down within the base to align with output holes A and B. Liquids will enter the internal cylinder from the top and then exit the base through holes A and B. Include as many holes in the internal cylinder as necessary to create the following liquid exit combinations:

**1** A open, B closed

**2** A open, B open

**3** A closed, B open

The internal cylinder is held in place by an alignment key and a stop button. The stop button is to be spring-loaded so that it will always be held in place. The internal cylinder will be moved by pulling out the stop button, repositioning the cylinder, and then reinserting the stop button.

Prepare the following drawings:

**1** Draw the objects as solid models.

**2** Draw an assembly drawing.

**3** Draw detail drawings of each nonstandard part. Include positional tolerances for all holes.

**4** Prepare a parts list.

### INTERNAL CYLINDER

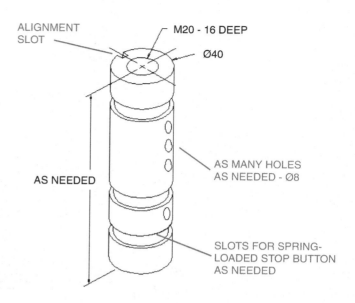

ALIGNMENT SLOT

M20 - 16 DEEP

Ø40

AS NEEDED

AS MANY HOLES AS NEEDED - Ø8

SLOTS FOR SPRING-LOADED STOP BUTTON AS NEEDED

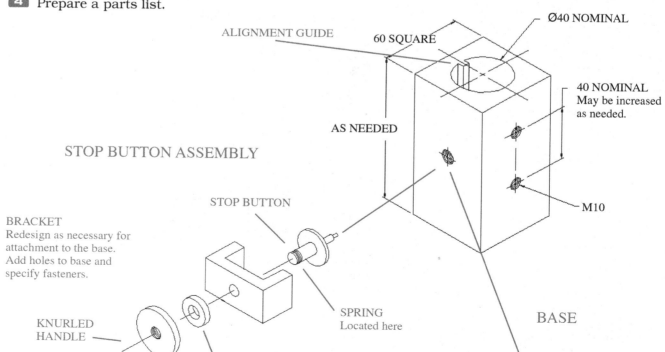

ALIGNMENT GUIDE

60 SQUARE

Ø40 NOMINAL

40 NOMINAL
May be increased as needed.

AS NEEDED

M10

STOP BUTTON ASSEMBLY

STOP BUTTON

BRACKET
Redesign as necessary for attachment to the base. Add holes to base and specify fasteners.

SPRING
Located here

BASE

KNURLED HANDLE

SPACER

MATCH TO STOP BUTTON

# EX15-61

Design a hand-operated grinding wheel specifically for sharpening a chisel. The chisel is to be located on an adjustable rest while it is being sharpened. The mechanism should be able to be clamped to a table during operation by two thumbscrews.

A standard grinding wheel is ⌀6.00 inch, is 0.5 inch thick, and has an internal mounting hole with a 50.00 ± 0.3 millimeter bore.

Prepare the following drawings:

**1** Draw the objects as solid models.

**2** Draw an assembly drawing.

**3** Draw detail drawings of each nonstandard part.

**4** Prepare a parts list.

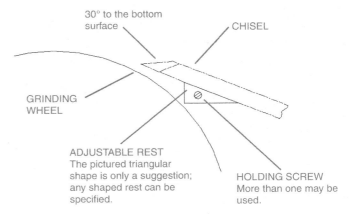

30° to the bottom surface

CHISEL

GRINDING WHEEL

ADJUSTABLE REST
The pictured triangular shape is only a suggestion; any shaped rest can be specified.

HOLDING SCREW
More than one may be used.

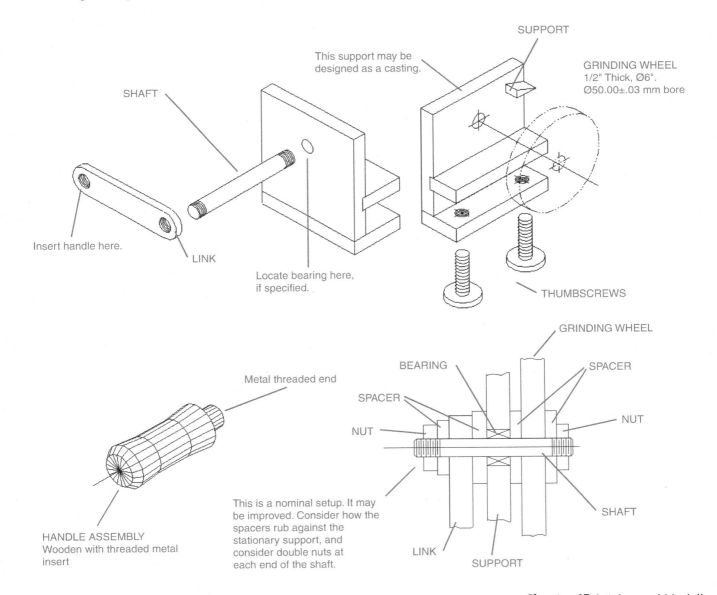

SUPPORT

GRINDING WHEEL
1/2" Thick, Ø6".
Ø50.00±.03 mm bore

This support may be designed as a casting.

SHAFT

Insert handle here.

LINK

Locate bearing here, if specified.

THUMBSCREWS

Metal threaded end

HANDLE ASSEMBLY
Wooden with threaded metal insert

This is a nominal setup. It may be improved. Consider how the spacers rub against the stationary support, and consider double nuts at each end of the shaft.

BEARING

SPACER

NUT

GRINDING WHEEL

SPACER

NUT

SHAFT

LINK

SUPPORT

## EX15-62

**1** Draw an assembly drawing of the given object.

**2** Prepare a parts list.

**3** Select appropriate fasteners to hold the object together.

**4** Define the appropriate tolerances.

C-BRACKET
SAE 1020 STEEL, 4 REQD
Part Number: AM311-1

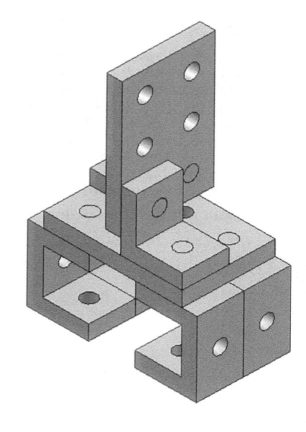

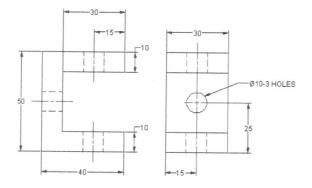

L-CLIP
SAE 1040 STEEL, 2 REQD
Part Number: AM312-4

SUPPORT PLATE
SAE 1040 STEEL, 2 REQD
Part Number: AM312-3

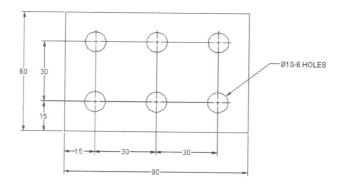

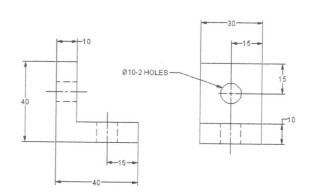

# EX15-63

**1** Draw an assembly drawing of the given object.

**2** Prepare a parts list.

**3** Select appropriate fasteners to hold the object together.

**4** Define the appropriate tolerances.

**5** Use phantom lines and define the motion of the center link and the rocker link if the drive link rotates 360°.

ROCKER ASSEMBLY

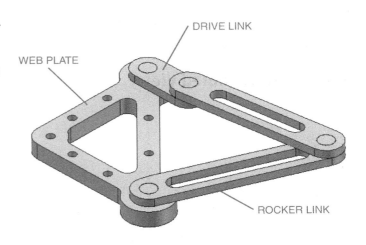

DRIVE LINK, SAE 1040 STEEL
Part Number: AM311-22A
5 mm THK

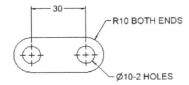

ALL FILLETS AND ROUNDS = R3

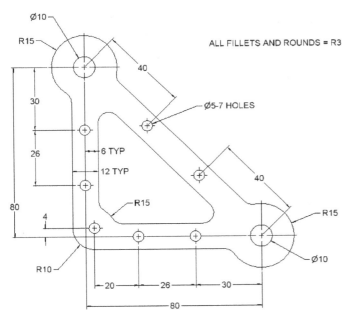

ROCKER LINK, SAE 1040 STEEL
Part Number: AM311-22C
5 mm THK

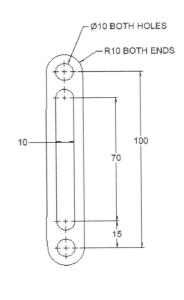

WEB PLATE, SAE 1040 STEEL
Part Number: AM311-22B
10 mm THK

CENTER LINK, SAE 1040 STEEL
Part Number: AM311-22D
5 mm THK

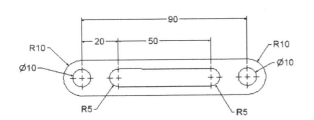

## EX15-64

**1** Draw an assembly drawing of the minivise.

**2** Prepare a parts list.

**3** Select the appropriate fasteners to hold the vise together.

**4** Redesign the interface between the drive screw and the holder plate.

## Minivise (Assembled View)

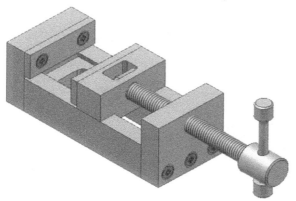

## Minivise-ISO (Exploded View)

### BASE

### SAE 1040 STEEL

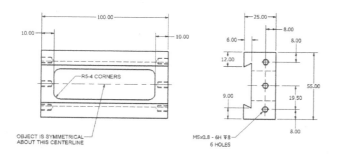

### END PLATE

### SAE 1040 STEEL

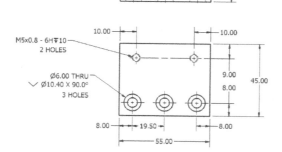

### DRIVE SCREW

### SAE 1040 STEEL

NOTE: ALL CHAMFERS = 1x45·

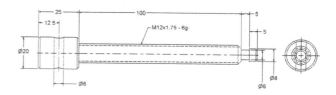

### SLIDER

### SAE 1040 STEEL

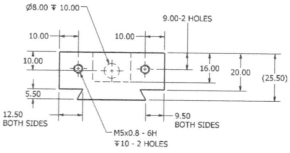

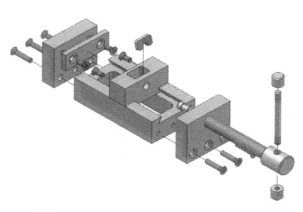

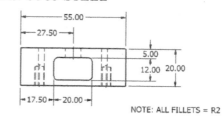

# EX15-64, continued

## HOLDER PLATE

### SAE 1040 STEEL

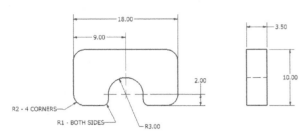

R2 - 4 CORNERS
R1 - BOTH SIDES
R3.00

## HANDLE

### SAE 1040 STEEL

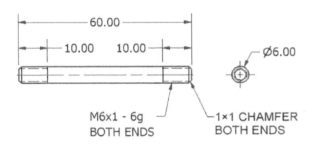

M6x1 - 6g
BOTH ENDS

1×1 CHAMFER
BOTH ENDS

Ø6.00

## DRIVE PLATE

### SAE 1040 STEEL

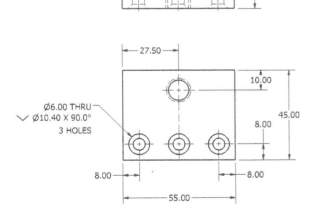

Ø6.00 THRU
∨ Ø10.40 X 90.0°
3 HOLES

M5 × 10 RECESSED COUNTERSUNK HEAD-STEEL

M5 × 22 RECESSED COUNTERSUNK HEAD-STEEL

## FACE PLATE

### SAE 1040 STEEL

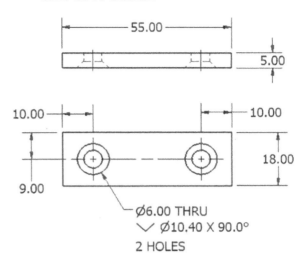

Ø6.00 THRU
∨ Ø10.40 X 90.0°
2 HOLES

## END CAP

### SAE 1040 STEEL

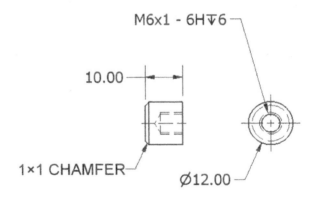

M6x1 - 6H⍗6

1×1 CHAMFER

Ø12.00

## EX15-65

Create the following for the slider assembly shown:

1. Select the appropriate fasteners.

2. Create an assembly drawing.

3. Create a parts list.

4. Specify the tolerance for the guide shaft/ bearings interface.

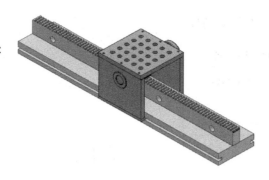

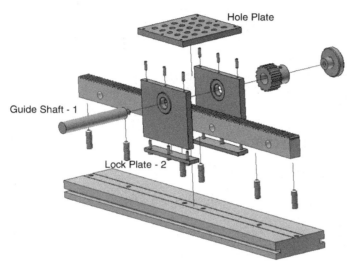

Hole Plate

Guide Shaft - 1

Lock Plate - 2

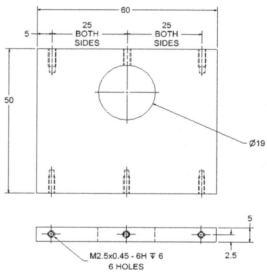

60

25 BOTH SIDES · 25 BOTH SIDES

5

50

Ø19

M2.5x0.45 - 6H ⊽ 6
6 HOLES

5

2.5

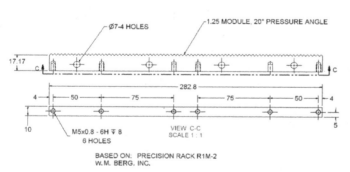

Ø7-4 HOLES

1.25 MODULE, 20° PRESSURE ANGLE

17.17

282.8

4 — 50 — 75 — 75 — 50 — 4

10

M5x0.8 - 6H ⊽ 8
6 HOLES

VIEW C-C
SCALE 1 : 1

5

BASED ON: PRECISION RACK R1M-2
W.M. BERG, INC.

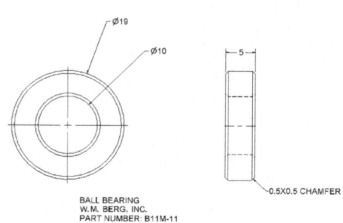

Ø19

Ø10

BALL BEARING
W.M. BERG, INC.
PART NUMBER: B11M-11

5

0.5X0.5 CHAMFER

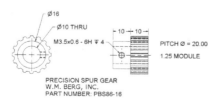

Ø16

Ø10 THRU

M3.5x0.6 - 6H ⊽ 4

10 — 10

PITCH Ø = 20.00

1.25 MODULE

PRECISION SPUR GEAR
W.M. BERG, INC.
PART NUMBER: PBS86-16

# EX15-65, continued

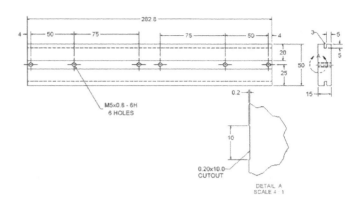

M5x0.8 - 6H
6 HOLES

0.20x10.0
CUTOUT

DETAIL A
SCALE 4 : 1

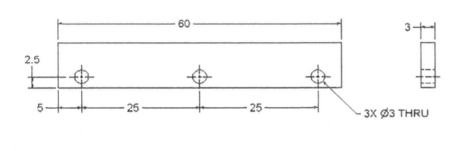

3X Ø3 THRU

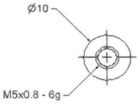

Ø10

M5x0.8 - 6g

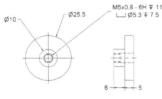

M5x0.8 - 6H ⍂ 11
⊔ Ø5.3 ⍂ 7.5

Ø10    Ø25.5

KNURLED THUMB NUT
W.M. BERG, INC.
STOCK NUMBER: PD1M-15

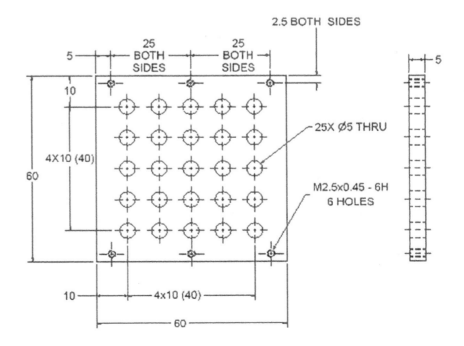

2.5 BOTH SIDES

25 BOTH SIDES    25 BOTH SIDES

25X Ø5 THRU

M2.5x0.45 - 6H
6 HOLES

4X10 (40)

10    4x10 (40)

60

# Index

**B**